Title I -

MENTAL RETARDATION

MENTAL

Edited by
HARVEY A. STEVENS
and
RICK HEBER

A REVIEW OF RESEARCH

RETARDATION

THE UNIVERSITY OF CHICAGO PRESS
CHICAGO AND LONDON

Library of Congress Catalog Card Number: 64-15808

THE UNIVERSITY OF CHICAGO PRESS, CHICAGO 60637
THE UNIVERSITY OF CHICAGO PRESS, LTD., LONDON W. C. 1

© *1964 by The University of Chicago. All rights reserved*
Published 1964. Fifth Impression 1969
Printed in the United States of America

DEDICATED TO

the scores of professional and lay individuals who have given unselfishly of themselves in behalf of the mentally retarded

and to

the memory of John Fitzgerald Kennedy, whose compassion, understanding, and leadership have brought new hope to the disadvantaged people of the world

FOREWORD

This document brings together the knowledge obtained from research in all of the major scientific disciplines which are contributing to a better understanding of the complex phenomena of mental retardation.

The manuscript for this publication was authorized by the American Association on Mental Deficiency Project on Technical Planning in Mental Retardation and was supported, in part, by Research Grant 3M-9103(C4) from the National Institute of Mental Health, Public Health Service, U.S. Department of Health, Education, and Welfare. It represents another attempt of the Project to bring about the integration and organization of new knowledge which has already been acquired from the field of mental retardation and related fields.

It is rare that a group of distinguished scientists, representing both the behavioral and the biological sciences, have been afforded the opportunity to bring the work from divergent fields into focus in a single volume. This extraordinary document promises to contribute substantially to the advancement of our knowledge of mental retardation. It should serve as a stimulus to future scientists, increase our capabilities to provide more adequately for the mentally retarded, and serve to stimulate the development of new programs whose purpose is to prevent or ameliorate the condition of mental retardation.

As in many projects of this nature, many indirect benefits should accrue which are not and will not be measurable. Among these might be the more rapid dissemination of new knowledge concerning mental retardation through the distribution of this document to libraries throughout the world. It could well serve as a text in universities and colleges concerned with training of personnel in the various professional disciplines. It should provide ample opportunity to stimulate discussions of the research findings reported. It will also be an invaluable aid to the graduate student who is about to embark upon his first research project.

No doubt it will serve as another reminder to parents that the problem of their mentally retarded child is also the deep concern of many others.

In the past decade there has been an almost incredible awakening of the public conscience concerning mental retardation. With this resurgence of concern, research has increased manyfold during this period. With the increased interest in mental retardation on the part of federal and state governments as well as numerous private foundations, the future for increased knowledge concerning mental retardation through research is insured.

This volume provides us with the pause that enables us to assess and reflect upon the progress we have made in the field of mental retardation toward the solution of the medical, social, educational, and welfare problems with which we as a society and a nation are confronted.

All of us who have a deep concern for the mentally retarded are deeply indebted to the Editorial Committee, the authors, and the editors for their efforts.

HERSCHEL W. NISONGER
Director
Project on Technical Planning
in Mental Retardation—
American Association
on Mental Deficiency

COLUMBUS, OHIO

PREFACE

The accumulation of knowledge concerning mental retardation during the past twenty-five years has been relatively meager when compared with advances in knowledge of other conditions which have afflicted mankind. The past decade has produced sufficient evidence to demonstrate the need for a bold attack on the multiplicity of problems generated by the mentally retarded.

It is now generally accepted that the resolution of the problems precipitated by the mentally retarded is no longer the sole responsibility of any single profession or discipline. It is one requiring the co-operative efforts and the pooling of knowledge and information of many, all directed toward the resolution of these problems.

The need for co-operative planning in the field of mental retardation was recognized by the National Institute for Mental Health in 1955 when it made a significant grant to the American Association on Mental Deficiency for a project entitled "Technical Planning in Mental Retardation."

> The basic purpose of this project was seen as the delineation of current needs, the stimulation of creative thinking, integration and organization of work which had already been done, the improvement of liaison between interested groups and individuals—professional, government, lay and parents. For functional and organizational structure the broad general problems were thought to fall into three categories: research, training of personnel, and programming (U.S. Department of Health, Education, and Welfare, p. 20).

The importance and the interrelationship of research in the biological, psychological, educational, and socio-cultural aspects of mental retardation were recognized by the project on Technical Planning in Mental Retardation when it granted support and financial assistance for the preparation of this manuscript. It is hoped that this document will, in no small measure, contribute to stimulating more effective interdisciplinary research.

The preparation of a document of this magnitude was not undertaken by the AAMD project without full knowledge and realization of the innumerable obstacles which might be (and were) encountered.

In order to facilitate the preparation of a manuscript for publication the project director, Mr. Herschel Nisonger, appointed an Editorial Committee. It was the Editorial Committee's responsibility to delineate the scope and direction the text was to take, to select appropriate authors and reviewers for each chapter and, finally, to secure a publisher. The Editorial Committee consisted of Samuel A. Kirk, Donald Jolly, Delton Beier, Rick Heber, and Harvey A. Stevens. The latter served as chairman of the Editorial Committee. Final editing of the manuscript became the responsibility of Stevens.

It was the responsibility of the Editorial Committee to delineate the major areas of research relating to mental retardation that could appropriately be reviewed and organized into a single volume. This was no small task. The Editorial Committee as well as the authors recognized that the reported research was meager in some areas, while numerous references were readily available in others. In some areas other authors have already published specialized summaries in scientific journals and reports. Reference is made to such summaries by the authors.

In reviewing the manuscripts of all authors, the editors became aware of some overlapping between one or more chapters. In one respect, one may view the obvious overlapping, not as a weakness nor as a duplication of reported research, but, rather, as a strength of the text. This overlapping clearly demonstrates the interrelationship and interdependence of research in this broad, complex field. It again highlights the importance and need for researchers in one field to familiarize themselves with the research being conducted and reported in related fields.

The significant increase in our knowledge concerning chromosomes and chromosomal aberrations is one such striking example. The reader will be aware of the differences in the styles of reporting employed by the authors as well as in the methods utilized in reviewing the relevant research in their particular fields of scientific interest.

This divergence of style and method of reporting might well be a strength rather than a weakness, since to a large degree it is a reflection of the obvious difference in the current status of the various fields of scientific inquiry as they relate to mental retardation.

The editors have assumed some responsibility for providing consistency in terminology, since the inconsistent use of terms is one of the major impediments in this field.

A cursory review of each chapter may help the reader to grasp the global aspects and complexity of the problem as well as to delineate the content of the specialized area of scientific inquiry reported by each author.

Stevens' chapter, entitled "Overview," familiarizes the reader with the nature and scope of mental retardation and indicates the responsibility that is and should be assumed by various levels of government for the mentally retarded.

Benton's chapter considers the literature on "Psychological Evaluation and Differential Diagnosis." Limitations of space have obviously necessitated omission of numerous studies in the general areas of his topic and those previously summarized in other publications. He points out the direction that future research in this area might take—particularly research which will provide basic knowledge to develop the usefulness of the psychological evaluation for prognostic purposes.

The review of the literature in "Research in Education" by Kirk is confined to the educational "treatment" of mental retardation. Despite the critical importance of education in the "treatment" of the retarded child, little attention has been paid in research to validating current educational methods and teaching procedures. Since studies on learning and motivation are discussed by Denny in his chapter on learning, Kirk has included only research relating to educational methodology and organization, particularly as it relates to the various phases of the school curriculum.

Denny's chapter on "Research in Learning and Performance" represents a comprehensive review of the literature relating to learning experiments. He does not relate his summary to those studies dealing with the motivational aspects of behavior. Studies relating to motivation are dealt with by Heber in his chapter on "Personality." Further research in those areas which attempt to identify the "fundamental deficit(s) in the retarded's learning" is suggested by Denny. This chapter appropriately points out some of the difficulties the researcher must be prepared to face in the field of mental retardation due to (1) definition, (2) etiology, and (3) problems of suitable controls. It is encouraging to note that Denny is of the opinion that "the outlook for the mentally retarded is surprisingly optimistic . . . and . . . it should be possible to develop appropriate motivational procedures and special training techniques to overcome an appreciable portion of the retardate's difficulties." (See Denny's chapter, Conclusion.) No doubt more research in basic learning and motivation and its practical application to specialized techniques of instruction is still required.

Heber's chapter, "Personality," reviews the substantial body of research on motivation and concludes that motivational deficits are principal secondary contributors to the inadequate performance of the retarded. With the exception of the work on motivation, little has been done on other aspects of personality development. As Heber points out, behavioral research in mental retardation has focused almost exclusively on the concept of intelligence. An added impediment to "giving the mentally retarded a personality" has been methodological; tests and measures devised for use with intellectually normal persons have usually been found inadequate for use with retardates.

McCandless has appropriately avoided the review of the literature dealing with prenatal environment of the individual and devoted his attention in his chapter, "Relation of Environmental Factors to Intellectual Functioning," to the research dealing with postnatal environment. He has concentrated his review of research on those studies relating to environmental influences on intellectual functioning and on research directly related to intellectual functioning of endogenous mentally retarded individuals. He concludes by raising a most thought-provoking and challenging question, ". . . if isolation and deprivation blunt the 'intelligence' of a rat or a dog what, then, must they do to a baby?" (See McCandless' chapter, page 175.)

Goldstein discusses the "Social and Occupational Adjustment" of the mentally retarded from four different aspects: (1) the early concepts of the adjustment potential of the mentally retarded, (2) the adjustment of institutional and non-institutional mentally retarded in the community, (3) the vocational status of the retarded, and (4) the occupational outlook for the retarded. Particularly alarming, yet challenging, is his observation that the effects of automation upon the mentally retarded have yet to be conclusively demonstrated. Goldstein stresses that "if the retarded are to compete with normal workers for unskilled positions, it will be necessary for them to be well prepared and well advised." This should serve as a point of departure for future researchers in this particular area. The significance of existing research findings and future findings may well usher in a new era of education for the older retardate.

Gruenberg's chapter on "Epidemiology" reviews the pertinent epidemiological studies which have been made of mental retardation. He stresses the fact that it should be viewed only as an introduction to the epidemiological literature, as an aid to those contemplating research, and as an aid to a better understanding of the social welfare problems generated by the mentally retarded. Dr. Gruenberg has appropriately left the comments on research in individual risks of illness to summaries already published and to relevant discussions in Anderson's chapter on genetics. The reader will be interested in learning the various ways in which epidemiological data can be used to throw light upon questions which the investigator did not have in mind when initiating his study.

Greatest progress in knowledge of the etiologies of retardation and in the capability to prevent mental retardation has come about through advances in biochemistry. Waisman and Gerritsen's chapter reviews the current status of biochemical understanding of retardation and delineates some of the more promising avenues of investigation.

Anderson's chapter on genetics clearly demonstrates the tremendous advance made during the past decade in the field of human genetics. No small part of this advance has been due to the development of highly specialized techniques.

It was Fraser's thought in orienting the direction of his chapter, "Teratogenesis of the Central Nervous System," that "a number of recent advances in genetics, embryology, and teratology [might in] some or many [ways] lead to a better understanding and perhaps control of prenatal factors that influence postnatal mental function." (See Fraser's chapter, p. 395, Conclusions.) He does suggest that much of the current knowledge concerning the teratogenesis of the central nervous system does not now have practical application to mental retardation. However, the possibility that, in time, a practical application of this knowledge will be achieved is raised. Fraser suggests many areas for further research in teratology.

The chapter "Neuropathology," by Malamud, emphasizes the need for an objective appraisal of the pathologic findings. He carefully analyzes the data in a series of unselected cases and compares them with those reported in the literature to demonstrate that such findings can provide a better understanding of the etiology and pathogenesis of mental retardation.

The chapter "Behavioral Disturbances," by Beier, presents the major considerations, trends, and points of view that are necessary for an understanding of severe behavior disorders in the mentally retarded. Beier, like many of the authors, encountered difficulty in reviewing the literature because of the problems in defining the population under consideration. This chapter again demonstrates that the mentally retarded cannot be viewed as a homogeneous group.

The Editorial Committee would be remiss in its duties if it did not applaud the assistance, and above all the patience, of Mr. Nisonger. The editors are particularly grateful to him for resolving the all-too-many production problems encountered. This manuscript is in no small way another example of his administrative skill and diplomacy.

One final note: If one measures the progress being made in all aspects of mental retardation by the passing of a decade rather than by a fleeting, single year, one will enthusiastically admit that progress is being achieved. There truly is hope for future generations!

HARVEY A. STEVENS
RICK HEBER
Coeditors

CONTENTS

OVERVIEW

Harvey A. Stevens

CONCEPT OF MENTAL RETARDATION

Mental retardation refers to subaverage general intellectual functioning which originates during the development period and is associated with impairment in adaptive behavior (Heber, p. 3).

This is the official definition adopted in 1959 by the American Association on Mental Deficiency. It is in the context of this definition that this text is oriented. For a more comprehensive discussion of definitions refer to Benton's chapter on psychological evaluation.

The term "mental retardation," as used in the above definition and in this text, also encompasses the meanings previously incorporated into both descriptive terms, such as mental deficiency, feeble-mindedness, and mental subnormality, and the historical terms—amentia, idiocy, and imbecility.

Heber stated that the "choice of the term 'mental retardation' was predicated on the basis that it appears, at present, to be the most preferred term among professional personnel of all disciplines concerned" (Heber, p. 3).

The definition recognizes that mental retardation is now viewed as a reversible condition. This is a departure from the classical and historical concept of "once mentally retarded, always mentally retarded." It is a term describing the current status of the individual in regard to his intellectual functioning as well as his adaptive behavior.

The *Manual on Terminology and Classification in Mental Retardation* concludes its discussion of definition by stating,

. . . an individual may meet the criteria of mental retardation at one time and not at another. A person may change status as a result of changes in social standards or conditions or as a result of changes in efficiency of intellectual functioning, with level of efficiency always being determined in relation to the behavioral standards and norms for the individual's chronological age group (Heber, p. 4).

EXTENT OF THE PROBLEM

Mental retardation affects and disables 10 times more individuals than does diabetes, 20 times as many as tuberculosis, 25 times more than muscular dystrophy, and 600 times more than infantile paralysis. Only mental illness, cardiac disease, arthritis, and cancer affect a greater number of individuals (President's Panel on Mental Retardation, p. 197).

It was estimated in 1962 that more than 5 million individuals were retarded. At the present birth rate and the rate of prevalence of mental retardation, it is estimated that 126,000 infants born each year will be classified as being mentally retarded sometime during their lifetime. It is also estimated that by 1970 there will be more than 6 million mentally retarded persons in the United States; more than half will be children. Over 200,000 persons—children and adults—were cared for in 124 state-supported residential facilities at a cost in excess of 300 million dollars. More than 250 million dollars was spent in support of special educa-

1

tional programs conducted by the public schools. In 1963 the national government will spend in excess of 128 million dollars in its programs to combat mental retardation (Secretary's Committee on Mental Retardation, p. 1).

Over 400,000 adults are so retarded that they are unable to participate in competitive or productive employment. The loss in economic output due to the total absence of productivity and underproductivity was estimated to be more than several billion dollars. During World War II, 716,000 men were rejected because of "mental deficiency" (President's Panel, p. 2).

About 96 per cent of the nation's mentally retarded people are cared for outside of residential facilities (Secretary's Committee, p. 11).

Of greater significance than the loss to our nation's security and economy is the untold and immeasurable suffering to the parents, brothers and sisters, relatives and friends of the mentally retarded individual. It is impossible to describe adequately the feelings of parents when they eventually realize that their mentally retarded child will never be capable of living a normal childhood or ever become, as an adult, a participating and contributing member of society!

It is a relatively simple task to elicit, from an "intellectually normal" blind, deaf, or physically handicapped person, his attitudes or his feelings toward his own handicapping condition as well as his own concept of its effect upon his parents, relatives, or friends. The retarded individual is incapable of making such observations or reaching such conclusions.

This brief discussion serves to highlight the magnitude of this problem. Concerted action is required in order for these individuals to take their rightful place in our society and, more important, to assume their full share of responsibilities in support of our democratic way of life.

WHAT IS MENTAL RETARDATION?

Mental retardation is a constellation of syndromes. It is not a disease, although it may be the result of a disease. It is more accurate to describe it as a condition that affects from 2 to 3 per cent of the total population. Its principal characteristic is retarded intellectual development and inability to adapt to demands of society.

Based on current knowledge, more than one hundred causes of retardation have been identified. It may be caused by factors which affect the embryo or fetus during development. It may affect the infant during the birth process, shortly after birth, or during the child's early years of growth and development. With present techniques of diagnosis it is possible to make a positive and precise identification of the cause of mental retardation in only 15 to 25 per cent of all cases. Our present state of knowledge does not permit definitive diagnoses in the remaining 75 to 85 per cent.

The discovery by Tjio in 1957 of the exact number of chromosomes in the human cell has renewed investigations into the genetic factors associated with the etiology of a variety of clinical entities. Mongolism is now the classical example of chromosomal aberration with mental retardation.

Lejeune of France identified, in 1959, the extra chromosome in mongolism and has further established that this chromosomal aberration is responsible for tryptophane metabolism observed in mongolism. There now exists the possibility that this discovery may open up an entirely new field of collaborative research, "human genetic biochemistry." The chapters dealing with genetics and biochemistry should be of particular interest to both the geneticist and the biochemist interested in this aspect of the problem.

There are numerous factors, in addition to the genetic components, which may affect the embryo or the developing fetus, including infections, poisons, and intoxications in the mother's body during pregnancy. Poor nutrition of the mother during pregnancy may later affect the intellectual development of her child.

It has been demonstrated, for example, that contraction of German measles during the first trimester of pregnancy, Rh blood factor incompatibility, lead poisoning, and such metabolic defects as phenylketonuria (PKU) and galactosemia may produce a relatively small number of mentally retarded individuals.

Many of these conditions have responded to specific modalities of treatment, and preventive therapeutic measures have been developed for others. Fortunately, some of these conditions are amenable to correction. However, additional preventive methods must still await discovery. The etiological aspects of these clinical entities are of particular significance to those interested in neuropathology and teratology.

Organic pathology occasionally may be demonstrated as the result of injury or disease occurring during or shortly after birth. In those instances where observable clinical evidence is present, there may be marked neurological damage which will result in profound or severe mental retardation. Trauma received during the birth process and oxygen deprivation due to delayed breathing following birth are frequent causes of mental retardation. Severe injuries to the brain following an accident, cardiac failure during or following surgery with restoration of life, and partial drowning with restoration of breathing have also produced profound and severe mental retardation.

Improved and new obstetrical and surgical techniques as well as improved highway safety measures will result in the reduction of the number of cases due to brain trauma.

There are a relatively small number of cases of mental retardation caused by abnormal tumor-like growths within the brain. Several of these entities are heredi-tary in origin. In a large number of cases, pathological conditions within the brain resulting in mental retardation are still of undetermined etiology. The exact relationship of these pathological conditions to mental retardation must await further research. Thus, post-mortem examination of these cases is most helpful to the neuropathologist interested in the etiological aspects of abnormal growth and development.

By far the largest group of the mentally retarded is composed of those individuals for whom there is no demonstrable pathology in the brain (at least with present techniques of identification). This group is usually classified as being mildly mentally retarded. There is some evidence to suggest that this group may be the result of yet to be determined or understood genetic factors. A number of these cases are born of mothers who lack adequate prenatal and postnatal care. A large number are born and reared in deprived environments. There is ample evidence to indicate that there is a positive correlation between the prevalence of mental retardation and the socio-economic status of the family and the community. Such conditions foster a lack of opportunities for learning that somehow interferes with normal intellectual development during the early developmental years.

Improved living conditions for a large segment of our society are necessary in order to reduce the causative factors leading to this type of mental retardation. The discussion in this text relating to personality development, learning, education and vocational rehabilitation, and environment is particularly meaningful to those concerned with increasing the effectiveness of the mildly retarded.

NATURE OF MENTAL RETARDATION

As a group, the mentally retarded are considered heterogeneous; therefore, the nature and degree of retardation vary considerably. To date, no system devised to classify the degrees or levels of retardation has been completely acceptable to all professional disciplines concerned. The official classification of the American Association on Mental Deficiency uses intelligence test scores as its basis for categorizing the degrees or levels of mental retardation (Heber, p. 57).

The degree of mental retardation suggests the probable level of functioning the individual is capable of achieving. It also suggests the kinds of problems that one might anticipate they will create and present to themselves, their families, and their communities. These levels of retardation become useful when attempting to select retarded individuals for participation in specialized programs of

TABLE 1

DEGREES OF MENTAL RETARDATION

Level	Descriptive Term	Intelligence Quotient (IQ) Range
Level I.........	Profound	Below 20
Level II........	Severe	20–35
Level III.......	Moderate	36–52
Level IV.......	Mild	53–68

care, treatment, education, and rehabilitation.

A brief discussion of the various levels of mental retardation is intended to show that mental retardation is a generic term describing four distinct groups. Each group possesses rather distinct characteristics and presents specific problems requiring specialized programs for their care and management. It should also be recognized that there is considerable variation between individuals, even within each group.

THE PROFOUNDLY MENTALLY RETARDED

Those individuals who classify as "profoundly mentally retarded" usually have considerable central nervous system impairment, and organic pathology is present to an unusual extent. Many present other types of handicapping con-

ditions in addition to mental retardation, such as blindness, deafness, epilepsy, and gross physical anomalies. Speech usually is absent. Their motor development is very poor. Frequently one may observe patterns of repetitive behavior such as rocking movements, head banging, biting of hands, and lip biting. Their life expectancy may be assumed to be far below average.

The profoundly retarded individual is considered, on the basis of current knowledge and practices, incapable of profiting from any type of training or education. Most of these individuals require lifelong supportive residential care. Many will be bedfast throughout their lives. Relatively few families are capable, physically or financially, to provide for this type of care and management in their own home.

When a profoundly retarded child is retained in his own home, it usually necessitates considerable alteration in normal family living and routines. Family plans must be made around this individual and not the needs of other family members, thus creating problems in the total family unit.

THE SEVERELY MENTALLY RETARDED

Those persons who are classified as being "severely mentally retarded" present some of the same characteristics and problems associated with the "profoundly mentally retarded," but to a lesser degree.

In a large number of cases there is considerable damage to the central nervous system as well as organic pathology and other handicapping conditions.

The severely mentally retarded may be viewed as being above the level of total dependency throughout their lifetime. Many require intensive and extensive medical and nursing care; while others, because of organic brain damage, are somewhat difficult to control. Motor development is retarded, as are language and speech.

A large number of the severely retarded will spend at least a portion of their lifetime in a residential facility. Lifelong supervision and support are required. Many, particularly those with intelligence quotients (IQ's) between 25 and 35 can respond to and profit from systematic training in self-help skills. With intensive and prolonged training, they may function in a highly controlled and supervised terminal sheltered workshop facility as adults.

Those severely retarded persons who do not present complicated problems of care and management may be fairly adequately cared for in their own home. Some, after reaching adulthood, may require residential care when one or both parents are no longer living.

THE MODERATELY MENTALLY RETARDED

The moderately retarded individual presents less complicated neuropathological conditions as contrasted with the profoundly and severely retarded. Fewer types of other handicapping conditions, such as blindness, deafness, epilepsy, and physical anomalies, are present. In most cases, motor development approaches normal. Language and speech can be developed. Those with organic brain damage and epilepsy may present objectionable social behavior patterns as well as difficult-to-manage behavior. Self-help skills in toileting, feeding, and, usually, bathing can be attained. As a group they may be viewed as being semidependent.

The moderately retarded are capable of profiting from organized formal programs of systematic training aimed at development of self-help skills and social awareness. The self-concept is capable of being developed at this intellectual level. A few are capable of attaining a minimal level of academic achievement, possibly third grade.

With careful training and supervision, many of the more physically and socially adequate moderately retarded are capable of achieving partial self-support in a sheltered employment situation, and a few are capable of maintaining a position in competitive employment. As adults most of them will require frequent supervision and guidance in many of their personal, social, and economic problems.

THE MILDLY MENTALLY RETARDED

The largest group of the mentally retarded (probably 85 per cent of all retarded) is represented by the mildly retarded. They approach the low average in terms of physical characteristics. They are usually slow in development in walking, talking, feeding themselves, and toilet training. Few observable physical signs are present to assist in etiological diagnosis. Other handicapping conditions appear in a frequency slightly higher than in the average general population. Motor development is relatively normal. Eye-hand co-ordination is somewhat retarded below normal expectancy. Identification of a child as a mild retardate is usually not made until after at least one, possibly two, years of regular school experience.

Social and communication skills may be developed in carefully structured special class and related educational programs. The mildly mentally retarded can also profit from systematic training in arts and crafts and arithmetic at the elementary education level. They are incapable of completing secondary school requirements, although many can participate in a special class program located in a secondary school. They are capable of competing, with a moderate degree of success, in selected non-academic subjects at the secondary school level, such as physical education, arts and crafts, manual arts, etc.

If the mildly retarded are educated in the regular classes, they will present a variety of problems to the regular teacher. Some of these problems are: (1) excessive amount of teacher-time for instructional purposes, (2) antisocial behavior, (3) objection to their presence in school by other teachers, and (4) inability to conform to social standards of the class. They frequently repeat one or more grades. Their peers will isolate and reject them.

Occupational skills may be developed, and, in a few cases, semiskilled job levels may be attained. Automation in industry may displace many of these individuals.

Some mildly retarded individuals have their problems of learning and adjustment further complicated by a serious social or emotional problem. As a result, some will require residential care in order to protect themselves, other family members, and society. Many of this latter group come into conflict with the authorities. The more serious offender may require care, education, treatment, and management in a security-type residential facility. The less serious cases may only require short-term placement in a regular residential facility for the mentally retarded.

Many of this group marry and have families. In such cases they usually encounter some difficulty in managing their own affairs. Frequent unemployment precipitates social welfare problems.

As adults, many are capable of sustaining themselves with only minimal assistance, particularly those having an intelligence quotient of 60 to 68.

EFFECTS OF THE MENTALLY RETARDED ON THE FAMILY

The presence of a retarded child in a home presents a variety of complex problems involving all facets of family life and all family members.

The nature and level of mental retardation of the child, the socio-economic status of the family, the emotional stability of the parents, the emotional climate the parents create in the home, as well as the level of community tolerance for the mentally retarded, all affect the manner in which the parents plan to meet the needs of their retarded child. These same factors will also determine how realistically the family accepts the child. Moreover, the constant presence in the home of a retarded child, who presents obvious physical stigmata, sometimes creates social rejection of the family by relatives and friends.

Many families, hoping for greater community acceptance, have moved to new communities, only to be disillusioned. Families frequently change physicians in the hope of obtaining additional or new medical information which is more acceptable to them.

The cost of medical and nursing care often is far beyond the financial abilities of families having a profoundly or severely retarded child. Many families maintain their child in private facilities at costs far beyond their means and, often, at great sacrifice to themselves and other children.

It must be recognized that the effect of family life on a profoundly retarded child reared in a high socio-economic status family will be totally different from that on a mildly retarded child reared in a family of low socio-economic status. The levels of aspiration of parents for their children greatly influence the attitudes the parents have for their children.

The lack of adequate parent counseling and lack of community services frequently complicate the family's ability to cope with the care and management of their child in their own home or to make realistic plans for their child's future.

EFFECTS OF THE MENTALLY RETARDED ON THE COMMUNITY

Individually and as a group, the mentally retarded present a wide variety of complex educational, social, and welfare problems to the community as well as to their families. The presence of even a small number of retarded persons in a given community is cause for concern and requires concerted action on the part of community leaders to plan for the needs of the individual and the family. The public, in general, is not always fully cognizant or understanding of the nature of mental retardation, nor is the public always aware of what can or needs to be done for the retarded individual or his family.

The profoundly and severely retarded do not always present to the public the same type of problems as do the moderately and mildly retarded. The former are usually retained at home or placed in residential facilities and, thus, do not come into frequent contact with the public; while the latter do make attempts to participate in a variety of community activities. It is at this point that community attitudes toward the retarded come into sharp focus.

While only limited data are available, it is known that many families disintegrate through separation and divorce because they are unable to effectively resolve their problems. This action precipitates many community problems; some are of a financial nature.

Not too infrequently one or more members of a family will require psychiatric services at community expense as a direct result of the presence of a retarded child in the family. The inability of a family to resolve emotional conflicts growing out of their inability to cope with the problems of acceptance, care, and management of the retarded child often requires a constellation of community services to help such families.

The sheer economic costs to states of providing adequate residential facilities for the ever increasing number of mentally retarded is reaching a level where many are now seeking alternate measures and placing greater responsibility upon the community and families to care for their retarded child. Long residential waiting lists are creating new kinds of problems for families and communities.

In many states the laws relating to the mentally retarded do not reflect current knowledge. This is particularly true in regard to guardianship, commitment to residential facilities, the right to make contract, protection of themselves as retarded individuals, criminal responsibility, and the like. The adult retardates who are employable may encounter long periods of unemployment during periods of economic decline, thus requiring community support and supervision.

Many communities, through public education, are attempting to support the families by creating a variety of community-centered services as well as by developing a more positive public awareness and tolerance for the mentally retarded.

CURRENT APPROACHES TO PROGRAMS AND SERVICES FOR THE MENTALLY RETARDED

Renewed efforts toward the resolution of the problems of the mentally retarded began following World War II. The year 1950 witnessed the creation of the National Association for Retarded Children. This organization, composed chiefly of parents of mentally retarded children, has done much to develop and stimulate a public awareness of the problems of mental retardation. It has also been most effective in urging state legislatures to enact laws fostering improved and new programs and services for the mentally retarded. It has been instrumental in creating several state commissions to delineate total, comprehensive, and state-wide plans of services for the mentally retarded. Increased interest on the part of the federal government is partly due to their efforts.

The American Association on Mental Deficiency, organized in 1876, whose members are from the professional disciplines of medicine, education, psychology, and social work and administration, has played an important role in this field. In recent years, through its committee for "technical planning in mental retardation," it has developed and conducted numerous conferences and studies in the broad areas of (1) research, (2) training of personnel, and (3) programming.

The Council for Exceptional Children of the National Education Association has stimulated the development of teacher-training programs, assisted in delineating the qualifications of teachers of the mentally retarded and, most important, encouraged the dissemination of scientific information in the broad field of special education through state, regional, and national conferences and publications.

Numerous private foundations and schools have also fostered and conducted a variety of programs and services. The 1962 International Achievement Awards in mental retardation, sponsored by the Joseph P. Kennedy, Jr. Foundation, is an excellent example of support given to stimulate public awareness of, and encourage increased professional participation in, the problems of mental retardation. The annual Wood School Conferences (Langhorne, Pennsylvania) have also contributed to a better understanding of the exceptional child, particularly the mentally retarded.

Efforts to develop a variety of programs and services (U.S. Department of Health, Education, and Welfare, pp. 7 and 8) to meet the multiplicity of needs of the mentally retarded are currently directed toward the following broad areas:

1. *Diagnostic and clinical services.*— There are over 90 clinics specializing in services to the retarded. Over half were established within the past five years. The 20,000 children and adults aided in 1960 represent only a small fraction of those who need the services.

2. *Care in residential institutions.*—Today there are over 200,000 mentally retarded patients in such institutions, approximately 10 per cent more than there were five years ago. The waiting lists continue to grow. Increases in both facilities and manpower are necessary.

3. *Special education.*—The number of mentally retarded enrolled in special educational classes has been doubled over the past decade. Less than 25 per cent of the retarded children have access to special education. Moreover, the classes need teachers specially trained to meet the specialized needs of the retarded. To meet minimum standards, at least 75,000 such teachers are required.

4. *Parent counseling.*—Counseling of parents is now being provided by private physicians, clinic staffs, social workers, nurses, psychologists, and school personnel. Although this service is still in an experimental stage, it offers bright prospects for helping parents to better understand their own social and emotional problems.

5. *Social services.*—Social services provided for mentally retarded children and adults include casework, group work, work placement, foster home care, and day care. These services are an integral part of clinical and rehabilitation programs. Social workers are also active in community organizations and parents' groups.

6. *Vocational rehabilitation.*—In the past five years the number of mentally retarded rehabilitated through state vocational agencies has more than tripled —from 1,094 in 1957 to 3,562 in 1961. In terms of the number who could benefit from rehabilitation services, this number is very small. New knowledge and new techniques are needed, for over 25 per cent of those leaving the special classes still cannot be placed in competitive employment.

7. *Preparation of professional personnel.*—The federal government is now promoting the training of leadership personnel as education, rehabilitation, research, and medical and welfare specialists. In addition, programs are being provided that will increase the competence of the

health professions in providing services for retarded persons. Nevertheless, shortages of qualified personnel remain one of the major obstacles to providing services to retarded individuals and their families.

8. *Research.*—Support for research into the causes, prevention, and amelioration of mental retardation has been greatly increased during the past five years. Considerable progress has been made in the biological aspects of this problem as well as in the behavioral areas. However, we must await major breakthroughs in several areas before we will be able to achieve a more intelligent understanding of the genetic, pathological, psychological, sociological, and environmental aspects of mental retardation.

An acceleration of programs in these broad areas may be achieved by developing a greater public awareness of the problems of mental retardation.

COMMUNITY RESPONSIBILITY FOR THE MENTALLY RETARDED

We are a society possessing strong motivations to assist individuals in need. The outstanding characteristic of our society is the high value we place upon the life of each individual. In this frame of reference, the dignity and the integrity of each individual must be preserved, sustained, and protected.

For a variety of reasons many are unable or cease to contribute and become dependent members of our society. Others, willfully or unknowingly, become a hazard or a threat, and, as a result, these individuals must be isolated for the good of society; thus they become dependent members.

In attempting to meet the needs of these dependent members, our society must recognize and observe the limitations upon infringements of the individual's initiative and freedom. Equally as important is the need to weigh such limitations against the justice and security of society as a whole.

It is important that we note that most members of our society are capable of meeting their own needs by themselves or in concert with members of their immediate families.

Society, then, has two basic functions in meeting the needs of its dependent members. First, it must so organize itself that opportunities are afforded each individual to meet his own needs, and, second, it must develop methods and techniques by which the members can efficiently and economically organize to meet the needs of the individual who is unable to meet his own needs.

The ultimate goal is provision of carefully designed, well-organized, and co-ordinated services and programs of a social welfare nature. The government is one agency that can accomplish these tasks. Many private agencies in our society are capable of fulfilling some of the same functions as government, particularly in the social welfare field.

The ultimate role that government is to play in meeting the social welfare needs is almost entirely dependent upon how our society wishes to view the government's role and the nature and extent of the responsibility it wishes to assign government. It must also consider how it views the capability of private agencies, as contrasted to government agencies, in meeting specific social welfare needs of the individual and the group.

It has been suggested that the government's role should not be determined by a set of "pious principles," but rather, the test should be: "Will the use of government yield advantages unobtainable through voluntary efforts?" "Will it, in the specific instance, damage essential qualities of health or welfare services so that the standards of performance will be impaired?" "Will it interfere unduly with the personal and economic freedoms and responsibilities of either the provider or the recipient of the services?" (U.S. President's Commission on National Goals, p. 252).

We live in an era when the public frequently looks to government—federal, state, and local—to assume an increased responsibility for the health, education, and welfare needs of an ever increasing number of its dependent citizens. This demand is being extended to various provisions for handicapped individuals. To an ever increasing degree, the responsibility is being accepted by government.

This development may be viewed as being both logical and practical, since government is able to attain goals not attainable by individuals, by small groups, or through isolated local efforts. It is, however, a widespread misconception that the problems and needs of the mentally retarded can be resolved merely by providing adequate financial support for the necessary services and needed research.

Providing all of the necessary services, per se, will not solve the multiplicity of problems for the vast majority of the mentally retarded. We are dealing with individuals who, as a group, are heterogeneous and demonstrate great extremes in abilities and needs. These individuals require an accepting environment in order to develop reasonably acceptable behavior patterns and acceptable levels of social and economic attainments. An environment typified by genuine public understanding and acceptance is required; positive attitudes, rather than those based on sympathy or misconceptions, must prevail. The community's threshold of tolerance for the mentally retarded must be raised.

The efforts of society on behalf of the retarded are purposeful insofar as they facilitate the individual to function in society to the maximum of his ability. The patterns of organization and administration of services for this group must be based on that criterion. The pattern calls for co-ordination and integration of efforts by the government and the community, with both sharing responsibility and active participation.

Community and individual citizen participation is necessary if acceptable public attitudes are to be developed and opportunities extended so that the retarded can demonstrate their ability to take their place in the life of a community.

Government has the resources, the administrative organization, and the technical staff to provide for such basic services in the areas of prevention, diagnosis, treatment, education, rehabilitation, care and management, and research. It lacks the general flexibility and sensitivity for creating effective personal involvement of the individual citizen to achieve the goals felt to be desirable.

Equally important in the provision of adequate services is the need, where practical, to make maximum use of existing resources within the community. What needs to be done can frequently be accomplished through already existing administrative units of government. Separate services—separate facilities—should be provided only for those individuals whose needs preclude services from already existing programs, public and private, for the non-handicapped individual. It must be recognized that community attitudes largely determine the degree to which the retarded—individually and as a group—are permitted to utilize these resources.

Because of the pressures of contemporary life and the intense efforts to capture the individual's interest, an individual seems to concentrate only on those social issues in which he has some kind of stake or is in some way personally involved. Where he senses that some other agency—such as government—gives support, he tends to turn his attention to other issues. We can no longer depend merely on publicizing a need and attracting attention via the mass media to gain the co-operation and support of the average citizen.

There is a great need for increased government support but there is a concomitant increased need for the community to create a positive social environment for greater integration of the mentally retarded into the community. The federal government has recognized mental retardation as one of our nation's major social welfare problems and is initiating numerous programs to assist communities in utilizing existing and new knowledge in the resolution of the problems of the mentally retarded.

THE ROLE OF THE FEDERAL GOVERNMENT IN MENTAL RETARDATION

One of the primary concerns of science is to increase man's understanding of his environment, and more important, of himself. In the past one hundred years, science, through research, has made possible an entirely new way of life and has more adequately explained man's place in nature. In the past twenty-five years the changes brought about by increased knowledge and technological advancements are legion! This new knowledge has made possible better control of our environment and improvements in man's physical well being. It has greatly extended both life itself and understanding of the nature of life.

The tremendous body of knowledge now available to the scientist and the array of technical tools suggest that many of the problems yet to be resolved can be resolved at a much more rapid pace than in the past. Such progress and advancement depends upon well-qualified research personnel and adequate research facilities. It is in this context that the federal governmnt has actively supported efforts in both the biological and behavioral aspects of mental retardation.

A review of the activities of the federal government in the field of mental retardation, as well as suggested plans for the future, appears to be in order.

ACTIVITIES OF THE DEPARTMENT OF HEALTH, EDUCATION, AND WELFARE IN MENTAL RETARDATION

Within the Department of Health, Education, and Welfare there are four agencies concerned with various aspects of mental retardation, namely, the Public Health Service, Social Security Administration, Office of Vocational Rehabilitation, and the Office of Education. In general, these agencies are concerned with (a) services, (b) construction of facilities, (c) professional preparation, (d) research studies, and (e) income maintenance.

The programs (U.S. Department of Health, Education, and Welfare, pp. 13 and 14) administered by these four agencies are as follows:

a) Services

(1) Consultation by the Office of Education to state and local school systems, educational personnel, and voluntary groups.

(2) Financial assistance to states under federal-state programs of public assistance.

(3) Benefit payments for the disabled under the federal program of old-age, survivors, and disability insurance.

(4) Consultation and technical services of Children's Bureau staff to state and local communities under the maternal and child health and the child welfare services programs.

(5) Consultation and technical services to state rehabilitation agencies under the Office of Vocational Rehabilitation programs.

(6) Collection and dissemination by the Office of Education of comprehensive basic statistics and reports concerning the education of exceptional children, including the mentally retarded, and

consultation, particularly to state departments of education and to national organizations.

(7) Consultation and technical assistance to state and local agencies provided by the National Institute of Mental Health through its regional office staffs.

(8) Activities relating to the application of knowledge to problems of mental retardation through the neurological and sensory disease service program of the Public Health Service.

b) Construction

(1) Facilities for the mentally retarded under the hospital and medical facilities construction (Hill-Burton) program.

c) Professional preparation

(1) Office of Vocational Rehabilitation grants to educational institutions for training of personnel for all phases of rehabilitation.

(2) Teaching and training grants of National Institutes of Mental Health and Neurological Diseases and Blindness.

(3) Intramural training programs of the Public Health Service.

(4) Office of Education training grants to colleges and universities and State educational agencies for leadership positions in education for the mentally retarded.

d) Research and studies

(1) Intramural and extramural support programs of the National Institute of Mental Health, the National Institute of Neurological Diseases and Blindness, and the Center for Research in Child Health of the Public Health Service.

(2) The Office of Education programs of studies, surveys, and co-operative research.

(3) Special project grants under the maternal and child health program of the Children's Bureau, Social Security Administration.

(4) Research and demonstration projects of the Office of Vocational Rehabilitation.

(5) Income maintenance

(a) Payments to mentally retarded persons under the public assistance program of aid to the permanently and totally disabled of the Welfare Administration (The Secretary's Committee on Mental Retardation, p. 3).

(b) Payments by the Social Security Administration from the old-age and survivors insurance trust fund in behalf of persons whose disability commenced before age 18 and continued thereafter (Secretary's Committee, p. 3).

FEDERAL EXPENDITURES FOR MENTAL RETARDATION PROGRAMS

The programs (Secretary's Committee, p. 1) to combat mental retardation under the authority of the Department of Health, Education, and Welfare for fiscal year 1963 and proposed for 1964 are summarized in Table 2.

The legislation proposed for 1964 represents an increase of 76,219,000 dollars over 1963. The amount allocated in 1963 more than doubles the expenditures of 1959 (Department of Health, Education, and Welfare, p. 17).

CO-ORDINATION OF ACTIVITIES OF THE DEPARTMENT OF HEALTH, EDUCATION, AND WELFARE

Activities in all areas relating to mental retardation are co-ordinated and planned through the Secretary of the Department. This office (Department of Health, Education, and Welfare, p. 17) is chiefly concerned with the following:

1. Serves as the principal adviser to the Secretary for improving the programs and activities of the Department related to mental retardation.

2. Provides staff co-ordination and direction to the staff offices of the Office of the Secretary and to operating agencies relative to the planning, execution, co-ordination, reporting, and evaluation of mental retardation activities.

3. Maintains liaison on behalf of the Department with the President's Panel on Mental Retardation, with other interested federal agencies, and with professional and other groups.

4. Provides leadership to the Department's Committee on Mental Retardation.

DEPARTMENT OF HEALTH, EDUCATION, AND WELFARE COMMITTEE ON MENTAL RETARDATION

The Committee on Mental Retardation of the Department consists of representatives from each of its agencies. The Committee serves in an advisory capacity to the Secretary and in an advisory capacity to the department as a whole (Department of Health, Education, and Welfare, p. 18). It also co-ordinates the activities and efforts of the President's Panel on Mental Retardation.

PRESIDENT'S PANEL ON MENTAL RETARDATION

Beginning in late 1961, the problem of mental retardation received attention from the highest level of the federal government, through the efforts of the "President's Panel on Mental Retardation."

In its report, "National Action to Combat Mental Retardation," to the President, the Panel summarizes its almost two hundred recommendations (President's Panel, pp. 14 and 15) in the following eight broad areas:

1. *Research* in the causes of retardation and in methods of care, rehabilitation, and learnings.

2. *Preventive health measures* includ-

ing (*a*) a greatly strengthened program of maternal and infant care directed first at the centers of population where prematurity and the rate of "damaged" children are high; (*b*) protection against such known hazards to pregnancy as radiation and harmful drugs; and (*c*) extended diagnostic and screening services.

3. *Strengthened educational programs generally and extended and enriched programs of special education* in public and

TABLE 2

PROGRAMS TO COMBAT MENTAL RETARDATION

PROGRAMS UNDER PRESENT AUTHORITY	APPROPRIATION	
	1963	1964
Research, training, services, and other activities relating to prevention and treatment	$ 31,704,000	$ 51,048,000
Public assistance and Social Security payments to persons disabled because of mental retardation	96,800,000	111,300,000
Activities for which new legislation is proposed	. . . .	42,375,000
Grand total.	$128,504,000	$204,723,000

private schools closely co-ordinated with vocational guidance, vocational rehabilitation, and specific training and preparation for employment; education for the adult mentally retarded and workshops geared to their needs.

4. *More comprehensive and improved clinical and social services.*

5. *Improved methods and facilities for care*, with emphasis on the home and the development of a wide range of local community facilities.

6. *A new legal, as well as social, concept of the retarded*, including protection of their civil rights; life guardianship provisions when needed; an enlightened attitude on the part of the law and the

courts; and clarification of the theory of responsibility in criminal acts.

7. *Helping overcome the serious problems of manpower* as they affect the entire field of science and every type of service through extended programs of recruiting with fellowships and increased opportunities for graduate students and those preparing for the professions to observe and learn at first hand about the phenomenon of retardation. Because there will never be a fully adequate supply of personnel in this field and for other cogent reasons, the Panel has emphasized the need for more volunteers in health, recreation, and welfare activities and for a domestic Peace Corps to stimulate voluntary service.

8. *Programs of education and information to increase public awareness* of the problem of mental retardation.

In addition to a strong emphasis on *research* and *prevention,* the report recommends the following:

1. That programs for the retarded, including modern day care, recreation, residential services, and ample educational and vocational opportunities, be *comprehensive.*

2. That they operate in or close to the communities where the retarded live— that is, that they be *community-centered.*

3. That services be so organized as (*a*) to provide a central or fixed point for the guidance, assistance, and protection of retarded persons if and when needed, and (*b*) to assure a sufficient array or *continuum* of services to meet different types of need.

4. That private agencies as well as public agencies at the local, state, and federal levels continue to provide resources and to increase them for this worthy purpose. While the federal government can assist, the principal responsibility for financing and improving services for the mentally retarded must continue to be borne by states and local communities.

There is no doubt that through the active and immediate implementation of the Panel's recommendations, one will witness increased co-ordinated efforts on behalf of the federal government, all directed toward "a search for solutions to the problems of mental retardation" (President's Panel, p. 196).

A FINAL NOTE

How, then, can we marshal the multiplicity of forces so necessary to resolve the problems growing out of, and associated with, this complex phenomenon we have so simply labeled "mental retardation"?

The present accumulation of knowledge relating to mental retardation is insufficient to immediately initiate effective programs of prevention, methods of treatment, and services to minimize the effects of mental retardation. Obviously this can only be accomplished through greatly expanded research efforts.

Yet the acquisition of new knowledge through research is insufficient unless there is widespread dissemination and utilization of research findings and information. The importance of immediate and accurate reporting of research, as well as the ease of retrieval, has long been recognized.

The communication of research findings and information from one professional discipline to another is basic to the resolution of the present problems confronting the scientist when he attempts to explore even a single aspect of the complex condition of mental retardation. Improvement in communication between the professional disciplines warrants consideration by the scientific community. This text is one attempt to foster interdisciplinary communication and collaborative research.

REFERENCES

HEBER, R. (ed.). 1958. A manual on terminology and classification in mental retardation. *Monogr. Suppl., Amer. J. Ment. Defic.,* **64,** No. 2.

THE PRESIDENT'S PANEL ON MENTAL RETARDATION. October, 1962. *Report to the President: A Proposed Program for National Action to Combat Mental Retardation.* Washington, D.C.: U.S. Government Printing Office.

THE SECRETARY'S COMMITTEE ON MENTAL RETARDATION. February, 1962. *Mental Retardation Program of the U.S. Department of Health, Education, and Welfare* *(Fiscal Year 1964).* Washington, D.C.: U.S. Department of Health, Education, and Welfare.

U.S. DEPARTMENT OF HEALTH, EDUCATION, AND WELFARE. May, 1962. Mental Retardation. *Activities of the U.S. Department of Health, Education, and Welfare.* Washington, D.C.: U.S. Government Printing Office.

U.S. PRESIDENT'S COMMISSION ON NATIONAL GOALS. 1960. Goals for Americans. *Report of the President's Commission on National Goals.* Prentice-Hall.

PSYCHOLOGICAL EVALUATION
AND DIFFERENTIAL DIAGNOSIS

Arthur L. Benton

Psychological evaluations are made for a variety of purposes in the field of mental retardation. Perhaps the most prominent of these purposes are: (1) to determine whether or not an individual should be classified in the broad category of the mentally retarded; (2) if it is concluded that he does belong in the category of mentally retarded, to determine the type or subgroup of the broad category in which he should be placed; (3) to make a prognostic evaluation in respect to course of development and response to special educational, psychotherapeutic, or physiotherapeutic measures; (4) if it is concluded that he does not belong in the category of mentally retarded, to determine whether he should be classified in a diagnostic category other than that of "normality" (i.e., problem of differential diagnosis).

The diagnostic procedures and judgments which are covered by the collective term "psychological evaluation" bear a reciprocal relationship to fundamental theory in the field of mental retardation. In clinical work, diagnostic practice is dependent upon, and, in large measure, determined by, prevailing theoretical assumptions about the nature of mental retardation. Thus the decision, on the basis of a psychological evaluation, that a given individual is or is not mentally retarded ultimately depends as much on the clinician's fundamental conception of the nature of mental retardation as it does on the specific findings of the examination. For example, the same findings (e.g., IQ 70 on the WISC) will lead the

examiner with a purely "psychometric" concept of mental retardation to make that inference and, at the same time, may lead the clinician whose concept of mental retardation implies etiological factors to conclude that, however handicapped or deprived the individual may be, he is not mentally retarded. Similarly, the initial postulation of specific types of mental retardation is a prerequisite for the assignment of an individual to one or another type on the basis of his psychological test performances or other aspects of his behavior. To take a final example, fundamental distinctions between mental retardation and other forms of behavioral maldevelopment (e.g., between "true" retardation and childhood autism) must be drawn before differential diagnosis by means of the psychological evaluation can be accomplished.

On the other hand, in investigative work, the relationship between basic theory and diagnostic practice is reversed. Here the psychological evaluation is utilized as an empirical test of the tenability of the theoretical formulation. For example, the validity of some aspects of the familiar dichotomy between "brain-damaged" and "familial," "exogenous" and "endogenous," and "neurological" and "non-neurological" types of mental retardation ultimately depends upon whether the psychological evaluation does disclose the behavioral differences predicted by this theoretical classification. Similarly, the distinction which is so often drawn between "true" and "pseudo" mental retardation will stand or fall on the empirical findings provided by the psychological evaluation. If the latter cannot provide the differential observations necessary to make the distinction in practice, the theoretical formulation is operationally meaningless.

Because of this close interdependence of fundamental theory and diagnostic practice, a review of research on psychological evaluation and differential diagnosis must concern itself with theoretical issues as well as with the findings of empirical studies in the field of diagnosis. For this reason, the present chapter will begin with a discussion of those aspects of the conceptual framework underlying current thinking about mental retardation which bear more or less directly on psychodiagnostic practice. In the light of this discussion, the empirical literature on psychological evaluation and differential diagnosis will be reviewed. Because of space limitations, this review is necessarily selective in nature and consequently must omit mention of many studies in the general area. Finally, an attempt will be made to indicate the directions which future developmental work might take.

As used in this chapter, the term "psychological evaluation" will refer primarily to objective procedures (usually, but not always, standardized) for the assessment of general intelligence, specific aspects of intellectual functioning (e.g., memory, conceptual thinking), language functions, personality, psychomotor skill, and sensory discriminative capacity. Studies based on interview findings, life-history studies, naturalistic observations, or special experimental procedures (e.g., conditioning) will not receive consideration, although reference to a few studies of this type will be made.

THEORETICAL CONSIDERATIONS

CONCEPT OF MENTAL RETARDATION

On first encounter, mental retardation may appear to be a fairly simple and straightforward concept. It is taken to denote a tye of social incompetence or behavioral maladaptation which is determined by a global developmental deficit in intellectual capacity. In turn, this developmental deficit is conceived to be a result of the operation of either hereditary or exogenous factors, the latter being of a congenital nature or having produced their effects in the early years of life. It is assumed that the intermediate element between the behavioral subnormality and the basic causative factor (whether it be hereditary or acquired) is defective cerebral structure and function. A fundamental distinction is drawn between the condition and other types of social incompetence or behavioral maladaptation such as psychosis, incapacitating neurosis, or antisocial personality development. Once the diagnosis is established and the severity of the intellectual deficit is determined, one feels able to predict a typical course and outcome with a fair degree of confidence.

Yet the apparent simplicity and clarity of the concept are deceptive. First, it is doubtful that any concept which possesses at the same time social, behavioral, developmental, etiologic, neuropathologic, and prognostic implications can be thought of as being a "simple" concept. Secondly, as a matter of empirical fact, one often finds that one or more features are not present, or at least not demonstrable, in individual cases. This finding, which holds for every feature with the exception of the developmental aspect, raises the question as to which features are to be considered as *definitive* characteristics. There is considerable disagreement among experts in the field on this question. Social incompetence or behavioral maladaptation is regarded by many, but not all, students as a basic criterion. Similarly, intellectual subnormality in the strict sense, i.e., defective "psychometric" intelligence, is generally (but not universally) accepted as a nuclear trait. From the etiologic standpoint, mental retardation is often assumed to imply defect or disease of critical cerebral mechanisms as the proximate cause of the behavioral inferiority, but, at least in the case of high-grade retardates, this proposition has been criticized as lacking a substantial empirical foundation and as being unduly restrictive. There is further lack of agreement concerning the logical status of the factors of course and outcome as defining characteristics of mental retardation. Some clinicians have included a poor prognosis as an essential characteristic, while others have held that a predicted future course and terminal status cannot provide a firm foundation for diagnosis. Even with respect to the idea that mental retardation is a developmental disorder, there is general agreement only with respect to the obvious denotation that the condition must be manifested at some time before maturity is reached. Beyond this, there is disagreement concerning the specific implications of the term and also criticism that, as a defining characteristic, it can be equally well applied to a variety of other behavioral disorders in both children and adults.

THE CRITERION OF SOCIAL INCOMPETENCE

There is, and has been for a long time, widespread acceptance of the proposition that the factor of social competence or over-all quality of behavioral adaptation is the ultimate determinant of the diagnosis of mental retardation. In essence, this proposition states that no matter what specific and striking behavioral weaknesses in the intellectual, affective, or conative spheres a person may show he can be considered to be mentally retarded only if his socio-economic and personal competence is significantly inferior to that shown by the great majority of his contemporaries. As long ago as 1890, the British psychiatrist Charles Mercier made this point, remarking that a man may be extremely dull and stupid, but if he can earn enough to permit him to maintain a standard of living appropriate to his social class and if his moral conduct is satisfactory, he cannot be considered to be mentally retarded. Only when his intellectual deficiency is so serious as to make him economically or morally incompetent can the judgment of mental retardation be passed upon him.

Modern authorities have continued to emphasize that the essence of mental retardation is gross behavioral maladaptation and not merely intellectual deficiency. The experts assembled at a White House conference on child health and protection drew a distinction between feeblemindedness and intellectual subnormality, characterizing the first as mental subnormality *with* social incompetence and the second as mental subnormality which is *not* necessarily accompanied by social incompetence (Ellis, 1933). Thus the mentally subnormal individual was viewed as one who was intellectually handicapped but not necessarily retarded. Similarly, A. F. Tredgold (1952), the author of the most influential English-language textbook in the field, rejected both educational achievement and performance on standardized intelligence tests as satisfactory criteria of mental retardation and considered that social competence was "not only the most logical and scientific concept of mental deficiency, but . . . the only criterion which the community can justly impose." Finally, Doll (1941) has been particularly insistent upon a basic distinction between mental deficiency and intellectual subnormality, the distinction resting on the issue of the social competence of the individual.

It is apparent that from this standpoint the diagnosis of mental retardation will depend in large part, if not exclusively, upon a broad social value judgment which assesses the adaptation of the individual to his milieu. Indeed, as Burt (1947) and McCulloch (1947) have pointed out, the concept then becomes essentially administrative in nature, implying the necessity for appropriate social action in the form of special appraisal, treatment, custody, and training.

This emphasis on social incompetence or behavioral maladaptation as the basically definitive characteristic of mental retardation has not escaped criticism. It has been pointed out that "social incompetence" is a frequent characteristic of all types of behavioral abnormality and hence cannot serve to distinguish mental retardation from other types of developmental deficit such as antisocial personality, psychosis, severe neurosis, and some forms of psychomotor epilepsy which are also associated with gross behavioral maladaptation. Thus, Tredgold's exclusive reliance on the criterion of social competence led him (quite logically) to include "moral imbecility" as a form of mental retardation, so that account could be taken of patients with adequate psychometric intelligence who showed antisocial or immoral behavior (i.e., the type of patient diagnosed by most psychiatrists as an antisocial or psychopathic personality). Another shortcoming of the criterion of social competence is that it represents a value judgment which is rather fluid and which necessarily varies with the nature and conditions of a society. According to McCulloch (1947), a society may be said to set up a "threshold of tolerance" which it employs to distinguish social competence and acceptable behavioral adaptation from incompetence and maladaptation; he further points out that a variety of social and economic factors may cause significant fluctuations in the threshold. Penrose (1949) has also emphasized that "social criteria are not only changeable; they are relative, not absolute." Hence, to make a diagnostic inference of mental retardation solely on the basis of a finding of social incompetence in a particular environment (e.g., a competitive urban setting) at a particular time is unjustified, since the same person might well be found competent "in a different environment or according to different standards." In support of this general thesis, Arthur (1947) has cited actual cases in which application of the criterion of social competence would place one in the awkward position of having to consider a person mentally retarded in one situation but not in another.

The emphasis on social incompetence or global behavioral maladaptation as a fundamental criterion arose in part as a reaction against the tendency to rely exclusively on scholastic or psychometric criteria of mental retardation. As such, it has no doubt played a very useful function by reminding workers in the field that in some respects the idea of mental retardation (as of any other behavioral abnormality) is a social, and not a theoretical, issue. However, while granting the essential validity of this point, one has the impression that at times there has been a somewhat excessive insistence on it, for the limitations of the concept of "social competence" as a theoretical criterion of mental retardation must also be taken into account. As has been seen, it provides no basis for differentiating between mental retardation and other forms of developmental behavioral maldevelopment, assuming that one is interested in making such a differentiation. Furthermore, its sensitivity to variation in social, economic, and geographic conditions makes it somewhat unstable from an operational standpoint. Perhaps it is best conceived as a frequent accompaniment, rather than a criterion, of mental retardation. Other distinctive behavioral characteristics must be demonstrable to establish the diagnosis.

THE CRITERION OF INTELLECTUAL SUBNORMALITY

It is generally considered that intellectual subnormality is the basic trait which defines the form of behavioral maladaptation known as mental retardation. As has been pointed out, there has not been complete agreement on this point. One exception to the rule is the concept of moral defect, advanced by Tredgold (1952), as a particular form of mental retardation. A moral defective, according to Tredgold,

differs from the ordinary type of defectives in that he is neither illiterate, deficient in his range of general knowledge nor lacking in understanding; but is defective in common sense or wisdom, and is at the same time possessed of strongly marked antisocial instinctive impulses. It is necessary to emphasize . . . that such a person is *mentally* defective.

This clinical picture of antisocial or immoral conduct within the setting of adequate psychometric intelligence corresponds to the diagnostic categories of antisocial personality and psychopathic personality of current psychiatric nosology, and Tredgold seems to have been virtually alone among American and British authorities in classifying it under the rubric of mental retardation. However, the concept has been held by a few Continental workers (e.g., Dubitscher, 1936).

A second exception to the idea that psychometric subnormality is a necessary characteristic of mental retardation is represented by the concept of "camouflaged mental deficiency" which has been postulated by Delay, Pichot, and Perse (1952a). Unlike "moral defect," this condition presents no question of serious antisocial or immoral conduct. Rather, it is the clinical picture presented by an individual with adequate psychometric intelligence who, however, clearly shows a lack of practical intelligence in his daily living, as manifested by an incapacity to meet successfully the intellectual problems inherent in the usual social situations, e.g., traveling in the city, making purchases at a store. Thus the twenty-seven-year-old woman described as an example of the condition had a Wechsler-Bellevue Full Scale IQ of 103 with a

Verbal Scale IQ of 121 and a Performance Scale IQ of 82. Brought up in an educated household, she was docile and pleasant, showed excellent conversational skill, and helped in household tasks as well as in the activities of a charitable organization. However, her scholastic progress had been extremely poor; she was incapable of self-directed action and behaved quite unintelligently in practical matters. The discrepancy between the Verbal and Performance IQ's and a relatively poor performance on the Comprehension subtest (weighted score = 6) are cited as pointing to an atypical type of mental retardation, which might well be missed on cursory examination because of the patient's excellent performance on tasks sensitive to the influence of cultural factors and rote learning.

Certainly it would be possible to explain cases such as these on bases other than that of "camouflaged mental deficiency." However, taken as it stands, the interpretation by Delay, Pichot, and Perse, that these cases represent a type of mental retardation without global intellectual subnormality, is a conceptualization of considerable theoretical importance and deserves careful analysis.

Finally, another exception to the principle that significant intellectual subnormality is a necessary ingredient of mental retardation is provided by the statistics of institutions for the mentally retarded, which almost invariably show a small proportion of patients with IQ of 80 or above. When these represent cases of sensorimotor deficit or convulsive disorder, the specific reasons for institutionalization are self-evident, and such cases obviously do not constitute exceptions to the rule. But even when these cases are excluded from consideration, there still remains a small number of patients without major physical handicap or significant intellectual subnormality whose behavioral maladaptation has been of such a nature as to cause them to be institutionalized as "mentally retarded." Thus, to take a single example, approximately 1 per cent ($N = 53$) of the patients in the public institutions for the mentally retarded of Massachusetts in 1940 had IQ's of 80 or above (Perkins and Dayton, 1940). Forty-four of these cases carried diagnoses of "familial" or "undifferentiated" mental retardation and were presumably free from significant sensorimotor handicap or epilepsy.

Despite these exceptions, there can be little doubt that intellectual subnormality *is* the most salient characteristic of mental retardation as a discriminable type of behavioral maladaptation. This subnormality is assumed to be pervasive in nature—extending over a wide range of intellectual operations—and a fundamental distinction is drawn between the global intellectual deficit of mental retardation and more specific deficits such as oral or written language disabilities and visuomotor impairments. One of the most important functions of the psychological evaluation is to aid in clarifying this distinction. However, while the subnormality is more or less global in character, all intellectual skills do not necessarily show an equal or near-equal level of development. A greater or lesser degree of irregularity, or "scatter," of function is likely to be manifested, and it is not unusual for a high-grade retardate to show an average development of ability in one or more aspects of intellectual activity. The extreme in this respect is represented by idiot savants with astoundingly high capacity in specialized operations such as rote memory, calculation, drawing, or music (cf. Anastasi and Levee, 1960).

The significance of irregularity in the development of various abilities has been interpreted in different ways. It is often conceived to be the result of the operation of more or less adventitious factors of a physical, psychological, or social nature and accepted as an expected natural variation. At the other extreme, there is the point of view of Jastak (1949) that all variation is quite significant and that general level of intellectual capacity should be indexed by a person's most highly developed abilities and not by a measure of central tendency which takes account of all abilities. This question of the diagnostic implications of irregularity in the development of various abilities will be considered in detail in a later section on the psychometric determination of mental retardation. Obviously, the greater the "scatter" of intellectual abilities into the average range, the less "pervasive" must be the person's intellectual subnormality. From both a theoretical and practical standpoint, the basic issue is how much of this type of irregularity can be present without invalidating an inference of the global intellectual subnormality which defines mental retardation.

PROGNOSIS

The last decade has seen a profound change in the conception of the role which course and outcome play in the concept of mental retardation. Until quite recently it was assumed, implicitly or explicitly, that a poor prognosis was a defining characteristic of the condition. The assumption was implicitly reflected in the fairly standard clinical practice of changing an original diagnosis of mental retardation in the case of a patient who was once judged to be defective but whose status at some later date no longer supported the diagnosis. In short, a change in a patient's status operated retroactively to revise the original diagnosis because of the dominating influence of the assumption, "once defective always defective." This principle was also explicitly stated in definitions of mental retardation such as, for example, the well-known "inclusive concept" of Doll (1941), in which a necessary criterion for the diagnosis was the qualification that the behavioral maladaptation must obtain at maturity. In Doll's view, the concept of the essential incurability of feeble-mindedness is part of the diagnostic picture. If the prognosis suggests a possibility of amelioration of symptoms amounting to prospects of ultimate normality, then a diagnosis of mental retardation is not warranted (Doll, 1947).

The same idea was expressed in the contention of Porteus (1941) that an individual who has been diagnosed as mentally retarded on the basis of a poor test performance and "who finally functions at a normal level proves thereby that he never was feebleminded."

The validity of this idea of a poor prognosis and "incurability," which was so integral a part of the concept of mental retardation, has come under sharp attack on both logical and empirical grounds, and a broader view, which leaves the question open to empirical study and therapeutic endeavor, has taken its place. Benton (1956a) has pointed out some of the logical objections to the employment of the criterion of "incurability" in defining mental retardation. In essence, it represents the last application of the old doctrine of "malignancy" (i.e., of a poor outcome being inherently characteristic of a disease and therefore essential for its diagnosis), which was characteristic of a bygone era of medicine. The course and outcome of any condition are, of course, a function of its nature. But they depend quite as much on the prevailing level of medical and educational technology. Since the efficiency of this technology changes with time, a diagnostic concept which is based on course and outcome, rather than on past and present conditions, is not only logically objectionable but is also untenable in suggesting the future impossibility of amelioration and cure with advances in therapeutic efficacy. Similarly, Clarke and Clarke (1955) have insisted that a condition of mental retardation may be impermanent and, hence, that a favorable course and

outcome do not necessarily invalidate the diagnosis. Cantor (1955) has also emphasized the disadvantages of a concept which includes incurability in its definition and has pointed out that it is possible to formulate an operationally satisfactory concept of mental retardation, which will permit prognostic statements on a probability basis.

Empirical studies of course and outcome in psychometrically defined mental retardation as well as the findings of the newer therapeutic procedures based on biochemical investigation (cf. the chaps. by McCandless, on the relationship of environmental factors to intellectual functioning, and by Waisman and Gerritsen, on the biochemistry of mental defect) have also impaired the cogency of the criterion of poor prognosis. For example, follow-up studies of high-grade defectives find that many individuals who were diagnosed in childhood as mentally retarded and who were treated as such (i.e., were institutionalized or placed in special classes) show adequate social competence and some improvement in intellectual level in adult life. In line with this, some observers (e.g., Pototzky and Grigg, 1942; Pflugfelder, 1949) have been impressed with the occurrence of a "late maturation" of intellectual functions in retardates. The reasons for such changes in intellectual level and behavioral adaptation remain a matter of conjecture. Whatever the determinants may be, the fact that such changes occur is incontrovertible.

Current thinking, then, does not consider that course and outcome represent an essential criterion of mental retardation. Prognosis is viewed as a variable factor which is open to investigation and modification. This view in no way denies the possibility of prognostic evaluations of an empirical nature, based on comparisons of present findings with past experience and consisting essentially of predictions of the most likely future state of affairs. One of the traditional functions of the psychological evaluation has been to provide the basis for such a prediction.

NEUROPATHOLOGIC ASPECTS

A detailed analysis of the neuropathology of mental defect is presented in the chapter by Malamud and has no place in the present section, the only purpose of which is to consider the logical status of neuropathologic factors in the concept of mental retardation. The basic question in this respect is whether mental retardation necessarily implies cerebral pathology in the clinical neurologic sense of that term, i.e., structural alteration leading to cerebral dysfunction.

The results of modern neuropathologic study in the field of mental retardation (e.g., Schob, 1930; Weygandt, 1936; Benda, 1952; Tredgold, 1952; Masland, 1958) may be summarized as follows: Central nervous system damage is usually encountered in low-grade defect. However, it has not been possible to demonstrate a close correlation between the extent of structural damage and the severity of the behavioral defect. In high-grade retardation the findings are somewhat different. While pathologic alteration is often shown, some cases present an apparently normal anatomy and histology, on the basis of current methods of investigation.

The interpretation of this last finding is discussed in Malamud's chapter. Here it is appropriate to point out that one's basic approach to the question depends upon one's convictions concerning the place which neuropathologic factors must be accorded in the concept of mental retardation. The traditional position is that mental retardation implies cerebral defect or disease as the proximate cause of the observed behavioral maladaptation. For example, according to Tredgold (1952),

the brain is the organ for the manifestations of mind [and] the material basis of mental deficiency consists in an inadequate develop-

ment, or persistent imperfection of function, of the neurones of the mantle of the brain . . . the general statement may be made that primary amentia is the result of an inherent incapacity of these neurones to attain an adequate degree of development and function, while secondary amentia is due to their development having been arrested by some external cause.

From this standpoint, it is assumed that the negative findings in neuropathologic studies of high-grade retardates reflect the limitations of current techniques of investigation and that improved methods of analysis would disclose the postulated cerebral defect.

This assumption is certainly quite tenable. However, a newer point of view questions the necessity for making it in the first place. This point of view acknowledges the possibility that the majority of cases of mental retardation are to be ascribed to cerebral disease or maldevelopment but rejects the assumption that *all* cases necessarily rest on this basis. This position finds support from current conceptualizations about the nature of behavioral disorders in general. It is not believed that neurosis, psychosis, or psychopathic personality development is necessarily based on cerebral defect (in the clinical neurologic sense of the term and ignoring the biophilosophic truism that disturbed behavior necessarily implies altered somatic structure and/or function). Griesinger's dictum that "all mental disease is brain disease" has long been abandoned. Hence, there is no compelling reason to maintain it as a fundamental assumption in the case of high-grade mental retardation. This more eclectic point of view also finds support in the evidence, provided by recent studies, that cultural and emotional factors can play a significant role in determining general level of intellectual function (cf. the chap. by McCandless, on the relation of environmental factors to intellectual functioning).

The concept of mental retardation held

by most clinicians in the field at the present time is that it is a form of behavioral maladaptation determined by structural cerebral deficit and that clinically similar behavioral pictures which are not ascribable to such defect do not represent instances of "true" mental retardation. However, the broader conceptualization steadily gains ground, and an increasing number of workers are prepared to admit the possibility of forms of mental retardation which are not primarily determined by structural cerebral alterations of the "classic" type. In any event, whether the latter type of case is viewed as belonging within the conceptual framework of mental retardation or not, an important goal of the psychological examination is to ascertain whether there are behavioral criteria which permit differentiation between the two types.

CONCEPT OF "PSEUDOFEEBLE-MINDEDNESS"

A clinician whose concept of mental retardation includes structural cerebral defect and a poor prognosis as necessary elements may encounter a patient who shows the behavioral characteristics of the condition (i.e., social incompetence by reason of developmental intellectual subnormality) but not the neuropathologic or prognostic features. When this occurs, his concept of mental retardation forces him to conclude that the patient does not belong in this diagnostic category. To take account of the similarities between the patient's condition and "true" mental retardation, he designates the former as "pseudofeeblemindedness." In so doing, the clinician is following a familiar practice in medical nosology (cf. the designation of "pseudobulbar palsy" to cover disorders of functions innervated by brain stem nuclei but caused by supranuclear lesions).

The concept of pseudofeeblemindedness has attained considerable importance in recent decades. Like many clini-

cal concepts, its limits have not been precisely defined, and it has been used in different senses by different people. The term was early used in the psychoanalytic literature to refer to conditions of mental retardation (from the behavioral standpoint) that were due to emotionally determined inhibitions of intellectual development (Bornstein, 1930; Bergler, 1932; Mänchen, 1936). It was employed by Bijou (1939) to designate both defective performance on intelligence tests of the verbal type by individuals with specific language handicaps and defective performance on non-verbal intelligence tests by individuals with "emotional instability." Arthur (1947) has utilized the concept to cover intellectual subnormality associated with a wide variety of factors—special disabilities, delayed speech, severe early illness, brain damage with selective effects on behavioral capacities, and physical handicaps. Finally, Delay, Pichot, and Perse (1952b) consider that schizoid personality developments which involve a passive and immature behavioral adaptation in association with adequate psychometric intelligence may be viewed as a form of "pseudofeeblemindedness."

Thus, pseudofeeblemindedness has come to mean many things. It has meant simply a mistake in diagnosis, as, for example, when mental retardation is confused with some specific disability. It has been used to refer to states of mental retardation ("real" or "apparent," depending upon one's assumptions) which show a favorable course and outcome. It has meant states of mental retardation which are determined by factors (physical, emotional, social) other than the traditional factor of structural cerebral defect.

Setting aside its unjustified application to cover errors in diagnosis, it is evident that the concept is required only by those clinicians whose concept of "true" mental retardation includes a distinctive pathogenesis and a poor prognosis as necessary features. On the other hand, those who have a broader concept, which allows for the operation of a number of causative agents in the production of mental retardation as well as for variation in course and outcome, feel no need for it. The latter hold that what has been called "pseudofeeblemindedness" simply represents specific forms of mental retardation. Hence, in the view of some workers (e.g., Cantor, 1955; Clarke and Clarke, 1955; Benton, 1956*a*), the concept serves no useful function and might well be discarded.

CLASSIFICATION

The grouping of observed phenomena into classes or categories is a practical activity, which is determined by prevailing interests and knowledge and which is designed to aid accurate recognition, advance fundamental understanding, and facilitate management and treatment. Since interests and the state of knowledge do not remain fixed, classifications are almost, by definition, of a tentative nature and subject to revision from time to time. Moreover, since they "are arbitrary language systems which vary according to their intended purpose" (Heber, 1959), more than one system of classification can be applied to the same phenomena at any one time.

Classification in the field of mental retardation has shown two salient characteristics. First, with advances in knowledge and new developments in therapeutic approach, there has been an evolution from extremely broad categorizations (e.g., hereditary vs. acquired) to systems with more numerous and more specifically defined categories. Secondly, corresponding to the respective interests of medical and psycho-educational personnel in the field, it has been typical for two types of classification to exist side by side—a medical classification, with etiologic and pathogenetic implications, and a behavioral classification, with implications for social adaptability, education, and vocational training.

The current thinking of professional workers in the United States on the problem of classification has been crystallized in the new system of terminology and classification adopted by the American Association on Mental Deficiency (Heber, 1959). The *Medical Classification* (Table 1) provides for eight broad cate-

TABLE 1

OUTLINE OF MEDICAL CLASSIFICATION
OF MENTAL DEFICIENCY

I. Diseases and conditions due to infection.
II. Diseases and conditions due to intoxication.
III. Diseases and conditions due to trauma or physical agent.
IV. Diseases and conditions due to disorder of metabolism, growth or nutrition.
V. Diseases and conditions due to new growths.
VI. Diseases and conditions due to (unknown) prenatal influence.
VII. Diseases and conditions due to unknown or uncertain cause with structural reactions manifest.
VIII. Due to uncertain (or presumed psychologic) cause with functional reaction alone manifest.

SUPPLEMENTARY CLASSIFICATION

1. With genetic component.
2. With secondary cranial anomaly.
3. With impairment of special senses.
4. With convulsive disorder.
5. With psychiatric impairment.
6. With motor dysfunction.

Adapted from Heber (1959).

gories which are defined essentially by etiologic or pathogenetic factors—infection, intoxication, trauma, metabolic disorder, undetermined prenatal influences of a physical nature, encephalopathy of undetermined origin, and familial or psychogenic determinants. Subgroups within each broad category are represented by the second digit of the diagnostic code (e.g., under Category I, prenatal infectious encephalopathy is 11, and postnatal infectious encephalopathy is 12). Specific diseases are represented by the third digit of the code (e.g., congenital rubella is 11.2, and congenital toxoplasmosis is 11.4). Finally, statements concerning six supplementary factors (genetic component, secondary cranial anomaly, sensory impairment, convulsive disorder, psychiatric impairment, motor dysfunction) are added to the basic classification but cannot be used as a primary diagnosis.

TABLE 2

BEHAVIORAL CLASSIFICATION
MEASURED INTELLIGENCE

LEVEL	SD RANGE	IQ RANGE		
		WAIS or WISC	Stanford-Binet	Arthur Scale I
VI...	<−1.01	>84	>83	>83
V....	−1.01 to −2.00	70–84	68–83	67–83
IV...	−2.01 to −3.00	55–69	52–67	50–66
III..	−3.01 to −4.00	40–54	36–51	33–49
II...	−4.01 to −5.00	......	20–35	16–32
I....	>−5.00	......	<20	<16

Adapted from Heber (1959).

Certain features of the classification may be remarked. First, prognostic considerations find no place in it. Secondly, the factor of heredity does not function as a primary principle of classification as it did in older systems. This is not to say that it is ignored, for when a genetic factor is known or suspected, provision is made for indicating its nature as a supplementary term in the diagnosis (e.g., dominant gene type transmission, etc.). However, in those conditions in which an hereditary factor is operative, the primary criterion for classification is the observed pathology rather than the specific nature of the genetic component. Finally, provision is made for psychogenic mental retardation, i.e., for forms of retardation that are not a result of structural defect of the central nervous system. That this concept is not viewed with confidence is suggested by the terminology employed in the title of this broad category, "Due to Uncertain (or Presumed Psychologic) Cause." Thus the

new medical classification accepts the possibility of psychogenic mental retardation but reserves judgment on the question of its actual existence.

The new *Behavioral Classification* describes mental retardation in terms of two positively correlated dimensions, *measured intelligence* and *adaptive behavior*. Despite the positive association of these two components, the possibility of a significant discrepancy between them in individual cases is believed to be of sufficient importance to warrant a dual classification. *Measured intelligence* (Table 2) is assessed objectively in terms of performance on an appropriate mental test battery and is described in terms of standard deviation units, thus eliminating a long-standing source of confusion and misinterpretation in the comparison of IQ scores derived from different tests or at different ages. Provision is made for classification into one of

TABLE 3

BEHAVIORAL CLASSIFICATION
ADAPTIVE BEHAVIOR

Level	Description	SD Range on Scales
V.....	No impairment	−1.00
IV....	Mild negative deviation	−1.01 to −2.25
III...	Moderate negative deviation	−2.26 to −3.50
II....	Severe negative deviation	−3.51 to −4.75
I.....	Profound negative deviation	>−4.75

Adapted from Heber (1959).

five levels of subnormal intelligence, ranging from mild retardation (1–2 SD's below the mean of the population and corresponding roughly to the "borderline" category of older systems) to profound retardation (more than 5 SD's below the population mean and corresponding roughly to the "idiot" category of older systems).

Adaptive behavior (Table 3) refers essentially to the degree to which the individual can maintain himself independently in the community as well as his ability to conform to established social norms of personal behavior. It is assessed on the basis of general observation and/or the use of such instruments as the Vineland Social Maturity Scale. Provision is made for classification of the individual into one of four levels of subnormality in this respect, ranging from mild inadequacy (1.0–2.25 SD's below the population mean) to profound incompetence (more than 4.75 SD's below the population mean). In addition, a supplementary classification records the status of sensory, motor, and articulatory speech functions and of some specific aspects of personal behavior.

In contrast to the medical classification with its emphasis on etiology or underlying pathology, the behavioral classification is essentially descriptive. The assessment of measured intelligence offers little practical difficulty in view of the availability of standardized test batteries and special tests (which is not to say that further development is not strongly indicated). The situation is somewhat different with respect to the direct evaluation of adaptive behavior. With the exception of the Vineland scale (which is often not applicable), no standardized procedures of a quantitative nature are available for clinical application, and evaluation must be based on general behavioral observation. The criteria suggested by Sloan and Birch (1955) for rating adaptive behavior at the preschool, school, and adult levels, which are included in the Behavioral Classification, provide useful anchoring points for such evaluations. However, the need for objective scales for the direct measurement of adaptive behavior is apparent, and a number of such scales are currently in process of development.

It will be noted that neither the medical nor the behavioral classification makes any major reference to a type of classification which has had a dominating in-fluence on clinical thinking and practice during the past twenty-five years, namely, the distinction between subcultural-endogenous-primary mental retardation and pathological-exogenous-secondary mental retardation. It is true that provision is made in the medical classification for the subcultural-endogenous-primary type under Class VIII, in which the category of "cultural-familial mental retardation" finds a place. However, it is explicitly stated (Heber, 1959, p. 40) with respect to this category that

there is no intent . . . to specify either the independent action of, or the relationship between, genetic and cultural factors in the etiology of cultural-familial mental retardation. The exact role of genetic factors cannot be specified . . . and there is no clear understanding of the specific manner in which environmental factors operate to modify intellectual functioning.

This recession in the importance of a basic distinction between subcultural and pathological mental retardation has been conditioned by a number of factors, among them being the failure to develop convincing evidence for the postulated genetic deficit in subcultural retardation, an increased awareness of the possible influence of cultural and emotional factors as determinants of this clinical picture, and the fact that predicted behavioral differences between the two groups have not always been demonstrable. The empirical evidence bearing on the last question is reviewed in a later section of this chapter.

MENTAL RETARDATION AND MENTAL DISORDER

All mental disorders (including mental retardation) represent, by definition, failure in adaptive behavior. In addition, there are some mental disorders (including mental retardation) which also involve intellectual impairment as a salient characteristic. The distinction between mental retardation and other forms of mental disorder also characterized by intellectual impairment is easily made when the latter occur only after maturity has been attained. Thus, even though there were no other differentiating features, the history alone would prevent a behavioral defect state referable to cerebral disease or to a schizophrenic process from being designated as mental retardation.

But this distinction is not always so easily made when such disorders occur during the early years of life. Behavior which is evaluated as neurotic, psychotic, or psychopathic is often observed in children with demonstrable intellectual subnormality. The nature of the association between these manifestations of psychopathology and the trait of intellectual subnormality in these children has been interpreted in a number of ways:

1. The association has been interpreted as being of a coincidental nature, i.e., as reflecting the occurrence of two independent pathologic processes in the same individual.

2. The association has been interpreted as the expression of a single basic process, e.g., brain disease leading both to intellectual subnormality and to defective emotional control, the latter in turn giving rise to antisocial, neurotic, or psychotic behavior.

3. The psychopathological traits have been interpreted as results of the primary intellectual deficit and as representing the reactions of the defective individual to adverse or stressful circumstances.

4. The intellectual deficit has been interpreted as a result of the primary psychopathologic process and as representing a particular form that the neurotic or psychotic reaction may take (cf. Benton, 1962).

Each of these points of view has its proponents; each carries its specific implications for management and treatment. The last interpretation (i.e., that a proportion of cases diagnosed as mentally retarded are, in essence, psychotic or severely neurotic) has received considerable support in recent years. In general, high-grade retardation has been equated with neurosis, low-grade retardation with psychosis. However, objections to this type of conceptualization have been raised on the ground that only confusion can result from attempts to merge conditions which are themselves heterogeneous (cf. Eisenberg, 1958).

The relationship between childhood autism and mental retardation has also been examined. While the two conditions are typically distinguished from each other, the prevalence of autistic features in the behavior of some retardates has been remarked, and the question as to whether such cases are not better classified as "autistic" rather than "retarded" has been raised.

These efforts to identify some cases of mental retardation with childhood neurosis or psychosis have had the effect of blurring conventional distinctions between the various forms of developmental behavioral disorder, of provoking a re-examination of present diagnostic habits, and of producing some degree of conceptual uncertainty and confusion in the field. The fundamental issues which are involved are considered in detail in Beier's chapter on mental retardation and behavioral disturbances.

EMPIRICAL STUDIES

PSYCHOMETRIC DETERMINATION

The trait of intellectual subnormality implies a global deficiency in intellectual skills, which is consistently manifested in the actual life behavior of the individual. It is standard practice to assess this intellectual subnormality in terms of psychometric test performance. Nevertheless, a psychometric test battery, however extensive it may be, can represent only a limited sampling of behavior. Hence, the interpretation of intellectual subnormality from the evidence provided by test performances is essentially an inference which is based on the assumption that the quality of behavior exhibited by a person under the special observational conditions of the test accurately reflects the quality of his behavior in daily life. The degree to which this assumption is tenable in the case of a given test or test battery is a measure of the *validity* of that instrument.

Considerable investigative work has been devoted to questions associated with the validity of psychometric testing procedures employed in the field of mental retardation. One major question has to do with the type of test which provides the most appropriate data for valid inference. Historically, psychometric assessment of persons in whom the question of mental retardation had been raised was first accomplished mainly by tests of a verbal nature, either of the Binet type or of the type (e.g., recent memory, information, calculation) to be found in the older manuals for psychiatric examinations. However, it was not long before clinical examiners, feeling that the Binet rating was more predictive of scholastic aptitude than of behavioral efficiency in "real life" situations, supplemented the verbal test with a battery of performance tests such as the tests of Healy and Fernald (1911), the Pintner-Paterson Scale (1917), the Porteus Mazes (1918), the Kohs Block Designs (1923), the Goodenough Draw-A-Man Test (1926), the Arthur Point Scale (1930), or the Cornell-Coxe Performance Ability Scale (1934). This conviction was strengthened by the finding that many, presumably normal, enlisted men in World War I made scores within the defective range on the Army Alpha Scale, a group intelligence test of the verbal type (Yerkes, 1921). In due time, the two types of scale, "verbal" and "non-verbal," were combined into a single instrument in the form of the Wechsler scales (Wechsler, 1939, 1949).

Until the advent of what may be called the "experiential deprivation" theory of mental retardation, most clinical examiners were satisfied that a combined battery of verbal and non-verbal tests provided a reasonably valid estimate of behavioral efficiency in everyday life. This theory, which holds that affective and intellectual deprivation in the earliest years of life is in large part responsible for the partial failure in the development of intelligence observed in the "non-neurological" high-grade mental retardate, raised many issues, among them being the question of whether such patients possess the familiarity with everyday objects and situations which is taken for granted when an intelligence test is given. It had long been appreciated that verbal tests were likely to underestimate the intellectual capacity of a culturally underprivileged child because of this factor. Moreover, since many performance tests assume an acquaintance with materials which are not necessarily part of the child's experiential history, it was realized that the typical non-verbal test battery also might not provide a valid estimate of his capabilities. With this consideration in mind, investigators have explored the application of "culture-free" or "culture-fair" test batteries in the psychological assessment of the mentally retarded, particularly those with a background of early cultural deprivation.

The "culture-fair" test batteries which probably have been applied most extensively are the Leiter International Performance Scale (1936, 1940, 1948), the IPAT Culture Free Intelligence Tests (Cattell, 1951), and the Davis-Eells Games (1953). When these tests have been given to mentally retarded persons, the general finding has been that their scores are *not* higher than those made by the patients on standard batteries such as the WISC or the Stanford-Binet (Bensberg and Sloan, 1955; Papania, Rosenblum, and Keller, 1955; Gallagher, Benoit, and Boyd, 1956; Alper, 1958). For example, in the study of Papania *et al.*, the performances of "non-neurological" retarded boys of lower-class social background on the Davis-Eells Games, WISC, Stanford-Binet, and California Test of Mental Maturity were investigated. The Davis-Eells scores of these presumably culturally handicapped subjects were not higher than their other test scores.

Thus the application of "culture-fair" tests in conjunction with standard test batteries has not produced evidence of specific handicap in retardates whose backgrounds might well have involved significant experiential impoverishment. This finding, as it applies to mental retardates, must be evaluated in the light of the more general finding that tests such as the Davis-Eells Games have not succeeded in their avowed aim of eliminating differences in test performance which presumably arise from socially determined differences in experience (cf. Knief, 1957; Drake, 1959). These results might be interpreted as indicating that differential experience plays no important role in determining the differences in test performance that are observed when children of differing social backgrounds are compared. An equally tenable conclusion is that experiential deprivation adversely affects the development of fundamental thinking abilities (e.g., conceptualization, facilitative verbal mediation of perceptual problem-solving) of a child and not merely his performances on certain tasks with "culture-related" content. If the latter conceptualization is correct, an experientially deprived child should do poorly on any valid intelligence test, "culture-fair" or not.

A second major question in the psychometric assessment of the mentally retarded concerns the diagnostic significance of irregularity of level of performance on a test such as Stanford-Binet, WAIS, or WISC. As was pointed out in the introductory section of this chapter, perfect evenness in performance is hardly to be expected. The observed irregu-

larity, which has been the subject of numerous studies, has been analyzed from two points of view: (1) purely quantitative analyses without regard to direction of deviation, i.e., estimates of amount of "scatter," and (2) analyses which take direction of deviation into account, i.e., determinations of "patterns" of performance.

With respect to scatter, clinical examiners have often been inclined to believe that unduly high scatter suggests a lower degree of social competence or behavioral efficiency than would be implied by the obtained IQ score alone. Thus, given two patients with WAIS IQ 75, who differ significantly with respect to the scatter of the subtest scores, it is expected that the patient with the more even profile will be better adjusted and achieve more in actual life situations than the patient with the less even profile. One facet of the reasoning behind this conclusion is that high scatter reflects the influence of non-intellectual factors such as anxiety, hostility, depression, and impulsivity and hence is a sign of emotional interference with behavioral efficiency. The same reasoning has led to another conclusion, namely, that the better subtest performances of a patient with high scatter would seem to be least affected by emotional factors and, hence, to be the most valid estimate of his intellectual potentiality. From this standpoint, the obtained IQ of such a patient may be a reasonably valid estimate of his current behavioral efficiency but is an underestimate of his "basic" intellectual level. The latter concept has been pushed to its logical limit by Jastak, who has suggested that a patient's intelligence level be estimated on the basis of his highest subtest score rather than on the basis of his composite score. With specific reference to the psychological evaluation of a person in whom the question of mental retardation has been raised, this means that "average achievement on any test, regardless of the ability tested, automatically excludes intellectual defect as a diagnostic possibility" (Jastak, 1949).

A review of the pertinent empirical evidence of this question discloses that it is quite inadequate to support these ideas about the diagnostic significance of scatter. In an early analysis of the importance of various measures of scatter on the Stanford-Binet, Harris and Shakow (1937) concluded that "research up to now has failed to demonstrate clearly any valid clinical use for numerical measures of scatter." With respect to test performance in mental retardation, this conclusion still seems to hold good today, despite the studies which have been done since 1937. The evidence that scatter per se has a specific significance apart from composite score is largely tangential in nature. The observation that various pathologic groups (including mental retardates) often show more scatter on test batteries than do normal control groups has led to the conviction that irregularity in performance *must* have something to do with behavioral maladjustment, in mental retardates as well as in other diagnostic groups. However, there is no direct evidence to support the idea. For example, in advocating the use of the highest subtest score as an index of basic intelligence, Jastak adduces no systematic evidence to support the recommendation.

There are a number of possible reasons for this failure to substantiate clinical impression about the diagnostic significance of scatter. Measures of scatter which have been utilized may be defective; they have been criticized repeatedly on a number of grounds (cf. Anastasi, 1954). Another possibility is that the important factor in scatter is not the mere occurrence of unevenness in level but rather the direction of deviation in test performances. Certainly the interest of the clinical examiner, when he examines a test record for scatter, is focused on the specific performances which are outstandingly good or poor and not on the mere fact of scatter itself, and it is from evaluation of these specific performances that his diagnostic assessment and special recommendations are derived.

A somewhat more positive picture emerges from empirical studies in which direction of deviation has been taken into account and pattern of performance on test batteries has been examined. A considerable number of investigators (e.g., Earl, 1938, 1940; Bijou, 1941, 1942, 1944; Bijou and McCandless, 1944; Abel, 1945a; Sarason and Sarason, 1946) are in accord in concluding that the relationship between verbal test and non-verbal test performances provides a significant predictive measure of behavioral achievement and adjustment in actual life, the specific finding being that either an even level of performance or a relative superiority in non-verbal task performance is associated with high behavioral efficiency.

Some of these studies may be briefly summarized. Earl (1940) gave his high-grade retarded subjects a verbal test battery consisting of the 1916 Stanford-Binet Vocabulary, the Stanford-Binet Absurdities (Year X), and another oral absurdities test (Weisenburg, Roe, and Mac-Bride, 1936), as well as a non-verbal test battery consisting of the Kohs Block Designs and a form-board test devised by Kent. Performance was then related to independent judgments of social competence. He found that both an unbiased profile and relative superiority on the non-verbal test battery were associated with good adjustment while relative superiority on the verbal test battery was associated with poor adjustment. These results have ben confirmed in a recent study by Gunzburg (1959). Essentially the same finding was reported by Bijou (1941) who gave his high-grade retarded boys the Stanford-Binet and the Arthur Performance Scale. A relative superiority on the Arthur was found to be positively associated with ratings of "good behavior" within the institutional environment. Abel (1945a), comparing the academic achievement of two groups of high-grade retarded girls who had been matched for age and Stanford-Binet IQ but who differed in respect to performance level on the Arthur Scale, found that the group whose non-verbal test scores were higher than their Binet scores were scholastically ahead of the other group. Among the tests of the Arthur Scale, the Porteus Mazes and the Healy Picture Completion I appeared to be the most discriminating measures. Sarason and Sarason (1946) divided a sample of high-grade familial, "non-neurological" retardates into one group whose Kohs Block Designs performance level was above Binet level and another in which this relationship was reversed. The "Kohs-below-Binet" group showed poorer work records and more antisocial behavior than the other group. However, a dissenting note is sounded by the negative results of Sloan and Cutts (1945) who found no difference in verbal-performance pattern on the Wechsler-Bellevue when institutionalized well-adjusted and delinquent retardates were compared. A possible reason for this failure of the Wechsler-Bellevue pattern to differentiate the two groups is offered by Sloan and Cutts. They point out that the "well-adjusted" group (mean IQ 69, range 49–85) was institutionalized, a fact which itself implies a failure in adjustment. Considering that a good number of these patients had IQ's above 75, the argument would seem to have some weight. Another possible reason for the discrepancy between these findings and those of the earlier studies is that the Wechsler Performance Scale is rather different from such non-verbal batteries as the Pintner-Paterson or the Arthur.

A review of these studies leaves little doubt that relatively good performance on non-verbal test batteries is associated with general behavioral efficiency. However, even cursory examination raises the question as to whether the association is really a matter of *pattern* of performance. Wherever the information is explicitly given (e.g., Bijou, 1944; Abel, 1945; Sarason and Sarason, 1946), it is apparent that the contrasting groups of subjects were at least roughly equal in respect to level of performance on the verbal test battery. It follows that if the verbal and non-verbal test batteries were combined to yield a single score, the group with "relatively high" non-verbal test levels would have higher total IQ's than the contrasting group. This means, of course, that groups of somewhat different mental levels were being compared in these studies, and the finding that the brighter group was more efficient and better adjusted is only to be expected. Alternatively, the results of these studies may mean simply that performance on certain types of non-verbal tasks is the best predictor of behavioral efficiency in high-grade retardates. In this regard, it is interesting that some writers (e.g., Earl) view the non-verbal tasks as procedures to elicit the overt expression of clinically significant personality traits and that Abel found the Porteus Mazes to be an excellent predictor of the academic achievement of her subjects. In any case, whatever may be the most reasonable interpretation of these results, it seems that performance on the non-verbal tests per se is the significant variable, rather than the *relationship* between verbal and non-verbal test levels.

A more or less direct measure of social competence is provided by the Vineland Social Maturity Scale (Doll, 1953), which has been the subject of numerous empirical studies (cf. Watson, 1951; Buros, 1959). In mental retardates the correlation between Vineland scores and mental-age scores derived from the Stanford-Binet or the WISC is typically rather high. The instrument has been criticized on a number of grounds, e.g., the "hearsay" nature of data based on the report of an informant rather than on direct observation, the possible dependence of score on more or less accidental characteristics of the child's environment, the restriction of consideration to only certain aspects of social competence, etc. Nevertheless, its clinical utility as a component of the psychological evaluation is undeniable. For example, an impressive inferiority of "social age" in relation to mental age immediately alerts the clinical examiner to the possibility of the operation of non-intellectual factors in determining an abnormally low level of behavioral efficiency and social adjustment.

ORGANIZATION OF ABILITIES

Alfred Binet pointed out that while intellectual level could be usefully expressed in terms of a mental-age score this did not mean that the mental organization of a retarded individual was the same as that of a normal child of the same mental age. A substantial amount of investigative work has been done to determine in what respects the pattern of intellectual performance of mental retardates does differ from that of normal individuals of either the same chronological or the same mental age (MA). Some of these studies may be reviewed and their implications considered.

Stanford-Binet.—Laycock and Clark (1942) compared the Stanford-Binet performances of contrasting groups of retarded (mean IQ–74) and very bright (mean IQ–123) children, members of each group having been individually matched with respect to MA, sex, socioeconomic status, and locality in which they lived. Mean MA for each group of forty subjects was nine years, five months. The proportion of successes on each subtest from Years VIII through XII of the Scale was determined, and it was found that the retarded children appeared to be relatively superior on eight subtests and the very bright children to be relatively superior on ten subtests, although most of the differences were not demonstrably significant. The retarded children excelled on such tasks as Vocabulary, Making Change, and Absurdities, a finding which Laycock and Clark were inclined to attribute to their longer life experience. In contrast, the very bright children excelled on rote and ideational memory tasks.

These findings of Laycock and Clark were confirmed to some degree in the much more extensive study by Thompson and Magaret (1947) of the Stanford-Binet performances of 441 mental retardates (mean IQ–63), the essential comparison being between this group and the group of 1326 children on whom the Scale was standardized. In seventy-three comparisons, twenty-nine consistently significant differences (.01 probability level) were found, the retardates being relatively superior on eleven items and the standardization group being relatively superior on eighteen items. Most of the subtests which had elicited some difference in performance in the Laycock-Clark study also differentiated in the same direction in this study, although not always to a statistically significant degree. Most notable, perhaps, was the finding in both studies of a relative superiority in rote memory task performance on the part of normal children. Thompson and Magaret made an attempt to test the traditional hypothesis (cf. Merrill, 1924; Wallin, 1929)—that mental retardates do relatively well on tasks in which length of life experience plays a differential role—by comparing individual subtest performance in the two groups with ratings by judges of the probable dependence of subtest response on past experience. There was no relationship between the relative success of the two groups and these ratings, and, hence, no support for the hypothesis was adduced. However, they did find that the subtests on which the children of the standardization group excelled were saturated more heavily with the "general factor," derived by McNemar (1942) in his factorial analysis of Stanford-Binet performance, than were the subtests on which the retardates excelled, the difference being significant at the .01 probability level.

In a subsequent study, Magaret and Thompson (1950) extended the comparison to include very bright children (IQ–120) and secured essentially similar results. The subtests on which the very bright children excelled, as compared to both average and retarded children, were more highly saturated with McNemar's "general factor." Rote memory tasks were done relatively well by the very bright children, as compared with the mental retardates, but there was no difference in this respect when very bright and average children were compared. Another finding of some interest was that the retardates were relatively superior on tests which required manual manipulation as well as on those which involved the use of test material.

Wechsler scales.—In discussing the performance characteristics of mental retardates on the W-B and the WAIS, Wechsler (1958) presents a characteristic subtest profile, the salient features of which are relatively high scores on Object Assembly, Comprehension, and Vocabulary and relatively low scores on Arithmetic and the digit-reversal aspect of Digit Span. Particular emphasis is placed on the Arithmetic Subtest, and the comment is made that relatively high Arithmetic and Block Design subtest scores argue against a diagnosis of uncomplicated mental retardation. Wechsler does not find a bias in favor of a relatively high Performance Scale level, which, in his experience, appears to be more closely associated with delinquency and antisocial trends.

The main features of Wechsler's test profile find empirical support in the study by Magaret and Wright (1943) of the Wechsler-Bellevue I performances of forty high-grade retardates. The highest mean scores of this group were on Vocabulary, Object Assembly, Comprehension, and Information while by far the lowest mean score was on Arithmetic. Subsequent studies (e.g., Cutts and Sloan, 1945; Sloan and Cutts, 1945; Cutts and Lane, 1947; Hays, 1950; Alderdice and Butler, 1952) are in agreement in finding Object Assembly quite easy, and Arithmetic quite difficult, for mental retardates. However, other features of the profile are not confirmed, and a number of studies report a significant trend for Performance Scale level to be higher than Verbal Scale level.

Another aspect of Wechsler test performance which has been studied is the application to mental retardates of the deterioration "quotient" or "ratio," which was designed to disclose acquired impairment in intellectual function in various disorders. The findings in the investigations of Boehm and Sarason (1947) and Sloan (1947) are unequivocal in their indications that a high proportion of mental retardates show quotients indicative of "deterioration." The Boehm-Sarason study is particularly noteworthy in this respect because it restricted consideration to retardates of the "non-neurological," familial type. These results, of course, impair the validity of the formula as a method for detecting relatively recently acquired loss of mental efficiency. However, in the present context their major interest lies in the implied similarity in pattern of performance between mental retardates (even of the "non-neurological" type) and patients suffering from other types of behavioral disorder.

Similar studies have been done on pattern of performance on the WISC (e.g.,

Sloan and Schneider, 1951; Sandercock and Butler, 1952; Kolstoe, 1954; Beck and Lam, 1955; Newman and Loos, 1955; Baroff, 1959). There is agreement that, in high-grade retardates of the familial or undifferentiated type, Performance Scale level is at least equal to, and usually higher than, Verbal Scale level. However, a curious contradictory note in this regard is sounded by the study of Atchison (1955) of eighty Negro mental retardates of the "non-neurological" type. The mean Verbal Scale quotient of these children was 66 while the mean Performance Scale quotient was 57. Atchison makes the pertinent comment that "it became obvious during the testing that the Ss had difficulty in understanding instructions," an observation which raises a number of questions. First, the rather obvious question of cultural determinants of differential performance on the Scales is raised. Secondly, while correlational analysis suggests that there is indeed a difference in the types of abilities sampled in the Verbal and Performance Scales, this does not necessarily mean that the difference is along the general dimension of "language," as implied by the names of the Scales. It may be along some specific dimension of language function and not along others or along dimensions which are essentially unrelated to language function. For example, Sarason (1959) has pointed out that "non-verbal" tasks may involve a considerable amount of implicit language activity and verbal mediation of performance, and he has characterized the distinction between "verbal" and "non-verbal" tests as being essentially one which divides tests into those which require the subject to talk to someone else ("verbal") and those which only require him to talk to himself ("non-verbal"). That the essential difference may still be ascribable to a language factor (i.e., level and quality of expressive speech) is certainly quite possible, but that affective and interpersonal variables may be playing the determining role would seem to be equally likely.

Other tests.—The many studies concerned with the performances of mental retardates on various other tests of intellectual function and mental efficiency cannot be systematically reviewed. However, to indicate the general trend of results, mention will be made of the findings of Bolles (1937) with respect to performance on the Babcock (1930) test for "mental deterioration" and the sorting tests of Goldstein (cf. Goldstein and Scheerer, 1941). Comparing mental retardates and normal children of about the same Stanford-Binet mental age, Bolles found that while Babcock test performance indicated normal functioning in the children, it indicated significant "mental inefficiency" in the retardates, as indexed by almost consistently negative "efficiency indexes," some of them of large magnitude. On a color-form sorting test of the Weigl type, the performances of the children were comparable to that of normal adults, while the performances of the retardates were more similar to those of brain-damaged and schizophrenic patients. Finally, on object-sorting tests involving classification according to essential similarity, Bolles noted that the retardates showed the same inability to make cogent classifications and to shift from one classification to another that has been observed in some brain-damaged and schizophrenic patients. The normal children showed no such difficulties. Her findings, insofar as they apply to color-form sorting, have been confirmed in a recent study by Halpin (1958).

Concluding comment.—A review of the relevant empirical studies suggests that the organization of abilities in mental retardates does differ from that of normal children of comparable mental level. This proposition that one is dealing, not with a simple retardation in behavioral development, but with defective or distorted development has been accepted for a long time. However, the nature of the factors which are responsible for the observed differences is still obscure, and a precise definition of the particular variables which account for them has still to be made. The similarity of some aspects of performance (e.g., significant "deterioration ratios" on the Wechsler-Bellevue and the Babcock) to the performances of patients in other neuropsychiatric categories, "functional" as well as "organic," has been observed repeatedly. On the other hand, the trend toward high "nonverbal" test scores, on the part of the "non-neurological" retarded at least, is not consistent with the performance pattern which is most frequently encountered in patients with cerebral or mental disease. Since the findings regarding the question of the behavioral differences which may exist between endogenous and exogenous mental retardation have a direct bearing on this issue, further discussion of it will be postponed until after this question has been considered.

LANGUAGE FUNCTIONS

An excessively high incidence of defects in speech articulation is a common finding in mental retardates (cf. Harrison, 1958; Penwill, 1958). The relative frequency of such defects varies inversely with mental age, but this fact does not serve as a sufficient explanation of the finding, since the incidence is decidedly higher than in normal children of comparable mental ages. Articulation can be improved by special training procedures (cf. Lubman, 1955; Mecham, 1955; Schlanger, 1958), although doubt has been expressed by some workers about how much can be accomplished with patients with IQ's under 50. A significant proportion of retarded children show hearing losses of one type or another (see below). Defective articulation is to be expected in cases of serious hearing loss, but it is of interest that Mecham (1955) found no relationship between auditory word discrimination level and severity of articulation deficit. Retardates of the familial type are likely to show better articulation than brain-damaged or mongoloid patients (Schlanger and Gottesleben, 1957).

Some children show a pronounced retardation in the development of understanding and/or expression of oral language. When this disability occurs within a setting of apparently adequate hearing capacity, general intelligence, and social competence, the child is considered to have a specific language retardation or "congenital aphasia" (cf. Benton, 1959b). However, the disability is more likely to occur within a setting of somewhat subnormal general intelligence and social competence, as measured by "non-verbal" tests and by such instruments as the Vineland Social Maturity Scale. The typical psychometric pattern of such a child shows a pronounced deficit on test performance requiring verbal response and (if the language disability extends to the understanding of oral speech which it usually does to a degree) on those non-verbal performances which involve relatively complex verbal instructions. On the other hand, non-verbal tests which involve pantomime or simple verbal instructions will be done on a higher, but still subnormal, level.

In the past, there has been much discussion about whether or not such a child should be considered mentally retarded. More recently, it has been appreciated that this is not a very important issue. By all behavioral criteria, the child is retarded, and the crucial question which arises is whether the language disability is merely one type of expression of a global mental retardation or whether it is in itself a major determinant of the observed global retardation. Many genetic psychologists have insisted upon the indispensable role of language in the ongoing process of mental growth in the child. For example, Luria and Yudovich

(1959) point out that language habits regulate behavior, stabilize perception, make possible abstract reasoning and the apprehension of complex relationships, and raise the level of the child's thinking "to a higher, qualitatively new stage." If this is so, it is only to be expected that a child with a severe language handicap will perform defectively, not only on verbal tests, but also on most non-verbal tasks, even when the latter do not require "understanding of language" in the usual sense of the term. Thus the question which the examiner must pose is, not whether the child is "defective" *or* "aphasic," but what is the role of the aphasia in producing his mental retardation. The answer to this question can be derived only from a relatively extensive sampling of his abilities, including assessment of behavior on tasks in which verbal mediation is presumably not an important determinant of level of performance. The relationship between his performance level on such tests and on other tests ("language" and "non-language") which do require verbal mediation for optimal performance should provide an indication of the part which language functions are playing in determining general behavioral level.

MOTOR PROFICIENCY

Motor skills can play a decisively important role as a determining factor in the behavioral and social efficiency of the intellectually subnormal person. A genius can afford to be a "motor imbecile," but a person with an IQ of 75 cannot. The latter's psychomotor ability may well determine whether he will attain a reasonable degree of social competence. For this reason, assessment of motor capacity is an aspect of the psychological evaluation which has significant implications for prediction, guidance, and training.

The most widely used standardized battery of tests of motor skills is that of Oseretsky, two American versions of which are the Vineland Adaptation (Cassel, 1949) and the Lincoln-Oseretsky Motor Development Scale (Sloan, 1955). A review of recent studies of various versions of the Oseretsky scale can be found in the paper of Rabin (1957); earlier work is covered in the annotated bibliography of Lassner (1948).

Motor proficiency, as measured by the Oseretsky, shows a high positive correlation with chronological age in both mentally retarded and normal children. It is significantly, but not closely, related to intelligence level in mental retardates, who show poorer performances than children of comparable chronological age. However, there is at best only a questionable association of small magnitude between motor proficiency and intelligence level in normal children (Malpass, 1960). There is no evidence that institutionalization is a determining factor in performance (Malpass, 1960). "Brain-damaged" patients do not perform as well as "familial" patients (Cassel, 1949), and the clinically observed motor awkwardness of mongoloids is reflected in a more marked retardation in performance than is found in other retardates (Pertego, 1950).

Other tests of motor proficiency, involving both fine movements and gross postural action, have been applied to the mentally retarded. Manipulative dexterity has been the subject of a number of studies (e.g., Tizard, O'Connor, and Crawford, 1950; Cantor and Stacey, 1951) with the general finding that the performances of retardates are significantly below normative standards. The Rail-Walking Test of Heath (1942), a measure of locomotor co-ordination, has also been found to discriminate between retardates and normal subjects as well as between "endogenous" and "exogenous" retardates.

These measures of motor proficiency would seem to have considerable face validity. However, not many empirical investigations of their predictive significance have been done. The most outstanding is the study by O'Connor and Tizard (1951) in which the performances of 104 high-grade retardates on an extensive battery of tests were correlated with ratings of their work success. Multiple correlation coefficients between parts of the battery and the ratings were about 0.65. Rail-Walking Test performance contributed quite significantly to the prediction of work success. Its correlation with the ratings was 0.44 and, when combined with score on a body-sway test, the multiple correlation coefficient was 0.52. Validation of the Oseretsky test with respect to the prediction of vocational adjustment must wait upon the collection of data on adult subjects.

SENSORY DISCRIMINATIVE CAPACITY

Audition.—It has already been mentioned in the discussion of language disorders that a relatively high proportion of the mentally retarded show evidence of hearing deficit (cf. Kodman, 1958). For example, Birch and Mathews (1951), comparing mental retardates with normative groups, found from two and a half to eighteen times as much hearing loss in the retarded, depending upon the particular groups being compared and the sound frequencies employed in the testing. Similar results were secured by Foale and Paterson (1954), who, however, did not find quite as high an incidence of deficit as did Birch and Mathews. The difference in this respect is quite possibly attributable, as Foale and Paterson point out, to the fact that their patients were somewhat more intelligent (mean IQ—66) than the Birch-Paterson group (mean IQ—49). Kodman *et al.* (1958) reported an incidence of hearing loss which was almost four times as high as that estimated to exist in school children. That a similarly high incidence of impairments in hearing exists in adult retardates has been shown by Siegenthaler and Krzywicki (1959).

Birch and Mathews mention some of the implications of these findings. There is no doubt that impairment in hearing in mental retardates often remains undetected. The retarded child's difficulties in understanding and expressing language, which are conditioned by the hearing loss, are likely to be accepted as a simple manifestation of low intelligence. It is also possible that some of the observed irregularity in test performance observed in retardates may be a function of unsuspected hearing loss.

Auditory performances that are more complex than those involved in the simple threshold determinations of audiometry have also been studied. Cantor and Girardeau (1959) investigated the ability of mongoloid patients and of normal children of average and superior intelligence to discriminate between the sounds produced by two metronomes beating at different rates (88 beats per minute and 120 beats per minute, respectively). The normal children proved to be superior to the retarded, but, since the groups were not equated for mental age and a positive correlation between performance level and mental age was observed, it is probable that no real difference exists. Blacketer-Simmonds (1953) explored more complex performances, such as the reproduction of heard rhythmic patterns and keeping in time to music, in mongoloid and non-mongoloid retardates and found that the mongoloids showed a slight (but not demonstrably significant) superiority. Both the Cantor-Girardeau study and that of Blacketer-Simmonds suggest that the allegedly superior development of the "rhythmic sense" in mongoloid patients is a fiction.

A still more complex type of auditory discrimination was the subject of a recent study by Hunt (1960), who investigated the performances of brain-injured and familial retardates on a task involving the comprehension of stories presented on phonograph records. Three groups of twenty children each were studied: (1) familial retardates, (2) brain-injured children who had been rated on the basis of classroom observation as having difficulties in auditory comprehension and reproduction but with no evidence of obvious hearing loss, and (3) brain-injured children who had received higher ratings of auditory comprehension with no evidence of obvious hearing loss. Her findings were that the patients with "classroom" difficulties showed a significantly lower performance level on the experimental task than either the familial patients or the brain-injured patients without such difficulties. The latter two groups did not differ from each other. Thus, in essence, this study consisted in a confirmation under controlled observational conditions of the impressions of classroom observers. One important implication of it is, in Hunt's words, "that a universal classification system wherein brain-injured children are considered as a generic class is not sufficient. They deviate in the type and severity of their disabilities." Secondly, following the reasoning of Gellner (1957), the findings suggest that differential teaching methods are required for brain-injured children with distinctive disabilities.

Vision.—The simple visual capacities have not received as much attention as has auditory sensitivity. An early study by Kempf and Collins (1929) of Illinois school children disclosed a higher incidence of defective visual acuity (6/10 or worse in one or both eyes) in dull children (IQ < 90) than in children of average intelligence, the ratio being 1.4:1. The relative incidence of strabismus was also higher in the dull children (ratio = 1.75:1). As compared with normative standards, color blindness is somewhat more frequent in male retardates of moderate retardation level but not more frequent in higher-grade male retardates (O'Connor, 1957).

With respect to some of the simpler visuoperceptive performances, Gordon (1944) found that mongoloid patients performed slightly below the level of normal children of comparable mental age on such tasks as brightness, size, form, and texture discrimination. The number of cases in each group was extremely small and the observed difference was not significant. Barnett and Pryer (1958) studied visual depth perception in mental retardates but did not include a comparison with the performance of a control group. Accuracy of depth perception was found to be unrelated to either mental age or IQ. However, intra-individual variability in performance was inversely correlated with both variables. When small matched groups of brain-damaged and familial retardates were compared, no differences in general accuracy of depth perception were demonstrable, although the brain-damaged patients showed a larger constant error.

More complex visuoperceptual and visuoconstructive behavior has been extensively studied. It is not clear from this work whether mental retardates actually perform on a lower level than normal children of comparable mental age. On the other hand, when brain-injured and familial retardates are compared, a difference in favor of the familial patients has often been reported. The interpretation to be placed on this finding is discussed in a later section and need not be considered here. However, the results of Hunt's recent studies on performance differences within a brain-damaged group as well as between it and a familial group deserve mention.

Hunt and Patterson (1958) investigated the performances of familial and brain-injured patients on visual picture arrangement tasks, verbal reproduction of orally presented stories, and a "combined" task involving picture arrangement in response to orally presented stories. The brain-injured children were inferior to the familial retarded on all three tasks. However, when the brain-injured children were classified on the basis of classroom observation as having primarily a psycho-visual or psycho-auditory deficit and the two subgroups compared, it was found that relative level of performance on the experimental tasks was closely related to the nature of the clinically observed disability. In addition, interesting qualitative differences in the performances of the brain-injured and familial children were observed on the task of arranging pictures to accord with an orally presented story, which involved a combination of both visual and auditory stimulation.

The examiner found that the familial children were able to rely on both visual and auditory cues, i.e., looking at the pictures and listening to the story simultaneously. On the other hand, many of the brain-injured children would tend to blot out one of the areas and rely entirely upon one cue. . . . For example, one child covered his ears and refused to listen to the story. He arranged the pictures according to the action of the characters. . . . On the other hand, there were children who spent little time looking at the pictures but listened carefully to the story and asked for it to be repeated. . . . On the whole, the brain-injured group seemed to have difficulty in co-ordinating the visual and auditory cues to derive full benefit from the combination. They were inclined to select one area as the dominating factor in their performance. The choice of area was usually based upon ability; the visually handicapped children favoring the stories, and those handicapped in the auditory area favoring the pictures (p. 76).

In a subsequent study, Hunt (1959) investigated the performances of these two types of brain-injured retarded children as well as familial retarded on a visuoconstructive task. The brain-injured children with clinically judged visuoperceptive disability performed more poorly than either the brain-injured children with clinically judged auditory disability or the familial cases. On the other hand, the brain-injured children with clinically judged auditory disability performed at a somewhat higher level than the familial cases. Some of

the theoretical and practical implications of this series of studies have already been mentioned. They argue against the tenability of the idea that brain-injured children can be considered as a relatively homogeneous group in respect to pattern of mental abilities and disabilities. The usefulness of certain types of tasks of a visuomotor nature for detecting "brain injury" in general is called into question. The presence of striking visuo-constructive deficit in some familial cases makes doubtful the validity of assumptions about evenness of level of performance in that diagnostic category. Perhaps most important are the implications for the special education of retarded children.

Somatosensory functions.—When seen in its totality, a considerable amount of investigative work on the status of the simpler somatosensory functions (e.g., thresholds for light pressure and pain, point localization, two-point discrimination) has been done. Some of this work dates back many decades. However, the findings of the early work are of dubious validity, and, in general, because of variation in the conditions of investigation, meaningful comparison of the results of different studies is quite difficult.

A number of recent studies have been concerned with the question of pain perception. Some of these are case reports of indifference or insensitivity to pain in mental retardates, usually of low or middle grade but occasionally of a higher level (e.g., Madonick, 1954). A more systematic study of reaction to pain in low-grade retardates has been reported by Stengel, Oldham, and Ehrenburg (1958). As a group, these patients responded (withdrawing or wincing) to pin prick as vigorously as did other types of patients. However, there was marked inter-individual variability in reaction and it would seem fair to classify some of the patients as having reduced sensitivity, if not insensitivity or indifference, to pain. There was a positive relationship between size of reaction to the painful stimuli and ratings of general activity level. On the other hand, no association between pain reaction under these controlled conditions and propensity to self-injury was observed.

In evaluating the findings in the literature and in planning investigations of the question, it is necessary to distinguish between *indifference* to pain in the presence of intact sensitivity and actual *insensitivity* (or reduced sensitivity) to pain. Ogden, Robert, and Carmichael (1959) provide a useful analysis of these two conditions, which are often confused with each other.

Gordon (1944), whose observations on visual discrimination in mongoloid patients have already been cited, also gave tests of tactual discrimination of size, form, and texture to his small group of cases. In contrast to the results with respect to vision, he found that tactual discrimination in the mongoloid patients was strikingly poor, as compared with the performances of normal children of similar mental age. Tactual form perception has also been studied by Sloan and Bensberg (1951). Utilizing a test of tactual recognition of common objects, which Benton and Schultz (1949) had devised to assess stereognostic capacity in preschool children, they found no difference in performance between brain-damaged and familial retardates. No control group was included in the comparison.

The status of more complex somatosensory performances, such as the identification of right and left body parts and finger localization, was first studied by Strauss and Werner (1938, 1939) and Spillane (1942) and has been the subject of a series of investigations by Benton and co-workers (Benton, 1955, 1959*a*; Benton, Hutcheon, and Seymour, 1951). The essential findings of these studies are that mental retardates show significantly poorer right-left discrimination and finger localization than do normal children

of comparable mental age. This generally lower performance level is determined, for the most part, by the occurrence of grossly defective performances by some retardates who show virtually complete right-left disorientation and finger agnosia. The two abilities are significantly related to each other, independent of the influence of chronological and mental age. The performances of familial retardates do not differ from those classified as brain-injured.

The clinical and educational significance of the status of these "body schema" performances still requires elucidation. Strauss and Werner attempted to relate defective finger localization and right-left orientation to arithmetic disability, and Spillane's case did show this association of deficits (as well as defective oral speech and writing). However, a critical study by Benton, Hutcheon, and Seymour (1951) could not confirm this relationship. Disturbances in right-left orientation have been related to reading disability by Harris (1957), Hermann and Norrie (1958), and Benton (1958; Benton and Kemble, 1960). In the latter two studies, it was found that children who show systematic reversal in right-left discrimination (e.g., consistently point to the left hand or leg when asked to point to the right, and vice versa) also show a relatively poor development of language functions and, conversely, that children with specific reading difficulty show a higher incidence of such systematic reversal than do children with average reading ability.

Another type of somatosensory performance that has been studied in mental retardates is responsiveness to double simultaneous tactual stimulation with particular reference to the phenomenon of "extinction" (Fink, Green, and Bender, 1953; Swanson, 1957; Pollack and Gordon, 1960). The general finding has been that lack of "extinction" (i.e., perception of both stimuli) is closely related to mental-age level in both normal and mentally retarded children. However, when mental-age level is controlled, retardates show a somewhat higher incidence of "extinction" than do normal children (Swanson, 1957). No differential responsiveness between brain-injured and familial retardates has been demonstrated.

PERSONALITY AND PROGNOSIS

One often encounters the statement that the assessment and investigation of personality factors in mental retardates have not received the attention which they deserve. The statement is only partially correct. Perhaps the field has been relatively neglected, but, nevertheless, a good many studies dealing with one or another aspect of personality in mental retardation have been reported during the past twenty years. The basic significance of these studies is another matter. As in most other areas of clinical assessment of personality, early hopes of achieving major insights into the relationship of personality structure and overt behavior have not been realized; the gains have been of a more modest nature.

That personality differences exist among mental retardates has always been apparent and classifications in terms of "torpid" and "excitable," "stable" and "unstable," and the like, based on general observation, were established for descriptive purposes and as a guide to management and training. Modern psychological assessment has favored the employment of formal test procedures over clinical observation for purposes of personality assessment. Not surprisingly, the projective techniques have been most frequently utilized.

Projective techniques.—The Rorschach test has been applied extensively for personality assessment and investigation in mental retardation (for reviews of the literature, see Benton, 1956*b* and Molish, 1958). As is true of Rorschach work in all clinical fields, the reports range from purely autistic productions, through single case studies (which are often quite interesting but necessarily of limited evidential value), to reasonably careful systematic investigations. The Rorschach performances of retardates show some decided group trends (i.e., low F+, M, W, and high A) which would seem to be more or less direct reflections of the nuclear trait of intellectual subnormality. However, as the early study of Beck (1932) showed, there is considerable interindividual variation in performance. One important clinical question is the relationship between such individual differences in Rorschach performance and personal adjustment. Consistently positive findings in this respect have been rather meager. The studies of Abel (1945*a*, *b*) and of Sarason and Sarason (1946) agree that the presence of FC responses and a high F+ in the protocol are indicators of good personal adjustment. Beyond this, their findings are not in agreement (e.g., with respect to productivity and movement responses) and the results of a later study of a similar nature by Sloan (1948) were completely negative.

The Thematic Apperception Test has also found wide application as a method of personality assessment in retardates. The opinion of many clinical examiners is that, in the individual examination, it provides valuable clues to areas of emotional disturbance and conflict. However, in contrast to the Rorschach, critical evaluations of the test by comparative analysis of the performances of defined groups differing in personal adjustment do not seem to have been carried out.

An investigation of one aspect of the validity of the Picture Frustration Study of Rosenzweig (1948) has been reported recently by Lipman (1959). Two contrasting groups of high-grade retardates, one consisting of socially well-adjusted, co-operative children and the other consisting of chronically aggressive, delinquent children, showed no differences on the various scores derived from test performance. Yet ability to complete the mirror drawing of a five-pointed star did discriminate between the two groups, a higher proportion of the aggressive children refusing to carry the task to completion. Callahan and Keller (1957) have reported rather encouraging preliminary results in the application of a picture interpretation test (Children's Anxiety Pictures) designed to permit inferences regarding the anxiety level of the subject. Response to the pictures significantly discriminated between contrasting groups of high-grade retardates with high and low digit-span performance levels.

Every year or two a study appears in which the Rorschach or the Thematic Apperception Test has been given to a group of mental retardates with the finding of a high incidence of textbook signs of "abnormality" on the Rorschach or of recurrent themes of "disgust," "disappointment," and "aggression" in the TAT productions. Without going to the trouble of investigating the performances of a control group or of attempting to relate these signs of abnormality to behavior within the retarded group, the author concludes forthwith that his results indicate that many individuals diagnosed as mentally retarded are not "true" retardates but rather victims of neurotic inhibition or some other form of psychogenic or sociogenic personality disturbance. The conclusion is usually accompanied by a blast at IQ testers, organicists, and hereditarians. Such reports are perhaps best ignored, but they do become part of the literature, are sometimes widely cited, and have to be dealt with. Hence, one welcomes the careful investigation of Klausmeier and Check (1959), which can serve well as a counterweight to these methodologically incompetent studies. In the Klausmeier-Check study, three groups of children within different WISC IQ ranges (55–80, 90–110, 120+) were compared on a variety of measures of physical development, scholastic achieve-

ment, and personality. The findings of particular interest in the present context were that, while there was a wide range of individual ratings in each group, the mean ratings by psychologists of emotional adjustment and of achievement in relation to capacity (based on Rorschach, TAT, figure drawing, and interview) did not differ in the three groups. Thus, there was no evidence that, as a group, the retarded, special-class children suffered particularly from emotional inhibition of intellectual function or interference with optimal achievement. Needless to say, this does not exclude the possibility that some children in the low-IQ group might have been suffering from such interference.

Non-projective techniques.—A number of recent studies have explored the application of the Children's Form of the Manifest Anxiety Scale (Castaneda, McCandless, and Palermo, 1956). In these studies, the items of the test are usually presented orally because of the limited reading ability of the subjects. Keller (1957) compared the Anxiety Scale scores of matched groups of high-grade retardates who differed with respect to digit-span test performance (presumably susceptible to the interfering effects of anxiety). No difference in the scores of the two groups was found. Similarly, Lipman (1959) in his study of groups of patients differing markedly in the expression of aggression found that the Anxiety Scale score did not discriminate the two groups. Lipman (1960) has also shown that, as a group, mental retardates do not have higher total scores than normal children of comparable mental ages. As he indicates, one implication of this negative finding is that no support is provided for the idea that the observed inferior learning ability of mental retardates (as compared with normal children of the same mental age) can be ascribed to a high anxiety level in the retardates.

Personality and clinical types.—Clinicians have long been impressed by the characteristic personality differences to be observed among the various clinical types of mental retardation, e.g., mongolism, microcephaly, cretinism, etc. The extreme in this respect is, of course, the mongoloid patient who is regarded as being extraordinarily docile, good-natured, sociable, and affectionate. Hence it would seem that comparative study of the personality traits of patients in the several diagnostic categories and correlation of these traits with physical variables should constitute a very promising investigative program that might provide findings with important implications for the general problem of the physical determinants of personality and temperament. Unfortunately, the results of recent studies give no support to such expectations. In this regard, the comprehensive investigation by Blacketer-Simmonds (1953) of personality differences between mongoloid and non-mongoloid retardates is particularly worthy of mention. One part of this study consisted of a review of the histories of 140 mongoloid and 100 non-mongoloid patients with special reference to remarks about fifteen personality traits (e.g., cheerfulness, sociability, docility, irritability, destructiveness). With respect to twelve of the traits, no differences in the proportions of patients in the two groups manifesting the trait were found. The direction of the differences with respect to the remaining three traits was opposite to that which would be predicted from textbook descriptions. Thus, as compared with the control group, the mongoloid retardates were noted *less* often to be docile (17 per cent vs. 31 per cent) and *more* often to be solitary (16 per cent vs. 5 per cent) and mischievous (38 per cent vs. 24 per cent).

A second part of the study compared nurses' ratings of sixty mongoloid and three hundred non-mongoloid patients with respect to twelve personality traits. Not a single noteworthy difference was found, the largest observed differences in incidence being 4 per cent. It seems clear from these findings either that a distinctive syndrome of personality traits does not exist in mongolism or that the syndrome has been misnamed.

Prognosis.—Earlier in this chapter it was pointed out that, although course and outcome in mental retardation are variables which are open to investigation and control, empirically based prediction of future status is still quite feasible. The psychological evaluation plays an important role in this prognostic function. The empirical relations which form the basis for the prediction of future level of behavioral function from an observed present level have been determined in the course of numerous studies concerned with the "constancy of the IQ." The results of these studies have been summarized by many writers (e.g., Thorndike, 1940; Goodenough, 1949; Freeman, 1950; Anastasi, 1958) and are generally well known. Mention need be made of only two well-established findings that are of special interest. The first is that intelligence ratings at the age of six years or higher show a correlation of moderately high magnitude with later ratings, the size of the correlation varying inversely with the length of the interval between test and retest. Applied to the clinical situation, this permits prognostic inferences of *some* validity to be made from the findings of the psychological evaluation, the content of these inferences being in the form of a statement about the "most probable" future level of function of the patient. A second finding of interest (which follows necessarily from the fact of an only "moderately high" correlation between test and retest) is that many children show a considerable change in relative level of function (e.g., gaining or losing 15–30 IQ points) during the course of the developmental period. This fact is obviously of the utmost clinical importance for the prognostic assessment of the high-grade retarded child, and, quite naturally, the question as to whether the psychological evaluation can be utilized to differentiate the "gainers" from "no-changers" and the "losers" has been raised.

While there is no dearth of unvalidated convictions about the matter, a review of the relevant literature offers no substantial support for the belief that current methods of assessment and analysis can play a role of this kind. The study of Guertin (1950) may be cited as an example. He compared (among other factors) the initial test performances of a group of patients whom he considered to be "pseudofeebleminded" (i.e., showed large gains in IQ in later years) with those of a group whose IQ's did not change. Apparently the only differentiating psychometric feature that was found was a higher relative superiority on the Wechsler-Bellevue Performance Scale, as compared to the Verbal Scale level, in the subjects who subsequently gained in intelligence level. Judgments of emotional interference with intellectual function derived from inspection of the test results did not discriminate between the two groups. On the other hand, such factors as very poor home conditions and the absence of a family history of mental retardation appeared to be characteristic of the group which made large IQ gains.

In this connection, it is noteworthy that recent studies of retardates who later showed significant gains in IQ (e.g., Clarke, Clarke, and Reiman, 1958; Craft, 1959) emphasize the importance of the social history as a factor in prognosis and pay little attention to specific features of the psychological test findings. An exhaustive review of the literature on the diverse factors associated with prognosis in mental retardation has recently been completed by Windle (1962). This review, which includes a section on "abilities and disabilities," provides a valuable source of references as well as a sober evaluation of the present state of knowledge regarding the relationship between assessed characteristics and future status.

CLASSIFICATION AND DIFFERENTIAL DIAGNOSIS

Endogenous and exogenous defect.— As was mentioned in the introductory section of the chapter, it has been typical for two kinds of classification to be utilized in the field of mental retardation— a classification which takes account of etiologic or pathogenetic factors and one which is based on behavioral characteristics. Another kind of classification, which is called "etiological" but which, in fact, combines etiologic and behavioral elements, is the distinction between endogenous (familial) and exogenous (brain-injured) types of mental retardation. This classification, introduced by Strauss and Werner (1941; Werner and Thuma, 1942a, b; Strauss and Lehtenin, 1947; Strauss and Kephart, 1955), has had a deep influence on clinical thinking and psychological evaluation in the field. The decision as to whether a retarded patient is endogenous or exogenous is based upon three criteria, two being historical in nature and the third being based on clinical assessment. One is a history of mental retardation in the family; a positive history indicates endogenous defect, and a negative history indicates exogenous defect. The second is a history of injury to the brain by one or another noxious agent; a negative history indicates endogenous defect, and a positive history indicates exogenous defect. The third criterion is derived from a neurological examination with special reference to the findings in respect to motor co-ordination; normal findings indicate endogenous defect, and abnormal findings indicate exogenous defect.

The exact weight which is given to each of these criteria, which are not necessarily in a consistent direction in the individual case, seems to vary from one investigator to another, but, in any event, a considerable number of studies which have compared performances in the two types indicate a distinctive difference. The major features of the differences are that the exogenously retarded child is likely to show a more uneven level of performance with specific deficit in visuo-perceptive and visuomotor behavior (e.g., block design construction, drawing, perception of hidden figures). However, some studies have failed to find this difference, and, in addition, some of the apparently positive studies, when critically examined, prove to be not as informative as they might appear at first glance. For example, Werner (1945), comparing the performances of the two types of retardates on the Rorschach (here viewed as a perceptual task rather than a "personality" test), reported characteristic differences in the records, e.g., a higher proportion of oligophrenic details, space and pure color responses, and a lower incidence of movement responses on the part of the exogenous group. Yet, as Sarason (1959) has pointed out, the study has such serious technical weaknesses that the reported findings have little meaning.

There are a number of considerations which tend to impair confidence in the validity and usefulness of a dichotomy between endogenous and exogenous types of mental retardation. First, the concurrent use of three criteria which may or may not be consistent in their indications poses difficulties. If a child has a negative history for brain injury and a positive history for familial incidence and positive signs on the clinical neurological examination, should he be considered endogenous or exogenous? Should a retarded child with a history of postnatal cerebral disease be counted as exogenous if his family history is positive for mental retardation and the neurological examination is negative? These difficulties are well illustrated in a study by Feldman (1953) of the Bender-Gestalt Test (Bender, 1938) performances of endogenous and exogenous defectives. Feldman first

selected his subjects on the criterion of incidence of mental retardation in the family and formed two groups of familial (N = 101) and non-familial (N = 142) retardates. The neurological examination of Strauss and Lehtinen (1947) was then given to these subjects. The proportion of subjects in each group showing positive neurological signs did *not* differ significantly in the two groups. For the purposes of the study, two subgroups, one consisting of subjects with a *positive* family history and *no* neurological signs (N = 54) and the other consisting of subjects with a *negative* family history and *positive* neurological signs (N = 56), were then formed. These groups did show differential performance on the Bender-Gestalt Test, the "non-neurological" familial patients being superior to the "neurological" non-familial patients. However, more than half of the patients in the original groups are not accounted for, and, further, one does not know whether the differential performances of the tested groups are related to the familial history, the positive neurological signs, or both factors.

In the study of Gallagher (1957), the performances of carefully matched groups of brain-damaged and familial children were compared on a variety of tasks. All the brain-damaged patients had histories suggestive of cerebral insult or maldevelopment, twenty of the twenty-four had positive neurological findings, and the EEG records of all cases examined (N = 22) showed deviant characteristics. On the other hand, the twenty-four familial cases seemed to have been selected primarily on the basis of the occurrence of mental retardation in other members of the family. The findings of the neurological and EEG examinations, if given, are not detailed. The two groups thus formed did not show the differences in visuoperceptive and visuomotor performance which had been predicted from established generalizations and the findings of earlier studies, nor was there a difference in pattern of performance on the Stanford-Binet.

Another consideration that throws doubt on the usefulness of the distinction between brain injury and familial types of defect is that, when familial cases are neurologically evaluated, signs indicative of brain damage are often found, in many instances not less frequently than in cases of brain injury (cf. Yakovlev and Farrell, 1941; Benda, 1944; Feldman, 1953). Coupled with this, there is the behavioral evidence of specific deficit (rather than simple retardation) in familial retardates. The behavior of the brain-injured retardate has often been compared to that of the adult patient with acquired cerebral disease, but, as has been seen, the performances of familial retardates show the same similarity (cf. Boehm and Sarason, 1947; Sloan and Bensberg, 1951; Benton, 1955, 1959a; Swanson, 1957; Hunt, 1959).

While the dichotomy proposed by Werner and Strauss has not proved to be a useful one, it did have the merit of showing that the pattern of behavioral abilities and disabilities differs significantly among the mentally retarded and that these differences in pattern must be considered in planning for management and education. Thus, one result of the investigative work which has been done on familial and brain-injured patients has been to emphasize the diagnostic significance of different patterns of performance in the psychological evaluation, independently of assumed etiologic differences. Feldman (1953) concluded from his study that features of the mental test performance may be more predictive of other behavior, educability, and prognosis than the utilization of neurologic criteria. Similarly, Gallagher (1957) has raised the question, "Does the educator not gain more information from the fact that the child is perceptually disturbed than from the fact that he is brain-injured?" He gives the answer that "it would seem reasonable to expect the educator to make his own educational diagnosis of each child's perceptual development, personality skills or language development and make his plans accordingly whether or not a diagnosis of brain injury has been medically determined." Finally, as has already been mentioned, Hunt (1959, 1960) has argued forcefully for the adaptation of special-education programs to the observed behavioral disabilities of the child rather than to his prior diagnostic classification.

Mental retardation and mental disorder.—Since global intellectual subnormality is the nuclear trait in mental retardation, its exclusion in the psychological evaluation is sufficient to indicate that a patient is not mentally retarded, however incompetent or maladjusted he may be. Moreover, in the case of an adult whose over-all level of function is low, it is usually possible to distinguish between mental retardation existing since childhood and a more recently acquired condition of mental incompetence. Difficulties arise when the psychological evaluation indicates a global intellectual subnormality in a child in whom the question of mental disorder (as distinguished from mental retardation) has been raised. The relationships between mental retardation and various other clinically differentiated forms of behavior disorder in children, such as childhood autism and antisocial conduct, are the subject of Beier's chapter and need not be considered in detail here. At this point, only one facet of the problem will be mentioned to illustrate its complexity from the standpoint of the psychological evaluation.

The relationship between childhood autism or schizophrenia and mental retardation is an unsettled question. Bender (1959, p. 85) has advanced the view that autistic thought and action can occur within the setting of different primary difficulties, such as mental retardation, brain damage, and disturbances in interpersonal relations, and that, for the most part, it is not a basic diagnosis but rather "a primitive form of behavior, a part of the normal developmental process which may persist and become exaggerated or represent by withdrawal, a defense against disorganization and anxiety in children with many different types of pathology in their genes, brains, perceptual organs or social relationships." Many clinicians disagree with this formulation, consider childhood schizophrenia to be a primary disorder, and insist that differential diagnosis between it and mental retardation is a necessity.

Empirical data bearing on this question of the relationship between childhood schizophrenia and mental retardation is provided by Pollack's (1958) discussion of psychological test performance in schizophrenic children, the main finding of which is that they show an excessively high incidence of low IQ scores. His review of the literature indicates that about 34 per cent of schizophrenic children score below IQ 70 and an additional 44 per cent score within the IQ range of 70–89, thus demonstrating "the marked overlap in intellectual functioning between schizophrenic children and those diagnosed as mentally retarded" (p. 423). Moreover, a comparison of schizophrenic children with children suffering from other types of behavior disorder showed a significantly higher incidence of subnormal IQ's in the schizophrenics. Further comparisons of performance on perceptual and motor tests indicated a similarity between the schizophrenic children and mental retardates. These findings led Pollack to conclude (p. 427) that

neither childhood schizophrenia nor mental retardation is a distinct clinical entity encompassing homogeneous groups. When severe behavior disorder coexists with intellectual defect in childhood, the altered behavior may be a reflection of cerebral dysfunction. Which aspect is stressed—the retardation or the behavior disorder—is, in part, a function of the observer's orientation rather than the child's behavior.

CONCLUDING REMARKS

The strengths and limitations of current psychodiagnostic practice in the field of mental retardation might be assessed as follows: There is a sufficient variety of procedures available to assure a comprehensive evaluation of abilities and a valid estimate of general intellectual level. This is not to deny that in any individual case extraneous factors (e.g., anxiety, hostility, simulation of stupidity, transient physical disability) may operate to depress level of performance in the examination situation itself and thus reduce the validity of inferences regarding intellectual capacity made from observation of test performance. However, this problem, inherent in all forms of clinical examination, does not necessarily reflect unfavorably on the assessment procedures themselves but, rather, calls for judgment on the part of the examiner.

Clinical investigation indicates that performance on certain types of nonverbal tasks (e.g., formboards, picture construction, mazes) has relatively high value for the prediction of behavioral efficiency and personal adjustment. In view of this, it is rather regrettable that some of these tasks have tended to fall into disuse for purposes of assessment, perhaps because the WISC covers some of these areas of performance. Maze tests of the Porteus type seem to be particularly useful in this respect. Although the WISC includes a maze subtest, it is an "optional" one and usually is not given. The predictive significance of tests of motor skills, such as the Oseretsky, has not received a great deal of critical evaluation, but they seem to have considerable face validity and to provide important implications for training and placement. Yet one's impression is that usually they are not part of the psychological assessment battery. Auditory and visual perception, on various levels of complexity, ranging from basic acuity to higher-level semantic performances, is an important determinant of behavioral development and efficiency in the subnormal individual. Again the typical test battery does not include direct assessment of these functions.

These considerations lead one to make a distinction between current psychodiagnostic practice and current psychodiagnostic possibilities and to conclude that, in general, the possibilities are not being fully exploited. If more comprehensive assessment batteries were the rule and if, in addition, some degree of standardization in content were established, not only would an immediate practical advance be achieved but also a good many questions about the clinical validity of various procedures could be answered rather quickly. In addition, the application of such a comprehensive battery to normal children and mental defectives should provide much-needed information regarding the organization of abilities in the two groups.

Turning to some of the more specific questions to which the psychological evaluation is often expected to contribute answers, one finds that there is very little evidence to support the practice of making inferences regarding the presence of emotional (or other non-intellectual) interference with intellectual function from observation of various features of test performance (e.g., scatter, digit-span performance, W:M ratio on the Rorschach). This general procedure is often conceptualized as drawing a comparison between "intellectual capacity" or "intellectual potential" and "actual level of intellectual functioning." Quite apart from the fact that the employment of the concepts of "capacity" and "potential" in this context requires fuller explication if the idea is to be a useful one, the conclusion that the observed performance of a high-grade retardate is an underestimate of "potential" is drawn so often that at times it becomes a non-discriminating "universal diagnosis." This propensity of clinical psychologists has not escaped the

notice of some physicians. Lauretta Bender (1959, p. 82) has had occasion to remark that "of late it has seemed that psychologists seek to find evidence of higher potentialities in all the deviate children they study, and rarely fail to do so. The mental defective who does not have some such evidence is also very rare." This uncritical handling of psychometric findings, which sometimes seems to represent no more than a generous impulse to temper justice with mercy, serves no useful purpose. Valid inferences regarding the effects of non-intellectual factors on overall intellectual functioning must wait upon, first, a more precise theoretical formulation of the basic issue than is represented by simply distinguishing "capacity" and "actual functioning" and, second, the determination of stable relationships between test factors and the relevant psychological variables. In view of the keen clinical interest in this issue at the present time, carefully conceived investigative work on it is of primary importance.

Another specific question for which the answer is sought primarily in the psychological evaluation is the differential diagnosis between mental retardation and specific language retardation. Sometimes the distinction is quite easily made on the basis of the test findings. However, as was suggested earlier in the chapter, when the findings indicate both a language handicap and a general mental retardation, a reformulation of the problem may be advantageous. In such cases, the examiner may ask whether or not the language handicap is playing a responsible mediating role in the appearance of the global defect state. As has been indicated, it may be possible to derive the answer from a comparative analysis of performances on tasks requiring varying degrees of language function (this latter term referring to capacity for symbolic formulation and expression rather than simply ability to understand and express spoken or written language). This requires a more precise knowledge than we now possess of the "verbal saturation," so to speak, of various tests. Hence, one direction which future investigative work might take is toward the development of such tests and the analysis of their diagnostic significance in mental retardation. In order to broaden the significance of the findings, such investigation should include consideration of the performances of various groups of subjects and maintain ties with current theoretical research on human abilities as well as clinical studies of patients with cerebral disease, particularly aphasic patients.

Prognosis is one of the traditional functions of the psychological evaluation. As we have seen, it can provide a valid, if somewhat gross, *general* prediction of future status (which, in most cases, consists simply in the statement that the observed intellectual level is the most probable future level). On the other hand, the psychological evaluation per se is not capable of providing a *specific* prediction in the sense of identifying those children who will show an atypical rate of development and whose final relative level of intellectual function will be significantly higher or lower than that shown at the time of examination.

Can the prognostic precision of the psychological evaluation be increased? One approach has been to analyze various aspects of test performance with the aim of identifying those features which correlate most highly with future level. While these attempts have not proved to be successful, the possibilities have not been fully explored, and it may be that further analysis of hitherto unconsidered aspects of performance on a comprehensive assessment battery will yield substantial results. However, it may be that this basic approach, which implicitly assumes that prognosis reflects a "destiny" that is relatively independent of the effects of future events, is sterile. As we have seen, the modern conception is that

course and outcome are variables and not constants—variables which are determined by many factors, some of which can be modified by deliberate biochemical, surgical, special educational, psychotherapeutic, and social efforts. From this standpoint, there is little hope of being able to achieve greater precision in the prediction of final status directly from present examination findings, since this assumes either a constancy of the future internal and external milieu or a resistance to changes in it. Instead, prognosis on the basis of the psychological evaluation becomes more complex and qualified and, at the same time, more meaningful in certain respects. The direct prediction of future status from the psychological findings may be schematized as simply, "if A, then Z." In contrast, a prediction which takes account of possibly modifiable factors (some of which might be disclosed by the psychological evaluation) requires rather more complex schemas such as, "if A, and if B and C can be changed, then Y; but if B and C are not changed, then Z." Thus, unlike the direct prediction, the qualified prediction may include important indications for special management and treatment.

Certainly an important task for future research is to provide the basic knowledge which is required to develop the usefulness of the psychological evaluation for such "qualified" prognosis. The work of Hunt on patients who show relatively specific psycho-visual or psycho-auditory handicap, with its indications for special educational procedures of a defined nature, suggests one direction of effort. The clinical and prognostic significance of specific somatosensory deficits in the mentally retarded is still an open question and deserves further exploration. Above all, language functions warrant intensive analysis because of their crucial role in mental development. There is a tendency to think of specific deficits, such as these, as relatively unmodifiable and to recommend the use of educational methods which in one way or another circumvent them. However, the degree to which some of them (e.g., auditory-verbal disability, right-left disorientation) can be influenced by special training has not been thoroughly studied. The results of such experimentation could have quite important clinical implications.

References

ABEL, T. M. 1945a. The relationship between academic success and personality organization among subnormal girls. *Amer. J. Ment. Defic.*, **50**:251–56.

——. 1945b. The Rorschach test and school success among mental defectives. *Rorschach Res. Exch.*, **9**:105–10.

ALDERDICE, E. T., and BUTLER, A. J. 1952. An analysis of the performance of mental defectives on the Revised Stanford-Binet and the Wechsler Intelligence Scale. *Amer. J. Ment. Defic.*, **56**:609–11.

ALPER, A. E. 1958. A comparison of the Wechsler Intelligence Scale for Children and the Arthur Adaptation of the Leiter International Performance Scale with mental defectives. *Amer. J. Ment. Defic.*, **63**: 312–16.

ANASTASI, A. 1954. *Psychological Testing.* New York: Macmillan.

——. 1958. *Differential Psychology.* 3d ed.; New York: Macmillan.

ANASTASI, A., and LEVEE, R. F. 1960. Intellectual defect and musical talent: a case report. *Amer. J. Ment. Defic.*, **64**:695–703.

ARTHUR, G. 1930. *A Point Scale of Performance Tests.* New York: Commonwealth Fund.

——. 1947. Pseudo-feeblemindedness. *Amer. J. Ment. Defic.*, **52**:137–42.

ATCHISON, C. O. 1955. Use of the Wechsler Intelligence Scale with eighty mentally defective Negro children. *Amer. J. Ment. Defic.*, **60**:378–79.

BABCOCK, H. 1930. An experiment in the measurement of mental deterioration. *Arch. Psychol.*, No. 117.

BARNETT, C. D., and PRYER, M. W. 1958. Note on depth perception in defectives. *Percept. Motor Skills*, **8**:130.

BAROFF, G. S. 1959. WISC patterning in endogenous mental deficiency. *Amer. J. Ment. Defic.*, **64**:482–85.

BECK, H. S., and LAM, R. L. 1955. Use of the WISC in predicting organicity. *J. Clin. Psychol.*, **11**:154–58.

BECK, S. J. 1932. The Rorschach test as applied to a feebleminded group. *Arch. Psychol.*, No. 136.

BENDA, C. E. 1944. The familial imbecile or oligo-encephaly as a morbid entity. *Amer. J. Ment. Defic.*, **49**:32–42.

——. 1952. *Developmental Disorders of Mentation and Cerebral Palsy.* New York: Grune & Stratton.

BENDER, L. 1938. A visual motor gestalt test and its clinical use. *Res. Monogr., Amer. Orthopsychiat. Assoc.*, No. 3.

——. 1959. Autism in children with mental deficiency. *Amer. J. Ment. Defic.*, **64**:81–86.

BENSBERG, G. J., and SLOAN, W. 1955. The use of the Cattell Culture-Free Test with mental defectives. *Amer. J. Ment. Defic.*, **59**:499–503.

BENTON, A. L. 1955. Right-left discrimination and finger localization in defective children. *Arch. Neurol. Psychiat.*, **74**:583–89.

——. 1956a. The concept of pseudofeeblemindedness. *Ibid.*, **75**:379–88.

——. 1956b. The Rorschach test and the diagnosis of cerebral pathology in children. *Amer. J. Orthopsychiat.*, **26**:783–91.

——. 1958. Significance of systematic reversal in right-left discrimination. *Acta Psychiat. Neurol. (Kbn.)*, **33**:129–37.

——. 1959a. *Right-Left Discrimination and Finger Localization: Development and Pathology.* New York: Hoeber-Harper.

——. 1959b. Aphasia in children. *Education*, **79**:408–12.

——. 1962. Some aspects of the concept of psychogenic mental deficiency. *Proceedings of the London Conference on the Scientific Study of Mental Deficiency, 1960*, pp. 243–50. Dagenham, England: May & Baker.

BENTON, A. L., HUTCHEON, J. F., and SEYMOUR, E. 1951. Arithmetic ability, finger localization capacity and right-left discrimination in normal and defective children. *Amer. J. Orthopsychiat.*, **21**:756–66.

BENTON, A. L., and KEMBLE, J. D. 1960. Right-left orientation and reading disability. *Psychiat. Neurol. (Basel)*, **139**:49–60.

BENTON, A. L., and SCHULTZ, L. M. 1949. Observations on tactual form perception (stereognosis) in preschool children. *J. Clin. Psychol.*, **5**:359–64.

BERGLER, E. 1932. Zur Problematik der Pseudodebilität. *Int. Z. Psychoanal.*, **18**:528–38.

BIJOU, S. W. 1939. The problem of pseudo-feeblemindedness. *J. Educ. Psychol.*, **30**:519–26.

———. 1941. The psychometric pattern approach as an aid to clinical analysis: a review. *Amer. J. Ment. Defic.*, **46**:354–62.

———. 1942. A genetic study of the diagnostic significance of psychometric patterns. *Amer. J. Ment. Defic.*, **47**:171–77.

———. 1944. Behavior efficiency as a determining factor in the social adjustment of mentally retarded young men. *J. Genet. Psychol.*, **65**:133–45.

BIJOU, S. W., and McCANDLESS, B. R. 1944. An approach to a more comprehensive analysis of mentally retarded pre-delinquent boys. *J. Genet. Psychol.*, **65**:147–60.

BIRCH, J. W., and MATHEWS, J. 1951. The hearing of mental defectives: its measurement and characteristics. *Amer. J. Ment. Defic.*, **55**:384–93.

BLACKETER-SIMMONDS, D. A. 1953. An investigation into the supposed differences existing between mongols and other mentally defective subjects with regard to certain psychological traits. *J. Ment. Sci.*, **99**:702–19.

BOEHM, A. E., and SARASON, S. B. 1947. Does Wechsler's formula distinguish intellectual deterioration from mental deficiency? *J. Abnorm. Soc. Psychol.*, **42**:356–58.

BOLLES, M. M. 1937. The basis of pertinence. *Arch. Psychol.*, No. 212.

BORNSTEIN, B. 1930. Zur Psychogenese der Pseudodebilität. *Int. Z. Psychoanal.*, **16**:378–99.

BUROS, O. K. (ed.). 1959. *The Fifth Mental Measurements Yearbook.* Highland Park, N.J.: Gryphon Press.

BURT, C. 1947. *Mental and Scholastic Tests.* London: Staples Press.

CALLAHAN, R. J., and KELLER, J. E. 1957. Digit span and anxiety: an experimental group revisited. *Amer. J. Ment. Defic.*, **61**:581–82.

CANTOR, G. N. 1955. On the incurability of mental deficiency. *Amer. J. Ment. Defic.*, **60**:362–65.

CANTOR, G. N., and GIRARDEAU, F. L. 1959. Rhythmic discrimination ability in mongoloid and normal children. *Amer. J. Ment. Defic.*, **63**:621–25.

CANTOR, G. N., and STACEY, W. L. 1951. Manipulative dexterity in mental defectives. *Amer. J. Ment. Defic.*, **56**:401–10.

CASSEL, R. H. 1949. The Vineland Adaptation of the Oseretsky tests. *Training Sch. Bull.*, Monogr. Suppl. Ser., No. 1, 1–32.

CASTANEDA, A., McCANDLESS, B. R., and PALERMO, D. S. 1956. The Children's Form of the Manifest Anxiety Scale. *Child Develop.*, **27**:317–26.

CATTELL, R. B. 1951. Classical and standard score IQ standardization of the I.P.A.T. Culture Free Intelligence Scale. *J. Consult. Psychol.*, **15**:154–59.

CLARKE, A. D. B., and CLARKE, A. M. 1955. Pseudo-feeblemindedness—some implications. *Amer. J. Ment. Defic.*, **59**:505–9.

CLARKE, A. D. B., CLARKE, A. M., and REIMAN, S. 1958. Cognitive and social changes in the feebleminded—three further studies. *Brit. J. Psychol.*, **49**:144–57.

CORNELL, E. L., and COX, W. W. 1934. *Performance Ability Scales: Manual of Directions.* Yonkers, N.Y.: World Book Co.

CRAFT, M. 1959. Personality disorder and dullness. *Lancet* (1), 856–58.

CUTTS, R. A., and LANE, M. A. 1947. The effect of hospitalization on Wechsler-Bellevue subtest scores by mental defectives. *Amer. J. Ment. Defic.*, **51**:391–93.

CUTTS, R. A., and SLOAN, W. 1945. Test patterns of adjusted defectives on the Wechsler-Bellevue test. *Amer. J. Ment. Defic.*, **50**:98–101.

DAVIS, A., and EELLS, K. 1953. *Davis-Eells Test of General Intelligence or Problem-Solving Ability.* Yonkers, N.Y.: World Book Co.

DELAY, J., PICHOT, P., and PERSE, J. 1952a. La notion de débilité mentale camouflée. *Ann. Medico-psychol.*, **110** (1):615–19.

———. 1952b. La notion de pseudo-débilité mentale par arriération affective. *Ibid.*, pp. 620–25.

DOLL, E. A. 1941. The essentials of an inclusive concept of mental deficiency. *Amer. J. Ment. Defic.*, **46**:214–19.

———. 1947. Is mental deficiency curable? *Ibid.*, **51**:420–28.

———. 1953. *The Measurement of Social Competence: A Manual for the Vineland*

Social Maturity Scale. Minneapolis: Educational Test Bureau.

DRAKE, R. M. 1959. Review of Davis-Eells Games of general intelligence or problem-solving ability. (See Buros, 1959, p. 326.)

DUBITSCHER, F. 1936. Der moralische Schwachsinn unter besonderer Berücksichtigung des Gesetzes zur Verhütung erbkranken Nachwuchses. *Z. Neurol. Psychiat.*, 154:408–57.

EARL, C. J. C. 1938. The performance test behavior of adult morons. *Brit. J. Med. Psychol.*, 17:78–92.

———. 1940. A psychograph for morons. *J. Abnorm. Soc. Psychol.*, 35:428–48.

EISENBERG, L. 1958. Emotional determinants of mental deficiency. *Arch. Neurol. Psychiat.*, 80:114–21.

ELLIS, W. J. 1933. *The Handicapped Child*. New York: Century.

FELDMAN, I. S. 1953. Psychological differences among moron and borderline mental defectives as a function of etiology. *Amer. J. Ment. Defic.*, 57:484–94.

FINK, M., GREEN, M. A., and BENDER, M. B. 1953. Perception of simultaneous tactile stimuli by mentally defective subjects. *J. Nerv. Ment. Dis.*, 117:43–49.

FOALE, M., and PATERSON, C. W. 1954. The hearing of mental defectives. *Amer. J. Ment. Defic.*, 59:254–58.

FREEMAN, F. S. 1950. *Theory and Practice of Psychological Testing*. New York: Holt.

GALLAGHER, J. J. 1957. A comparison of brain-injured and non-brain-injured mentally retarded children on several psychological variables. *Monogr. Soc. Res. Child Develop.*, 22, Ser. No. 65, No. 2.

GALLAGHER, J. J., BENOIT, E. P. and BOYD, H. F. 1956. Measurement of intelligence in brain-damaged children. *J. Clin. Psychol.*, 12:69–72.

GELLNER, L. 1957. The pathology of mental defects. *Proc. First Int. Cong. Neurol. Sci.*, 5:103–8. London: Pergamon Press.

GOLDSTEIN, K., and SCHEERER, M. 1941. Abstract and concrete behavior: an experimental study with special tasks. *Psychol. Monogr.*, 53, No. 239.

GOODENOUGH, F. L. 1926. *Measurement of Intelligence by Drawings*. Yonkers, N.Y.: World Book Co.

———. 1949. *Mental Testing: Its History, Principles and Applications*. New York: Rinehart.

GORDON, A. M. 1944. Some aspects of sensory discrimination in mongolism. *Amer. J. Ment. Defic.*, 49:55–63.

GUERTIN, W. H. 1950. Differential characteristics of the pseudo-feebleminded. *Amer. J. Ment. Defic.*, 54:394–98.

GUNZBURG, H. C. 1959. Earl's moron-battery and social adjustment. *Amer. J. Ment. Defic.*, 64:92–103.

HALPIN, V. G. 1958. The performance of mentally retarded children on the Weigl-Goldstein-Scheerer color form sorting test. *Amer. J. Ment. Defic.*, 62:916–19.

HARRIS, A. J. 1957. Lateral dominance, directional confusion and reading disability. *J. Pyschol.*, 44:283–94.

HARRIS, A. J., and SHAKOW, D. 1937. The clinical significance of numerical measures of scatter on the Stanford-Binet. *Psychol. Bull.*, 34:134–50.

HARRISON, S. 1958. A review of research in speech and language development of the mentally retarded child. *Amer. J. Ment. Defic.*, 63:236–40.

HAYS, W. 1950. A comparison of scatter patterning for mental defectives on the Wechsler Forms I and II. *Amer. J. Ment. Defic.*, 55:264–68.

HEALY, W., and FERNALD, G. M. 1911. Tests for practical mental classification. *Psychol. Monogr.*, 13, No. 2.

HEATH, S. R. 1942. Rail-walking performance as related to mental age and etiological type among the mentally retarded. *Amer. J. Psychol.*, 55:240–47.

HEBER, R. (ed.). 1959. A manual on terminology and classification in mental retardation. *Monogr. Suppl., Amer. J. Ment. Defic.*, 64, No. 2.

HERMANN, K., and NORRIE, E. 1958. Is congenital word-blindness a hereditary type of Gerstmann's syndrome? *Psychiat. Neurol.* (Basel), 136:59–73.

HUNT, B. M. 1959. Performance of mentally deficient brain-injured children and mentally deficient familial children on construction from patterns. *Amer. J. Ment. Defic.*, 63:679–87.

———. 1960. Differential responses of mentally deficient brain-injured children and mentally deficient familial children to meaningful auditory material. *Ibid.*, 64:747–53.

HUNT, B. M., and PATTERSON, R. M. 1958. Performances of brain-injured and familial mentally deficient children on visual and auditory sequences. *Amer. J. Ment. Defic.*, **63**:72–80.

JASTAK, J. 1949. A rigorous critique of feeble-mindedness. *J. Abnorm. Soc. Psychol.*, **44**:367–78.

KELLER, J. E. 1957. The relationship of auditory memory span to learning ability in high grade mentally retarded boys. *Amer. J. Ment. Defic.*, **61**:574–80.

KEMPF, G. A., and COLLINS, S. D. 1929. A study of the relation between mental and physical status of children in two counties in Illinois. *Public Health Rep., U.S. Public Health Service,* **44** (2):1743–84.

KLAUSMEIER, H. J., and CHECK, J. 1959. Relationships among physical, mental, achievement, and personality measures in children of low, average and high intelligence at 113 months of age. *Amer. J. Ment. Defic.*, **63**:1059–68.

KNIEF, L. M. 1957. "An Investigation of the Cultural Bias Issue in Intelligence Testing." Ph.D. dissertation, State Univ. Iowa.

KODMAN, F. 1958. The incidence of hearing loss in mentally retarded children. *Amer. J. Ment. Defic.*, **62**:675–79.

KODMAN, F., *et al.* 1958. An investigation of hearing loss in mentally retarded children and adults. *Amer. J. Ment. Defic.*, **63**:460–63.

KOHS, S. C. 1923. *Intelligence Measurement.* New York: Macmillan.

KOLSTOE, O. P. 1954. A comparison of mental abilities of bright and dull children. *J. Educ. Psychol.*, **45**:161–68.

LASSNER, R. 1948. Annotated bibliography on the Oseretsky tests of motor proficiency. *J. Consult. Psychol.*, **12**:37–47.

LAYCOCK, S. R., and CLARK, S. 1942. The comparative performance of a group of old-dull and young-bright children on some items of the Revised Stanford-Binet Scale, Form L. *J. Educ. Psychol.*, **33**:1–12.

LEITER, R. G. 1936. The Leiter International Performance Scale. *Univ. Hawaii Bull.*, **15**:1–42.

———. 1940. *The Leiter-International Performance Scale,* Vol. 1. Santa Barbara, Cal.: Santa Barbara State Coll. Press.

———. 1948. *Leiter International Performance Scale: Revised Manual.* Washington, D.C.: Psychological Service Center Press.

LIPMAN, R. S. 1959. Some test correlates of behavioral aggression in institutionalized retardates with particular references to the Rosenzweig Picture-Frustration study. *Amer. J. Ment. Defic.*, **63**:1038–45.

———. 1960. Children's manifest anxiety in retardates and approximately equal M.A. normals. *Amer. J. Ment. Defic.*, **64**:1027–28.

LUBMAN, C. G. 1955. Speech program for severely retarded children. *Amer. J. Ment. Defic.*, **60**:297–300.

LURIA, A. R., and YUDOVICH, F. IA. 1959. *Speech and the Development of Mental Processes in the Child.* London: Staples Press.

McCULLOCH, T. L. 1947. Reformulation of the problem of mental deficiency. *Amer. J. Ment. Defic.*, **52**:130–36.

McNEMAR, O. 1942. *The Revision of the Stanford-Binet Scale.* Boston: Houghton Mifflin.

MADONICK, M. J. 1954. Insensitiveness to pain. *Neurology*, **4**:554–57.

MÄNCHEN, A. 1936. Denkhemmung und Aggression aus Kastrationsangst. *Z. psychoanal. Pädagogik,* **10**:276–99.

MAGARET, A., and THOMPSON, C. W. 1950. Differential test responses of normal, superior and mentally defective subjects. *J. Abnorm. Soc. Psychol.*, **45**:163–67.

MAGARET, A., and WRIGHT, C. 1943. Limitations in the use of intelligence test performance to detect mental disturbances. *J. Appl. Psychol.*, **27**:387–98.

MALPASS, L. F. 1960. Motor proficiency in institutionalized and non-institutionalized retarded children and normal children. *Amer. J. Ment. Defic.*, **64**:1012–15.

MASLAND, R. 1958. The prevention of mental retardation: a survey of research. *Amer. J. Ment. Defic.*, **62**:991–1112.

MECHAM, M. F. 1955. The development and application of procedures for measuring speech improvement in mentally defective children. *Amer. J. Ment. Defic.*, **60**:301–6.

MERCIER, C. 1890. *Sanity and Insanity.* London: Walter Scott.

MERRILL, M. A. 1924. On the relation of intelligence to achievement in cases of mentally retarded children. *Comp. Psychol. Monogr.*, No. 10.

MOLISH, H. B. 1958. Contributions of projective tests to problems of psychological diagnosis in mental deficiency. *Amer. J. Ment. Defic.*, **63**:282–92.

NEWMAN, J. R., and LOOS, F. M. 1955. Differences between Verbal and Performance IQ's with mentally defective children on the Wechsler Intelligence Scale for Children. *J. Consult. Psychol.*, **19**:16.

O'CONNOR, N. 1957. Imbecility and color blindness. *Amer. J. Ment. Defic.*, **62**:83–87.

O'CONNOR, N., and TIZARD, J. 1951. Predicting the occupational adequacy of certified mental defectives. *Occup. Psychol.*, **25**:205–11.

OGDEN, T. E., ROBERT, F., and CARMICHAEL, E. A. 1959. Some sensory syndromes in children: indifference to pain and sensory neuropathy. *J. Neurol. Neurosurg. Psychiat.*, **22**:267–76.

PAPANIA, M., ROSENBLUM, S., and KELLER, J. E. 1955. Responses of lower social class, high-grade mentally handicapped boys to a "culture fair" test of intelligence—the Davis-Eells Games. *Amer. J. Ment. Defic.*, **59**:493–98.

PENROSE, L. S. 1949. *The Biology of Mental Defect*. New York: Grune & Stratton.

PENWILL, M. 1958. Speech disorders and therapy in mental deficiency. In CLARKE, A. M., and CLARKE, A. D. B. (eds.). *Mental Deficiency: The Changing Outlook*, pp. 393–421. Glencoe, Ill.: Free Press.

PERKINS, C. H., and DAYTON, N. A. 1940. Annual Report, Commissioner of Mental Health, Commonwealth of Massachusetts, P.D. No. 117.

PERTEGO, J. 1950. La "Escala metrica de Oseretzky" para el examen de la motorica. *Rev. Psicol. Gen. Apl.*, **15**:539–53.

PFLUGFELDER, G. 1949. Uber intellektuelle spätreife bei zerebraler Kinderlähmung. *Schweiz. Arch. Neurol. Psychiat.*, **63**:294–99.

PINTNER, R., and PATERSON, D. 1917. *A Scale of Performance Tests*. New York: Appleton-Century-Crofts.

POLLACK, M. 1958. Brain damage, mental retardation and childhood schizophrenia. *Amer. J. Psychiat.*, **115**:427–28.

POLLACK, M., and GORDON, E. 1960. The face-hand test in retarded and non-retarded emotionally disturbed children. *Amer. J. Ment. Defic.*, **64**:758–60.

PORTEUS, S. D. 1918. The measurement of intelligence: 653 children examined by the Binet and Porteus tests. *J. Educ. Psychol.*, **9**:13–31.

———. 1941. *The Practice of Clinical Psychology*. New York: American Book.

POTOTZKY, C., and GRIGG, A. E. 1942. A revision of the prognosis in mongolism. *Amer. J. Orthopsychiat.*, **12**:503–10.

RABIN, H. M. 1957. The relationship of age, intelligence and sex to motor proficiency in mental defectives. *Amer. J. Ment. Defic.*, **62**:507–16.

ROSENZWEIG, S., FLEMING, A. F., and ROSENZWEIG, L. 1948. The children's form of the Rosenzweig Picture-Frustration Study. *J. Psychol.*, **26**:141–91.

SANDERCOCK, M. G., and BUTLER, A. J. 1952. An analysis of the performance of mental defectives on the Wechsler Intelligence Scale for Children. *Amer. J. Ment. Defic.*, **57**:100–105.

SARASON, S. B. 1959. *Psychological Problems in Mental Deficiency*. 3d ed.; New York: Harper.

SARASON, S. B., and SARASON, E. K. 1946. The discriminatory value of a test pattern in the high grade familial defective. *J. Clin. Psychol.*, **2**:38–49.

SCHLANGER, B. 1958. Speech therapy with mentally retarded children. *J. Speech Dis.*, **23**:298–301.

SCHLANGER, B., and GOTTESLEBEN, R. H. 1957. Analysis of speech defects among the mentally retarded. *Training Sch. Bull.*, **54**:5–8.

SCHOB, F. 1930. Pathologische Anatomie der Idiotie. In BUMKE, O. (ed.). *Handbuch der Geisteskrankheiten*, **7**:779–995. Berlin: Springer.

SIEGENTHALER, B. M., and KRZYWICKI, D. F. 1959. Incidence and patterns of hearing loss among an adult mentally retarded population. *Amer. J. Ment. Defic.*, **64**:444–49.

SLOAN, W. 1947. Validity of Wechsler's deterioration quotient in high-grade mental defectives. *J. Clin. Psychol.*, **3**:287–88.

———. 1948. Prediction of extramural adjustment of mental defectives by use of the Rorschach test. *J. Consult. Psychol.*, **12**:303–9.

———. 1955. The Lincoln-Oseretsky Motor Development Scale. *Genet. Psychol. Monogr.*, **51**:183–252.

SLOAN, W., and BENSBERG, G. J. 1951. The stereognostic capacity of brain-injured as compared with familial mental defectives. *J. Clin. Psychol.*, 7:154–56.

SLOAN, W., and BIRCH, J. W. 1955. A rationale for degrees of retardation. *Amer. J. Ment. Defic.*, 60:258–64.

SLOAN, W., and CUTTS, R. A. 1945. Test patterns of defective delinquents on the Wechsler-Bellevue test. *Amer. J. Ment. Defic.*, 50:95–97.

SLOAN, W., and SCHNEIDER, B. 1951. A study of the Wechsler Intelligence Scale for Children with mental defectives. *Amer. J. Ment. Defic.*, 55:573–75.

SPILLANE, J. D. 1942. Disturbances of the body scheme: anosognosia and finger agnosia. *Lancet* (1), 24–44.

STENGEL, E., OLDHAM, A. J., and EHRENBURG, A. S. C. 1958. Reactions of low-grade mental defectives to pain. *J. Ment. Sci.*, 104:434–38.

STRAUSS, A. A., and KEPHART, N. C. 1955. *Psychopathology and Education of the Brain-Injured Child, Vol. 2: Progress in Theory and Clinic.* New York: Grune & Stratton.

STRAUSS, A. A., and LEHTINEN, L. E. 1947. *Psychopathology and Education of the Brain-Injured Child.* New York: Grune & Stratton.

STRAUSS, A. A., and WERNER, H. 1938. Deficiency in the finger schema in relation to arithmetic disability (finger agnosia and acalculia). *Amer. J. Orthopsychiat.*, 8:719–25.

———. 1939. Finger agnosia in children: with a brief discussion on defect and retardation in mentally handicapped children. *Amer. J. Psychiat.*, 95:1215–25.

———. 1941. The mental organization of the brain-injured mentally defective child. *Ibid.*, 97:1194–1203.

SWANSON, R. 1957. Perception of simultaneous tactual stimulation in defective and normal children. *Amer. J. Ment. Defic.*, 61:743–52.

THOMPSON, C. W., and MAGARET, A. 1947. Differential test responses of normals and mental defectives. *J. Abnorm. Soc. Psychol.*, 42:285–93.

THORNDIKE, R. L. 1940. "Constancy" of the IQ. *Psychol. Bull.*, 37:167–86.

TIZARD, J., O'CONNOR, H., and CRAWFORD, J. M. 1950. The abilities of adolescent and adult high-grade male defectives. *J. Ment. Sci.*, 96:889–907.

TREDGOLD, A. F. 1952. *A Textbook of Mental Deficiency (Amentia).* 8th ed.; Baltimore: Williams & Wilkins.

WALLIN, J. E. W. 1929. A statistical study of the individual tests of the Stanford-Binet scale. *Ment. Meas. Monogr.*, No. 6.

WATSON, R. I. 1951. *The Clinical Method in Psychology.* New York: Harper.

WECHSLER, D. 1939. *The Measurement of Adult Intelligence.* Baltimore: Williams & Wilkins.

———. 1949. *Wechsler Intelligence Scale for Children.* New York: Psychological Corp.

———. 1958. *The Measurement and Appraisal of Adult Intelligence.* 4th ed.; Baltimore: Williams & Wilkins.

WEISENBURG, T., ROE, A., and McBRIDE, K. 1936. *Adult Intelligence.* New York: Commonwealth Fund.

WERNER, H. 1945. Perceptual behavior of brain-injured, mentally defective children: an experimental study by means of the Rorschach technique. *Genet. Psychol. Monogr.*, 31:51–110.

WERNER, H., and THUMA, B. B. 1942a. A deficiency in the perception of apparent motion in children with brain injury. *Amer. J. Psychol.*, 55:58–67.

———. 1942b. Critical flicker-frequency in children with brain injury. *Amer. J. Psychol.*, 55:394–99.

WEYGANDT, W. 1936. *Der jugendliche Schwachsinn.* Stuttgart: Enke.

WINDLE, C. D. 1962. Prognosis of mental subnormals. *Monogr. Suppl., Amer. J. Ment. Defic.* Pp. 180.

YAKOVLOV, P., and FARRELL, M. J. 1941. Influence of locomotion on the plantar reflex in normal and in physically and mentally inferior persons. *Arch. Neurol. Psychiat.*, 46:322–30.

YERKES, R. M. 1921. *Psychological Examining in the United States Army.* ("Memoirs, Nat. Acad. Sci.," Vol. 15.) Washington, D.C.

RESEARCH IN EDUCATION

Samuel A. Kirk

Educational research is generally applied, or engineering, research. Just as medicine relies on the basic sciences for the improvement of its practice, so education likewise relies primarily on the social sciences for the improvement of its procedures. A complete review of the research that has implications for education would include many experiments in learning, the field of personality or social adjustment, measurement, sociology, and related disciplines. The present volume, however, includes chapters on the contributions of the basic sciences to the field of mental retardation. For that reason, these areas have not been included in this review. Instead, research which is related more directly to educational practice and which would not ordinarily be included in other sections has been covered here. This chapter includes a review and an evaluation of investigations on (1) special classes for the educable mentally retarded, (2) education of trainable mentally retarded children, (3) modifying intelligence through education, (4) reading, (5) arithmetic, (6) language and speech, (7) art and music, and (8) physical education as well as a summary statement. The fields dealt with are the general fields of concern to educators of the mentally retarded. A substantial number of investigations have been made in these areas.

SPECIAL CLASSES FOR THE EDUCABLE MENTALLY RETARDED

Special classes for mentally retarded children in public day schools have been organized in many countries of the world (International Bureau of Education,

1960). In the United States, the first classes in public schools were organized in 1896. The growth of special classes since that date has been slow but steady. An indication of the growth of classes in the United States, as taken from statistics which have been gathered approximately every five years since 1922 by the U.S. Office of Education, is shown in Table 1.

SPECIAL CLASSES VERSUS REGULAR GRADES

The increases in special schools and classes have been accomplished on the basis of logic and the belief that placing retarded children in special classes is more beneficial to them than retaining them in the regular grades. As will be noted later, there is little empirical evidence to demonstrate clear-cut benefits of special-class placement. The empirical evidence is as yet inconclusive and, in a sense, contradictory. The following experiments bear on the general issue.

Bennett (1932) compared fifty retarded children in special classes with fifty retarded children in the regular grades of the same city. All children were within the twelve- to thirteen-year age group, and the two groups were matched for CA, MA, and IQ. The average IQ was about 73. Bennett reported that in educational achievement and in physical characteristics (such as vision, speech defects, and motor co-ordination) the special-class children were inferior to the retarded children who remained in the regular grades.

Bennett recognized the effect of differential selection of children in the special classes, i.e., mentally retarded children

57

who are inferior educationally and physically are the ones who are most apt to be referred to special classes, while those with similar IQ's but with less severe educational retardation or fewer behavior problems are less frequently referred for special-class placement. Because this selection factor was not controlled, the Bennett study does not answer the question of whether or not special classes are beneficial. Its results indicate, rather, that retarded children referred to special classes are inferior to retarded children retained in the regular grades.

TABLE 1

ENROLMENT IN SPECIAL CLASSES
1922–58

1922	23,252
1927	51,814
1932	75,099
1936	99,961
1940	98,416
1948	87,030
1952	113,565
1958	196,785

Data for this table were obtained from the *Biennial Survey* of the U.S. Office of Education (1950, chapter v), which covered the periods 1922 to 1948, from the *Biennial Survey* (1954, chapter v), which included the data for 1952, and from the work of Mackie and Robbins (1960), which included the data for 1958.

Pertsch (1936) conducted a similar study in New York City. He paired 278 children in the regular and special classes for CA, MA, IQ, sex, and racial extraction. Measures were obtained on educational achievement, mechanical aptitudes, personal adjustment, father's occupation, and personal and educational data. Pertsch also concluded that those remaining in the regular grades were superior in educational achievement and personal adjustment to those placed in the special classes. In addition, Pertsch retested the children after six months to determine the relative progress of the two groups. He again found that the "non-segregated" group was superior in progress in reading comprehension, arithmetic computation, arithmetic reasoning, and in personality adjustment. Pertsch tended to ignore the facts that selection for special classes is often made on the basis of the failure to adjust to the regular class and that children with greater problems are probably more frequently referred for special-class placement.

Cowen (1938) re-evaluated the Pertsch study, questioning the selection factor as an error in methodology. Using Pertsch's own data, Cowen calculated the percentage of mean gain in achievement, demonstrating that this percentage was actually greater for the special-class children (except in arithmetic computation) than for the retarded children left in the regular grades. Thus Cowen reversed Pertsch's conclusions.

Blatt (1958), recognizing that the selection factor in the previous studies invalidated any definitive conclusions, attempted to control this factor by another procedure. He matched seventy-five children placed in special classes in one school system with children of similar CA, MA, and IQ in the regular grades of another school system which did not have any special classes. In this study, he found no difference between the groups in educational achievement, personality, or physical status, except that the special-class children had more uncorrected or permanent physical defects.

Although Blatt partially controlled the selection factor, he did not succeed in eliminating this very important factor, since his two groups are still not comparable. One group contained the obvious cases who were referred to special classes, and the other group contained both the obvious cases who would have been referred had there been special classes in that community and also the less obvious cases who normally would have remained in the regular class. By thus partially controlling the selection factor, he found no difference between the groups.

Cassidy and Stanton (1959), using a

design similar to that of Blatt, compared the performance of ninety-four educable mentally retarded children in regular grades in Ohio school systems which had no special classes with children in special classes in other cities. The results again indicated the superiority in academic achievement of those enrolled in the regular grades. The special-class pupils, however, were superior in some aspects of personality and in social adjustment. This superiority in social adjustment reflected the goals of the special-class teachers, who, on a questionnaire, indicated that they were more interested in effecting social adjustment than academic achievement.

Cassidy and Stanton noted that other selective factors besides the IQ were operating in the referral of retarded children to special classes. This study, like many others, leaves open the question of the efficacy of special classes.

Elenbogen (1957) compared the achievement of mentally retarded children in special and regular classes in the Chicago elementary schools. The mean CA of each group was 13.46, and the mean IQ was 70.5. The children in the special classes had been thus enrolled for about two years. Elenbogen's results were similar to other studies. In academic achievement, the retarded children in the regular grades were superior to those in the special class. On the other hand, the special-class teachers rated their children higher in social adjustment than did the regular-class teachers. Again, the selection factor was not controlled.

Thurstone (1959) conducted a comparative study of retarded children in special classes and similar children in regular grades in the state of North Carolina. A total of 1273 children with IQ's between 50 and 79 were identified. Of these, 769 were in special classes, and 504 were in regular grades. The results of this experiment may be summarized as follows:

1. On the first evaluation with the Stanford Achievement Test, the children in the regular grades scored significantly higher than those in the special classes on all measures except arithmetic computation.

2. When the tests were repeated the second year and gain scores calculated, there was no significant difference between the gains of those in the special-class group and those in the regular grades. Neither were there any signif icant differences in gains between sexes or races. The only significant difference shown was for the lower IQ (50 to 59) group. For this group, the gains (except in arithmetic computation) were consistently in favor of the special-class children.

3. Sociometric and teacher ratings of the social acceptance and adjustment of the retarded children in the regular grades and in the special classes showed a superiority of the special-class retardates. As in a study by Johnson (1950), the children in the regular grades tended to be isolated. In commenting on the teacher ratings, Thurstone (1959, p. 170) states:

If their ratings are sound, mentally handicapped children in special classes are emotionally better adjusted, have a higher regard for their own mental ability, participate more widely in learning and social activities, and possess more traits desired by their peers than do their counterparts in regular grades.

The Thurstone study, like the others, did not control the selection factor. Its results inform us that those who are mentally retarded and also educationally retarded below their capacity are more apt to be placed in special classes. It indicates that gain scores of the two groups do not differ except for the more extreme deviates. With respect to the sociometric ratings, these and teacher ratings should be checked with the adjustment of these children at home and in the neighborhood, rather than in their own classes, where they were rated by Thurstone.

Ainsworth (1959) compared three

groups of mentally retarded children under differing treatment conditions: (1) special classes, (2) regular grades, and (3) regular grades plus an itinerant teacher. The special-class group included forty-eight children with a mean CA of 126.8 months and a mean Wechsler Intelligence Scale for Children (WISC) IQ of 63.9; the seventy-eight children in the regular-grade group had a mean CA of 123.7 months and a mean IQ of 65.7; the number in the itinerant group was 48; the mean CA was 127.6 months, and the mean IQ was 62.3.

The children in the three groups were given a series of educational achievement tests in February, 1958, and again one year later. In addition, they were rated and observed on behavior and social adjustment before and after the year's interval. The results indicated that all three groups made progress in educational achievement in the one-year period but that there were no significant differences among the three groups in achievement, in social adjustment, or in behavior.

This study shows that gains made by retarded children whose training began at about the age of ten are similar under three forms of management. It should not be expected that gains would be different in a one-year period. Actually, such a study should be continued for five years before any definite results, if any, could emerge.

Wrightstone et al. (1959) compared mentally retarded children under three different types of grouping. One group was classed as high educable with IQ's roughly between 60 and 75; another group was classed as low educable, with IQ's of 50 to 59; and a third group of controls contained both low and high educable children.

In academic achievement, there appeared to be no clear-cut pair-wise differences between groups. In some intangible areas, such as social adjustment and speech, the homogeneous low-edu-cable children showed significant growth over their heterogeneous counterparts.

The Wrightstone comparison suffers from the general methodological weaknesses of in situ experiments of this type. First, the children in the experiment were approximately thirteen years of age; most of them had been placed in one of the special classes around the age of nine or ten, after they had failed in the regular grades. Second, the high- and low-educable categories were not discrete, since the high-educable classes contained 15 per cent low-educable, while the low-educable classes contained 5 per cent high-educable children. Of the 3627 pupils assigned to the experimental and control populations, two-thirds were lost to the experiment through attrition during the first year of evaluation. The pupil turnover in this year demonstrates the erratic nature of special-class enrolment. Actually, such experiments will require their initiation at the beginning of a child's school career, rather than in the middle, and more discrete and continuous education over some period of time will be required before definitive conclusions can be made.

Mullen and Itkin (1961), using a matched-pair technique, compared 140 mentally retarded children in special classes with another 140 retarded children who were in regular grades by matching them on seven variables: age, IQ, sex, socio-economic community ratings, reading achievement, school attendance in the rural south, and foreign language spoken in the home. The subjects ranged in age from seven to thirteen years, and in IQ from 50 to 74.

From the analysis, two significant findings resulted. The first followed an analysis of factors associated with achieving and non-achieving mentally retarded children in both groups. This part of the study showed that, although the mental ages of the two groups were the same, the achieving group (1) had in their records more questions about the validity of the IQ rating, (2) tended to come from more stable homes, (3) tended to receive higher adjustment ratings, (4) were distinguishable from the poor achievers by fewer cases of public assistance, and (5) received on the average significantly higher scores on general information and comprehension tests and on tests of ethical comprehension.

The second finding related to the comparison of the mentally retarded in the regular grades with matched controls in the special classes on pre- and post-tests after a one-year period. This comparison, as in previous studies, indicated no differences in academic achievement gains between the two groups except that the retarded children remaining in the regular grades showed superiority in arithmetic gains. In spite of the matching on relevant variables, the authors concluded that a selective factor still operated. They state:

Although bias in the comparison of the progress of special class and regular class groups was decreased in the present experiment, selective factors determining placement remained and influenced the comparisons made.

This study's major contribution, according to this reviewer, points clearly to the major methodological problems involved in *in situ* research. It points out that even when known predictive variables are carefully controlled as in this study, other variables not easily controlled can affect the comparisons. The study should end further attempts to compare children in regular grades with those in special classes in an ongoing service program.

Goldstein, Jordan, and Moss (1962) report a current research project which compares the progress and adjustment of educable mentally handicapped children in regular grades with those in special classes. This experiment, still in progress, selected 120 retarded children in first grades in communities which had no spe-

cial classes. They were divided into two groups by random numbers. Sixty children were placed in four special classes, while the other sixty children remained in the grade in which they were tested. The children in both groups are being observed and tested annually on different dimensions of development, and the study is to continue for at least four years. When completed, this study should answer basic questions concerning the benefits or detriments of special classes, since it is not handicapped by the selection factor which has plagued previous studies.

ADJUSTMENT IN SPECIAL CLASSES AND REGULAR GRADES

Another type of study relating to the adjustment of mentally retarded children has been concerned with the effects of regular-class placement. Johnson (1950) studied the acceptance of mentally retarded children in the regular grades through the use of sociometric techniques. In his study, he selected communities that had no special classes. By testing six hundred children in two communities in the first through fifth grades, he found thirty-nine children who had IQ's, on the Stanford-Binet Scale, of 69 and below—his definition of mental retardation. A sociometric study of these six hundred children showed that the mentally retarded children in the grades tended to be isolated and rejected by the other children in the classes.

To determine whether the results obtained by Johnson were peculiar to traditional school systems, Johnson and Kirk (1950) repeated the study in a progressive school system and found similar results. Mentally retarded children in the regular grades were isolated and rejected by their peer groups even though an attempt was made by the teachers to integrate them into the regular classroom. Johnson and Kirk concluded that the physical presence of a mentally retarded child in the regular grades does not assure social integration.

Baldwin (1958) conducted a similar experiment in a school system that had special classes. In this system, she compared those retarded who remained in the regular grades with non-retarded children in the same grades. Her results were similar to those of Johnson. In this connection, reference should be made to the Thurstone study (1950), which not only confirmed the results of other studies on academic progress but, in addition, related the sociometric data of children in the regular grades to those of children in the special class. Baldwin points out that there exist among the mentally retarded many "stars" in the special classes, but very few "stars" in the regular grades.

Jordan and deCharms (1959) conducted a different comparison of children in special classes with retarded children in the regular grades. They compared forty-two mentally retarded children in special classes with sixty mentally retarded children in the regular grades on the n-achievement motive (a measure of achievement motive derived from a content analysis of a modified TAT). On the n-achievement motive the retarded children in the special classes (although significantly lower in academic achievement) appeared to have less fear of failure than the mentally retarded children in the regular grades. In this study, as in others, Jordan and deCharms did not control for the selection factor. If their data are substantiated, it might mean that the pressure for academic achievement in the regular grades is producing fear of failure, while lack of emphasis on academic achievement in the special classes decreases the fear of failure.

COMMENTS

Special classes for educable mentally retarded children in the United States increased in enrolment nearly tenfold between 1922 and 1958. This increase would indicate an acceptance of the advantages of special classes over the retention of the mentally retarded in the regular grades. To date, however, research has not justified the faith on which this acceptance is based. Such research is surrounded by many pitfalls.

The efficacy of special-class placement has been studied in the main by comparing retarded children placed in special classes with retarded children left in the regular grades. The results of these numerous investigations have indicated that (1) the children left in the regular grades are, on the whole, superior academically to the children assigned to special classes, (2) possibly the children at the lower range of educability (low-educable) show equal or superior academic achievement in the special class, (3) children assigned to special classes appear to be superior in social adjustment to those left in the regular grades, and (4) the retarded children in the regular grades tend to be isolated and rejected by their normal peers.

All of the completed studies suffer from the problems of *in situ* investigation. None controlled the essential variables needed for adequate inferences. First, the selection factor in the assignment of children to special or regular grades was not controlled in any of the investigations. No investigator was able to assign children to the two treatment groups randomly.

Second, the children in the investigations attended regular grades for a number of years before they were assigned to special classes. Actually, the comparisons of the regular and special classes were made between children who remained in the regular grades and children who had failed in the regular grades from anywhere from two to five years and were then assigned to special classes. Many of the children in the experiments had been in special classes for only one year.

Third, there has not been a clear-cut delineation of a special class, the curriculum, or the qualifications of special teachers. Special classes vary widely in organization and in curriculum and teaching methods. Qualifications of teachers vary from well-trained teachers to those subjected to short-term summer courses taught largely by instructors who have had little training or experience with special classes. The administrative labeling of a group of retarded children as a special class for the purpose of receiving state subsidy does not assure its being a *special class* for experimental purposes.

Fourth, another important factor hinges on the reliability and validity of the measuring instruments used in the comparative studies. The important goals of a special class are in intangible areas, such as social adjustment, motivation, self-concepts, and so forth. Many of the studies improvised their own focus of measurement for these facets of development.

From a review of these studies, one can only conclude that, until we obtain well-controlled studies of a longitudinal nature, our opinions about the benefits or detriments of special classes will remain partly in the realm of conjecture.

EDUCATION OF TRAINABLE MENTALLY RETARDED CHILDREN

Until recently, educational programs and educational research with the mentally rearded have been concerned with the educable retarded child who has an IQ roughly between 50 and 75. During the last decade, however, there have arisen considerable interest and some controversy concerning the educability of children in a public school situation for those under an IQ of 50.

Kirk (1957, p. 13) has summarized the legislative definitions of severely retarded or trainable children and states:

For school purposes a trainable or severely retarded child is one: (1) who is of school age; (2) who is developing at the rate of one-third to one-half that of the normal child (IQ's on individual examinations roughly between 30 and 50); (3) who, because of retarded mental development, is ineligible for classes for the educable mentally retarded who will, however, probably not be custodial, totally dependent, or require nursing care throughout his life; (4) who has potentialities for self-care tasks (such as dressing, eating, toileting), and who can learn to protect himself from common dangers in the home, school, or neighborhood; (5) who has potentialities for social adjustment in the home or neighborhood and can learn to share, respect property rights, cooperate in a family unit and with the neighbors; and (6) who has potentialities for economic usefulness in the home and neighborhood—by assisting in chores around the house, or in doing routine tasks for remuneration in a sheltered environment under supervision—even though he will require some care, supervision, and economic support throughout his life.

Using previous surveys, Kirk estimated that the prevalence of such school-aged children in a community's school population is about two per thousand.

Because of public interest, a number of states enacted laws, sometimes rather hastily, authorizing and supporting school and community classes for trainable retarded children. This movement was not without opposition by groups insisting that school programs are not necessarily beneficial to such children. For these reasons, investigations were initiated in a number of states for the purpose of determining the effects of such organized school programs on the development of trainable children. These studies are reviewed below.

THE MINNESOTA STUDIES

Reynolds and Kiland (1953) reported on a study by Lorenz, which is one of the few longitudinal studies in the literature. St. Paul had maintained classes for the severely retarded since 1934. Of the eighty-four children graduating from these classes, sixty-six were still in Minnesota and could be followed up twenty years later. The individuals of this group had remained in the special class for an average of five years. They had left the class for varying reasons; seventeen had been excluded after a trial period, forty had remained in the school until they reached the upper age limit of sixteen to twenty-one, and the others had dropped out for differing reasons. The average of their latest IQ's was 36. The follow-up study of these individuals may be summarized as follows:

1. Forty-seven per cent of the children were institutionalized immediately after leaving the special class. Boys had a higher percentage of institutionalization than girls.

2. Ten per cent of the children were deceased.

3. About 45 per cent (forty children) were at home.

4. In general, those who remained at home came from families of higher socio-economic status. Those institutionalized tended to come from average or below average socio-economic levels.

5. Of those who remained at home, two-thirds of the children were reported to be well accepted in the community. Ten were reported as making few service contacts.

6. Ten of the individuals (all males) had some history of employment in their home community. Only four of them, however, were working at the time of the study. Two males were working full-time, and the other two, part-time. One full-time worker was employed washing pots and pans in a department store. The IQ's he had obtained earlier were 62, 55, 48, 44, and 46. Another male was working as a janitor with a friend. His IQ was 55. The two part-time workers were doing yard work and golf-caddying.

THE ILLINOIS STUDIES

Goldstein (1956) summarized a two-year study in Illinois on a project for trainable children authorized by the state legislature. Data were obtained from 22 classes with 24 teachers and 173 children during the first year of the study, and on 125 children during the second year of the study. The major conclusions of this study were:

1. On psychometric tests, the children showed no acceleration in mental growth during the two-year period.

2. Parents and teachers rated the level of development of the children on an extensive check list of behavior traits before and after training. The children made some progress during the first year of the program but did not show gains during the second year.

3. Approximately 7 per cent of the children admitted to the classes were transferred to classes for the educable mentally handicapped after one year. These were children who had IQ's that averaged 52 upon admission and whose IQ's were higher at the end of the study. They tended to show more gains than did the rest of the group.

4. Twenty-two children were excluded from the program after a trial period of from six weeks to two years. These children tended to have IQ's below 35, mental ages below two years, and social quotients below 35. Practically all of the children with Kuhlmann Tests of Mental Development IQ's below 25 were excluded as not profiting from the program.

5. The parents tended to become more realistic about their children's abilities and limitations. While they felt that the children improved in self-care skills, they did not continue the expectation that the children would become self-supporting.

THE MICHIGAN STUDY

A three-year project, reported by Guenther (1956), was conducted in Michigan with the support of the Kellogg Foundation.

The purpose of this project was to study three aspects of the problem through the operation and evaluation of three programs: (1) a school for a heterogeneous age group in a relatively rural community, (2) a school for young severely retarded children between the ages of four and eight in an urban area, and (3) a program for adolescents and adults (ages sixteen years and above) for training in economic usefulness in the home or in a sheltered environment under supervision.

The rural school was located in a farmhouse several miles from a city of six thousand population. Fifteen children, ranging in age from five to seventeen and in IQ from 25 to 52, were enrolled. Six of the fifteen children were mongoloid. A study of the cases showed that out of the fifteen children admitted, nine remained in the school for over two years. According to the teachers' reports and behavior rating scales, all of the nine children made from slight to considerable progress in the school. Only one child, who had an IQ of 52, was given a prognosis of ability to work in the community on part-time routine jobs under supervision. The others were believed to be children who might help at home but who would require supervision throughout their lives.

The school for young children was much more difficult to manage. Of the thirty-two children who were referred to the center, eleven were considered untrainable. Sixteen children were enrolled, but four of them were later excluded because they were unmanageable in a group situation. Over a three-year period, only nine remained for more than one year. The turnover in this school and the number of children referred who were classified as custodial made the operation and management difficult. It raised the question of the feasibility of operating schools for young severely retarded children in smaller communities.

THE NEW YORK STUDY

Johnson and Capobianco (1957) studied seventeen classes for severely retarded children. Some of the classes were half-day classes, some were in institutions, and some were in public day schools. They re-evaluated the children after a two-year training period by comparing their initial tests with final tests on: (1) a behavior check list, (2) the Vineland Social Maturity Scale, (3) articulation tests, (4) a language test, and (5) the Fels Child Behavior Rating Scale.

The results of the study indicated the following:

1. There was no marked change in the over-all social quotient of the children after training. Those with IQ's below 30 tended to drop in SQ, while those above 30 tended to rise slightly.

2. On the behavior check list, there was some increase in favorable ratings for those above an IQ of 31, but no increase for those below 30 IQ.

3. On the language test, a matched control group was established. These were tested and retested at the same intervals as the group under training. The results indicated no statistically significant difference between the two groups.

On other ratings, and in general, the two-year training program did not demonstrate that the small improvements obtained were sufficiently significant to warrant a change in prognosis.

THE TEXAS STUDY

Peck (1960) compared different organizations for the management of trainable children. Four groups were identified: (1) a class in the public schools, (2) a segregated class in the community, (3) an institutional class, and (4) a control group residing at home without training. The training programs continued for two nine-month periods. The experimental groups, beginning with nine children each, had nine, six, and eight children at the termination of the experiment. The controls had seven.

A curriculum with seven areas was organized, and a rating scale was constructed to measure progress in the various skills and abilities within the curricular areas. The performance of the experimental groups was rated six times during the two years, and the controls were rated three times during this period.

The general results of this experiment indicated the following:

1. The experimental groups made more progress in learning as measured by most of the rating scales than did the control group which received no school training.

2. There were no significant differences between the public school group, the segregated class, and the institution group.

3. There were no significant changes in IQ or SQ in any of the four groups.

THE TENNESSEE STUDY

Hottel (1958) reported a controlled experiment with trainable children in Tennessee. This investigation studied pairs of trainable children with one of each pair obtaining day class training, while the other member of the pair, serving as a control, lived at home without the benefits of a special class. The problem was to determine whether a special class could improve the development of children more than the training they obtained from their parents. Twenty-one pairs were matched for sex, clinical type, chronological age, and mental age. The mean age of the experimental group was 8.7 years, and the mean IQ was 41.1. The control group had a mean age of 8.6 years and a mean IQ of 39.9.

The evaluation measures included the Stanford-Binet Scale (Form L), the Vineland Social Maturity Scale, a modified version of the Fels Parent Behavior Rating Scale, and an especially constructed Rating Scale of Child Behavior. The results of this one-year experiment were as follows:

1. There were no statistically significant differences in change-scores between the experimental and control groups in mental age, IQ, social age, social quotient, behavior rating, or on the Fels Parent Behavior Rating Scale. Apparently, in a one-year period, day class training does not produce significant changes in the behavior of the children themselves or in the parent behavior toward the children.

2. When the groups were subdivided into low (IQ's between 30 and 40) and high (IQ's between 40 and 50) groups, it was found that the high-IQ training group (ten pairs) gained significantly in IQ over both the home-group counterpart and the low-IQ training group. Similar results were not obtained on social age or social quotients.

The Tennessee study is one of the more carefully controlled studies on the effects of training severely retarded children. Its major defects lie in the short-term (one year) evaluation and in the practical difficulty of describing the training program and having it managed by highly trained and experienced teachers.

Cain and Levine (1963) studied the development of social competence of 182 trainable children in (1) institutions and (2) communities. In each setting an experimental group consisting of children in classes for trainable retarded children was compared with a control group which remained in the wards or at home. The results of the experiment over a two-year period indicated the following:

1. The community groups made significantly greater progress than the institution groups. This finding, however, was contaminated by the fact that the community group was higher in initial status than the institution group.

2. Both the school and non-school institution and community groups made gains on pre- and post-ratings in social competency.

3. There were no significant differences in gain scores in social competency between the experimental (training group) and the controls in either the institution or community settings.

4. Observation and analysis of the instructional program in the community experimental classes showed that the training program devoted a small portion of the classroom time to the devel-

opment of social competence. Furthermore, the observations showed that a major portion of the class time was devoted to non-instructional activities—rest periods, recess, and free activity. These observations led the authors to conclude that placement in a special class for trainable children did not necessarily insure a systematic developmental and instructional program. This is due to the newness of the programs for trainable children and to the lack of knowledge on the part of teachers and others concerning this group of children.

COMMENTS

With the exception of the Minnesota follow-up study by Lorenz (Reynolds and Kiland, 1953), all of the evaluations of the effects of day training programs for trainable mentally retarded children have been short-duration studies. On the whole, investigators have had a difficult time establishing the benefits of special-class training for this group. Many difficulties are encountered in studies of trainable children. First, evaluation instruments, including intelligence tests, have been devised primarily for school children over the age of five. Many of the trainable children have mental levels below the age of five, which tends to restrict standardized instruments for pre- and post-testing to a relatively limited group of tests. Many of the common intelligence tests, such as the Wechsler Intelligence Scale for Children (WISC), are not applicable to this group. Instruments for the measurement of self-care, social adjustment, and economic usefulness have been improvised by the investigators. Second, because of the small numbers of such children in communities (two per thousand school population), it has been difficult to conduct experiments with randomized groups. And third, the heterogeneity of etiology found within this group makes matched-pair comparisons questionable. The diagnosis of brain injury, for example, is

not a valid factor for matching, since brain-injured children vary widely in behavior and prognosis.

The question of the improvement of trainable mentally retarded children through classroom training programs is still a major problem. Attempts at research with this group have netted relatively negative results. Although we have tended to attribute these negative results to the lack of adequate measuring instruments, lack of controlled experimentation, lack of experienced teachers, and short-term research, it might be necessary to find new approaches to the educational programs for these children. For the present, more adequate insights may be obtained from intensive case studies on a longitudinal basis, similar to Itard's classic experiment with a sample of one.

MODIFYING INTELLIGENCE THROUGH EDUCATION

Early efforts to educate retarded children were directed primarily toward curing or alleviating the disability. The pioneers in this field—Itard, Seguin, Montessori, and Decroly (cf. Kirk and Johnson, 1951)—were interested in remedies for mental retardation. All of these physicians made their contributions, not in the field of medicine, but in the development of educational methods and systems. Their efforts were stimulated and influenced by the prevailing sensationalist philosophy that the training of the senses had a direct influence on the central nervous system and, consequently, on the development of retarded children.

Binet (1909, pp. 140–61), who is considered the inventor of the modern age-scale of intelligence, did not hold the view that the retarded child's rate of development, as measured by his tests, remained constant. On the contrary, he attempted to dispel the prejudice against the educability of intelligence. Although he furnished no empirical evidence for his training method, which he called "mental orthopedics," he stated in 1909

(p. 140): "After the evil, the remedy; after exposing mental defects of all kinds, let us pass on to their treatment."

American psychologists and educators reacted enthusiastically to the testing movement initiated by Binet. Few, however, followed Binet's ideas on the educability of intelligence. Instead, there arose a pessimistic attitude toward the training of intelligence. This pessimism arose because of three trends.

The first influence resulted from the studies of Goddard (1914) which purported to show that mental deficiency is largely inherited along recessive Mendelian lines. This research implied that a genetic component was unalterable through education. In the United States, concentration of effort was directed primarily toward eugenic lines, through the control of the mentally retarded by segregation in institutions and preventing mental retardation by sterilization.

The second influence resulted from the concept of pseudofeeblemindedness. This concept implied that the rate of mental growth is constant and that if a retarded child appeared to change his rate of growth or IQ, the original diagnosis was incorrect. This concept was introduced to explain deviations in rate of growth which is alleged to be constant. It assumes that any apparent change cannot be an actual change, since education or environment cannot produce change.

The third influence stemmed from a widely accepted definition of mental deficiency proposed by Doll (1941), who stated that mental deficiency (1) is developmental arrest, (2) of constitutional origin, (3) obtaining at maturity, and (4) essentially incurable. This is a fatalistic definition and does not encourage efforts toward educational procedures for the purpose of accelerating mental development.

Efforts to evaluate growth among the mentally retarded have been confined largely to the measurement of progress in reading, arithmetic, and other school subjects, as well as to the effects of education on social and vocational adjustment. There have been some attempts, however, to evaluate the effects of special educational procedures on the development of mental ability in retarded children. The studies reported below deal with mentally retarded populations, rather than with the wider populations of the nature-nurture studies.

Kephart (1939) organized activities to stimulate the thinking ability of sixteen adolescent mentally retarded children in a "self-determining cottage" of an institution for high-grade defectives. The IQ's of this group increased from an average Stanford-Binet Scale IQ of 66.3 to an average of 76.4 in a period of three years. He compared this group with twenty-six boys living in the traditionally operated cottages and found that the IQ's of the contrast group showed an average increase of only 1.9 IQ points during the same period. Kephart attributed the difference in increase to the educational program in the self-determining cottage. The selection of the cases was not randomized in this study, and the results may reflect an unknown selection factor in the self-determining cottage.

A most impressive study of young mentally defective children was reported by Skeels and Dye (1939). These investigators transferred thirteen young children under three years of age from an orphanage to an institution for retarded children. The average IQ of these children on the Kuhlmann Test of Mental Development at the time of admission to the institution for defectives was 64, and the range in IQ was 35 to 89. These babies were placed in different wards of the institution where older retarded girls were housed. The children received a great deal of attention and stimulation from the attendants and girls on the ward. After a year and a half, the IQ's of these children had increased 27.5 points. Skeels and Dye compared these increases in IQ's with the changes in IQ's of twelve children with somewhat higher original IQ's (ranging from 50 to 103) who remained in the orphanage. This group of orphanage children dropped 26.2 points during the same period. These results could not be explained on the basis of the unreliability of infant scales, since a contrast group was used.

In a follow-up study, Skeels (1942) retested the experimental and control groups two and one-half years following the experimental period. The mean IQ of the thirteen experimental children was 95.9, four IQ points higher than at the close of the experimental period. Eleven of the thirteen experimental children had been taken out of the institution and placed in adoptive homes. One stayed in the institution and one was returned to the orphanage. The mean IQ of the adoptive children was 101.4, with no child having an IQ below 90. The contrast group, which showed an initial IQ of 86.7 and an IQ of 60.3 at the end of the experimental period, now showed a mean IQ of 66.1. There had been a rise of 5.6 IQ points, but, in general, those who remained in the unstimulating environment of the orphanage continued to show retardation.

The most sensational study on the effects of education was reported by Schmidt (1946). She described an eight-year study on 245 children in special classes in Chicago. The initial average IQ was reported as being 52.1. At the completion of three years of school, it was stated that their average IQ had risen to 71.6; at the completion of five years of postschool experience, the average IQ has risen to 89.3. Twenty-seven per cent of the group graduated from high school, and 5.1 per cent continued beyond high school training. The increases in IQ and achievement were attributed to the special-class training. These results were in such sharp contrast to professional opinion that the editors of *Psychological Monographs* felt it necessary to explain the publication of the study in a prefatory statement.

In an investigation of the Schmidt study, Kirk (1948) checked the records of the children in Schmidt's special classes in Chicago by visiting the schools where the classes were held and tabulating the test scores from the files of the Chicago Bureau of Child Study. He found the mean IQ on admission to Schmidt's class to be 69 instead of the 52 reported by Schmidt. Schmidt's highest reported IQ on admission was 69. According to Kirk, 50 per cent of the children in Schmidt's classes had IQ's above 69. The lack of correspondence between the data found in the files of the Bureau of Child Study and the tabulated data reported by Schmidt tended to throw doubt on the authenticity of the report and to invalidate the study.

A longitudinal study of the effects of preschool training on the social and mental development of young retarded children in an institution and in a community was conducted by Kirk (1958). He identified eighty-one retarded children between the ages of three and six with IQ's generally between 45 and 80. These eight-one children were placed in four groups. Twenty-eight received training in a specially designed community preschool and were restudied after the preschool experience. Twenty-six children, serving as a contrast group with similar ages and level of development, were tested at the same intervals but were not given the opportunities of preschool education. Fifteen children were given preschool education in an institution, while twelve other children, serving as an institutional contrast group, remained in the wards during the preschool period and were restudied after the preschool period. This experiment was presented in the form of case studies and statistical results. The evaluation of rates of development was in terms of results of intelligence tests and other tests and observations on social development.

The children were classified before, during, and at the conclusion of the experiment under six categories: average, low-average, borderline, high-educable, low-educable, questionable educability, and uneducable. Any change of one or more classification levels upward or downward was considered a significant change.

One part of the experiment dealt with a comparison of differing degrees of stimulation change. In this part of the experiment, (1) four children were taken out of inadequate homes and placed in foster homes and were also enrolled in the preschool, (2) twelve children from inadequate homes stayed in their own homes but were given preschool education, and (3) fourteen sibling and twin controls (of the twelve children) who did not receive preschool education were evaluated and compared with the twelve experimental children during and after the preschool period. The results showed:

1. The four children who were taken out of their inadequate homes by social agencies and placed in foster homes all increased their rate of development. Two increased one level in classification, one increased two levels, and one increased three levels.

2. Of the twelve children who remained in their psycho-socially deprived homes but received the benefits of preschool education, two-thirds increased their rate of development one or more classification levels, one-third retained their rate of development, and one dropped a classification level. The latter child attended the preschool only 50 per cent of the time.

3. Of the fourteen twin and sibling controls (those who did not attend the preschool but later attended regular schools or special classes), only two children, or one-seventh, increased their rate of development; seven, or one-half, retained the same rate of growth; and five, or nearly one-third, dropped in classification as they grew older. The dif-

ferences in development between the twelve experimental children and the fourteen sibling and twin controls were statistically significant at the 0.02 level.

Kirk concluded from these data that children from psycho-socially deprived homes tend to retain their rate of development or to drop in rate of development as they grow older. Preschool opportunities for these children tend to reverse this tendency by assisting more of them to increase their rate of development. When more drastic changes of environment, such as both a foster home and preschool, were introduced, more of the children increased in rate of development. These results lend support to the proposition that educational opportunities at an early age can accelerate the rate of mental growth of children reared in psycho-socially deprived homes.

Another aspect of the experiment compared fifteen institutionalized preschool children, who had intensive training at the preschool level, with twelve children who remained in the wards of the institution and did not attend school until the age of six. From age four years, four months to age seven years, four months, the fifteen children in the training group increased from an average IQ of 61 to 71 on the Stanford-Binet, from 57 to 67 on the Kuhlmann Tests of Mental Development, and from 72 to 82 on the Vineland Social Maturity Scale. In contrast, the twelve children who did not receive preschool training dropped in Stanford-Binet Scale IQ's from 57 to 50, on the Kuhlmann Tests of Mental Development from 54 to 50, and on the Vineland Social Maturity Scale from 73 to 61. These differences were all statistically significant. In addition, six of the fifteen children in the training group were paroled from the institution, while none of the twelve children without training was paroled. These data are further evidence that educational treatment at an early age is effective in increasing the rate of development of institutionalized mental defectives.

Other results of the experiment showed: (1) that preschool education was less effective with children with organic involvements than with those without a definitive diagnosis of organicity and (2) that children from relatively adequate homes tended to increase in rate of social and mental development in the first grade without preschool education. These results indicate that, for children from relatively adequate homes, the age of six is not too late to expect accelerated development as a result of schooling.

Lyle (1959, 1960) compared the performance of imbecile children in day schools and hospitals on verbal and non-verbal intelligence. He administered the verbal and non-verbal parts of the Minnesota Preschool Scale to samples of institutionalized and day-school imbeciles. Seventy-seven children were at the Fountain Hospital in London where they attended an Occupation Center. One hundred and seventeen children lived at home and attended special training schools in Middlesex. The ages of the two groups ranged from six years, six months to thirteen years, six months. All were within the range of the Minnesota Preschool Scale.

On non-verbal tests, the 77 hospital and 117 day-school children showed grand means of 35.05 and 35.34, respectively. However, on the verbal scale "there were highly significant differences between the C-score means . . . between the Day School and Institution groups for both mongols and non-mongols, in favor of the day school group." Lyle concluded that "It seems likely that long residence in the institution retards verbal intelligence much more than non-verbal intelligence."

Gallagher (1960) conducted a three-year experiment of the effects of tutoring brain-injured children on the development of intellectual functions, on social maturity, and on personality development. In this experiment, forty-two institutionalized brain-injured children, ages eight to twelve, were identified and divided into experimental and control groups of twenty-one each, matched on Stanford-Binet Scale MA scores, and placed in the experimental and control groups randomly. The experimental group received tutoring on intellectual tasks one hour a day for two years, and no tutoring for one year. The controls, who were not tutored during the first two years, received tutoring during the third year of the experiment. Comparing test-retest results on a variety of measures, Gallagher summarized his results as follows:

1. Improvement in the intellectual development of some brain-injured, mentally retarded children can be obtained through the tutoring methods described here.

2. The children who responded to the tutoring achieved more in the area of verbal skills than non-verbal skills, but all of the children had extreme difficulty at the higher abstract levels of conceptualization.

3. The younger children (ages 8–10) in the study showed significant improvement over the older children (ages 10–12).

4. Certain behavioral changes were noticed during tutoring; principally, an increased ability to pay attention.

5. When the tutoring procedures were removed from the life of the child, there was a tendency for his development to regress to lower levels or become arrested.

6. There was an impressive range of individual differences both in the characteristic of the children prior to tutoring and in their response to tutoring (p. 151).

Gallagher feels that the modest results which he obtained under institutional living could possibly be made more substantial under a "total push" program. He concluded by stating that:

It is quite likely that history will also record that we have been entirely too pessimistic about the possible training potential of brain-injured children and that this pessimism has prevented us from giving them the intellectual and educational stimulation that we would wish for all of our children (p. 168).

Cruickshank *et al.* (1961) conducted an experiment on methods of teaching brain-injured and hyperactive children. Although the children in this experiment were not designated as mentally retarded, the mean IQ's for the four groups ranged from 78 to 82. In this experiment two experimental classes of children were taught by a modified Strauss-Lehtinen technique using principles of (1) reduction of environmental space, (2) reduction of visual and auditory environmental stimuli, (3) establishment of a highly structured daily program, and (4) increasing the stimulus value of instructional materials. The two matched control classes were organized according to conventional methods. The results of this experiment over a one- and two-year period indicated:

1. The children in the four experimental and control classes made significant academic progress.

2. There was no significant difference in gains in academic achievement between the experimental and control classes.

3. There were no significant increases in IQ or in other psychological factors except in the ability to differentiate figure from background. In the latter the experimental subjects exceeded the controls.

Many programs have been organized for the training of brain-injured children, but none of the programs have been subjected to more than minimal experimental evaluation. The studies of Gallagher and Cruickshank are the only ones that have subjected a training program to an experimental design.

COMMENTS

The few studies on the effects of educational procedures on the educability of intelligence of retarded children have been sporadic and, in general, short-term studies. There are many reasons for the paucity of such studies. One reason has been the prejudice against the possibility of developing intelligence through educational procedures. Another reason is related to the length of time needed to produce reliable results. A third reason is that the factors of control, attrition, and reliability of measurement tend to discourage experimenters from launching a controlled longitudinal experiment of an educational nature.

The evidence presented indicates some positive results of educational treatment, especially with young retarded children. These results do not agree with the statement of Masland, Sarason, and Gladwin (1958, p. 158), who state: "It is our opinion . . . that educational retardation is not likely to be significantly decreased by building new and more schools and hiring more teachers." They ascribe the retardation to cultural settings and indicate that schooling per se will have little effect unless cultural changes are made. However, from a theoretical point of view, our task is to determine (1) whether environment, including schooling, can displace the rate of development of retarded children, (2) the age at which this change is most effective, and (3) the variables within a family, or the instructional program, which can determine the change in rate of growth. The problem for research on the educability of intelligence is to identify more specifically the factors in the *nature* of the child and the variables in the *nurture* provided by the environment which effect changes in rate of growth, both positively and negatively.

READING

Research on reading constitutes by far the largest bulk of educational literature concerning the education of the mentally retarded and covers such topics as: (1) reading capacity and achievement, (2) comparative studies of the mentally retarded, normal, and gifted, (3) mental age and beginning reading, and (4) factors relating to the reading process of the mentally retarded. Studies in these areas have been exhaustively reviewed by Dunn (1956). Readers are referred to Dunn's review for a more complete coverage of the research literature on reading up to 1956.

READING CAPACITY AND ACHIEVEMENT

Investigators have been interested in determining the potential reading achievement of the mentally retarded and have made numerous investigations on reading achievement as related to mental age and other capacity measures.

Merrill (1918, 1921) conducted two studies on the relation of reading achievement to mental age. The first study was conducted in Minnesota, and the second in California. In both of these studies Merrill found that the reading achievement of mentally retarded children in special classes was generally below that achievement expected for their mental age.

Renshaw (1919), Hoyt (1924), Witty and McCafferty (1930), Kelly (1934), and Hill (1939) made investigations independently in different areas of the country using different achievement tests. All of these investigators reported similar results, namely, that mentally retarded children read below their mental ages.

During the postwar period similar investigations were made by Scarborough (1951) and Mullen (1952) in Chicago. In the Scarborough study, records of 1182 mentally retarded children were selected at random from the files of the special classes. She found the mentally retarded children to be one year retarded in reading below their Binet mental ages. The Mullen study dealt with 570 adolescent children enrolled in special classes. This group was 1.4 years retarded below their mental ages in reading.

Bennett (1929), Chapman (1939), and Ring (1951) studied the reading achievement of mentally retarded children in New York, Oregon, and Massachusetts. These investigators found that, in their samples, mentally retarded children read up to, or in excess of, their mental ages.

In reviewing these and other studies, Dunn (1956, p. 15) concluded:

With 11 studies finding the mentally retarded in special classes to read below mental age expectancy level, and only three studies finding this group to read at, or above, expectancy, the following conclusion seems warranted: In general, mentally retarded children in special classes tend to read below expectancy. In cases where special attention is given to reading, however, it would seem reasonable to expect these pupils to attain reading ages up to, or even beyond, their mental age. No clearcut pattern can be established from the preceding 14 studies on relative achievement of the mentally retarded in the various school subjects (pp. 12–15).

COMPARISON OF RETARDED, NORMAL, AND GIFTED CHILDREN

The studies cited in the previous section indicated that mentally retarded children in general read below their mental-age–reading-grade expectancy. This leads to the question of whether normal or superior children read up to, in excess of, or below their mental ages.

Merrill (1924) compared the school achievement of retarded, average, and superior children of the same mental ages as determined by the 1916 Stanford-Binet Scale. Three-hundred and seven retarded pupils enrolled in special classes were matched with normal children of the same mental ages (IQ's 90–110), and with one hundred superior children, whose IQ's were above 140 but whose mental ages were similar to the mental ages of the retarded group. On some reading tests the retarded children were below the normal children in achievement. On the Stanford Achievement Tests, however, the retarded and the superior groups both read up to their mental ages.

Similar studies have been reported by

Wilson (1926), Torgerson and Shuman (1925), Lewis (1944), and Brown and Lind (1931). All of these studies indicate that when mental age is controlled, retarded children tend to be closer to their mental ages than do superior children. This is understandable from a number of points of view. The retarded child who can learn to read is under pressure to achieve because, on the basis of his CA, he is retarded. The gifted child, on the other hand, is not under the same pressure to achieve, since, on the basis of his CA, he is accelerated.

MENTAL AGE AND BEGINNING READING

One of the major problems in the teaching of reading to mentally retarded children is determining the mental-age level at which reading instruction should be introduced. In practice many retarded children are faced with reading tasks as they enter school at the age of six, even though their mental age may be four or five. If reading instruction were to be delayed until they are mentally six or six and one-half years of age, they would be nine or ten years of age and have attended school from two to four years.

Davidson (1931) investigated experimentally the learning of words of thirteen children whose mental ages were four years. Three groups of four or five children each were used. One group was of superior intelligence with CA's of three, and MA's of four, and a third group was of dull intelligence with CA's of five and MA's of four. Individual reading lessons of a developmental nature were given to each child for ten minutes a day for a six-week period. The results indicated that all groups were able to learn words but that the superior child learned and retained the most words, while the dull group was the most inferior.

Melcher (1940) and Weiner (1954) reported on a prolonged pre-academic program of the Wayne County Training School. In Melcher's group, reading instruction was delayed until the subjects reached a mental age of eight. When reading instruction was introduced, these subjects learned more rapidly than previously. Weiner (1954) followed up thirty-seven of the boys in the Wayne County Training School experiment and compared their achievement with thirty-one boys who were admitted to the school's regular program without the delay in formal pre-academic instruction. The two groups were approximately fifteen years, six months old at the last testing. Upon admission to the school's program at the age of eleven, the control group was significantly superior to the pre-academic group. On the final tests, however, the pre-academic group caught up with the control group, both testing at the fourth-grade level in reading and arithmetic.

TEACHING METHODS

Methods of teaching reading to retarded children have also been investigated. Braem (1931) asked one first-grade teacher to emphasize the phonic method with a group of retarded children in a state residential institution and compared their progress with another first-grade group in which the sight-reading method had been emphasized. According to Braem, the sight-reading group made three times as many errors and took three times as long to read the Gray Oral Reading Paragraphs Test as did the phonic group.

Hegge (1934) reported on the progress made by thirteen youths at the Wayne County Training School, who, in addition to being mentally retarded, were also reading-disability cases. By the use of the Hegge, Kirk, and Kirk (1936) *Remedial Reading Drills*, which is a systematic phonic method, the youths progressed from a mean grade of 1.6 to a mean grade level of 4.2 in a one-year, ten-month period. This is considered a gain in reading above that expected of normal children in the same time interval.

McIntyre (1937) and French (1950) also applied systematic phonic instruction to older retarded children who were significantly below their mental ages in reading achievement. The progress under this type of remedial instruction was marked.

Coleman (1938) and Storey (1936) each applied a varied remedial program to retarded children who were below their mental age in reading achievement. Both authors report good results with a varied method, but with emphasis on word recognition. Like the other studies reported, this study used varied methods with retarded children who were also reading disability cases and did not compare methods with retarded children during their developmental period in school.

Kirk (1933) compared the kinesthetic or manual-tracing method with the sight method in teaching word recognition with six subnormal boys over a fourteen-day period. There was no significant difference in learning between the two methods, but there was a significant difference in favor of the manual-tracing method in the retention scores.

Studies on methods of teaching reading have been made largely on remedial cases, those who have became educationally retarded below their mental age. In general, remedial reading has been quite successful. The phonic method appears to have its advocates, but some also stress an eclectic approach. Unfortunately, only one controlled experiment on the kinesthetic method was reported. It is likely that this approach may be more beneficial than the sight or phonic method with some retarded children.

RATE OF PROGRESS IN READING

Of interest to research workers has been the question of the rate of progress of mentally retarded children in reading as well as a comparison of progress in reading with that in other school subjects.

Murdoch (1918) was one of the first to compare the rate of progress of retarded children in reading, arithmetic, spelling, and composition by means of standardized achievement tests. She studied twenty-one mentally deficient children who were in the highest grades of a state residential school. The average chronological age of the group was sixteen years, four months, and their average intelligence quotient was 61. She found that the subjects were working slightly above expectancy level on arithmetic fundamentals but were below their expectancy level in spelling and language achievement. As measured by retests one year later, they made a slight average gain in each area. In no case did these gains parallel the gain in mental age.

Bradway (1939) reported on the achievement of fifty-three mentally retarded subjects in a private residential school. The children had no marked physical or sensory defects, no extreme neurotic conditions, and no history of brain involvement. Their program consisted of intensive instruction in reading. She found that the mean reading-comprehension age exceeded the mean mental age by one year. In spelling the mean age exceeded the mean expectancy level by two years, but in arithmetic they approximated their mental age. In calculating the rate of progress of this selected group, Bradway found that the subjects had made from one-half year to two-thirds year improvement in the various school subjects.

Nemzek and Meixner (1939) reported on the rate of progress made by 326 mentally retarded pupils in Detroit special classes, as measured by the Stanford Achievement Tests. They estimated that over a period of four years the yearly gain in reading was roughly two-fifths of a grade. The arithmetic fundamental scores (arithmetic computation) exceeded the reading scores. A similar study was reported by Engel (1942) on the progress of 3169 pupils in special classes in the Detroit Public Schools. She obtained the same results as Nemzek and Meixner: namely, two-fifths of a grade per year.

Janes (1953) reported on the reading progress of children in special classes in Camden, New Jersey. He stated that during the first two years in the special class, the children made nine and ten months progress, respectively, while during the last two years, they made six and four months progress. Janes commented that these results could be explained by their school history. Before placement in a special class, they had vegetated in a regular classroom; thus, their progress in the special class was similar to remedial reading experience for normal children. In the special class, they made up for the previous lack of efficient instruction.

In summarizing these and similar studies Dunn comments as follows:

The studies on the rate of reading gain show conflicting findings. It is probable that under average conditions the increase in reading age parallels the increase in mental age. However, when mentally retarded children who are reading considerably below their expectancy level are given intensive remedial instruction, gains may, at first, be quite rapid. This pattern probably ceases ɛs reading age begins to exceed mental age (Dunn, 1956, pp. 24–29).

THE READING PROCESS OF THE MENTALLY RETARDED

In addition to studies of reading achievement, there have been some studies related to specific factors and processes that may be uniquely characteristic of the reading of mentally retarded children. These studies deal with reversal errors, other errors in reading, and the effects of brain injury on the reading process of the mentally retarded.

Mintz (1946) studied the relationship between reversal errors and lateral preferences of a group of ninety-five mentally retarded boys. He found no clear-cut relationship between reversals and lateral preference.

Kirk (1934b) reported a study of the relation of ocular and manual preference to reading in a group of sixty-one older mentally retarded subjects (ages twelve to fourteen) at a residential school. These children scored between grades 1.4 and 4.0 on the Gray Oral Reading Paragraphs Test. He had the subjects read paragraphs reprinted in mirror writing. Two groups of retarded children were compared. The thirty-one subjects of one group were left-eyed (and largely right-handed) and the thirty subjects of another group were right-eyed and right-handed. He found no difference between the groups in mirror reading. This was contrary to the results of Monroe (1932), who found that pure and mixed sinistrals (right-eyed and left-handed or left-eyed and right-handed) were more fluent in mirror reading than were the pure dextrals.

In addition to studies of mirror reading, Kirk and Kirk (1935) reported on a study dealing with reversal tendencies in writing. They found that the teacher's handedness did not influence reversal errors in writing, as postulated by Dearborn (1930), but that young superior children with mental ages of six made more reversal errors in writing than did older mentally retarded children whose mental ages were six. In addition, there seemed to be no differences in reversal errors in writing of the older mentally retarded children, whether they were left-handed or right-handed.

A comprehensive process study was conducted by Dunn (1956). In this study he compared twenty mentally retarded boys in special classes with thirty normal boys of the same mental age who were selected randomly from the regular classes of the public elementary schools in the same school systems. In addition to general reading tests, the children were given a series of analytical tests which, among other things, analyzed the errors in reading by the Monroe (1932) system.

The results of the Dunn study may be summarized as follows:

1. The retarded group was retarded in reading about one year below the normal children of the same mental age.

2. On the patterns of reading errors, equated for grade level, the retarded group showed significantly excessive errors over the normal children in faulty vowels, omission of sounds, and words aided and refused. There were no significant differences in other types of errors, such as faulty consonants or reversals. Interestingly, the retarded group showed fewer repetitions in oral reading than the normals. Dunn explained this by observing that the retarded tended to be word-by-word readers with less concern for meaning.

3. There was no significant difference between the retarded and normals on sound-blending tests.

4. On tests of handedness, there were more left-handed boys among the retarded, but the difference was not statistically significant. More of the retarded, proportionately, had mixed lateral dominance in eyedness and handedness, but the difference between groups was not statistically significant.

5. On all other tests, the normals were significantly superior to the retarded. These included (1) a special test of context clues, (2) tests of timed and untimed tachistoscopically presented words and phrases, (3) auditory acuity tests, (4) visual acuity tests, (5) a teacher questionnaire determining social and emotional adjustment, and (6) studies of economic status, social class, and emotional atmosphere of the homes.

This study of the reading process along with other factors in retarded boys assigned to special classes is very revealing. It showed that the retarded boys were inferior, not only in some aspects of the reading process, but also in visual and auditory abilities and in social adjustment and home conditions. It should not be surprising that children with multiple handicaps are poor achievers in relation to their tested mental level.

Vance (1956) matched brain-damaged with non-brain-damaged institutionalized children on CA, MA, and IQ. The IQ's ranged from 40 to 70, and the CA's from 7 to 13. A prescribed educational program was administered to the group three days a week for one and one-half hours each day over an eight-month period. The children were tested before the initiation of the prescribed educational program, after the eight-month treatment period, and after a three-year period. There were no significant differences between the groups on reading and reading readiness tests.

Capobianco and Miller (1958) conducted a study similar to that of Dunn (1956) on the process of reading, but used exogenous and endogenous institutionalized children as subjects. They matched a group of twenty exogenous with a group of twenty-nine endogenous subjects on CA and IQ, using the Riggs and Rain classification system and the Syracuse Visual Figure Background Test. It has been assumed that exogenous (brain-damaged) children have perceptual problems which will interfere with their ability to learn to read. A comparison of the reading achievement of the two groups, as well as the pattern of reading errors on faulty vowels, consonants, reversals, and so forth, may be summarized as follows:

1. On silent-reading achievement, word discrimination, word recognition, and oral reading, the exogenous group scored higher than the endogenous group, but the differences were not statistically significant.

2. On the ten error types analyzed (including faulty vowels, faulty consonants, reversal errors, omission and addition of sounds or words, repetitions, and words

aided or refused), no significant differences were found.

3. On auditory acuity and visual perception tests, no significant differences were found.

This study casts doubt on the assumption that "organicity" and perceptual disturbances as measured by psychological tests are factors which inhibit the retarded child's ability to read.

Further light on this important problem has been shed in a study by Frey (1961). He selected a group of children who had been diagnosed as brain injured on the basis of neurological tests, who exhibited perceptual disturbances on psychological tests, and who had been under a special educational program using the Strauss and Lehtinen techniques for brain-injured children.

Twenty brain-injured children in the special class were matched on CA, IQ, and MA with twenty non-brain-injured children from the special or regular classes in the same public school system. The mean CA's of the two groups were ten years, five months for the brain-injured and ten years, three months for the non-brain-injured. The mean IQ's on the WISC were 78.8 for the brain-injured group and 79.45 for the non-brain-injured group. The MA's were eight years, two months and eight years, one month, respectively.

Using the same tests for quantitative and qualitative analysis of the reading process as were used in the study by Dunn (1956) and Capobianco and Miller (1958), Frey obtained the following results:

1. The brain-injured group was significantly superior to the non-brain-injured group on the Gray Oral Reading Paragraphs Test, the Monroe Word Recognition Test, the Gates Primary Reading Test, and the Monroe Word Discrimination Test.

2. On the Monroe Sound Blending Test, the brain-injured group was signif-icantly superior to the non-brain-injured group.

3. On the Monroe Visual Memory Test and on the Gates Reversible Words Test, there were no significant differences between the two groups

4. On the analysis of errors in reading, the brain-injured group showed a normal profile. The non-brain-injured group showed significantly excessive errors as compared to the brain-injured group in faulty vowels, faulty consonants, omission of sounds, and substitution of words. There were no significant differences between the brain-injured and non-brain-injured subjects in reversal errors, addition of sounds, repetition of words, addition of words, omission of words, and words aided or refused.

Results of studies on the reading achievement and reading process of brain-injured children are contrary to expectation in view of the numerous studies which have tried to differentiate brain-injured from non-brain-injured children on the basis of psychological tests. It has been assumed that distortions of perception and of conceptualization will interfere with school progress. The results of the studies reported above indicate that reading achievement can be attained by brain-injured retarded children and that the important variable is instructional procedure. When instruction is similar, as was the case in the Vance and in the Capobianco and Miller studies, no significant differences are found between the brain-injured and non-brain-injured groups. When there is systematic and intensive instruction for brain-injured children (as in the Frey study, 1961), as compared to ordinary school instruction, the brain-injured of the same mental age exceed the non-brain-injured in reading achievement and show normal errors for their level in the process of reading. It would appear from these studies that systematic education is the variable which compensates for deficits within children. Signs of "organicity" on psychological tests may not, as is commonly assumed, have a direct relationship to the process of learning to read.

REMEDIAL READING AND PERSONALITY MALADJUSTMENT

Kirk (1934a), using a case-study method, investigated the effects of remedial reading on the personality and social adjustment of ten mentally retarded children in an institution. Success in reading was associated with better adjustment in the classroom and tended to diminish signs of personality maladjustment, such as negativism and daydreaming.

Miller (1921) gave intensive training to four cases for a five-week period. All four showed improvement in reading and in attitudes toward reading.

Ewerhardt (1938) reported on a group of retarded children who were referred to a psychiatric clinic for both reading and emotional problems. His observations led him to the conclusion that the reading failures were caused by the emotional problems. In addition, remedial reading alone was not successful, but the treatment of the emotional problem followed by reading instruction led to better results.

Rabinovitch (1956) differentiated between "primary reading disabilities," related to brain damage; and "secondary reading disability," associated with personality maladjustment. He found that remedial instruction was more successful with the secondary form of reading disability.

On the other hand, Axline (1947), working with normal and dull-normal children, advocated play therapy as a method of correcting emotional disturbance. She concluded that emotional factors are the cause of reading retardation and that removal of the emotional factor will free the child to learn to read.

COMMENTS

These studies furnish considerable information about the reading ability of mentally retarded children and about some of the factors which influence their ability to achieve.

First, it appears clear that mentally retarded children in special classes do not read up to their mental-age–reading-grade expectancy. This is understandable, since those children referred to special classes are the ones who are most retarded mentally and educationally. In addition, special-class teachers tend to de-emphasize acadamic learning, since their interest is in the reduction of frustration and in the social and emotional development of the children.

Second, the research on teaching methods has not clearly demonstrated the superiority of one method over another. The phonic method has its advocates, while others report success with varied methods. It is likely that the enthusiasm of the experimenter for one method is a determining variable. It is also likely that retarded children can learn by various modes of presentation, provided the methods are presented systematically and enthusiastically.

Third, there are reports of methods which show excellent results with retarded children who are below expectancy in reading. In general, the children respond with rapid progress during the initial stages and taper off as they approach, or exceed, their mental level.

Fourth, the studies on the quantitative and qualitative aspects of reading of brain-injured children give us new insights into the interpretation of psychological tests of disturbances of perception. Originally, psychologists were interested in finding psychological correlates of brain damage. Some now infer brain damage from psychological test performances. The inference, however, that these psychological disturbances will interfere with school progress must be questioned. From the studies reported, it appears that brain-injured children with perceptual difficulties achieve similarly to non-brain-injured children under conventional methods of instruction. Under more systematic methods of instruction, the brain-injured children progressed faster than non-brain-injured children receiving conventional special-class or regular-class instruction.

Fifth, the studies on the relationship between reading disabilities and emotional disturbance are not in agreement. To some, reading failure is the primary cause of maladjustment. To others the maladjustment is the cause of the reading difficulty. It is likely that there are cases of both kinds and that neither generalization is applicable to all cases. It is also possible that both factors contribute to each other and that one difficulty accentuates the other. Research in this area has not pointed out the specific relationship of the two factors.

ARITHMETIC

Among the studies on school subjects, arithmetic has attracted only a few workers. The literature on the teaching of arithmetic is largely confined to courses of study and descriptions of programs. The few studies available concern (1) the relation of arithmetic to mental ability, (2) process studies, and (3) the comparison of different methods of teaching.

RELATION OF ARITHMETIC ACHIEVEMENT TO MENTAL AGE

Cruickshank (1948b, c) compared fifteen normal boys with fifteen high-grade mentally retarded boys in an institution. The mean MA of the retarded children was 10.06, and that of the normal sample, 9.96. The mean IQ of the retarded group was 73.33, and that of the normal group, 110.4. On the Stanford Achievement Arithmetic Test, the retarded group obtained a mean arithmetic age of 9.73, while the normal group obtained a mean arithmetic age of 9.84 on the same test. These results indicate that in arithmetic achievement, there is no significant difference between Cruickshank's normal and retarded groups and that the arithmetic age corresponds closely to the mental age.

Dunn (1956) compared twenty retarded and thirty normal children of the same mental ages in a public school. He found that there was no significant difference between the retarded and the normal groups in arithmetic computation but found a significant difference in arithmetic reasoning as measured by the Progressive Achievement Tests. He cites agreement with the findings of Witty and McCafferty (1930), who found that the mentally retarded achieved at a higher level in arithmetic fundamentals than in any other school subject, and with Ring (1951), who found the mentally retarded working at the same level as their mental ages in arithmetic fundamentals.

In arithmetic reasoning, Dunn's retarded group worked twenty-four months below their mental-age–expectancy level. Dunn states (p. 76): "These findings are as expected when one considers that tests of arithmetic reasoning involve both reading and reasoning—both processes in which the retarded appear to be deficient."

Bensberg (1953), using the American School Achievement Tests, studied the achievement of the retarded at an institution. He found that their mean arithmetic achievement was within one month of their mental age, a non-significant difference. He used a large sample of 504 mentally retarded subjects ranging in IQ from 38 to 87. He further found that females, matched with males on CA and MA, achieved significantly higher than the males. No differences were found between etiological types or between those who attended the institution school for five years and those who attended public school prior to admission to the institution.

Klausmeier *et al.* (1959) compared retarded, average, and superior children of the same chronological age on several variables. His hypothesis, that superior children learn rapidly and forget rapidly while low IQ children learn slowly but forget less, was not supported by the data.

In summary, the results of survey research on the relationship of mental age to arithmetic achievement indicate that, basically, retarded children appear to achieve in harmony with their mental-age expectancy in arithmetic fundamentals but are below their expectancy in arithmetic reasoning problems requiring reading. Although there are some discrepancies in the results, these discrepancies can be accounted for by (1) differences in groups studied, such as public-school samples versus institution samples, (2) differences in IQ levels, and (3) differences in the methods of comparison. Some investigators take the arithmetic age from the norms in the test, while others (Dunn and Capobianco, 1956) assume year-by-year progress, i.e., an MA of seven years is the equivalent of grade two, an MA of eight is equal to grade three, etc. This does not always harmonize with an age equivalent which is determined empirically.

STUDIES OF PROCESSES IN ARITHMETIC

Capobianco (1956) gave a battery of arithmetic tests to two groups (exogenous and endogenous) of mentally retarded children, matched for CA and MA, in an institution. By the use of covariance for the control of length of institutionalization, he found no significant differences on the battery of arithmetic tests between the endogenous and exogenous groups in general achievement in arithmetic, rigidity, reversal errors, zero errors, and habits.

The significance of Capobianco's negative findings is related to the assumptions that have been made concerning perceptual and conceptual problems of brain-injured children. It has been assumed that children with perceptual and conceptual disorders, as determined by test results, should have difficulty in learning to read and to achieve in arithmetic. If Capobianco's results are confirmed, the assumption of a direct relationship between tested perceptual problems and learning is contraindicated.

One of the more extensive analyses of processes in arithmetic was made by Cruickshank (1948c). He presented retarded and normal subjects with three kinds of problems. The first problem consisted of presentation of necessary facts with many superfluous facts; the second problem presented only the needed facts; and the third, just the computational facts, such as $5 \times 2 = ?$ He found that the retarded were (1) significantly less able to extract the needed facts for a problem from superfluous material, (2) significantly less able to solve arithmetic problems when given the necessary facts in verbal form, and (3) more nearly like the normal in straight arithmetic computation. These findings correspond to the findings of other studies in which the retarded do better in arithmetic computation than in written reasoning problems.

In another aspect of the same experiment, Cruickshank (1948c) found that the retarded, as compared to the normals, had difficulty in naming the process involved in solving a problem when it was presented to them in printed form.

In another report, Cruickshank (1948a) used the Buswell-John Diagnostic Chart for Fundamentals in Arithmetic. As the subject worked on the problems, the examiner recorded the errors made. He found that the retarded had (1) an excess of primitive habits, such as counting on fingers, (2) inadequate technical habits, such as lack of understanding of the process, (3) carelessness, and (4) errors in reading.

In still another report, Cruickshank (1946) studied the arithmetic vocabulary of the retarded as compared to that of normals. He found that the retarded defined 49 per cent of the words, while the normals of the same mental age defined 62 per cent. The difference was significant at the 0.01 level. The author pointed out that the words which were concrete and related to activities in daily living are most familiar to retarded children, while the most abstract terms of mathematics, space, time, or quantity are most difficult.

An interesting, but inconclusive, report was made by Werner and Garrison (1942) on a finger schema test and its relation to arithmetic achievement. They found some suggestion of a relationship between finger localization and arithmetic retardation. Benton, Hutcheon, and Seymour (1951) also made studies relating to finger localizing ability and arithmetic achievement, but found no significant relationship. They did find, however, that there was some relationship between finger localization and right-left discrimination in some of the subnormal children.

Gothberg (1949), following Piaget's lead, studied the concept of time in three groups of retarded: 155 school children ranging in age from five to nineteen years with mental ages of two years, nine months to twelve years, six months; 42 adult defectives with ages of twenty to thirty; and 11 parolees, aged twenty-four to forty-five, with mental ages of seven through ten. She interviewed each subject by means of three pictures, a questionnaire, and sheets of paper upon which were drawn faces of clocks with the hands in various positions. Measures were obtained on clock time, age relationships, time periods, sequence dura-

tion, and historical time. She found that a mental age of twelve had to be reached before 50 per cent of the institutionalized defective children could tell time but that 80 per cent of the adult defectives at mental age twelve could tell time. The parolees could tell time at a lower mental age. Gothberg concluded that within these groups, the concept of time is closely related to mental age. Chronological age, experience, and special interest were also determinants. Further, the mentally retarded have little conception of sequence, relativity, or historical time. She suggested that teaching should be confined to concrete terms within the child's experience.

COMPARISON OF TEACHING METHODS

There have been few studies which compared different methods of teaching arithmetic to the mentally retarded. One such study has been made by Costello (1941). She used 271 subjects in a special school for mentally retarded children, the majority of whom were Negro. In addition, this group showed emotional instability in 52.8 per cent of the cases, and 39 per cent of the families were on relief. The mean CA was eight years, nine months, and the mean IQ was 74.2.

Three methods of teaching were used: (1) the socialization, or experience, method, (2) the sensorization method (an adaptation of the Montessori techniques), and (3) a verbalization method (the conventional approach).

The results of this experiment indicated that the socialization method produced the greatest gains on the Philadelphia Inventory Test of Arithmetic; sensorization, the next order of gains; and verbalization, the least gains. The author noted that there was greater variance in the socialization and verbalization methods than in the sensorization method and suggested that although the sensorization method did not show the most marked gains it showed the least pronounced losses.

Werner and Garrison (1942) selected children who were deficient in finger localization and in arithmetic and administered remedial instruction to them for five hours a week for a period of five months. Their results (using special devices such as finger abacuses, peg boards, and marble boards) indicated rapid learning under such remedial instruction. Control groups were not used.

As indicated earlier, there has been little systematic research on the teaching of arithmetic to mentally retarded children. The studies have been sporadic and discrete. In general, it can be stated that the mentally retarded achieve at a higher level (according to present methods of teaching) on the more mechanical, computational skills than on reasoning problems involving reading. This fact probably reflects the methods of teaching arithmetic in classrooms, since it is easier to drill on computational problems than it is to develop quantitative concepts.

The processes that have been studied indicate some differences between the normals and the retarded. These differences, again, may reflect the efficacy of teaching methods rather than special characteristics of subnormal intelligence.

The few studies on brain-injured children appear contradictory and confusing. While one author finds a relation between finger-localizing ability and arithmetic retardation, another author was unable to find this relationship. While it is expected that exogenous mental defectives would have difficulty in learning arithmetic, Capobianco's study (1956) could not find a difference between exogenous and endogenous retardates in arithmetic achievement. These studies should not discourage researchers from seeking relationships, since in some cases clinicians have found clear-cut cases of acalculia in children with brain damage. It is likely that categories, such as exogenous, brain-damaged, or organic, are not discrete or adequate enough to reveal such relationships.

The needed research in this area is the study of instructional procedures by which quantitative thinking ability can be developed in mentally retarded children.

One of the major diagnostic characteristics of mentally retarded children is delay in speech and language development. The factors relating to this fundamental characteristic have been the subject of many articles. The major research obstacles to adequate studies in this field are its complexity and the inadequacy of measuring instruments. One author utilizes a particular criterion for evaluating speech and language, while another one may use another criterion. In the following, an attempt is made to differentiate studies in *speech defects*, which may occur at an automatic, less meaningful, level of functioning, from *language*, which is primarily a part of the representational level of operation.

The incidence of speech defect among the mentally retarded has been surveyed by Goertzen (1957). As would be expected, different investigators had found that there are considerably more speech defects among the mentally retarded than among the normal population; but the prevalence was dependent upon the population studied, the degree of defect, the age, and so forth. He cites, for example, Kennedy (1930) as giving the following percentages of speech defects among the mentally retarded: morons, 42.6 per cent; imbeciles, 96.9 per cent; and idiots, 100 per cent.

Sirkin and Lyons (1941) examined 2522 cases in an institution and stated that speech defects existed in 42 per cent of the higher grades of morons and borderline children, 74 per cent of the imbecile group, and 100 per cent of the idiots. These figures agree with Kennedy's results, except for the imbecile group. Undoubtedly, different standards were used by the different investigators.

One of the earlier studies on speech defects was conducted by Town (1912). By her method of observation, she categorized the development of speech of idiots into five levels of development: (1) understanding of gestures, (2) imitation of gestures, (3) voluntary gestures, (4) understanding of words heard, and (5) sounds and attempts at articulation. She found a higher level of language among the imbeciles, which increased with increasing mental age. Echolalia was present in 19 per cent of the low-grade imbeciles while only 2 per cent of the high-grade imbeciles showed echolalia.

Bangs (1942) analyzed the articulatory deficiencies of the mentally retarded and attempted to relate these to intelligence levels. His subjects were fifty-three mentally retarded children in an institution. He found, in an analysis of the initial, medial, and final positions of the sounds, that the rank order of sounds avoided was not significantly different from those of normal children of the same mental age. The consonants most easily articulated seemed to be the ones preferred. One of the differences found was that the consonants in the final position were the ones most omitted by the retarded. Bangs concluded (1) that the retardates lack power of concentration to finish a verbalized idea, (2) that they lack the motor co-ordination of the normal, (3) that they have faulty habit patterns, and (4) that the best predictor of speech is the mental age.

Schlanger (1953a) investigated the speech development of seventy-four children in a private institution, between the ages of eight and sixteen, and with IQ's over 40. He found that 62 per cent had voice defects, 57 per cent had articulatory defects, and 20 per cent were stutterers. The mean number of sentences per hour was 88.8, the mean number of words per minute was 50, and the mean sentence length was 3.96 words. According to Schlanger, these were significantly below the speech performance of normal children of five and a half, six and a half, and nine and a half years of age. The mental age correlated higher with speech performance than did the CA. Schlanger ascribes low oral expression to social inhibition of language caused by slow speech development.

Batza (1956) evaluated the speech and oral language development of 108 retarded children in the Chicago public school's special classes. He compared three groups: (1) IQ's 59 and below, (2) IQ's 60 to 69, and (3) IQ's 70 and above. He found that the higher the IQ, the better the child was in articulation, oral language, auditory discrimination, motor co-ordination, and memory span. In view of the similarity of ages of the groups, this result is similar to other studies showing a relationship between mental age and speech development.

A similar study was made by Donovan (1957) in the New York City public schools. She examined two thousand children with IQ's between 50 and 75 to determine their needs for speech training. She found that 8 per cent of them had severe speech defects such as lisping, lalling, sound substitutions, stuttering, and speech defects due to cerebral palsy, brain injury, cleft palate, and impaired hearing. She also stated that almost all of the children had developmental speech problems. This included retarded language development, which appears to be a definite characteristic of the mentally retarded.

It appears from surveys that the kinds of speech defects found in the mentally retarded are similar to the speech problems of other children but that these defects are more frequent in the mentally retarded.

The effects of speech correction or

speech therapy (as it is sometimes called) with the mentally retarded have been studied by a few workers. Since strictly objective tests of speech are not readily available, the evaluation is dependent upon the judgment of the speech correctionist. Whether the progress a child makes is a factor of maturation or the result of speech therapy is sometimes difficult to establish. Few studies have used control groups.

Sirkin and Lyons (1941) studied the effects of speech therapy on a group of defective children. From clinical evaluations they found that 52 per cent showed satisfactory response to treatment. A follow-up study showed that 63 per cent of those who had improved had retained the correction. No control groups were used in this study.

Schlanger (1953*b*) compared the test results of sixty-two speech-defective children before and after speech correction. The children were trained in groups of three to five, two to three times a week for the school year. Schlanger reported that the children made significant gains in speech skills and verbal output but showed no improvement in sound discrimination. Since no control group was used in this experiment, it is difficult to tell whether this improvement was due to speech training or to maturation.

Schneider and Vallon (1954) gave a one-year program of speech therapy to thirty-four children in a school for trainable children. They classified the defects as delayed language development, insufficient language development, articulatory disturbances, vocal disturbances, and disturbances of speech perception. At the end of the year, the therapists felt improvement had been made; but these judgments were subjective, and no control group had been used.

One study using a control group was conducted by Mecham (1955). He developed tests of articulation, auditory discrimination, auditory digit span, and oral language development. He adminis-

tered the test to three groups of retarded children at the Columbus State School. The experimental group consisted of twenty-one children, ages nine to eighteen years, with an IQ range of 41 to 75 (mean 58.5). Ten children selected at random from the same classes, ages nine to fifteen, and IQ's 55 to 81 (mean 67.9), served as a control. Ten other children were matched for CA, IQ, and sex, and served as a second control. The experimental group and first control group were tested before and after the therapy period, while the second (matched) control group was tested only at the end. Speech therapy was given by two speech therapists to the twenty-one children in the experimental group. Split-half tests of reliability for the tests showed adequate reliability. The experimental group showed significant improvement on all four tests as a result of speech therapy. Subjects who did not receive therapy made no significant improvement during the eight-week period except for one instance of improvement in auditory memory span. Mecham stated that there was a selection factor operating, since the experimental children were selected on the basis of need for speech correction, and the controls scored higher on initial tests.

In summary, research has shown (1) that speech defects are more prevalent among the mentally retarded than among normal children, (2) that the greater the mental defect, the greater the prevalence of speech defects, and (3) that the effects of speech therapy have not been adequately determined. Those who work with the children report they have made progress. Whether the improvement is confined to the speech-correction session or is transferred to a life situation has not been proven. As indicated above, only one study used a control group in the measurement of improvement. Even in this study, the control group was only a contrast group, since the children selected for speech correction were the

most needy, and these were not randomized into an experimental and control
group. Instead, other retarded children
were selected as a control.

It is difficult to separate studies in
speech correction from those in language
development, since speech is a part of
the total language process. Speech correction, however, deals primarily with
vocal encoding, the end result of the language process. Learnings preceding the
vocal response may be the other facets
of language behavior.

Like speech, language development
appears to be related to mental age; the
higher the mental age, the better the language. Karlin and Strazzulla (1952),
working in a medical clinic, surveyed
fifty retarded children, ranging in age
from three to fourteen. The histories of
these children indicated that the lower
the IQ, the later the children began to
talk. The greatest retardation in growth
was in the speech and language area.

Griffith and Spitz (1958) studied ab-
stracting ability in relation to word
meaning of mentally retarded adolescents. The twenty-six boys were presented with twenty-four groups of three
nouns and asked to name the common
characteristic. In another session, the
subjects were asked to define these nouns
along with several new words. The correct abstractions of the triads were then
compared with the definitions of the
words to see if the definition combined
the characteristics given in the abstraction. The results showed that the proportion of abstractions attained increased
sharply when at least two of the words
of the triad were defined in common.
The authors felt that the identical element in the descriptions mediated abstraction and that rigidity was evidenced,
because these subjects could not easily
go beyond their immediate verbal description to find a common quality.

Bijou and Werner (1944) matched nineteen brain-injured children with nineteen
non-brain-injured children on the variables of CA and MA. On a vocabulary
test, the brain-injured were found to be
superior in range and quality of correct
definitions. The non-brain-injured gave
answers in terms of use, while the brain-
injured were inclined to define words
in terms of their independent properties.

Mein (1961) reports studies of the oral
vocabulary of severely subnormal patients at the Harperbury Hospital in
London. He found significant differences
between mongoloids and non-mongoloids
in the percentage of nouns used in an
interview. He concluded that mongoloids
function at a lower level than non-mongoloids in the percentage of nouns used,
even though the classified and unclassified vocabulary of the two groups was
the same.

Speidel (1958) studied the language
abilities of mentally retarded children in
special classes in Boston. A series of
standard and clinical tests of listening,
reading, speaking, and writing were
given to 67 retarded children in the primary grades and to 142 children in the
intermediate grades. On the Durrell-Sul-
livan test of listening comprehension,
Speidel found that the retarded in the
primary grades were fourteen months
higher than their mental age and sixteen
months higher than their reading age. In
the intermediate grades, their listening
comprehension was eight months higher
than their mental age and twenty-three
months higher than their reading age. In
speaking, writing, and oral recall, the
retarded children were fairly competent.
In the intermediate grades, the retarded
children did not show the advance which
would be expected. The author suggested
a more systematic program of language
instruction for mentally retarded children.

One of the major theoretical questions
is whether lack of language development
among mentally retarded children is an
inevitable consequence of mental retar-

dation or whether intensive training can improve the rate of language development.

Lyle (1960) studied the effects of institutionalization on the development of language. In general, he found that *ad hoc* language tests tended to correlate highly with verbal intelligence tests such as the Minnesota Preschool Scale. Thirty-two young imbeciles from a hospital were randomized, and sixteen of them, who served as an experimental group, were removed from the hospital and placed in a small resident nursery school under relatively intensive instruction. After twelve months of education, the two groups (experimental and control) were compared on gains. The experimental children gained eight months in mental age on the verbal part of the Minnesota Preschool Scale, while the controls gained four months. This difference was statistically significant at the 0.05 level. A test of speech sounds and word-naming also showed significant differences in favor of the experimental group. Eighteen months after the initiation of the experiment, both groups were again tested. At this point, significant differences in favor of the nursery-trained group were again evident in verbal intelligence, word-naming, comprehension, complexity of language, and speech sounds. No differences were found on non-verbal intelligence or on word definition.

Kolstoe (1958) paired thirty mongoloids in an institution on the basis of mental age and randomly selected fifteen for training in language by a tutorial system, leaving the other fifteen in the wards as controls. The mean mental age on the Kuhlmann Test of Mental Development was two years, two months. The IQ's of the subjects ranged from 19 to 36 with a mean of 24.53 for the experimental group and 23.07 for the controls. The training group received tutoring forty-five minutes a day, five days a week, for five and one-half months. The teaching

procedures involved the securing of attention, repetition of symbols used, reward, and reinforcement.

On the Kuhlmann Test of Mental Development test-retest scores, the experimental group lost 1.2 IQ points, while the control group lost 2.78 points. This difference was statistically significant at the 0.05 level. On five subtests of the Illinois Language Scale, the experimental group gained significantly over the controls during the same period. On observational rating scales, no differences were observed. An analysis of the data indicated that a minimum mental age of two was necessary for the instruction to be profitable.

A negative report on training was made by Johnston and Farrell (1957). They gave special work in auditory training, lip reading, and speech correction to hard-of-hearing retarded children. They used control groups and obtained no improvement of the experimental children over the controls.

COMMENTS

The review of research on language and speech with the mentally retarded is not dissimilar to that in other areas of interest. Most of the studies are of a survey type, attempting to determine prevalence and to relate speech defects to CA, IQ, MA, and other variables. The kinds of speech defects and their development or lack of development have been the concern of some workers.

There have been few studies on the effects of therapy in speech correction or of educational programs on the development of speech and language. Only one study used randomized control groups, and few researchers have tested the reliability of their measuring instruments. Reports in many journals typically consist of a brief description of an educational program and a report that improvement was observed by the teachers or by others on a subjective basis. This procedure, however unscientific, does not differ radically from the many subjective reports on the effects and values of techniques in such areas as psychotherapy or general education, where evaluation with adequate controls is most difficult.

ART AND MUSIC EDUCATION

The utilization of arts and crafts and music as media of instruction is a standard part of the curriculum in the educational program for the mentally retarded. This aspect of the curriculum is difficult to evaluate, and the design of research which subject this part of the curriculum to controlled experimentation is likewise difficult. This is represented by the paucity of well-designed research studies.

ART

Observations on a "sample of one" are usually not considered research. Yet rare cases of performance in single individuals are worthy of report in research literature. Such a case is the noted artist Kiyoshi Yamashita of Japan who has won renown as a modern Van Gogh. In spite of this fame, he is considered mentally retarded. Dr. Ryuzabura Shikiba, a Japanese psychiatrist who knew him well, reported (1956) that Yamashita was born in Tokyo in 1922. His mother parted with her husband, who was reported to be an alcoholic. Yamashita was a backward child in school. On a Japanese translation of the Stanford-Binet Scale, he obtained an IQ of 68. Because of his school failures, feelings of inferiority, ridicule by his classmates, broken home, and behavior problems, he was placed in an institution. Here he was tutored by an instructor who specialized in making a type of collage, technically known in Japan as *hari-e*. This process consisted of pasting together small bits of colored paper torn with the fingers or cut with scissors. Yamashita became quite proficient in this activity and introduced techniques of his own. He finally left the institution and became a wanderer, producing works of art sporadically. In 1949, he began to paint in oils. He continued to be considered mentally retarded by psychiatrists and psychologists in Japan.

The present reviewer has consulted personally with Japanese psychologists who knew and had examined Yamashita and feels that this is a case of a famous artist who is deficient in verbal learning and in social relations but is a genius in a specific area. The Japanese psychologists, however, are convinced that Yamashita is mentally retarded. They feel that he is mentally retarded according to all measures and observations but that he has a specific and special ability in one phase of artistic behavior which is not related to our concepts of intelligence. Is this a case of a retarded individual who, through concentrated and intensive training in a special field, developed an ability in a specific area; or is he a case of a genius who has disabilities in the verbal and personality areas?

Vaughn and Hoose (1936) reported a case of a mentally retarded boy in an institution who was able to look at a complex picture for fifteen seconds and reproduce it in detail. On psychometric tests and on a series of tests of visual imagery, he showed great variation. On Memory for Designs in the Detroit Tests of Learning Aptitude, he scored at the eighteen-year level when he was fourteen years of age. His IQ on the Stanford-Binet Scale at the age of seven years, ten months, was 98; at nine years, nine months, 79; at fourteen years, 64; at fourteen years, six months, 67. He scored at the 94th percentile rank on the Stenquist Mechanical Assembly Test. On the Grace Arthur Point Scale of Performance Tests, his IQ was 104. He did not show creativity. It would appear from his record that this boy was not mentally retarded but had a personality disturbance and was educationally retarded.

Spoerl (1940) studied (1) the developmental tendencies of retarded children, (2) the comparative performance of normal and retarded children of the same mental age (six years, one month), and (3) the distinguishing characteristics of the work of retarded children. Spoerl used thirty children in a special class with IQ's of 42 to 97, MA's ranging from three years, one month to nine years, six months, and CA's ranging from seven to fourteen. Drawings were secured from the children in free and structured situations. The pictures were scored using the McCarty Scales, for houses and compositions, and the Goodenough Intelligence Test, for human figures.

The retarded children showed consistent development in art, corresponding to increases in mental age. They did best in unstructured situations, while the borderline over age ten and the dull-normals did better in more structured or directed situations. When compared with the normals (only six pairs), who showed steady advance with mental age, the retarded showed more fluctuations after the age of ten. The retarded had greater ability in copying, which was accounted for by the author on the basis of advanced chronological age. Some of the items that distinguished the drawings of the retarded from the normal were: short arms in relation to the rest of the figure, frequent clichés, meticulous workmanship, automatism, lack of proportion between parts, a large amount of asymmetry, and a tendency to give undue attention to detail.

Patterson and Leightner (1944) compared the spontaneous paintings of normal and mentally retarded children. The retarded children were residents of the Wayne County Training School, while the normal children of the same mental age were selected from the neighboring public schools. The mean mental age of both groups was seven years, two months. In this experiment, paintings of twenty-five mentally retarded children were compared with those of the normal group on recognizability, technique, integration, number of objects shown in single pictures, and range of subjects chosen. Three judges compared the paintings of both groups.

The researchers concluded that the similarities between the normal and retarded groups were more numerous than the differences. However, the mentally retarded had a larger percentage of pattern paintings (rhythmic design) and the normal group had a higher percentage of paintings with filled-in contours. The authors felt that the mentally retarded continued to respond to sensory stimuli of color and form without ideational content longer than the normal children and that they were more easily satisfied with simple techniques.

Schaefer-Simmern (1948) conducted an art-training program for adult retardates at the Southbury Training School. He postulated that artistic activity is a function of general human activity and that there are various stages of visual conception which form the mental foundation of artistic activity. Artistic development must start from the individual's stage of visual conception. Schaefer-Simmern illustrates results with a case study of Selma, who was thirty years old and had a mental age of six years, nine months. Her first artistic activity consisted of drawing with many repetitions, like a six-year-old. According to Schaefer-Simmern, she showed lack of visualization of the whole but, nevertheless, developed mental concentration and longer attention. Observation indicated that she underwent a change in personality and in emotional and physical behavior.

Gaitskell and Gaitskell (1953) studied the artistic expression of mentally retarded children. They analyzed the art work of 514 children enrolled in fifty-five schools. The children ranged in CA from seven years, six months to sixteen years, and in IQ from 10 to 89. Twenty of the children were paired with normal children on the basis of MA and CA.

The Gaitskells concluded: (1) both the retarded and the normal begin with manipulation, but the retarded children stay at this stage longer; (2) the retarded tend to repeat symbols which, in a sense, retards their progress to the next stage; (3) the meanings of symbols are shown in exaggerated marks; and (4) the retarded may reach the schematic and realistic stages, but their work is usually poorer than that of normal children.

A second experiment by the Gaitskells (1953) attempted to discover the effects of dictatorial teaching methods on habits of work and the output of art. Eighty-two retarded children (IQ's 52 to 86, and ages eight to fifteen), who had been taught by an authoritarian method, were encouraged to do art work of a creative nature for nine days. For the next twenty-one weeks, the group was divided into two groups. One group was again taught in a dictatorial fashion, while the other group continued to work creatively. After this period, the group taught by a dictatorial method was asked to work creatively for six days. From the observations made, the Gaitskells concluded that the work of the children who were taught by the dictatorial method became stereotyped and irrelevant. Those who had continued to work creatively had developed some ability to express themselves.

In an attempt to determine the lowest level of intelligence needed for artistic expression, the Gaitskells gave wax crayons and newsprint to forty-four children with CA's of six to twelve and IQ's of below 50. They concluded that children with IQ's lower than 40 derived little or no profit from art activities.

MUSIC

Carey (1958) surveyed music education in cities over 25,000 population in an attempt to determine the effective and profitable types of music education for the mentally retarded. In addition to surveying cities, nine field situations were established in northern Illinois with seven classes from primary to junior high school. Music activities were conducted under the supervision of the investigator and classroom teachers for a four-month period.

Carey found: (1) music was included in the curriculum for the mentally retarded in 458 of the 465 cities included in the study; (2) the same methods of teaching music used with normal children were utilized with the mentally retarded, with a slower pace and more repetition; (3) activities included rote singing, listening, free and controlled rhythmic activities, creativity, and playing percussion instruments; and (4) the progress appeared to be similar to the rate found in academic studies.

Research on the evaluation of music programs, like research in art, is generally conducted on a subjective basis. Weigl (1959) described the procedures used in a hospital clinic school for mentally retarded children for a period of four years. Weigl obtained ratings on the children at the beginning and at the end of each ten-week period. He stated that on the evaluation of adjustment and attitudes, 10 per cent showed no change, 20 per cent some change, and 70 per cent showed improvement which carried over to the home and school.

Murphy (1957) observed the responses to music of low- and middle-grade retarded children in an institution. She compared thirty-two subjects who expressed rhythm with rocking movements with thirty-two subjects who expressed rhythm with clapping movements. Murphy concluded that "rockers" appeared to represent a solitary, self-absorbed, infantile level of social-emotional development. They also represented the lowest mental age and the most primitive motor level. The "clappers" appeared to engage more in socialized group activity.

COMMENTS

Some forms of art and music activities are usually standard practices in educational programs for the mentally retarded. Research and evaluation of the effects of such activities are meager. The most insightful results come from special case studies of children. The information obtained from survey and case-study material indicates that competencies in art and music are related largely to the mental development of the child. The mentally retarded are slower to learn and remain longer at each stage. The effects of these activities (art therapy and music therapy) on personality or intelligence are still in the realm of conjecture.

MOTOR AND PHYSICAL EDUCATION

The effects of physical education on the development of mentally retarded children have not attracted many research workers. The philosophies behind physical education or physical activity follow two points of view. The first stems from the efforts of Seguin (1907), who developed a physiologic method of teaching the mentally retarded. He postulated that specific training of the peripheral nervous system through muscle and sense training would strengthen the receptors, bombard the central nervous system, and stimulate the cortex to greater mental functioning. The other purpose of physical education used by modern educators is to develop the co-ordination and personality of the child without any expectation of developing intelligence.

Since the time of Seguin, only one report has been made showing some effects of physical education on tested intelligence. Oliver (1958) matched two groups of educationally subnormal boys, and gave a ten-week course of physical conditioning to one group in addition to regular schooling, while the control group received only schooling. Both groups were tested before and after the experiment on a series of intelligence tests. According to Oliver, the experimental group gained 4.26 IQ points on the Revised Stanford-Binet Scale, while the control group gained 0.9 IQ points. The difference was significant to the 0.01 level. On the Goodenough Draw-a-Man Test and on the Porteus Maze Test, the differences in favor of the experimental group were also significant. There were no significant differences on Raven's Progressive Matrices or on the Seguin-Goddard Formboard.

The author explains these increases in test scores for the experimental group on the basis of the effects of continued successful experience, improved social adjustment, improved physical condition, and the effects of feeling important.

This study is the only piece of research the reviewer was able to find on the effects of physical education on intelligence since Seguin presented his theory in 1846. This kind of research is quite feasible in schools, and the results should be checked with other experiments before acceptance.

The studies on physical activities of the mentally retarded have been confined largely to a comparison of normals and subnormals on tests of physical proficiency. Sloan (1951) compared twenty normal and twenty mental defectives on the Lincoln Adaptation of the Oseretsky Tests of Motor Proficiency. The mean CA of his two groups was ten years. The mean IQ of the mentally retarded males was 54.2 and the mean IQ of the normal male was 105.8. For the females (one-half of each group), the mean IQ of the retarded was 56.2, and of the normal females, 99.2. Sloan concluded that mental defectives are significantly inferior in motor proficiency to children of average intelligence. Sloan made no attempt to train the defectives in motor proficiency to determine whether such deficits can be developed through training.

Rabin (1957) also used the Lincoln Adaptation of the Oseretsky Test on institutionalized mental defectives. He found motor proficiency to have a significant relationship to CA. He found no significant relationship to IQ, contrary to Sloan's results.

Malpass (1960) compared institutionalized mental retardates with normal children and with mentally retarded children in special classes in the public schools. He found a significant difference on the Oseretsky test between the normals and the retarded but no difference between the institutionalized and non-institutionalized children.

Francis and Rarick (1960) tested 284 mentally retarded boys and girls in special classes on a battery of eleven gross motor tests. They found that the special-class mentally retarded were markedly inferior to normal children in all of the motor performance tests. The mentally retarded were from two to four years below the published age norms for normal children. The motor proficiency of the children was not related to educational programs.

Howe (1959) conducted a similar study in which he compared forty-three normal boys and girls with forty-three mentally retarded boys and girls on eleven motor tasks. On all tests—Sargent-Jump, balancing on foot, tracing speed, dotting speed, and so forth—the normal children were significantly superior to the mentally retarded.

In addition to testing the two groups, Howe (1960) gave instruction to both the retarded and the normals for a two-week period on three motor skill tasks. Both groups showed the same significant gains on the "squat thrust." On the other two tasks both groups showed only moderate gains.

Shotick and Thate (1960) initiated a program of physical education for seven children in a class for the mentally retarded. For three months, observers anecdotally recorded the performances and reactions of the children. They tabulated the responses as "Enthusiastic," "Response to Instruction," and "Reaction to Other Children." No statistical analysis was made of the study, but the activities that showed more enthusiastic response and those showing adequate response to instruction were noted.

COMMENTS

The foregoing review of literature reveals (1) that there have been some survey studies which show that retarded children are inferior to normals in motor proficiency, and (2) that the effects of physical education programs with the retarded have not been evaluated. In view of the repeated sporadic efforts throughout the history of the education of the mentally retarded to emphasize physical and motor training, further research efforts along this line may be worthwhile.

SUMMARY STATEMENT

Educational research with the mentally retarded, as reviewed in this chapter, has been limited primarily to research on the achievement and development of retarded children in the various phases of the school curriculum. This review leads to the following comments:

1. The practice of organizing special classes for the educable mentally retarded increased tenfold between 1922 and 1958. In spite of this rapid increase in special provisions, as contrasted to leaving the children in the regular grades, there is only sporadic research evidence which justifies this increase. Although over a dozen research studies have been conducted in this area, definitive conclusions cannot be made. The general impressions derived from these studies are that (1) the children assigned to special classes are equal to or inferior in academic achievement to those remaining in the regular grades, (2) the children at the lower range of educability show equal or superior academic achievement to similar children left in the regular grades, (3) in social adjustment the special-class groups appear superior to those left in the regular grades, and (4) the retarded children in the regular grades tend to be isolated and rejected by their normal peers. Any generalizations made from the studies are questionable, since the studies suffered from the *in situ* na-

ture of the investigations, lack of control of the selection factor, the short period of time the children were enrolled in special classes after failure in the regular grades, little definition of the programs of the special classes, and the questionable reliability and validity of the instruments used to measure achievement and adjustment. What is needed is a comprehensive longitudinal study of the effects of special classes beginning when children are six years of age. The development of a special-class group should be compared with that of a randomized group of retarded children remaining in the regular grades. Such an experiment is now under way.

2. The interest in community classes for the trainable retarded child (IQ's below 50) during the postwar period has generated a series of short-term studies on the effects of training in self-care, social adjustment, and economic usefulness on the development of such children. Of the seven studies reported, only one extended for a number of years, and only two used a contrast group. In general, the results did not show significant benefits from the special-class programs, which were hurriedly assembled with staff which had had little previous training or experience with this type of child. The instruments of measurement were generally improvised by the investigators. It is the reviewer's opinion that research in this area was initiated without adequate preparation in terms of structure, theory, adequate hypotheses, or adequate measuring instruments. It is possible that intensive case studies, even with a sample f one in some cases, would have seived a better purpose at this stage of development than the attempt to use complex statistical procedures on uncontrolled variables.

3. The studies on the effects of educational procedures on the development of intelligence with retarded children (a topic which has remained dormant for many years) have recently attracted some attention. The prejudice against the theory that intelligence is educable (resulting from certain views on heredity, the constancy of the IQ, and the static nature of mental retardation) tended to shelve the topic as an area worthy of investigation. Sporadic research studies present positive evidence that educational treatment tends to displace the rate of growth, especially when cultural and educational programs are provided at a young age. The present problem for research on the educability of intelligence is to identify more specifically the factors in the *nature* of the child and the variables in the *nurture* provided by the environment which effect change in rate of growth, both positively and negatively.

4. Studies on reading with the mentally retarded have attracted more authors than all other areas combined. Of particular interest are the studies which show that the mentally retarded are generally reading below their mental-age–reading-grade expectancy. Where they are up to or above their expectancy, a special emphasis on reading instruction has been made. No special methods were found superior to others in teaching reading to retarded children. One surprising result of several studies points out that children with brain damage and with perceptual disturbances are not necessarily defective in reading if special methods and emphasis have been given to this process. If the studies reported are confirmed by future research, it would appear that brain-injured children achieve similarly to non-brain-injured children under conventional methods of instruction but that brain-injured children under more systematic methods of instruction can progress faster than non-brain-injured children under conventional special-class or regular-class instruction. These results, together with others, point to the importance of research on systematic methods of instruction with retarded children.

5. The area of quantitative thinking

abilities and arithmetic achievement has not been the subject of many experiments. In general, the mentally retarded achieve at a higher level in arithmetic computation than in arithmetic reasoning. Also, some differences in the process of computation have been found between normals and subnormals. Both of these findings, however, probably reflect the methods used in instruction rather than a specific characteristic of subnormal intelligence. The needed research in the area of arithmetic is the study of instructional procedures by which quantitative thinking ability can be developed in the mentally retarded child.

6. Most of the studies on speech and language of the mentally retarded are of a survey type. These tend to relate speech defects to CA, MA, and IQ. There were few studies which attempted to evaluate the effects of speech correction or language instruction. Of the few studies reported, only one study (on the training of language of mongoloid children) used a randomized control group. Much of the literature on language instruction deals with a description of the procedures used and a report that improvement was observed by the teachers or others on a subjective basis. Since deficits in language facility in all of its phases are traditionally correlated with subnormal intelligence, this area is deserving of more research than is presently evident. It is likely that our psychological theories of language and thought processes have not progressed sufficiently for us to conduct applied research in educational programs with the mentally retarded.

7. Art and music activities are usually standard practices in educational programs for the mentally retarded. From the few studies reported, there is an indication that competency in art and music is related to mental development. The mentally retarded are slower to learn and remain longer at each stage. The effects of art and music therapy on personality or intelligence are still in the realm of conjecture.

8. Surveys on motor proficiency show quite clearly that retarded children are inferior to normal children in this so-called non-intellectual ability. The effects of training in physical education or motor proficiency have not yet been determined. In view of Seguin's earlier efforts with the physiological method of training defectives and the sporadic attempts to use physical activity as an educational media, research in this area may be worthwhile. This is an area of research that has been seriously neglected. With the recent interest in the concepts of Piaget and the methods of Montissori, a fresh approach to this question should be in the making.

REFERENCES

AINSWORTH, S. H. 1959. *An Exploratory Study of Educational, Social and Emotional Factors in the Education of Mentally Retarded Children in Georgia Public Schools.* ("U.S. Office of Education Cooperative Research Program," Project No. 171 [6470].) Athens, Georgia: University of Georgia.

AXLINE, V. M. 1947. Nondirective therapy for poor readers. *J. Consult. Psychol.,* **11**: 61–69.

BALDWIN, W. D. 1958. The social position of the educable mentally retarded in the regular grades in the public schools. *Except. Child.,* **25**:106–8.

BANGS, J. L. 1942. A clinical analysis of the articulatory defects of the feebleminded. *J. Speech Dis.,* **7**:343–46.

BATZA, E. M. 1956. Investigation of the speech and oral language behavior of educable mentally retarded children. *Diss. Abstr.,* **17**:299.

BENNETT, A. 1929. Reading ability in special classes. *J. Educ. Res.,* **20**:236–38.

———. 1932. *A Comparative Study of Subnormal Children in the Elementary Grades.* New York: Teachers College, Columbia University, Bureau of Publications.

BENSBERG, G. J. 1953. The relationship of academic achievement of mental defectives to mental age, sex, institutionalization and etiology. *Amer. J. Ment. Defic.,* **58**:327–30.

BENTON, A. L., HUTCHEON, J. E., and SEYMOUR, E. 1951. Arithmetic ability, finger localization capacity, and right-left discrimination in normal and defective children. *Amer. J. Orthopsychiat.,* 21:756–66.

BIJOU, S. W., and WERNER, H. 1944. Vocabulary analysis in mentally deficient children. *Amer. J. Ment. Defic.,* **48**:364–66.

BINET, A. 1909. *Les idées modernes sur les enfants.* Paris: E. Flemmarion.

BLATT, B. 1958. The physical, personality, and academic status of children who are mentally retarded attending special classes as compared with children who are mentally retarded attending regular classes. *Amer. J. Ment. Defic.,* **62**:810–18.

BRADWAY, K. P. 1939. Academic achievement in a group of mentally retarded subjects. *Proc. Amer. Assoc. Ment. Defic.,* **44**:154–62.

BRAEM, H. R. 1931. An experiment in the methodology of teaching reading to mental defectives of moron and borderline level. *Proc. Amer. Assoc. Stud. Feebleminded,* 36:92–99.

BROWN, A., and LIND, C. 1931. School achievement in relation to mental age—a comparative study. *J. Educ. Psychol.,* **32**:561–76.

CAIN, L. F., and LEVINE, S. 1963. *Effects of Community and Institutional School Programs on Trainable Mentally Retarded Children.* CEC Research Monographs, Series B, No. B-1. Washington, D.C., 1963, pp. 56.

CAPOBIANCO, R. J. 1956. A comparison of endogenous and exogenous mentally retarded on arithmetic processes. *In:* L. M. DUNN and R. J. CAPOBIANCO, Studies of reading and arithmetic in mentally retarded boys. *Monogr. Soc. Res. Child Develop.,* **19** (1954), No. 1: 100–140. Lafayette, Indiana: Child Development Publications.

CAPOBIANCO, R. J., and MILLER, D. Y. 1958. *Quantitative and Qualitative Analyses of Exogenous and Endogenous Children in Some Reading Processes.* ("U.S. Office of Education Cooperative Research Program.") Syracuse, N.Y.: Syracuse University Research Institute.

CAREY, M. A. 1958. Music for the educable mentally handicapped. *Diss. Abstr.,* **19**: 2967.

CASSIDY, V. M., and STANTON, J. E. 1959. *An Investigation of Factors Involved in the Educational Placement of Mentally Retarded Children: A Study of Differences between Children in Special and Regular Classes in Ohio.* ("U.S. Office of Education Cooperative Research Program," Project No. 043.) Columbus: Ohio State University.

CHAPMAN, C. S. 1939. "A Study of the Reading Ability of Special Class Pupils." Unpublished Master's thesis, University of Oregon.

COLEMAN, M. U. 1938. Remedial reading for special groups. *Proc. Amer. Assoc. Ment. Defic.,* **43**:123–27.

COSTELLO, H. M. 1941. "The Responses of Mentally Retarded Children to Specialized Learning Experiences in Arithmetic." Unpublished Ph.D. dissertation, University of Pennsylvania.

COWEN, P. A. 1938. Special class vs. grade groups for subnormal pupils. *Sch. and Soc.,* **48**:27–28.

CRUICKSHANK, W. M. 1946. Arithmetic vocabulary of mentally retarded boys. *Except. Child.,* **13**:65–69, 91.

———. 1948a. Arithmetic work habits of mentally retarded boys. *Amer. J. Ment. Defic.,* **52**:318–30.

———. 1948b. Arithmetic ability of mentally retarded children, I. *J. Educ. Res.,* **42**: 161–70.

———. 1948c. Arithmetic ability of mentally retarded children, II. *Ibid.,* **42**:279–88.

CRUICKSHANK, W. M., BENTZEN, FRANCES A., RATZEBURG, F. E., and TANNAHAUSER, MIRIAN T. 1961. *A Teaching Method for Brain-Injured Hyperactive Children.* Syracuse, New York: Syracuse University Press.

DAVIDSON, H. P. 1931. An experimental study of bright, average, and dull children at the four year mental level. *Genet. Psychol. Monogr.,* **9**:110–20.

DEARBORN, W. F. 1930. The nature of special abilities and disabilities. *Sch. and Soc.,* **31**:632–36.

DOLL, E. A. 1941. The essentials of an inclusive concept of mental deficiency. *Amer. J. Ment. Defic.,* **46**:214–19.

DONOVAN, H. 1957. Organization and development of a speech program for the mentally retarded in the New York City Public Schools. *Amer. J. Ment. Defic.*, **62**:455–59.

DUNN, L. M., 1956. A comparison of the reading processes of mentally retarded boys of the same mental age. *In:* L. M. DUNN and R. J. CAPOBIANCO, Studies of reading and arithmetic in mentally retarded boys. *Monogr. Soc. Res. Child Develop.*, **19** (1954), No. 1: 7–99. Lafayette, Indiana: Child Development Publications.

ELENBOGEN, M. L. 1957. A comparative study of some aspects of academic and social adjustment of two groups of mentally retarded children in special classes and in regular grades. *Diss. Abstr.*, **17**: 2497.

ENGEL, A. M. 1942. A study of 3,169 retarded pupils in the Detroit Public Schools. *Amer. J. Ment. Defic.*, **46**:395–401.

EWERHARDT, P. J. 1938. Reading difficulties in subnormal children. *Proc. Amer. Assoc. Ment. Defic.*, **43**:188–93.

FRANCIS, R. J., and RARICK L. 1960. *Motor Characteristics of the Mentally Retarded.* ("Coop. Res. Monogr.," No. 1.) Washington, D.C.: U.S. Department of Health, Education, and Welfare, Office of Education.

FRENCH, E. L. 1950. Reading disability and mental deficiency: a preliminary report. *Training Sch. Bull.*, **47**:47–57.

FREY, R. M. 1961. "Reading behavior of public school brain-injured and non-brain-injured children of average and retarded mental development." Unpublished Ph.D. dissertation, University of Illinois.

GAITSKELL, C., and GAITSKELL, M. 1953. *Art Education for Slow Learners.* Peoria, Illinois: Charles A. Bennett Co.

GALLAGHER, J. J. 1960. *Tutoring of Brain-Injured Mentally Retarded Children.* Springfield, Illinois: C. C Thomas.

GODDARD, H. H. 1914. *Feeblemindedness: Its Causes and Consequences.* New York: MacMillan.

GOERTZEN, S. M. 1957. Speech and the mentally retarded child. *Amer. J. Ment. Defic.*, **62**:244–53.

GOLDSTEIN, H. 1956. *Report Number Two on Study Projects for Trainable Mentally Handicapped Children.* Issued by Vernon L. Nickell, Superintendent of Public Instruction. Springfield, Illinois.

GOLDSTEIN, H., JORDAN, L., and MOSS, J. W. 1962. *Early School Development of Low IQ Children: A Study of Special Class Placement.* ("U.S. Office of Education Cooperative Research Program," Project SAE 8204, Interim Report.) Urbana, Illinois: University of Illinois, Institute for Research of Exceptional Children.

GOTHBERG, L. C. 1949. The mentally defective child's understanding of time. *Amer. J. Ment. Defic.*, **53**:441–55.

GRIFFITH, B. C., and SPITZ, H. H. 1958. Some relationships between abstractions and word meaning in retarded adolescents. *Amer. J. Ment. Defic.*, **63**:247–51.

GUENTHER, R. J. 1956. *Final Report of the Michigan Demonstration Research Project for the Severely Retarded.* Lansing, Michigan: Department of Public Instruction.

HEGGE, T. G. 1934. Special reading disability with particular reference to the mentally deficient. *Proc. Amer. Assoc. Ment. Defic.*, **39**:297–343.

HEGGE, T. G., KIRK, S. A., and KIRK, W. D. 1936. *Remedial Reading Drills.* Ann Arbor: George Wahr.

HILL, I. 1939. "A Survey of Reading Difficulties of Mentally Retarded Children in Schenectady, New York." Unpublished Master's thesis, New York State College for Teachers, Albany.

HOTTEL, J. 1958. *An Evaluation of Tennessee's Day Class Program for Severely Mentally Retarded Trainable Children.* Nashville, Tennessee: State Department of Education.

HOWE, C. E. 1959. A comparison of motor skills of mentally retarded and normal children. *Except. Child.*, **25**:352–54.

———. 1960. Compensation or correlation. *Education*, **80**:1–3.

HOYT, M. 1924. Mental age and school attainment of 1007 retarded children in Massachusetts. *J. Educ. Psychol.*, **15**:297–301.

INTERNATIONAL BUREAU OF EDUCATION. 1960. *Organization of Special Education for Mentally Deficient Children.* UNESCO, Publication No. 214. Place De Fontenoy, Paris.

JANES, H. P. 1953. Is remedial reading effective with slow learners? *Training Sch. Bull.*, **50**:51–53.

JOHNSON, G. O. 1950. A study of the social position of mentally handicapped children in the regular grades. *Amer. J. Ment. Defic.*, **55**:60–89.

JOHNSON, G. O., and CAPOBIANCO, R. J. 1957. *Research Project on Severely Retarded Children.* Albany, New York: Interdepartmental Health Resources Board.

JOHNSON, G. O., and KIRK, S. A. 1950. Are mentally handicapped children segregated in the regular grades? *Except. Child.*, **17**:65–68, 87–88.

JOHNSTON, P. W., and FARRELL, M. J. 1957. An experiment in improved medical and educational services for hard of hearing children at the Walter E. Fernald State School. *Amer. J. Ment. Defic.*, **62**:230–37.

JORDON, T. E., and DECHARMS, R. 1959. The achievement motive in normal and mentally retarded children. *Amer. J. Ment. Defic.*, **64**:457–66.

KARLIN, I. W., and STRAZZULLA, M. 1952. Speech and language problems of mentally deficient children. *J. Speech Hearing Dis.*, **17**:286–94.

KELLY, E. M. 1934. The improvement of reading in special classes for mentally retarded children. *Proc. Amer. Assoc. Ment. Defic.*, **39**:67–73.

KENNEDY, L. 1930. "Studies in the Speech of the Feebleminded." Unpublished Ph.D. dissertation, University of Wisconsin.

KEPHART, N. C. 1939. The effect of a highly specialized program upon the IQ in high grade mentally deficient boys. *Proc. Amer. Assoc. Ment. Defic.*, **44**:216–21.

KIRK, S. A. 1933. The influence of manual tracing on the learning of simple words in the case of subnormal boys. *J. Educ. Psychol.*, **24**:525–35.

———. 1934*a*. The effects of remedial reading on the education progress and personality adjustment of high-grade mentally deficient problem children: ten case studies. *J. Juv. Res.*, **18**:140–62.

———. 1934*b*. A study of the relation of ocular and manual preferences to mirror reading. *Pedagog. Sem. J. Genet. Psychol.*, **44**:192–205.

———. 1948. An evaluation of the study by Bernadine G. Schmidt entitled: Changes in personal, social, and intellectual behavior of children originally classified as feebleminded. *Psychol. Bull.*, **45**:321–33.

———. 1957. *Public School Provisions for Severely Retarded Children.* Albany, New York: Interdepartmental Health Resources Board.

———. 1958. *Early Education of the Mentally Retarded.* Urbana, Illinois: University of Illinois Press.

KIRK, S. A., and JOHNSON, G. O. 1951. *Educating the Retarded Child.* Boston, Massachusetts: Houghton Mifflin.

KIRK, W. D., and KIRK, S. A. 1935. The influence of the teacher's handedness on children's reversal tendencies in writing. *Pedagog. Sem. J. Genet. Psychol.*, **47**:473–77.

KLAUSMEIER, H. J., FELDHUSER, J., and CHECK, J. 1959. *An Analysis of Learning Efficiency in Arithmetic of Mentally Retarded Children in Comparison with Children of Average and High Intelligence.* ("U.S. Office of Education Cooperative Research Program.") Washington, D.C.

KOLSTOE, O. P. 1958. Language training of low grade mongoloid children. *Amer. J. Ment. Defic.*, **63**:17–30.

LEWIS, W. D. 1944. The relative intellectual achievement of mentally gifted and retarded children. *J. Exp. Educ.*, **13**:98–109.

———. 1959. The effect of an institution environment upon the verbal development of imbecile children, I: Verbal intelligence. *J. Ment. Defic. Res.*, **3**:122–28.

LYLE, J. G. 1960. The effect of an institution environment upon the verbal development of imbecile children, III: The Brooklands residential family unit. *J. Ment. Defic. Res.*, **4**:14–23.

McINTYRE, E. 1937. Teaching of reading to mentally defective children. *Proc. Amer. Assoc. Ment. Defic.*, **42**:56–67.

MACKIE, R. P., and ROBBINS, P. B. 1960. Exceptional children in local public schools. *Sch. Life*, **43**:14–16.

MALPASS, L. F. 1960. Motor proficiency in institutionalized and non-institutionalized retarded children and normal children. *Amer. J. Ment. Defic.*, **64**:1012–15.

MASLAND, R. L., SARASON, S. B., and GLADWIN, T. 1958. *Mental Subnormality.* New York: Basic Books.

MECHAM, M. J. 1955. The development and application of procedures for measuring speech improvement in mentally defective children. *Amer. J. Ment. Defic.*, **60**:301–6.

MEIN, R. 1961. A study of the vocabularies of severely subnormal patients, II: grammatical analysis of speech samples. *J. Ment. Defic. Res.*, **5**:52–59.

MELCHER, RUTH T. 1940. Developmental progress in young mentally handicapped children who received prolonged pre-academic training. *Amer. J. Ment. Defic.*, **45**:267–73.

MERRILL, M. A. 1918. The ability of the special class children in the three R's. *Pedagog. Sem. J. Genet. Psychol.*, **25**:88–96.

———. 1921. The relation of intelligence to ability in the three R's in the case of retarded children. *Ibid.*, **28**:249–74.

———. 1924. On the relation of intelligence to achievement in the case of mentally retarded children. *Comp. Psychol. Monogr.*, **2**:1–100.

MILLER, L. W. 1921. "A Study of the Reading of a Group of Subnormal Children." Unpublished Master's thesis, University of Chicago.

MINTZ, A. 1946. Reading reversals and lateral preferences in a group of intellectually sub-normal boys. *J. Educ. Psychol.*, **37**:487–501.

MONROE, M. 1932. *Children Who Cannot Read.* Chicago, Illinois: University of Chicago Press.

MULLEN, F. A. 1952. The Reading Ability of the Older Ungraded Pupil. Chicago, Illinois: Bureau Mentally Handicapped Children, Chicago Public Schools.

MULLEN, F. A., and ITKIN, W. 1961. *Achievement and Adjustment of Educable Mentally Handicapped Children.* ("U.S. Office of Education Cooperative Research Program," Project SAE 6529.) Chicago, Illinois: Board of Education, City of Chicago.

MURDOCH, K. 1918. Rate of improvement of the feebleminded as shown by standardized educational tests. *J. Appl. Psychol.*, **2**:243–49.

MURPHY, M. M. 1957. Rhythmical responses of low grade and middle grade defectives to music therapy. *J. Clin. Psychol.*, **13**:361–64.

NEMZEK, C. L., and MEIXNER, B. 1939. Academic progress of subnormal pupils. *Sch. and Soc.*, **50**:806–8.

OLIVER, J. N. 1958. The effects of physical conditioning exercises and activities on the mental characteristics of educationally subnormal boys. *Brit. J. Educ. Psychol.*, **28**:155–65.

PATTERSON, R. M., and LEIGHTNER, M. 1944. A comparative study of spontaneous paintings of normal and mentally deficient children of the same mental age. *Amer. J. Ment. Defic.*, **48**:345–53.

PECK, J. R. 1960. *A Comparative Investigation of the Learning and Social Adjustment of Trainable Children in Public School Facilities, Segregated Community Centers, and State Residential Centers.* ("U.S. Office of Education Cooperative Research Program," Project No. SAE 6430.)

PERTSCH, C. F. 1936. *A Comparative Study of the Progress of Subnormal Pupils in the Grades and in Special Classes.* New York: Teachers College, Columbia University, Bureau of Publications.

RABIN, H. M. 1957. The relationship of age, intelligence and sex to motor proficiency in mental defectives. *Amer. J. Ment. Defic.*, **62**:507–16.

RABINOVITCH, R. D. 1956. A research approach to reading retardation. *Neurol. Psychiat. Child.*, **34**:353–96.

RENSHAW, S. 1919. The abilities of pupils in Detroit prevocational classes. *J. Educ. Psychol.*, **10**:83–94.

REYNOLDS, M. C., and KILAND, J. R. 1953. *A Study of Public School Children with Severe Mental Retardation.* St. Paul: State Department of Education, Research Project No. 8.

RING, S. B. 1951. "A comparison of achievement and mental ages of ninety-eight special class children." Unpublished Master's thesis, Boston University.

SCARBOROUGH, W. H. 1951. *The Incidence of Reading Retardation among 1,182 Mentally Handicapped Children.* Paper read at Amer. Assoc. Ment. Defic., Fall.

SCHAEFER-SIMMERN, H. 1948. *The Unfolding of Artistic Activity.* Los Angeles: University of California Press.

SCHLANGER, B. 1953a. Speech measurement of institutionalized mentally handicapped children. *Amer. J. Ment. Defic.*, **58**:114–22.

———. 1953b. Speech therapy results with mentally retarded children in special classes. *Training Sch. Bull.*, **50**:179–86.

SCHMIDT, B. G. 1946. Changes in personal, social, and intellectual behavior of children originally classified as feebleminded. *Psychol. Monogr.*, **60:**1–144.

SCHNEIDER, B., and VALLON, J. 1954. A speech therapy program for mentally retarded children. *Amer. J. Ment. Defic.*, **58:**633–39.

SEGUIN, E. 1907. (First published in 1846.) *Idiocy and Its Treatment by the Physiological Method.* Albany: Columbia University, Brandow Printing Company.

SHIKIBA, R. 1956. *Works of Kiyoshi Yamashita.* Japan.

SHOTICK, A., and THATE, C. 1960. Reactions of a group of educable mentally handicapped children to a program of physical education. *Except. Child.*, **26:**248–52.

SIRKIN, J., and LYONS, W. F. 1941. A study of speech defects in mental deficiency. *Amer. J. Ment. Defic.*, **46:**74–80.

SKEELS, H. M. 1942. A study of the effects of differential stimulation on mentally retarded children: a follow-up report. *Amer. J. Ment. Defic.*, **46:**340–35.

SKEELS, H. M., and DYE, H. B. 1939. A study of the effects of differential stimulation. *Proc. Amer. Assoc. Ment. Defic.*, **44:**114–36.

SLOAN, W. 1951. Motor proficiency and intelligence. *Amer. J. Ment. Defic.*, **55:**394–405.

SPEIDEL, E. B. 1958. Language achievements of mentally retarded children. *Diss. Abstr.*, **19:**3180.

SPOERL, D. T. 1940. The drawing ability of mentally retarded children. *J. Genet. Psychol.*, **57:**259–77.

STOREY, B. L. 1936. "Analytical Appraisal of a Remedial Program in Reading for Pupils with an IQ of 90 or Below." Unpublished Ph.D. dissertation, University of Pittsburgh.

THURSTONE, T. G. 1959. *An Evaluation of Educating Mentally Handicapped Children in Special Classes and in Regular Grades.* ("U.S. Office of Education Cooperative Research Program," Project No. OE SAE-6452.) Chapel Hill: University of North Carolina.

TORGERSON, T. L., and SHUMAN, I. 1925. The variability of the accomplishments of pupils of the same mental level. *J. Educ. Res.*, **11:**132–36.

TOWN, C. H. 1912. Language development in 285 idiots and imbeciles. *Psychol. Clinic,* **6:**229–35.

U.S. OFFICE OF EDUCATION. 1950. Statistics of special education for exceptional children, 1947–1948. *Biennial Survey of Education in the United States.* Washington, D.C.: Superintendent of Documents, U.S. Government Printing Office.

———. 1954. Statistics of special education for exceptional children, 1952–1953. *Biennial Survey of Education in the United States.* Washington, D.C.: Superintendent of Documents, U.S. Government Printing Office.

VANCE, H. S. 1956. Psychological and educational study of brain-damaged and non-brain-damaged mentally retarded children. *Diss. Abstr.*, 17:1033.

VAUGHN, C. L., and HOOSE, E. S. 1936. Special abilities in a mentally deficient boy. *Proceedings and Addresses of the Sixtieth Annual Session of the American Association of Mental Deficiency*, 197–207.

WEIGL, V. 1959. Functional music, a therapeutic tool in working with the mentally retarded. *Amer. J. Ment. Defic.*, **63:**672–78.

WEINER, B. B. 1954. A report on the final academic achievement of thirty-seven mentally handicapped boys who had been enrolled in a prolonged pre-academic program. *Amer. J. Ment. Defic.*, **59:**200–219.

WERNER, H., and GARRISON, D. 1942. Measurement and development of finger schema in mentally retarded children. *J. Educ. Psychol.*, **33:**252–64.

WILSON, F. T. 1926. Some achievements of pupils of the same mental ages but different intelligence quotients. *J. Educ. Res.*, **14:**43–53.

WITTY, P. A., and McCAFFERTY, E. 1930. Attainment by feebleminded children. *Education*, **50:**588–97.

WRIGHTSTONE, J. W., FORLANO, G., LEPKOWSKI, J. R., SONTAG, M., and EDELSTEIN, J. D. 1959. *A Comparison of Educational Outcomes under Single-Track and Two-Track Plans for Educable Mentally Retarded Children.* ("U.S. Office of Education Cooperative Research Program," Project No. 144.) New York: New York Board of Education.

RESEARCH IN LEARNING
AND PERFORMANCE

M. Ray Denny

This chapter represents a fairly complete review of the experiments on learning in the mentally retarded, leaving large blocks of material on motivation and performance to other chapters. The plan is to deal first with the basic operations in learning and then to cover the material on verbal and mediational learning. Wherever relevant, studies using infrahuman subjects will be cited.

Data on learning in the mentally retarded are not abundant, but the studies that have been done suggest that this is a field of great potential interest. This means that little of a definitive nature can be said about learning in the retarded. Yet, in the interest of stimulating thought and research in the area, a number of trends or hypotheses are definitely indicated, and speculation, though guarded, is the keynote of this chapter. So when the reader stumbles over what is, in his judgment, an overly hasty interpretation it is hoped that he will remember this objective. One problem which demands its share of speculation is untangling the data so as to identify the fundamental deficit(s) in the retarded persons' behavior. Much of the theorizing and suggestions for research will be directed to this end.

Many difficulties, such as delineating the mentally retarded group, confront the researcher on mental retardation as well as the reviewer who attempts to generalize from the data reported. Insofar as it is possible, many of these complications will be discussed or dismissed now, so that the remainder of the text will not be overburdened with distracting qualifications.

Individuals classified as mental retardates generally include those ranging in IQ all the way from 0 to 75; and, for a specified level of IQ, the within-group variance for performance on a variety of tasks is often greater in the mentally retarded than in normal or superior individuals at the same MA level. In addition, some of the retarded have obvious physical defects while others are normal in this respect. Thus, it is clear that we are not talking about a unitary phenomenon. To simplify the present presentation and fit the practice of most learning experiments, the term "mentally retarded," unless otherwise indicated, will refer to individuals within an IQ range of approximately 30–70 who are free from obvious sensory or motor impairment. In keeping with current practice, the terms "moron" (50–75 IQ), "imbecile" (25–50 IQ) and "idiot" (0–25 IQ) will be used sparingly.

Another complicating factor is etiology. Yet from the available data (Pascal, Stolurow, Zabarenko, and Chambers, 1951; Gallagher, 1957; Schucman, 1957; Swanson, 1957; Barnett, Ellis, and Pryer, 1960) it appears that retarded individuals, when contrasted according to the loosely and broadly defined categories of organic and familial, perform essentially the same on a wide variety of learning tasks. However, the so-called organics do perform more poorly in reaction-time (Bensberg and Cantor, 1958) and drawing tests (Halpin, 1955), in olfactory discrimination (Adis-Castro and Berger, 1955), depth-perception judgments (Barnett and Pryer, 1958), and tactual-kinesthetic localization (Satter and Cassel, 1955).

Given these data and the hodgepodge categories, it might be tentatively held that the "organic's" special disability, if he has one, is more likely to be motor or sensory than purely associative. Thus, except where indicated, this distinction will be ignored. As is consonant with the rest of the book, the definition of mental retardation is strictly behavioral.

Another difficulty arises from the fact that the mentally retarded who serve as subjects in learning experiments usually live in institutions, while the normal subjects with whom they are compared live at home and attend public schools or lead a normal adult existence. Again, unless contraindicated, this state of affairs obtains, and the data should be interpreted accordingly.

Further, some of the research, particularly the earlier work, has involved poorly specified categories of mental retardation, little if any intelligence test data, very few subjects per group, and no inferential statistics. Much of this is often true of the Russian research, at least as reported or summarized. Such data, however, will be referred to only when supported by replications. Thus, all the data to be discussed in the present chapter have approximately equal footing, except when qualified.

Finally, let us discuss the problem of control groups. A sizable number of studies have used normal controls matched on MA with the mentally retarded; i.e., the normals have a higher IQ and a lower CA. A mixture of results evolves from such studies. Many of these studies indicate that the learning differences between the normal and retarded are slight or non-existent; a few indicate superiority for the mentally retarded; and the remaining minority indicate inferior learning performance by the retarded.

We can label this last result the LOW-IQ deficit; such a deficit is due specifically to a low IQ, since MA is held constant. Opposed to this is the LOW-MA-LOW-IQ deficit, which refers to the poorer performance of the mentally retarded when they are compared with normal controls who have been equated with them on CA. (By definition the retarded have both a lower MA and a lower IQ.) This means that a learning deficit exists *only* when the retarded have both a lower MA and lower IQ than the normal. The more critical defect, obviously, is the LOW-IQ deficit. The best way to pinpoint the deficit even into these rough categories is to run two control groups, one equated on MA and one equated on CA with the mentally retarded. Ordinary practice has been to use only one control. Consequently, the nature of the deficit is indeterminate and the meaning of the results blurred.

The ordinary research strategy seems inefficient. If two controls were used instead, it would be possible to determine whether there were a LOW-MA-LOW-IQ deficit, a more basic LOW-IQ deficit, or no deficit at all and whether the deficit present was independent of CA. The import of this information would also spread to general psychology. By always having control groups at different age levels we would be adding considerably to our present inadequate knowledge of how learning and performance vary with age. A similar technique would be to use an extended range of MA's and CA's in both the normal and retarded groups and evaluate the effect of MA and CA by analysis of covariance.

At various points in the chapter, reference will be made to the two types of deficit described above and to the recommended strategy for research.

CLASSICAL CONDITIONING

With but few exceptions (Mateer, 1918; Cornil and Goldenfoun, 1928; Marienesco and Kreindler, 1933; Melhado,

1949) classical conditioning in the mentally retarded has been the exclusive area of the Russian investigator. This fact when viewed in the light of the interesting and consistent results obtained seems quite surprising. Krasnogorski, back in 1913, was the pioneer in the area (Mateer, 1918; Razran, 1933). He adapted the salivary conditioning situation to children, using a conditioned stimulus–unconditioned stimulus (CS-US) interval of ten seconds, candy or honey as the US, and a tambour attached to the hyoid bone to measure the conditioned response (CR), swallowing and mouth movements. He found that the CR was more difficult to establish in imbeciles and morons than in normals—and even harder to extinguish. In differential conditioning and the establishment of conditioned inhibition the retarded were even more inferior. In turn, conditioned inhibition and differential responses were quite unstable. This picture is essentially what Florence Mateer found in this country in 1918—at least to the extent to which she repeated Krasnogorski's work. Mateer did a pretty careful job of experimenting and of classifying her mentally retarded subjects, though she used only fourteen retardates (twelve boys and two girls) as compared with fifty normal children (twenty-four boys and twenty-six girls). The retarded ranged in age from three years to seven years, nine months, and in mental age from approximately one to seven. As then classified, half were idiots or low-grade imbeciles and half were high-grade imbeciles, morons, or dull-normals. The normal children ranged in age from two to seven years, but nine subjects below twenty-nine months had to be eliminated from the extinction phase of the experiments because of marked emotional reactions to the omission of candy. In other words, the mentally retarded and normals were much more closely matched on CA than MA.

The simple, even crude, conditioning set-up consisted merely of sliding a blindfold down over the subject's eyes (CS), waiting 10 seconds and placing a small piece of chocolate candy in his mouth (US), and recording kymographically the CR (opening of the mouth before the ten seconds had elapsed). The intertrial interval was three minutes and was filled with tests and other activities. The criterion of conditioning was two CR's in succession. Twenty-four hours later, conditioning continued to the same criterion (retention), followed immediately by extinction to a criterion of failing to make the CR twice in a row, followed terminally by reconditioning to the original criterion.

The results indicated that such conditioning is extremely rapid (somewhat faster than found by Krasnogorski) and that it occurs just about as quickly with the less severely retarded as with normal children. The retarded required a mean of 6.4 trials to criterion, including criterion trials, and the normals a mean of 5.1 (range = 3–13 and 3–8, respectively). For the more severely retarded the mean was approximately 11 (range = 5–18).

For extinction, the picture is considerably different: the mean number of trials to extinction for the high-grade defectives was 12.3 (range = 8–16), and for the normals was 7.4 (range = 3–12). With a t test computed by the present author the mean difference of 4.9 is statistically significant at the 0.001 level of confidence. This contrasts with the non-significant difference of 1.3 trials between the less severely retarded and normals during acquisition ($t = 1.1$). Because the overlap of extinction scores is slight (the youngest normal extinguished more quickly than the oldest retardate), the suggested inhibition deficit seems to represent a LOW-IQ deficit as well as a LOW-MA-LOW-IQ deficit. On the developmental level this finding is consistent with Bekhterev's assertion (1928) that CR's are difficult to extinguish in normal infants.

Retention over twenty-four hours for

all subjects studied was usually perfect (two trials to criterion) and was the same for both retarded and normals. Reconditioning after extinction took a minimum of three trials for all retardates but slightly longer in a number of normals. (Range = 3–8; mean = 3.5.)

Among the normal children the correlation between speed of conditioning and CA was 0.57, and between conditioning and MA it was 0.59, while between conditioning and extinction the correlation was negative ($r = -0.45$). This last correlation in particular is discontinuous with the data for the mentally retarded. The retardates who learned somewhat more slowly than the normals also extinguished more slowly than normals, rather than rapidly—as the negative correlation between extinction and conditioning among the normals would seem to imply.

To summarize, the mentally retarded acquired and retained a positive, appetitive CR about as well as the normals yet extinguished more slowly than the normals. Further, the inhibition when it did develop seemed more labile: reconditioning was uniformly rapid among the retarded.

These data have stood up well over the years, particularly in regard to the inhibition deficit. When checked with Razran's review of the Russian studies (1933), with Luria's early report (1932), and with Luria's more recent summary (1959), there are no apparent discrepancies. As long as the US is positive the results of conditioning in the mentally retarded are nicely consistent. The CR is not too difficult to establish, and inhibition, except for external inhibition, is impaired: extinction is retarded; differential conditioning is poor; delayed CR's and conditioned inhibition cannot be established, or only with great difficulty; and disinhibition occurs very readily.

Marinesco and Kreindler (1933) have related the inhibition deficit to poor attention or distractibility. This same hypothesis has prevailed from 1904 (Kuhl-

mann) until today (Zeaman, 1959) as a way to account for the retardate's difficulty in discrimination-learning (specifically, to explain the retardate's ignoring of relevant stimuli). But the question which must be asked is this: Is the inability to attend caused instead by the inability to inhibit? May not the retardate's failure to inhibit the effects of extraneous stimuli account for his inability to attend to the particular task? Perhaps, the inhibition deficit is the more basic (Berger, 1954). Luria, for one, lumps together distractibility, impulsiveness, and inhibitory defect in his discussions. Luria (1959) described one situation in which the retarded child is presented with a balloon and is instructed to press the balloon when the green light comes on. Although he is less able to inhibit indiscriminate pressing than a normal child of the same CA, he has more difficulty in learning a discrimination, namely, to press when the green light comes on but not to press when the red light comes on or vice versa. But, for the most part, the retarded are distinguished from the normal by the fact that the differentiation once formed is easily disinhibited. Sounding a bell or interrupting the task destroys the discrimination. The normal child is virtually unaffected by such extraneous events.

Regardless of the consistency of the results presented so far it is not clear what they mean. Only more research will tell. Moreover, as soon as one turns to the few conditioning studies using an aversive US, the data no longer remain consistent and the scattered findings are at times opposite to the findings with a positive US. As a matter of fact the most extensive and convincing study (Osipova [Razran, 1933]) gives just such results. Using the familiar shock and finger withdrawal technique, Osipova conditioned 58 mentally retarded boys, including only a few idiots, and 116 normal boys and girls of approximately the same CA (7–14) as the retarded. The mentally retarded reached criterion in a mean of 5.53 trials as compared with a mean of 11.76 trials for the normals. The normal boys and girls performed essentially alike. The retardates' superiority is statistically significant ($cr = 3.44$) and appears in a situation where a LOW-MA-LOW-IQ deficit could obtain. The correlations between speed of conditioning and MA and CA were negative (approximately -0.50). Assuming these data are reliable, it is possible that they are an artifact based on the mental retardate's poor verbal control of his own behavior. For example, the retardate's difficulty in the balloon-pressing experiment is referred to by Luria as a deficit in the second-signal system or a dissociation of the verbal sphere from the motor. The point is that normal subjects, particularly males, frequently inhibit anticipatory finger-withdrawal responses in order to demonstrate their fortitude. Perhaps it is only the absence of such voluntary verbal control in the retarded which accounts for their superiority. In the same vein is an early exploratory study done in France by Cornil and Goldenfoun (1928), which showed that the greater the mental retardation, the better the knee-jerk conditioning. (The reaction, however, was more diffuse in the more retarded children.) Here again the response being conditioned is normally capable of verbal control. In other words, both finger withdrawal and the patellar reflex are ordinarily inhibitable. Therefore, it is possible that both studies are examples of the retardates' ubiquitous inhibition deficit, which, in this instance at least, may be a result of their inability to control the motor system with the verbal system.

A slightly later study by two other French investigators (Marinesco and Kreindler, 1933) appears to contradict these findings. Using Bekhterev's technique, with strong shock as a US and leg or arm flexion as the CR, Marinesco and Kreindler found very poor conditioning in four retardates, together with slow extinction, poor differential CR's, and an absence of delayed CR's. These investigators, however, specifically mentioned the reflexive or uncontrollable character of their response. Their results are qualified by the fact that the subjects appeared to be profoundly retarded.

Whether the retarded actually condition faster than the normal when a noxious US is used certainly needs to be checked; this should be a simple matter. Through the use of GSR, vasoconstriction, or eyelid conditioning procedures, verbal control can be greatly minimized or eliminated, permitting the direct study of simple conditioning together with all the related conditioning phenomena. To the author's knowledge there are two studies along this line using mentally retarded subjects, and both are relatively inaccessible. One on eyelid conditioning by Cromwell, Palk, and Foshee (1961) is unpublished and has been summarized as indicating that eyelid conditioning is independent of IQ and only marginally related to MA ($r = +0.29$); extinction trials were not included in the study. The other is Russian (Gakkel, Mololkova, and Trofimov, 1957) and includes the conditioning of vasomotor and eyelid reactions. According to this study, conditioning above the idiot category is not especially impaired but neither is it facilitated, and extinction is, as usual, retarded. Thus, it seems that an aversive US does not necessarily yield faster conditioning in the retarded than in normals.

A very recent study by Franks and Franks (1962), using an eyelid conditioning technique, indicates that retarded adults, who are not brain-injured or who make a good work adjustment, condition faster and show greater resistance to extinction than the brain-injured or poor adjusters, irrespective of IQ. Such findings complicate the interpretation of the conditioning data, particularly with respect to extinction.

The picture with respect to extinction is further complicated in a study by Vinogradova (1956). Here, for the first time, appears a report of faster extinction in the retarded than normals. Vinogradova, however, conditioned vasoconstriction-orienting responses to words as conditioned stimuli by means of instructions; the use of verbal techniques is probably the clue to her unusual finding. If verbal-motor connections in the mentally retarded are defective, then the CR would be weak and would undergo rapid extinction. In another part of her study Vinogradova found just such evidence. Unconditioned vasoconstriction took place to all kinds of words in normal adolescents and took a long time to adapt, whereas reactions to words in retarded adolescents were highly restricted and adapted immediately. That the mentally retarded may condition poorly to verbal stimuli and may fail to inhibit because of lack of verbal control appears to strike at the heart of the mental retardation problem. Yet we are only groping in the dark until more research is done. Also, it would be unwise to imply that the inhibition deficit is necessarily a function of poor verbal control, for in lower animals the juvenile organism exhibits an inhibition deficit as compared with the mature adult (Thompson, 1941; Panchenkova, 1956; Vince, 1959). The deficit is reflected in slow extinction, poor differential learning, and perseverative behavior. The parallel with the mentally retarded would seem to be more than coincidental. Moreover, natal or prenatal anoxia in rats, to be discussed later, results most clearly in impairment in the inhibition sphere.

Although the data on classical conditioning are sparse they certainly offer a number of promising leads. We will return to these data in the next section when we attempt to relate them to discrimination-learning.

INSTRUMENTAL LEARNING

OPERANT CONDITIONING

There are at least five studies using the free operant conditioning technique with mentally retarded subjects. The earliest study was by Mitrano (1939) and was primarily concerned with determining whether certain standard conditioning phenomena would be displayed in a rather severely retarded male population (CA = approximately 10; IQ = approximately 30; N = 86). Mitrano employed two manipulanda in his operant situation: a machine which yielded poker chips upon the insertion of marbles (marble-chip machine) and a machine which yielded chocolate candy upon the insertion of poker chips (chip-candy machine). In all experiments the subject was first run through the behavior sequence of putting a marble into the marble-chip machine, receiving a chip, putting a chip into the chip-candy machine, and receiving candy for a total of *ten reinforcements*. Extinction was then carried out in a variety of ways for various groups and usually after the subject had been out of the experimental room for a few minutes.

From the data the following conclusions seem warranted: (1) Extinction on either machine with the other one absent results in the generalization of inhibition to the other machine when the machines are switched. (2) The inhibition generated by extinction at Step 2 in the sequence (chip-candy machine) is greater than that generated by extinction at Step 1. (3) Extinction takes place slowly (mean trials to extinction with both machines present and when only the chip-candy machine failed to operate was 94; range = 1–779). (4) The correlation between MA and number of responses to extinction is negligible. (5) The response tendency at Step 2 is stronger than at Step 1 [many subjects persisted in responding to the candy machine when extinguished on the marble-chip machine as in (2) above]. (6) Spontaneous recovery occurs over as short an interval as five minutes or as long an interval as four months.

Since this study is non-comparative perhaps its main contribution is to indicate the feasibility or even desirability of doing basic learning research with mentally retarded subjects.

Another fairly early study by Fuller (1949), with only one subject, is peripheral to our major concern. But it does demonstrate an important point rather conclusively, namely, that the severest case of vegetative retardation is capable of learning. In this demonstration-experiment a hungry, severely retarded eighteen-year-old who was incapable of coordinated movement or meaningful speech was administered a liquid diet each time he raised his right arm to a vertical position. By the fourth experimental session the subject was performing at a near maximal rate of three responses per minute. With the omission of the food the response gradually extinguished.

Skinner and Lindsley (1954) in their operant conditioning studies with psychotic patients included a few retarded adults and children, frequently with psychotic symptoms. The main finding is that these retarded individuals learned and responded at typical rates (reinforcements were typically candy, gum, and cigarettes).

A more extensive investigation, using a large sample of rather severely retarded children is one by House, Zeaman, and co-workers (1957). In a preliminary study a dozen children (MA = 2–6) pulled a lever for immediate candy reinforcement. The results indicated that retarded children condition quickly under 100 per cent reinforcement, maintain a stable rate of response for at least one-half hour, and continue to respond appropriately when gradually shifted to a one-minute variable interval schedule. In the larger, as yet uncompleted study, forty-five boys and girls (MA = 3–7) were left alone in a cubicle to play a candy game. The reinforcements included "M & M's," chocolate chips, candy corn, and miniature marshmallows; no more than forty reinforcements were given per session. The manipulanda in the cubicle consisted of a left-lever and a right-lever, one of which delivered candy in the reinforcement tray; the tray lighted up as the candy dropped down, providing immediate secondary reinforcement. When the number of correct responses minus the number of incorrect responses exceeded 80 per cent of the total, reversal training was begun. Reinforcement was not shifted to the opposite lever at the beginning of a session; three reversals were given. Of twenty-two subjects on which data have been reported, twenty learned the original position discrimination and the three reversals, taking less than a mean of two fifteen-minute sessions for all problems. How these children would compare with normal MA and CA control groups is not known. In view of the classical conditioning data, such comparisons, especially on straight extinction and reversal learning, should be illuminating.

The most recent published study by Ellis, Barnett, and Pryer (1960) employed severely retarded individuals with IQ's below 30 (N = 12) as well as individuals with IQ's in the 30–70 range (N = 26). All subjects were Negro teenagers or adults. A straight Skinnerian approach with a single Lindsley manipulandum was used with "M & M" candies or cigarettes as reinforcers. The subjects were switched to fixed-ratio 10 (FR 10) after a minimum of continuous reinforcement and maintained on FR 10 for eleven days at which point a variety of schedules was introduced. The results indicated that even most of the "untestable" retarded were sensitive to schedule changes, though their response records contained pauses like those of the psychotic (Skinner and Lindsley, 1954). The subjects with the higher MA's performed at consistently higher rates than the low-MA group. The authors suggest the operant technique holds promise for training the severely retarded. Unfortunately, data on experimental extinction and on normal children are lacking.

MAZE LEARNING

Despite the scarcity of experiments there is a good opportunity to compare normals and the mentally retarded on maze learning. Two main types of maze learning are represented. One type allows the subject to see and apprehend the entire maze as he works. The other type, which is more analogous to the problem posed to the rat, requires the subject to be blindfolded or for a screen to shield the maze pattern. The paper and pencil maze of DeSanctis (1931) and the stylus maze (Lafayette Instrument Co.) of Sloan and Berg (1957) are examples of the former.

DeSanctis worked with twelve retarded children (CA = 7–13), only one of whom was severely retarded, and all except the severely retarded child solved the rather difficult maze problem, eight learned rapidly, and three slowly. The study was distinguished from others by the use of two normal groups, approximating an MA and a CA control. Excluding the severely retarded child, the retarded behaved more like the older normals showing visual apprehension—a sizing up of the maze before starting the trial—which was characteristic of the older but not the younger normals. In short, there was little if any evidence of even a LOW-MA-LOW-IQ deficit in the retarded sample.

Although the Sloan and Berg study did not include normal comparison groups, its sample of retarded adults covered a wide range of IQ values (MA = 8.2; IQ = 57; SD = 11.3). Ten trials were given on the maze; performance was evaluated in terms of a time measure, and trial to trial performance was reliable. When maze learning was correlated with MA, r was low and non-significant. As in the previous study, this first type of maze learning appears to be relatively independent of intelligence (no LOW-MA-LOW-IQ deficit).

When we consider the second type of maze learning, the results are quite different, at least so far as a single study can carry the burden of evidence. This study, however, is an extensive investigation by Ellis, Pryer, Distefano, and Pryer (1960), employing a total of 151 male and female subjects and a wide range of IQ values (40–139). All subject groupings were roughly matched on CA; the subjects were older adolescents or young adults. A shielded, high relief finger maze with eight choice points (R L R R L L R L) was used. Prior to the regular maze trials, the subjects were given trials on a practice maze which they viewed for fifteen seconds during an initial demonstration. Twenty-two subjects (fifteen from the 40–59 IQ category) were eliminated on the practice maze for not attaining the criterion of nine out of ten errorless trials. During the regular maze trials, the intertrial interval was twenty seconds, and the criterion of learning was two consecutive errorless trials or a maximum of one hundred trials. As customary for multiple unit mazes, a "correction" procedure was used. Figure 1 presents the mean number of trials to criterion for five IQ groupings. Here it is obvious that IQ made a difference in speed of learning; the greatest improvement was from the 50–79 range to 80–99 ($p = 0.01$), i.e., when leaving the mental retardation category. There was no significant sex difference.

A slight but significant correlation was also found between IQ and trials to criterion in the subnormal groups ($r = -0.24$; $p = 0.05$). Since the CA's were essentially the same, all the data taken together only made it possible to identify a LOW-MA-LOW-IQ deficit; the possibility of a LOW-IQ deficit is indeterminate. The above receives added weight from the fact that high-IQ college students performed better than low-IQ college students on a similar maze when blindfolded (Spence and Townsend, 1930).

The superiority of the normals on this

learning task appears reliable and can be viewed as being consistent with the major trends thus far mentioned. It is known that subjects on such a maze as used by Ellis and his co-workers do best if they use a verbal or partially verbal method of learning rather than straight kinesthesis or visual imagery. This is particularly true when trials are relatively massed, as in the present study. Since we have already emphasized that the retardate is characterized by inability to mediate his behavior verbally, it is consistent for the

but not on learning a simple T-maze. However, it did impede learning a reversal of the simple position response (inhibition deficit) and was related to "stereotypy" of a position response in discrimination tasks (inhibition deficit). Prenatal anoxia also impaired retention of the maze problem.

The genetic manipulation of "maze-learning ability" in the rat is another and, perhaps, more familiar way to simulate the mental deficiency problem. Recent research on the "bright and dull" strains

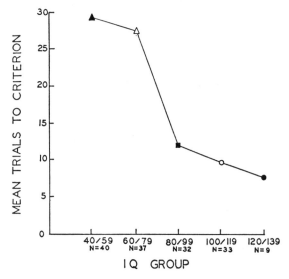

Fig. 1.—Mean trials to criterion on the maze task for five IQ groupings. (From Ellis *et al.*, 1960.)

normals to be superior on the *shielded* maze. On the other maze, the task is primarily visual, and there is no special reason for expecting an appreciable difference between intelligence groups.

It seems appropriate to conclude our discussion of maze learning by referring to a few maze studies with rats. In a certain sense, mental retardation has been artificially produced or simulated in the rat by use of natal or prenatal anoxia (Meier *et al.*, 1960). In this study, sixty minutes of oxygen deprivation following birth had a deleterious effect on the subsequent learning of a multiple-unit maze,

of the McGill group (Thompson, Heron, and Kahn, 1955; Cooper and Zubek, 1958), together with research in progress at Michigan State University, places a new slant on the interpretation of this kind of data. When "bright" rats explore a Y-maze for six minutes, they explore a good deal to begin with, but over the whole period, explore less than "dull" rats (Thompson, Heron, and Kahn, 1955). The "bright" rats, in other words, are fast satiaters (show rapid stimulus satiation), and the "dull" rats are slow satiaters. That the mentally retarded have also been classified as slow satiaters (Spitz and Blackman, 1959; Blackman, 1960), though in a rather different context, will be mentioned later. It is possible to begin with an unselected group of rats and divide them into fast and slow satiaters on the basis of an exploration test ("IQ test" for rats). Experiments of this type are being performed in our Michigan State University laboratory. We expect, when all the data are collected, to find that the slow satiaters will perform, if anything, better than the fast satiaters on a simple T-maze where the task is to visit the same place each trial (all trials free). But in a complex maze, where the true path represents stimulus change and the cul-de-sacs represent stimulus repetition, the fast satiaters should be the better learners. The data so far support these hypotheses. And in the genetic studies the "bright" and "dull" rats have been the fast and slow learners, respectively, on a complex maze. Here again we seem to be referring to a type of inhibition deficit. The "dull" rats satiate or inhibit slowly; the "bright" satiate or inhibit quickly. That all of this ties in with the results of the Meier *et al.* study on the effects of early anoxia on learning in the rat should also be pointed out. Here the deleterious effect was restricted to the learning of the *complex* maze and appeared in *stereotypy* on discrimination problems.

DISCRIMINATION-LEARNING

This area contains an abundance of studies, and the data are rather illuminating. In 1904 Kuhlmann pointed out that the mentally retarded (CA = 8–14) had difficulty in matching dominoes according to numbers of spots. Ordahl and Ordahl in 1915 found that as MA increased among retardates, ability to learn a color-sequence discrimination improved. Woodrow (1917), however, using the retarded (CA = 13–14; MA = 8–9) and normal controls matched on MA, found no significant differences between them on over-all performance,

amount of improvement, and transfer in a variety of sorting tasks. The measure of performance was speed of sorting, and in no case did a task seem to pose a new discrimination-learning problem for the sample of retarded that he used. That is, they were able to distinguish sticks of varying lengths, pegs of different colors, letters of the alphabet, and simple geometric forms from the very beginning.

It seems more than likely that Woodrow's study tells us about performance on a simple motor skill rather than about discrimination-learning. Other investigators have found little difference between normals and defectives on learning simple motor skills, especially with respect to amount of improvement (see, for example, Johnson, 1919; Wilson, 1928; and Reynolds and Stacey, 1955). The fact that retardates discriminate well between familiar stimuli, e.g., between shades of gray (Ordahl and Ordahl, 1915), is in agreement with this analysis. If the mentally retarded have difficulty in discrimination-learning, it does not appear to be a matter of sensory capacity. Rather, as will soon be discussed, the difficulty appears to be inherent in the *methodology* of the discrimination-learning experiment.

At the core of the modern studies on discrimination-learning in the mentally retarded is a group of studies by Betty House and David Zeaman and associates. Probably the most dramatic of these experiments (House and Zeaman, 1958*a*) shows that imbeciles (MA = 2–4) learn amazingly slower than naïve monkeys (Harlow, 1945) and by inference slower than two- to four-year-old normal children. For normal two- to four-year-olds learn discrimination problems as well as or better than monkeys and chimpanzees (Gellerman, 1933*b*; Weinstein, 1941; Hayes, Thompson, and Hayes, 1953). A LOW-IQ deficit in the area of discrimination-learning is clearly suggested.

Let us examine the evidence in detail. House and Zeaman employed subjects with a mean IQ of 31—a more severely retarded group than is typically used. The experiment was a close replica of Harlow's monkey study (1945), using a modified Wisconsin General Test Apparatus—two food wells covered with erect tridimensional stimulus forms differing in both shape and color, e.g., red triangle vs. black cross (2 inches high, 2 inches wide, and ½ inch thick). The cup under

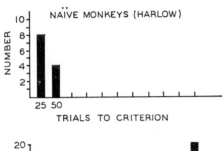

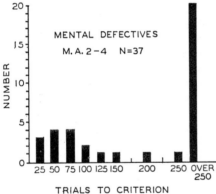

Fig. 2.—A comparison of performance of mentally defective subjects and monkeys on a color-form discrimination problem. (From House and Zeaman, 1958a.)

the positive stimulus was baited with candy and varied randomly from left to right. Twenty-five massed trials were given daily until the criterion of 20 out of 25 correct was attained. Ten subjects were given non-correction trials like Harlow's monkeys while the remainder, who learned neither better nor worse, were allowed to correct an error. The comparison between the mentally retarded and the monkeys is presented graphically in Figure 2. The median number of errors

for the retarded subjects was 119, for the monkeys, 4.

Such results are, to say the least, clearcut, but the possibility exists that the differences were due to side variables such as poor motivation and "not having the idea of the game." A follow-up study by Zeaman, House, and Orlando (1958) seems to answer both objections rather satisfactorily. Subjects (IQ = 28) failing the color-form discrimination were then presented a much easier discrimination, using junk stimuli that differed multidimensionally, e.g., a red plastic soap dish, a toy guitar. Seven of the eight subjects run learned this discrimination easily but again failed to learn when retrained on the color-form problem. These results indicate that the severely retarded can learn in the situation, i.e., are motivated sufficiently, pay attention sufficiently, and are sufficiently interested in the candy reinforcers. Secondly, they show that catching on to the game cannot reasonably be used as an explanation of the original results.

House, Zeaman, Orlando, and Fischer (1957) then went ahead to present the same problem to a large group of retardates (N = 66) with a wider range of MA's, 2–6 (IQ = 37), in order to make a correlational analysis. Holding CA constant, MA and IQ correlated —0.54 and —0.47, respectively, with errors on the task ($p = 0.01$). IQ also correlated significantly with errors when MA was held constant ($r = 0.20$, $p = 0.05$), yielding additional support for positing a LOW-IQ deficit in discrimination-learning. Further evidence for this comes in their next study (House and Zeaman, 1958b) where thirty normals (MA = 4 years to 6 years, 2 months) were compared directly with thirty-two retardates of the same mental age. Two MA-IQ level splits (MA = 4–5; IQ = 40.4; N = 17 vs. MA = 5–6; IQ = 51; N = 15) in the retardates were independently compared with a similar MA split in the normals. At the 4–5 MA level the retardates made significantly more errors than the normals but at the 5–6 MA level, learning was so rapid in both groups that any difference was undetectable. The last item points up the fact that the LOW-IQ discrimination-learning deficit seems most pronounced at IQ levels around 50 and below. Stevenson and Iscoe (1955) found a LOW-IQ deficit in discrimination-learning in the mentally retarded (CA = 9–40; IQ = 40) matched at an MA level of 7 years with normals. (Subjects with IQ's below 40, did so poorly in preliminary tests that they were excluded.) The subjects were trained to choose the smaller of two white squares (2 inches vs. 4 inches); the retarded took a mean of 41.9 trials to reach the criterion of nine out of ten correct as compared with 28.6 trials for the normals.

Other studies which tend in varying degrees to indicate a LOW-IQ discrimination-learning deficit include Doll and Aldrich (1932), Gardner (1945), Jacobs (1950), Girardeau (1959), Luria (1959), and O'Connor and Hermelin (1959a). Probably the most convincing is the Girardeau study (1959) which is primarily on learning sets and will be considered later in this context. His ten normal children matched on MA with ten mongoloids (IQ approximately 40) were significantly superior on the first two of five distinct object-quality discriminations. In fact, if it were not for a floor effect, the normals would probably have been clearly superior on all five problems (see Fig. 3).

There are also at least three studies (Plenderleith, 1956; Stevenson and Ziegler, 1957; Stevenson, 1960) which do not show a difference between the mentally retarded and normals in discrimination-learning, when matched on MA. This is true even though the MA or IQ levels of the mentally retarded subjects in these three studies are no higher or not appreciably higher than in studies which get positive results. There are some procedural differences, however, which may

account for the negative findings and at the same time shed light on the discrimination deficit. Stevenson and Zigler (1957), instead of presenting two stimuli to the subject to choose between, present three gray blocks varying along a size dimension; the subject must select one. Position of the correct block varies randomly, and no block is ever in the same position more than two consecutive times. This procedure seems innocuous enough, but it may be a key to the whole affair. First, let us assume that the discrimination-learning deficit is basically an inhibition deficit, as Zeaman (1959) has suggested and as we previously interpreted the data on differential conditioning. Second, the one response that is bound to be reinforced and yet must be eliminated prior to learning the discrimination is the position response. When there are only two stimuli each position (left or right) is reinforced 50 per cent of the time and occasionally, à la Gellerman (1933a), three times in a row. A subject is likely to have an initial position preference to boot, and the position responses are the easiest for the defective to learn, per House and Zeaman et al. (1957). When there are three stimuli any one position is *only* reinforced one-third of the time and, at the most, never more than twice in a row, and any initial position preference is probably weaker. In short, an interfering position habit should be considerably less when three stimuli are employed, vitiating the need for its extinction. Simply strengthening the approach to the positive stimulus should be sufficient to mediate the learning of the discrimination. In the two-stimulus situation, on the other hand, extinguishing or inhibiting a position response should greatly facilitate the learning process. Thus if the mental retardate has an inhibition deficit he should learn more slowly, as reported in two-stimulus situations.

Stevenson (1960), in one of two discrimination problems studied, again used three stimuli (3-inch, 2½-inch, and 2-inch black squares) and again obtained no significant differences between normals and the retarded (MA = 7.3; CA = 15.8) when matched on MA, though there was a significant correlation ($r = 0.79$, $p = 0.01$) between MA and number of correct responses in the mentally retarded group. In other words, he found a LOW-MA-LOW-IQ deficit but no LOW-IQ deficit.

In the third study, by Plenderleith (1956), pairs of stimuli were used, but the problem was quite different from the standard discrimination task. It was quite similar, however, to a learning-set experiment. The subject was presented with the same pair of stimulus pictures for six trials only, then presented with a new pair for six trials, and so on until he learned that the first one chosen of a newly presented pair was always incorrect and that for the next five trials the other picture would always be correct (five correct out of six—three pairs in a row was the criterion). "Charms" and candy served as rewards and position varied randomly. Although eliminating a position response would help in this situation, it was probably clear to most subjects that in a series of new problems the same response is not going to be correct over and over again, or, to put it more objectively, each change of problem was likely to bring about the external inhibition of prior response tendencies.

In the other discrimination problem studied, Stevenson (1960) again found no significant difference between retarded and normal groups and no correlation between learning and MA. In this experiment seven different pairs of *familiar* animal pictures were presented *one above another* instead of left and right and no two in succession. Thus these findings appear consistent with the discussion above.

Zeaman and House have accepted the existence of a LOW-IQ deficit in discrimination-learning in the retarded and have been concerned with identifying the nature of this deficit in a number of studies (House, Orlando, and Zeaman, 1957; House, Zeaman, and Fischer, 1957; House and Zeaman, 1958c; House and Zeaman, 1959). In effect, they found little to support the hypothesis that the negative stimulus in the two-choice discrimination-learning paradigm plays a minor role compared to the positive stimulus. That is, they found no clear-cut evidence here of an inhibition deficit. The present author, teamed with Robert Boice, has attempted to determine whether strong position habits are critical in the retardate's discrimination-learning deficit. In a series of experiments completed in June, 1962, a variable other than position fixation came forward as a possible explanation of the LOW-IQ deficit as found by House and Zeaman. Although position fixations were more pronounced in the retarded than the normal it was found that the LOW-IQ deficit nearly vanished when certain methodological changes were introduced. When the impersonal, unattended learning situation of the Wisconsin General Test Apparatus (WGTA) was replaced by a face-to-face experimenter with subject situation the institutionalized retarded ($\overline{CA} = 13.6$; $\overline{IQ} = 35$; $N = 24$) now learned the form-color discrimination much faster than reported by House and Zeaman (mean = 55 trials to a 9 out of 10 criterion) and nearly as well as normal nursery school children ($\overline{CA} = 4.5$; $N = 12$), though the latter difference was significant at the 0.05 level. And when non-institutionalized retarded ($\overline{CA} = 17$; $\overline{IQ} = 35$; $N = 14$) were compared with the normal children, both run in the face-to-face situation, there was no significant difference between groups (means = 41 and 32 trials, respectively). With IQ partialed out, CA was not significantly correlated with the discrimination-learning scores of the retarded, as has also been found by House and Zeaman using the WGTA (1960).

These results seem clear in implication, stressing the importance of an attention deficit in the learning performance of the retarded. When there is no experimenter immediately present, as with the WGTA, the retardate is much more likely to show lack of attention and low motivation for the task and consequently unusually poor performance even when compared to monkeys. For monkeys come to the WGTA learning situation with a much more appropriate life-history than would socially dependent retardates. These results provide an alternative or additional explanation of Stevenson's results with three-choice discriminations as well as Plenderleith's results, for it seems clear from the procedures described in these studies that the learning took place in an informal, face-to-face situation.

A short note is in order here. It appears that a discrimination deficit may extend to "mentally defective rats." Auerbach, Waisman, and Wyckoff (1958) have produced phenylketonuria in the rat by means of a special diet, and such animals are significantly poorer in learning a temporal discrimination than normal controls. The discrimination was part of an operant conditioning procedure in which the rat learned to lick a dry dipper on a two-minute fixed interval schedule, with water as a reinforcement.

The few remaining studies on discrimination-learning in the mentally retarded deal largely with special training conditions. Ellis and Pryer (1958) compared the effectiveness of jelly beans and 1-inch squares of yellow paper as reinforcers in two equal groups of male and female mentally retarded ($\overline{MA} = 5.2$; $\overline{CA} = 15.7$; $N = 70$). The stimulus objects to be discriminated were a 2-inch square block and a cylinder 2 inches in diameter and 2 inches long (both painted flat blue). There was no significant difference in the learning over fifty training trials though the yellow squares of paper produced the better performance. In

the context of the instructions given the subjects, both reinforcing objects had equivalent informational value, and the authors had no real basis for positing jelly beans as primary and yellow paper as secondary reinforcement. In fact, the jelly beans could distract from the set to learn as appeared the case from the candy groups' behavior during the intertrial intervals. In the context of modern contiguity theory which emphasizes the importance of consistent responding in learning (Denny and Adelman, 1955), the results are not unexpected.

Cantor and Hottel (1955) also found that four peanuts were no better than one peanut as rewards in learning a form discrimination, which is similar to results on lower animals (Reynolds, 1949). In the same study they did find, however, a LOW-MA-LOW-IQ deficit, as twenty-four adult subjects with IQ's above 50 (median = 56.5) learned significantly better than twenty adults with IQ's below 50 (median = 36). Barnett and Cantor (1957) then took one-half of the retarded who could not learn this form discrimination, upright vs. inverted triangle, and trained them on a black-white discrimination, semicircular disks. When returned to the form discrimination these subjects did significantly better than the control half which had simply been color-naming in the interim. Such results are contradictory to those of Zeaman, House, and Orlando (1958) where pre-training on junk stimuli did not mediate the color-form discrimination. A possible difference between the two studies is the number of stimulus dimensions present in the pre-training stimulus. Perhaps, the main thing that transfers positively is getting the subject to orient to a single or restricted stimulus dimension, as was the case in the Barnett and Cantor study (1957). In this connection, the first part of the Zeaman, House, and Orlando study (1958) is relevant, for here they found that learning the verbal labels for color stimuli (color-naming) facilitated the subsequent color-form discrimination. Jacobs (1950), who used institutionalized orphans as normal controls, also found a trend in this direction; labeling three ambiguous shapes "bird, dog, and shoe" tended to facilitate a discrimination for these stimuli, though more so for normals than the retarded.

Cantor and Hottel (1957) found that training the retarded to learn nonsense syllable labels for each of two similar cross-like figures facilitated the learning of a subsequent discrimination between the two figures. The two open-line drawings had the continuous bar oriented horizontally in one instance and vertically in the other. In a partial replication of the study, Smith and Means (1961) controlled for the possibility that the positive transfer due to learning nonsense syllable labels for visual stimuli may have been due to the experience gained by simply looking at the stimuli. They found that visual inspection, provided by a matching technique, was indeed as effective as labeling with nonsense syllables. Theoretically, such a result is not surprising. Learning meaningful verbal labels or relevant motor responses (appropriate hand movements), on the other hand, did provide significantly greater positive transfer than matching or learning nonsense syllable labels. Their subjects were thirty-seven male and forty-eight female retardates ranging in age from thirteen to forty-five and in IQ from 35 to 85.

In addition, Bensberg (1958) has studied "attention sets" in learning to associate nonsense names with stimulus forms. Retardates who first learned to press buttons to form stimuli learned the name-form associations better than retardates without the facilitating set training; and those who first learned to press buttons to color stimuli did worse on name-form learning than either of the other two groups (interfering set). Thus the variable of stimulus orientation appears relevant to a full understanding of learning

and performance in the mentally retarded.

Another note about discrimination-learning in the mentally retarded stems from Barnett's Ph.D. thesis (1958). Briefly, he found that the stimulus-generalization gradients for spatial stimuli were essentially the same for normals and the retarded (IQ = 50). Thus flatter stimulus-generalization gradients in retardates as an explanation of their discrimination-learning deficit does not appear to be a tenable hypothesis, at least for the present. A more fruitful approach seems to be along the line of an inhibition or attention deficit. Consonant with the retardate's difficulty with language, however, Bialer (1961) has shown that secondary or verbally mediated stimulus generalization is greater the higher the intelligence level.

Finally, there are two interlocking studies which seem to bear on the matter of an attention deficit in a rather different way (Foshee, 1958; Gardner, Cromwell, and Foshee, 1959). By means of a ballistograph, Foshee divided adult mental defectives (mean IQ slightly less than 50) into a high-active group and a low-active group (N = approximately 24 in both the top and bottom quarters). They were then presented with a simple card-sorting discrimination task involving the differentiation of two geometric forms and a complex sorting task employing eight different geometric forms. On both tasks the low-active group was superior—a result which may or may not fit with the Hullian drive concept but makes sense if the high-active group is considered especially inattentive or distractible. Such an interpretation appears reasonable in light of the second study, which showed that both groups were significantly less active under increased visual stimulation and that this effect was greater for the hyperactive group than the hypoactive group. Presumably, when there was something to attend to besides a blank wall the mentally retarded engaged in less stimulus-searching activity. In other words, activity as a rough index of inattentiveness is, as Foshee found, negatively correlated with discrimination-learning. This would mean, everything else being equal, that retardates should learn a discrimination better when the surroundings are homogeneous and the discriminative stimuli are prominent or multidimensional. To the extent that the work of House, Zeaman, and Fischer (1957) is relevant here their results are compatible with this hypothesis.

To sum up, discrimination-learning problems can readily be arranged to expose a basic LOW-IQ deficit in the mentally retarded with IQ's around 50 or less. This appears to be related to a deficit in the inhibition sphere, including an inability to maintain an orientation for the relevant stimuli. The similarity between these data and those of classical conditioning is striking.

COMPLEX INSTRUMENTAL LEARNING

Learning set.—The type of complex learning closest to discrimination-learning is the learning-set problem (learning successive discriminations more rapidly with the successive presentations of discrete two-choice problems). Here again a deficit in the mentally retarded seems indicated, though the data are fewer and less clear-cut than in simple discrimination-learning.

One way to view learning set, similar to the way suggested by Restle (1958), is to assume that a series of two-choice problems involves learning to make a choice-response on the basis of a consistent information cue. As a child, the human being has not yet learned in a two-choice situation that "wrong" means the other alternative is almost invariably right or that "right" means that this choice is going to remain right. Once he has learned this, most two-choice problems become one-trial learning affairs as is true in naïve monkeys after rewards ("right") and non-rewards ("wrong")

eventually acquire the same kind of cue value (learning set).

On the basis of such an analysis the main clue as to why the mentally retarded might be inferior in learning set is that it is quite similar to the kind of learning involved in verbally mediated behavior. By implication then, the retarded individual's presumed deficit in the verbal control of behavior, as discussed in the section on classical conditioning, might be more basic than language per se.

Possibly the earliest indication of something resembling learning set in the mentally retarded was the classical trial-and-error study by Hamilton (1911) where the task was to learn, in a four-choice situation, that the last correct response was never correct on the next trial (using reward as a cue with a reverse twist). Two retardates, a man and a boy, performed almost as well as normals, better than a twenty-six–month infant, and better than monkeys, cats, dogs, and horses.

Other early evidence came in a study by Doll and Aldrich (1932). Given a series of size-discrimination reversals, two idiots out of ten showed a clear tendency to learn faster after the first reversal. The results also imply a deficit, for five out of seven who learned the first size discrimination did not exhibit learning set. House and Zeaman (1958) likewise found little evidence of learning set in retarded children (IQ = 28) in a series of thirty two-choice problems using junk stimuli, whereas monkeys in a comparable situation (Harlow, 1950) clearly evidenced learning set.

The remaining studies nevertheless show that the formation of learning set is common in retardates and that the speed of acquisition seems directly related to MA level. Quite convincing in both of these directions is a study by Kaufman and Peterson (1958). The retarded children (N = 8) had IQ's ranging from 50 to 75 and were matched on CA and sex with six normals (CA = 9–12). As usual, the Wisconsin General Test Apparatus was employed and forty-eight different problems from a pool of four hundred pairs of objects were presented. Three trials were permitted per problem, eight problems were given per day, left and right positions were equated for being correct in any one day, and chocolate chips served as reinforcers. The criterion of learning set was 90 per cent correct on the second trial. Five out of six normals and only one retardate met the criterion within forty-eight problems. Given another forty-eight problems a total of five

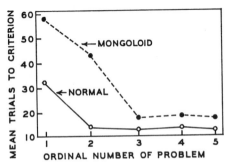

Fig. 3.—Mean trials to criterion for the mongoloid and normal groups. (From Girardeau, 1959, p. 568.)

out of eight retardates reached criterion. The retarded scored significantly more perseverative errors than the normals, i.e., more errors following an error. Since the groups were matched on CA the deficit is a LOW-MA-LOW-IQ deficit, which is about all that can be safely inferred from any study in this area.

Ellis (1958) compared fifty high MA subjects ($\overline{MA}$ = 8; $\overline{CA}$ = 14.75) with forty low MA subjects ($\overline{MA}$ = 5; $\overline{CA}$ = 13.6) on ten successive object-quality discrimination problems, where each problem was learned to a criterion of twenty successive correct responses. Learning sets developed quickly in both groups. The high-MA group acquired them more rapidly and attained more efficient sets than the low-MA group. The F based on errors to criterion was significant at the

0.001 level of confidence. Selecting subjects from each group to achieve a more exact CA match did not alter the results.

Stevenson and Swartz (1958) studied two levels of mental deficiency and one normal level on a series of object discriminations. The higher deficient group ($\overline{IQ}$ = 53.5; CA = 11.5; N = 10) was matched on CA with the normal (N = 10) but was younger than the lower group ($\overline{IQ}$ = 33.4; CA = 14.2; N = 10) and not much higher in MA (5.7 vs. 4.1). Even so, the higher deficient group performed strikingly better than the low group as eight of ten attained the learning-set criterion of learning in one trial within twenty-four problems while only one S in the low group did so. Such data hint at a LOW-IQ deficit in the learning-set area. Performance on the very first problem also indicated a discrimination deficit in both mentally retarded groups.

Girardeau (1959) used mongoloids matched on MA with normal children in a series of five object-quality discriminations learned to criterion. The mongoloids (IQ = approximately 40) improved significantly from Problem 1 to Problem 3 and from Problem 2 to Problem 3 (learning set occurred), and though it looks as if the retarded subjects would level off at an inferior level of learning when compared with normals, too few problems were given to justify any such conclusion (see Fig. 3). Research is badly needed to determine whether or not there is a LOW-IQ deficit in the mentally retarded with respect to acquiring learning sets.

The only other study where retardates were matched on MA with normals does not indicate any learning-set deficit. This is Plenderleith's (1956) study which was described earlier and as previously indicated was not classified as a learning-set experiment by the experimenter. Probably the most appropriate qualification to make about the Plenderleith study is that her subjects had relatively high IQ's

(IQ = 56–69). It is true they were of the same CA and IQ range as the Kaufman-Peterson study, but the latter used a CA control. It is quite possible that the same problem administered to more retarded subjects would reveal a LOW-IQ deficit.

When House and Zeaman (1959) simplified the learning-set problem for their severely retarded subjects ($\overline{MA} = 3$ years, 2 months, IQ = 30) they found clear-cut evidence of learning set. They copied a left-right position reversal study with rats (Dufort, Guttman, and Kimble, 1954) using the Wisconsin General Test Apparatus. The results compared with the rat data are presented in Figure 4. That the retardates did not do appreciably better than the rats is at least suggestive of a LOW-IQ learning-set deficit in the severely retarded. Longnecker and Ferson (1961), however, recently found that mongoloids achieved one-trial reversal better than the rat.

In a recent study with normal and mildly retarded children Wischner and O'Donnell (1962) have found that the *concurrent* type of learning-set experiment yields superiority for the normals, but that both groups establish sets quickly and efficiently. In the concurrent technique each of several different object-quality pairs was presented only once until all pairs had been presented, and then the pairs were repeated in exactly the same order. A series of discriminations learned to criterion was followed by four more problems or series; learning set was reflected in improved performance on succeeding problems. The retarded group also showed a more pronounced serial position effect within a series of discriminations than did the normal children. Paradoxically the very first series of discrimination problems was learned faster by the retarded than the normals. Here is a technique like Plenderleith's (see page 112) which probably prevents the establishment of position habits. If so, these data are in accord with the prior interpretation which

explained the discrimination-learning deficit in the retarded in terms of an inhibition deficit and the customary methodology of discrimination-learning experiments.

Other studies in this area are unpublished and for the most part are noncomparative. Wischner and his associates (Wischner, Braun, and Patton, 1960), however, have found that of all categories of organic deficiency studied, cerebral palsy in children seems to impair learning-set formation least. DeHaan (1960), working in the same laboratory, has found no difference in learning-set

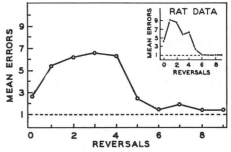

Fig. 4.—Mean errors for successive reversals of a position discrimination for imbecile children and rats. (From House *et al., J. Comp. Physiol. Psychol.,* **52** [1959], 565.)

formation when tridimensional objects versus flat photographs were used as the discriminative stimuli. If the main cues in learning set are the occurrence or nonoccurrence of reinforcement, then such a result is not surprising.

Transposition.—Again one of the earliest bits of information on the phenomenon comes from the two-choice size discrimination experiment of Doll and Aldrich (1932). When, for example, the initially larger positive box was made the smaller of the two stimuli, most of their subjects (ten retardates) showed transposition by selecting the new, larger box.

Stevenson and Iscoe (1955) have performed a more recent and more extensive study, which was described in part in the section on discrimination-learning. After the subjects learned the size discrimination they were given transposition tests at a distance of one, two, or four steps from the original pair of 2-inch vs. 4-inch squares. Similar to the results on lower animals the mental retardates showed transposition from 65 to 75 per cent of the time; however, they transposed about the same amount for all steps (significantly above chance). Transposition occurred despite the fact that only three of the forty-four subjects were able to verbalize the relationship and even though the test for transposition came immediately after the subject had reached criterion. Stevenson and Langford (1957) found more transposition in children after a twenty-four–hour delay.

Delayed response.—Harlow and Israel (1932) studied delayed reaction in twenty-five severely retardated subjects (CA = 5–60; MA = 1–3), using a candy reward and opaque containers. As long as the period of delay was not more than fifteen seconds the retardates performed successfully with a minimum of practice. Errors increased rapidly when the period was thirty seconds or more. The retardates compared favorably with subhuman primates on the shorter, simple delays but showed no superiority on longer or more complex delay problems. Within the restricted sample there did not appear to be any relationship between length of a successful delay and MA or language facility.

On the other hand, data collected with a wider range of MA values (MA = 2 years, 1 month, to 7 years, 1 month) by Pascal *et al.* (1951) show a positive relationship between MA and capacity to delay. For twenty-seven male retardates (CA = 5 years, 11 months, to 31 years, 10 months) the rank order correlation between maximum delay and MA was +0.68 and between delay and IQ was +0.60 ($p = 0.01$). There was no significant correlation between delay and CA and between delay and medical classification. The delayed response was for

place and was tested in a five-choice situation, using candy as a reward. A maximum delay was the longest delay in which the subject made three successive correct responses. The maximum delay interval for the twenty-seven subjects varied from two seconds to fourteen days; most subjects beyond an MA of 2 years, 10 months could delay responses for minutes, hours, or days.

These data on delayed reaction for place were contrasted with delayed reaction for form (five common geometrical figures randomly situated) in the same subjects by Pascal and Stolurow (1952). Form is the more difficult problem. Six subjects were unable to solve the problem with a one-second delay and fewer negotiated delays greater than thirty seconds than was true for place. The maximum delay for form correlated +0.88 with MA ($p = 0.01$) and +0.38 with CA ($p = 0.05$).

Amos (1960) compared three-year-olds with and without anoxic conditions at birth on delayed response, for delays of one, two, three, four, five, and ten minutes. The twenty controls were significantly superior to the nineteen anoxics on the ten-minute interval ($p = 0.05$). The anoxics got progressively worse as the interval increased, while this tendency was less marked in the controls. The anoxics had a significantly lower IQ than the controls ($p = 0.01$); and IQ in the anoxics was related to delayed-response performance (rho = 0.69), though not so in the controls.

Although normal controls of the same MA are lacking in delayed-response experiments with retardates, there are separate data by Skalet (1931) on normal children of approximately the same MA range as studied by Pascal *et al.* (CA = 2 years to 5 years, 6 months). In a three-choice situation, the shortest maximum delay for place for the normal children was one day and the longest was at least thirty-four days (N = 46). This contrasts with two seconds and fourteen days found by Pascal *et al.* in the mentally re-tarded. In a six-choice situation using familiar forms (Kiddie car, rabbit, auto, etc.) the maximum delays were exactly the same, one to thirty-four days (N = 27). When six geometrical forms were used, a situation quite comparable to one found by Pascal and Stolurow to be very difficult for many retardates, the normal children had maximum delays which ranged from ten minutes to four days (N = 37). All in all, a LOW-IQ deficit is certainly suggested. Skalet also found significant correlations between maxi-mum delay and MA and CA but, in agreement with Amos' normals, not much correlation with IQ.

Recent research on object discrimina-tion learning in monkeys with frontal le-sions by Mishkin, Prockop, and Rosvold (1962) suggests that the reason frontal lesions may impair spatial delayed re-sponses is because frontal lesions pro-duce an inhibition deficit. Because mon-keys with frontal lesions cannot readily learn to suppress a prevailing position habit they show a deficit in delayed re-sponse. Thus it might be argued that the ubiquitous inhibition deficit may, in fact, underlie the delayed response deficit in the mentally retarded.

Finally, Barnett, Ellis, and Pryer (1959) have shown that training the re-tarded to attach appropriate names to the discriminative stimuli will improve delayed-response performance and some-what more so for those with higher MA's. More research is certainly needed to round out the picture and to relate de-layed response to other learning data. What about the retardate who can nego-tiate long delays successfully? Is he supe-rior on other tasks? It would seem, for example, that poor judgment, which characterizes the retarded, is at least partly a function of an inability to delay responses successfully.

Double alternation.—In the sense that the individual must, in both cases, make an appropriate response to cues that have passed him by there is a similarity be-tween double alternation and delayed response. Thus, it is not surprising that Pascal and Zak (1956) and Stolurow and Pascal (1950) have found fairly high correlations ranging from 0.64 to 0.83 be-tween double alternation performance and IQ, both in cerebral palsied children (IQ = 35–111) and unselected mental defectives. The double alternation task which these investigators used required subjects to select the extreme door at one end of a line of five doors twice in suc-cession and then select the door at the other end twice in succession (all four responses rewarded). Their clear-cut re-sults suggest including the double alter-nation task as part of any new process-oriented or theory-based method of assessing intelligence. Added weight is given this recommendation by the recent finding that double alternation is one of two out of seven learning tasks on which familials excel organics (Barnett, Ellis, and Pryer, 1960).

Problem-solving (non-verbal).—Here we have a dearth of experimental work. Except for a recent oddity-problem ex-periment by Ellis and Sloan (1959), the total contribution to the reviewer's knowl-edge, came thirty years ago (Aldrich and Doll, 1931*a, b*) and was limited to the performance of a handful of retard-ates. Aldrich and Doll (1931*a*) stud-ied the problem of stacking boxes to reach a lure, using eight subjects. Six of their subjects solved the problem of "stacking" one box and five solved the stacking of both two boxes and three boxes. The criterion of success was three successive solutions, and individual dif-ferences in attaining this were marked. Their behavior to the point of initial so-lution was considered very similar to the behavior of the great apes, but on subse-quent trials the retardates were reported to achieve solution more quickly than the typical chimpanzee. Switching incentives was necessary to achieve solution in some subjects. Some solved it with a bell but not a cookie and vice versa.

In their other experiment, Aldrich and Doll (1931b) studied problem-solving with implements; the problem was to use a rake or two sticks to reach a lure behind a partition. Seven subjects (MA = 19–38 months, IQ = 14–35, CA = 8.6–11.9) were given four different problems: (1) rake outside partition, (2) rake just inside partition, (3) two sticks, the one which was too short being outside the partition, (4) two short sticks which could be stuck together. The subjects with the four highest MA's solved three or four problems. The other three solved one, two, or more. The trial-and-error behavior of the lowest retardates approached pure randomness. The authors concluded that the retardates' performance fell between the apes and preschool children (see also McPherson, 1948).

Ellis and Sloan (1959) tested 139 mentally retarded and 40 normal children, grouped according to MA, on a form-oddity problem. The mean MA's for four levels of mental deficiency were 4.1, 6.1, 7.7, and 9.7 ($\overline{CA}$'s = 14–20), and two normal-MA control groups had mean CA's of 6.2 and 7.3.

From two different pairs of objects three were "randomly" presented with the odd or unpaired one always hiding a marble. There were no extrinsic rewards given; the marble just designated a correct choice. All subjects were given two hundred trials or brought to a criterion of twenty successive correct. The higher the MA among the retarded, the better the learning, both in terms of asymptote and rate of approaching asymptote. Learning in the 4.1-MA group was negligible, while learning in the 9.7-MA group was fast and went to a high level. The learning curves for the three highest MA groups of retardates, which definitely showed learning, were negatively accelerated; whereas the curves for the younger normals were quite recti-

linear, lagging behind the retardates with the same MA in early trial blocks but attaining the same level at the end of practice. The product-moment correlations between number of correct responses and MA and IQ in the retarded sample were, respectively, 0.48 and 0.55. Except possibly for the extremely poor performance of the lowest MA group there is no evidence of a LOW-IQ deficit in the oddity-learning area, but a LOW-MA-LOW-IQ deficit is quite apparent. In fact, a recent preliminary report by Hill (1962) argues against any sizable LOW-IQ deficit. Her normal children were unable to solve oddity problems until three to six years of age.

In summary, the mentally retarded rather consistently show a deficit in the area of complex learning, though not necessarily a LOW-IQ deficit. This appears to be associated with a lessened ability to use less obvious or less available cues, as characteristic of learning set, delayed response, double alternation, oddity problem, and even problem-solving with implements. (The problem with the stick or rake inside the partition gave the most difficulty.) These findings are congruent with a discrimination-learning deficit.

ROTE LEARNING

Pictorial.—Bernice Lott (Eisman, 1958) has probably conducted the most thought-provoking study in the area of rote learning in the mentally retarded. In essence, she found no significant difference between the retarded and superior normals in the learning and retention of paired-associate material, *when the groups were matched on CA.* Let us examine her study in more detail. A total of sixty-nine subjects was used, twenty-three (nine male and fourteen female) in each of three groups (CA's = 12 years, 2 months to 17 years, 2 months). The mentally retarded group was from a special class in a public junior high school and ranged in IQ from 46 to 77 (median = 68). An average normal group had IQ's from 91 to 108 (median = 80) and the superior normals ranged from 120 to 134 (median IQ = 123). Since a number of the retarded were non-readers or poor readers, the learning materials consisted of seven pairs of pictures of common objects such as basket-hammer and suitcase-flower. These were presented on cards at a slow controlled rate until the criterion of four consecutive correct trials was reached. Stimulus generalization was then tested with pictures similar to the stimulus figures. (In agreement with the findings of Barnett [1958] there was no significant difference between the normals and retarded in degree of generalization.) Thirty-six subjects were given a retention test approximately one week after learning and thirty-three were given the test after approximately one month.

Although there were no significant differences between groups on any measure, the differences were in every instance, except one, in favor of the normals, and the 0.05 level was approached on the short-term retention test. This is mentioned because it is quite possible that Eisman's findings may be due to positive transfer effects (use of highly familiar material) which tend to erase any basic learning difference. This possibility is reinforced by the fact that Wilson (1928), using less familiar or more difficult material (memorizing multiplication tables and shorthand characters), found a significant difference between non-institutionalized "bright" and "dull" children, all of whom were within normal range. It still remains true, however, that given well-differentiated stimuli and responses, the association is established about as readily in the retarded as in the normals; and the importance of this finding should not be underestimated.

Further, two other studies using pictorial stimuli or the like, as well as CA controls, provide support for Eisman's results. Akutagawa and Benoit (1959), like

Wilson, did not work with a truly retarded population, but, unlike both Wilson and Eisman, they used subjects who were all institutionalized. Average IQ children (CA's = 8–10 and 11–13) were compared with subaverage children in the same CA categories (IQ = 70–89; mean = 84.5) on learning three different paired-associate lists of varying difficulty, each containing eight pairs of pictures. They found that the lists were sufficiently sensitive to differentiate the CA levels (better learning by the older subjects), even though they did not differentiate according to MA. As such, these findings add to the generality of Eisman's results. Whether these findings would hold up with a list of about sixteen pairs of pictures within a truly retarded population would seem to be a question of considerable interest.

The other study (Berkson and Cantor, 1960) is more difficult to assess because the stimulus member of the paired-associate pairs was generally an odd or even number while the response member was either a picture of a common object or a hexagon of one of six different colors. In the complete experiment, to be referred to again later, three lists of six pairs each were presented as a test of a mediation hypothesis. On the first list presented there was no significant difference between the public school retardates (CA = 9–12; IQ = 69.6) and normals just a few months younger, and this finding substantiates Eisman's. But by the third list the normal were significantly superior at the 0.05 confidence level. That this may be due to a superiority in learning set or learning how to learn in the normals seems quite a reasonable hypothesis, particularly since the specific mediation effect that was tested and noted was found to be independent of IQ level.

An exception to the Eisman finding is the recent replication of her study by Ring and Palermo (1961). Unlike Eisman they presented the picture associates in a mechanical apparatus which markedly reduced the presentation time from the "informal" seven seconds used by Eisman. Under these new conditions the normal children now learned significantly faster in the *second half* of the learning session (fourteen trials). Perhaps the normal children's superiority is related to the fact that the retarded do well only in a relaxed, face-to-face situation as found in two-choice discrimination-learning; perhaps it indicates the retardate's greater susceptibility to proactive interference under a rapid presentation rate; or perhaps both.

One aspect of Eisman's study as well as Berkson and Cantor's which should be underlined is that the mentally retarded groups were non-institutionalized. Since Badt (1958) has found a significant negative correlation (−0.61) between length of institutionalization and abstraction scores on the vocabulary list of the Stanford-Binet (Form L) and a non-significant r or 0.24 between MA and the abstraction score, this variable cannot be overlooked. Yet in view of the Wilson study and the Akutagawa-Benoit study it is doubtful that this is a crucial variable. It would seem more profitable, for the time being at least, to entertain the notion that, when the presentation of the material is unhurried and informal, the connections between readily distinguishable stimuli and common responses are established as readily in the retarded with IQ's above 50, if not below, as they are in normals. Such an assumption actually does not run counter to the facts of classical conditioning or our interpretations of the facts of discrimination-learning and seems to be supported by the maze-learning experiments of DeSanctis (1931) and Sloan and Berg (1957). Within a reasonable stretch of the imagination, visible maze patterns qualify as non-verbal visuomotor rote-learning tasks, and, as you may remember, the learning of such mazes was relatively independent of MA level.

Verbal.—When we turn to the verbal rote-learning studies with groups matched on CA the results, however, are distinctly different. McCulloch, Reswick, and Roy (1955) did not study normals but did compare two MA levels (MA = 6 years ± 6 months vs. MA = 9 years ± 6 months) matched on two different CA levels (16 and 48 years). Lists of from three to nine common words were delivered individually by means of a tape recorder with words spaced at intervals of one and one-half seconds. Three seconds of time per word to repeat the list were allowed at the end of each list. Each list was repeated five times and the next list, containing one more word (all new words), was presented in the exact same manner and so on until all seven lists were given. The MA-9 group both on the initial repetition and all five repetition attempts was significantly superior to the MA-6 group.

Sloan and Berg (1957) replicated the McCulloch *et al.* study in a correlational design with a single group of retardates (MA = 8.2; IQ = 57; and SD = 11.3) and found a significant correlation between gain and MA. So in general "word-learning" seems directly related to MA level.

A more recent and extensive investigation by Ellis, Pryer, Distefano, and Pryer (1960) compares five MA-IQ levels, as presented in Figure 5, effectively matched on CA ($\overline{CA}$ = approximately 17), on the serial learning of a list of ten commonly used nouns. Only those who could read the list were used as subjects. The words were presented at a two-second rate and the intertrial interval was twenty seconds. The criterion of learning was one errorless trial. As can be seen in Figure 5 there is a substantial relationship between test intelligence and verbal rote-learning. The sharpest drop in trials to criterion, which is significant at the 0.01 level, comes at the customary dividing line between mental retardation and dull-normal.

Only in the mentally retarded groups was there a significant correlation between IQ and trials-to-criterion ($r = 0.49$). All groups had similar learning curves and showed serial position effects; the learning rate was simply faster and the bow-shaped serial position curve flatter as IQ increased.

Using the same list of nouns Pryer (1960) found that normals learned nearly twice as fast as retardates and that the correlation between IQ and trials-to-criterion was -0.64. The retarded

and non-familial, with a group of normals on serial verbal-learning ($CA = 20$, and $N = 26$ in each group). On an initial practice list of only three words the normals were superior. But with lists six words long there were no significant differences between groups on an original list, an interpolated list, and a relearning list (a retroactive inhibition design). All groups showed a significant amount of retroactive inhibition, and familials and organics performed alike. Despite the absence of significant differences (0.05

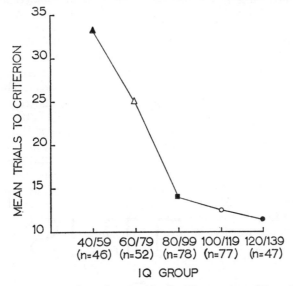

FIG. 5.—Trials to criterion in serial rote learning for five IQ groupings. (From Ellis *et al.*, 1960.)

showed typical serial position effects as well as retroactive inhibition but less retroactive inhibition than normals—though not significantly less. On the basis of these four studies it seems safe to conclude that there is a LOW-MA-LOW-IQ deficit in the retarded with respect to verbal rote-learning.

When we look at verbal rote-learning studies in which normals and retardates are matched on MA the results are somewhat inconsistent, indicating either a small LOW-IQ deficit or no deficit at all. Cassel (1957) compared two mentally retarded groups ($MA = 9+$), familial

level), it should be noted that the normals did take fewer trials to criterion and that one hundred aments were initially eliminated from the experiment because they could not read the words (no normals were eliminated on this basis). A selection bias, inherent with verbal materials, might be attenuating a real difference in Cassel's study.

The most comprehensive study of verbal rote-learning where groups are matched on MA has been reported in a book by Johnson and Blake (1960). The mentally retarded sample ranged in IQ from 50 to 75 and included both institutionalized and public school children. On the serial learning of a six-item list of easily pronounced nonsense syllables there was no significant difference between public school retardates and normals. There also was no significant difference one week later on relearning; but on a recognition test just preceding the relearning the normals were significantly superior, though the absolute difference was rather small.

On the other hand, on paired-associate nonsense syllable–learning using only three pairs (*bip-juf, kej-pop, zab-rix*) the mentally retarded were slightly but significantly inferior. In a test for stimulus generalization with slightly changed stimulus words (*bep, kaj, zub*) there were no significant differences between normals and retardates, as is consistent with Barnett (1958) and Eisman (1958). The apparent discrepancy between serial- and paired-associate learning is difficult to interpret because custodial cases rather than public school children served as subjects in the latter experiment.

The picture is further obfuscated by the fact that public school defectives (IQ = 68.6) in the Johnson and Blake (1960) investigation learned a letter-digit substitution task (like the digit-symbol test) better than the normals. When the letter-digit relations were shifted the normals exhibited more retroactive inhibition than the defectives, as found by Pryer (1960), but the same amount of proactive inhibition.

To summarize, as long as the rote-learning materials are non-verbal and familiar there is insufficient evidence of a learning deficit in the mentally retarded with IQ's of 50 and above. As soon as a verbal or *symbolic* element is introduced there is consistent evidence of a sizable LOW-MA-LOW-IQ deficit and rather tenuous evidence for a small LOW-IQ deficit.

VERBAL MEDIATION

Verbal conditioning.—There are at least two studies modeled on the Hum-

phrey guessing experiment. Metzger (1960), used retardates, MA = 6 and MA = 9 (CA = 16–35), matched with normals on MA. The probabilities in a light-guessing experiment were 70–30 per cent. The retardates' final mean per cent corresponded with Estes' probability matching law but differed somewhat from the normals in that less than 25 per cent fell between 65 per cent and 75 per cent. The retarded, however, were significantly more rigid than the normals à la Kounin (1941, 1948). Metzger's stereotypy score yielded significant negative correlations with MA within the retarded sample (r = approximately −0.50).

Shipe (1959) asked thirty educable retarded and thirty normal children to guess the size of color patches presented two hundred times. The probabilities for half the subjects were 80 per cent "big" and 20 per cent "little," and for the other half, 60 per cent "big" and 40 per cent "little." There was no significant difference between the guessing behavior of the mentally retarded and normal for 80 per cent "big," as both groups rapidly approached the 80 per cent level. With 60 per cent "big" the retarded did a significantly better job of approaching the 60 per cent asymptote. Since it is unclear psychologically, if not mathematically, what this type of verbal conditioning involves we are reluctant to hazard any interpretation of these interesting findings.

Verbal control of motor behavior.—Luria (1959) and Luria and Vinogradova (1959) emphasize a dissociation between verbal and motor systems in the mentally retarded. Presumably in the retarded child language does not develop sufficiently to assume a regulating function. The previously mentioned balloon-pressing experiment (p. 103) and the vascular reactions studied by Luria and Vinogradova furnish evidence for this assertion. In the latter set of studies educable mental retardates and trainable mental retardates (CA = 15–17) were presented with the task of pressing a button to a signal word "koshka" (cat) and tested with words of similar sound, e.g., "okoshko" (window), and words of similar meaning (dog, kitten, etc.). Although the educable retardates only pressed the button to the signal word, the *tendency* to press was identified by means of vascular-orienting reactions. Borderline retardates showed generalization to both words of similar meaning and similar sound; whereas normals generalized almost exclusively on the basis of meaning. Rather low educable retardates showed semantic generalization only to "kitten" and a great deal of generalization to sound. Trainable retardates, on the other hand, frequently pushed the button to similar sounding words despite contrary instructions. Generalization here was specifically along the sound dimension and was more extended for vascular reactions than for overt button-pressing. Borderline retardates, at least, were capable, with continued reinforcement, of learning increased semantic generalization and decreased sound generalization. But fatigue in these subjects brought about a disinhibition of the inhibited generalization to sound. An interesting sidelight to the study was that placing "okoshko" (window) in a verbal context of "house, door, wall, etc." inhibited generalized orienting reactions to it.

The British psychologists O'Connor and Hermelin have attempted to test Luria's views in a number of studies. O'Connor and Hermelin (1959a) ran two discrimination reversal experiments using retardates ($\overline{CA} = 11.5$; $\overline{MA} = 4.9$) and normal school children (CA = 5.1). In the first experiment ten retardates were compared with ten normals on learning a size discrimination (black squares of 5:8 ratio on a red background) and an immediate reversal of this discrimination. Both problems were learned to a criterion of 10 consecutive correct trials with candy as a reward. On original learning the normals were superior but not significantly superior. On the reversal the re-

tardates learned significantly faster: the retarded needed a mean of 11 trials as compared with 25.4 for the normals. Eight of the ten normal children verbalized a principle of size discrimination; whereas only one retardate, despite prompting, did so.

The hypothesis is that the discrimination is not under verbal control in the retarded, and consequently a strong generalized verbal habit does not have to be extinguished in the reversal problem. In the normal five-year-olds, however, there is sufficient verbal control to occasion negative transfer but insufficient verbal facility to analyze the situation and change set. This is rather a roundabout interpretation but appears fundamentally sound, and the part about the normal five-year-olds' level of verbal development for shifting set coincides with the experimental data of Kendler and Kendler (1959).

The second experiment was an empirical check of this interpretation. Ten more retardates matched with the previous group were given the same problem except that now each correct discrimination response was verbally reinforced by identifying the correct stimulus as "the big one" or "the little one" and having the subject verbalize this relationship after each correct response throughout the original size discrimination. (No comments were made or solicited during reversal training.) Whereas in the first experiment the retardates took many fewer trials to reverse than to learn, they now took more (39.6 vs. 25.1) and significantly more than the first group of retardates ($p = 0.1$). Thus the interpretation of the first experiment and with it Luria's basic premise was upheld. Also, the data now come more closely in line with the notion of an inhibition deficit or of greater rigidity in the mentally retarded (Kounin, 1941, 1948).

Two discrimination-reversal studies actually preceded the one by O'Connor and Hermelin (1959a) and have been partially discussed under the topic of discrimination-learning, Stevenson and Zigler (1957) and Plenderleith (1956). Both found no significant difference between normals ($\overline{\text{CA}}$ between 5 and 6) and retardates of the same MA on reversal learning. As such this finding does not necessarily contradict O'Connor and Hermelin because, everything else being equal, the retarded, according to Kounin's rigidity hypothesis and an inhibition deficit hypothesis, should reverse more slowly than the normals. In view of Luria's chronology of verbal control in the normal child it may also be relevant to point out that the normal children were several months older in the Plenderleith and Stevenson and Zigler studies than in the O'Connor and Hermelin study. In other words, if six-year-old controls and retardates with an MA of 6 were run in the O'Connor and Hermelin experiment there might not be a significant difference on reversal learning, as the investigators themselves intimate; that is, some of the normal six-year-olds might begin "to catch on and change set" as found by Kendler and Kendler (1959).

Another study getting at the connection between the verbal and motor systems in the mentally retarded is quite different in format (Hermelin and O'Connor, 1960). Forty retardates lacking motor defect and having some speech ($\text{CA} = 12$ years, 6 months, $\text{IQ} = 41.5$) were matched on MA with twenty normals and each group was divided into four sub-groups. The stimulus for two groups was one or two pencil taps and for the other two the stimulus was counting "one" or "one, two." On Trials 1–10 one sub-group from each pair of sub-groups responded for each stimulus by tapping, and the other two sub-groups responded by counting. On Trials 11–30, all subjects both tapped and counted together, and Trials 31–40 were identical with 1–10. Per initial instructions and repeated instructions after every 10 trials, all subjects throughout the experiment

had to make two responses if one signal was given and one response if two signals were given. That is, the responses to be made in accordance with the general verbal instructions were in direct contrast to the number of stimulus impulses.

Whereas normals performed essentially the same under all conditions, the retarded had considerable difficulty under the conditions where the stimulus and response were the same (like modality conditions). At these points they were significantly inferior to normals and to themselves under cross-modality conditions. Specifically, the defectives had great difficulty responding correctly (oppositely) if the stimulus and response were both tapping or both counting but, when stimulus and response differed, did about as well on the first set of five trials after instructions as did the normals. On the second set of five trials after instructions cross-modality performance fell off significantly, while no such trend was present in the normals.

In summary, a lack of verbal control over motor behavior in the mentally retarded is manifested in a variety of ways: (1) Retardates often fail to follow verbal instructions explicitly (balloon-pressing and button-pressing). (2) Responses to verbal signals show more generalizations to words of similar sound than to words of similar *meaning*. (3) Retardates ordinarily do not verbalize about the size of the stimuli in a size-discrimination experiment. Consequently, they learn a size reversal as quickly as, or more quickly than, five- to six-year-old normals. (4) In the face of opposing instructions, the mentally retarded fail to inhibit the influence of *direct* stimuli when the response to be made is of the same modality as the stimulus. (5) The effect of verbal instructions which had been initially effective fades away with the passing of time. The cue to training retarded would be to repeat instructions frequently. Slight discrepancies in the above (as in 1 and 5) might be accounted for by our interpretations of the Russian categories of mental retardation.

Mediation of verbal and abstract behavior.—A third study by O'Connor and Hermelin (1959*b*) is concerned with the problem of meaningful-word associations in moderately retarded children. The upshot of this fairly complicated study is that semantic generalization can be arranged to occur in a verbal-learning experiment and, if this is done, that *three months* later generalized meaningful associations will predominate on a relevant word-association test. Yet, when not preceded by specific training, meaningful associations occur no more often than unconnected associations, and "clang" associations are rare. This last set of findings is close to what has been reported in other word association experiments with defectives (Otis, 1915; Horan, 1956). If the above findings hold up, the implications for training the retarded are clear: meaningful mediators can be established and can be expected to last.

Closely related to this last study is one by Berkson and Cantor (1960) already referred to under pictorial rote-learning. They also found that the mentally retarded benefited from mediational training and that the amount of benefit was not particularly related to IQ level, which was true in the restricted IQ range of the O'Connor-Hermelin study too. In the Berkson-Cantor study the experimental groups learned three lists of paired associates according to the paradigm (A-B, B-C, A-C) in contrast with the control groups' paradigm (X-B, B-C, A-C). In line with a mediation hypothesis, the experimentals learned the third list, A-C, significantly faster than did the controls. The authors mention as a flaw in their design the fact that odd numbers were used more often as stimuli in the experimental groups than in the controls. Nevertheless, it seems unlikely that such a slight procedural difference could have generated their results. Furthermore, Bensberg (1957), as mentioned earlier,

was also successful in getting the mentally retarded to acquire and use mediators.

Griffith and Spitz (1958) and Griffith, Spitz, and Lipman (1959) have elucidated the role of verbal mediators in concept formation in the mentally retarded. Given an abstraction test involving triads of nouns such as carrots, peaches, meat and elephant, mountain, whale, seventeen-year-old retardates, in general, fail to achieve an acceptable abstraction unless they also use the appropriate abstraction in subsequent definitions of at least two of the three words of a triad (both the abstraction test and the following definition test contained decoy words). On the other hand, normal children matched on MA with the adolescent retarded (MA = 9–10) were highly successful in making an abstraction when only one word of a triad was subsequently defined in terms of the abstraction. When seven-year-old normals were compared with the same group of retardates, however, there was essentially no difference. In point of language development the retarded seem about three years behind their MA. When the brighter half and the lower half of the retarded group were considered separately the high group was frequently capable of making an abstraction when only one or even zero words were defined by a possible abstraction, though it was still inferior to the normal.

In a follow-up of the foregoing study Miller and Griffith (1961) gave retarded adolescents specific training in giving associations to the four concepts which had given the most difficulty on the abstraction task. Regardless of whether the associations elicited were differentially reinforced or relevant to the eventual abstraction task, the training had a facilitative effect on an abstraction test given seven days later. But this was true only for the words specifically covered in training; there was no general transfer effect.

For the most part, without having explicit mediators available to him the retarded cannot abstract. In this sense there is a similarity to O'Connor and Hermelin's finding that retardates make predominantly meaningful associations only when meaningful associates are previously made available to them. This notion of availability will be reconsidered when the problem of retention is discussed.

Two studies by Osler and Firel (1961) and Osler and Trautman (1961) also show that among a normal population the ability to learn a concept and use a concept plus the degree to which verbal mediation is used for coping with a complex stimulus situation is directly related to intelligence. Superior individuals excel over normals.

Most of the remaining studies in this area (Dolphin and Cruickshank, 1951; Stacey and Portnoy, 1951; Stacey and Cantor, 1953; Korstevdt, Stacey, and Reynolds, 1954; McMurray, 1954; Levy and Cuddy, 1956; Siegal, 1957; and Weatherwax and Benoit, 1958) have used sorting tests or categorizing tasks and frequently the subjects have been required to verbalize a concept. On the whole, the mentally or educationally retarded are more concrete in their approach, show greater rigidity, and make more errors than normals, at least of the same CA. This fits with Thompson's normative data on sorting tasks for normal children through the first six grades (1941). The oldest children formed the most acceptable categories and generalizations while the youngsest classified things concretely or not at all. The organic retardates do not always come out at the bottom and might benefit from training on conceptualizing (Weatherwax and Benoit, 1958).

Verbal reasoning or problem-solving in the mentally retarded is practically an untouched area, but Johnson and Blake (1960) have given a series of pictorial analogy problems to normals and retard-

ates (CA = 13) matched on MA (8–10). Five series of ten problems each were presented, with the first five problems of each series corrected as the subject proceeded. For each series a different principle was capable of being abstracted and applied. For example, for each problem there were three pictures: the key-picture with two figures, the test-picture with but one figure, and the answer-picture with three alternative figures. Assume that in the key-picture the figure on the right is large, the one on the left is small, and shape is irrelevant. Then for the test-picture the mate to be selected from among the three alternatives should maintain this size relationship. Despite the similarity of this task to the concept-formation task of Griffith and his co-workers, there was no significant difference between normals and retarded in the number of correct solutions, and though normals, according to a behavioral criterion, abstracted the principle more frequently (mean of 2.48 vs. 1.96 out of a possible 5), the difference was not significant. Rather the data lean a bit toward the oddity-problem data of Ellis and Sloan (1959) where the normals' final performance was comparable to the retardates' (groups matched on MA). Taking all the data into account, the Johnson-Blake analogy tests appear to fall between the concept formation problem and the oddity-problem with regard to degree of verbalization required and thus with regard to difficulty for the retarded.

All in all a LOW-IQ deficit in the area of verbal mediation receives considerable substantiation.

PERFORMANCE

MOTOR SKILLS

In 1917 Woodrow found that mentally retarded adolescents with IQ's of 50 and above were not inferior to normals of the same MA on sorting and cancellation speed tests. In another early study with retardates the amount of improvement in learning to throw darts was not related in any simple way to MA level (Johnson, 1919). Let us first examine the few data where the retarded have been matched with normals on MA.

Johnson and Blake (1960) using public school retardates (MA between 50 and 75) matched on MA with normal school children actually found that the retarded did significantly better than the normals on a simple card-sorting task. The subjects distributed thirty-two shuffled cards containing four different geometrical designs into four separate boxes. On all five trials given, the retarded sorted faster but the slopes of the learning curves for the two groups were parallel. In such a simple situation it appears that the older, more muscularly mature retarded school children have an advantage over the younger normals. That the learning curves of both groups leveled off by the third trial but at significantly different levels suggests both the simplicity of the task and a differential age factor of motor co-ordination (speed). When these groups learned puzzle-assembly tasks the retarded also did as well as if not better than the normals.

By virtue of the developmental rotary-Pursuit data on normals, collected by Ammons, Alprin, and Ammons (1955), it is possible to compare retarded and normals on rotary-pursuit performance when matched on MA (rotary-pursuit data are typically quite stable and relatively independent of laboratory and experimenter differences). When the rotary-pursuit data of Ellis and Sloan (1957) on retardates with mean MA's of 6.3 and 9.4 years are compared with the data on eight- to nine-year-old normals under comparable practice conditions, the match is excellent. The Ammons, Alprin, and Ammons data fall just about in the middle of the two performance curves for the retarded group, which themselves are quite close together. Thus, when an MA control is used or available there appears to be no evidence for a LOW-IQ deficit in motor-learning.

The remaining studies compare the retarded and normals when matched on CA- or correlate MA-level with performance in adult or adolescent retardates. If the task is at all difficult this type of study indicates a LOW-MA-LOW-IQ deficit. But probably of greater moment are two related trends that stand out: (1) Mental retardates, excluding the severely retarded, initially exhibit a deficit but with practice improve more rapidly than normals and sometimes catch up with them. (2) As the difficulty of the task increases, the importance of intelligence increases, and despite faster improvement the retarded are unable to make up the difference.

One of the earliest studies to bring the first point to light was that of Holman (1933), using a ball and slot test which emphasized kinesthetic control (tipping a board to aim the ball into the correct slot). She compared thirteen-year-old normals (IQ = 103; N = 18) with thirty-three mental retardates of the same CA (IQ = 58) on learning this task over a four-week period (four practice periods of two hundred shots each per week). At the beginning of practice, the difference in favor of the normals was large and significant but, by the fourth day, was small and non-significant and, by the third week, was practically gone. The retardates who started as well as the normals attained a higher final score than the normal group, and normals who started as poorly as the retardates did not reach as high a final score as the retarded group.

As indirect evidence in support of the same point, Brace (1948), in a physical education setting, evaluated well-practiced athletic skills in mentally retarded girls and found a negligible r with IQ.

Boldt (1953) compared sixty defectives, thirty males and thirty females (CA = 15–30; IQ = 50), with sixty college students, thirty males and thirty females, on a block-turning task which consisted of turning over ten blocks for thirty consecutive trials. Subjects were run either under massed or spaced practice with differently weighted blocks. The superiority of the college students under all conditions was marked but under spaced practice where improvement occurred, the retarded *improved* faster and more than the college student. Weighting the blocks was an irrelevant variable.

Tizard and Loos (1954) had six adult retardates practice for eight trials on each of the four boards of the Minnesota Spatial Relations Test and compared their initial and final performance with the published norms. By the third trial the mean time on the first board had been more than halved, cut by 815 seconds, and dropped 191 more by the eighth trial. Performance on the fourth board practiced was best of all. When retested one month later on all four boards under standard test-administration conditions, the retarded did only slightly poorer than at the end of original practice and when compared with the norms now did as well as the normal population.

The results of Reynolds and Stacey (1955) for a mirror drawing experiment are in the same vein. Sixty normals, 30 male and 30 female, were compared with 108 retardates divided into three groups of 36, 18 male and 18 female, on the basis of IQ. The three groups had IQ ranges of 50–59, 60–69, and 70–79. All subjects were between fifteen years and fifteen years, six months old. A six-pointed star made up of sixty small circles was used with instructions to hit all the circles with the pencil. On the very first trial (non-preferred hand) the lowest IQ group took more than three times as long to traverse the star as the normal group (over seven hundred seconds), and the females of the 60–69 group took over twice as long as the normals. After this first trial, all groups were split in two, one-half of the group receiving ten trials with the preferred hand (experimentals)

and the other half receiving a rest (controls). All groups then received a second trial with the non-preferred hand. The 50–59 control group's time on the second trial was almost one-fifth of the first trial while the normals' time was a little less than one-half of the first trial. The 70–79 group of experimental males whose time at the start was about double that of the normal males actually ended up on the transfer test to the non-preferred hand as slightly superior to the normal males (fifty-four vs. fifty-seven seconds). Admittedly, these comparisons are selected as the more startling but they serve to highlight the general picture. The above is best summarized by two correlation coefficients which held for the total sample: $r = -0.54$ between IQ and time taken on the very first trial (non-preferred hand), $r = +0.98$ between time on first trial and gain in seconds (drop). At this point it is pertinent to mention a seeming discrepancy between the findings of Ellis, Barnett, and Pryer (1957) in another mirror drawing experiment and those of Reynolds and Stacey. In the former study they found no correlation between time taken on first trial and IQ ($r = 0.01$) but a significant r with errors. A procedural difference is quite crucial however. Ellis, Barnett, and Pryer used a simple pathway and cautioned their subjects to stay on the path. With such a procedure, in the reviewer's experience, time does not reflect errors (proficiency); whereas if the subject is required to touch each 4-cm. circle as in the Reynolds-Stacey experiment, then time is an accurate reflection of errors. Thus there is no real discrepancy between the two studies.

In a practical setting, Clarke and Hermelin (1955) have observed the same sort of improvement. Retardates given adequate training can learn such tasks as folding cardboard boxes, cutting insulated wire to exact lengths, and soldering four different colored wires to the terminals of an eight-pin television plug.

They work for long periods at these tasks, even without supervision, contributing substantially to their keep.

Closely related to this improvement phenomenon are the data on motivation and incentives in the performance of the mentally retarded. A number of studies demonstrate that setting goals for the subjects and providing praise and encouragement result in heightened performance and continued improvement (Gordon, O'Connor, and Tizard, 1954; O'Connor and Claridge, 1955; and Ellis and Distefano, 1959).

The second point, on the interaction of task difficulty and intelligence, is nicely illustrated by the comparison of two rotary-pursuit studies. Barnett and Cantor (1957) studied rotary pursuit performance in a single group of mental retardates (CA = 14–48 and mean = 27.4; MA = 5 years, 7 months, to 10 years, 2 months, mean = 7 years, 1 month) and found no relationship with MA level. The effects of massing and spacing and rest were also investigated, and the retarded exhibited all the typical rotary-pursuit phenomena except warmup: better performance under spaced conditions, clear-cut reminiscence, and shifting of performance levels when conditions of massing and spacing were switched. The main point, however, is that the turntable in this experiment rotated at only 30 rpm, one-half the customary speed. With 30 rpm the task is extremely simple; for example, the retardates after ten minutes of spaced practice were on target 67 per cent of the time, while with the rotor moving at 60 rpm, college students under comparable conditions only attain about 25 per cent time on target. In effect, if the task is simple enough, retardates do not even appear to exhibit a LOW-MA-LOW-IQ deficit.

These data stand in sharp contrast to those of Ellis and Sloan (1957*b*) where the pursuit rotor traveled at 60 rpm. Here there is a sharp difference between MA groupings; and the *r* between MA and rotary-pursuit performance with CA partialed out is 0.43. These investigators studied three MA levels with equal CA (MA's = 3.6, 6.3, and 9.4). Given twenty-second trials with twenty-second inter-trial intervals, the lowest group showed no learning whatsoever while the groups comparable to Barnett and Cantor's on MA level, though they showed continued improvement, reached only 5 per cent time on target in six minutes and forty seconds. This compares with at least 20 per cent for typical normal data and an estimated 50 to 60 per cent for the 30-rpm data on the retarded.

In other words, when the task is fairly difficult, there is now clear evidence of a LOW-MA-LOW-IQ deficit but, as discussed previously, the very same data assert no LOW-IQ deficit.

Probably the most straightforward analysis of the difficulty issue is presented by Annett (1957). Using information theory and the concepts of time and motion study, he varied the information load on the reach element in a peg-board task. Based on the number of alternatives from which the subject must choose to select the correct peg, four different conditions prevailed (from easiest to hardest): no bits of information (no choice), one bit (two alternatives), two bits (four alternatives), and three bits (eight alternatives). A total of seventy-two male retardates from sixteen to twenty-one years of age was divided equally into three IQ levels: IQ 60 and over, IQ 40–59, IQ below 40. Under the zero-bit condition there were no significant differences in time to complete the reach element, though the times ordered themselves according to IQ level (shortest time for highest IQ). As the number of bits increased, time to reach increased linearly for all groups but at different slopes, increasing most for the most severely retarded group and least for the high-grade group. That is, the performance curves diverged and, over-all, the low-grade group did more poorly than the high-grade group. The slopes differed significantly, or, to put it another way, there was a significant interaction between intelligence and difficulty.

Annett then used the same task in a learning experiment on thirty-six of the same subjects. Because of the small N per IQ level, the data are only suggestive; but, in accord with our first point, the most retarded showed the greatest degree of improvement of all three groups, and this was true for all elements of the task, reach, grasp, transport, and assemble. Yet after a great deal of practice the groups at the end were still apart.

Standardized performance tests also demonstrate the interaction of task difficulty and level of intelligence. The more operations involved in the Purdue Pegboard task, the more the adult retarded sample deviates from the published norms (Cantor and Stacey, 1951). On the Oseretsky Tests of Motor Proficiency as the task becomes more complex or requires more integrative activity, as rationally determined, there appears to be a greater relationship with IQ level (Sloan, 1951). On both the Purdue Pegboard and the Oseretsky Tests of Motor Proficiency the adult retardates were generally and significantly below the adult norms.

REACTION TIME AND BASAL
SKIN CONDUCTANCE

The data are almost completely consistent in pointing to a reaction-time deficit in the mentally retarded. As early as 1915, Ordahl and Ordahl had noted a negative correlation between simple reaction time (RT) and MA. Pascal (1953) testing twenty retardates ranging in CA from 5 years, 11 months, to 30 years, 10 months, and MA from 2 years, 1 month, to 7 years, 1 month, found an r of −0.61 between MA and reaction time. Ellis and Sloan (1957a) tested seventy-nine retardates (CA = 10.3–19.5; MA = 3.7–12.2)

and found a correlation of −0.54 between MA and reaction time. The relationship was linear and independent of CA. Reaction time was more variable for the lowest MA's. Bensberg and Cantor (1958) found a negative r between MA and reaction time in twenty-four organic subjects but it was not significant. But in twenty-four familials the r between MA and RT and the r between MA and disjunctive reaction time were −0.57 and −0.64, respectively. The familials were superior to the organics on simple-reaction time and disjunctive-reaction time and significantly more so on the latter. Others, using normal populations as well (Peak and Boring 1926; McFarland, 1930; Scott, 1940), have gotten substantially the same results. The only exception is a recent study by Wolfensberger (1960) who reports no significant r between simple reaction time and IQ. A possible reason for this discrepancy is that Wolfensberger's sample presumably included few retarded with MA's below six or seven years. His sixty subjects ranged in CA from eleven to fifty with a mean age of twenty-four and had a mean IQ of 59. According to both Pascal (1953) and Scott (1940) the relationship between MA and reaction time is curvilinear leveling off at MA's above six or seven, though Ellis and Sloan report a rectilinear relationship. It is also quite possible that many of the older subjects had the higher IQ's, which would effectively camouflage a negative correlation between reaction time and IQ, since reaction time increases with age. Wolfensberger also reports that prizes or poker chips or their removal had no noticeable effect on speed of reaction time, in contrast to the positive findings of Heber (1957).

According to Travis and Young (1930) there is no correlation between speed of reflex (patellar and Achilles) and IQ. Thus what does a slow reaction time in the retarded mean? For one, we know, that a fast reaction time requires maintaining good attention or an appropriate set. Thus to the extent the mental retardate has an attention and/or inhibition deficit reaction time would be longer and more variable, per Ellis and Sloan. In fact, Cruse (1961) has recently supplied us with experimental data which clearly support this position. Therefore, the reaction-time data may well relate to the findings on conditioning, discrimination-learning, etc.

In 1956 O'Connor and Venables (1956) reported a significant negative correlation of −0.40 between Binet IQ and the basal level of skin conductance (GSR) in forty retarded women. Eighteen male retardates also had a significantly higher conductance level than normals. Ellis and Sloan (1958) countered with the finding of no significant correlation between MA or IQ and basal conductance in the mentally retarded (IQ = 25–83), but they did find a significantly higher conductance in retardates than normals. Then Collman (1959) entered the fray, testing 827 thirteen- and fourteen-year-old children ranging in IQ from 45 to 140, and stated that *both* the retarded and the bright have lower conductance than the dull-normal range but presumably for different reasons (maximum GSR was estimated at 90 IQ). The psychological significance of all these data is certainly not very clear but one hypothesis that could be offered, similar to Collman's, is based on how people of different IQ levels might interpret the elaborate testing procedure and equipment involved in measuring skin conductance. The retardate is likely to be nonplused by it all and therefore not particularly anxious; the average normal and dull are likely to recognize the electrical paraphernalia and be frightened; and the bright, because they understand pretty well what is going in, are relatively calm, yielding the Collman cycle of low GSR, high GSR, low GSR.

ATTEMPT AT INTEGRATION AND
SUGGESTIONS FOR
RESEARCH

Since an attempt to integrate has been going on throughout the chapter, only integrative material that has so far been omitted or is directly related to research suggestions will be dealt with in this section.

The performance-learning data have interesting implications tying in with the earlier material and demand early attention. If the retarded individual is capable of learning so well (Reynolds and Stacey, 1955; Tizard and Loos, 1954) why is he so bad at the start? One obvious answer is because of poor retention, at least long-term retention. Since the data on long-term retention in the retarded are practically nil it is hard to answer this question; but when the few studies which include retention data are reviewed a retention deficit is either non-existent or fairly small, for instance, Eisman (1958), Tizard and Loos (1954), Gordon, O'Connor, and Tizard (1954), O'Connor and Claridge (1955), Johnson and Blake (1960), Wischner, Braun, and Patton (1962), and Ellis, Pryer, and Barnett (1960). Let us look a bit more closely at the last two studies, until now unmentioned, as illustrative of the indeterminate status of a retention deficit in the mentally retarded.

The long-term retention study of object-quality learning sets by Wischner, Braun, and Patton indicated fairly good retention by retarded (IQ = 68) over a 6 month period but there was no comparison with normals. When transferred to an oddity learning-set problem these subjects did not do significantly better than naïve subjects of the same CA-MA-IQ level. Ellis, Pryer, and Barnett measured retention on the rotary pursuit task in both normals and mentally retarded after 1 and 28 days and, though the normals retained relatively more after 28 days than did the retardates, the difference was not marked.

Heber in an as yet unpublished study, using nonsense form stimuli and nonsense syllables for responses (paired-associates), has found that a retention deficit in the retarded shows up more markedly over a long retention interval than a short interval but that this differential can be significantly reduced by having all subjects overlearn the original material.

To the extent a retention deficit may exist in the mentally retarded the present reviewer favors a "peanut brittle hypothesis" over a "leaky bucket hypothesis." That is, the defective probably *has* the associations but they are not available to him as well differentiated or appropriate responses (all stick together). This is illustrated by the occurrence of frequent unconnected responses on word-association tests (Otis, 1915; Horan, 1956) and by the fact that the retarded do significantly poorer than MA controls on recognition but not on relearning of a nonsense syllable list (Johnson and Blake, 1960).

Before any opinions can legitimately be held about a retention deficit, a great deal of research, particularly on long-term retention, must be done. Yet in view of the fact that what data there are do not support any sizable retention deficit, another possibility does gain priority. Perhaps, the retarded are poor performers because they are much poorer incidental learners than normals. Perhaps they learn little in the ordinary course of events, requiring special stimulation, guidance, and motivation to learn effectively. To the reviewer's knowledge very few studies have been done specifically on incidental learning in the mentally retarded. Otherwise, the closest thing to incidental learning studies is the learning-set experiments where the retarded do manifest a deficit, but even here what the subject is learning is closely related to the task at hand. Thus with

hardly a shred of direct evidence we suggest an incidental learning deficit, which in turn may be basically an attention deficit. It sounds so conveniently plausible.

Experimental tests of this hypothesis should not be difficult, although arranging a situation which is sufficiently ordinary for the retardates so as not to possess extra attention value may pose a problem. For instance, by using an orientation task in which the retarded and CA and MA controls sort a variety of forms according to color we could then test them on the recall or recognition of shapes.[1] Closer to everyday incidental learning might be the following: While the subject is playing or otherwise engaged in a room, about a dozen people walk into the room individually, stay for thirty seconds being sure to be perceived by the subject and then leave. Young boys who enter wear white shirts, men wear blue shirts, girls all have plain dresses, and the women all have on jackets. This is followed by an immediate recognition test with boys in blue shirts, women in plain dresses, etc., plus the original dozen. Ask the subjects which people had previously walked into the room.

In a modification of this design using female college students as incidental stimuli and then photographs for the recognition test, the present author found that the hypothesized incidental learning deficit showed up in educable retarded significantly or most clearly after a two-week retention period. Goldstein and Kass (1961) in a recent study, comparing the educable retarded with the gifted, found that the mentally retarded chil-

[1] In a very recently published study, where such a design was used by Hetherington (formerly Plenderleith) and Banta (1962), it was shown that non-institutionalized educable organics (IQ 50 and above) manifested a significant incidental learning deficit when compared with normals, whereas educable familials did not. On intentional learning of the object-picture material all three groups performed essentially alike, à la Eisman (1958).

dren were quite capable of incidental learning but were significantly less accurate than nursery school gifted of the same MA, that is, made more incorrect responses though the same number of correct responses as the gifted child.

Further support for an incidental learning deficit actually exists in the literature on the normal college student. According to Plenderleith and Postman (1956), IQ is more clearly correlated positively with measures of incidental learning than with measures of intentional learning.

The incidental learning hypothesis seems closely related to a suggestion of Benoit (1957), which stems from a Hebbian analysis. Benoit says that the retarded lack integrative sets or phase sequences and need to be guided gradually into formal training. Or, as we are saying it, if the retardate fails to learn many things incidentally he is not going to be ready at eight years of age for formal schooling. He needs to learn what the normal three- and four-year-olds have already learned before he is ready.

In Benoit's framework the retardate tends to be a stimulus-bound organism—responding to the stimulus of the moment rather than to internal maintaining stimuli or sets. Thus, if this is the case, he will not respond *consistently* or repeatedly in an ordinary situation. Since, according to Denny and Adelman, *consistent* responding is necessary for differential learning it follows from the elicitation framework that little incidental learning will take place in the retarded. On the other hand, with a definite US, with an appropriate set of instructions, or with rewards, consistent responding should occur and the retardate should now learn a specific response. Furthermore, since there is evidence that he does not satiate (fatigue, adapt) along a number of dimensions as rapidly as the normal (Kounin, 1941; Zigler, Hodgden, and Stevenson, 1958; Spitz and Blackman, 1959; Blackman, 1960; Lipman and Spitz,

1961; Stevenson and Knight, 1961) it follows that his learned responses will often become fixated (per data on perseveration, position habits, high resistance to extinction) or continue to improve (per motor-skills data). That is, once a response is learned in the retarded it may be more impervious to the inhibitory effects of repeated stimulation or repeated responding. This last bit of speculation means you are still left with an individual who is different from the normal but not as different as if he had hardly learned at all.

The paradox that the retardate seems to have an attention deficit and yet satiates more slowly to stimuli than the normal is not irreconcilable. Perseveration seems to be characteristic of the retarded only after the response is well learned or when the response is dictated by instructions which the retarded can follow. Without a special set, which he typically lacks, the retarded individual appears to be at the beck and call of the stimuli around him, even though he may satiate slowly to them.

SUMMARY

A review of the literature indicates rather conclusively the following performance deficits in the mentally retarded:

1. An inhibition deficit is manifested by increased resistance to extinction in classical conditioning, difficulty in discrimination-learning (including differential conditioning), and special susceptibility to disinhibition or distraction.

2. A defect in complex learning is exhibited in poor performance on learning set, delayed reaction, and double alternation.

3. Difficulty in verbal learning is reflected in poor performance in verbal rote learning and abstraction tasks.

4. A lack of verbal control of the motor sphere is congruent with poor semantic conditioning, difficulty in following verbal instructions, ease of learning and

lack of verbalization in discrimination reversal, possibly with poor performance on a shielded maze, and possibly with the ease of conditioning finger withdrawal.

On the positive side of the ledger we note the following:

1. When matched on CA with normals, retardates do very poorly at the outset on motor skill tasks but with continued practice show a rapid rate of improvement and, if the task is not too difficult, may even catch up with the normals (can learn if properly motivated or make the required responses).

2. In rote learning, if familiar nonverbal material is used, an association seems to be established as quickly and retained about as well as in the normals, at least for non-institutionalized subjects.

3. There is little evidence of an appreciable retention deficit in any performance area.

4. The retarded can learn to use verbal mediators when specifically trained to do so.

The outlook for the mentally retarded is surprisingly optimistic—at least theoretically. It should be possible to develop appropriate motivational procedures and special training techniques to overcome an appreciable portion of the retardates' difficulties, at least to the extent that they relate to the closely connected deficits in incidental learning, attention, and verbal control. These defects might be amenable to correction by (1) long-term training to attend or orient to stimuli, especially verbal stimuli, and (2) motivating the retarded children sufficiently and building in what they failed to learn incidentally during the early years, as, for example, with specially designed and programmed teaching machines.

REFERENCES

ADIS-CASTRO, G., and BERGER, A. 1955. Olfactory discrimination of three etiological groups of mental deficients. *Training Sch. Bull.*, **52**:24–30.

AKUTAGAWA, D., and BENOIT, E. 1959. The effect of age and relative brightness on associative learning in children. *Child Develop.*, **30**:229–34.

ALDRICH, C. G., and DOLL, E. A. 1931a. Problem solving among idiots, *J. Comp. Physiol. Psychol.*, **12**:137–69.

————. 1931b. Problem solving among idiots: the use of implements. *J. Soc. Psychol.*, **2**:306–36.

AMMONS, R. B., ALPRIN, S. I., and AMMONS, C. H. 1955. Rotary pursuit performance as related to sex and age of pre-adult subjects. *J. Exp. Psychol.*, **49**:127–33.

AMOS, I. E. 1960. "Delayed response performance at 3 years of age among children with anoxic and non-anoxic experiences at birth." Unpublished Ph.D. dissertation, Louisiana State University; *Diss. Abstr.*

ANNETT, J. 1957. The information capacity of young mental defectives in an assembly task. *J. Ment. Sci.*, **103**:621–31.

AUERBACH, V. H., WAISMAN, H. A., and WYCKOFF, L. B. 1958. Phenylketonuria in the rat associated with decreased temporal discrimination learning. *Nature*, **182**:871–72.

BADT, M. I. 1958. Levels of abstraction in vocabulary definitions of mentally retarded school children. *Amer. J. Ment. Defic.*, **63**:241–46.

BARNETT, C. D. 1958. "Stimulus generalization in normals and retardates on a visual-spatial task requiring a voluntary response." Unpublished Ph.D. dissertation, George Peabody College for Teachers.

BARNETT, C. D., and CANTOR, G. N. 1957. Discrimination set in defectives. *Amer. J. Ment. Defic.*, **62**:334–37.

————. 1957. Pursuit motor performance in mental defectives as a function of distribution of practice. *Percept. Motor Skills*, **7**:191–97.

BARNETT, C. D., ELLIS, N. R., and PRYER, M. W. 1959. Stimulus pre-training and delayed reaction in defectives. *Amer. J. Ment. Defic.*, **64**:104–11.

————. 1960. Learning in familial and brain-injured defectives. *Ibid.*, **65**:894–901.

BARNETT, C. D., and PRYER, M. W. 1958. Note on depth perception in defectives. *Percept. Motor Skills*, **8**:139.

BEKHTEREV, V. M. 1928. *General Principles of Human Reflexology: An Introduction to the Objective Study of Personality.* Translation from 4th ed.; New York: International Publications.

BENOIT, E. P. 1957. Relevance of Hebb's theory of the organization of behavior to educational research on the mentally retarded. *Amer. J. Ment. Defic.*, **61**:497–506.

BENSBERG, G. J., JR. 1957. Concept learning in mental defectives as a function of appropriate and inappropriate "attention sets." *J. Educ. Psychol.*, **48**:137–43.

BENSBERG, G. J., and CANTOR, G. N. 1958. Reaction time in mental defectives with organic and familial etiology. *Amer. J. Ment. Defic.*, **62**:534–37.

BERGER, A. 1954. Inhibition of the eyelid reflex in three etiologic groups of mentally retarded boys as compared with normals. *Training Sch. Bull.*, **51**:146–52.

BERKSON, G., and CANTOR, G. N. 1960. A study of mediation in mentally retarded and normal school children. *J. Educ. Psychol.*, **51**:82–86.

BIALER, I. 1961. Primary and secondary stimulus generalization as related to intelligence level. *J. Exp. Psychol.*, **62**:395–402.

BLACKMAN, L. S. 1960. Fatigue processes: their role in theory unification and understanding mental retardation. *NARC Conference on Learning in Mental Retardation,* Los Angeles.

BOLDT, R. F. 1953. Motor learning in college students and mental defectives. *Proc. Iowa Acad. Sci.*, **60**:500–505.

BRACE, D. K. 1948. Motor learning in feeble-minded girls. *Res. Quart.*, **19**:269–75.

CANTOR, G. N., and HOTTEL, J. V. 1955. Discrimination learning in mental defectives as a function of magnitude of food reward and intelligence level. *Amer. J. Ment. Defic.*, **60**:380–84.

———. 1957. Psychomotor learning in defectives as a function of verbal pretraining. *Psychol. Rec.*, **7**:79–85.

CANTOR, G. N., and STACEY, C. L. 1951. Manipulative dexterity in mental defectives. *Amer. J. Ment. Defic.*, **56**:401–10.

CASSELL, R. H. 1957. Serial verbal learning and retroactive inhibition in aments and children. *J. Clin. Psychol.*, **13**:369–72.

CLARKE, A. D. B., and HERMELIN, B. P. 1955. Adult imbeciles: their abilities and trainability. *Lancet*, **2**:337–40.

COLLMAN, R. D. 1959. The G.S.R. of mentally retarded and other children in England. *Amer. J. Ment. Defic.*, **63**:626–32.

COOPER, R. M., and ZUBEK, J. P. 1958. Effects of enriched and restricted early environments on the learning ability of bright and dull rats. *Canad. J. Psychol.*, **12**:159–64.

CORNIL, L., and GOLDENFOUN, F. 1928. Sur les réflexes associatifs chez les enfants anormaux. *C. R. Soc. Biol.*, **99**:406–9.

CROMWELL, R. L., PALK, B. F., and FOSHEE, J. G. 1961. Studies in activity level: V. Relationship of eyelid conditioning to intelligence and activity level. *Amer. J. Ment. Defic.*, **65**:744–48.

CRUSE, D. B. 1961. The effects of distraction upon performance by brain-injured and familial retarded children. *Amer. J. Ment. Defic.*, **66**:86–92.

DEHAAN, H. J. 1960. "An experimental evaluation of two methods for the formation of learning sets in retarded children." Unpublished Ph.D. dissertation, University of Pittsburgh.

DENNY, M. R., and ADELMAN, H. M. 1955. Elicitation theory: I. An analysis of two typical learning situations. *Psychol. Rev.*, **62**:290–96.

DESANCTIS, S. 1931. Visual apprehension on the maze behavior of normal and feeble-minded children. *J. Genet. Psychol.*, **39**:463–67.

DOLL, E. A., and ALDRICH, C. G. 1932. Simple conditioning as a method of studying sensory discrimination among idiots. *J. Gen. Psychol.*, **39**:104–42.

DOLPHIN, J. E., and CRUICKSHANK, W. M. 1951. Pathology of concept formation in children with cerebral palsy. *Amer. J. Ment. Defic.*, **56**:386–92.

DUFORT, R. H., GUTTMAN, N., and KIMBLE, G. A. 1954. One-trial discrimination reversal in the white rat. *J. Comp. Physiol. Psychol.*, **47**:248–49.

EISMAN, B. S. L. 1958. Paired associate learning, generalization and retention as a function of intelligence. *Amer. J. Ment. Defic.*, **63**:481–89.

ELLIS, N. R. 1958. Object-quality discrimination learning sets in mental defectives. *J. Comp. Physiol. Psychol.*, **51**:79–81.

ELLIS, N. R., BARNETT, C. D., and PRYER, M. W. 1957. Performance of mental defectives on the mirror drawing task. *Percept. Motor Skills*, **7**:271–74.

———. 1960. Operant behavior in mental defectives: exploratory studies. *J Exp. Anal. Behav.*, **3**:63–69.

ELLIS, N. R., and DISTEFANO, M. K. 1959. Effects of verbal urging and praise upon rotary pursuit performance in mental defectives. *Amer. J. Ment. Defic.*, **64**:486–90.

ELLIS, N. R., and PRYER, M. W. 1958. Primary versus secondary reinforcement in simple discrimination learning of mental defectives. *Psychol. Rep.*, **4**:67–70.

ELLIS, N. R., PRYER, M. W., and BARNETT, C. D. 1960. Motor learning and retention in normals and defectives. *Percept. Motor Skills*, **10**:83–91.

ELLIS, N. R., PRYER, R. S., DISTEFANO, M. K., and PRYER, M. W. 1960. Learning in mentally defective, normal and superior subjects. *Amer. J. Ment. Defic.*, **64**:725–34.

ELLIS, N. R., and SLOAN, W. 1957a. Relationship between intelligence and simple reaction time in mental defectives. *Percept. Motor Skills*, **7**:65–67.

———. 1957b. Rotary pursuit performance as a function of mental age. *Ibid.*, **7**:267–70.

———. 1958. The relationship between intelligence and skin conductance. *Amer. J. Ment. Defic.*, **63**:304–6.

———. 1959. Oddity learning as a function of mental age. *J. Comp. Physiol. Psychol.*, **52**:228–30.

FOSHEE, J. G. 1958. Studies in activity level: I. Simple and complex task performance in defectives. *Amer. J. Ment. Defic.*, **62**:882–86.

FRANKS, V. and FRANKS, C. M. 1962. Classical conditioning proceduress as an index of vocational adjustment among mental defectives. *Percept. Motor Skills*, **14**:241–42.

FULLER, P. R. 1949. Operant conditioning of a vegetative human organism. *Amer. J. Psychol.*, **62**:587–89.

GAKKEL, L. B., MOLOLKOVA, I. A., and TROFIMOV, N. M. 1957. Experimental study of nervous processes in oligophrenics. *Zhurnal Visshei Nervnoi Deyatelmosti*, **7**:495; *Psycol. Abst.*, **32**:5649.

GALLAGHER, J. T. 1957. A comparison of brain-injured and non-brain-injured mentally retarded children on several psychological variables. *Monogr. Res. Child Develop.*, **22**, Ser. No. 65, No. 2.

GARDNER, L. P. 1945. The learning of low grade aments. *Amer. J. Ment. Defic.*, **50**:59–80.

GARDNER, W. I., CROMWELL, R. L., and FOSHEE, J. G. 1959. Studies in activity level: II. Effects of distal visual stimulation in organics, familials, hyperactives, and hypoactives. *Amer. J. Ment. Defic.*, **63**:1023–33.

GELLERMAN, L. W. 1933a. Change orders of alternating stimuli in visual discrimination experiments. *J. Genet. Psychol.*, **42**:206–8.

———. 1933b. Form discrimination in chimpanzees and two-year-old children. I. Form (triangularity) per se. *Ibid.*, **42**:3–27.

GIRARDEAU, F. L. 1959. The formation of discrimination learning sets in mongoloid and normal children. *J. Comp. Physiol. Psychol.*, **52**:566–70.

GOLDSTEIN, H., and KASS, C. 1961. Incidental learning of educable mentally retarded and gifted children. *Amer. J. Ment. Defic.*, **66**:245–49.

GORDON, S., O'CONNOR, N., and TIZARD, J. 1954. Some effects of incentives on the performance of imbeciles. *Brit. J. Psychol.*, **45**:277–87.

GRIFFITH, B. C., and SPITZ, H. H. 1958. Some relationships between abstraction and word meanings in retarded adolescents. *Amer. J. Ment. Defic.*, **63**:247–51.

GRIFFITH, B. C., SPITZ, H. H., and LIPMAN, R. E. 1959. Verbal mediation and concept formation in retarded and normal subjects. *J. Exp. Psychol.*, **58**:247–50.

HALPIN, V. C. 1955. Rotation errors made by brain-injured and familial children on two visual-motor tests. *Amer. J. Ment. Defic.*, **59**:485–89.

HAMILTON, G. V. 1911. Trial and error reactions in mammals. *J. Anim. Behav.*, **1**:33–66.

HARLOW, H. F. 1945. Studies in discrimination learning in monkeys: V. Initial performance by experimentally naïve monkeys on stimulus-object and pattern discriminations. *J. Genet. Psychol.*, **33**:3–10.

———. 1950. Analysis of discrimination learning by monkeys. *J. Exp. Psychol.*, **40**:26–39.

HARLOW, H. F., and ISRAEL, R. H. 1932. Comparative behavior of primates: IV. Delayed reaction tests on subnormal humans. *J. Comp. Psychol.*, **14**:253–63.

HAYES, K. J., THOMPSON, R., and HAYES, C. 1953. Discrimination learning set in chimpanzees. *J. Comp. Physiol. Psychol.*, **46**:99–107.

HEBER, R. F. 1957. "Expectancy and expectancy changes in normal and mentally retarded boys." Unpublished Ph.D. dissertation, George Peabody College for Teachers.

HERMELIN, B., and O'CONNOR, N. 1960. Like and cross modality responses in normal and subnormal children. *Quart. J. Exp.*, **12**:48–53.

HETHERINGTON, E. M., and BANTA, T. J. 1962. Incidental and intentional learning in normal and mentally retarded children. *J. Comp. Physiol. Psychol.*, **55**:402–4.

HILL, S. D. 1962. Chronological age levels at which children solve three problems varying in complexity. *Percept. Motor Skills*, **14**:254.

HOLMAN, P. 1933. The relation between general mental development and manual dexterity. *Brit. J. Psychol.*, **23**:279–83.

HORAN, E. M. 1956. Word association frequency tables of mentally retarded children. *J. Consult. Psychol.*, **20**:22.

HOUSE, B. J., ORLANDO, R., and ZEAMAN, D. 1957. Role of positive and negative cues in the discrimination learning of mental defectives. *Percept. Motor Skills*, **7**:73–79.

HOUSE, B. J., and ZEAMAN, D. 1958a. Visual discrimination learning in imbeciles. *Amer. J. Ment. Defic.*, **63**:447–52.

———. 1958b. A comparison of discrimination learning in normal and mentally defective children. *Child Develop.*, **29**:411–16.

———. 1958c Reward and nonreward in the discrimination learning of imbeciles. *J. Comp. Physiol. Psychol.*, **51**:614–18.

———. 1959. Position discrimination and reversals in low-grade retardates. *Ibid.*, **52**:564–65.

———. 1960. Visual discrimination learning and intelligence in defectives of low MA. *Amer. J. Ment. Defic.*, **65**:51–58.

HOUSE, B. J., ZEAMAN, D., and FISCHER, W. 1957. *Learning and Transfer in Mental Defectives*. Progress Report No. 1. Research Grant M-1099 NIMH.

JACOBS, A. 1950. "Performance of children in a discrimination problem." Unpublished Ph.D. dissertation, State University of Iowa.

JOHNSON, B. 1919. Practice effects in a target test, a comparison of groups of varying intelligence. *Psychol. Rev.*, **26**:300–316.

JOHNSON, G. O., and BLAKE, K. A. 1960. *Learning Performance of Retarded and Normal Children*. Syracuse: Syracuse University Press.

KAUFMAN, M. E., and PETERSON, W. M. 1958. Acquisition of a learning set by normal and mentally retarded children. *J. Comp. Physiol. Psychol.*, **51**:619–21.

KENDLER, T. S., and KENDLER, H. H. 1959. Reversal and nonreversal shifts in kindergarten children. *J. Exp. Psychol.*, **58**:56–60.

KORSTEDT, A., STACEY, C., and REYNOLDS, W. 1954. Concept formations of normal and subnormal adolescents on a modification of the Weigl-Goldstein Scheever Color Form Sorting Test. *J. Clin. Psychol.*, **10**:88–90.

KOUNIN, J. S. 1941. Experimental studies of rigidity in normal and feeble-minded persons. *Char. Pers.*, **9**:251–73.

———. 1948. The meaning of rigidity: A reply to Heinz Werner. *Psychol. Rev.*, **55**:157–66.

KUHLMANN, F. 1904. Experimental studies in mental deficiency. *Amer. J. Psychol.*, **15**:391–446.

LEVY, N. M., and CUDDY, J. M. 1956. Concept learning in the educationally retarded child of normal intelligence. *J. Consult. Psychol.*, **20**:445–48.

LIPMAN, R. S., and SPITZ, H. 1961. The relationship between kinesthetic satiation and inhibition in rotary pursuit performance. *J. Exp. Psychol.*, **62**:468–75.

LONGNECKER, E. D., and FERSON, J. 1961. Discrimination reversal learning in mongoloids. *Amer. J. Ment. Defic.*, **66**:93–99.

LURIA, A. R. 1932. *The Nature of Human Conflicts*. Translated by W. H. GANTT. New York: Liveright.

———. 1959. Experimental study of the higher nervous activity of the abnormal child. *J. Ment. Defic. Res.*, **3**:1–22.

LURIA, A. R., and VINOGRADOVA, O. S. 1959. An objective investigation of the dynamics of semantic systems. *Brit. J. Psychol.*, **50**: 89–105.

McCULLOCH, T. L., RESWICK, J., and ROY, I. 1955. Studies of word learning in mental defectives: I. Effects of mental level and age. *Amer. J. Ment. Defic.*, **60**:133–39.

McFARLAND, R. 1930. An experimental study of the relationship between speed and mental ability. *J. Genet. Psychol.*, **3**:67–95.

McMURRAY, J. 1954. Rigidity in conceptual thinking in exogenous and endogenous mentally retarded children. *J. Consult. Psychol.*, **18**:366–70.

McPHERSON, M. W. 1948. A survey of experimental studies of learnings in individuals who achieve defective ratings on standardized psychometric measures. *Amer. J. Ment. Defic.*, **52**:232–54.

MARINESCO, G., and KREINDLER, A. 1933. Des réflexes conditionnels. *J. Psychologie*, **30**:855–86.

MATEER, F. 1918. *Child Behavior*. Boston: The Gorham Press.

MEIER, G. W., BUNCH, M. E., NOLAN, C. Y., and SCHEIDLER, C. H. 1960. Anoxia, behavioral development and learning ability: a comparative-experimental approach. *Psychol. Monogr.*, **74**:1–48.

MELHADO, J. 1949. "Irradiation and Generalization in Aments." Unpublished Master's thesis, University of New Hampshire.

METZGER, R. 1960. Probability learning in children and aments. *Amer. J. Ment. Defic.*, **64**:869–974.

MILLER, M. B., and GRIFFITH, B. C. 1961. The effects of training verbal associates on the performance of a conceptual task. *Amer. J. Ment. Defic.*, **66**:270–76.

MISHKIN, M., PROCKOP, E. S., and ROSVOLD, H. E. 1962. One-trial object-discrimination learning in monkeys with frontal lesions. *J. Comp. Physiol. Psychol.*, **55**:178–81.

MITRANO, A. J. 1939. Principles of conditioning in human goal behavior. *Psychol. Monogr.*, **51**, No. 230.

O'CONNOR, N., and CLARIDGE, G. S. 1955. The effect of goal setting and encouragement on the performance of imbecile men. *Quart. J. Exp. Psychol.*, **7**:37–45.

O'CONNOR, N., and HERMELIN, B. 1959a. Discrimination and reversal learning in imbeciles. *J. Abnorm. Soc. Psychol.*, **59**: 409–13.

———. 1959b. Some effects of word learning in imbeciles. *Sp. Lang.*, **2**:63–71.

O'CONNOR, N., and VENABLES, P. H. 1956. A note on the basal level of skin conductance and Binet I.Q. *Brit. J. Psychol.*, **47**: 148–49.

ORDAHL, L. E., and ORDAHL, G. 1915. Qualitative differences between levels of intelligence in feeble-minded children. *J. Psycho-Asthen.*, *Monogr. Suppl.*, **1**:3–50.

OSLER, S. F., and FIREL, M. W. 1961. Concept attainment: I. The role of age and intelligence in concept attainment by induction. *J. Exp. Psychol.*, **62**:1–8.

OSLER, S. F., and TRAUTMAN, G. E. 1961. Concept attainment: II. Effect of stimulus complexity upon concept attainment at two levels of intelligence. *J. Exp. Psychol.*, **62**:9–13.

OTIS, M. 1915. A study of association in defectives. *J. Educ. Pyschol.*, **6**:271–88.

PANCHENKOVA, E. F. 1956. The ontogenetic development of conditioning in the white rat. *Zh. Vssh. Nerv. Deiat.* **6**:312–18.

PASCAL, G. R. 1953. The effect of a disturbing noise on the reaction time of mental defectives. *Amer. J. Ment. Defic.*, **57**: 691–99.

PASCAL, G. R., and STOLUROW, L. M. 1952. Delayed reaction for form and place contrasted. *J. Comp. Physiol. Psychol.*, **45**: 294–99.

PASCAL, G. R., STOLUROW, L. M., ZABORENKO, R. N., and CHAMBERS, K. S. 1951. The delayed reaction in mental defectives. *Amer. J. Ment. Defic.*, **56**:152–60.

PASCAL, G. R., and ZAX, M. 1956. Double alternation performance as a measure of educability in cerebral palsied children. *Amer. J. Ment. Defic.*, **59**:658–65.

PEAK, H., and BORING, E. G. 1926. The factor of speed in intelligence. *J. Exp. Psychol.*, **9**:71–94.

PLENDERLEITH, M. 1956. Discrimination learning and discrimination reversal learning in normal and feebleminded children. *J. Genet. Psychol.*, **88**:107–12.

PLENDERLEITH, M., and POSTMAN, L. 1956. Discriminative and verbal habits in incidental learning. *Amer. J. Psychol.*, **69**: 236–43.

PRYER, R. S. 1960. Retroactive inhibition in normals and defectives as a function of temporal position of the interpolated task. *Amer. J. Ment. Defic.*, **64**:1004–11.

RAZRAN, G. H. S. 1933. Conditioned responses in children—a behavioral and quantitative critical review of experimental studies. *Arch. Psychol.* No. 148.

RESTLE, F. 1958. Toward a quantitative description of learning set data. *Psychol. Rev.*, **65**:77–91.

REYNOLDS, B. 1949. The acquisition of a black-white discrimination under two levels of reinforcement. *J. Exp. Psychol.*, **39**:760–69.

REYNOLDS, W. F., and STACEY, C. L. 1955. A comparison of normals and subnormals in mirror drawing. *J. Genet. Psychol.*, **87**: 301–8.

RING, E., and PALERMO, D. S. 1961. Paired associate learning of retarded and non-retarded children. *Amer. J. Ment. Defic.*, **66**:100–107.

SATTER, G., and CASSEL, R. H. 1955. Tactual-kinesthetic localization in the mentally retarded. *Amer. J. Ment. Defic.*, **59**:652–57.

SCHUCMAN, H. 1957. A study in the learning ability of the severely mentally retarded child: A method for obtaining a quantified index of educability for severely retarded children. *Diss. Abstr.*, **17**:2692.

SCOTT, W. S. 1940. Reaction time of young intellectual deviates. *Arch. Psychol.*, No. 256, 36.

SHIPE, D. M. 1959. A comparison of probability learning in mentally retarded and normal children. Minor Research Project. George Peabody College for Teachers.

SIEGAL, S. M. 1957. Discrimination among mental defective, normal, schizophrenic and brain-damaged subjects on the Visual-Verbal Concept Formation Test. *Amer. J. Ment. Defic.*, **62**:338–43.

SKALET, M. 1931. The significance of delayed reactions in young children. *Comp. Psychol. Monogr.*, **7**, No. 4.

SKINNER, B. F., and LINDSLEY, O. R. 1954. Studies in behavior therapy, status reports II and III. Office of Naval Research Contract N5 ori-7662.

SLOAN, W. 1951. Motor proficiency and intelligence. *Amer. J. Ment. Defic.*, **55**: 394–406.

SLOAN, W., and BERG, I. 1957. A comparison of two types of learning in mental defectives. *Amer. J. Ment. Defic.*, **61**:556–66.

SMITH, M. P., and MEANS, J. R. 1961. Effects of type of stimulus pretraining on discrimination learning in mentally retarded. *Amer. J. Ment. Defic.*, **66**:259–65.

SPENCE, K. W., and TOWNSEND, S. 1930. A comparative study of groups of high and low intelligence in learning a maze. *J. Gen. Psychol.*, **3**:113–30.

SPITZ, H. H., and BLACKMAN, L. S. 1959. Figural aftereffects and reversible figures in retardates. *J. Abnorm. Soc. Psychol.*, **58**:105–10.

STACEY, C. L., and CANTOR, G. N. 1953. The use of Zaslow's test of concept formation on a group of subnormals. *J. Clin. Psychol.*, **9**:51–53.

STACEY, C. L., and PORTNOY, B. 1951. A study of concept formation by means of the object sorting tests with subnormals. *Amer. J. Ment. Defic.*, **56**:169–73.

STEVENSON, H. W. 1960. Learning of complex problems by normal and retarded subjects. *Amer. J. Ment. Defic.*, **64**:1021–26.

STEVENSON, H. W., and ISCOE, I. 1955. Transposition in the feebleminded. *J. Exp. Psychol.*, **49**:11–15.

STEVENSON, H. W., and KNIGHT, R. M. 1961. Effect of visual reinforcement on the performance of normal and retarded children. *Percept. Motor Skills*, **13**:119–26.

STEVENSON, H. W., and LANGFORD, T. 1957. Time as a variable in transpositions by children. *Child Develop.*, **28**:365.

STEVENSON, H. W., and SWARTZ, J. W. 1958. Learning set in children as a function of intellectual level. *J. Comp. Physiol. Psychol.*, **51**:755–57.

STEVENSON, H. W., and ZIGLER, E. F. 1957. Discrimination learning and discrimination reversal in normal and feebleminded individuals. *J. Pers.*, 699–711.

STOLUROW, L. M., and PASCAL, G. R. 1950. Double alternation behavior in mental defectives. *Amer. Psychol.*, **5**:273–74 (abstract).

SWANSON, R. 1957. Perception and simultaneous tactual stimulation in defective and normal children. *Amer. J. Ment. Defic.*, **61**:743–52.

THOMPSON, J. 1941. The ability of children of different grade levels to verbalize on sorting tests. *J. Psychol.*, **11**:119–26.

THOMPSON, W. R., and HERON, W. 1954. The effects of early restriction on activity in dogs. *J. Comp. Physiol. Psychol.*, **47**: 77–82.

THOMPSON, W. R., HERON, W., and KAHN, A. 1955. Retroaction in the exploratory activity of 'bright' and 'dull' rats. *Canad. J. Psychol.*, **9**:173–82.

TIZARD, J., and LOOS, F. M. 1954. The learning of a spatial relations test by adult imbeciles. *Amer. J. Ment. Defic.*, **59**:85–90.

TRAVIS, L. E., and YOUNG, C. W. 1930. The relations of electromyographically measured reflex times in the patella and achilles reflexes to certain measurements and to intelligence. *J. Genet. Psychol.* **3**:374–400.

VINCE, M. A. 1958. "String-pulling" in birds. II. Differences related to size in greenfinches, chaffinches, and canaries. *Anim. Behav.*, **6**:53–59.

———. 1958. Effects of age and experience on the establishment of internal inhibition in finches. *Brit. J. Psychol.*, **50**:136–44.

VINOGRADOVA, O. S. 1956. Orientational reflexes in the mental defective. *Voprosy Psykhologii*, **2**:101–9.

WEATHERWAX, J., and BENOIT, E. P. 1958. Concrete and abstract thinking in organic and non-organic mentally retarded children. *Amer. J. Ment. Defic.*, **62**:548–53.

WEINSTEIN, B. 1941. Matching-from-sample by rhesus monkeys and by children. *J. Comp. Psychol.*, **31**:195–213.

WILSON, F. T. 1928. Learning of bright and dull children. *Teachers' College Contributions to Education*, No. 292.

WISCHNER, G. J., BRAUN, H., and PATTON, R. 1960. Progress reports learning set projects. University of Pittsburgh, U.S. Public Health Service.

———. 1962. Acquisition and long-term retention of an object-quality learning set by retarded children. *J. Comp. Physical Psychol.*, **55**:518–23.

WISCHNER, G. J., and O'DONNELL, J. P. 1962. Concurrent learning-set formation in normal and retarded children. *J. Comp. Physiol. Psychol.*, **55**:524–27.

WOLFENSBERGER, W. 1960. Differential rewards as motivating factors in mental deficiency research. *Amer. J. Ment. Defic.*, **64**:902–6.

WOODROW, H. 1917. Practice and transference in normal and feebleminded children. Part I: Practice. *J. Educ. Psychol.*, **8**:85–96.

ZEAMAN, D. 1959. Discrimination learning in retardates. *Training Sch. Bull.*, **56**:62–67.

ZEAMAN, D., HOUSE, B. J., and ORLANDO, R. 1958. Use of special training conditions in visual discrimination learning with imbeciles. *Amer. J. Ment. Defic.*, **63**:453–59.

ZIGLER, E. F., HODGDEN, L., and STEVENSON, H. W. 1958. The effect of support on the performance of normal and feebleminded children. *J. Pers.*, **26**:106–22.

PERSONALITY

Rick Heber

This chapter reviews research aimed at elucidation of the relationship between intellectual defect and personality. The limited nature of the literature concerned with this relationship attests to a traditional tendency to regard all behavior of the mentally retarded as attributable to intellectual defect.

Theoretical formulations of personality have given minimal consideration to the mentally retarded while personality researchers have usually restricted their investigation to subjects of normal intelligence. Sarason (1957), in commenting upon this lack of theoretical concern, states ". . . that theorists assume that the behavior and development of the retarded child requires no special explanation, that is, that the theory is applicable to all forms of human behavior and there is no reason to assume that in the case of the retarded child the theory is not sufficient" (p. 6).

An exception to this general statement was Lewin's (1935) formulation in 1930 of a "dynamic theory of the feeble-minded." As a direct outgrowth of this theory, Kounin (1941a) formulated the rigidity hypothesis as an explanation of the behavior of the retarded. This concept was a productive one in that it generated a substantial number of studies described later in this section. More recently, a number of studies of the mentally retarded have been stimulated by Rotter's (1954) social learning theory of personality.

Other conceptualizations of the behavior of the mentally retarded from a personality frame of reference have been attempted. Williams and Belinson (1953) have undertaken an analysis of neurotic behavior in the retardate in terms of perceptual development. The concept of pseudofeeblemindedness, as espoused by Kanner (1949) and others, was offered as an explanation of mental retardation occurring secondary to, and as a symptom of, personality pathology. Kirk and Johnson (1951) have discussed the differing experiences of retarded children in school and the potential consequences of these experiences on behavioral deviations. Dexter (1958) has proposed a social theory of mental retardation in which he attempts to explain the effects on the retarded of their continuously being confronted with unattainable goals in an essentially competitive society. He states:

> The self-image of the mentally defective in a society which stresses aptitude at intellectual achievement is likely to be negative because the "looking-glass self" principle operates and they learn from their social contacts and experiences to look down upon and distrust themselves [p. 924].

Pearson (1942) has interpreted mental retardation from a psychoanalytic frame of reference. Retardation is regarded essentially as a defect in *ego* function which results in malfunction of the *superego*. The *id* remains intact. Because of the ego defect, the retarded person is unable to repress, inhibit, or find adequate outlets for id urges. Pearson predicts from this analysis that the dreams of retardates would be subject to less superego distortion than would those of normals. Goldstein (1959), Frankenstein (1958), and Hirsch (1959) are other recent authors who have proffered

143

explanations of the relationship between personality traits or disorders and mental retardation.

None of these theoretical formulations appear to have stimulated any substantial amount of research on the interrelationship of intellectual defects and personality characteristics. Aside from the lines of investigation stimulated by the *rigidity* concept and by *social learning theory*, most of the personality research in mental retardation has been concerned with the prevalence of particular personality disorders and traits or has been stimulated by the availability of a particular research technique. The organization of this chapter follows those areas or problems which have received major attention.

PREVALENCE OF BEHAVIOR DISORDERS AND
PERSONALITY TRAITS IN THE
MENTALLY RETARDED

A number of studies have been concerned with the prevalence of behavior disorders or particular personality traits among the mentally retarded. These studies have been directed at one or more of the following questions:

1. What is the prevalence of behavior disorders among the mentally retarded?

2. Are there certain types of personality disorders which are characteristic of the mentally retarded or of subgroups of the mentally retarded?

3. Are there particular personality traits which are characteristic of the retarded?

Most attention has been directed to the question of the prevalence of severe behavior disorders and psychoses (particularly infantile autism and schizophrenia) in the mentally retarded. These studies are reported in the chapter on behavioral disturbances and will not be repeated here. The general consensus of such studies is that the incidence of severe behavior disorders including psychoses is considerably higher among *institutionalized* retarded persons than in the general population. This finding cannot be generalized to the population of non-institutionalized retarded persons since the presence of a behavior disorder is, no doubt, a variable in institutionalization. Studies of military personnel have yielded some of the most informative data pertaining to the personal adjustment of the total population of retarded.

Weaver (1946) conducted a survey to determine the adjustment of mental retardates in military service. Subjects for the study were eight thousand military inductees who had either successfully completed the special training program or who had bypassed the program by achieving a critical score on one or more of the classification tests. Of the eight thousand subjects studied, 56 per cent of the males and 62 per cent of females were found to have made a satisfactory adjustment to the demands and stresses of the military environment. Forty-four per cent of the males and 38 per cent of the females became psychiatric or psychosomatic problems or committed repeated acts of misconduct. Eight per cent of the white and 25 per cent of the Negro inductees were discharged because of inability to meet the requirements of adaptation for military service. Three per cent of white and 11 per cent of Negro inductees were discharged because of undesirable habits or traits of character (categorized by the investigator as psychopathy). Six and four-tenths per cent of whites and 1.3 per cent of the Negroes were committed for further rehabilitation following severe antisocial behavior but were finally discharged when such restoration to military duty was deemed impossible. Thirteen per cent of the white and 6.5 per cent of the Negro inductees were discharged because of severe psychiatric and psychosomatic conditions.

This pessimistic picture of the personal-social behavior of adult mentally retarded was confirmed in a study by

Dewan (1948) of emotional instability in retarded and non-retarded Canadian army recruits. Recruits, passing through an induction center, were assessed on intellectual ability (Canadian Army "M" Test) and emotional stability. Each recruit was given a psychiatric examination, and a social history was also obtained. On the basis of these evaluations it was found that better than 47 per cent of the retarded were considered to be emotionally unstable, as opposed to approximately 20 per cent in the non-retarded group.

Typical of the literature on institutionalized retardates is O'Connor's report (1951) on 104 young men (mean CA = 20.9 years) admitted consecutively to a British institution. On the basis of a large battery of tests, 12 per cent of O'Connor's group were classifiable as neurotic and 44 per cent as emotionally unstable.

With respect to school adjustment of children, Blatt (1958) reports a greater frequency of personality maladjustments among retarded pupils remaining in regular classes, as well as among those placed in special classes, as compared with typical children.

Inconsistent with the general trend in the literature is Enos' (1961) recent report on the emotional adjustment of 120 bright, average, and retarded children. The children (mean CA = 9 years, 4 months) all attended public school classes. Their emotional adjustment was estimated by the average rating of two or three clinical psychologists who based their opinion on the results of a clinical interview and a number of projective tests. On the basis of these ratings Enos concluded that girls were better adjusted than boys; that among girls, bright girls made the best, and retarded girls the poorest adjustment; that among boys, retarded boys made the best, and average boys the poorest over-all adjustment. Enos does not offer any statement regarding the inter-rater reliability or the validity of the ratings.

A number of investigators (e.g., Jolles, 1947; Sloan, 1947) have administered projective tests, notably the Rorschach Ink Blot Test and the Thematic Apperception Test, to institutionalized retardates in the effort to determine (1) the prevalence and nature of personality deviations in the institution population or (2) the existence or extent of mental retardation caused by, and secondary to, personality disorder. In general, these studies, discussed in the chapter on psychological evaluation, suggest a high prevalence of personality disorders among the population of *institutionalized* retardates.

That this is so is not surprising, since the major factor precipitating institutionalization frequently is the presence of a behavior disorder (Saenger, 1957). Since only a relatively small proportion of the mentally retarded are institutionalized, results of these studies cannot be generalized to the total population of the mentally retarded. The retardates identified in the Weaver and Dewan studies are more nearly a representative sample of the population of non-institutionalized retarded, and these studies confirm the high prevalence of maladjustment.

Hirsch (1959) explains the high frequency of personality disorders among the mentally retarded on the following basis:

. . . The retarded child does not function in accordance with the same psychological principles or with the same need systems as the normal child. The knowledge that the intelligence is dulled seems to carry with it the false implication that the retarded child is less sensitive to hurt, less responsive to disappointment, and not in need of gratifications which come with the knowledge that one's efforts are appreciated. The major difference between the retarded child and his normal peer rests in the retarded child's ego limitation. This limitation seriously interferes both with his capacity to obtain, through his own efforts, optimal needed satisfaction, as well as with his capacity to meet environmental demands. He needs to depend much more on help from others. To the extent that he is surrounded by lenient, supportive adults, he may make an adequate emotional adjustment. To the extent that important adults are inconsistent in their attitudes, overly demanding, undependable, and non-supportive of his efforts, the retarded child's needs emerge with greater urgency. When he finds the demands made upon him confusing or impossible to meet, and when his necessarily limited accomplishments are unappreciated or ridiculed, his symptomatic behavior may become increasingly intensified [p. 639].

In view of the intellective limitations in the capactiy of the retarded person to gratify basic needs in a socially approved manner within a highly competitive culture, it would be rather remarkable if the mentally retarded did not show a heightened susceptibility to personal and social maladjustment. It is unfortunate that knowledge of this high prevalence of personality disorders has not stimulated much in the way of research on the specific development and nature of these disorders.

There are numerous, widely held beliefs regarding common personality characteristics or traits in the retarded, such as, for example, that they are highly suggestible and lack persistence. Few of these notions have received research verification. Brady (1948) compared suggestibility in mentally retarded (N = 106; CA = 17–59; IQ = 50–70), epileptic, hysteric, and neurotic subjects. Suggestibility was measured by the Hull Body Sway Test. This is a test in which the subject, while standing still and relaxed, listens to a repeated suggestion that "he is falling forward." Amount of body sway of the subject is measured in inches and constitutes the suggestibility score. The test of persistence used was one in which the subject is seated in a chair and instructed to hold one of his legs extended above the seat of another chair as long as possible. Persistence was measured in terms of the length of time the subject was able to hold his leg above

the chair. The persistence and suggestibility scores of both the retarded and epileptic groups were not significantly different from those of the normal group and were better than those for either the hysteric or neurotic groups. Here, then, are two commonly assumed traits of the retarded which have no experimental verification and, indeed, some evidence in refutation.

SELF-CONCEPT

Central to a number of contemporary theories of personality is a global concept which, in general, refers to the sum total of all of the characteristics a person attributes to himself, and the positive and negative values he attaches to these characteristics. Rogers (1947) has termed this the *"self-concept."* It is referred to by Snygg and Combs (1949) as the *"phenomenal self."* Jahoda (1958) believes that positive mental health can be measured in the attitudes of the individual toward his own self, and Rogers (1947) states that:

It would appear that when all of the ways in which an individual perceives himself—all perceptions of the qualities, abilities, impulses and attitudes of the person, and all perceptions of himself in relation to others are accepted into the organized conscious concept of the self then this achievement is accompanied by feelings of comfort and freedom from tension which are experienced as psychological adjustment [p. 364].

Guthrie, Butler, and Gorlow (1962) have studied the patterns of attitudes toward self among institutionalized and non-institutionalized retarded girls (CA = 14–18; IQ = 50–80) through administration of a self-attitude questionnaire constructed by Guthrie *et al.* Factor analyses of the questionnaire indicated seven general self attitudes: there is nothing wrong with me; I do as well as others do; I don't give trouble; I act hastily; I am shy and weak; and I am useless and nobody likes me. Interestingly, the institutionalized retarded girls admitted to fewer negative statements about self than the non-institutionalized girls.

Ringness (1961) investigated the reality of retarded children's estimates of their achievement in eight areas: success in learning arithmetic, success in English, spelling and writing, success in reading, acceptance by peers, acceptance by adults, success in sports, leadership of peers, and intelligence. Retarded, normal, and superior children of fourth-grade age estimated their achievement in these areas in each of three consecutive years. The California Achievement Tests, a sociogram, and teachers' ratings were used to obtain actual measures of the children's achievement. Based on analyses of the discrepancies between these measures and children's estimates, Ringness drew the following conclusions:

1. Mentally retarded children more generally tend to overestimate success than do average or bright children.
2. Bright children tend to rate themselves more highly than retarded and average children, following in that order.
3. Mentally retarded children have a less realistic self-concept than bright or average children.
4. The self-estimate varies not only with the child, but with intelligence, sex, and situation.
5. Self-ratings of mentally retarded children are less reliable than those of average or bright children [p. 459].

Ringness' use of the term self-concept is idiosyncratic; what was evaluated was the child's ability to judge his performance objectivity and/or the child's aspiration level rather than the child's own feelings about himself.

This reviewer was unable to discover any additional studies relevant to the retardates' concept of self. Despite the importance of global concepts of "feelings about one's self" in contemporary personality theory, one can only speculate about the self-concept of the mentally retarded.

FRUSTRATION AND AGGRESSION

The concept of frustration plays a major role in most of the contemporary theories of personality. One of the best-known points of view is that of Dollard *et al.* (1939) who define frustration "as that condition which exists when a goal-response suffers interference." They believed that hostile or aggressive behavior ". . . is always a consequence of frustration" (p. 11). Rosenzweig (1945) extended the frustration-aggression theory by classifying the various types of behavior which occur in a frustrating situation. His categories were: *extrapunitive,* characterized by the person blaming the external world and reacting with anger; *intropunitive,* whereby the individual blames himself and reacts with feelings of remorse and guilt; and *impunitive,* in which the person passes over frustrating situations lightly as if they represented unavoidable accidents for which no one was to blame.

Dollard *et al.* (1939) considered the relationship of intelligence to frustration:

Not only would low intelligence seem likely to increase the amount of frustration experienced by an individual; it would also be expected to diminish the effectiveness of socializing forces in that it would imply a lowered capacity to appreciate the consequences of specific acts. . . . But since the normally intelligent man is instigated both by needs which are actually present and also, perhaps to an even greater extent, by anticipated wants, the person with blunted capacity for looking into the future is likely to have a relatively low level of aspiration and to find acceptable a life status which would be intolerable to a more intelligent person. The same limitation of intelligence which restricts an individual's learning and earning capacities may also make the ensuing low level of accomplishment far less frustrating than it would otherwise be [pp. 116–17].

Interest in the reactions of mentally retarded to frustration, however, has been based on the assumption that retarded persons are subject to *more* rather than *less* frustration as a consequence of a reduced ability to achieve desired goals. This assumption was lent some support by Sherman and Bell's (1951) study which reported a significant correlation between the Ohio Mental Ability Tests and a paper and pencil test of frustration. Several studies of the reactions of the mentally retarded to frustration have utilized the methodology of the Rosenzweig Picture-Frustration Study (Rosenzweig, 1945; and Rosenzweig, Fleming, and Rosenzweig, 1948). The children's form of this projective test consists of cartoon-like drawings which depict everyday situations. The cartoons include figures of adults and children with facial expressions omitted but with enough figure and background to suggest the overall situation. Each cartoon presents both a source of frustration and a victim which can be easily identified. The subject is requested to give the response he thinks the thwarted person in the cartoon would make. Subjects' responses are scored according to the *direction of aggression* (extrapunitive, intropunitive, or impunitive) and the *type of reaction* (obstacle dominance, ego defensive, or need persistence).

Angelino and Shedd (1956) administered the children's form of the Rosenzweig Picture-Frustration Study to 102 retarded children (California Test of Mental Maturity IQ's below 80) in public schools and compared their responses to Rosenzweig's norms. In analyzing the data by age levels it was found that the retarded group basically responded in the same way to frustration as normal children, moving from extrapunitive to intropunitive with increasing age, except that they appeared to reach each level of reaction about two years later than the normal group. A specific finding of interest, however, was that Angelino and Shedd's twelve- to thirteen-year-old subjects were more intropunitive than those in Rosenzweig's normal group.

Portnoy and Stacey (1954) utilized the children's form of the Picture-Frustration Study to study aggression in thirty Negro and thirty white institutionalized retardates. For both groups the extrapunitive response dominated, with the impunitive and intropunitive following in that order. The Negro group was more impunitive than the white group. Both groups of retardates, however, were more impunitive and less ego-defensive than the normal youngsters comprising the Rosenzweig norms. Casting doubt on the validity of the Rosenzweig technique is a more recent study by Lipman (1959) designed to validate the Picture-Frustration Study, The Children's Form of the Manifest Anxiety Scale, and a mirror drawing test as measures of aggression. These tests were administered to two groups of subjects selected from an institutionalized population: behavior problems (students who habitually acted in a destructive and aggressive manner) and behavior models (students who got along well with peers and supervisors and who complied with institutional rules). No differences between groups were obtained on any of the measures. This finding raises serious question as to the validity of these measures as predictors of aggression in view of the fact that the two groups represented the extremes of the continuum of overt aggression.

Aggressive behavior has emerged as a major factor in a number of studies of institutional populations. Rudolph (1958), for example, reported that television-viewing in an institution resulted in a great increase of behavior incidents. The greatest increase ". . . occurred in incidents relating to objects, and disobedience or surliness." Greene (1945), in comparing adjusted and unadjusted retarded girls within an institution, found, among other factors, that the unadjusted group ". . . was more aggressive in social situations, and tended to take things more personally" (p. 474). In studies of elopements from institutions, Gothberg (1947) found that the TAT responses of runaway girls indicated they were reacting to restrictions by aggressive attitudes, and Thorne (1947) found elopement to be a frequent reaction to frustration. Culbertson *et al.* (1961) studied the motivation behind aggressive behavior in a group of fifty institutionalized retarded women (CA = 18–22; IQ = 50–80) who were administered a test constructed by the authors. Factor analysis of the test responses suggested six factors: intropunitive and impunitive defense against hostile expression, defensive denial of hostility, conscious defense against expression of hostility, extrapunitive response to frustration, concern with hostile defenses, and choice of hostile function determined by situation. Culbertson *et al.* concluded that, as with other persons, different dimensions of aggression may serve quite different functions for various retarded persons.

Miller (1961) has related the problem of aggression to the "interrupted task resumption" phenomenon. Previously, Bialer and Cromwell (1960) and Spradlin (1960) had found that choice of an interrupted task for repetition, in preference to an uninterrupted task, was more likely in brighter and older retardates. These findings were consistent with those obtained earlier with normal children (Rosenzweig, 1933, 1945). Bialer (1961) later found choice of the interrupted versus the uninterrupted task to be more a function of mental than of chronological age. Miller (1961) speculated that the child's ego-involvement in the situation and his "rebelliousness" may be an important variable in interrupted task repetition choice. He presented the interrupted task paradigm to fifty-two retarded pupils in public school special classes (CA = 4 years, 1 month to 17 years, 7 months; IQ = 49–77). One-half of the subjects performed under an ego-involving condition, and the other half under a non-ego-involving condition.

Twenty-two of the twenty-six subjects returned to the interrupted tasks under the non-ego-involving condition whereas only ten of twenty-six did so under the non-ego-involving condition. However, tendencies toward aggressiveness, as measured by a "rebellious pupil" scale, were found to be related to tendencies to choose the interrupted task under the ego-involving condition.

In view of the common assumption that the mentally retarded tend to be subjected to more frustration than other persons, it is rather remarkable that so few studies of frustration and its effects have been conducted. Little evidence is available to support this assumption, nor is there much evidence to suggest that the retarded respond any differently (as one might expect if they, in fact, are more continuously frustrated) or are any less tolerant of frustration than non-retarded persons. Indeed, validity of the technique used in the major studies of reactions of retarded persons to frustration appears to be in question (Lipman, 1959). Aggressivity, as a factor associated with institutionalized retardates, is fairly well documented. That aggressive behavior is a major problem among institutional populations is not surprising, since such behavior is known to precipitate institutionalization.

RIGIDITY

One of the most common and widely accepted descriptions of the characteristic behavior of retarded persons has been in terms of rigidity. Lewin, in 1936, published a "dynamic theory of feeblemindedness" based on a concept of "rigidity." Lewin's formulation proved to be of great heuristic value in that it stimulated a number of alternative conceptual explanations of rigid behavior in the retarded, and a series of studies to determine whether, and under what conditions, the behavior of the retarded was, in fact, rigid. The rigidity controversy and the ensuing research have been reviewed in detail by Zigler (1962).

In Lewin's general theory, individual differences are attributable to differences in the structure, state, and meaningful content of the "dynamic system" of the person. With respect to mental retardation, structure was viewed as of major importance. Lewin regarded the skill structure of the retardate as less differentiated with fewer regions than the structure of the non-retarded child of the same age. Thus, an older retarded child would be comparable to a younger normal child in degree of structural differentiation. Further, given an older retarded and a younger normal child, of equal differentiation, Lewin pointed out that the boundaries between the differentiated regions would be less fluid and more rigid in the case of the retarded. Frequently overlooked in considering Lewin's formulation is the fact that he regarded two other variables as related to rigid behavior—life experience and the psychological situation. An individual continually confronted with failure in problem-solving could adopt a life-style characterized by rigid behavior. Differences in rigid behavior between people may also be a function of a lack of psychological equivalence of the given situation in which the rigid behavior is observed. Lewin's conception of retardation in terms of rigidity was based on his observations of the behavior of retarded and normal ten-year-olds in a satiation-type task (drawing moon faces).

As pointed out by Zigler (1962), much of the difficulty in understanding Lewin's theory and the behavioral predictions to be derived therefrom grew out of his failure to clearly distinguish between his theoretical concept of rigidity and rigid behavior. While rigid behavior could be a function of differences in the permeability of the boundaries between regions (the rigidity concept), it could also be a function of degree of structural differentiation, life experience, or the individual's perception of the behavioral situation. Kounin (1941a, b), in attempting to clarify and extend Lewin's concept, posited that rigidity was a positive, monotonic function of chronological age. He reasoned that rigidity (the concept) could be directly related to certain behaviors under conditions where the variable—degree of differentiation—was controlled. Kounin even utilized the rigidity concept as an explanation of the inadequate intellectual development in retarded persons as follows: (1) Rigidity makes the occurrence of change more difficult. Assuming that mental growth involves change, rigidity thus operates to retard the rate of growth of individuals to be characterized as more rigid. (2) Assuming that environmental differentiation plays a role in mental growth, it can be concluded that the same situation is less stimulating for feebleminded individuals than for normal individuals. (3) Assuming that integration and restructuring (reorganization) play a role in mental growth, one is enabled to derive the slower rate of growth of the feebleminded individual from the theories which state that the normal individual more readily restructures a given field, and is more likely to attain integrated and unified structures.

Kounin (1941a, b) offered the results of five experiments in support of his formulation of the rigidity concept. In addition to the theorem that rigidity is a positive monotonic function of age, he also posited that rigidity is a positive, monotonic function of the degree of mental retardation. From this conception Kounin predicted that the older and/or more retarded a person, (1) the less effect a change of state in one region would have upon the state of neighboring regions, (2) the less likely he would be in an overlapping situation, (3) the more difficulty he would have in the performance of a task which required him to be influenced by more than one region, (4) the more he would be likely to structure a new, perceptually ambiguous field into a relatively large number of separate, independent regions, and (5) the less he would be able to perform a task which required restructuring of a given field.

These predictions were tested in five studies conducted using three groups of twenty-one subjects—an older retarded group (mean CA = 41.7 years), a younger retarded group (mean CA = 14.5 years), and a younger normal group (mean CA = 6.8 years). The three groups were matched on mental age as a control for the "degree of differentiation" variable. In the first study on satiation and co-satiation, subjects were instructed to draw cats, bugs, turtles, and rabbits, with each new drawing introduced when subjects were satiated on the previous figure. As Kounin predicted the least amount of co-satiation was found in the older retarded group. In a second study, subjects were given three series of thirty trials in which they were required to *depress* a lever which thereby released a marble. Subjects were later required to *raise* the lever to obtain a marble. It was found that with this shift in the required response, the young normal group made the most, and the older retarded group the fewest, errors (depressing the lever). This finding supported Kounin's contention that the retarded were less likely to be in an overlapping situation because of the relative impermeability of the boundaries between regions. This notion was lent further support in the third study in which subjects learned three simple card tasks and were then required to perform a task in which all components were involved. In this situation, involving overlapping of regions, the older retarded group performed the poorest. In the final two studies both of which called for the subject to make shifts in the basis of sorting cards (color to form), the normal group performed best and the older retarded group the poorest.

Kounin's findings provided strong support to his formulation of the rigidity concept: tasks facilitated by a lack of communication (rigidity) between neighboring regions would be performed more efficiently by older and/or more retarded persons; the reverse would be true for tasks facilitated by an interaction between regions. However, the Kounin formulation of the rigidity conception was quickly questioned, while the supporting studies were subjected to serious methodological criticisms. Prior to the experiments, Kounin had interacted at length with his subjects and allowed them to engage in the future experimental activities in order to insure their security and confidence. Further, both of Kounin's retarded groups were institutionalized and consequently, institutionalization and length of institutionalization were uncontrolled variables.

The first major criticism of Kounin's work was rendered by Goldstein (1943) who, while acknowledging the presence of rigidity behavior in the mentally retarded, objected to the Lewin-Kounin explanation. He maintained that "rigidity occurs when an organism is unable to come to terms with its environment in an 'adequate' way" (p. 225). Zigler (1962) has noted that Goldstein's failure to understand correctly Kounin's definition of rigidity caused what is seemingly a misdirected criticism of the Kounin position. Goldstein's error seemed to be his insistence on interpreting Kounin's concept of rigidity as referring to a type of behavior rather than a hypothesized qualitative aspect of the boundaries between cognitive regions (Zigler, 1962).

In place of the Lewin-Kounin concept Goldstein presented a two factor theory of rigidity. He felt *primary* rigidity involved "an abnormality of the Einstellung mechanism, most frequently observed in lesions of the subcortical ganglia" (p. 225) and advanced the position that *primary* rigidity is independent of an impairment of higher mental processes, manifesting itself in a lack of ability to change "from one set to another." Goldstein viewed *secondary* rigidity as being "due to a primary defect of the higher mental processes occurring in cortical damage and cortical malformations, such as feeblemindedness" (p. 225). Underlying *secondary* rigidity is an impairment of abstract thinking. Goldstein apparently makes no distinction between retardation with and without demonstrable organic impairment; his explanation of rigid behavior derives from a conception of all retardation as being due to a common organic impairment. (Lewin and Kounin apparently restricted their formulation to the "familial retarded.") More cogent is Goldstein's criticism of Kounin's interpretation of which tasks do and do not involve a shifting of regions: "It is difficult for Kounin to show that drawing bugs after drawing cats requires the individual to move to a new region" (p. 218).

Werner (1946, 1948), like Goldstein, acknowledged rigid behavior as a characteristic of the retarded but took issue with the concept of rigidity. In particular, he rejected Kounin's hypothesis that rigidity is a positive monotonic function of age. Also, as with Goldstein's, Werner's objections seem to be based on a misunderstanding of Kounin's definition of rigidity, and, consequently, he seemingly failed to differentiate between "rigid behaviors" and the Kounin definition of rigidity. Werner explains Kounin's findings on the satiation–co-satiation experiment on the basis that ". . . since feebleminded children possess a considerable tolerance to monotonous work, it is probably easy to persuade them to draw bugs after cats, and turtles after bugs" (pp. 44–45). Werner, like Goldstein, argues for a multiple conception of rigidity in discussing *subnormal* and *abnormal rigidity.* Kounin (1948) replied to Werner's criticisms by pointing out that Werner offered no evidence in support of his opinions other than general descriptive statements based on subjective impressions. In sum, the Goldstein (1943) and Werner (1946, 1948) discus-

sions do not call into question the existence of behavior describable as rigid, but rather present alternative conceptualizations in vague, undefined terms less susceptible to experimental verification than the Lewin-Kounin concept.

As mentioned earlier, a major variable clouding interpretation of results of the classic Kounin investigation was the failure to control the variables of institutionalization and length of institutionalization. Brand, Benoit, and Ornstein (1953) attempted to evaluate the role of length of institutionalization in the production of rigid behavior. Rigidity, CA, MA, and length of institutionalization were intercorrelated for fifty-two institutionalized retarded subjects (mean CA = 23.5 years; mean MA = 7.6 years; mean length of institutionalization = 11.5 years). Rigidity was measured by the latency in time taken by the subject to change his response (tapping) rate with a change in the stimulus (metronome) rate. Significant correlations were obtained for age and rigidity and for age and length of institutionalization. A correlation approaching significance ($0.10 > p > 0.05$, df 50) was obtained for mental age and rigidity. It was not possible for Brand *et al.* to evaluate the relative influence of age and length of institutionalization on rigid behavior because of the high correlation obtained between the two variables. An opportunity to do this, however, was made available to Solomon (1954) with the opening of a new public institution. The population of this facility became comprised of a combination of transfers from other institutions and new admissions from the community. Solomon, like Brand *et al.*, used the Rhythm Tapping Test devised by Luchins (1947) as the measure of rigidity. Solomon compared a group of twelve newly institutionalized (less than three weeks) subjects with a group of twelve subjects who had been institutionalized for more than five years. The two groups were matched on sex, CA, IQ, and etiology. Solomon found no significant difference between the groups and concluded that length of institutionalization was not related to rigidity. The major defect in the study was, of course, the small number of subjects employed. Solomon raises the interesting speculation that the retardate getting along well in the community may differ in rigidity from the retardate who must be institutionalized, suggesting the possibility that institutionalization per se may be a variable relevant to rigidity.

A major contradition to the rigidity concept is represented in Plenderleith's (1956) findings. She hypothesized that, if the Lewin-Kounin rigidity notion was valid, retarded subjects would have great difficulty in learning a discrimination reversal problem. Thirty normal and thirty retarded subjects, of comparable mental age, were trained on the experimental task which consisted of learning the correct member of pairs of pictures. The reversal problem, in which the previous incorrect response became the correct response, was administered twenty-four hours or six weeks after original learning. Contrary to predictions, no significant differences between retarded and normal subjects in solving the reversal problem were obtained. Zigler and Unell (1962) have criticized the methodology of the Plenderleith study on the basis of the extreme simplicity of the experimental task and the failure to match carefully on certain relevant variables.

Stevenson and Zigler (1957) conducted a study similar to Plenderleith's but employed a number of tasks. In the first experiment, retarded children and adults, and normal children (with the three groups matched on mental age) were trained on a size-discrimination problem and, subsequent to varying degrees of training, were switched to a new size-discrimination problem involving smaller stimuli. The three groups did not differ significantly in their performance on either the first or second problem;

nor were there any differences as a function of degree of training. In a second experiment, retarded children and adults and normals (with groups matched on mental age) were trained on the same size-discrimination task as used in the first experiment but this time were switched to a *position*-discrimination task. Once again, the three groups did not differ significantly in their performance on either problem. Consequently, the findings of both experiments fail to support the hypothesis that the retarded exhibit more rigid behavior than normal persons of comparable mental age.

As a result of this finding, inconsistent with Kounin's original work, Stevenson and Zigler (1957) proposed the motivational hypothesis as an explanation of the differences in rigidity behavior reported in previous studies, that is, that the differences in performance between retarded and normal subjects are attributable to differences in motivation. They point out that, in their study, tasks were used which required the subject to learn two successive discriminations with a minimal amount of instruction and a minimal amount of interaction with the experimenter. Whereas in Kounin's (1941a, b) studies, the subject was required to perform a response in compliance with instructions rather than to learn a response. Stevenson and Zigler speculated further that institutionalized retarded persons may be more highly motivated to interact with the experimenter and comply with instructions than normal persons of the same mental age. To investigate the explanation of rigid behavior in the retarded in terms of motivation, Zigler, Stevenson, and their associates initiated a sequence of studies.

The first of these was conducted by Zigler, Hodgden, and Stevenson (1958). Wishing to employ tasks similar to those used by Kounin (1941a, b), these investigators constructed three simple motor, instruction-initiated satiation tasks.

Each task consisted of two parts. On Part I, the subject was instructed to make one response and was allowed to continue until satiated; on Part II, the subject was instructed to make a new response to the same or highly similar stimuli and was again allowed to perform until satiated. Two conditions of reinforcement were introduced: in one condition, the experimenter maintained a non-supportive role and did not reinforce the subject's performance; in the second condition, the experimenter made positive comments and in general reinforced the subject's performance. These two conditions were introduced to test the predictions that (1) support has a reinforcing effect which results in an increment in performance over that found in a non-support condition and (2) interaction with an adult and adult approval are more reinforcing to retarded than to normal subjects. Based on the assumption that institutionalized retarded children would be relatively deprived of adult contact and approval, Zigler *et al.* predicted that retarded subjects would perform longer than normals under both support and non-support conditions, and that the difference between support and non-support conditions would be more marked in the case of the retarded subjects.

The twenty institutionalized retarded subjects (mean CA = 12.5 years; mean MA = 5.9 years) and twenty normal (nursery school) subjects (mean CA = 4.8 years; mean MA = 6.1 years) were matched on mental age. The three experimental tasks were extremely simple so that the successful performance was dependent upon compliance with instructions. The findings, in general, supported the motivational hypothesis in the following ways:

1. The retarded subjects performed significantly longer under the support than under the non-support conditions, whereas the normal subjects did not.

2. The retarded subjects spent a great-er amount of time at each game than the normal subjects under both conditions.

3. The difference in performance under support and non-support conditions was greater for the retarded than for the normal subjects.

4. There was little difference in the co-satiation effect for normal subjects as a function of support and non-support conditions. For the retarded subjects, however, support not only resulted in less co-satiation but in an actual increase in length of time spent on Part II of the game.

5. The co-satiation effect was significantly less for the retarded than for normal subjects on three of the four measures.

6. The proportion of errors made by the normal subjects was not significantly greater than the proportion of errors made by retarded subjects. In fact, the tendency was for the retarded subjects to make the greater proportion of errors.

7. More retarded subjects than normals stopped the task they were performing on when the experimenter asked if they wanted to play other games. This was viewed by the experimenter as evidence of the greater compliance with instructions on the part of retarded subjects.

These findings supported the assumption that institutionalized retardates tend to have been relatively deprived of adult contact and approval and, consequently, have a higher motivation to obtain such contact and approval than do normal children. Other studies by Gewirtz and Baer (1958a, b) add further support to the view that reported differences in rigidity between normals and retardates may be due to greater social deprivation in the retardates rather than to any inherent rigidity.

Zigler (1961) attempted to test this view further by reasoning that, should this explanation be correct, a relationship should exist between the degree of deprivation experienced and the amount of rigid behavior manifested. Sixty cultural-familial institutionalized retarded children (CA = 8–14 years, MA = 4–8 years) were rated on a social deprivation scale which ranged from very protected to very deprived. All subjects played a two-part simple monotonous game; following satiation on Part I of the game, the subject played Part II until satiated. Half of the subjects played Part I of the game under a non-support condition and Part II under support condition. The remaining subjects performed Part I under a support condition and Part II under non-support. The findings confirmed the predictions that the more socially deprived subjects would spend more time on the game, more frequently make the maximum number of responses possible, and show a greater increase in time spent from the first to the second part of the game.

Further evidence supporting the Zigler motivational hypothesis is provided in a study by Green and Zigler (1962). Three groups of subjects, normals, institutionalized retarded, and non-institutionalized retarded, were equated on mental age, with the two retarded groups also being equated on chronological age. As with the study (Zigler, 1961) above, subjects were allowed to become satiated on both parts of a two-part game, with one-half the subjects receiving a support to non-support condition from Part I to Part II and the remaining subjects receiving the reverse. No differences were found between the performances of the normal and the non-institutionalized retarded groups; the institutionalized retarded group, however, spent significantly more time at the task. Presumably, the institutionalized retarded child has experienced greater social deprivation than the non-institutionalized retardate, either as a function of institutionalization or in pre-institutional life.

Shallenberger and Zigler (1961) in a further study of satiation–co-satiation phenomena have extended the motiva-tional hypothesis to include the concept of "negative and positive reaction tendency." Subjects in this study were given pre-experimental games under either a negative or a positive reinforcement condition. Both retarded and normal subjects receiving negative reinforcement on the pre-experimental games evidenced significantly higher co-satiation scores than subjects receiving positive reinforcement. The retarded subjects receiving negative reinforcement on the pre-experimental games produced significantly higher co-satiation scores than did normal subjects receiving negative reinforcement. Shallenberger and Zigler concluded that social deprivation results both in an increased desire to interact with an adult and in a reluctance to do so.

Shepps and Zigler (1962) have suggested that the motivational hypothesis may also be applicable to the explanation of the rigidity of brain-damaged retardates. In comparing twenty organic and twenty familial retardates on three measures of rigidity under two conditions of reinforcement (support and non-support) no differences emerged between the brain-damaged and familial groups. Both groups were equally responsive, however, to differences in reinforcement conditions. Shepps and Zigler consequently reject the prevalent view that inherent rigidity of behavior is a frequent concomitant of exogenous retardation. The Shepps and Zigler finding, however, contrasts with McMurray's (1954) study in which a brain-damaged and a familial retarded group equated on age and intelligence were compared in their ability to shift their principle of sorting cards using a modified Wisconsin Card Sorting Test. The greater rigidity of the brain-damaged retarded group was apparent on the three different measures employed.

On the basis of the extensive work of he and his associates, Zigler (1962) concludes that the rigid behavior observed in the mentally retarded may most usefully be viewed as stemming from a variety of motivational factors. Zigler summarizes these as follows:

1. Institutionalized feebleminded children tend to have been relatively deprived of adult contact and approval and hence have a higher motivation to secure such contact and approval than do normal children.

2. While feebleminded children have a higher positive reaction tendency than do normal children, due to a higher motivation to interact with an approving adult, they also have a higher negative reaction tendency. This higher negative reaction tendency is the result of a wariness of adults which stems from the more frequent negative encounters that feebleminded children experience at the hands of adults.

3. The positions of various reinforcers in a reinforcer hierarchy differ as a function of environmental events. Due to the environmental differences experienced by institutionalized feebleminded children, the positions of reinforcers in their reinforcer hierarchy will differ from the position of the same reinforcers in the reinforcer hierarchy of normal children [pp. 159–60].

In summary, it appears that the observed differences in "rigid" behavior between normal and retarded persons can more adequately be explained on the basis of motivational factors than in terms of the Lewin-Kounin concept. Further, with the exception of satiation–cosatiation phenomena, which appear to be directly susceptible to motivational influences, there is more evidence in refutation (Plenderleith, 1956; Stevenson and Zigler, 1957; Zigler and Unell, 1962) than in support of the widely held belief that rigid behavior is characteristic of the mentally retarded.

MOTIVATION

The vague and elusive concept of motivation has received more attention than any other variable subsumed under personality theory. Most of this research has been directed at the study of external reinforcers with relatively few studies from the viewpoint of "need" or "deprivation."

Achievement motivation.—One method of studying *need* which has been used with the retarded is the evaluation of achievement motivation based on the modified projective techniques of McClelland. Tolman and Johnson (1958) studied thirteen pairs of organic and familial children (MA range = 5–7 to 8–0) in an institutional population using TAT cards and the McClelland scoring system. Contrary to the experimenters' expectations, the familial retardates indicated greater needs for achievement and affiliation than organic subjects. In both groups, the need for achievement diminished as the length of institutionalization increased. Jordan and deCharms (1959) utilized McClelland's technique in the attempt to differentiate achievement motivation between normal (N = 60; mean CA = 15.7 years; IQ > 75) and retarded children and between retarded children enrolled in special classes (N = 47; CA > 13 years) and those retarded pupils (N = 42; mean CA = 15.2 years; IQ < 75) remaining in regular classes. The experimenters hypothesized that the mentally retarded would show less achievement motivation than normal children and that retarded pupils in special classes would show less anticipation of failure than retarded pupils remaining in regular classes. The authors hypothesized, further, that a relationship would be obtained between achievement motivation and academic achievement. In general, no difference between groups in need achievement emerged, nor did that variable show any relationship to intelligence or academic grade placement within groups. An interesting finding, however, was that only 13 per cent of retarded children in special classes showed any fear of failure, whereas 36 per cent of retarded children in regular classes and 38 per cent of normal children did so. Apparently, the special class does, indeed, shelter the retarded pupil from failure. On the basis of these essentially negative findings, Jordan and deCharms concluded that the McClelland methodology was not yet ready to deal with intellectual differences.

With the exception of the above studies the experimental approach to the problem of motivation has been through manipulation of incentives. This, of peanuts versus one peanut) may not have been sufficient to make a difference to these subjects. In a follow-up on the Cantor and Hottel study, Heber (1959) had subjects drawn from the same institution and scaled a number of potential rewards in terms of the personal preference of the subject. Subjects were then assigned to a high- or low-incentive con-

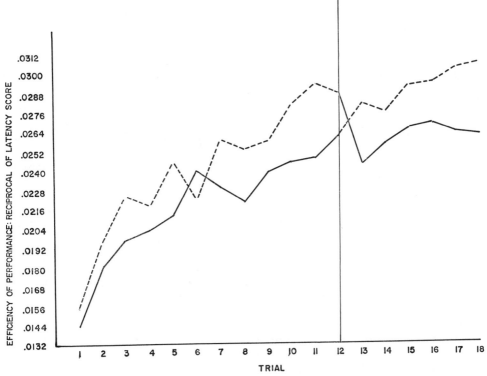

FIG. 1.—Performance curves under high and low preference incentive conditions

course, is not surprising since it is much simpler to manipulate reward than need.

Manipulation of tangible rewards.— Cantor and Hottel (1955) studied the performance of institutionalized male retardates (N = 44; 24 subjects had IQ's above 50, and 20 subjects had IQ's below 50) on a simple discrimination learning problem as a function of two magnitudes of reward. No differences in performance emerged as a function of the incentive difference. It was pointed out that the difference in incentive magnitude (four dition with the subject's own reward-preference ranking determining his particular high or low incentive. Using a simple motor task, it was found that the high-incentive group performed the task more efficiently than the low-incentive group. Further, as can be seen in Figure 1, a "Crespi effect" was manifest in that when the original "higher-preferred incentive" group was shifted to the "less-preferred incentive" there was a rapid, substantial decrease in performance efficiency. With a shift to a higher-preferred

incentive condition, the original less-preferred incentive group showed an immediate increase in performance efficiency.
It should be recognized that the incentives in the Heber study varied in kind
rather than in actual magnitude as in the
Cantor and Hottel study. Heber found,
however, that the Cantor and Hottel incentive (peanuts) was almost the least
preferred incentive for his subjects, sub-
stantiating the notion that the difference
in magnitude was not sufficient to make
any difference to the subject. Nonetheless, the Heber and the Cantor and Hottel results support the role of magnitude
of incentive as a determinant of performance rather than learning per se.

Wolfensberger (1960) utilized the
Heber incentive preference ranking technique to study the effectiveness of various incentives in inducing behavior
changes in retarded subjects. Sixty institutionalized retarded subjects (CA =
11–50 years; IQ = 50–74) were divided
into five groups: concrete reward (highly
preferred prize), symbolic reward
(chips), control (no reward), concrete
punishment (prize taken away), and
symbolic punishment (chips taken
away). No differences between groups
were obtained in performance on a simple reaction time task. Such a finding, if
confirmed, would raise a question as to
the efficacy of the common techniques of
reinforcement employed in studies of
performance with retarded subjects. The
lack of differences may, however, be accounted for on the bases of the Zigler
(1962) "social deprivation" hypothesis—
the presence of the experimenter and his
attention may have been so reinforcing
as to overshadow any differences which
might otherwise have emerged as a function of the incentive variable. The failure
to obtain significant differences could
also be attributed to the typically large
subject variability in reaction-time performance and the relatively small number of subjects (twelve) per treatment
condition.

Ellis (1962) has studied the effect of
incentive magnitude on operant behavior. Seventy-four institutionalized male
retarded subjects (IQ = 11–86) were
assigned randomly to high- (three cigarettes) and low- (one cigarette) reward
groups. Subjects were required to depress a lever for the reward under an increasing ratio schedule of one, four,
eight, twelve, etc. There were no significant differences between groups in rate
of conditioning or in time to extinction.
In a second phase of the study, subjects
were allowed to choose either candy or
cigarettes as a reward, but again there
were no differences between high- and
low-reward groups. As in the Cantor and
Hottel (1955) study, one could speculate
that the incentive value of cigarettes or
candy for these subjects may have been
so minimal and the differences in magnitude so slight as to preclude the possibility of a performance differential as a
function of incentive magnitude.

Manipulation of social reinforcement.—
A number of studies conducted in Britain
have investigated the effects of verbal reinforcement on performance of moderately and severely retarded subjects.

Gordon, O'Connor, and Tizard (1954)
have studied the effects of various incentives upon the performance of motor
tasks. In the first study, adult male subjects (CA = 17–35; IQ = 25–48) performed the leg-persistence test, a task on
which the subjects were assumed to have
had little, if any, experience. The control
and reinforcement groups were matched
on the basis of pre-experimental performance on the leg-persistence test. One reinforcement group was given verbal encouragement by the experimenter while
the other was given a goal by setting a
visible indicator at a level which was
10 per cent higher than the subject's best
previous performance. The introduction
of incentives effected striking differences
between the three groups. The performance of the goal group was superior to
that of the encouragement group, and

both incentive groups were superior to the control group. In a second phase of the study, the same subjects were shifted to different incentive conditions. The sequence in which the incentives were presented to the subject was found to be a critical factor in determining performance level; performance went from best to worst in the following order: (1) the group which continued on a goal incentive, (2) the group shifted from goal to encouragement, (3) the group shifted from encouragement to goal, (4) the group shifted from control to goal, (5) the group continuing under encouragement, and (6) the group continuing under the control condition.

In a third phase of the study, subjects were re-administered the leg-persistence test under the original incentive. The retention performance of the subjects tended to correspond to their level of performance under the original incentive condition rather than the incentive condition to which they were transferred. These findings emphasize the significance of initial achievement level.

In a similar study by Gordon *et al.* (1955), subjects (CA = 17–35; mean IQ = 36) were required to perform a task which entailed inserting small nails into holes. Subjects performed the task initially under a goal condition, a team-competition condition, a competition condition with one rival, or a control-incentive condition. After the initial performance all subjects, except for those in the goal group, had their incentive changed. In a final phase, subjects performed under the original incentive condition. Again, the goal-incentive condition was found to produce superior performance, and the control condition the worst performance. The performance of subjects under the team-competition and competition with one rival conditions was intermediate between the goal and control conditions with very little difference between the two. Shifting the incentive condition to a goal condition produced sharp increases in performance proficiency, with the control group showing the greatest improvement.

Following the lead of these studies are two by O'Connor and Claridge (1955, 1958). In the first study, subjects were divided into three reinforcement groups: a non-reinforcement control group, a goal-with-encouragement group, and a goal-with-indifference group. The control group was set only to the task; the encouragement group was given encouragement and a goal by the experimenter; and the goal-with-indifference group was given a goal but without further comment from an experimenter. Encouragement produced performance superior to that of either of the other two groups, which did not differ significantly from one another. On the basis of this finding, O'Connor and Claridge concluded that the performance level, obtained in the previous study by Gordon *et al.* (1955), which was attributed to establishment of the goal incentive, was largely due to factors other than those associated with goal striving. In the second study, O'Connor and Claridge (1958) used a routine motor task (Nail Frame Task) to study the effects of shifts in incentive level. Forty male institutionalized retardates (CA = 18–45; mean IQ = 41) were divided into four groups matched on the basis of pre-experimental performance on a task comparable to the experimental task. One group performed under a goal condition throughout, a second group under the control-incentive condition throughout. A third group was shifted from an initial goal-incentive condition to a control condition, and a fourth group was shifted from an initial control-incentive condition to a goal-incentive condition. Subjects shifted from the initial control condition to the goal-incentive condition showed a typical Crespi type "elation" effect, that is, their performance following the shift exceeded that of the group which was maintained throughout under the goal-incentive condition. No depression effect was found when subjects performing under the goal-incentive condition were shifted to the control-incentive condition. This latter finding confirms findings of the earlier studies suggesting that the achievement level attained under an initial, highly effective incentive condition is relatively permanent.

Walton and Begg (1958) compared the performance of four groups of institutionalized retarded subjects (CA = 17–35; mean IQ = 36) on the leg-persistence test under four incentive conditions: a control incentive, a goal incentive, a competition incentive, and an encouragement incentive. Contrary to the previous British studies, there was no difference in performance between any of the incentive conditions.

The British studies demonstrate that moderately and severely retarded subjects can respond differentially in terms of motor proficiency on simple and routine motor tasks. These subjects appear to respond to goal setting and verbal encouragement in a manner similar to normal persons. Further, the achievement level attained under highly effective incentive conditions appears to be relatively permanent in that it tends to persist over a period of time and is apparently not subject to any significant depression effect with shifts from high- to low-magnitude incentives.

In the United States, Ellis and Distefano (1959) have studied the effect of verbal encouragement on rotary-pursuit performance in institutionalized retardates (N = 28; mean CA = 17 years; mean IQ = 51). All subjects were told their scores at the end of each trial and those in an encouragement group were given added comments of praise for their performance. No comments of praise were given control subjects. Consistent with the British studies reported above, verbal reinforcement in the form of praise and urging produced superior performance to that of control subjects per-forming in the absence of an experimentally defined reinforcer.

The effects of verbal or social reinforcement have been studied extensively by Zigler, Stevenson, and their colleagues in a series of systematic investigations growing out of the "social deprivation" hypothesis (see Zigler, 1962). Some of these studies were reviewed in the discussion of rigidity, above.

Zigler, Hodgden, and Stevenson (1958) compared the effect of verbal plus nonverbal social reinforcement in normal and retarded children. The groups were first satiated under a control reinforcement condition on a task similar to the experimental task. The groups, matched on mental age, performed on a simple, monotonous motor task. On both the pre-experimental and the experimental task, the retarded subjects performed for a longer time before satiating. Normal subjects did not respond to the verbal-social reinforcement in terms of increased resistance to satiation, whereas the retarded subjects did so to a marked degree. Zigler *et al.* explain this differential effect of verbal-social reinforcement on the basis that the retardates had been more deprived of adult-child contact, thereby increasing their response to such reinforcement. In evaluating the results of this study, it is to be noted that the retarded subjects were more than twice as old as the normal youngsters and that the normal subjects were not *average . . .* hasty reference to Stanford-Binet tables suggests a mean IQ of over 130.

Tending to confirm the greater reinforcement value of "attention from an experimenter" for retarded than for normal children is a study by Bijou and Oblinger (1960) of the performance of retarded and normal children on a simple, repetitive motor task. Groups of normal subjects (CA = 2 years, 6 months, to 6 years, 6 months) were drawn from a university preschool and from a co-operative and private day-care center. Retarded subjects (CA = 6 years, 1 month, to 11 years,

7 months; IQ = 24–70) were institutionalized. The subject was instructed on performance of the task and was allowed to continue until he failed to make a response in a one-minute period. The experimenter remained passively in the background during the subject's performance. It was found that the retarded subjects made a greater number of responses than the normals; among the normal subjects, both groups of day-care center children made more responses than university preschoolers. Evidently, retarded subjects found the experimental situation the most reinforcing, and university preschoolers found it the least reinforcing. Confounding interpretation of the study is, of course, the factor of the older age and the institutionalization of the retarded subjects.

On a further investigation of the validity of the "social deprivation" hypothesis, Stevenson and Knights (1962) studied the effect of social reinforcement on performance of retarded children immediately after their return to the institution following a summer vacation with their families and again after a period of several months back in the institution. Sixty familial retardates (mean CA = 14.2 years; mean IQ = 60.4) were administered an experimental task which required the subject to sort marbles varying in color into appropriate holes under either an attentive but non-reinforcing condition or a verbally reinforcing condition in which the experimenter made supportive statements about the subject's performance. One-half of the subjects were administered the task within two days after their return to the institution and again twelve and thirty weeks later. The remaining subjects were administered the task twelve and thirty weeks after their return to the institution. The significant and interesting finding of the study was that the performance of the boys under both experimental conditions and in both groups was more comparable than was that of the girls. The author in

attempting to interpret this unusual finding speculated that the sex of the experimenter had a differential effect on the performance of boys and girls; that is, that social reinforcement delivered by the male experimenter was more effective in modifying the performance of girls than of boys. This hypothesis was supported in another study by Stevenson (1961) in which a differential effect of social reinforcement provided by male and female experimenters was found. The supportive reinforcing comments made by the experimenter did facilitate the performance of those girls tested two days after their return to the institution; no such effect was noted for those subjects who were not tested until twelve weeks after their return to the institution. This finding was contrary to the experimenter's original hypothesis that the amount of social reinforcement available from adults would be increased during the child's stay at home, making the attention of an experimenter less reinforcing upon return to the institution.

Stevenson and Cruse (1961) studied the comparative effectiveness of social reinforcement with normal and retarded children. Thirty institutionalized retarded children (mean CA = 14.2 years; mean MA = 6.1 years) and thirty normal children (mean CA = 5.2 years; mean MA = 6.1 years) were administered a simple experimental task which required the subject to place marbles varying in color into appropriate holes. Subjects were instructed to put as many marbles in the holes as they wished and to advise the experimenter when they wished to terminate the game. The subjects performed the task under one of three experimental conditions: a reward condition in which the experimenter made supportive comments concerning the subject's performance, a condition in which the experimenter was attentive but silent, and a condition in which the experimenter instructed the subject and left the room.

A large proportion of the retarded children either performed for the maximum time limit of thirty minutes or inserted all of the marbles available on all of the five consecutive days of the experiment. By contrast, performance of the normal children differed as a function of the three experimental conditions. The normal youngsters showed a significant decrease in the number of marbles sorted from the first to the fifth day of the experiment. By contrast, retarded subjects in the reinforcement and attention groups actually showed a slight, though not significant, increase from the beginning to the termination of performance. The failure to find differences in the performance of the retarded as a function of social reinforcement does not support the "social deprivation" hypothesis. However, as Stevenson and Cruse point out, such differences possibly may not have emerged because of the fact that a large number of retarded subjects in all groups spent the full time allotment on the task, thereby creating an artificial ceiling on performance. In a second study, using an experimental procedure identical to that reported above, Stevenson and Cruse added a negative social reinforcement condition in order to determine whether this would suppress performance to a greater degree in retarded than it would in the normal subjects. In addition to retarded and normal youngsters matched on mental age, a group of normal subjects equivalent in chronological age to the retarded subjects was utilized. The negative reinforcement in the form of critical comments by the experimenter affected the performance of all three groups. The performance of both the younger normal and the retarded groups was decreased under the punishment (criticism by the experimenter) condition, whereas performance was increased with criticism in the older normal group. Under reinforcement and attention conditions, older normal subjects were actually found to perform more poorly than

younger normal subjects. Stevenson and Cruse interpreted this finding on the basis that older normal subjects were less dependent upon adults for social reinforcement than younger subjects and that, consequently, supportive comments by an attentive experimenter were less reinforcing for older normal subjects.

A major defect of the studies of effectiveness of social reinforcement discussed thus far lies in their utilization of institutionalized retarded subjects in comparison with non-institutionalized normal youngsters. Consequently, it was not determined in these studies whether the differential performance of the retarded and normal subjects was attributable to institutionalization or to mental retardation per se. However, Stevenson and Fahel (1961) have attempted to clarify this question through utilization of institutionalized and non-institutionalized subjects, both retarded and normal. The normal, institutionalized subjects were drawn from a state orphanage. Subjects performed a simple motor task under either a neutral condition (in which the experimenter refrained from comments) or a reward condition (in which the experimenter made supportive comments about the subject's performance). The performance of institutionalized subjects was significantly greater (in terms of number of marbles sorted) than that of non-institutionalized subjects. Contrary to predictions, the social reinforcement condition did not produce a higher level of response than the neutral condition. The most important implication of the Stevenson and Fahel study is that previous findings of a differential in performance between retarded and normal subjects as a function of social reinforcement may be more a function of institutionalization than of the variable of retardation.

Visual reinforcement.—Stevenson and Knights (1961) investigated the comparative reinforcing value of visual stimuli for retarded and normal subjects. Sixty-four retarded (mean CA = 12.8 years; mean

MA = 5.4 years) and sixty-four normal children (mean CA = 4.5 years; mean MA = 5.6 years) were exposed to a device which resulted in the appearance of a pictorial stimulus (a common animal such as an elephant, a bear, etc.) when the subject depressed a response button. The retarded and normal groups were each subdivided in eight groups to permit manipulation of the following variables: the number of pictures (one or five), the number of response buttons (one or five), and the length of exposure (0.5 or 2.0 seconds). A variable ratio reinforcement schedule was employed such that a visual reinforcer was illuminated on an average of every tenth response. Though the initial rate of response was higher for normal subjects, it declined to a level below that for retarded subjects suggesting that visual stimuli maintain their reinforcing value for retardates for a longer period than for normals. Normal subjects had higher response rates with five response buttons; retarded subjects, with one.

Primary and secondary reinforcement. —Ellis and Pryer (1958) have attempted to compare primary and secondary reinforcement in mental retardates. On a discrimination-learning task, it was found that subjects performed more efficiently for the secondary reinforcer than for the primary reinforcer. However, it should be noted that "jelly beans" were utilized as the primary reinforcer and "yellow paper squares" as the secondary reinforcer. In attempting to account for their unusual findings, the authors suggested that the "jelly beans" had been too distractible for the retarded subjects. However, Ellis and Pryer do not indicate that the paper squares had any acquired association with the jelly beans or with any other concrete reward. In effect, they were actually comparing two types of primary reward. It is entirely possible that mentally retarded subjects may not place jelly beans very high on the hierarchy of desired rewards, in which case

the greater effectiveness of "paper squares" could well be understood.

Negative reinforcement.—Stevenson and Snyder (1960) studied the interaction effects of incentive conditions utilizing institutionalized retarded boys and girls (N = 90; mean CA = 13.5 years; mean MA = 6.5 years). Subjects performed a simple marble-sorting task under one of three incentive conditions (reward, neutral, or punishment) and were then switched to an alternate incentive or were maintained on the same incentive. Reward consisted of supportive comments and punishment of critical comments by the experimenter. On the first phase it was found that the neutral incentive condition produced performance superior to that under the reward condition which, in turn, was superior to the punishment condition. On phase two, however, the effects of a particular incentive were dependent upon the incentive condition under which the individual has worked in the first phase. For groups that had performed under a neutral condition in the first phase, neutral, reward, and punishment conditions were effective in that order on the second phase. However, for groups who had performed under either reward or punishment on the first phase, reward, neutral, and punishment were effective in that order on the second phase. The results indicated that the effect of a particular incentive condition is not independent; it is influenced by the condition that precedes it. Further, it was found that the subjects with higher mental ages were more susceptible to the effects of the incentive condition than were subjects with lower mental ages, suggesting that sensitivity to verbal reinforcement is, at least in part, a function of mental age.

In summary, the studies of incentive-manipulation suggest, to use Hullian terms, that the concept of "drive" has relevance to the problem of mental retardation, as well as the concept of "habit strength." The research is consistent in suggesting that even severely retarded subjects are responsive to variations in type and magnitude of incentive. Studies which failed to find differences as a function of magnitude of incentive (Cantor and Hottel, 1955; Ellis, 1962) may have used a type of incentive and a difference in magnitude that were simply inappropriate for their subjects. There is some evidence to suggest that social (verbal and non-verbal) reinforcement may be particularly valued by retarded subjects and to a greater extent than is the case with normal subjects, though the relationship between the institutionalization variable and social reinforcement has not yet been defined.

ANXIETY

Part of the folklore concerning mental retardation is the reputed increased anxiety of the mentally retarded as a group. Clinical studies (Feldman, 1946; Beier et al., 1951; DeMartino, 1954; Stacey, 1955); have tended to confirm this presumed attribute. Recently, anxiety has been brought within the scrutiny of experimental investigation, largely, as a result of the outgrowth of a specific index of anxiety, the Taylor Manifest Anxiety Scale, and an adaptation for children, The Children's Form of the Manifest Anxiety Scale.

Lipman (1960), on the basis of his review of anxiety, indicates that, in general, increased anxiety enhances learning performance when the correct response is dominant for the subject but hinders it when the response is not dominant, as in complex learning. Lipman compared the performance of retarded children with that of normals (as run by Castaneda et al., 1956; Hafner and Kaplan, 1959) on The Children's Form of the Manifest Anxiety Scale and concluded that "anxiety . . . cannot account for performance differences between high-grade retardates and roughly equal MA normal males" (p. 1028). Consistent with this

report, Kitano (1960) found no relation between measured intelligence and scores on the CMAS (Children's Form of the Manifest Anxiety Scale).

Malpass et al. (1960), however, found institutionalized retarded children to be more anxious than non-institutionalized retarded children, as measured by the CMAS, and both groups to be more anxious than normals. There was, again, no relation between CMAS scores and intelligence within groups.

Lipman and Griffith (1960) studied the effect of anxiety level on concept formation. A form of the CMAS, modified for the mentally retarded, was given to 115 institutionalized retardates. The results were found to be negatively related to the anxiety scores. This is interpreted to support one aspect of the earlier generalization, i.e., increased anxiety produced poorer performance in the complex learning situations.

Wiener et al. (1960) divided a group of adolescent male retardates into three levels on the basis of scores on a school achievement test. Each subject was administered a general-anxiety test, a test-anxiety test, and a visual-motor test. Poor school achievement was found related to high *test* anxiety, but not to high general anxiety. The visual-motor scores were found to be related inversely with both types of anxiety and positively with school achievement scores.

Departing from the test measures of anxiety (of questionable validity), Cantor (1960) evaluated the effect of competition with members of the same and opposite sex on motor performance. He assumed that heterosexual competition would be anxiety-inducing for retarded persons who had limited experience with the opposite sex. From the "drive" concept Cantor predicted that this anxiety would interfere with performance on a complex task. Using a subtest of the Minnesota Rate of Manipulation Test on institutionalized adult retardates, Cantor found no differences in performance as a function of competition with a member of the same or the opposite sex.

To sum, there is an almost complete lack of evidence to indicate that increased anxiety is more prevalent in retarded persons or that it is a major factor interfering with performance. A major problem is, of course, the unknown validity of the one or two test measures of anxiety available. Though extremely difficult to undertake, studies of the effects of experimentally induced anxiety, such as attempted by Cantor, would undoubtedly prove to be a more profitable approach.

SOCIAL LEARNING THEORY

Rotter's (1954) social learning theory has provided the conceptual framework for the most systematic sequence of studies on personality aspects with the possible exception of the work stimulated by the Zigler-Stevenson (see Zigler, 1962) social deprivation hypothesis. In social learning theory, two major constructs, expectancy and reinforcement value, mediate the measurement and prediction of behavior in any given situation. *Reinforcement value* is "the individual's degree of preference for any reinforcement to occur if the probabilities of their occurring were all equal" (Rotter, 1954, p. 107). *Expectancy* refers to the subjective probability held by an individual that a particular reinforcement will occur as a function of specific behavior on his part. Theoretically, expectancies may vary from 0 per cent expectancy of occurrence of an event to 100 per cent expectancy of occurrence. An individual's successful attainment of a reinforcement in a behavioral situation leads to an increment in expectancy while his failure to do so leads to a decrement. With other variables held constant, the greater the expectancy, the greater the potential for the occurrence of a given behavior. The theory assumes that the behavior which has the greatest potential at any instant will be the one which occurs. In the studies reported below it is assumed further that the greater the potential of a given behavior, the more efficient that behavior will be when it does occur, as efficiency may be assessed through quantitative and qualitative measures of performance. It is possible, then, to make differential predictions about behavior knowing the differences in expectancies held by different persons.

The expectancy held by an individual in any given situation at any given time is determined (1) by his specific success-failure experiences in that particular situation and (2) by the broad range of experiences which the individual has had in a wide variety of prior life situations. Thus, when an individual is placed in a novel situation, his expectancy is initially determined by a generalized expectancy based on his past success-failure experiences in goal attainment in other situations. As experience is gained in the situation, the expectancy increasingly comes to be specifically determined by actual success-failure experiences in that situation and the weight of the prior experience in other situations gradually decreases.

Considering mental retardation within the framework of social learning theory, circularity becomes involved in the behavior or performance of the mentally retarded. As a result of limited intellectual abilities, the mentally retarded person in competition with his fellows of normal or superior intellect is likely to fail in much of his goal-seeking activity. With many failures and few successes in a wide variety of life situations, the mentally retarded person should come to hold a very low generalized expectancy of goal-attainment. Since expectancy is one of the variables mediating behavior potential, the performance of the retarded child should show a further qualitative and quantitative decrement with the acquisition of a low expectancy for success. This reduction in performance efficiency would result in further failure leading to even lower expectancies and so on, in circular fashion. This reasoning suggests that life experiences of failure may accentuate performance deficits attributed to intellectual defect.

Expectancy.—This line of reasoning led to an investigation of expectancy changes in retardates and normals by Heber (1957). He assumed that when retarded

pectancy would be discrepant from the initial expectancy held prior to the success experiences would depend on the level of the initial expectancy. The change from initial to final expectancy would be directly reflected by a corresponding change in behavior potential or performance. Since both normal and retarded children should come to hold an

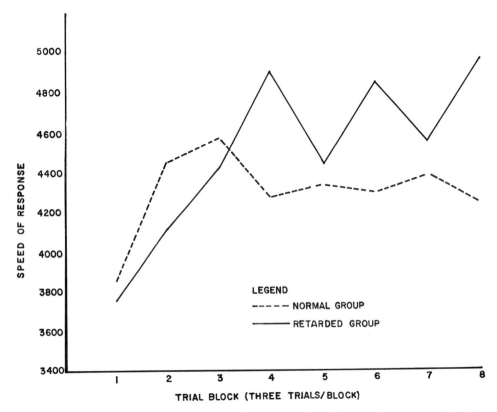

FIG. 2.—Mean reaction-time performance under a series of predominantly success trials. *Note:* speed of response measure is based on the reciprocal of the latency score.

and normal children are equated on initial task performance, the retarded actually have a higher performance potential in terms of constitutional ability because their initial matching performance is depressed by a low generalized expectancy. Following a large number of success experiences on a task, subjects would come to hold a very high expectancy on that task. The amount by which this final ex-

approximately equal, high final expectancy, the increment from initial to final performance level would be greater for the mentally retarded subjects if they, in fact, entered the task with a lower generalized expectancy. Similarly, with a series of failure experiences on a task, retarded subjects should show less decrement in performance since their final expectancy based on failure trials would be less discrepant from the initial, low, generalized expectancy. These predictions were tested by Heber on sixty mentally retarded (CA = 9 years, 6 months, to 15 years, IQ = 51–75) and sixty normal boys (CA = 7 years to 9 years, 6 months, IQ ≥ 94), using a simple reaction time device. As can be seen from Figure 2 and as predicted, retarded subjects receiving

onset of a decrement in performance during the last half of the failure trials.

The changes in performance with success support the notion that retardates enter novel task situations with a relatively low generalized expectancy which depresses initial performance. The initial rapid increment in performance efficiency was suggested as being a function of the

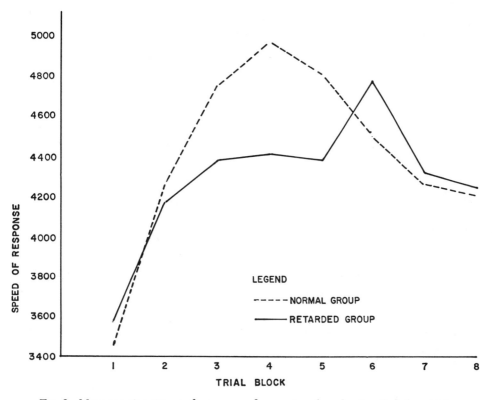

FIG. 3.—Mean reaction-time performance under a series of predominantly failure trials

a series of nineteen of a possible twenty-one successes showed a significantly greater improvement in performance than normals with whom they were matched in initial performances. Contrary to predictions, terminal performance of retarded and normal subjects under failure conditions was almost identical, with the groups showing an increment rather than the predicted decrement. Figure 3, however, suggests the

negative reinforcement value of failure and consequent failure avoidant behavior which took the form of increased effort on the task.

Gardner (1958) undertook a further analysis of reactions to experimentally induced failure. Sixty retarded and sixty normal subjects (previously matched on a task similar to the experimental task) were administered a simple card-sorting task under a neutral or "no reinforcement" condition. Forty normal and forty retarded subjects then received either "total failure" or "partial failure" on an interpolated task; the remaining twenty subjects in both the normal and retarded groups performed the interpolated task under "no reinforcement" conditions. Subjects were then readministered the original card-sorting task. Reactions to the interpolated failure, measured in terms of

spective of the direction of change in performance. These findings supported Gardner's speculations that failure had a greater magnitude of effect for normals as a function of its unexpectancy and that more normals than retardates had learned to achieve ultimate success by increasing effort when threatened by failure.

Closely allied to the Heber and Gardner studies is Ringelheim's (1958) in-

REACTIONS TO INTERPOLATED FAILURE EXPERIENCE

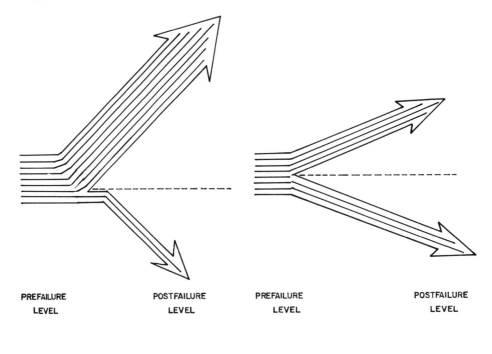

PREFAILURE   POSTFAILURE   PREFAILURE   POSTFAILURE
LEVEL   LEVEL   LEVEL   LEVEL

NORMALS   RETARDATES

Fig. 4.—Illustration of Gardner's hypotheses

performance shifts from first to second administration of the card-sorting task, are indicated in Figure 4. Though most subjects showed an increment in performance from pre- to post-failure performance, as in the Heber (1957) study, a greater proportion of normals increased their performance level following failure, and the magnitude of shift in performance level was greater for normals irre-

vestigation of the verbal reactions (betting behavior) of retarded and normal subjects to success and failure. Ringelheim used a vertical lift apparatus which was rigged so as to enable the experimenter to control success or failure of the subject's performance. Unlike the Heber and Gardner findings, the reactions of retarded and normal subjects to success and failure sequences in terms of betting on their performance on the subsequent trial were highly similar. Apparently, verbal statements of expectancy (which could in themselves be regarded as behaviors determined by expectancies) do not measure the same thing as motor-performance measures.

Directly concerned with the effects of success and failure on performance, though not conceived within a social learning theory frame of reference is a study by Kass and Stevenson (1962). Retarded (N = 51; mean CA = 11.4 years; mean MA = 5.1 years) and normal (N = 51; mean CA = 4.7 years; mean MA = 5.0 years) subjects were given a series of predominantly success or failure experiences on three pre-training games prior to administration of a discrimination-learning task. The rate of learning with prior failure or a control condition was the same for both retarded and normal subjects. The facilitating effect of the success experiences was, however, greater for normal than for retarded subjects, a finding directly opposite to that reported by Heber (1957). Kass and Stevenson explained the lesser degree of facilitation of success for retarded subjects as being due to greater difficulty in reducing their anxiety as a result of a long history of failure in learning tasks.

A recent study by Simpson (1962) investigated the effect of failure on retention. Following learning of a paired-associates task using the adjusted learning method, one-half of the group of normal subjects and one-half of the group of retarded subjects were led to believe they had failed the task. The remaining subjects were given an indication of their success through a monetary reward. On a twenty-four-hour retention test it was found that, for normal subjects, failure produced retention superior to that which occurred following success; for retarded subjects, however, the reverse was true. Studies, then, of motor performance, simple discrimination-learning, and

retention of paired associates all tend to suggest a differential effect of success and failure for normal and retarded subjects. Speculatively, it can be be stated that the performance levels of a retarded person appear to be depressed by expectancies of failure and comparatively fewer retarded than normals tend to use failure as a cue to increase effort. The basic social learning theory conception of the performance of retardates has been extended with the introduction of the concept of success-striving and failure-avoiding modes of reaction to failure by Moss (1958) and Bialer and Cromwell (1959), and by application of the concept of locus of control by Bialer (1961) and Miller (1961).

Summary and Conclusions

The extreme paucity of experimental data bearing on the relationship between personality variables and behavioral efficiency of the retarded person is indeed remarkable in view of the generally acknowledged importance of personality factors in problem-solving. Textbooks are replete with statements describing the retarded as passive, anxious, impulsive, rigid, suggestible, lacking in persistence, immature, and withdrawn, and as having a low frustration tolerance and an unrealistic self-concept and level of aspiration. Yet not one of these purported attributes can be either substantiated or refuted on the basis of available research data.

It is apparent that the mentally retarded and particularly those who are institutionalized have a substantially higher prevalence of psychotic and psychoneurotic disorders than the general population. The Zigler (1962) explanation of certain "rigid" behaviors on the bases of "social reinforcement" effects appears to be a more satisfactory explanation than the theoretial concepts offered by Lewin and Kounin. It should be pointed out, however, that the studies conducted by

Zigler and Stevenson and their colleagues have focused on satiation effects wherein subjects were assessed in terms of their persistence on a task which *remained appropriate*. A more common definition of "rigid" behavior refers to persistence of a particular behavior or response beyond the point where it is appropriate or correct. This latter conception of rigidity has not been subjected to systematic investigation.

The three or four studies of frustration do not support the notion that the retarded as a group are less able to tolerate frustration than normals, or that they respond in a different manner. Only one study has been specifically directed to self theory, and that study utilized a rather atypical conception of "self-concept." Other concepts from general personality theory such as defense mechanisms, superego development, psychosexual development, identification, etc., have had no application in mental retardation research.

The few striking and consistent findings from the meager investment in "personality research" with the retarded converge in highlighting the importance of motivational variables. Even severely retarded persons appear to be responsive to variations in incentive conditions; social reinforcement in the form of verbal praise and encouragement or just simple attention appears to be at least as effective as with normal persons. There is a strong suggestion that the performance of retardates may be depressed as a function of generalized expectations of failure and that proportionately more retarded than normals may respond to the threat of failure with decreased rather than increased effort.

Four major methodological problems or pitfalls emerge in considering the research to date: (1) rather naïve comparisons of institutionalized retardates and non-institutionalized normal persons on variables obviously related to why retarded persons become institutionalized, (2) comparisons of retarded and normal groups matched for mental age, without chronological age controls, on variables related to age, (3) enforced utilization of rating scales, questionnaires and projective tests, of questionable validity for use with retarded persons, because of unavailability of more appropriate tools of measurement, and (4) as in all areas of personality research, the lack of clearly defined terms and constructs and utilization of such undefined labels as "phlegmatic-labile dimension" and "psychodynamic principles," etc.

Though not explicitly stated as such, past research has tended, perhaps, to search for personality characteristics which would be universally descriptive of the mentally retarded. In the judgment of the present writer, a more profitable approach would focus on those aspects of the life experience of a retarded child which may be expected to produce deficits in personality development. For example, a large percentage of retarded children are reared in culturally deprived homes by parents who may be indifferent. What effect does this have on personality development? What etiological circumstances, biological and social, may produce personality deviations *and* intellectual defects? How do parents, siblings, and peers react to the child as a retarded person in a way that is different and how do these reactions affect his personality development? How do continuing experiences of failure in goal-seeking behavior affect the retarded person? Finally, the importance of emphases in two directions cannot be overstated: (1) toward the development of techniques, both observational and standardized, for more effective assessment of various aspects of personality and (2) toward the initiation of comprehensive, longitudinal studies of personality development in retarded children.

REFERENCES

ANGELINO, H., and SHEDD, C. L. 1956. A study of the reactions to "frustration" of a group of mentally retarded children as measured by the Rosenzweig Picture-Frustration Study. *Psychol. Newsletter,* 8:49–54.

BEIER, E. G., GORLOW, L., and STACEY, C. L. 1951. The fantasy life of the mental defective. *Amer. J. Ment. Defic.,* 55:582–89.

BIALER, I. 1961. Conceptualization of success and failure in mentally retarded and normal children. *J. Pers.,* 29:303–20.

BIALER, I., and CROMWELL, R. 1959. Failure as motivation with mentally retarded children. *Abstracts of Peabody Studies in Mental Retardation, 1955–1960,* 1. Division of Human Development, George Peabody College for Teachers.

———. 1960. Task repetition in mental defectives as a function of chronological and mental age. *Amer. J. Ment. Defic.,* 65:265–68.

BIJOU, S. W., and OBLINGER, B. 1960. Responses of normal and retarded children as a function of the experimental situation. *Psychol. Reports,* 6:447–54.

BLATT, B. 1958. The physical, personality, and academic status of children who are mentally retarded attending special classes as compared with children who are mentally retarded attending regular classes. *Amer. J. Ment. Defic.,* 62:810–18.

BRADY, M. 1948. Suggestibility and persistence in epileptics and mental defectives. *J. Ment. Sci.,* 94:444–51.

BRAND, H., BENOIT, E. P., and ORNSTEIN, G. N. 1953. Rigidity and feeblemindedness: an examination of the Kounin-Lewin theory. *J. Clin. Psychol.,* 9:375–78.

CANTOR, G. N. 1960. Motor performance of defectives as a function of competition with the same and opposite-sex opponents. *Amer. J. Ment. Defic.,* 65:358–62.

CANTOR, G. N., and HOTTEL, J. V. 1955. Discrimination learning in mental defectives as a function of magnitude of food reward and intelligence level. *Amer. J. Ment. Defic.,* 60:380–84.

CASTANEDA, A., PALERMO, D. S., and McCANDLESS, B. R. 1956. Complex learning and performance as a function of anxiety in children and task difficulty. *Child Develop.,* 27:327–32.

CULBERTSON, E., 1961. Patterns of hostility among the retarded. *Amer. J. Ment. Defic.,* 66:421–27.

DeMARTINO, M. F., 1954. Some characteristics of the manifest dream content of mental defectives. *J. Clin. Psychol.,* 10:175–78.

DEWAN, J. G. 1948. Intelligence and emotional stability. *Amer. J. Psychiat.,* 704:548–54.

DEXTER, L. A. 1958. A social theory of mental defieciency. *Amer. J. Ment. Defic.,* 62:920–28.

DOLLARD, J., DOOB, L. W., MILLER, N. E., MOWRER, D. H., and SEARS, R. R. 1939. *Frustration and Aggression.* New Haven: Yale University Press.

ELLIS, N. R. 1962. Amount of reward and operant behavior in mental defectives. *Amer. J. Ment. Defic.,* 66:613–17.

ELLIS, N. R., and DISTEFANO, M. K. 1959. Effects of verbal urging and praise upon rotary pursuit performance in mental defectives. *Amer. J. Ment. Defic.,* 64:486–90.

ELLIS, N. R., and PRYER, M. W. 1958 Primary versus secondary reinforcement in simple discrimination learning of mental defectives. *Psychol. Reports,* 4:67–70.

ENOS, F. A. 1961. Emotional adjustment of mentally retarded children. *J. Ment. Defic.,* 65:606–9.

FELDMAN, A. 1946. Psychoneurosis in the mentally retarded. *Amer. J. Ment. Defic.,* 51:247–54.

FRANKENSTEIN, C. 1958. Low level of intellectual functioning and dissocial behavior in children. *Amer. J. Ment. Defic.,* 63:294–303.

GARDNER, W. 1958. "Reactions of intellectually normal and retarded boys after experimentally induced failure." Unpublished Ph.D. dissertation, George Peabody College for Teachers.

GEWIRTZ, J., and BAER, D. 1958a. The effect of a brief social deprivation on behaviors for a social reinforcer. *J. Abnorm. Soc. Psychol.,* 56:49–56.

———. 1958b. Deprivation and satiation of social reinforcers as drive conditions. *Ibid.,* 57:165–72.

GOLDSTEIN, K. 1943. Concerning rigidity. *Char. Pers.,* 11:209–26.

———. 1959. Abnormal mental conditions in infancy. *J. Nerv. Ment. Dis.,* 128:538–57.

GORDON, S., O'CONNOR, N., and TIZARD, J. 1954. Some effects of incentives on the performance of imbeciles. *Brit. J. Psychol.*, **45**:277–87.

———. 1955. Some effects of incentives on the performance of imbeciles on a repetitive task. *Amer. J. Ment. Defic.*, **60**:371–77.

GOTHBERG, L. C. 1947. A comparison of the personality of runaway girls with a control group as expressed in the themas of Murray's thematic apperception test. *Amer. J. Ment. Defic.*, **51**:627–31.

GREEN, C. G., and ZIGLER, E. 1962. Social deprivation and the performance of retarded and normal children on satiation type task. *Child Develop.*, **33**(3):499–508.

GREENE, C. L. 1945. A study of personal adjustment in mentally retarded girls. *Amer. J. Ment. Defic.*, **49**:472–76.

GUTHRIE, G. M., BUTLER, A., and GORLOW, L. 1962. Patterns of self attitudes of retardates. *Amer. J. Ment. Defic.*, **66**:222–29.

HAFNER, A. J., and KAPLAN, A. M. 1959. Children's manifest anxiety and intelligence. *Child Develop.*, **30**:269–71.

HEBER, R. 1957. "Expectancy and expectancy changes in normal and mentally retarded boys." Unpublished Ph.D. dissertation, George Peabody College for Teachers.

———. 1959. Motor task performance of high grade mentally retarded males as a function of the magnitude of incentive. *Amer. J. Ment. Defic.*, **63**:667–71.

HIRSCH, E. A. 1959. The adaptive significance of commonly described behavior of the mentally retarded. *Amer. J. Ment. Defic.*, **63**:639–46.

JAHODA, M. 1958. *Current Concepts of Positive Mental Health.* New York: Basic Books.

JOLLES, I. 1947. A study of mental deficiency Rorschach technique. *Amer. J. Ment. Defic.*, **52**:37–42.

JORDAN, T. E., and DECHARMS, R. 1959. The achievement motive in normal and mentally retarded children. *Amer. J. Ment. Defic.*, **64**:457–66.

KANNER, L. 1949. Child psychiatry; mental deficiency. *Amer. J. Psychiat.*, **105**:526–28.

KASS, N., and STEVENSON, H. W. 1962. The effect of pretraining reinforcement conditions on learning by normal and retarded children. *Amer. J. Ment. Defic.*, **66**:76–80.

KIRK, S. A., and JOHNSON, G. O. 1951. *Educating the Retarded Child.* Boston: Houghton Mifflin.

KITANO, H. H. L. 1960. Validity of the children's manifest anxiety scale and the modified revised California inventory. *Child Develop.*, **31**:67–72.

KOUNIN, J. 1941a. Experimental studies of rigidity. I. The measurement of rigidity in normal and feebleminded persons. *Char. Pers.*, **9**:251–73.

———. 1941b. Experimental studies of rigidity. II. The explanatory power of the concept of rigidity as applied to feeblemindedness. *Ibid.*, pp. 273–82.

———. 1948. The meaning of rigidity: a reply to Heinz Werner. *Psychol. Rev.*, **55**:157–66.

LEWIN, K. 1935. *A Dynamic Theory of Personality: Selected Papers.* Translated by A. K. ADAMS and K. E. ZENER, New York: McGraw-Hill.

———. 1936. *A Dynamic Theory of Personality.* New York: McGraw-Hill.

LIPMAN, R. S. 1959. Some test correlates of behavioral aggression in institutionalized retardates with particular reference to the Rozenzweig Picture-Frustration Study. *Amer. J. Ment. Defic.*, **63**:1038–45.

———. 1960. Children's manifest anxiety in retardates and approximately equal MA normals. *Ibid.*, **64**:1027–28.

LIPMAN, R. S., and GRIFFITH, B. C. 1960. Effects of anxiety level on concept formation: a test of drive theory. *Amer. J. Ment. Defic.*, **65**:342–48.

LUCHINS, A. S. 1947. Proposed methods for studying degrees of rigidity in behavior. *J. Pers.*, **15**:242–46.

MCMURRAY, J. G. 1954. Rigidity in conceptual thinking in exogenous and endogenous mentally retarded children. *J. Consult. Psychol.*, **18**:366–70.

MALPASS, L. F., MARK, S., and PALERMO, D. S. 1960. Responses of retarded children to the Children's Manifest Anxiety Scale. *J. Educ. Psychol.*, **51**:305–8.

MILLER, M. B. 1961. "Locus of control, learning climate, and climate shift in serial learning with mental retardates." Unpublished Ph.D. dissertation, George Peabody College for Teachers.

———. 1961. Rebelliousness and repetition choice in adolescent retardates. *Amer. J. Ment. Defic.*, **66**:428–34.

Moss, J. 1958. "Failure-avoiding and success-striving behavior in mentally retarded and normal children." Unpublished Ph.D. dissertation, George Peabody College for Teachers.

O'Connor, N. 1951. Neuroticism and emotional instability in high-grade male defectives. *J. Neurosurg. Psychiat.*, **14**:226–30.

O'Connor, N., and Claridge, G. 1955. The effect of goal-setting and encouragement on the performance of imbecile men. *Quart. J. Exp. Psychol.*, **7**:37–45.

———. 1958. A "Crespi effect" in male imbeciles. *Brit. J. Psychol.*, **49**:42–48.

Pearson, G. 1942. The psychopathology of mental defect in the nervous child. *Nerv. Child.*, **31**:9–20.

Plenderleith, M. 1956. Discrimination learning and discrimination reversal learning in normal and feebleminded children. *J. Genet. Psychol.*, **88**:107–12.

Portnoy, B., and Stacey, C. L. 1954. A comparative study of Negro and white subnormals on the children's form of the Rosenzweig Picture-Frustration Test. *Amer. J. Ment. Defic.*, **59**:272–78.

Ringelheim, D. 1958. "Effects of internal and external reinforcements on expectancies of mentally retarded and normal boys." Unpublished Ph.D. dissertation, George Peabody College for Teachers.

Ringness, T. A. 1961. Self-concept of children of low, average, and high intelligence. *Amer. J. Ment. Defic.*, **65**:453–62.

Rogers, C. 1947. Some observations on the organization of personality. *Amer. Psychologist*, **2**:358–68.

Rosenblum, S., and Callahan, R. J. 1958. The performance of high-grade retarded, emotionally disturbed children on the Children's Manifest Anxiety Scale and Children's Anxiety Pictures. *J. Clin. Psychol.*, **14**:272–75.

Rosenzweig, S. 1933. Preferences in the repetition of successful and unsuccessful activities as a function of age and personality. *J. Genet. Psychol.*, **42**:423–40.

———. 1945. The Picture-Association Method and its application in a study of reactions to frustration. *J. Pers.*, **14**:3–23.

Rosenzweig, S., Fleming, E. E., and Rosenzweig, L. 1948. The Children's Form of the Rosenzweig Picture-Frustration Study. *J. Psychol.*, **26**:141–91.

Rotter, J. 1954. *Social Learning and Clinical Psychology*. New York: Prentice-Hall, Inc.

Rudolph, G. deM. 1958. The effect of children's television on behavior. *Mental Health*, **17**:55–60.

Saenger, G. 1957. *The Adjustment of Severely Retarded Adults in the Community*. A report to the New York State Interdepartmental Health Resources Board, Albany, New York.

Sarason, S. B. 1957. In: C. L. Stacey and M. F. DeMartino (eds.), *Counseling and Psychotherapy with the Mentally Retarded*. Glencoe, Illinois: The Free Press.

Shallenberger, P., and Zigler, E. 1961. Rigidity, negative reaction tendencies, and cosatiation effects in normal and feebleminded children. *J. Abnorm. Soc. Psychol.*, **63**:20–26.

Shepps, R., and Zigler, E. 1962. Social deprivation and rigidity in the performance of organic and familial retardates. *Amer. J. Ment. Defic.*, **67**(2):262–68.

Sherman, M., and Bell, E. 1951. The measurement of frustration: an experiment in group frustration. *Personality*, **2**:44–53.

Simpson, N. 1962. "Short-term retention of paired associates by mentally retarded and normal children as a function of success or failure in original learning." Unpublished Master's Thesis, University of Wisconsin, Office of Special Education.

Sloan, W. 1947. Mental deficiency as a symptom of personality disturbance. *Amer. J. Ment. Defic.*, **52**:31–36.

Snygg, D., and Combs, A. V. 1949. *Individual Behavior: A New Frame of Reference for Psychology*. New York: Harper.

Solomon, P. 1954. A note on rigidity and length of institutionalization. *J. Clin. Psychol.*, **10**:391–92.

Spradlin, J. E. 1960. Task resumption phenomena in mentally retarded Negro children. *Abstracts of Peabody Studies in Mental Retardation, 1955–1960*, **1**, No. 40. George Peabody College for Teachers.

STACEY, C. L. 1955. Worries of subnormal adolescent girls. *Except. Child.*, **21**:184–86.

STEVENSON, H. W. 1961. Social reinforcement with children as a function of CA, sex of E, and sex of S. *J. Abnorm. Soc. Psychol.*, **63**:147–54.

STEVENSON, H. W., and CRUSE, D. B. 1961. The effectiveness of social reinforcement with normal and feebleminded children. *J. Pers.*, **29**:124–35.

STEVENSON, H. W., and FAHEL, L. S. 1961. The effect of social reinforcement on the performance of institutionalized and non-institutionalized normal and feebleminded children. *J. Pers.*, **29**:136–47.

STEVENSON, H. W., and KNIGHTS, R. M. 1961. The effect of visual reinforcement on the performance of normal and retarded children. *Percept. Motor Skills*, **13**:119–26.

————. 1962. The effectiveness of social reinforcement after brief and extended institutionalization. *Amer. J. Ment. Defic.*, **66**:589–94.

STEVENSON, H. W., and SNYDER, L. C. 1960. Performance as a function of the interaction of incentive conditions. *J. Pers.*, **58**:1–11.

STEVENSON, H. W., and ZIGLER, E. F. 1957. Discrimination learning and rigidity in normal and feebleminded individuals. *J. Pers.*, **25**:699–711.

THORNE, F. C. 1947. The problems of institutional elopements. *Amer. J. Ment. Defic.*, **51**:637–43.

TOLMAN, N. G., and JOHNSON, A. P. 1958. Need for achievement as related to brain-injury in mentally retarded children. *Amer. J. Ment. Defic.*, **62**:692–97.

WALTON, D., and BEGG, T. L. 1958. The effects of incentives on the performance of defective imbeciles. *Brit. J. Psychol.*, **49**:49–55.

WEAVER, T. R. 1946. The incidence of maladjustment among mental defectives in military environment. *Amer. J. Ment. Defic.*, **51**:238–46.

WERNER, J. 1946. Abnormal and Subnormal rigidity. *J. Abnorm. Soc. Psychol.*, **41**:15–24.

————. 1948. The concept of rigidity: a critical review. *Psychol. Rev.*, **53**:43–52.

WIENER, G., CRAWFORD, E. E., and SNYDER, R. T. 1960. Some correlates of overt anxiety in mildly retarded patients. *Amer. J. Ment. Defic.*, **64**:735–39.

WILLIAMS, J. R., and BELINSON, L. 1953. Neuroses in a mental defective. *Amer. J. Ment. Defic.*, **57**:601–12.

WOLFENSBERGER, W. 1960. Differential rewards as motivating factors in mental deficiency research. *Amer. J. Ment. Defic.*, **64**:902–6.

ZIGLER, E. 1961. Social deprivation and rigidity in the performance of feebleminded children. *J. Abnorm. Soc. Psychol.*, **62**:413–21.

————. 1962. Rigidity in the feebleminded. In: E. P. TRAPP and P. HIMELSTEIN (eds.), *Readings on the Exceptional Child*, pp. 141–62. New York: Appleton-Century-Crofts.

ZIGLER, E. F., HODGDEN, L., and STEVENSON, H. W. 1958. The effect of support and non-support on the performance of normal and feebleminded children. *J. Pers.*, **26**:106–22.

ZIGLER, E., and UNELL, E. 1962. Concept-switching in normal and feebleminded children as a function of reinforcement. *Amer. J. Ment. Defic.*, **66**:651–57.

RELATION OF ENVIRONMENTAL FACTORS TO INTELLECTUAL FUNCTIONING

Boyd R. McCandless

INTRODUCTORY REMARKS

This chapter does not pretend to be an inclusive review of *all* the literature that has been published dealing with relations between environment and intellectual functioning. Such literature would take the reviewer along a range from conception to the grave and from intellectual levels corresponding essentially to IQ = 0 to IQ = genius. In terms of academic disciplines, it would range from physics and biochemistry through sociology and history.

Rather, the author has chosen to concentrate on the postnatal environment, ignoring the extensive literature on prenatal environments almost entirely. The population with which the author chiefly concerns himself is the "endogenous" mentally retarded population—i.e., the population with no obvious somatic involvements associated with mental retardation, e.g., no mongolism, no Tay-Sachs disease, no cretinism. The tested IQ of this endogenous population typi-

Some of the organization of this chapter, as well as much of the text, follows that of Boyd R. McCandless, *Child and Adolescent Behavior and Development* (New York: Holt, Rinehart, and Winston, Inc., 1961), chap. vii: Intelligence: its measurement and educational treatment, and chap. viii: Sources of variation in measured intelligence. The author appreciates the courtesy of Holt, Rinehart, and Winston, Inc., for permission in this matter. Because of the author's residence overseas, this chapter has not been updated since its original draft, as have certain other chapters.

cally ranges between 50 and 70 to 75, whether a Stanford-Binet Scale or a Wechsler test is used. Preponderantly, members of this population come from the lower socio-economic status groups. Numerically, it composes the bulk of what is considered the mentally retarded population of the nation. Dingman and Tarjan (1960, p. 933), for example, while stating that "The true number of mentally retarded can only be estimated in the crudest fashion," extrapolate, using hospital populations and common-sense extensions of figures from these and a United States population base of 175 million to arrive at a population estimate of 5,276,755 for the number of persons having an IQ between 50 and 70. An informal survey of the literature indicates that, of this number, probably three-fourths or more are endogenous, i.e., have as a group no more deviant somatic accompaniments than a population selected in the 90–110 range. Dingman and Tarjan's estimates of the number of mentally retarded below 50 IQ are 437,500—87,500 between 0 and 20 IQ and 350,000 between 20 and 50 IQ.

The present author suggests that from the endogenous population of three or four million come the most, and the most serious, social problems that our culture associates with mental retardation; he believes that this group of children has been heavily affected—and retarded—by the forces of our culture and that, for practical reasons if no other (we can *do* something about cultural conditions; little or nothing about genetic conditions), this is the group that merits a major social-psychological-medical "attack."

Hence, this chapter is devoted almost entirely to research concerning the endogenous mentally retarded or to research that throws suggestive light on their development and condition. Some of the research reviewed here has been done with the population considered endogenous mentally retarded, some with dull normal (70–90 IQ) populations, and some with bright young adults; still other research deals with subhuman species.

By environment, the present author refers to the most conspicuous and (hopefully, quantifiable) *effective* set of learning conditions to which the developing organism is exposed postnatally. The outline of this chapter presupposes that endogenous mentally retarded children have been exposed to environments malignant in a number of ways: financially and culturally deprived, lacking in respect for these children as individuals, barren for them of what is ordinarily considered intellectual stimulation, often ethnically discriminatory against them, and so on. Studies in Newcastle-on-Tyne, England (Spencer *et al.*, 1954; Miller *et al.*, 1960), have analyzed in great detail the interrelations of factors like these and their effect on child development.

Clarke and Clarke (1960) have considered especially the factors of deprivation and have presented us with an analysis of the conditions of deprivation which is more sophisticated than most. They consider the major dimensions of early childhood deprivation to be (1) social isolation, (2) cruelty and neglect, (3) institutional upbringing, (4) adverse child-rearing practices, and (5) separation experiences across a wide range of severity. They also consider socio-economic and cultural deprivations, placing them somewhere with points (2) and (3) above, and believe that the dimension of sensory deprivation in infancy

and early childhood probably deserves special consideration.

The problem of environment has been approached in many ways. The sociologists have given us the useful (although often cloudy) notion of social class, sometimes simply defined by contrasting blue- and white-collar families; sometimes more elaborately classified by criteria of "family income, paternal occupation, paternal place of residence, paternal education," or home furnishings and possessions into subdivisions of upper, middle, and lower classes. Others have defined social class by educational level alone or by paternal occupational level considered by itself, while others ascertain values and assign respondents "psychologically." Attempts have been made to assess environment by interview (e.g., Baldwin, Kalhorn, and Breese, 1945; Sears, Maccoby, and Levin, 1957).

All investigators of environment seem to be seeking the answer to the same questions the present author asks: What are the *learning* experiences through which the child goes, how can these be quantified, and what relations do they have to his development, intellectual and otherwise?

DEFINITION OF INTELLIGENCE

The technology of measuring intelligence appears to be better developed than is theory about intelligence. Many attempts have been made to treat the concept of intelligence logically and theoretically (e.g., Ferguson, 1954, 1956; Haggard, 1954; Spiker and McCandless, 1954). Attempts at definition range from stating that "intelligence is what intelligence tests measure," through definitions such as "intelligence is the ability to do abstract thinking."

Early (Thorndike *et al.*, 1926) and recent (Ferguson, 1954, 1956) students of the topic hold that there are many intelligences or argue for a factor theory of intelligence, factors being more or less individually "pure" and independent of each other (Thurstone and Thurstone, 1950). The Thurstones have standardized tests for children and adults designed to isolate primary factors in intellectual functioning, such as vocabulary, ability to deal with spatial concepts, and number ability. Spearman (1927) postulated a general or "g factor." Some types of test were heavily dependent on g (e.g., vocabulary), while other s (for special ability) factors were only slightly related to g (for example, music ability and motor skill).

The last twenty years have seen little original "theory" of intelligence. From the writer's point of view, the most influential work has come from Hebb and those who have been stimulated by him (such as Ferguson, 1954, 1956). Ferguson (1954) writes:

At present no systematic theory, capable of generating fruitful hypotheses about behavior, lies behind the study of human ability. Current approaches are largely empirical. . . . The concept of intelligence . . . is no longer a useful scientific concept except as subsuming some defined set of clearly distinguishable abilities (p. 95).

Ferguson proceeds to develop a theory of intelligence based more on learning than genetics. To Ferguson, "ability" (intelligence), as measured by our current tests, is composed of correlated overlearnings. These, in interaction with the genetic heritage, result in the separate abilities which, when grouped (as in intelligence tests), reach their asymptotes as a result of the individual's social learning, which may vary widely according to the culture in which he develops.

The most conspicuous characteristic of the United States' (and Britain's) intelligence tests is that they are remarkably efficient in predicting groups' academic achievement, particularly groups at the younger age levels, such as elementary school pupils. Ferguson's argument is that, in such cultures as the United States and Britain and for groups, the abilities tapped by these tests have reached a stage of overlearning such that (like the ability to swim or ride a bicycle) time has little influence on either their decline or gain. The predictive efficiency for school performance that such tests possess results from the "transfer" between performance on the test tasks and school performance. For individuals, however, such tests are likely to be less efficient in predicting the future than for groups, since individual intellectual growth is not often linear with time (e.g., Dearborn and Rothney, 1941).

For "intellectual" tasks that are valued by a culture or subculture, growth (Ferguson believes) probably continues to age seventeen; for "intellectual" tasks that are not valued, growth may terminate much earlier or be much slower in rate. Thus, he accounts for differences in intelligence and intelligence test patterns for children growing up in different cultures, different social classes, rural as contrasted to urban areas, institutions rather than the free community, and so on. Clarke, Clarke, and Reiman (1958), for example, report data concerning Wechsler IQ changes for twenty-five mentally retarded subjects from "very bad" homes over a test-retest period of approximately three years, and compare them with thirty-four subjects (Ss) from less adequate homes, committed to the same hospital. Presumably the contrast in circumstances involved in transfer to a hospital (including values attached to "intellectual" behaviors) would be greater for the former than for the latter group. Average IQ change for the "bad home" group was 9.7 points, for the "not so adverse" group, 4.1 points. A greater interval between tests (approximately six years), and enriched experiences (work in the community) did little to change the average difference between two such groups (numbering eleven and ten only), although the average gain was increased so that the net gain for the "bad homes" group was 14.1 points, for the "less adverse homes" 10.4.

To anticipate material included later in this chapter, it has been shown that children who develop in culturally isolated rural areas (the mountains of eastern Tennessee, for example) decline progressively in intelligence as measured by standard intelligence tests: older brothers and sisters have lower measured intelligence than their younger sibs. Ferguson would say that the skills measured by a standard United States' intelligence test are not particularly important in adapting to life in the Tennessee mountains and thus decline (or at least develop less rapidly) with age.

A study by Havighurst and Hilkevitch (1944) relates to this point—one of profound importance in considering the training of endogenous mentally retarded children. These authors found that a sample of Hopi Indian children living quite remote from the usual United States' culture tested substantially higher on a performance intelligence test than Indian children living closer to the "standard" culture: indeed, their mean score was 115 compared with the approximate mean of 100 for the original standardization group of white children. This group of youngsters also tested much higher than a group of more acculturated Shiprock Navaho children, who averaged 96.

Following Ferguson, one might speculate that the highly organized tribal structure and ritual, the high artistic level, the architectural skills, and the tribe's dependence on an environment so harsh that survival demands that it be studied in exquisite and painstaking detail all go to develop high performance skills among the Hopi. The Navahos are herders rather than farmers, are architecturally and artistically less proficient, and thus may have less opportunity (and need) to develop the skills measured by such a performance test. Midwestern children, such as those in the standardization sample, live in moderately comfortable, undemanding surroundings and

may, like the Navahos, have neither as much need nor opportunity to practice skills that make for high scores on performance tests.

Ferguson's statement illuminates these results: "Presumably children reared in different environments, which demand different types of learning at different ages, develop different patterns of ability" (1954, p. 99). Different abilities, Ferguson believes, come into play and are required at different stages of learning a task. "An individual might possess the ability to improve rapidly in the early stages of learning, but might lack the abilities necessary to attain high proficiency at the stage of high habituation or overlearning." In other words, most of us can learn the elements of golfing, but few of us become champions. In support of this differential entry of skills into learning a task, Ferguson (1956) cites a study of young men who, in their early stages of learning a visual-motor task, were superior or inferior according to their spatial and verbal abilities. Early learning was fastest for those who were facile in verbal skills and who could manipulate spatial concepts. But the final, polished performance was dependent on reaction time and the rate at which the individual moved. Similar phenomena have been shown with animals. Ritchie, Aeschliman, and Pierce (1950) worked with rats in a maze-learning situation. The first stages of learning mazes seemed to depend on the acuity of the animals' visual discrimination. But final, efficient running of the maze seemed to depend on whether the animals could utilize motor and kinesthetic cues.

Bayley (1955) has been a leader in longitudinal studies of human development. Her interests have been mainly in intellectual and physical development. Concerning intellectual development, her conclusions differ little from Ferguson's theories. She says:

I see no reason why we should continue to think of intelligence as an integrated (or simple) entity or capacity which grows throughout childhood by steady accretion. . . . Intelligence appears to me, rather, to be a dynamic succession of developing functions, with the more advanced or complex functions in the hierarchy depending on the prior maturing of earlier simpler ones given, of course, normal conditions of care (p. 807).

Whether or not material on the topic of this chapter concerns the endogenous mentally retarded, the normal, or the gifted, it is well (for practical reasons if no other) to think of intelligence as *problem-solving ability.*

The ability to solve problems is no simple process but, rather, incredibly complex. It involves concentration, speed, depth or power, breadth, and so on. Some problems involve only the use of words; others use words to mediate motor pressures; others involve numbers and space. One man can be an excellent farmer but a poor geometrician. Some of the most gifted teachers of arithmetic in the elementary grades do poorly at college algebra. A brilliant physicist may be a poor farmer. Yet there is an amount of generality to problem-solving ability: were the physicist as motivated to farm as he was to study atom splitting, he would probably have been a good farmer.

THE QUESTION OF NATURE AND NURTURE

Through the thirties and forties of this century, the relative importance of nature and nurture for the development of intelligence was debated by psychologists and child developmentalists. At times, the debate more resembled a street fight than the resolution of a scientific issue. While, for the most part, the issue has been reduced to data and common sense concerning the range of normal intelligence, considerable heat can still be engendered by asking the question: Is the endogenous (or garden variety) mental retardate a product of his genes or his postnatal environment? Or, the unan-

swerable question: What relative contributions are made by nature and nurture?

Some time ago (1948) Anastasi and Foley suggested a sensible analysis of the question: they suggest that our first approach should be to decide whether *structure* or *function* is the matter being discussed, then to ask whether it is *hereditary* structure or function or *environmental* structure or function that is the issue.

Most people agree that, under normal circumstances, a child's physical growth pattern, his height, his prepotency toward one or another body build, and his hair and eye colorings are structural characteristics at least partially determined by his genes. On the other hand, starvation alters body build, can stunt growth, and can alter structure (as in rickets). So the environment, too, can alter structure. But encephalitis associated with whooping cough or measles or serious head injury can alter function (as well as structure) and render a previously normal child mentally retarded. In this case, no one argues the responsibility of genes: environment has changed structure *and* function. Amaurotic family idiocy, apparently clearly genetic, alters function as well as structure.

Functional-structural characteristics such as near- or far-sightedness are probably partially determined by heredity; on the other hand, such visual functions as reading have never resulted genetically. With such possible exceptions as Tarzan, everyone else has been taught to read: reading is an environmentally determined function.

Clear-cut answers about the inheritance or acquisition through learning of such complex traits as intelligence and personality adjustment are unavailable. In at least one sense, the whole nature-nurture debate is scientifically meaningless, if for no other reason than that when each of two conditions or states is required to produce a phenomenon—a child, an IQ—neither can be said to be more important than the other. Both heredity and environment begin to operate at the moment of conception, and they cannot be meaningfully separated. A geneticist, Stern (1956) has said that the environment comprises

all that is not genetic. It means the intrauterine surroundings of the embryo and fetus, the food and climate which impinge on the child and adult, and the psychological and cultural influences of home, school and society in their complex reactions upon the personality (p. 48).

Both nature and nurture, in their most extreme forms can, of course, be *totally* responsible for arrested mental development, and there are one or two extremely well-documented cases where children have been brought up in a social vacuum and, on discovery, have been functioning at a very severely retarded level (see Davis, 1940, 1947). Occasionally this developmental arrest has been shown to be reversible, suggesting that the child was potentially normal. Probably the main difficulty in separating the effects, on the one hand, of heredity and, on the other, of environment is that *within most groups which have been studied, the environmental variable is somewhat attenuated.* For example, the Clarke and Clarke studies (e.g., 1954, 1958) concerned children most of whom came from very bad homes; yet others have studied those who have enjoyed specially stimulating experiences; or again, the famous studies of identical twins reared apart only found minor differences in environment (e.g., town versus country). Thus, since the whole gamut of environmental effect is limited in such research, its influences tend to have been underestimated.

Heredity and environment—nature and nurture—interact. The traditional literature has tended to overlook this interaction: in the Kallikak family, for example (Goddard, 1912), Martin Kallikak begot an illegitimate male baby by a pre-

sumptively mentally retarded barmaid during Revolutionary times. Later and more respectably, other children were born to a wife of his own social status. The descendants of the first boy produced remarkable records of criminal behavior, begot many illegitimate children, were often mentally retarded and were, in general, wretched citizens. Some of our best people are descended from the second family. Reports of these two families overlooked the fact that the environments of the two father-related clans differed to an even greater extent than their heredities, which, at least for the first generation following Martin, overlapped genetically by 50 per cent. The children of intelligent, successful parents ordinarily grow up in security. They are well fed and well educated. The children of dull parents, who are typically rather unsuccessful in making their economic way through life, mature in a setting of deprivation, uncertainty, and depressed neighborhood conditions.

Human family histories are so fragmentary that accurate assessment of the attributes of ancestors is impossible, except in certain rare cases—for example, some royal families—and only partially so for them. Intelligence tests have been in use only since the middle of the second decade of this century; it is doubtful whether many royal children have been subjected to the Stanford-Binet. Also, family histories are really only useful when a quality which marks out its possessor sharply from others who do not possess it (e.g., hemophilia) can be discerned. Compared with most lower species of animals, the span between human generations is so great that any one scientific worker can ordinarily encompass no more than two generations in his professional life. Psychology and human genetics are new sciences, whose progress is so rapid that techniques useful for assessing one generation are outmoded by, and not comparable with, techniques available for the second generation. Actually, techniques applicable in one decade are frequently transcended by techniques developed in the second. This fact has added greatly to the difficulty of longitudinal research in many areas, including intelligence, but particularly in the emotion-personality area.

An adequate study of heredity and environment necessitates control over mating as well as rather extreme manipulation of the environment. In a Western society such as ours controlled mating is impossible. People marry whom they will. Manipulation to produce extreme environmental circumstances is, for good reasons, socially and legally impossible. (We cannot, for example, place the very superior two-year-old of very privileged parents in a situation where he would have no contact with humans.) Yet to study environment and heredity in any conclusive fashion, extreme manipulations of heredity (mating of one mentally retarded and one very superior person, for example) and of environment (as in the example given above) are necessary. It is for such reasons that some of our best information in this area comes from studies of animals, for which it is possible to manipulate both the genetic pool and the surroundings. Some of these animal studies are reviewed later in the chapter.[1]

[1] One reader believes that this chapter has neglected studies of disastrous social isolation, such as those by Davis (1940, 1947) which represent "extreme manipulations of environment" by accident. Hence, there results underestimation of what can be, or has been, gleaned from studies of gross deprivation. This reader also urges that qualification should be made that animals have no speech and are rigid, pointing out that, in his judgment, "more has been gained by studying individual humans who, as adults, gained their sight than by artificially blinding many apes."

"Animal studies," this reader continues, "although of tremendous importance, must be severely limited in their applications to man, particularly where subprimates are concerned." The author of this chapter has attempted to introduce appropriate cautions in the introductory paragraphs of the section of "Animal Research."

SIGNIFICANCE OF THE NATURE-NURTURE QUESTION

The nature-nurture question is discussed at some length, even though it is *logically* unclear, and scientific answers to it are difficult, if not impossible. There are several reasons why it merits full discussion, of which the least important is that it has been historically and is currently a matter of preoccupation in the study of child development. More important are the facts that heredity is heavily weighted in placing babies for adoption and that any information that we can obtain about contribution to the variance of human intelligence is important information. There exist very real reservations, possibly but not clearly justified by evidence, about placing for adoption babies whose parents are mentally retarded or borderline in intelligence or who are psychotic and even neurotic. Yet the evidence for the inheritance of these traits is not clear-cut. Rather impressive evidence exists (e.g., Skeels and Harms, 1948; Skodak and Skeels, 1949) to show that, given a good environment, many children who might have become simple mental retardates had they stayed in their true homes turn out to be typical prospects of normality, superiority, or inferiority when placed in good adoptive homes. Little or no evidence exists about the effects of adoptive placement on children of psychotics or neurotics.

When an issue intimately affects the lives of many children and, in addition, has numerous other broad social implications, this issue and the evidence with reference to it should be examined. Because the data currently available are inconclusive, few scientists today are willing to take an extreme position. One widely accepted viewpoint has been advanced by Stern (1956).

The genetic endowment in respect to any one trait has been compared to a rubber band and the trait itself to the length which the rubber band assumes when it is stretched by outside forces. Different people initially may have been given different lengths of un-stretched endowment, but the natural forces of the environment may have stretched their expression to equal length, or led to differ-ences in attained length sometimes corre-sponding to their innate differences and at other times in reverse of the relation (p. 53).

REVIEW OF RESEARCH

It has been mentioned earlier that this review of research is not intended to be all-inclusive. It includes many studies dealing with normal populations of chil-dren and adults, as well as studies em-ploying animals as subjects. It omits many studies, some of them classic. The studies selected for review seem to the present author to shed light on *principles* that are important in understanding and working with endogenous mentally re-tarded children and adults. This litera-ture review consists of seven sections: (1) endogenous mentally retarded chil-dren and their families, (2) studies of adopted children, particularly those of "inferior" social stock, (3) school attend-ance and intelligence, (4) language, (5) social class, isolation, ethnicity, and mi-gration, (6) deprivation, and (7) studies of animals.

THE ENDOGENOUS (OR SUBCULTURAL, OR SIMPLE) MENTALLY RETARDED

This group of endogenous mentally re-tarded has been previously defined as consisting of neurologically and physical-ly normal children testing below about 70 IQ on standard intelligence tests. When they are dressed well and silent they cannot be distinguished from nor-mal children. Ordinarily, their IQ's are not below 50, and the overwhelming ma-jority of them come from the most dis-advantaged of the social classes (Sara-son, 1953). They comprise perhaps 2+ per cent of the American population—a relatively small percentage, but a tre-mendous number—somewhere between three and six million persons if we use as our base a United States census of 185,-

000,000 population (see Introduction to this chapter). From their ranks comes a disproportionate number of relief, char-ity, delinquent, criminal, and promiscu-óus persons, although (see, e.g., Charles, 1953) even in this marginal group most, apparently, come to be self-supporting and law-abiding.

Intimate experience with and deep in-terest in this group have earlier led the present author (McCandless, 1952, pp. 684–85) to say that two learning hypoth-eses may be formulated to bear, in a gen-eral way, on the question of how subcul-tural mental retardation develops:

First, the environment from which the subcultural mentally retarded person comes is one providing minimal opportu-nity for the learning of the skills sub-sumed under the term *intelligence*.

Second, the environment from which the subcultural mentally retarded person comes is one in which he has had maxi-mal opportunity to learn "self-defeating" techniques—expectancies of failure, abso-lute as opposed to relative thinking, con-crete as opposed to abstract thinking, be-lief in his essential worthlessness, and so on. Ferguson's thinking (1954, 1956) is also relevant in this connection.

Study after study (see, McCandless, 1952; Sarason, 1953) reveals the hopeless-ness of the environments from which such children come: stark poverty, pa-rental abandonment, social humiliation, rejection and defeat, parental drunken-ness, feeblemindedness, and psychosis, school failure and rejection by peers pro-gressively increasing with age, malnutri-tion, cultural barrenness of the home, pa-rental indifference to the child's educa-tional progress and community success, poor health, bad teeth, retarded growth.

It has been demonstrated that a rela-tively simple and circumscribed experi-ence of failure can prevent children from taking advantage of practice that, under ordinary circumstances, would improve their score on intelligence test items (Lantz, 1945). Such failure had the greatest influence on items that test the thinking process. When such experiences of failure and frustration can interfere so markedly with intellectual performance, it seems plausible that a lifetime of frustration will interfere far more. Such experiences characterize the lives of children and adults who belong to the group of subcultural mental retardates. In addition, of course, their lives are impoverished in terms of sheer cultural opportunities to learn.

Kephart (1940) has demonstrated that the longer the time (simple) retardates spent in their homes, the lower their IQ's were likely to be. Upon transfer to a relatively privileged institution, where there were about two employees to every seven children, the pattern of IQ change reverses itself, particularly during the first year of their residence in the institution. However, it should be stated that many of the children were tested under conditions of stress before being admitted to the institution. This fact would accentuate the picture of their steadily dropping IQ while in the community and in their own homes and exaggerate the gain they made while in the institution, where tests were given by highly skilled examiners under standard and relaxed conditions after the children had begun to feel at ease.

However, the influence of the environment varies according to the type of child. Kephart and Strauss (1940), in another study of children at the Wayne County Training School, separated children who were brain-damaged from those who were neurologically normal and checked the rate of mental growth they had shown before and after admission to the institution. They concluded that neurologically normal mentally retarded children are more sensitive to environmental influence than are children of about the same IQ level who have suffered neurological damage.

Clarke and Clarke (1954) and Clarke, Clarke, and Reiman (1958) present evidence based on tests and retests with the Wechsler I that, for their British population of committed defectives, those from "very bad homes" increase more in IQ than those from "less adverse homes" (see p. 177 of this chapter). Homes were judged "very bad" when independent raters assigned to them two or more of the following indicators: N.S.P.C.C. (National Society for Prevention of Cruelty to Children) intervention, parental attitude antagonistic, no fixed abode, "Fit Person" order, home conditions bad, considerable neglect, irregular school attendance due to neglect, home dirty and neglected, gross poverty, crime in the parents, rickets, and child found begging. The Ss in these studies judged to have developed in "less adverse homes" came from homes to which only one, or none, of the above criteria applied.

Mundy (1957), in a study done in Britain, supplies evidence that the stimulation provided by community living results in more intellectual gain then residence in an institution for the mentally retarded. She matched twenty-eight mentally retarded women between eighteen and fifty years of age who had left the institution with twenty-eight who remained and found that, over about a two-year period, those residing in the community had gained about 11 points in intelligence quotient, whereas those who remained in the institution had gained only about two points.[2]

---

[2] One of the readers of the manuscript of this chapter has pointed out that "Mundy's (1957) study can unfortunately hardly be quoted without criticism; her case for response to present environmental differences rests upon whether control and experimental groups were in fact initially equal in all respects. There is considerable internal evidence that this was not so, and in any case the control group contained extraordinarily atypical patients who showed a stability of IQ over a two-year period of such an order that has never before been reported (for details, see Clarke and Clarke, 1958, pp. 113–14). Other studies on similar patients do not support her conclusions; they suggest that re-

How do subcultural mentally retarded children function as adults? A number of studies, of which one by Charles (1953) is representative, indicate that although they do not do well, they do much better than might be expected, although outcome varies immensely from individual to individual. Charles traced 127 children from an earlier study of opportunity-room children, all of whom had tested below 70 IQ (the average was about 60) and made as full an investigation as possible of them when they were from their mid-thirties to their late forties. A disproportionate number of the group had died—over 15 per cent (twice as many as the national average)—and of those dead, almost one-third, mostly males, had died violently. More than one-third had been entirely self-sufficient economically during their adult lives; fewer than half had assistance from public relief funds. A smaller percentage than would be expected on the basis of national average had married, although this was partly attributable to the fact that a number of the group were or had been institutionalized. (About 18 per cent either were in institutions for the mentally retarded or psychotic, or had been institutionalized and then discharged.) Those who had married averaged 2.03 children, a figure slightly lower than the national average. Those children of the original group who could be reached for testing (73 in number) ranged in IQ from 50 to 138, with an average of 95. Only two of these children were so retarded that they had to be institutionalized.

The divorce rate was about the same as that for the nation; a greater percentage of the group than of the population as a whole lived in single-family houses; and over half of them owned or were buying their own homes (about the same as the national average). The men were,

for the most part, laborers, the women housekeepers. Of the sample that could be reached, about 40 per cent had been involved in some breach of the law. Twenty of the 127 were retested for IQ. When scores from the same test that had originally been used were averaged, the figure was 58 (about the same as the original score), but this particular test places adults at some disadvantage. A more modern and widely used test gave an average IQ of 81 for these 20 subjects.

As is typical of subcultural mentally retarded persons, an IQ based on verbal items was far inferior to one based on performance items (the respective IQ's were 72 and 88).

Krishef (1959) reports that the type of placement after release from an institution affects success of adjustment (his criterion of successful adjustment was non-return to the institution, and his sample was small—twenty-nine in each of two differentially placed groups). But Ss placed in rural settings appeared to adjust better than those placed in urban settings. An interesting sidelight on institutionalization is the negative relation Krishef reports between institutional behavior and community success: "acting-out behavior and runaways, when they were combined revealed that more wards in the unsuccessful adjustment group neither acted out, ran away, or did both" (p. 864).

Probably more mothers belonging to the group called endogenous mental retardates have illegitimate babies than is true for the general population. It is also likely that their babies are more likely to be placed for adoption than are the babies of mothers intellectually and economically more advantaged. Are such babies in turn, mentally retarded? Evidence is reviewed later in this chapter that this is not the case. The average of the children of retardates who could be tested in Charles's study approached normal IQ and ranged as high as 138 IQ (very

covery processes from past damage are responsible for, rather than response to present environment."

bright, or superior). In another study involving 312 children separated from their mothers before they were four years of age (Snygg, 1938), the children of the 98 mothers whose IQ's were less than 70 averaged 91 IQ (low normal), even though their foster-home placements were not in any sense ideal. The over-all correlation between the IQ's of children and their true mothers was 0.13. Such a correlation accounts for less than 2 per cent of the variance.

Speer (1940) studied a group of children whose mothers' average IQ was 49. The IQ's of children separated from their mothers before they were two years of age averaged normal. The mean IQ for a group of sixteen children who stayed with their mothers before they were two years of age averaged normal. The mean IQ for this small group (twelve children) was 100.5. The average IQ for a group of sixteen children who stayed with their mothers until they were from twelve to fifteen years of age was 53.

Another study (Stippich, 1940) reports the results from an investigation of children born to forty-eight mentally retarded mothers with IQ averages between 60 and 63 (depending on which of three intelligence tests was used in computing IQ). All the mothers had been legally declared mentally retarded and all had been institutionalized. The children had been separated from their families before they were one year of age and placed in boarding homes or institutions that offered less than ideal care for them. Even under such unfavorable circumstances, the children averaged 83 IQ at an average age of five years—at least 20 IQ points higher than their mothers. This study also included the similarly separated children of twenty-nine mothers whose IQ's averaged 102. These youngsters' IQ's averaged 97. Since it has not usually been found that environments other than rigorously depriving ones (such as impersonal institutional life) affect children before the age of about

eighteen months, this study provides some support for a genetic point of view: in similar but deprived environments, children of brighter mothers are brighter at the age of five than the offspring of duller mothers. Even so, the children of the mentally retarded mothers were a good 20 points higher in IQ than their mothers. Non-assortative mating seems often to occur with women of this type. Hence, paternal genetics may account partly for the higher IQ of the children (although Skeels and Harms [1948] present data suggesting that this is not likely the case).

This section has offered evidence indicating that the longer children live in very depressed environments (including homes where the mother is mentally retarded), the lower is their average IQ. There are indications that environmental reversal can change this developmental direction, although some of the evidence is weak. Several studies report normality or near-normality for children of mentally retarded parents placed early in foster homes and report that there is no significant relation between the IQ's of the mothers and their true children when the children are separated early from the mothers. The most pessimistic of the studies reveals a differential upward level of a full 20 points between the IQ's of the retarded mothers and their children, even though the children had been less than optimally placed.

STUDIES OF ADOPTED CHILDREN

There is a limited number of studies of the intellectual development of children of mentally retarded mothers and/or fathers since, traditionally, agencies have been reluctant to place such children, at least until after allowing extensive periods of time for observation following birth. These extensive periods of time, rather typically, have been spent in traditional infant-child institutions. Such institutions, according to the literature reviewed in a later section of this chapter, tend to retard children's intellectual development; hence, reports on intellectual development of children studied under such circumstances afford us little sound information about the later careers of children born to retarded parents. The last three studies cited in the preceding section have presented a moderately optimistic picture of children separated early from retarded mothers and placed in environments ranging from mediocre (at best) to adequate.

Other studies reported in this section bear out this trend. Some of the major studies reported here come from the Iowa Child Welfare Research Station, in conjunction with which the Iowa Board of Control of Institutions formerly worked. Data on which the studies were based were made possible because of the (probably accidental) tendency for Iowa adoptive placements to be made in a fashion such that selective placement (babies from "good" parents to "good" homes, and vice versa) was minimized, at least in comparison with placement policies in operation at the time.

A first conclusion to be drawn from a study of the literature concerning the intelligence of adopted children is that they are above the national average in IQ. For example, Skodak and Skeels' study (1949) of a group of 100 adopted children tested at an average age of thirteen years and six months showed them to have an average IQ of 117, whereas, for the nation, the figure is 100. This same group, containing a number of children who later dropped out of the study, had tested 117 on their first test at the age of two years and two months. There were 180 children in this initial group. For the 152 who took a second test, average IQ was 112 at four years and three months; and for the 139 who took a third test, the average was 115 at seven years of age.

Another study (Skeels and Harms, 1948) reports on the average IQ's of three groups of adopted youngsters, all of whose true parents were inferior in social history, i.e., mothers were mentally retarded, or fathers were in the lowest possible occupational bracket (unskilled labor), or both. Most of these children were tested at about kindergarten age; one group of 87 tested 105.5; and the other group of 111 tested at an average of 110. These findings are representative of what has been found in other studies. There are at least three reasons for the above-average IQ's of adopted youngsters: the *first* is that all obviously retarded children are screened out before adoption, so that there are few, if any, retarded youngsters to pull down the average. The *second* is that adopted children, by definition, are badly wanted by their parents and consequently probably get more than an average amount of love, attention, and stimulation. *Finally,* since the majority of children are probably placed by social agencies, only the "better" homes are given babies for adoption.

Although intelligence scores of adopted children do not correlate highly, if at all, with the intelligence quotients or education of their foster parents, the average level of their intelligence is about the same as would be predicted for the true children of their foster parents.

The pioneering Skodak and Skeels (1949) study mentioned above demonstrated that the IQ's of adopted children averaged either 20 or 30 points higher than those of their true mothers. The difference in these figures is due to the fact that two different tests were used for the children. The authors took a sample of 180 children and followed them from the time they were placed in their adoptive homes, which in all cases was before the age of six months. Although not all the mothers had taken intelligence tests (63 had), there was a correlation of 0.44 between the IQ's of the true mothers and the IQ's of the children at the time the children were more than thirteen years of age. Such a correlation, of course, accounts for less than one-fifth of the variance in children's IQ (19 per cent). One striking aspect of this study is the elevation of the children's IQ over that of their mothers: whereas the mothers functioned on the whole at a borderline level, the children were significantly superior to the national average in intelligence.

The study has been severely criticized. It is maintained that the mothers were tested under disadvantageous conditions (i.e., fairly soon after they had had their babies and usually after they had decided to give them up). There is little doubt that these factors operated to lower the intelligence-test scores of the mothers. Emotional upset, unusual conditions, and so on contribute to errors in measuring intelligence. But the biographies of these 63 mothers indicated that they were marginal social persons, whereas the children, on the whole, were successful adolescents. Thirty-one per cent of the children had IQ's higher than 99 per cent of the true mothers. Seventy per cent of the true mothers had IQ's below 95; only 16 per cent of the children fell so low. Whereas 25 per cent of the true mothers had IQ's below 75, only 4 per cent of the children did. One evaluator of the study (Honzik, 1957) makes much of the correlation between the IQ's of the true mothers and the IQ's of the children but partially ignores the fact that the level of intellectual functioning of the children is a socially and functionally important level above that of the mothers.

The striking Skeels and Harms study (1948) concerns the intelligence of children whose true parents were socially disadvantaged. Skeels and Harms studied three groups of adopted children. The mothers of the 87 children in the first group all had intelligence test scores of less than 75. The putative fathers of the 111 children in the second group were at the lowest occupational levels (semi- and unskilled laborers). A third group of 35 children was made up of children whose mothers tested below 75 IQ *and* whose fathers were at the bottom of the socio-economic ladder in terms of their occupations. About 80 per cent of the children in this study were illegitimate. The IQ's of these three groups of children were 105.5, 110.3, and 104, respectively. In other words, all three groups tested above the national average, yet their true parents were, at the very best, marginal members of society in terms of intelligence and occupation. The correlations between the intelligence of the three groups of children and their true mothers were, respectively: 0.23 (significant at the 0.05 level), 0.22 (just missing significance by the 0.05 level), and 0.12 (a statistically insignificant figure). It can be noted that for none of the groups does the intelligence of the true mothers account for more than about 5 per cent of the variance in child intelligence.

In the Pine School, a "total push" program has been conducted in which the families of older (five years and more) and younger (less than five years) "socially disadvantaged" children have been served by social workers, psychologists, pediatricians, nurses, nutritionists, and so on, while the children attended nursery school and kindergarten.[3]

The gain in IQ for the younger and total group was significant at less than the 0.05 level. The younger group gained significantly more than the older group, while the gain for the older group was not significant.

The implications to be drawn from the study (necessarily tentative, since these are preliminary data based on a small number of Ss) are, first that a "total push" program works. An interesting, informal sidelight of the study is that the investigators are "running themselves out of subjects." The younger children in the families, whom they had assumed might

[3] Unpublished data from Theron Alexander, Robert Kugel, and Lowell Schoer.

serve as later subjects for study, all test much brighter than their older sibs. The second implication from these preliminary data is that the younger a child is when he undergoes such experiences, the greater the effect they have on the child's development. Chambers and Zabarenko (1956) report results that, for the most part, agree with those from this preliminary study (and also find no effect of glutamic acid on intelligence change). Their conclusion seems also to be the sense of a review of literature on this subject made by Astin and Ross (1960). More controversially, Chambers and Zabarenko report more IQ gain by their brain-damaged than by their non-brain-damaged subjects.

One interesting study (Worbois, 1942) used as its subjects elementary school children and tested the differential effects of attending a rural consolidated or a rural one-room school. The different populations studied were rather closely matched for all factors but the type of school attended. The study was carried on for two years. The first group of children reported on experienced their first year of school while the study was in progress. Children attending a rural one-room school gained an average of 1 IQ point (from 105 to 106); rural consolidated-school children gained 5 points (106 to 111). The difference in these gains was significant. A second group whose first two years of school coincided with the period of the study, showed a 16-point gain for consolidated children (from an average of 105 to 121); the one-room children moved from 104 to 108. This difference is highly significant. A third group of youngsters had their second and third years of school during the experimental period. The consolidated children changed from 112 to 116, and the one-room children from 105 to 103. This was the smallest of the groups, and the difference in changes did not quite reach significance. Worbois believes that differences in the teachers' training together with the richness of experiences provided account for these differential intelligence gains.

LANGUAGE

While our present tests of intelligence are very useful, they also have obvious defects, and their results are frequently misapplied. The definition of intelligence adopted for this chapter is the traditional one of problem-solving ability. This ability, at least in conventional school programs, depends on being able to handle abstractions. Abstractions, in turn, are best dealt with by children who are high in verbal and number ability. Most of our current intelligence tests include many—even a majority of—items involving these abilities. Of eight "primary abilities" selected by Thurstone, two concern words and word usage: the factor V (verbal comprehension) and the factor W (word influency). Wechsler (1944), the author of probably the most widely used individual test of intelligence for adults and one of the more widely used tests for children, reports that scores from the vocabulary subtest of the total scale, composed (for the adult scale) of 42 words that the subject is asked to define, correlate 0.85 with the entire scale. Such a correlation accounts for almost three-fourths of the variance of the full-scale IQ (72 per cent). Substantial evidence exists to indicate that performance (non-verbal) problems are solved better by those who put verbal labels on different portions of their efforts. It has been clearly demonstrated (e.g., Spiker, 1956) that children learn new tasks more efficiently when they have names for the elements of the process or for the pieces of equipment that must be manipulated successfully in order to demonstrate learning. In other words, we are quite safe in saying that anything which affects the use of words probably has an effect on intelligence as it is now measured.

Vocabulary and the general adequacy and completeness of speech vary by socio-economic class. Speech is poorer in form and articulation, less in amount, and less precise for children at lower socio-economic levels than for those at higher social levels (e.g., Irwin, 1948). The only glimmer of hope we have for predicting the later intelligence of children tested as infants seems to lie in measuring their speech sounds (Catalano and McCarthy, 1954). Children reared with scant adult attention, who are relatively isolated or who live in institutions, are retarded even more in their speech than in their general IQ level. This retardation has been shown to exist as early as two months of age. Children who, at elementary school ages, test at the mentally retarded or borderline level started talking later than children who measure normal or bright. At least during the early years of their lives (presumably because they communicate primarily with each other and depend to a lesser degree on "socialization" with adults), twins and triplets test lower in both speech and intelligence than singletons, although much of this lag is overcome by school age. Their speech seems to be even more retarded than can be accounted for by their somewhat lower intelligence test scores. While the evidence is not entirely clear-cut, children who are bilingual during the preschool years—that is, typically, whose homes use one language while their schools use a different one—test lower than monoglots. Although social class is involved, since children from such homes are rather more frequently from lower- than from upper-class homes, the effect seems greater than can be accounted for by social class alone.[4]

As will be seen in the next subsection of the chapter, social class seems to be directly related to vocabulary level; yet children from some middle-class homes have been shown to have low vocabularies, while children from some lower-

class homes have relatively good vocabularies. One author (Milner, 1951) provides evidence indicating why there are such exceptions (at the same time presenting data to show that the child's language status and his socio-economic status correlate somewhere between 0.78 and 0.86, depending on which of two statistical techniques is used).

The twenty-one high-scorers in Milner's study of forty-two Negro first-graders came from homes ranging from upper-lower to lower-upper, this latter being the highest social class included in the study. They were distinguished as a group from the twenty-one low-scorers by such factors as eating breakfast and dinner with their families and engaging in conversation during these times. Their discipline inclined more toward guidance and prohibition, whereas physical discipline was more characteristic for the low-scoring children. High-scorers were more frequently expected to look after their own possessions and/or room and received more praise and affection. More high- than low-scorers had been exposed to baby sitters, and they went to bed later, frequently as late as ten at night. Low-scorers were "bribed" with small gifts of money more frequently than high-scorers. The high-scorers, as might be expected, possessed more books and indicated that their mothers and fathers more frequently read to them. More low-scorers said they could not recall ever feeling "real happy" and were more infrequently able to recall instances or situations where they had felt happy. Low-scorers more frequently possessed as reading material only funny books and/or schoolbooks.

Such factors as those listed above are, of course, strongly related to social class; but where there are variations in language within a social class, it is plausible that such variables as parental conversation, attention, praise, and so on, could produce the difference between the low- and the high-scorers.

[4] For a comprehensive review of this area, see McCarthy (1954).

Peck and Stephens (1960), using a very small sample of ten mentally retarded children and their families, report results (based on individual case analysis) that are congruent with Milner's:

. . . [T]he parent's willingness to answer his child's questions had a direct relationship to an exploring, questioning attitude in the child. Affectionateness, understanding, and rapport between the parents and their mentally retarded child were reflected in the child's ability to relate successfully with other adults (p. 843).

Such a state of affairs, it may be presumed, will further augment the child's intellectual eagerness and self-confidence. Parenthetically, Peck and Stephens found a correlation of 0.83 between the father's acceptance (or rejection) of his child and the amount of acceptance or rejection within the over-all home situation: Fathers set the pattern?

The hypothesis that parental reinforcement builds language is supported by an unpublished study of Irwin's (1960). Irwin secured the co-operation of a large group of mothers whose husbands were mostly skilled, semi-skilled, and unskilled laborers. Ordinarily such mothers do little reading to their children at any age and almost certainly none in the first year or so of their babies' lives. He persuaded fifty-five mothers to read aloud for at least ten minutes a day to their children from the time they were little more than babies (one year old). The participation in the study of another, control group of mothers was elicited by offers to check on the development of their babies. Otherwise no change was made in the interaction between them and their children.

Irwin measured the youngsters' speech development regularly and found great differences in all phases of speech by the time the children were twenty months of age. These differences appear to be highly significant statistically, although analysis of data has not been completed. This study is especially provocative when we consider the relations that have been found between speech and intelligence. Irwin reports the experimental mothers' amazement and chagrined amusement: "You asked us to read ten minutes a day," some exclaimed, "but I can't get away from that kid. He wants me to read to him all the time."

Once established during the preschool years, can a child's language level be changed? Since language is so closely related both to intelligence and to school achievement, the answer to this question is important. Dawe (1942) attempted to answer the query in a study that involved eleven pairs of children residing in an orphanage. When she began her study, the children ranged in age from three years, seven months to six years, ten months. Her experimental, or trained children were very carefully matched with the control children for school group attended, sex, chronological and mental age, IQ, and vocabulary. All children were attending either the orphanage nursery school or kindergarten, and she did her speech and language training on weekends for a total of ninety-two hours over a period of about seven and a half months.

At the begining of her study, her experimental group averaged low-normal (IQ = 80.6) as did her control group (IQ = 81.5). She trained the children in understanding words and concepts, looking at and discussing pictures, and listening to poems and stories. Occasionally she took them on short excursions, although this proved difficult within the framework of the orphanage.

Dawe's experimental group of children gained an average of more than 14 points in IQ during the training period, whereas the controls dropped an average of 2 points. At the beginning of training, average IQ's of the two groups were almost identical. At the end of the study they differed markedly, not only on the test originally given to them, but on another form of the test. Even on a performance test there was an average difference of 5.5 points in favor of the experimental children, although language presumably does not greatly affect the way children succeed on such a test (an assumption which is rather dubious). This difference, however, was not a significant one. Dawe's training did not include test-coaching, although her method of teaching may have helped the experimental children to be more efficient in approaching problems with elements similar to those included in intelligence tests.

Both groups of children gained in vocabulary, the experimentals 17.5 score points (words), the controls 10 score points. The experimentals gained significantly more than the controls. Information test scores also increased significantly more for the experimental than for the control children. Dawe made measures of such factors as attentiveness and intellectual interest. Dramatic improvements in almost all aspects of these important traits occurred for the experimental group. Such measures were not available for the controls.

Closely linked to Dawe's study, although not involving any specific training of the children, is a study performed by Badt (1958). She used as her Ss sixty inpatients in a school for mentally retarded children, who ranged in age from seven to fifteen years, all of whom were diagnosed as endogenously retarded, and whose IQ's ranged from 50 to 75. Stanford-Binet vocabulary scores for these children were weighted by 5 for abstract, 3 for use, and 1 for descriptive definitions of each word. For the word, *orange, abstract* was scored if, for example, the child defined it as a fruit or a color; *use* was scored if the definition was, "To eat"; and *descriptive* was scored if the child said, "It's round and yellow." She secured unanimous, three-judge agreement on classification of responses in 83 per cent of her definitions.

As might be expected, there was a low positive correlation between both chronological age and mental age and abstraction level (0.34 and 0.24, respectively). But the first-order correlation between length of institutionalization and abstraction score was a startling —0.61. When MA and CA were held constant, the length of institutionalization correlated —0.71 with level of abstraction (a concept corresponding rather closely to problem-solving ability). Badt's conclusion is that such a relation is due to lack of a mother figure. To the present writer, this seems an oversimplification (or overcomplication) of the case. But her results fit well with the evidence presented later in this chapter on general social deprivation, including lack of intellectual stimulation.

Griffith and Spitz (1958) have published a germinal study dealing with the ability to abstract verbally among a population of twenty-six boys, average IQ 66 (range 48–83), average age seventeen years, two months (range 14–20). Griffith and Spitz's findings fit well with those of Badt: those boys who gave abstract definitions for words in a vocabulary test were better able later to solve the problem of fitting a common principle to sets of three words in a test of "common properties" than boys who gave concrete definitions.

The authors' techniques for testing abstraction are interesting: six groups of three words each were given the Ss. The simplest set, for which all the boys induced a common property, was "coffee, tea, cocoa." The most difficult set, for which only 19 per cent induced the common property, was "pill, mosquito, pin." In the vocabulary test, the eighteen "conceptual" words had been imbedded in the total vocabulary list. Abstractions—inductions—were most likely when at least two of the three test words had been defined abstractly. The authors argue that this demonstrates rigidity on the part of their subjects and deduce at a speculative level certain training principles designed to control unsocial behavior, e.g., teaching the children abstract definitions and direct consequents for such words as fighting, lying, and stealing: these are all punishable; each can result in your being returned to the institution.

Theoretical contributions related to the role played by social class and language as factors predisposing individuals to think in a concrete manner have been made by Basil Bernstein (1958, 1959, 1960). Bernstein has attempted, in these papers, to show a relationship between two forms of linguistic expression and the manner in which relationships to objects are established. One form of language use, a *public language,* is commonly used by the unskilled and semi-skilled strata of society. This form of language use facilitates, according to Bernstein, "thinking of a descriptive order and sensitivity to a particular form of social interaction" (1959, p. 311). Because of this sensitivity to content, "only the simplest logical implications or boundaries of the structure will be cognized," i.e., "certain aspects of an object will not register as meaningful cues; or, if they do, the verbal response will be inadequately determined" (1958, p. 169). On the other hand, a *formal language,* the use of which is common to the middle class, "facilitates the verbal elaboration of subjective intent, sensitivity to the implications of separateness, and difference, and points to the possibilities inherent in a complex conceptual hierarchy for the organization of experience" (1960, p. 271).

The implications of this analysis are significant. Users of the public language (the lower class) are predisposed to "low levels of conceptualization—an orientation to a low order of causality, a disinterest in processes, a preference to be aroused by and respond to that which is immediately given rather than to the implications of a matrix of relationships" (1959, p. 318). The empirical support of this position is weak, consisting of two

minor investigations which show that the non-verbal intelligence of lower-class males in England is much higher than their verbal intelligence. If Bernstein's analysis is correct, it could be used to afford insight into the "conceptual rigidity" of the retardates in the Griffith-Spitz investigations.

Further evidence related to this point has been provided by M. L. Kellmer Pringle and his associates (Pringle and Bossio, 1958; Pringle and Tanner, 1958). In extensive investigations of the effects of early deprivation on the language development of children, he found that children who had resided in residential nursery schools and had experienced deprivation "were retarded in the formal aspects of language" (1958, p. 285). The nursery school children "lacked the ability for verbalizing phantasy and for using speech in making social relationships with contemporaries" (p. 286). Pringle believes that the results of his investigations support Goldfarb's assertion that deprivation is more detrimental to a child's language development than to any other aspect of his personality. This evidence might be used to account for the low performance of culturally deprived children on verbal intelligence tests and their high levels of ability on performance type tests.

EFFECTS OF SOCIAL CLASS AND OTHER SOCIAL FACTORS

A most comprehensive review of research on social class and intelligence is provided by Jones (1954, pp. 645–59). The evidence for social-class differences in intelligence is very clear-cut; the evidence is also clear that environmental opportunities substantially influence intellectual development. The social implications of such findings are readily apparent. No sensible person denies the important influence of heredity on all phases of human development, but the precise degree to which it affects so complex a phenomenon as intelligence is unknown. Likewise, no sensible person denies the influence of environment, although questions about the extent of its contribution to intellectual development are not yet answered. But we can *do something* about environment, little or nothing about heredity. Consequently, detailed studies of the range and type of environmental effects and developing courses of action built upon the results of such studies are of utmost social importance.

Dozens of studies (see, e.g., Jones, 1954) have been made of the resemblance in intelligence between parents and their offspring living in their own homes. Regardless of social class, level of parents' education, or parental intelligence, the correlation between measures of parental social status and children's intelligence is about 0.50. It is ordinarily a little lower than this for social class as measured, for example, by occupation; often a little higher when parental intelligence or educational level is used as a criterion. Some studies show that fathers' intelligence is more closely related to children's IQ than mothers'; other studies show the reverse. The safest conclusion is that both parents contribute about equally. Kagan and Moss, for example (1959), find that the median correlation between the IQ's of boys (measured at ages between three and ten) and their fathers is 0.39, and between boys and their mothers is 0.41. Girl children's IQ's correlate 0.51 with fathers' IQ's, with mothers' IQ's 0.48. Fathers' educational level has a median correlation of 0.24 with their boys' intelligence, and 0.39 with their girls'; mothers' educational level has a median correlation of 0.45 with their sons' IQ's, 0.57 with their girls. This suggests that the mothers have more to do with the pattern of family stimulation, and that the parents (as would be expected) contribute equally genetically to intelligence.

The correlation between parental social status and children's intelligence is,

as we have implied, remarkably stable. For studies of our highly complex human nature and behavior, a correlation of 0.50 is high (although it accounts for only 25 per cent of the variance in children's intelligence). Yet it represents the *combination* of parental genes and the environment provided by the parents. We must look elsewhere—no one knows precisely where—to account for the other 75 per cent of this variance: studies of the intelligence of grandparents, aunts, uncles, and great-grandparents may account for a larger share of the variance of children's intelligence than is usually considered likely. More sophisticated studies of motivation, personality, and *effective* environment should help still further in predicting children's intelligence.[5]

One of the more common ways of determining social class is by level of the father's occupation. In one such classification system Class I is made up of professional men (lawyers, conventionally educated ministers, physicians, and so on) and Class VII comprises unskilled laboring men. The 1937 revision of the Stanford-Binet Scale (Terman and Merrill, 1937) provided norms for 831 children between two and one-half years and five years of age, classified according to their social status. Class I children averaged 116 IQ; Class II children (whose fathers were semi-professional and managerial) averaged 112; Class III (fathers clerical and skilled-trades and retail workers) averaged 108; Class IV (rural owners) averaged 99; Class V (semi-skilled, minor clerical, and small-business) averaged 104; Class VI (slightly skilled laborers) averaged 95; and Class VII (urban and rural day laborers) aver-

[5] The child of wealth, whose nursery is crammed with toys and books, may be said to have an intellectually stimulating *objective* environment; yet if his contacts with adults are confined to a nurse of borderline mentality, who is not literate enough to read him the books or interested enough to stimulate him in play with his toys, his *effective* environment is poor.

aged 94. Similar results were obtained for other age levels up to the ages of fifteen to eighteen.

This large study was somewhat unrepresentative of the national population, since rural and unskilled laboring groups were not fully represented. But here and in other studies, an average difference of about 20 IQ points was found between the children of parents at the lowest and the highest social-class levels, regardless of the index used to measure social class.

This finding supports conclusively neither a hereditary nor an environmental point of view. It can be argued, probably legitimately but somewhat circularly, that people who "don't get ahead" are of inferior genetic stock, hence pass along a less adequate intellectual endowment to their children. That they provide less adequate intellectual stimulation is clear.

Our conclusion must be that the higher the socio-economic class of the parents, the brighter, on the average, the children will be. One ambitious study has gathered together intelligence test records of 45,000 children, fourth- through eighth-graders, from 455 schools in 310 communities in 36 of the (then) 48 United States (McGehee and Lewis, 1942). The upper 10 per cent of these children were classified as superior, the lower 10 per cent as retarded. Fathers' occupations were scaled from I (professional) through V (unskilled, day labor). Class I produced 2.4 times as many superior children as would be expected, whereas Class V produced only 0.3 as many as expected statistically; for the mentally retarded group, Class I parents produced only 0.14 times as many retarded children as would be expected, and Class V produced more than 1.5 times as many as expected statistically. Yet, in terms of sheer *numbers*, groups II, III, and IV (as the authors call them, the "great middle class") produced more than four-fifths of the total (84 per cent) of superior children and about two-thirds of the "retarded" children. It should be

noted that this study included as its subjects only those children actually enrolled in public school. Children of extremely low intelligence are thus not included. Some evidence exists (Halperin, 1946) to indicate that the higher socioeconomic classes produce more than their share of such children, perhaps because they can afford better medical care so that a larger proportion of severely handicapped children born to them survive.

In general, urban children do better on intelligence tests than rural children, although much of this difference in test quotients results from performance on certain types of items: urban children do better than rural children on verbal items. Yet, since much of the manifest functioning of intelligence in our society is verbal, this is an important difference. Several studies exist (see McCandless, 1952; Jones, 1954) which demonstrate that children who mature in depressed rural areas, where schools are poor and there is a minimum of stimulation, decline progessively in intelligence as they grow older. Studies of Tennessee mountain children reported by Wheeler (1942) demonstrate the effect of a barren environment on children's intellectual development, yet contrast current tendencies with the more depressing picture that existed ten years before he gathered his data. In 1930, six-year-olds from this region tested an average 95 IQ. In 1940 they tested an average 103. Older children tested lower, both in 1930 and 1940, than six-year-olds, so that in 1930 sixteen-year-olds averaged only 73.5 IQ; in 1940, 80.

This study is representative of many which demonstrate that prolonged residence in a depressed socio-economic–educational environment retards measured intelligence and that, despite the warnings of geneticists, children tend to measure higher in intelligence from one decade to another. The tentative conclusion is that this increase in measured, functioning intelligence is the result of better schools for more people. Increased test sophistication, in an era when most children are exposed to tests from their early school years, may also have something to do with the results.

It has been demonstrated that the closer to New Orleans they dwell, the higher Negro children from Louisiana measure in IQ. Presumably, New Orleans has the best schools in the state, and the influence of the New Orleans school program diminishes with distance. Klineberg (1935), the author of this study, has also demonstrated that the longer Negro children from the South live in New York City and attend New York schools, the higher are their IQ's. By the third emigree generation, they test about the same as their non-Negro peers, whereas genetically similar Negro children in the deep South test substantially lower than the national average. This difference shows up even for first-generation emigree children: those who have been in New York City for a short period of time test 81 IQ; those who have been there for two to three years test 84.5, and those who have lived there for longer than four years test 87 IQ. Klineberg offers some evidence to demonstrate that selective migration (i.e., that the brighter Negroes move out of the South) is not responsible for this phenomenon. Certain of his more crucial findings have been independently verified for a population of Negro emigree children in Philadelphia, Pennsylvania (Lee, 1951).

Knobloch and Pasamanick (1960) find no differences in infant intelligence test scores between white and non-white babies at forty weeks of age, but find that (for example) their language intelligence scores differ by 16 points at the age of three, in favor of the white youngsters. The major difference, they believe, is due to socio-economic influence: the non-white youngsters have had fewer advantages and less stimulation.

Kent and Davis (1957), in a very different type of study, find that different types of parental discipline are associated with different child IQ levels. They separated a sample of the parents of 213 children into four categories of family discipline: (1) *Demanding* parents who

set high standards ... which take the child's weakness too little into account. . . . They provide good opportunities for the child to learn, and the home is a stimulating one, but they expect him to conform to a model of what they think he should be. This model is inflexible and they are intolerant of any departure from it (pp. 27–28).

(2) *Overanxious* parents who

tend to be ambitious for their child, but in particular they are ceaselessly anxious lest he fall short of what they expect. . . . Their model is inconstant, although it may be emphatic. Also, they tend to be inconsistent in their use of reward and punishment; they are sometimes indulgent and sometimes intolerant, because they are apprehensive and uncertain. They sap the child's confidence . . . (p. 28).

(3) *Normal* parents who "are tolerant and patient, although firm. . . . They placidly enjoy each of their children and are affectionate toward them" (p. 28). (4) *Unconcerned* parents are content if their child keeps out of trouble and does not make demands on them. They are haphazard and inconsistent in their use of punishment.

The authors report no particular relation between fathers' occupations and discipline category, although there was a slight but non-significant tendency for fathers in the overanxious class to be in the lowest occupational category.

Kent and Davis administered the Binet test of intelligence (among other tests) to these children, and found that the IQ's of the children of demanding parents average 124, of overanxious parents 107, of normal parents 110, and of unconcerned parents 97. Tests of statistical significance showed the demanding parents' children to be significantly brighter and the unconcerned parents' children significantly less bright than the children of "normal" parents.

In other words (although perhaps at a severe emotional cost), effectively "driving" and highly stimulating parents "produce" bright youngsters.

INSTITUTIONAL LIVING AND ISOLATION

Most studies of the effects of isolation and institutional living (e.g., Goldfarb, 1945) show that IQ's of children so brought up are quite low. A few studies of dubious scientific merit concern children reared by animals. These children are reported to behave, not like human beings, but like animals. However, folklore plays more part than science in relaying the data about these children (Dennis, 1951); for example, we do not know whether they may not have been abandoned in the first place because they were feebleminded.

Another study (Spitz, 1945, 1946) of children reared in an institution found that during the first year of life their developmental quotient dropped from an initial level of 124 to 72—or from a classification of superior to one that could be considered retarded. This study has been severely criticized (Pinneau, 1955a, b) on the basis of its methods, and the criticisms are so severe and apparently well founded that only limited confidence can be placed in its results. However, more careful studies by Goldfarb (1945) and Levy (1947) obtained similar results, as did a study of Chinese infants (Hsu, 1946) in which it was found that the longer the infants had been in a baby ward, the lower their developmental quotient was likely to be. Spitz maintains that the effects of such deprivation are irreversible, and the evidence of Goldfarb and Levy bears him out to some degree.

Pasamanick (1946) found that baby-ward living had severely retarding effects but implies that when the condition is remedied the babies come back to normal.

A more recent study (Dennis, 1960) is pertinent to this question. In an investigation of the motor retardation of institutionalized children in Teheran, Dennis compared children between the ages of one and three who had been placed in two publicly supported institutions and a private institution in Teheran. He found that the children residing in the public institutions were strikingly retarded in their motor development. These children, who received only minimal environmental stimulation due to overcrowded and understaffed conditions in the public institutions, sat, crawled, stood, and walked at a considerably later age than did those children of similar age who were reared in the private institution which provided extensive fondling and stimulation (e.g., none of the public institution children studied walked prior to the age of two, and only 8 per cent walked between the ages of two years and two years, eleven months, while 15 and 94 per cent of the private institution children walked at these same ages). Dennis ascribes these differences to the differential kinds of learning opportunities provided for the children in the different institutional settings. Although he could not determine precisely how permanent these defects were, Dennis did take the position, contrary to that of Spitz, Goldfarb, and Levy, that these motor deficiencies were not permanent. He observed that many children between the ages of six and fifteen who had been raised in the same public institutions, under conditions the same (supposedly) as those prevailing at the time of his investigation, exhibited ". . . nothing in their general behavior to suggest that any permanent consequences issued from the extreme retardation in motor development during their early years" (p. 57).

A study by Beres and Obers (1950) of eighteen-year-olds who had spent much of their early life in institutions indicates that a substantial number of them (about one-half) were normal emotionally (and presumably intellectually). Rheingold (1956) has demonstrated that one interested, around-the-clock "mother figure" can improve the social responsiveness of institutionalized infants.

Of course, there are institutions and institutions. Unpublished data (Harms, 1957) indicate that babies resident in a nutrition ward with many nurses' aides and a warm motherly chief nurse, who are fed in the laps of adults and who have convalescent children running in and out of the ward, approach normal mental and emotional development even though many of their parents are of socially inferior stock.

Pringle and Bossio (1960) have studied two small groups of eight-, eleven-, and fourteen-year-olds (eleven included in a severely maladjusted group, five in a "notably stable" group), all of whom had been separated in relatively early childhood from their parents. In line with research reviewed earlier in the chapter, the greatest differences between the groups occurred in indexes of symbolic behavior and at the age and under the circumstances with which parental separation occurred. The "severely maladjusted" group tested much lower on the British Mill Hill Vocabulary Scale (their scores average 72.9, while the "notably stable" group averaged 93.6) and on reading scores from the Schonell Silent Reading Test B, where the mean for the maladjusted was 75.2, and for the stable 98.2. WISC IQ scores, while favoring the stable group, were not greatly different between groups. Age of separation from parents "favored" the stable group: for them, separation had occurred from twelve to forty-six months of age, and some relative (parents or other) had maintained consistent contact with them. The maladjusted group had, in all cases but two (of eleven), been separated from their parents before twelve months of age, and little family contact had been maintained.

Some of the studies mentioned above imply or state that the indisputable developmental retardation of infants brought up in baby wards where only routine attention is given by a large number of adults is due to the lack of a "significant and consistent mother figure." It might also be suggested that this retardation is due simply to lack of adequate sensorimotor stimulation. But the questions of the factors responsible and the degree of irreversibility remain open. Speaking from a social welfare point of view, enough evidence has accumulated to indicated that group living for babies in a baby ward where only routine care is given is sufficiently damaging (whether temporarily or permanently) to justify recommendations against such arrangements.

Scott and his colleagues (1959) have performed an interesting sensory deprivation study with Canadian male college undergraduates. While not directly applicable to the present topic, the results of the study are suggestive, and support the notion that sensory deprivation, even of short duration (three and four days) is rather profoundly disturbing to intellectual *function*. The implication drawn here is that it is equally or more disturbing to intellectual *development*. Scott *et al.* paid their subjects to lie for twenty-four hours a day in a comfortable bed in a lighted, semisoundproofed cubicle. During the experiment the Ss wore translucent goggles that admitted diffuse light but prevented pattern vision. Except when they were eating or toileting, they wore cotton gloves and cardboard cuffs extending from below their elbows to beyond their fingertips. A U-shaped foam-rubber pillow and the monotonous hum of air-conditioning and other equipment limited their auditory perception. In general, the young men could put up with this situation for only about three or four days.

The experimental subjects (the total number was twenty-nine, but not all completed all the tests) were tested before the experiment and at different times during it. Similar tests were given to control subjects, who had been isolated. In general, when compared with the controls, the experimental subjects, following as little as twelve hours of isolation, slowed down greatly in their performance of intelligence test items, made many more errors, and (in a test of susceptibility to propaganda) changed their opinions more in the direction of a propaganda recording, manifested more interest in the propaganda, and gave a higher ranking of importance to its topic (psychic phenomena).

In other words, isolation and deprivation studies indicate that both intellectual development and (even after stable establishment) function may be disturbed by circumstances of inadequate stimulation.

ANIMAL RESEARCH

It has been pointed out that, for practical reasons, studies using humans as subjects cannot throw definitive light on the relative influence of environment (social learning) and heredity on the variance in development of human intelligence or any other complex psychological trait. The research worker cannot subject his human subjects to extreme environmental or hereditary variations; nor, indeed, can he exercise any very rigorous control over his subjects' environment or heredity. These considerations apply much less to research work done with animals.

It is unusual to include animal studies in an article dealing with children. It has been done here, however, because of the practical social importance of knowing to what degree the environment can modify the organism. No *direct translation* or *application* can be made to human beings of research results or theories based on animals, but *suggestions* about human development may and frequently do arise from such results. Further, if one makes the reasonably tenable assumption that animals are simpler organisms and are more "genetically and instinctually bound" than man, then we can argue with some force that if environment affects an animal to some degree, it is not unlikely that it can affect the more complicated, self-determining, adaptable child or man to an even greater degree. Selected studies of animals will be reviewed and general conclusions drawn concerning the effects of early experiences on later animal development—emotional, social, and physical, as well as intellectual. Most of these research studies have been suggested by the work of Hebb (1949, 1955), whose theories have already been discussed.

Isolation and problem-solving.—One of the most elaborate experiments, although not the earliest in the Hebbian series, was done by Thompson and Heron (1954). They used as subjects twenty-six Scottish terriers, all of them descendants of one litter and, hence, genetically quite similar. Thirteen of the animals were reared as pets, in private homes or in the laboratories, from weaning time (at about four weeks of age) until they were about eight months of age, when they were put in ordinary dog cages. During this period the dogs were exercised outdoors every day that the weather permitted, were well fed, and had a moderate amount of experience with humans.

Thirteen of their brothers, sisters, and cousins were reared very differently after weaning. Three conditions of isolation were imposed on them: (1) Two experienced *severe isolation,* spending all their time up to seven to ten months of age in one of two types of rather small cages (30 × 40 × 60 in.). Every day they changed cages through a sliding door. One cage was kept in darkness, whereas light entered the other so that the dogs spent every other day in the dark. (2) Eight pups experienced *moderate restriction,* two to three of them per group living for eight to ten months in ordinary dog cages whose walls were cardboard covered so that they could not see out. Light came in from the top of the cage. They had contact with humans about ten minutes a day while the cages were cleaned. (3) Three pups were *slightly restricted* and lived for about seven months in cages similar to those of the moderately restricted group, except that the cardboard was removed from the front and top of their cages. They thus had considerable perceptual experience, but only of the environment immediately outside their cage.

Following this "experimental treatment" period, the restricted animals were handled precisely like the normally reared ones. The experimental animals were reported to be quite hyperactive after release from their restriction and, for the first few weeks to months, demonstrated considerable sensorimotor disturbance: they bumped into things, had trouble with stairs and steps, and so on. After this time, however they seemed normal enough. The experimental and control group lived under similar conditions for somewhat more than a year after the end of the period of isolation. At this time, "intelligence" testing of the animals was begun.

Although very simple from a human adult point of view, these tests fit well enough with our definition of intelligence as problem-solving behavior. Six tests were given the animals, an orientation test, I and II, a barrier test, I and II, an attention test, and a maze test that consisted of eighteen different arrangements of wire panels within a seventeen-foot square maze. The arrangement of the panels was from a very simple problem to rather complex ones.

For the first orientation test the animal was placed in corner *D* of an eight-foot square shown in Figure 1. He was given ten trials on which he ran to food at corner *A*. All of the animals that were given this test—eight normals, three slightly restricted, five moderately re-

stricted, and two severely restricted—easily acquired this habit in ten trials. After the habit had been learned and while the animal was watching, the food pan was switched 90° to corner *C* (to the left rather than to the right of the dog). Attention was further brought to the food by banging the pan on the floor and holding the food out so that the dog could see it. Five trials were then run for all animals. The pan was then changed to corner *B*, and another five runs were made by the animals; after this another trial from *D* to *C* was given; then two trials from *D* to *A*; and a final trial using corner *B* as a starting point, requiring the animal to move to corner *A* to get his food. An error was scored when a dog did not go directly from his starting corner to the food.

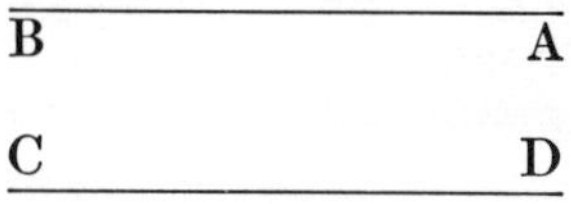

B		A
C		D

FIG. 1.—A diagram of the testing situation for Thompson and Heron's orientation tests, I and II.

The average number of correct trials out of 14 tests was 13.7 for the normally reared (control) animals, but only 5.9 for the restricted (experimental) dogs. The poorest of the control animals did better than the best of the experimental group. The difference was highly significant; *p* was less than 0.001. All the experimental animals continued to go to corner *A* first before proceeding to the new position, although they were able to locate the food.

Orientation test II was slightly more complicated: a starting box, open on one side, was placed in the middle of the square so that its opening faced wall *AB*, as shown in Figure 1. The animal went to food located in corner *A* for 10 trials. The box was then rotated to face in turn walls *BC*, *AD*, and *CD*. One trial was given in each position. The starting box was then rotated back to its first position for three trials. After that the food was moved to corner B for one trial, and the dog, before being placed in the starting box, was taken to it and allowed to sniff it. From these 7 test trials the control dogs averaged 5.1 correct runs (i.e., ran directly to the corner where the food had been placed rather than to an incorrect corner); but the experimental animals averaged only 2.7 correct trials (p for this difference was again less than 0.001). Only one of the experimental animals did better than the poorest control, doing as well as three other controls. The least efficient control dog had experienced the shortest period of time living as a pet.

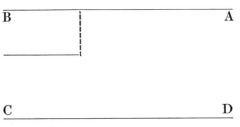

FIG. 2.—A diagram of the testing situation for Thompson and Heron's barrier tests, I and II.

In barrier test I, a chicken-wire barrier was extended at right angles from wall BC about two feet from corner B, as shown by the solid line in Figure 2. The food was placed behind it as the dog watched, and after he had had 5 trials of going from corner C to get the food before the barrier was put in place. A correct trial consisted of the dog's avoiding an error zone—that is, the dog was correct if he angled from corner C out past the end of the barrier and then went directly in to get the food. Control animals averaged 6.75 correct runs out of 10 trials; experimental animals, 2.4. This difference was significant at less than the 0.001 level. The experimental animals again manifested behavioral rigidity, frequently moving straight forward from corner C to the barrier, then circling it.

For barrier test II an addition was made to the barrier, as represented by

the dotted line in Figure 2. The animals were placed, one at a time, in this partial enclosure after having been allowed first to sniff the food outside the barrier. Time for reaching the food was measured for each trial. To get at the food, of course, the animals had to turn their backs on it, run through the opening, and around. The average time for the control animals was 29.4 seconds. The experimentals on the average required 72.1 seconds. This difference is significant at less than the 0.05 level, and there was only one case of overlap between the groups.

Another test involved the dogs' attention span. After they had learned to go immediately to the one of two doors behind which they had watched the experimenter place a pan of food, they were tested to determine how long they could "keep this in mind." That is to say, they were required to wait behind a door for periods of time ranging from five to three hundred seconds before being allowed to run to the easily opened door behind which they had watched the placement of the food. Even without delay, six of the seven experimental dogs were never able to handle this problem, and the one successful dog solved the problem for a delay only as long as twenty-five seconds. The *least* apt of the five control animals that were tested handled a fifty-second delay. These differences are obviously highly significant.

The final test was the maze test. All dogs were given five easy trials to get them accustomed to the maze, then were given progressively more difficult problems. There were no group differences for the easy problems, and the average controls dogs' score was lowered by one pregnant female who tired easily and gave up. Even when her scores were included, the controls averaged a total of 237 errors, while the experimentals made an average of 344 mistakes. This difference is significant at less than the 0.01 level. All dogs learned in a similar fashion: that is, both groups steadily improved performance, and the learning curve showing the effects of practice was the same in shape for the two groups, although at all points on the curve the experimentals did less well than the controls.

This striking study has been reviewed in detail because it has so many implications concerning the influence of early stimulus or environmental deprivation on later problem-solving behavior. Dogs reared in isolation as puppies, even when given a long period (more than a year) of living in a relatively normal environment, clearly do less well than dogs reared as pets on a series of tasks that seem to involve a factor which we would call intelligence. It has been pointed out that we cannot apply animal research directly to human beings. On the other hand, the implications of this study (done with higher mammals) are too striking to be completely ignored or dismissed. The authors describe the deficit of the dogs "as a lack of ability to discriminate relevant from irrelevant aspects of the environment, or to adapt to changes made in the experimental situation. There also seems to be some disturbance in the attention processes of the restricted animals" (p. 29). Hofstaetter (1954), in an analysis of common factors in intelligence test items for infants and preschoolers, found that the items thought to measure intelligent behavior before the age of speech are characterized by a factor he calls "sensorimotor alertness." This factor is of great importance up to twenty months of age. As speech begins, intelligence test items seem to involve a factor of "persistence," or "a tendency to act in accordance with an established set rather than upon interfering stimulation" (p. 162). This factor seems to be the major one for intelligence test items appropriate for children from about twenty to forty months. Certainly, the deficiencies of the restricted dogs in the Thompson and Heron study could be described by Hofstaetter's words. In fact,

the two descriptions are almost interchangeable.

Results of the same type have been obtained (see, e.g., Bingham and Griffiths, 1952; Thompson, 1955) using rats as subjects and employing similar research techniques.

Special stimulation in infancy.—Other investigators have secured results congruent with those reported above. In one study (Gibson and Walk, 1956) rats were reared in identical surroundings and with identical treatment, except that on the walls of the experimental animals' cages hung pieces of black metal cut into the shapes of equilateral triangles and circles. The cages of the control animals had blank walls. For most of the white rats used in this study, hereditary influences were controlled by splitting litters, putting half of one litter in an experimental and half in a control group. At ninety days of age and without any "meaning" (special learning) ever having been attached to circles and triangles, the animals were set to learn a discrimination problem involving these two geometric shapes. The rats exposed to the two stimuli proved far superior to the control group in learning the problem, this difference between groups being significant at much less than the 0.01 level.

Forgus (1956) has done several studies along the same general lines. One of these exposed groups of eleven baby rats to cutout forms—a circle, a triangle, a cross, and a square. The cages of the animals were blanked in, so that the forms were the conspicuous elements in the environment. These forms were placed on the walls of their cages as soon as their eyes opened (at sixteen days of age) and moved around from time to time to avoid any direct association ("meaning") between them and obtaining food and water. The forms were kept in cages until the rats were forty-one days of age.

Another group of rats was similarly reared, except that the forms were not put into their cages until they were forty-one days old and were left there until the animals were sixty-six days of age. Appropriate groups of control animals (in most cases, members of the same litter as the experimental animals) were reared identically, except that they were not exposed to the forms.

The rats that had been exposed to the forms from infancy were placed in a discrimination situation similar to that discussed above when they were forty-one days of age. The animals used as controls for this group also started to learn the

TABLE 1

NUMBER OF TRIALS REQUIRED TO LEARN A DISCRIMINATION PROBLEM BY RATS EXPOSED EARLY AND LATER IN LIFE TO FORMS*

	Number of Trials Required for Learning	Number of Errors Made on Generalization Test
Forms at infancy.....	33.8	4.7
Forms at forty-one days..............	39.4	11.1
Early controls........	48.2	19.7
Late controls........	46.5	19.6

*Adapted with permission from Forgus, 1956, *Canad. J. Psychol.* Courtesy of the University of Toronto Press.

discrimination (between a triangle and a cross) at this age. Animals who had been exposed to the forms only from the time they were forty-one days old and their controls began the discrimination problem when they were sixty-six days old. After the problem had been learned, the forms were rotated 90° to see how well the rats could generalize. Table 1 shows the results for the four different groups.

The statistical-significance figures for this table indicate clearly that an advantage, both in learning and in generalizing, accrues to the rats that were exposed to the forms early. They do better in learning and generalizing than rats who are exposed later in life, and the late-exposed rats in turn do better than rats never exposed to the forms before discrimination-testing. The early and late

controls show no difference in their discrimination-learning, although the animals tested later moved through each discrimination problem faster than those tested earlier: they seemed more confident or less fearful.

In another interesting study, Forgus (1954) reared rats in three different types of environment. Group I lived in a good-sized cage painted black, in which a number of white objects, such as blocks, alleys, tunnels, elevated platforms, and inclined planes, were placed around the walls so that the animals had free access to them. Group II rats lived in a similar cage, but a clear plastic frame was placed so that they could see but not reach the playthings. Group III lived in small, black, unfurnished boxes.

On various tests, Forgus found that group I and II animals moved around faster than group III animals, were less emotional and frightened, and showed much more varied behavior. They were also much more efficient at a problem that involved insight. But where visual discrimination was necessary to solve a problem, group II (the group that had looked but not manipulated) usually did somewhat better than group I. Forgus reasoned that this was because group II animals had spent their lives being able to do nothing *but look.* Consequently, when problem-solving depended on using their eyes, they did better than animals reared like group I, but group I animals would do better than animals who grew up under conditions similar to those of group II at problems demanding manipulation and in situations that involved no visual cues.

Forgus tested this reasoning in an experiment (1955) in which his group I and group II animals were reared in a fashion just described. They then started discrimination-learning in a maze that provided visual cues. These were removed before learning was complete; and the experiment was continued to see which group learned faster and made fewer errors. Group I, the "visuomotor" group, learned in an average of 19.5 trials and made an average of 60.5 errors during the learning. But group II (visual only) required an average of 26.6 trials and made 83.1 errors on the average. These differences are statistically significant.

Forgus, with Luchins (Luchins and Forgus, 1955), has performed another experiment of the same general type. In this study the experimental animals were brought up in cages equipped with blocks, alleys, and elevated platforms and were played with by humans for about an hour a day. The controls lived in a barren cage without much contact with people. Experimental tests showed that in a new situation the experimentals were much more confident: they moved around far more. They explored their environment more (a greater number of alternate routes to a goal was used by them than by the controls). They showed more insightful and efficient behavior in solving problems than the controls, and they showed that they could more rapidly drop an old method of problem-solving that had become inefficient.

Handling and gentling.—Another investigator (Levine, 1956) studied the effects of handling rats (1) very early in their lives (from the day after birth through twenty days of age), (2) later in their lives (from fifty through seventy days), and (3) not at all. When all the animals were seventy-one days of age, they were subjected to training designed to teach them to avoid an electric shock. The early-handled differed consistently from the non-handled group in the speed with which they learned to do this (they were faster and made fewer errors) and in the indications of emotional disturbance they showed (they were less emotional, that is, they defecated less and fewer of them "froze"). (Freezing is a frequent but maladaptive reaction of rats to stress.) On the whole, the later-handled group fell in efficiency between the early-

and the non-handled groups. On most measures it was not significantly different from either.

Weininger, whose work springs from Hebb's thinking, has published three papers, one of them with co-workers, on the effects of gentling white rats in infancy (Weininger, 1953, 1956; Weininger *et al.*, 1954). His technique of gentling, typically, is to take a rat from about the time of weaning (approximately twenty-one days) for ten minutes per day in his left hand, holding the rat gently against his chest and stroking it with the thumb of his right hand from the head to the base of the tail at the rate of about fifty times per minute. Weininger has found consistently that the gentled animals gain weight faster and to a higher eventual level than do non-gentled rats. This is a symmetrical weight gain in that the gentled rats are not only heavier but longer and bigger. They did not, however, actually eat more than the controls but presumably utilized their food better.

Weininger's gentled rats showed less fear of open spaces: they ventured farther and more frequently into the middle of a six-foot metal enclosure, where the light was brightest (rats fear open spaces and light). They hugged the walls of this open cylindrical space much less than the non-gentled rats. When placed under severe stress (immobilized by bandages without food or water for 48 hours), more of the non-gentled showed heart damage on autopsy and suffered more extensive duodenal and stomach bleeding. The non-gentled rats seemed to have enlarged adrenal glands *after* this experience of stress; another group failed to show this differential enlargement *before* stress. Still another group, exposed to even more severe (120 hours) stress consisting of immobilization, food and water deprivation, and marked, though accidental, heat deprivation, showed the same symptoms on autopsy. More of the non-gentled rats than of the gentled ones died under such circumstances. Levine and Otis (1958) also found that the earlier the albino-rat subjects were handled, the more resistant they were to stress.

At least three other studies (Bernstein, 1952; McClelland, 1956; Morgenson *et al.*, 1957) using rats as subjects support the findings reported above, including one which demonstrates that consistently handled animals learn faster than non-handled ones and that early handling is superior to later handling. The author of this last study (Bernstein, 1952) emphasizes that his results may be caused by not just an enriched objective environment but the building of a positive "emotional" relationship between the investigator and the animal.

Gentling, then, as done in the studies reported above, seems to produce important differences in animal behavior. However, one apparently carefully done study (Scott, 1955), using the same gentling techniques as those used by Weininger, found no behavioral or weight differences between gentled and ungentled rats. There is no obvious explanation for this difference in results, and we must, at present, rest content with the conclusion that the bulk of the evidence favors positive results from gentling but that some important research exists to discount its importance.

Isolation and emotionality.—The influences of restriction (as described in the 1954 Thompson and Heron study) on the emotional responses of dogs have also been studied by Canadian investigators. Melzack (1954) studied Scottish terriors, eight of them reared from puppyhood to maturity in homes, nine reared for a similar period in the restriction cages described earlier. They were released from the cages and tested after one month, during which time they lived relatively normally, and again after about one year from this. During the year all had been normally handled. In tests, Melzack exposed them to a mannequin head, bear and chimpanzee skulls, a toy car, a balloon, an umbrella, and a live rabbit. After an animal had been in the experimental room for one minute, one of these objects was moved toward him in zigzag fashion for one minute. The umbrella was opened to a thirty-six-inch spread, and the balloon blown to a ten-inch diameter over a thirty-second period before being moved toward the dog. Recording for behavior concerning the rabbit was not made until it had made its first move.

Table 2 shows the frequency of behavior of different sorts between the two groups of dogs. The third and last columns show the significance of differences between the two groups.

These differences are striking. The normally reared dogs show relatively more adaptive behavior (attacking or getting out of the way), while the restricted dogs behave in an "immature," excited, non-adaptive fashion. These differences decreased with time, as can be seen from Table 2, but were still in evidence nearly a year later. The same dogs had also been tested for intelligence in about the same fashion as Thompson and Heron's dogs. Like them, they had been found less apt at problem-solving behavior.

It may be that "intellectual" differences account for some of Melzack's findings, although there seems to be very little element of problem-solving involved in the emotional tests given to the animals. The study is not contaminated, that is, the experimenter did not know which dogs had been reared free and which under restricted circumstances. Melzack states, in conclusion:

When the restricted dogs were first released, their level of excitement was higher than any yet observed in the normal controls and was maintained for longer periods of time. . . . (The Study) adds further support to the view that diffuse emotional excitement is a primitive disturbed response out of which avoidance and other forms of emotional behavior develop. It demonstrates, however, that this behavior is primitive only insofar as it appears prior to integrated forms of emotional behavior. It may appear at any stage of the animal's life when the situation differs greatly from any that the animal has already encountered.[6]

Melzack reports in another study (1952) that the restricted dogs showed remarkably maladaptive reactions to pain in that they were much slower in learning to avoid an electric shock. Two of his seven restricted subjects never learned to do so during the experiment. In this situation (the experimenter was directing a mobile toy car that administered a shock to the dog), the control experimenter *after* he had burned or pricked them than they had done before, whereas the control dogs shied away from him. Some of the experimental dogs came snuffling back up to the fire immediately after having been burned by it.

Melzack and Thompson (1956) tested dogs reared under the same circumstances as those reported above for the adequacy of their social behavior. When the restricted animals were put into competition for a plate of food with normally reared animals of the same age, they lost consistently. The normal dogs scored

TABLE 2

DIFFERENCES IN TYPES OF EMOTIONAL BEHAVIOR SHOWN BY MELZACK'S SCOTTISH TERRIERS, RAISED UNDER NORMAL AND RESTRICTED CONDITIONS, TESTED SOON AFTER RELEASE FROM RESTRICTION AND ABOUT ONE YEAR LATER*

BEHAVIOR	AVERAGES					
	Test at 3–5 Weeks		*p*	Test 10–12 Months Later		*p*
	Restricted	Free		Restricted	Free	
Excitement..........	3.9	0.5	0.001	1.6	0.2	0.045
Avoidance..........	1.9	5.5	0.001	4.0	3.5	NS (non-significant)
Aggression..........	0	0.2	NS	0	2.2	0.03
No emotional response.	1.3	0.8	NS	1.3	1.2	NS

* Reproduced with permission from Melzack, 1954.

dogs were smooth and co-ordinated in their avoidance responses, the experimental dogs wild and haphazard. A retest two years later showed that the experimental dogs were still much less adroit at this avoidance than the control dogs had been at about nine months of age. The experimental dogs also used very little "sense" in avoiding lighted matches or pinpricks or in moving from the "hot" or electrically charged side of an apparatus to the safe side. They actually spent much more time around the

[6] Quoted, with permission of the American Psychological Association and R. Melzack, from Melzack, 1954, p. 197.

fifty-seven wins, i.e., drove the other dog away, the experimentals only seven wins. This difference is significant at the 0.001 level. Even when the normals were substantially younger, the experimental animals lost. Their social curiosity, when exposed to a strange dog on the other side of a chicken-wire fence, was less adaptive. Whereas the normal dogs soon tired of sniffing and exploring the other dog through the fence, the experimental dogs showed the opposite tendency. The experimental animals also showed less adaptive reactions to a human experimenter playing the part of a friendly, a timid, and a bold man.

Early experience, aggression, and sexual behavior.—Aggression is often thought to be an inborn trait for all species. We know that in man, learning influences its expression strongly, but it might be considered relatively unmodifiable in lower species. However, one study (Kahn, 1951) demonstrates that mice subjected while young to a severe beating by other mice grow up to be relatively timid and unaggressive. Evidence also exists that mice reared in groups are more aggressive as adults than mice reared alone (King and Gurney, 1954).

The future of any species depends upon its adequate sexual behavior. Such behavior should presumably be the least modifiable by environment, particularly in the lower species. Yet three representative studies illustrate how profoundly this presumably instinctual behavior may be modified by social learning. In one study (Kagan and Beach, 1953) rats were separated from their kind just before puberty. At the time of their separation, their behavior with the opposite sex had been primarily playful. Males so separated and replaced at adulthood in cages with females in heat behaved inefficiently, consistently interrupting their adaptive sex behavior with the play behavior that had been appropriate during their "pre-adolescence." In another study Hayward (1957) found that male rats which, before pubescence, had been consistently shocked in the presence of adult female rats in heat but not shocked in the presence of adult males avoided, as adults, the estrus females much more than a control group that had not been shocked in pre-adolescence. The experimental rats behaved inefficiently when they came into the presence of the female and spent far more time with the available adult male rats than did the controls, although they did not show homosexual behavior. However, actual ejaculation did not occur for either the control or experimental rats in this study (although the controls showed much more typical sexual behav-

ior). The author entertains the thought that the electric shock may have disorganized both groups. Rats reared in litters of six (Seitz, 1954), when contrasted with those reared in litters of twelve, seem emotionally more secure, are less fearful, eat more, but compete less effectively both for food and for sex objects.

Male guinea pigs with previous sexual experience (Riss and Goy, 1957) have been found to show much more sex behavior with an estrus female following periods when they have been living socially than they do following periods when they have been living in isolation. Where males were separated from other animals very early in life, the disturbance of sexual function was more profound than when separation occurred later (Valenstein, Riss, and Young, 1955).

To summarize this section on animals, research that has been done to test the effects of early experiences on the later behavior of a wide variety of animals— dogs, rats, guinea pigs, mice—demonstrates that such experiences exert profound effects on problem-solving behavior ("intelligence"), social behavior, including aggression, responses to pain, sex behavior, and even such presumably genetically determined phenomena as weight and size.

GAPS IN RESEARCH INFORMATION

It has become obvious to the writer, in preparing this chapter, that the gaps in the research literature are almost as conspicuous as the solid contributions, although, were the research literature thoroughly disseminated to workers in the field, considerable improvement of practice would likely occur.

Several questions immediately strike the reviewer of research in this field, for example:

Are the endogenous mentally retarded confined almost entirely to children of the lower-lower socio-economic classes?

The literature indicates this, but does not provide conclusive evidence.

Is it "safe" to place for adoption the children of endogenously mentally retarded mothers and fathers?

What is the frequency with which abnormal EEG's are found in presumably endogenous mentally retarded children and adults, and how does this frequency compare with controls matched for age, sex, and socio-economic status? And how does such frequency of abnormality vary by social class?

What are the ethnic-socio-economic-language interactions in relation to endogenous mental retardation? (For example, we know that a relatively high proportion of Negro and Puerto Rican children receive diagnoses of borderline and retarded intelligence, without accompanying diagnoses of somatic involvement.)

If we adopt a modified social-learning point of view about endogenous mental retardation (which the present author believes is made necessary, at least as an hypothesis, by the research literature already existing), what effective action programs can society take? Would high-grade, compulsory nursery schools for children of two and above in blighted urban and rural areas alleviate the problem?

Should legislation be urged to separate newborns from their endogenously retarded parents?

Are there ways (as suggested by Milner and Irwin) by which we can brighten the prospects for children born into intellectually low-level homes, in the sense that we add to their capacity for symbolic behavior, particularly in the speech and reading areas, without disrupting the home by withdrawing the children?

Even children with low IQ's, when motivated, make far from hopeless school pupils and succeed relatively well in the community. But the lack of achievement motivation is characteristic of endogenously retarded children (and of lower-

and, particularly, lower-lower-class children in general). What can be done to inculcate achievement motivation? Can this be accomplished as late as the kindergarten or elementary school years? Or must it be started earlier? How much earlier? And, in Anastasi's (1958) word, "How?"

It can be seen from the incomplete list of questions above that problems of "gaps in research information" are not greatly different, even in social urgency, for retarded children from what they are for normal or superior children. The gaps are those that exist for psychology in general, not simply for psychology (or social work, or medicine, or psychiatry) as it attempts to deal with the mentally retarded. The author should like to restate (McCandless, 1959) an earlier plea that the *science* be our first concern, the *nature of subject* secondary. At the same time it should be firmly borne in mind that "retarded children, particularly the large institutionalized population, provide for us one of our most intriguing subject pools" (p. 268).

DIMENSIONS FOR FUTURE RESEARCH

Anastasi (1958), in her article, "Heredity, Environment, and the Question, 'How?'" has, literally, written this section for the author. Appreciation must be extended to her for her contribution, not only to the area of mental retardation, but to the general psychology of human development. Like the author, she believes that important theoretical and practical contributions to theory and practice can be made by research with animals and recommends, as one of the seven hopeful lines of research effort, an extension of selective breeding studies to facilitate identifying specific hereditary variables underlying observed behavior characteristics.

Second, she proposes more intensive exploration of relations between behavioral characteristics and physiological variables, which may, in turn, be related to genetics. The studies in phenylketonuria provide a case in point, since they have been recently followed by nutritional research that, for the first time, provides hope that retardation no longer need accompany phenylpyruvic acid in the urine.

A third area in which research efforts should be intensified is in the study of prenatal environmental factors—e.g., threatened miscarriage, or poor maternal nutrition—as they relate to later intellectual (and personal-social) function.

Fourth, Anastasi urges more research on the influence of early experience on later development. A number of such studies, particularly in the section on animal research, have been summarized earlier in this chapter. Their potential usefulness is obvious.

Fifth, well-controlled, cross-cultural studies should prove useful. Earlier in the chapter, some validation of this point has been provided by the reviews of intelligence test results of Hopi and Navaho children, and isolated rural children. Extensions of such studies, including more imaginative social-class comparisons, should prove profitable. In the area of social class, for example, Findley and McGuire (1957), in an ingenious experiment suggested by the proponents of "culture-free" or "culture-fair" intelligence tests, have reasoned that, if a population of lower-class children were matched in IQ according to a standard test of intelligence, the "potential" on new, non-culture-related problem-solving tasks would be higher for the lower-class children. They found the opposite, providing support for the oft-documented observation that lower-class children simply do not receive the stimulation which results in the learning necessary for effective manipulation of symbols.

Sixth, Anastasi believes that research on somatopsychological relations should be intensified.

Finally, she urges that we focus more attention on studies comparing dyzygotic twins with non-twin siblings, with an emphasis on longitudinal studies. To the present writer, these last two areas of research seem less urgent than those listed earlier, although this is perhaps nothing more than a matter of taste.

SUMMARY

This chapter concentrates on research related to environmental influences on intellectual functioning, concentrating, insofar as possible, on research related directly to intellectual functioning of endogenous mentally retarded but drawing on research from other intellectual classifications as well as on research employing animals as subjects. The question of the contributions to variations of measured intelligence of nature and nurture is considered, although stress is laid on research related to nurture. The relative contributions of nature and nurture cannot, of course, ever be clearly assessed scientifically, because no organism can function without both a heredity and an environment, but the debate over the relative contributions to intelligence has practical implications such as, for example, on placement of children for adoption.

The author takes a somewhat environmentalistic position, because he believes that the contribution of environment and learning to intellectual development and function has, traditionally, been neglected. Environment and learning also deserve special attention because, practically speaking, they can be manipulated and changed, while heredity cannot.

This chapter reviews seven areas of research: (1) endogenous mentally retarded children and their families, (2) studies of adoption, (3) effects of differential school attendance, (4) studies of language and symbolic behavior, (5) relations of intelligence to social class, including cultural isolation, ethnicity, and migration, (6) deprivation studies, and (7) animal studies. The section on animal studies includes, in addition to studies of "intellectual behavior," investigations of the effects of early experiences on emotional and social behavior.

The preponderance of evidence indicates the crucial importance of learning opportunity in normal intellectual development and function. Environment undoubtedly interacts in complex and variable ways with heredity, but a stimulating environment appears, for example, to be a condition sufficient to assure normal development to children who, given environments characteristic for their true mothers and fathers, would have been predicted to be (at best) of borderline intelligence.

Studies of the development of problem-solving behavior and of emotional "adjustment" of animals indicate even more strikingly than studies using human beings as subjects the role that learning opportunities play. One can ask: if isolation and deprivation blunt the "intelligence" of a rat or a dog what, then, must they do to a baby?

REFERENCES

ANASTASI, A. 1958. Heredity, environment, and the question, "How?" *Psychol. Rev.*, 65:197–208.

ANASTASI, A., and FOLEY, J. P., JR. 1948. A proposed reorientation in one heredity environment controversy. *Psychol. Rev.*, 55:239–49.

ASTIN, A. W., and Ross, S. 1960. Glutamic acid and human intelligence. *Psychol. Bull.*, 57:429–34.

BADT, M. I. 1958. Levels of abstraction in vocabulary definitions of mentally retarded school children. *Amer. J. Ment. Defic.*, 63:241–46.

BALDWIN, A. L., KALHORN, J., and BREESE, F. H. 1945. Patterns of parent behavior. *Psychol. Monogr.*, 58: No. 3.

BAYLEY, N. 1955. On the growth of intelligence. *Amer. Psychologist*, 10:805–18.

BERES, D., and OBERS, S. J. 1950. The effects of extreme deprivation in infancy on psycho structure in adolescence: a study in ego development. *The Psychoanalytic Study of the Child*, Vol. 5. New York: International Universities Press.

BERNSTEIN, B. 1958. Some sociological determinants of perception: an inquiry into sub-cultural differences. *Brit. J. Sociol.*, 9:159–74.

———. 1959. A public language: some sociological implications of a linguistic form. *Ibid.*, 10:311–26.

———. 1960. Language and social class. *Ibid.*, 11:271–76.

BERNSTEIN, L. 1952. A note on Christie's "Experimental naïveté and experiential naïveté." *Psychol. Bull.*, 49:38–40.

BINGHAM, W. E., and GRIFFITHS, W. J., JR. 1952. The effect of different environments during infancy on adult behavior in the rat. *J. Comp. Physiol. Psychol.*, 45:307–12.

CATALANO, F. L., and McCARTHY, D. 1954. Infant speech as a possible predictor of later intelligence. *J. Psychol.*, 38:203–9.

CHAMBERS, G. S., and ZABARENKO, R. N. 1956. Effects of glutamic acid and social stimulation in mental deficiency. *J. Abnorm. Soc. Psychol.*, 53:315–20.

CHARLES, D. C. 1953. Ability and accomplishment of persons earlier judged mentally deficient. *Genet. Psychol. Monogr.*, 47:3–71.

CLARKE, A. D. B., and CLARKE, A. M. 1954. Cognitive changes in the feebleminded. *Brit. J. Psychol.*, 45:173–79.

———. 1960. Some recent advances in the study of early deprivation. *Child Psychol. Psychiat.*, 1:26–36.

CLARKE, A. D. B., CLARKE, A. M., and REIMAN, S. Cognitive and social changes in the feebleminded—three further studies. *Brit. J. Psychol.*, 49:144–57.

CLARKE, A. M., and CLARKE, A. D. B. 1958. *Mental Deficiency: The Changing Outlook*. London: Methuen.

DAVIS, K. 1940. Extreme social isolation of a child. *Amer. J. Sociol.*, 45:554–65.

———. 1947. Final note on a case of extreme isolation. *Ibid.*, 52:432–37.

DAWE, H. G. 1942. A study of the effect of an educational program upon language development and related mental functions in young children. *J. Exp. Educ.*, 11:200–209.

DEARBORN, W. F., and ROTHNEY, J. W. M. 1941. *Predicting the Child's Development*. Cambridge, Mass.: Science-Art Publishers.

DENNIS, W. 1951. A further analysis of

reports of wild children. *Child Develop.*, **22**:153–58.

DENNIS, W. 1960. Causes of retardation among institutional children. *J. Genet. Psychol.*, **96**:47–59.

DINGMAN, H. F., and TARJAN, G. 1960. Mental retardation and the normal distribution curve. *Amer. J. Ment. Defic.*, **64**: 991–94.

FERGUSON, G. A. 1954. On learning and human ability. *Canad. J. Psychol.*, **8**:95–112.

———. 1956. On transfer and the abilities of man. *Ibid.*, **10**:121–31.

FINDLEY, D. C., and McGUIRE, C. 1957. Social status and abstract behavior. *J. Abnorm. Soc. Psychol.*, **54**:135–317.

FORGUS, R. H. 1954. The effect of early perceptual learning on the behavioral organization of adult rats. *J. Comp. Physiol. Psychol.*, **47**:331–36.

———. 1955. Influence of early experience on maze-learning with and without visual cues. *Canad. J. Psychol.*, **9**:207–14.

———. 1956. Advantage of early over late perceptual experience in improving form discrimination. *Ibid.*, **10**:147–55.

GIBSON, E. J., and WALK, R. D. 1956. The effect of prolonged exposure to visually presented patterns of learning to discriminate them. *J. Comp. Physiol. Psychol.*, **49**:239–42.

GODDARD, H. H. 1912. *The Kallikak Family.* New York: Macmillan.

GOLDFARB, W. 1945. Effects of psychological deprivation in infancy and subsequent stimulation. *Amer. J. Psychiat.*, **102**:18–33.

GRIFFITH, B. C., and SPITZ, H. H. 1958. Some relationships between abstraction and word meaning in retarded adolescents. *Amer. J. Ment. Defic.*, **63**:247–51.

HAGGARD, E. A. 1954. Social-status and intelligence: an experimental study of certain cultural determinants of measured intelligence. *Genet. Psychol. Monogr.*, **49**: 141–86.

HALPERIN, S. L. 1946. Human heredity and mental deficiency. *Amer. J. Ment. Defic.*, **51**:153–63.

HARMS, I. 1957. "Development of intelligence in infancy." Unpublished manuscript, State University of Iowa, Iowa Child Welfare Research Station.

HAVIGHURST, R. J., and HILKEVITCH, R. R. 1944. The intelligence of Indian children as measured by a performance scale. *J. Abnorm. Soc. Psychol.*, **39**:419–33.

HAYWARD, S. C. 1957. Modification of sexual behavior of the male albino rat. *J. Comp. Physiol. Psychol.*, **50**:70–73.

HEBB, D. O. 1949. *The Organization of Behavior: A Neuropsychological Theory.* New York: Wiley.

———. 1955. The mammal and his environment. *Amer. J. Psychiat.*, **111**:826–31.

HOFSTAETTER, P. R. 1954. The changing composition of "intelligence": a study in T-technique. *J. Genet. Psychol.*, **85**:159–64.

HONZIK, M. P. 1957. Developmental studies in parent-child resemblance in intelligence. *Child Develop.*, **28**:215–28.

HSU, E. H. 1946. On the application of Viennese Infant Scale to Peiping babies. *J. Genet. Psychol.*, **69**:217–20.

IRWIN, O. C. 1948. Infant speech: the effect of family occupational status and of age on use of sound types. *J. Speech Hearing Dis.*, **13**:224–26.

JONES, H. E. 1954. The environment and mental development. *In:* L. CARMICHAEL (ed.), *Manual of Child Psychology*, pp. 631–96. New York: Wiley.

KAGAN, J., and BEACH, F. A. 1953. Effects of early experience on mating behavior of male rats. *J. Comp. Physiol. Psychol.*, **46**:204–8.

KAGAN, J., and MOSS, H. A. 1959. Parental correlates of child's IQ and height: a cross-validation of the Berkeley Growth Study results. *Child Develop.*, **30**:325–32.

KAHN, M. W. 1951. The effect of severe defeat at various age levels on the aggressive behavior of mice. *J. Genet. Psychol.*, **79**:117–30.

KENT, N., and DAVIS, D. R. 1957. Discipline in the home and intellectual development. *Brit. J. Med. Psychol.*, **30**:194–201.

KEPHART, N. C. 1940. Influencing the rate of mental growth in retarded children through environmental stimulation. *NSSE, Thirty-ninth Yearbook*, Part II, pp. 223–30.

KEPHART, N. C., and STRAUSS, A. A. 1940. A clinical factor influencing variations in IQ. *Amer. J. Orthopsychiat.*, **10**:343–50.

KING, J. A., and GURNEY, N. L. 1954. Effect

of early social experience on adult aggressive behavior in C57BL/10 mice. *J. Comp. Physiol. Psychol.*, 47:326–30.

KLINEBERG, O. 1935. *Negro Intelligence and Selective Migration*. New York: Columbia University Press.

KNOBLOCH, H., and PASAMANICK, B. 1960. Exogenous factors in infant intelligence. *Pediatrics* (in press).

KRISHEF, C. H. 1959. The influence of rural-urban environment upon the adjustment of discharges from the Owatonna State School. *Amer. J. Ment. Defic.*, 63:860–65.

LANTZ, B. 1945. Some dynamic aspects of success and failure. *Psychol. Monogr.*, 59. Pp. 40.

LEAHY, A. M. 1935. Nature-nurture and intelligence. *Genet. Psychol. Monogr.*, 17:235–308.

LEE, E. S. 1951. Negro intelligence and selective migration: a Philadelphia test of the Klineberg hypothesis. *Amer. Sociol. Rev.*, 16:227–33.

LEVINE, S. 1956. A further study of infantile handling and adult avoidance learning. *J. Pers.*, 25:96–114.

LEVINE, S., and OTIS, L. S. 1958. The effects of handling before and after weaning on the resistance of albino rats to later deprivation. *Canad. J. Psychol.*, 12:103–6.

LEVY, R. J. 1947. Effects of institutional vs. boarding home care on a group of infants. *J. Pers.*, 15:233–41.

LUCHINS, A. S., and FORGUS, R. H. 1955. The effect of differential post-weaning environments on the rigidity of an animal's behavior. *J. Genet. Psychol.*, 86:51–58.

McCANDLESS, B. R. 1952. Environment and intelligence. *Amer. J. Ment. Defic.*, 56:674–91.

———. 1959. Measurement problems in research. *Ibid.*, 64:265–68.

McCARTHY, D. 1954. Language development in children. *In:* L. CARMICHAEL (ed.), *Manual of Child Psychology*, pp. 492–630. New York: Wiley.

McCLELLAND, W. J. 1956. Differential handling and weight gain in the albino rat. *Canad. J. Psychol.*, 10:19–22.

McGEHEE, W., and LEWIS, W. D. 1942. The socio-economic status of homes of mentally superior and retarded children and the occupational rank of their parents. *J. Genet. Psychol.*, 60:375–80.

MELZACK, R. 1952. Irrational fears in the dog. *Canad. J. Psychol.*, 6:141–47.

———. 1954. The genesis of emotional behavior: an experimental study of the dog. *J. Comp. Physiol. Psychol.*, 47:166–68.

MELZACK, R., and THOMPSON, W. R. 1956. Effects of early experience on social behavior. *Canad. J. Psychol.*, 10:82–90.

MILLER, F. J. W., COURT, S. D. M., WALTON, W. S., and KNOX, E. G. 1960. *Growing Up in Newcastle upon Tyne*. London: Oxford University Press.

MILNER, E. 1951. A study of the relationship between reading readiness in grade one school children and patterns of parent-child interaction. *Child. Develop.*, 22:95–112.

MORGENSON, G. J., McMURRAY, G. A., and JAQUES, L. B. 1957. Effects of stress and administration of cortisone on weight gain in gentled rats. *Canad. J. Psychol.*, 11:123–27.

MUNDY, L. 1957. Environmental influence on intellectual function as measured by intelligence tests. *Brit. J. Med. Psychol.*, 30:194–201.

PASAMANICK, B. 1946. A comparative study of the behavioral development of Negro infants. *J. Genet. Psychol.*, 69:3–44.

PECK, J. R., and STEPHENS, W. B. 1960. A study of the relationship between the attitudes and behavior of parents and that of their mentally defective child. *Amer. J. Ment. Defic.*, 64:839–44.

PINNEAU, S. R. 1955a. The infantile disorders of hospitalism and anaclitic depression. *Psychol. Bull.*, 52:429–52.

PINNEAU, S. R. 1955b. Reply to Dr. Spitz. *Psychol. Bull.*, 52:459–62.

PRINGLE, M. L. K., and BOSSIO, V. 1958. A study of deprived children. Part I. Intellectual, emotional and social development. Part II. Language development and reading attainments. *Vita Humana*, 1:142–70.

———. 1960. Early, prolonged separation and emotional maladjustment. *Child Psychol. Psychiat.*, 1:37–48.

PRINGLE, M. L. K., and TANNER, M. 1958. The effects of early deprivation on speech development: a comparative study of four year olds in a nursery school and in residential nurseries. *Language and Speech*, 1:269–87.

RHEINGOLD, H. L. 1956. The modification of social responsiveness in institutional babies. *Monogr. Soc. Res. Child Develop.,* **21**:3–48.

RISS, W., and GOY, R. W. 1957. Modification of sex drive and oxygen consumption by isolating and grouping male guinea pigs. *J. Comp. Physiol. Psychol.,* **50**:150–54.

RITCHIE, B. F., AESCHLIMAN, B., and PIERCE, P. 1950. Studies in spatial learning. VIII. Place performance and the acquisition of place dispositions. *J. Comp. Physiol. Psychol.,* **43**:73–85.

SARASON, S. B. 1953. *Psychological Problems in Mental Deficiency.* New York: Harper.

SCOTT, J. H. 1955. Some effects at maturity of gentling, ignoring or shocking rats during infancy. *J. Abnorm. Soc. Psychol.,* **51**: 412–14.

SCOTT, T. H., BEXTON, W. H., HERON, W., and DOANE, B. K. 1959. Cognitive effects of perceptual isolation. *Canad. J. Psychol.,* **13**:200–209.

SEARS, R. R., MACCOBY, E. E., and LEVIN, H. 1957. *Patterns of Child Rearing.* Evanston, Ill.: Row, Peterson & Co. Pp. 549.

SEITZ, P. F. D. 1954. The effects of infantile experiences upon adult behavior in animal subjects: I. Effects of litter size during infancy upon adult behavior in the rat. *Amer. J. Psychiat.,* **110**:916–27.

SKEELS, H. M., and HARMS, I. 1948. Children with inferior social histories: their mental development in adoptive homes. *J. Genet. Psychol.,* **72**:283–94.

SKODAK, M., and SKEELS, H. M. 1949. A final follow-up study of one hundred adopted children. *J. Genet. Psychol.,* **75**:85–125.

SNYGG, D. 1938. The relation between the intelligence of mothers and of their children living in foster homes. *J. Genet. Psychol.,* **52**:401–6.

SPEARMAN, C. 1927. *The Abilities of Man.* New York: Macmillan.

SPEER, G. S. 1940. The mental development of children of feeble-minded and normal mothers. *NSSE, Thirty-ninth Yearbook,* Part II, pp. 309–14.

SPENCER, J., WALTON, W. S., MILLER, F. J. W., and COURT, S. D. M. 1954. *A Thousand Families in Newcastle upon Tyne.* London: Oxford University Press.

SPIKER, C. C. 1956. Stimulus pretraining and subsequent performance in the delayed reaction experiment. *J. Exp. Psychol.,* **52**: 107–11.

SPIKER, C. C., and McCANDLESS, B. R. 1954. The concept of intelligence and the philosophy of science. *Psychol. Rev.,* **61**:255–66.

SPITZ, R. A. 1945. Hospitalism: an inquiry into the genesis of psychiatric conditions in early childhood. *In:* O. FENICHEL *et al.* (eds.), *The Psychoanalytic Study of the Child,* 1, 53–74. New York: International Universities Press.

———. 1946. Hospitalism: a follow-up report on investigation described in Vol. I, 1945. *In:* O. FENICHEL *et al.* (eds.), *The Psychoanalytic Study of the Child,* 2, 113–17. New York: International Universities Press.

STERN, C. 1956. Hereditary factors affecting adoption. *In:* M. SCHAPIRO (ed.), *A Study of Adoption Practice,* 2, 47–58. New York: Child Welfare League of America.

STIPPICH, M. E. 1940. The mental development of children of feebleminded mothers: a preliminary report. *NSSE, Thirty-ninth Yearbook,* Part II, pp. 337–50.

TERMAN, L. M., and MERRILL, M. A. 1937. *Measuring Intelligence: A Guide to the Administration of the New Revised Stanford-Binet Tests.* Boston: Houghton Mifflin.

THOMPSON, W. R. 1955. The heredity-environment problem. *Bull. Marit. Psychol. Assoc.,* 30–40.

THOMPSON, W. R., and HERON, W. 1954. The effects of restricting early experience on the problem-solving capacity of dogs. *Canad. J. Psychol.,* **8**:17–31.

THORNDIKE, E. L. *et al.* 1926. *The Measurement of Intelligence.* New York: Teachers' College, Columbia University.

THURSTONE, L. L., and THURSTONE, T. G. 1950. *Primary Mental Abilities Scales: Primary, Elementary, and Intermediate.* Chicago: Science Research Associates.

VALENSTEIN, E. S., RISS, W., and YOUNG, W. C. 1955. Experimental and genetic factors in the organization of sexual behavior in male guinea pigs. *J. Comp. Physiol. Psychol.,* **48**:397–403.

WECHSLER, D. 1944. *The Measurement of Intelligence.* Baltimore: Williams & Wilkins.

WEININGER, O. 1953. Mortality of albino rats under stress as a function of early handling. *Canad. J. Psychol.,* **7**:111–14.

———. 1956. The effects of early experience on behavior and growth characteristics. *J. Comp. Physiol. Psychol.*, **49**:1–9.

WEININGER, O., McCLELLAND, W. J., and ARIMA, R. K. 1954. Gentling and weight gain in the albino rat. *Canad. J. Psychol.*, **8**:147–51.

WHEELER, L. R. 1942. A comparative study of east Tennessee mountain children. *J. Educ. Psychol.*, **33**:321–34.

WORBOIS, G. M. 1942. Changes in Stanford-Binet IQ for rural consolidated and rural one-room school children. *J. Exp. Educ.*, **11**:210–14.

SOCIAL AND OCCUPATIONAL
ADJUSTMENT

Herbert Goldstein

From the time of the first treatment center for the mentally retarded in the mid-nineteenth century, the major goal of interested disciplines and services has been to help the mentally retarded individual achieve social and occupational adequacy at maturity. Over the years, the context within which such help was rendered expanded to include the state-operated institution for the retarded, the public schools, and, more recently, public and private habilitation agencies and clinics.

In addition to providing diagnostic, treatment, and placement services commensurate with its unique structure, each organization has conducted research designed to improve and/or expand its contribution. Some research has been intramural, as in the case of studies on selection for training and placement. Some has been extramural, such as studies of the status of former inmates, students, or clients.

It is the purpose of this chapter to discuss the research relative to the social and occupational adjustment of the mentally retarded in society under the following topics: (1) the early concepts of the adjustment potential of mentally retarded persons, (2) the adjustment of institutional and non-institutional mentally retarded persons in the community, (3) the vocational status of mentally retarded persons, and (4) the occupational outlook for the retarded.

The mentally retarded persons referred to in this chapter will be, for the most part, the higher grade type—those considered educable by the standards of the public schools—or the analogous mild and moderate retarded as classified by the American Psychiatric Association.

EARLY CONCEPTS OF THE ADJUSTMENT POTENTIAL OF MENTALLY RETARDED PERSONS

Attitudes of professional and lay persons toward the potential for social and occupational adjustment of mentally retarded persons have been very influential in the development of services for the retarded. The extreme optimism of pioneers in the field motivated a reform movement which culminated in the existing public institutional program for the mentally retarded. Those inspiring the provision of state-operated schools for the mentally retarded anticipated that, following a period of training and education, most would return to their homes and communities to function at a level approaching normalcy. This expectation was comparatively short-lived, mainly because of two factors. First, the absence of discriminatory methods of evaluation and classification permitted the admission to the state schools of many children who were not amenable to instruction. Second, it was found that the depressed family status of many of those children who could be returned prohibited their discharge or parole.

As a result of these limiting factors, the goal of the public institution was modified in the direction of intramural adjustment and service of its inmates. Fernald (1893) estimated that less than

15 per cent of Waverly's inmates had the potential for social and occupational adequacy but that over 50 per cent could learn to perform service tasks within the institution and, in this way, contribute to their upkeep.

Thus, the dynamic role of the public institution did not materialize, and the institutions settled into a pattern of care and training with comparatively few cases of extra-institutional placement occurring. More and more, the mentally retarded were referred to as a burden to society. Soon, however, an additional descriptive term began to appear in the literature—the term "menace."

This marked change in attitude stemmed from two theories: (1) that mentally retarded persons were predisposed to a life of crime and depravity and (2) that mental retardation was almost entirely a hereditary phenomenon. Since both theories had far-reaching effects on social action in this area, it might be profitable to review some of the occurrences and their results.

PREDISPOSITION TO CRIME

The belief that the higher grade mentally retarded person was an incipient criminal became very common among both professional and lay persons. Statements such as "The brighter class of the feebleminded, with their weak will power and deficient judgment, are easily influenced for evil, and are prone to become vagrants, drunkards, and thieves" (Fernald, 1893) and "Quite a large per cent of our criminal class today were among those backward children of a generation ago" (Bancroft, 1901) began to appear more and more frequently.

With the arrival of the mental-test movement, such statements were augmented by statistics. Moore (1911), in reporting on Binet tests administered to new admissions to the New Jersey Reformatory, stated, "Nearly every young man who has entered our institution in the last 18 months has been tested by this system, and the result has shown that at least 46 per cent were mentally subnormal." Other studies by Goddard and Hill (1911), Morrow and Bridgeman (1912), Enyon (1913), Knollin and Terman (1918), and others showed that a large percentage of the criminals and delinquents were mentally retarded. Goddard (1914a) reported data obtained from sixteen institutions for delinquent boys and girls and showed that the percentage of inmates who were mentally retarded ranged from 28 per cent to 89 per cent. The median group numbered 70 per cent of its members as mentally retarded. Thirteen of the institutions reported that at least 50 per cent of their inmates were mentally retarded. In most cases, the Binet test was used to determine mental status. Of this fact Goddard wrote, "It is most discouraging to discover that the more expert is the examiner of these groups, the higher is the percentage of feebleminded found [among delinquents]" (p. 8). In commenting on this statement, Merrill (1947) pointed out that many testers, inexpert and poorly trained, attempted to demonstrate their expertness by the large number of cases they found to be mentally retarded. As early as 1916, Crafts (1916) had amassed a bibliography of some 206 items on mental retardation and its relationship to juvenile delinquency.

While the proportion of juvenile delinquents and criminals who were mentally retarded appeared to be unusually high, the refinement and broadening of the psychological evaluation together with the development of more meticulous criteria for juvenile delinquency and mental retardation contributed to a more realistic appraisal of the problem. Sutherland (1931) discussed 342 psychometric studies involving some 175,000 delinquents completed in the period 1910–28. Grouping the studies in five-year periods starting with 1910, he showed that the percentage of mentally retarded in the median study in each five-year group decreased from 51 per cent in 1910–14 to 20 per cent in 1925–28. Sutherland next grouped the studies in five-year blocks according to types of institutions holding the delinquents. Again, he found that in each case the trend was in the direction of a reduction in the proportion of mentally retarded in the institutional population. He concluded that this trend was, in great part, due to improvements in methods of mental measurement and in the standardization of psychometric instruments. He further contended that "... feeblemindedness has not been demonstrated to be a generally important cause of juvenile delinquency" (p. 363).

Zeleny (1931), in a similar analysis of studies of the relationship between mental retardation and criminal conduct from 1910 to 1930, suggested that variability in the proportion of mentally retarded in the institutional population might be due to the variations in criteria for mental retardation typical of that period. He found that upper limits for IQ's varied from 50 to 80; mental age from eight years to thirteen years.

Merrill points out that variation between studies can be due to alterations in institutional policy between studies. She cites the studies of Williams (1919) and Fenton et al. (1935) at Whittier State School in California. Williams found that 35 per cent of the delinquents at Whittier were mentally retarded, while Fenton found only 4 per cent in that classification. Both psychologists used the same Stanford revision of the Binet. In the interval between studies, however, institutional policy had been altered to preclude the admission of mentally retarded boys, thus affecting Fenton's results.

More recent studies conform to the conservative end of the trend suggested by Sutherland. Kvaraceus (1945) found that 10.4 per cent of the total delinquent group studied were mentally retarded. Healy and Bronner (1926) found 13.5 per cent of juvenile court cases to be

mentally retarded. Glueck and Glueck (1934) studied a similar population and found 13.1 per cent to be mentally retarded. Merrill studied County Juvenile Court records of five hundred consecutive cases and found 11.6 per cent to be mentally retarded. Burt (1938) tested juvenile delinquents and reports that 7.7 per cent were mentally retarded. In summarizing five studies accomplished in different parts of the country and employing varying definitions of delinquency, Kvaraceus reported that the studies tended to show that approximately 12 per cent of the delinquent populations were mentally retarded.

While recent studies of juvenile delinquents reveal a relatively greater consistency in reporting the proportion of mentally retarded in the study populations, it should be noted that there are still noteworthy differences between studies. It is also noteworthy that the proportion of mentally retarded in the delinquent populations ranges from over two to almost five times the proportion of mentally retarded in the total school-age population. The question is then raised: What factors underlie these differences?

In the case of the discrepancies between studies, part of the difference may be accounted for by (1) differences in psychometric instruments, (2) differences in criteria of mental retardation, (3) differences in concept or definition of delinquency, and (4) statutory factors.

Differences in psychometric instruments.—In Merrill's study, the Stanford-Binet was employed; Kvaraceus' test data were obtained in some cases with the Stanford-Binet and in others with the Kuhlman-Anderson; Burt employed the Binet-Simon; Glueck and Glueck found that the Stanford-Binet was used in most cases, Yerkes-Bridges tests in others, and that some twenty delinquents lacked test data.

Differences in criteria of mental retardation.—In most cases, mental retardation was reported only in terms of IQ. Merrill, Kvaraceus, Glueck and Glueck, and Burt established an upper limit of IQ 70. Healy and Bronner used a ceiling of IQ 75. While there is majority agreement on the IQ as a criterion, there is no indication in the report of other criteria applied by the examiner. This unstated aspect of the testing might be considered critical because of the clinical differences built into the testing situation by the attitude of the delinquent as compared with that of the member of the standardization population.

Differences in concept or definitions of delinquency.—Carr (1940) and Barron (1954) indicated that definitions of delinquency are quite varied and may be based on either moral, legal, psychological, or social concepts. The aforementioned studies represent a cross-section of concepts of juvenile delinquency with emphasis, however, on the legally defined or court-adjudged delinquent. The populations studied by Kvaraceus using the Binet test were comprised of both adjudicated and agency-referred delinquents. Merrill studied adjudicated delinquents only. Healy and Bronner also studied adjudicated delinquents but only those with records of repeated offenses. While Kvaraceus and Burt studied what appeared to be similarly defined populations, there is a notable difference in the proportion of mentally retarded in the delinquent populations. By the same token, Healy and Bronner found more mentally retarded among their repeaters than did Merrill, who did not differentiate between repeaters and first offenders.

Statutory factors.—State and local regulations and provisions directly and indirectly affect prevalence data on mentally retarded in the juvenile-delinquent population. Not infrequently, mentally retarded youths apprehended as juvenile delinquents may find themselves committed to an institution for the mentally retarded rather than to a correctional institution. In states where this is the practice, it may be assumed that the population in correctional institutions will be relatively free of mentally retarded youth as compared with corrective institutions in states where this practice is not followed. At the same time, commitment based on mental retardation may appear as such in the court records rather than as juvenile delinquency. Both of the foregoing tend to reduce the proportion of mentally retarded in the delinquent population.

Studies of the prevalence of mentally retarded in the juvenile-delinquent population indicate that the proportion is considerably less than that suggested by Goddard. As to Goddard's contention that mental retardation was the prime contributory condition to delinquency, most authorities take a more cautious stand and state that the exact relationship of mental retardation and juvenile delinquency is unknown.

THE CONCEPT OF THE HEREDITARY NATURE OF MENTAL RETARDATION AND ITS EFFECT ON THE SEGREGATION-STERILIZATION MOVEMENT

The belief that the condition of mental retardation was almost entirely hereditary stimulated the efforts of authorities toward methods of social control. In the last quarter of the nineteenth century, the search for the causes of mental retardation inevitably led to the study of families and the incidence or coincidence of mental retardation within a particular strain.

The revival of Mendelism provided a prestige vehicle for studies purporting to show that mental retardation was not only hereditary but that it was basic to many of man's physical and social ills. Bicknell (1896) reported a study of family trees of mentally retarded persons and found that as high as 80 per cent of the offspring were mentally retarded. Goddard (1914*b*), Dugdale (1877), Estabrook (1915), and others studied family histories and presented masses of data which were widely accepted as concrete evidence of the fact that mental retardation was a strong hereditary trait. Davenport (1911), a geneticist, used Goddard's data to illustrate that:

Low mentality is due to the absence of some factor, and if this factor that determines normal development is lacking in both parents it will be lacking in all of their offspring. . . . Probably no imbecile is born except of parents who, if not mentally defective themselves, both carry mental defect in their germ plasm (pp. 66–67).

The flood of literature dwelling on the hereditary nature of mental retardation and its threat to the well-being of society obliterated counter-evidence such as that presented by Pearson and Jaederholm (1914), who examined Davenport's thesis of mental retardation as a "unit character" and his assertion that it is a Mendelian recessive. Some 300 mentally retarded children in Stockholm classes for the mentally retarded were compared with 250 normal children according to their performance in various items of the Binet-Simon to ascertain that the characteristics imputed to mental retardation were exclusive to this group as claimed by the geneticists. They drew the following conclusions:

1. That there exists an absolute continuity of intelligence in the mentally defective group, with an even greater range of variation than occurs in the normal population.
2. That the grades of intelligence of the mentally defective children of the special schools largely overlap the grades of normal intelligence. As far as intelligence is concerned, there is no boundary whatever between the normal population and the population of children segregated as "mentally defective."
3. That no justification whatever can be derived from our data for talking of the mentally defective as lacking a "factor necessary for full mental development," or speaking of a "unit character upon which normal development depends," or of feeble-mindedness as due to germ plasm lacking a unique "determiner" (p. 36).

Nevertheless, studies and surveys (Grant, 1921; Wiggam, 1924; East, 1927; Pitkin, 1928; Gosney and Popenoe, 1929) were presented as evidence that the proportion of mentally retarded in the total population was on the increase. They suggested segregation and sterilization as the most efficient counter-measures.

Laughlin (1922) presented a historical review and analysis of legislation of sterilization in this country. He revealed that protagonists of this movement had no easy time selling their proposal to state legislatures despite the accumulation of evidence in their favor.

Landman (1932) reported that while thirty states adopted sterilization statutes at one time or another in the twenty-five-year period of this movement, only some twelve thousand persons had been sterilized within the framework of this legislation by 1932. Of this number, approximately one-third were mentally retarded. Landman suggested the futility of controlling the mentally retarded through sterilization and estimated that only about 11 per cent of the mentally retarded in any one generation might be eliminated. Tredgold (1948) estimated that no more than 10 per cent of the cases of mental retardation were inherited.

The multiplicity of factors relative to mental retardation began to penetrate through the arguments for sterilization. Doll (1929) pointed out the following:

There is ordinarily but little value in the eugenic sterilization of the low-grade feeble-minded who rarely mate and who seldom present sexual problems. There is theoretically no value in sterilizing the non-hereditary types. There are numerous technical difficulties in establishing the hereditary nature of feeble-mindedness where both parents are not themselves feeble-minded. There are objections to sterilizing borderline cases which may represent frank problems of diagnosis (p. 172.)

Coupled with these problems were the legal arguments against the sterilization laws (Landman, 1932) and the realization that the state laws did not provide for a means for reaching into the community for those mentally retarded persons who seemingly constituted a greater threat to the well-being of society than did their institutionalized counterparts. As Justice Holmes (Supreme Court Report, 1927) observed in affirming the constitutionality of the Virginia sterilization law:

The principle that sustains compulsory vaccination is broad enough to cover cutting the Fallopian tubes. . . . Three generations of imbeciles are enough. But . . . if this reasoning were applied generally it fails when it is confined to the small number who are in the institutions named and is not applied to the multitude outside.

The obvious ineffectiveness of a generalized sterilization program led to a more conservative approach to this mode of social control—that of selective sterilization. Watkins reported the results of a questionnaire study of members of the American Association for the Study of Feebleminded concerning their attitudes toward sterilization. Eighty per cent of the total membership responded. Of these, 94 per cent indicated that they approved of sterilization of the mentally retarded. Ninety-seven per cent of those favoring sterilization preferred selective sterilization. In states with sterilization laws, members were unanimous in holding that they did not want the law abandoned.

Selective sterilization.—Under the program of selective sterilization, the rate of sterilization of mentally retarded persons increased in public institutions in the thirty states legalizing this procedure. By 1935, the proportion of mentally retarded in the total sterilized in this country had increased to 44 per cent; by 1946

the proportion was 69 per cent. The rate of sterilizations per 100,000 persons showed a marked acceleration through 1937 and a slight leveling off through 1942. The shortage of medical personnel occasioned during the war years caused a slight decrease in the rate. Indications are, however, that the rate is increasing once again. In the majority of cases, those sterilized were of the higher grade mentally retarded destined for parole to community placement. Gamble (1951) reported that approximately 26,000 such persons were rendered parolable by sterilization by 1950.

Selective sterilization appears to be the pattern followed in institutions where state laws provide for this means of social control. Insofar as decision-making is concerned, practices vary from complete electivity on the part of the inmate and his family to complete control by the institutional authority. The criteria for sterilization generally appear to be sexual promiscuity for females and aggressiveness for males. Up to 1949, sterilization of females was almost double that of males in the United States.

Follow-up studies.—Follow-up studies of sterilized male and female mentally retarded parolees generally indicate that the operation results in an improvement in the social adjustment of the parolee. Craft (1936) studied 269 patients sterilized in North Dakota and found the following: (1) Those who were married at the time of the operation and those married subsequently were, in the main, happily married. (2) None of the patients experienced sexual changes following the operation. (3) Incidence of sex offenses decreased markedly after the operation. The ratio of offenses before and after the operation was seven to one.

Johnson (1946) studied the extra-institutional careers of 264 sterilized inmates in New Hampshire, 180 females and 84 males. She found the following: (1) Forty per cent of the girls and 63 per cent of the boys were self-supporting.

(2) Fifty-nine percent of the girls and 25 per cent of the boys have married since parole. (3) Twenty-three per cent of the girls and 19 per cent of the boys have been divorced. (4) Forty-two per cent of the girls and 43 per cent of the boys appear to be making a satisfactory adjustment to marriage.

Whitney and Schick (1931) reported that the general conduct of over 70 per cent of the cases sterilized at Elwyn had shown considerable improvement. Popenoe (1926) reported on a study of the records of 605 discharged or paroled inmates of a California institution who had been sterilized before separation. He found little correlation between success on parole and age, intelligence, socioeconomic status, family history, or length of time spent outside the institution. He found that two-thirds have been reasonably successful in their communities and concluded that sterilization is a valuable adjunct to parole.

Other reports (Pritchard, 1949; Hill, 1950) contend that the parolability of sterilized inmates of institutions for the mentally retarded has saved the states bed space and funds. Gamble (1951) estimated that continued institutionalization of the 26,000 patients parolable because of sterilization would have amounted to 336,000 inmate years at a total cost to the states of some 117,000,-000 dollars. These estimates are based on the life expectancy of patients of this type in institutions at a cost of 350 dollars per patient per year.

Gamble (1952) estimated that sterilization of the mentally retarded will reduce the prevalence of mental retardation in the following generations by 15 per cent. This estimate is an extrapolation of data obtained in restricted studies by Southwick (1939) and Johnson (1946). For the most part, the extrapolations are based on the prior record of the patient as compared with the birth rate of other mentally retarded family members.

Since selective sterilization as a means of social control appears to be an established fact in thirty states, there is little merit in devoting much space to the pros and cons of the issue. Suffice it to say that there is little doubt that sterilization contributes to the community adjustment of those mentally retarded persons who demonstrate a lack of control or a predisposition to problems in sexual behavior. At the same time, there is considerable doubt that sterilization has wrought all of the advantages imputed to it by the aforementioned studies. For one, these studies have involved persons who have been out of the institution as long as thirty years and some who have been out only a few years. The studies do not take into consideration the economic, environmental, and maturational differences within the group effected by time. Nor do they appear to consider the effect on behavior of supervision following parole as compared with the lack of supervision prior to institutionalization.

The limited application of this means of social control can be seen in the fact that between 1907 and 1949 only 24,957 mentally retarded persons were sterilized in thirty states. Of this total, over one-fourth of the operations took place in California. It is interesting to note that the most recent legislation permitting this treatment was passed in Georgia in 1937. Since that time Washington, one of the first states to legalize the operation in 1907, had its law declared unconstitutional by the State Spreme Court in 1942. Thus, while sterilization of the mentally retarded appears to be a legal procedure in a majority of states, practice shows that it has not been as effective as anticipated at the time that it was proposed as a method of social control.

THE ADJUSTMENT OF THE MENTALLY RETARDED IN THE COMMUNITY

With the implementation of the policy of segregating the mentally retarded into public institutions came a reduction in the mobility of institutional populations. Despite the diligence of institutional personnel, however, there was a continuous but small seepage of inmates out of the institutions and back to the communities. Some escaped while others were discharged in the custody of their families, who had exerted legal pressure on the institution.

During the period 1890–1924 some 1537 inmates escaped or were reluctantly discharged from one institution, Waverly State School in Massachusetts. It was an investigation of the status of departed inmates by the superintendent of Waverly, Walter E. Fernald, that stimulated a long line of follow-up studies, most of which emulated the pattern of inquiry established in his study, i.e., the gathering of information from community agencies and services that reflects the frequency with which the subjects depend upon or offend society.

Not long after the public schools began to provide special educational facilities for the educable mentally retarded, they, too, followed their graduates into the community to ascertain their status.

Since the environment and type of training of persons paroled from institutions differ in some degree from that of persons educated in the community, studies will be presented in two categories: (1) studies of persons paroled from institutions for the mentally retarded and (2) studies of non-institutionalized persons.

STUDIES OF MENTALLY RETARDED PERSONS PAROLED FROM INSTITUTIONS

Fernald's study of discharged inmates from Waverly.—Dr. Walter E. Fernald (1919) conducted the first recorded investigation on the careers of all those who had left Waverly State School in the twenty-five year period, 1890–1914. It is important to keep in mind the fact that the majority of the cases studied were discharged under protest of the institu-

tion management. This is significant since it demarcates the Waverly population from that of other studies in that the following studies dealt mostly with parolees who were prepared for placement and supervised in some degree after placement, while the Waverly dischargees were predominantly on their own.

Of the 1537 persons discharged from Waverly in the twenty-five year period, Fernald found that 612 had been transferred to other institutions for the mentally retarded, hospitals for the mentally ill, or to other custodial institutions, and 279 could not be located. Letters of inquiry were sent to friends or relatives of the remaining 646 dischargees. A social worker then visited the community and questioned others in the community such as agency personnel, police, and ministers. The letters and interviews netted data on 176 females and 470 males.

The data on the females showed that 62 (35 per cent) had been readmitted to Waverly or had been committed to other institutions, and 24 (14 per cent) had died. Ninety females (51 per cent) had remained in the community. Of those in the community, 52 (58 per cent) of this group had no record of difficulty: 11 had married and were keeping house; 8 were totally self-supporting and independent; 20 worked at home; and 13 lived at home without making a noteworthy contribution to the family. The community records of the remaining 38 females (42 per cent) were negative for the most part, involving sexual offenses, alcoholism, and theft. Even so, only 4 of this group had been committed to correctional institutions in the course of the twenty-five years.

In comparing the well-adjusted females with the poorly adjusted, it was found that the distinguishing differences appeared to be the amount of acceptance each received. The successful were counseled and aided by friends and relatives who supervised their activities and channeled them in socially acceptable directions. In contrast, there were very few instances of benign guidance and supervision among the unsuccessful females. Fernald concluded, "Apparently women who have friends capable of understanding them and properly protecting them did not have illegitimate children and did not become sex offenders" (p. 3).

Information was obtained on 470 males. The data on the males showed that 111 (24 per cent) had been readmitted to Waverly or had been committed to other institutions, and 54 (12 per cent) had died. Three hundred and five males (64 per cent) remained in the community. In this group only 13 had married. In most cases, wives were adjudged normal. Twelve children, all normal, were born of these unions. Twenty-eight of the total group were self-supporting and living independently; 86 were employed but living at home; 77 worked at home; and 59 lived at home but made no noteworthy contribution to the family.

In the twenty-five-year period, 23 of the males had been arrested for crimes or misdemeanors but had not been sentenced; 32 others had been arrested and had been committed to a penal institution soon after discharge from Waverly —8 of these to juvenile detention homes or reformatories.

In terms of occupation and income, jobs held by the males were predominantly in the unskilled category—laborer, factory hand, farm worker, and elevator man. There were some instances of semiskilled and skilled occupations among the single men such as painter, baker, printing pressman, brakeman, machinist, and barber. Earnings ranged from 8 to 36 dollars per week (pre–World War I). One man owned his own home, and savings among the married males were not uncommon. Those with occupations were, for the most part, higher grade mentally retarded; the 77 males who helped at home were in the moderately retarded range and the 59 males who lived at home and did little to contribute to the

family were in the low moderate–severe range.

The data on the males were far more encouraging than those on the females. Antisocial behavior was proportionately less, while extent of community adjustment appeared to be greater. As in the case of the females, the roles of friends and relatives in guiding and supervising the dischargees appear to be the deciding factors in the adjustment or maladjustment of the discharged males.

Fernald made two contributions to the study of the social adjustment of paroled or discharged inmates of institutions for the mentally retarded. The first contribution was one of methodology. The sequence of study from locating to reporting employed by Fernald has been the pattern of most studies which followed. Other studies have improved on various elements of the sequence by lending a preciseness to such variables as definition of mental retardation and components of adjustment and by becoming more detailed in such elements as levels of occupation and job tenure.

Fernald's second contribution was more in the direction of administration than science. The results of his study were diametrically opposed to the commonly held expectations of administrators, including Fernald. As Davies (1930) related, "Dr. Fernald told the writer that he had hesitated for two years to publish the results of this study because they seemed so much at variance with the then accepted theories dealing with mental deficiency" (p. 196). Once the study was published, administrators and workers in institutions were faced with a serious question: If some mentally retarded persons with serious records of misbehavior who have been discharged from the institution under protest of the administration can make adequate adjustment in their communities despite minimal training, chance placement, and chance supervision, what might be expected of those who receive relevant training, selective placement, and supportive supervision?

The nature of the response to this question can be seen in the programs of many state institutions for the mentally retarded (Ellis, 1941; Meece, 1946; Pero, 1955). A perusal of these programs shows an increasing tendency to train higher grade mentally retarded for community placement and to correlate the efforts of institutional workers toward the most suitable placement with the required supervision. Toward this end, more and more institutions are creating the position of educational director to co-ordinate all training and placement activities, as the clinical director correlates medical and psychiatric activities and services. In a few institutions, the position of superintendent has recently been held by educators rather than by physicians as in the past.

Matthews' follow-up of adolescents discharged from Waverly.—Shortly after the publication of Fernald's study, Matthews (1922) traced the careers of one hundred boys paroled from Waverly. This sample differed from Fernald's in that:

1. They were selected on the basis of their proximity to the institution.

2. They had all participated in an organized training program.

3. All but two were placed (two escaped but were permitted to go on parole), and all were supervised in the community by a social worker.

The boys in this study lived in the community from ten months to five years. Most had been out of the state between two and three years.

Briefly, all but three boys were making a satisfactory adjustment to community life; seven boys were completely self-supporting and living independently, while the rest lived under family or social-worker supervision. Of the three boys returned to the institution, one committed an indecent assault, one could not or would not keep a job, and one had not completed his training. His family requested that he be taken back for further work.

Matthews found that there was some relationship between mental age and income. She found that in grouping the boys by mental age (MA) there was a differential of two dollars per week in income for each year of MA.

Types of occupations were influenced by chronological age, with the younger boys relegated to messenger and office-boy jobs, while the older boys were laborers and crafts helpers.

Matthews concluded that the success of these boys was due to the constructive training received while in Waverly and the supervision given them for placement.

While Matthews' study presents little in the form of data, it was a suitable follow-up to Fernald's study, since it embodies the recommendations implicit in Fernald's findings. Her sample, while selected on the basis of expediency, was similar to Fernald's in that a good proportion of her subjects had court records of misdemeanors or worse leading to institutionalization. The sample was dissimilar to Fernald's in terms of chronological age, amount of preplacement training, and extent of postplacement supervision. Since there are no data relevant to psychometric status in either study, no comparison may be made.

Without pressing the scientific stature of Matthews' study, one might be justified in accepting that she accomplished her task of establishing the role of an institutional program in a parole system. In this respect, her study is a valuable adjunct to Fernald's work.

A study of discharged and paroled adults from Rome State School.—Foley (1929) studied the extra-institutional status of 636 inmates paroled from Rome State School during the twenty-year period 1905–24. In order to present a clearer picture of the community adjustment of these paroled patients, Foley's data have been converted into percentages as shown in Table 1.

The data on the 636 cases show that of the 375 males all but 76 were employed with some degree of success. Approximately two-thirds held unskilled laboring and factory jobs. The rest held a variety of positions including salesmen, gas station employee, and newspaper sales. Among the 76 who had no work record were 29 males who were not able to work because they were either of the lower grade classification of mentally retarded, physically handicapped, or too young.

TABLE 1

PAROLEES FROM ROME STATE SCHOOL, 1905–24

	MALES (375)		FEMALES (261)	
	No.	%	No.	%
Remuneratively employed............	299	80	163	62
Committed to other institutions.......	46	12	24	9
Charity cases.......	20	5	19	7
Court records.......	78	21	19	7
Nuisance records....	16	4	23	9
Married............	34	9	160	61
Divorced or separated	3	9*	11	7*

* Value represents the percentage of the total who are married.

One hundred sixty-three females were remuneratively employed. For the most part, they held jobs as domestic and restaurant workers or as factory and mill workers or were working at home. Only six females were incapable of holding a job. Extent of self-support might be inferred from the fact that only 20 males and 19 females required charitable assistance from welfare agencies in the twenty-year period.

Over the twenty-year period of the study, 46 males and 24 females were committed to other institutions for varying terms. A majority of such commitments were to county homes or hospitals.

There were 48 records of commitments to penal or reformatory institutions. It is noteworthy that 90 per cent of the total number of dischargees in the study had no record of having been committed to any type of institution.

Records reveal that 21 per cent of the males and 7 per cent of the females appeared in court at one time or another during the twenty-year period. For the most part, court appearances were for minor offenses. There were few instances of charges such as petty larceny and theft. Vagrancy, disorderly conduct, and a variety of non-criminal incidents comprised the majority of offenses. Other unacceptable behavior drawing complaints of nuisance was noted in the case of 4 per cent of the males and 9 per cent of the females. Such complaints ranged from sex perversion to foolish looks and unpleasing personality. No court action was taken in the nuisance cases.

A rating of the homes of the study group showed that the large majority of males and females lived in "good" or "very good" homes; less than 13 per cent lived in homes that were below the average for laborers in their community.

Nine per cent of the males and 61 per cent of the females had married. Together, these 110 families had 236 children. There was a total of 10 cases of separation and 4 of divorce. Mates of the females were predominantly laborers or unskilled workers, although some did marry skilled and professional persons.

The data in Table 1 show that the community adjustment of the 636 male and female dischargees was, on the whole, quite good at least insofar as the criteria for adjustment applied in the study are operative. There is no way of telling how the rates shown in Table 1 compare with those of the general population. Compared with Fernald's findings and the opinions commonly held by other administrators at this period, Foley's sample produced encouraging results.

While this study represents a marked improvement over its predecessors, it still leaves serious gaps in terms of data, description, and definition, as follows:

1. Foley does not describe his sample in terms of age, psychometric status, amount of training, length of time in institution, time in community, or type of supervision. It would be important to know the relationships, if any, of these variables to adjustment.

2. The criterion of remunerative occupation is too gross to adequately describe the extent of occupational adjustment. Unstated here are such critical variables as term of employment, relationship of employer, record of job efficiency, record of attendance and punctuality, relationship between job requirement and mental level of employees, and so forth.

3. Court records reveal only one aspect of behavior in the community. Unspecified here is the quantitative and qualitative nature of interpersonal relationships of this sample with its families and outsiders. One cannot perceive of the relationship, if any, between leisure-time activities and court of nuisance records.

4. Marital adjustment as signified by prevalence of divorce or separation tells only a small part of the total story. Family cohesiveness as measured by common interests, activities, and values might be a more profitable approach toward judgments in this area. Parent-child relationships, home management, and period of marriage are other variables that might help to clarify marital status.

Despite the shortcomings listed above, Foley's study was a substantial contribution to this area of research. It represents the first attempt at a comprehensive treatment of a problem with many ramifications. To the extent that he did identify elements of community adjustment, Foley helped set the pattern for the majority of studies that followed, up to the present.

A study of paroled adults from Letch-worth Village.—In the same year, Storrs (1924) reported on a study of parolees from Letchworth Village. Like Foley, he employed occupational record, police and complaint record, marital record, and the like, as indexes of community adjustment. Parolees were considered to have made poor adjustment if their records showed conflict in the areas listed and to have made good adjustment if they did not.

Storrs reported on all dischargees prior to 1927. After culling out those who had been transferred to other institutions, were dead, or could not be found, he had a sample of 620. Of these, 433 were males and 187 were females.

Generally, the data presented by Storrs are in agreement with Foley's. He found that 73 per cent of the males and 75 per cent of the females were successfully adjusted in their communities. Storrs reported data other than those presented by Foley in that he included tables on the sex and mental status of the dischargees as related to adjustment, conditions of discharge, age at discharge, and period of residence in the community at the time of the study. Essentially, his data on these factors indicate, for the males: (1) The largest proportion of dischargees, 55 per cent, was in the mildly retarded class. Moderately retarded individuals comprised 23 per cent of the group; severely retarded, 10 per cent. (2) Approximately 40 per cent of the successful group were in the mildly retarded class, 17 per cent were moderately retarded, and 8 per cent severely retarded. (3) In each class, the ratio of successes to failures was three to one. (4) A study of the conditions of discharge showed that there were five times as many escapees among mildly retarded than the next group, the moderately retarded. (5) In terms of age at time of discharge, there were twice as many mildly retarded as moderately retarded or severely retarded discharged under fifteen years of age. Between the ages of fifteen and twenty, the ratio of mildly retarded to moderately retarded was almost three to one, and of mildly retarded to severely retarded almost ten to one. Over twenty years of age, the mildly retarded outnumbered the moderately retarded by two to one and the severely retarded by twenty-nine to one. (6) Among the successful males, 18 per cent were over twenty years of age at discharge. Fifty-six per cent were between fifteen and twenty years, and 26 per cent were under fifteen. (7) Forty-five per cent of all successful dischargees had been living in their communities for over three years; of these one-half were in the mildly retarded group. Forty-two per cent had been in their communities from one to three years; of these 58 per cent were mildly retarded. Thirteen per cent had lived in their communities less than one year; of these 53 per cent were mildly retarded.

The data on the successfully adjusted females follow a similar pattern. They show the following: (1) The largest proportion of dischargees, 58 per cent, were in the mildly retarded class. Moderately retarded individuals comprised 21 per cent of the group; severely retarded, 9 per cent. The remaining 12 per cent were not mentally retarded or were undiagnosed. (2) Forty-five per cent of the successfully adjusted females were in the mildly retarded class. Sixteen per cent were moderately retarded, and 7 per cent were severely retarded. (3) By class, the ratio of success to failures was three to one in the mildly retarded and moderately retarded and seven to two in the severely retarded class. (4) A study of conditions of discharge showed that all escapees were mildly retarded. Twenty-five mildly retarded, four moderately retarded, and one non-retarded completed parole. (5) Age data at time of discharge show that 50 per cent of the successful females were between the ages of fifteen and twenty years, 34 per cent were over

twenty, and 10 per cent were dischargees before reaching age sixteen. (6) Thirty-three per cent of the females had been living in their communities for over three years at the time of the study; 50 per cent, from one to three years; and 17 per cent, under one year.

Storrs found that length of residence in the institution of both males and females was a critical variable if related to the period of special training. We found that those who had completed the program of training in the institution were universally successful regardless of the length of residence in the institution.

In terms of occupation, he found that the males had a remarkably stable record: 78 per cent of those able to work were employed steadily with few job changes, 10 per cent worked steadily but with many job changes, and 12 per cent worked intermittently. Almost all jobs were of the unskilled type. Only seven of the males were married and all maintained reasonably satisfactory homes.

Among the females, thirteen severely retardates excluded, 44 per cent were totally self-supporting, 7 per cent partially self-supporting, and 49 per cent were dependent on others. Of the dependent females, 22 per cent were supported by their husbands, and 77 per cent by their families. Thirty-eight females had married with twenty-six children resulting from these marriages.

Most of those employed were in domestic services or in factories. Almost all worked steadily with few job changes; only five worked intermittently.

It is interesting to note that about two-thirds of the unsuccessful males and one-half of the unsuccessful females were returned to the institution. There is no way of knowing what factor or factors precipitated institutionalization, nor is there any indication of the role of community and family tolerance.

Like preceding studies, Storrs applies gross measures in evaluating community adjustment. His inclusion of descriptive data, however, gives a clear picture of the population investigated.

It is very obvious, thus far, that there is a selective factor operating in the placement of inmates of institutions for the mentally retarded. From Storrs's data, it can be seen that mildly retarded appear to be the most frequently chosen class. Not unexpectedly, self-support and long-term residence in the community occur more frequently in this class. They also hold the better jobs and earn more. Incidences of return to the institution increase among the classes below mildly retarded and with increasing age of the individual. From this, one might infer the extent to which supervision contributes to keeping the moderately retarded and severely retarded at home or in the community.

Storrs's study represents another step forward in improving the methodology of this type of research. While his data are generally supportive of previous studies, the additional descriptive data showed that descriptive as well as comparative data were important.

Follow-up studies of parolees from institutions since 1930.—Little and Johnson (1932) studied the adjustment of 113 persons paroled from Laconia State School in the period July 1, 1925 to July 1, 1930. In order to facilitate comparison of results with prior studies, they employed the criteria used by Foley and by Storrs. They found that 84 per cent of their males were successful as compared to Storrs' 72.75 per cent and that 82.54 per cent of the females were successful as compared with Storrs's 75 per cent.

There was little basis for comparing these groups because of the marked differences that existed between them. Little and Johnson's aim was to demonstrate that the large majority of a trained group can make successful community adjustment.

Kinder, Chase, and Buck (1941) compared the records of fifty girls paroled from an institution for the mentally re-tarded with those of fifty girls paroled from a correctional school. The girls from the correctional school averaged 84.5 in IQ with a range of 52 to 126. Eighteen (36 per cent) of this group had IQ's between 52 and 80. The institutional group averaged 63.2 in IQ with a range of 50 to 80. Comparative data show that both groups had been out of the institution for the same period of time, eight years. The correctional school girls ranged in age from twenty-two to thirty years at the time of the study; the institutional, from twenty-four to forty. The period of institutionalization was greater for the institutional group—from seven months to twelve years as compared with from fifteen months to four years for the correctional school group.

The data show that more of the girls in the institutional group than in the correctional group made satisfactory community adjustments. At the same time, those of the correctional group who adjusted to their communities did so at a higher level of operation. Relationships established by the institutional girls were more stable. Only two institutional girls were sent to penal institutions as compared with nine of the correctional group.

Comparison by IQ showed that, among the 38 per cent of the correctional group with IQ's below 80, 28 per cent made successful community adjustment and 72 per cent failed. Sixty per cent of the institutional group were successful in their communities, while 40 per cent failed.

Johnson (1946) studied the records of 180 parolees of Laconia State School for the period 1924 to 1934. Applying criteria of adjustment comparable to those of previously mentioned studies, she found that 46 per cent of the females made successful adjustment in their communities, 37 per cent made borderline adjustment, and 17 per cent failed. Among males, 67 per cent made adequate adjustment, 9 per cent were borderline, and 24 per cent failed. In both sexes, those sterilized appeared to have a slightly, though not significantly, better record of adjustment.

Wardell (1946) described the group placement of inmates of Sonoma State Home. Patients were placed in groups in order to give them a ready-made community within a community and to facilitate supervision. Case reports show that the males were placed in jobs in a county hospital over a period of time. Of these, 80 per cent made a satisfactory adjustment, both occupationally and socially.

Wardell's recommendation for group placement and her arguments in favor of this technique were later supported by Harmes (1949) and by Cate and Gegenheimer (1950). Chandler and Shafter (1955), however, took exception to the positive factors posited by the above and suggested that they were outweighed by the following possible outcomes of grouping parolees: (1) Establishing the group may hinder or stop assimilation of its members into the community. (2) Leadership arising in the group may just as well lead the group into difficulties as assist its adjustment. (3) Group placement minimizes the possibility of treating patients on individual basis without making exceptions. (4) Poor adjustment of one parolee may result in a reputation which diffuses to the others.

At this time, there is no objectively derived information to support either of the above positions. It is not unlikely that the argument will be settled by the fact that comparatively few possibilities for group placement are available at any given time.

Coakley (1945) and Hegge (1944) reported on follow-up studies of institutionalized mentally retarded youths and adults placed in the community during a period of national emergency in 1944 and 1945. Coakley's sample of thirty-seven were individuals from twenty-one to forty-six years of age, with seventeen between ages twenty and thirty, sixteen between ages thirty and forty, and four between forty and forty-seven years old.

Twelve were females and twenty-five were males. The average period of institutionalization prior to placement was 6.2 years, with a range of from 4.2 to 25.7 years. The range of IQ's was from 40 to 75.

Prior to 1940, the work records of this group were spotty in terms of periods of employment and type of job. Because of the manpower shortage caused by the draft, however, this group was able to get and hold jobs for the duration of the war.

Coakley found no relationship between intelligence and wages. Most of the jobs obtained by individuals in this study were in the unskilled category; there were a few instances of semiskilled jobs spread through the entire IQ distribution. Most of the individuals obtained their jobs through the United States Employment Service or independently. Many were participating in a savings plan.

Hegge (1944) reported on 177 parolees all of whom were paroled in 1941 and 1942. Their average age at time of parole was seventeen years and the average IQ was 71.8 with a range of from 50 to 96 and over. He found that 88 per cent of the parolees were employed. Two-thirds of the males were either in the service or working in defense plants. A majority of the girls were employed in their own homes or in civilian jobs. From the capable manner with which these parolees handled their duties, Hegge felt that they were employable under normal conditions; they were not merely stopgapping. He further found that a large proportion worked above the unskilled level. Most were capable of finding their jobs independently. In agreement with Coakley, Hegge found no relationship between IQ and income.

Wolfson (1956) reported on the careers of 223 inmates of Newark State School who had been discharged during 1946. Of these, he was able to locate 89 males and 119 females. Data on these persons were obtained through correspondence with their families and employers and through various social agencies who had had contact with some of the dischargees.

Community adjustment was judged under four headings: (1) "continuous good adjustment"–a high level of adjustment marked by independence of operation vocationally and socially, (2) "satisfactory continuous adjustment"–a lower level of adjustment wherein supervision and support are necessary, (3) "temporary misconduct"–behavior requiring temporary return to the institution or to a correctional institution, and (4) "serious maladjustment or personality disorder"–behavior or characteristics requiring return to the institution.

Wolfson found that 59 males were mildly retarded. Of these, 36 (62 per cent) made a continuous satisfactory social and economic adjustment in the community. Of the 99 mildly retarded females, 72 (73 per cent) made satisfactory adjustment.

Windle, Stewart, and Brown (1961) studied three groups of patients released from Pacific State Hospital on different types of leave. There were 48 patients on vocational leave, 84 on home leave, and 164 placed on family-care leave. Each patient was followed for a four-year period. The authors studied the reasons for community failure and found substantial differences among the three types of leaves. They found that failure on vocational leave was most frequently accounted for by inadequate work performance, inadequate interpersonal relations, and voluntary departure from the leave situation. Patients on home leave were reported to fail predominantly for antisocial behavior. Patients who were placed on family care generally failed because of lack of environmental support for health or because of intolerable behavior. Although the reasons for failures were markedly different for the three groups, it was found that the percentage of failure was about the same in all groups. All groups averaged about 50 per cent failure.

Considering the data presented in the foregoing studies, only one broad generalization may be derived with any degree of confidence, that is, the probability is that the majority of higher grade mentally retarded inmates of public institutions will make a relatively successful adjustment in their communities when training, selection, placement, and supervision are all at an optimum.

Generalizations in terms of age, sex, mental status, length of institutionalization, and prior record would be hazardous because of the marked differences in the samples studied, the absence of relevant data in some cases, and the obscure nature of the data in others.

Following are certain inferences that might be drawn from the data and might, upon further study, lead to hypotheses: (1) There seems to be little relationship between mental status of the higher grade mentally retarded workers and their earning capacity. (2) Length of institutionalization appears to have little relationship to level of adjustment unless training for adjustment is a part of the institutional program. (3) Parolees are more frequently placed in urban settings than in rural.

Two areas of study are consistently absent from follow-up studies of parolees from institutions for the mentally retarded. These are (1) the relationship of community tolerance to success or failure in community adjustment and (2) the changes, if any, effected by a non-institutional environment on parolees.

The study of community tolerance is, of course, a vast undertaking. It is only by ascertaining levels of tolerance for certain types of behavior, however, that institutions can make their training programs meaningful, their screening techniques more effective, and their placement procedures more efficient.

With respect to the changes wrought in parolees by their experiences in the community, subjective evaluation by supervising personnel seem to indicate that improvement is evident in both behavioral and intellectual status. Other than a preliminary investigation by Marchand (1956), there are no objective data to support these observations.

Marchand compared the preparole and parole status of 123 ex-inmates of Newark State School in terms of chronological age, mental age, and intelligence quotient. Eighty-eight were females and 35 were males. The female paroleees were in three types of extra-institutional setting —colony, employment parole, and home care. The males were in employment parole and home care. His data showed that, after an average of eleven years, (1) the average change in IQ for the females was 8.9, for the males 10.2, for the total group 9.2 and (2) 88 per cent of the total group gained in IQ following extra-institutional experiences, 50 per cent gained from one to nine points, and 38 per cent gained from 10 to 31 points.

These data were compared with those derived from an institutional control group of ten males and ten females. The data from the control group show that these subjects, on the average, lost 1.4 IQ points.

Marchand points out that this study does not establish a causal relationship between parole and rise in IQ. While Doll (1947) raised the question of late maturation and its effect on mental status, the consistent trend toward positive change in intellectual status suggests that there might also be factors operating in the paroleees' environment which have positive effect on mental development. When identified, these may have some implication for institutional treatment even for those not destined for parole. This might further be supported by Charles (1963) who found that a representative sample of twenty subjects drawn from his study population had gained an average of 22.9 points in IQ in

the more than thirty years since leaving school.

Marchand's study is reminiscent of the foster home research of Freeman, Holzinger, and Mitchell (1928) and the Iowa studies of Skeels, Skodak, and Wellman (Skeels, 1936, 1942; Skodak, 1939, 1945; Wellman, 1944). These studies, together with those of Kephart (1939, 1940) and Kephart and Strauss (1940) and, more recently, Kirk (1959), emphasize the influence of environment on the mental status of children. Generally, they show that activity and stimulation in the environment appear to be related to a positive change in mental status while the impoverished, stultifying environment appears related to negative change. Marchand's findings indicate that there may be factors operating in the adult's environment with similar or comparable effect—an indication that is worthy of further study in terms of amount of change as well as factors contributing to change.

CRITERIA FOR SELECTION, TRAINING, AND
PLACEMENT OF INSTITUTIONAL
PAROLEES

In the vast majority of cases, criteria applied by institutional personnel for selection for training and subsequent parole of inmates are experientially and subjectively derived. Workers observe and study inmates in the institution and on parole and compare the pre- and post-institutional behavior and characteristics of successful parolees with unsuccessful ones (Deardon, 1961; Mickelson, 1951; Shafter, 1957). This procedure is the only alternative to random selection at this time. While prediction of behavior has been a broad field of study during the past half-century (Vold, 1935; Burgess and Cottrell, 1939; Ohlin, 1951), little that impinges directly on the area of mental retardation has come from this research. Likewise, studies of the intramural adjustment of institutionalized mentally retarded have contributed very little that is applicable to prediction of extra-institutional placement and management (Thomas, 1943; Greene, 1945; Whitcomb, 1945).

Only recently, with the population movement studies at Pacific State Colony, has a concerted long-term effort been made to analyze factors associated with the movement of patients in and out of state hospitals. Windle (1962) cites 112 different research studies which give information on the prognosis for adjustment of dischargees.

The problem of ascertaining criteria for selection and parole has been studied within a psychological frame of reference. Studies by Brill (1935) and Kinder and Hamlin (1937) have pointed up the inadequacy of a single measure (the IQ) in predicting vocational adjustment.

Hamlin (1938) and Earl (1940) studied the relationship between psychometric and behavior patterns of mentally retarded individuals to determine whether or not categories of behavior could be differentiated by this process. Both found that individuals classed in the more advanced adjustment or behavior groups had higher psychometric patterns.

Few studies of the appropriateness or effectiveness of the projective test as a screening device for parolees have been assayed. Sarason (1943) administered the Thematic Apperception Test to high-grade mentally retarded boys and concluded that, ". . . the data derived from the Thematic Apperception Test can be of value in the all-important task of placement" (p. 173). The extent or nature of the contribution of this test, however, was not determined.

Sloan (1948) administered the Wechsler-Bellevue and the Rorschach Ink Blot Test to parolees from Lincoln State School who, in the opinion of their supervisor, were making a successful adjustment in their communities. He applied the same measures to a comparable group of inmates who had been unsuccessful on parole and had been returned to the institution. Sloan found that statistical comparisons failed to distinguish between the successful and unsuccessful parolees on the basis of the Rorschach. He concluded that the value of the Rorschach as an instrument for predicting extramural adjustment was not demonstrated.

Fry (1956) studied the relationship between mental status, attitude, ability to perform, and personality of institutionalized females in Manitoba. She concluded from her results that the performance efficiency quotient derived from the Wechsler-Bellevue was the best measure for predicting work success. Fry found that 71 per cent of the girls with performance efficiency quotients of 60 or over were classified as satisfactory in their jobs.

Criteria for selection, training, and placement—other than psychometric or projective data—include such subjectively determined characteristics as ability to get along with others, attitude, personal appearance, personality, interests, and others. Usually chronological age, length of institutionalization, and commitment records are considered along with the above.

Shafter (1957) studied the relationship between parole criteria in public institutions in this country and the adjustment of parolees for the purpose of ascertaining the characteristics of parolees which might be used to predict success in future placements. He compiled characteristics noted at time of parole as described in the literature and as communicated to him by other institutions and found that he could objectify sixty-six characteristics such as age, type of admission, father's occupation, previous residence, IQ, educational attainment, sterilization, etc. Two hundred and five persons, of whom 111 had been successful and 94 unsuccessful in adjusting to their communities, comprised the study sample. Successful adjustment was defined as complete discharge from the hospital; unsuccessful adjustment was defined as return to the hospital after placement due to some fault on the part of the parolee. Comparisons were possible on fifty-six of the sixty-six objectified release characteristics.

Shafter found that thirty-eight characteristics contributed nothing toward predicting successful adjustment on parole. These included: clinical impressions of the examining psychologist, family characteristics, IQ, age at discharge, behavioral record while an inmate, self-care attributes, and length of institutionalization.

Shafter found that the following twelve release characteristics significantly differentiated successful from unsuccessful parolees as groups: (1) record of behavior, (2) record of escapes, (3) record of quarrelsomeness in the institution, (4) predisposition toward quarrelsomeness, (5) aggressiveness in the institution (successful group was found less likely to fight), (6) truthfulness, (7) ambition, (8) obedience, (9) attention to details and personal habits (carelessness), (10) five-year record of punishments in the institution, (11) history of stealing, and (12) quality of work in the institution.

It is certainly noteworthy that while the above characteristics differentiated between successful and unsuccessful parolees as discrete groups, seven do not discriminate between the successful and unsuccessful males. These were: behavior problem, escapes, quarrelsome, ambition, punishment record, stealing, and quality of work. While the data are not too clear, it appears that the discriminating ability of these characteristics is little better in differentiating between successful and unsuccessful female parolees.

Shafter employed the above twelve discharge characteristics in formulating a prediction table. Applying a discrimination equation, Shafter found that persons obtaining the highest possible behavior score stood sixty-six chances out of one

hundred of succeeding in extra-institutional placement.

The major contribution of this study can be seen in the extent to which it points up the problems in establishing criteria for selection, training, and parole. Together with the previously mentioned studies, it reveals that traditional methods have not resulted in reliable measures of evaluation and that there are serious gaps of information yet to be filled.

Kolstoe and Shafter (1961) point out that one of the serious research problems in the prediction of occupational success has been the indiscriminate way in which all occupations are grouped together. They point out that characteristics which make for success on one type of job might lead to failure on another. It would therefore seem important to study the predictability of success for specified types of jobs rather than simply "successful placement." Indications are that a molecular study of behaviors has thus far been unprofitable. Comparing an arbitrarily designated successful patient with one who has been unsuccessful on the sole basis of pre-admission and institution-based behavior might be considered somewhat unrealistic, particularly when one does not know the conditions stimulating the behavior or the values of the observer rating the behavior.

A more restricted psychometric approach was employed by Gunzburg (1959) who compared psychographic profiles of forty-four former inmates of an institution with their social status at least six years and up to nine years following parole. Gunzburg applied a testing pattern established by Earl (1940) in a study designed to identify a profile which would reflect the degree of instability of emotionally abnormal retardates. The profile was comprised of data derived from a battery of verbal and performance tests.

Applying the prediction profiles designated by Earl, Gunzburg found that there were only five cases (11.4 per cent) where the profile type disagreed with the patient's history. In twenty-seven cases (61.4 per cent) the prediction of social adjustment based purely on the psychograph was clearly a fact. In twelve cases (27.2 per cent), the psychograph was not in disagreement with the clinical picture of the inmate. Of the twelve cases, some were predicted as good placement risks but were not paroled because of limitations such as epilepsy. Others, unfavorable prognostic cases, were discharged with some misgivings.

Both Shafter's and Gunzburg's studies resulted in devices for predicting social adjustment in extra-institutional placement at a better than chance level. Both devices, however, would probably have under-predicted the number of patients making successful adjustment had they been employed by Fernald, Foley, and others.

The results of these studies indicate that neither descriptive nor psychometric data based on intra-institutional behavior are sufficient for predicting extra-institutional adjustment with the necessary reliability. Some supplementary information about the characteristics of the community and the occupational setting is necessary. Variations in community criteria for adjustment may very well have differential effect on prediction, but only to the degree that these criteria are known and incorporated into the prediction scheme.

FOLLOW-UP STUDIES OF NON-INSTITU-
TIONALIZED PERSONS

It is generally accepted that approximately 10 per cent of the total mentally retarded population in this country are cared for in institutions. The studies in this section refer to mentally retarded persons drawn from the estimated 90–95 per cent who have received treatment or training in their communities as opposed to public institutions. While these persons are of comparable mental status

with the higher grade persons in public institutions, their behavior or the relationship between their behavior and the level of community tolerance for certain behaviors has been such as to permit their continuance in the community.

In a majority of cases, studies will refer to mentally retarded persons who have participated in special classes in the public schools. In a few cases, the studies will refer to persons identified as mentally retarded as a result of clinic or guidance-center treatment.

Follow-up studies of special-class students.—Like the institutional studies, the early follow-up studies of boys and girls leaving special classes in the public schools were straightforward reports of the status of the ex-students in various roles such as those associated with marriage, police record, and employment.

Thomas (1943) reported on the employment histories of 142 persons, 54 females and 88 males, who left the special classes in the Springfield, Massachusetts schools between 1923 and 1928. Of the 142, only 4 had not worked. About one-third of the boys and one-sixth of the girls got jobs immediately after leaving school. The boys averaged two and one-half jobs each over the five-year period. Over one-third, however, held one job throughout the study period. The 54 girls averaged approximately three jobs each over the five-year period with about one-third holding one job during this period.

Seventy-seven per cent of the jobs held by girls were in factories and were largely unskilled. The remaining 23 per cent of the jobs were divided between working in stores, laundry work, and domestic work.

Forty per cent of the jobs held by boys were unskilled factory jobs, 12 per cent were errand or messenger jobs, and the balance were office helper, laborer, truck helper, machine helper, shoeshine boy, and the like.

There is little doubt that results of this study and others in this period were instrumental in focusing the attention of the schools on the need for preplacement preparation. Thomas' data show that, when untrained and left on their own to find employment, mentally retarded boys and girls wander aimlessly from job to job.

Bigelow (1921) reported on the results of a special class organized in New Haven especially to prepare mentally retarded girls for work in the rubber factories in the community. The girls selected for this class had reached the drop-out age in the schools and had not been able to find employment on their own. Over the nine-month period covered by the experiment, some twenty-three girls had been enrolled in the class. The girls were trained in jobs specific to the rubber industry and were paid commensurate with the type of job they filled. All but two of the girls were successful in acquiring skills specific to a particular task. Some of the lower grade girls could do no better than pick the paper from certain parts of rubber shoes, a necessary task. The higher grade girls could fulfil more complex tasks such as preparing various parts of the rubbers for assembly.

The adjustment of graduates of a training program designed to fit them for work in the garment industry was reported by Abel and Kinder (1942). The eighty-four retarded girls in this study had one to two years of training in special classes before being placed in factory jobs. A follow-up of the subjects during their first year of work showed that 35 per cent were unable to meet the work requirements and were dismissed within two weeks of their placement. By the third year, slightly over half of the girls remaining were employed, but only half of these were engaged in the work for which they had been trained. The remainder were occupied in comparatively simple tasks such as wrapping and packaging. Approximately 30 per cent were employed in factories other than their original placement and were working at substandard rates. Approximately 20 per cent had failed to meet work standards for any type of job in the garment trades.

Abel and Kinder concluded that IQ, personality factors, and employees' tolerance and understanding were critical factors determining the tenure of subjects in their jobs. Further, they felt that more extensive training might have achieved better results.

Duncan (1942) studied the records of former students in a British residential school for Educable Subnormal Children. Over a twenty-year period, almost 80 per cent of all graduates had become totally independent and self-supporting.

Haskell and Strauss (1943) reported on the adjustment to army life of one hundred dischargees from a county training school. Despite admission records of delinquency and antisocial behavior in some 60 per cent of this group's history, almost 90 per cent had acceptable army records with some 30 per cent also receiving promotions.

McKeon (1946) also reported on the war-time adjustment of 210 boys graduated from a special class during the ten-year period, 1932–42. He found that 36 per cent were employed and 54 per cent were on active duty in the armed forces. Only one former student had been discharged from the service, and 4 per cent were institutionalized.

Follow-up studies of persons treated in community clinics.—Kinder and Rutherford (1941) studied the status of sixty-eight mentally retarded children five years after their association with a psychiatric clinic. The children ranged in age from two to fifteen years at the time of their first visit to the clinic and ranged in IQ from below 50 to 90. They found that:

1. There was relatively little correlation between the degree of mental retardation and social adjustment as shown by a classification scheme of environment and social adaptation.

2. Children who had been placed in

superior environments had made satisfactory adjustments.

3. Children in very poor or poor homes without improved environments did not make satisfactory adjustments.

4. Over one-half of the cases became institutional inmates; eighteen were corrective and ten were custodial.

The authors concluded that, "The child's environment must be considered as an important contributory factor in any study of the social adaptation of retarded children" (p. 833).

Shimberg and Reichenberg (1933), in a study of 189 mentally retarded children seen at the Judge Baker Foundation over a period of five and one-half years, found that:

1. There was a slight correlation between economic status and adjustment.

2. A positive relationship was found between good personality traits and success.

3. Supervision played a key role in effecting adjustment.

4. The background of the individual, home conditions, race, siblings, and so forth, had little relationship to success and failure.

It is interesting to note that these studies disagree as to the relationship between the environment of the child and adjustment. A perusal of the studies shows, however, that the disagreement may stem from the differences in the ages of the persons studied and the resulting differences in criteria for adjustment. In contrast with the relatively young children studied by Kinder and Rutherford, this study set a lower age limit of eighteen years.

Lurie, Schlam, and Frieberg (1932) studied the progress of fifty-five school-age children with IQ's ranging from under 25 (one case) to 80, who had been referred to the neuropsychiatric clinic of the United Jewish Social Agencies in Cincinnati. This study showed that:

1. Sixty per cent of the children made complete social adjustment; 13 per cent made partial adjustment; 16 per cent made no adjustment.

2. The largest number of adjustments were made in those cases where clinic recommendations were carried out.

3. Personality of the child played a key role in adjustment.

4. Good home influences were found to be a distinct factor in effecting social adjustment.

5. There was an inverse relationship between intelligence and adjustment. The lower grade children were universally tractable and socially immobile.

The fact that Lurie *et al.* and Kinder and Rutherford found that the home environment had some effect on social adjustment while Shimberg and Reichenberg found that it had little effect draws attention to how differences in criteria for adjustment can affect conclusions in a study of this type. Certainly, judging the social adjustment of young children and more mature persons involved observation of two different types of behavior. The small child behaves in an environment that is relatively restricted and his repertoire of roles is relatively small. In contrast, the more mature individual has a more extended environment in which he interacts with a greater variety of persons under more varied conditions. It would seem, then, that the effects of the home environment would be less and less obvious as the person moves further into society.

In all three studies, social adjustment was defined grossly as lack of police record, lack of nuisance reports, and no record of sexual promiscuity. In the study of older children, self-support was an added basis for judgment. The results of these studies tend to substantiate the findings of prior work. There is some question about the frequency with which researchers contend that they found little relationship between intelligence and social adjustment in the studies of this type. A perusal of the studies shows that this conclusion is very likely an artifact arising out of the crude methods of judging social adjustment. It would not be illogical to expect that a more perceptive objective measure would present results that would correlate highly with intelligence. This will be seen more clearly in the section on vocations and vocational guidance.

Collman and Newlyn (1956) reported the employment histories of 106 normal and 200 mentally dull male and female ex-pupils in England some two to three and one-half years after these pupils had left school. They found that there was a positive relationship between IQ and performance of skilled jobs. The authors also found that sex differences were not significant in employment success of both normal and dull. Failure in occupations was negligible in both groups. Where failure did occur, it was linked with character defects, unstable temperament, inefficiency on the job, and poor home conditions. These applied to both the normal and dull subjects.

Very similar conclusions were reported by Phelps (1956) who studied the records of 105 male and 58 female graduates of special classes. The author found that 68 per cent were employed at the time of the study, 11 per cent were in the armed services, 11 per cent were housewives, and 11 per cent were unemployed. A study of factors critical to successful adjustment indicated that IQ and success were related and that efficiency at work and behavior that would permit acceptance by peers were characteristics of the successful. Since this study took place in an industrial center, union membership was also important.

Lee, Hegge, and Voelker (1959) completed a study of adequacy and failure of retarded youth. Three samples were studied—two from special classes and one non-retarded group drawn from the middle 60 per cent of the IQ distribution of the school population. The special-class groups comprised two hundred youths from public school classes and two hundred from special classes in a county training school. The normal sample consisted of one hundred youths.

The groups were compared on school histories, family background, vocational attainment, types of jobs held, police and social competence records, and service records in the armed forces.

The major findings in this study indicate that many of the retarded sample were not identified early enough in their school career; over half of the city special-class group were ten years of age or older when first referred for testing, and more than a year passed before the child was admitted to the special class. The average length of stay in the special classes was relatively short, slightly more than three and one half years in the city classes and four years in the county school. More of the retarded than normal youths had physical defects which, going uncorrected, affected their vocational adjustment.

With regard to general social adjustment of the two groups, the data showed that the retarded had poorer military records with greater incidence of discharges for inaptitude or unacceptable behavior. At the time of the study, the retarded groups were more unstable vocationally. They had experienced longer periods of unemployment, more frequent changes in jobs, and lower salaries. Over a three-year period, 33 per cent of the retarded had been discharged or quit because of unacceptable behavior.

In terms of violations of the law, the proportion with police records in the two groups of retarded ranged from 31 per cent to 71 per cent. In many cases these were serious offenses, including more than ten arrests per individual, culminating in prison or correctional school confinement.

The percentage of retarded girls who became pregnant out of wedlock varied from 26 per cent to 60 per cent. By contrast, illegitimate pregnancy occurred among 15 per cent of the normal girls.

The authors conclude that what has been done educationally for the retarded in this study is correct but inadequate. They suggest that earlier referral, diagnosis, and placement concomitant with relevant ancillary services to the students and families might have netted more optimistic results.

Kolstoe (1961) followed the progress of forty-one successful and non-successful trainees who had been through the Southern Illinois University Employment Evaluation and Training Project Center. He found that the vocationally successful group was clearly superior to the unsuccessful group in physical, social, and work characteristics. Although intelligence did not seem to be a relevant variable, the successful group was better looking, healthier, seemed to have better social graces, and came from better homes.

DISCUSSION OF FOLLOW-UP STUDIES

On the surface, the follow-up study of the retarded appears to ask a simple and straightforward question as to the status of the subjects some years after they have participated in a program of preparation for community life. If the data from Fernald's study on the follow-up of discharged inmates from Waverly are reliable, it would appear that the large majority achieve some measure of self-subsidy and concomitant independence.

It is important to note, however, that the subjects in the early studies were not participants in organized programs of preparation for community adjustment, while studies of more recent vintage treat with subjects who have been active in elaborate and expensive programs involving specially trained personnel, special facilities, and a broad application of ancillary services.

Since the proportion of those making acceptable adjustment from non-program and program settings in institutions and public schools is essentially similar, one might be justified in raising the question concerning the wisdom of investing so much time, money, and effort in a habilitation program. If those from a predominantly custodial setting do as well as those who have been taught academic subjects, counseled, and placed on jobs, why hire special teachers, psychologists, social workers, and rehabilitation experts? The answer to this question does not lie in the merits of program versus non-program. Rather, the answer lies in the social change that has occurred since the beginning of the twentieth century in terms of mores and technology—changes that have increased and complicated the "ways for doing things" in everyday life at home and work.

The years during, and some years following, Fernald's researches might be characterized as the comfortable years for the retardate, since this was the era of hand work and limited mobility. In contrast, the past decade or two have been stressful for the retardate because of the trend toward mobility and mechanization.

Where once the retardates could live well-circumscribed lives, they must now be as mobile as their peers in going from home to work to recreation and the like. Further, the know-how necessary to mobility have become more numerous and complex: bus schedules, fares, traffic rules, and courtesies are but a few of the everyday hurdles that the present-day retardate must take in his stride.

A possibly more critical example may be found in differences in the problems inherent in self-management. The early subjects had fewer decisions to make with respect to the disposition of income than do contemporary graduates. The retarded of today, while earning less than his normal peers, as will be seen in the next section, has the same number of outlets for his income. In addition, he is subject to the same pressures to fill his home with devices and appliances as his wealthier peers.

In effect, then, decision-making is more critical now, and there are more decisions to make. Preparation for, and counseling in, making decisions relevant to work and home are more necessary for this generation of retardates than they were for its earlier counterparts.

Finally, as will be seen in a subsequent section, the traditional "hand work" of the retarded in the city and on the farm is rapidly disappearing from the occupational scene. Brush-making, chair-cleaning, clothes-washing, and the like are now mechanized operations requiring technical skills. Furthermore, many of these occupations are centralized in large, heavily populated factories and shops where adjustment to fellow workers is as important as mastering the job skills.

In all probability, the data on the social adjustment of the retarded would take a different shape if it were not for the practice of educating and counseling the mentally retarded over the past three decades. More likely than not, the proportion adjusting adequately would be considerably less than in the past.

The question as to the relevance of the criteria for social adjustment is yet to be answered. The fact that there is some consistency in the results of investigations applying the same criteria in different places and at different times and under different conditions indicates that there is some merit in making judgments based on occupational record, police and social welfare data, marital adjustment, and the like. These criteria are drawn into more critical perspective in the next section, wherein the adult retarded are compared to normal peers of similar derivation and/or location.

COMPARATIVE FOLLOW-UP STUDIES

Because of the rigors of sampling and matching, few studies attempt to compare mentally retarded with normal persons in analogous roles. Three studies stand out in this area: those of Fairbanks

(1933), Baller (1936), and Kennedy (1948).

Fairbanks first reported on community adjustment of 122 of the original 166 mentally retarded children located in the 1914 survey who had been tested with the Huey Revision of the Binet and had received a thorough psychological workup. Seventeen years after the survey, Fairbanks found that data on these graduates of special classes for the mentally retarded show that (1) alcoholism was less of a problem with these persons than it was with their parents at the time of the survey, (2) over two-thirds of the group were in comfortable circumstances and almost half of these were buying their own homes, and (3) the remaining one-third were marginal financially and almost half of these were being helped by welfare agencies.

All three of the studies have been reviewed totally or in part in various publications (Sarason, 1943; Kirk, 1951; Wallin, 1955). In all cases, the results of the studies have been treated individually and within a predominantly psychological frame of reference. Considerable emphasis has been placed on the relationship between the conditions involved in the original diagnosis of mental retardation and the performance of the study group at maturity. Generalizations from these studies are frequently based on a one-to-one relationship between the mental status of persons in the study and their occupational attainment. It might therefore be more profitable to deviate from the traditional in presenting these studies by drawing them into a perspective on the basis of the variables of social adjustment measured in each.

Certainly, ecology plays as vital a role in determining the qualitative and quantitative nature of behavior. Consideration of conditions in the environment of these persons might help to account for many similarities and differences in the results and thereby help to stabilize generalizations.

TABLE 2

A Comparison of the Findings of Three Studies on the Basis of Social Adjustment

	Fairbanks (1931)		Baller (1935)		Kennedy (1948)	
Study..................	Fairbanks (1931)		Baller (1935)		Kennedy (1948)	
Locale...............	Locust Point, dist. Baltimore, Md.		Lincoln, Neb.		Millport,* Conn.	
General Economic Conditions	General employment		Severe depression		General employment	
Number of Mentally Retarded...............	122 (72 males, 50 females)		206 (126 males, 80 females)		256 (159 males, 97 females)	
Number of Controls......	90 (39 males, 51 females)		206 (126 males, 80 females)		129 (80 males, 49 females)	
	M/R	Controls	M/R	Controls	M/R	Controls
EMPLOYMENT STATUS						
Gainful employment......	95%	96%	20.00%	50.00%	75.00%	65.6%
Temporary employment...	....	....	71.00%	44.00%	10.30%	29.6%
Never employed..........	5%	4%	9.00%	....	14.70%	4.8%
ECONOMIC STATUS						
Owns home.............	30%	24%	....	....	9.20%	13.0%
MARRIED STATUS						
Married................	79%	58%	42.86%	54.95%	51.60%	45.0%
DEPENDENCY AND RELIEF						
Relief received..........	25%	7%	38.46%	15.58%	86.20%	65.5%
KINDS OF AID						
Cash....................	27%	0	....	....	64.90%	56.6%
Work relief.............	13%	0	....	....	70.10%	64.5%
COURT RECORDS						
Never arrested..........	75%	90%	57.14%	89.61%	78.90%	94.6%
Jail sentences, etc........	....	....	9.69%	1.43%	2.42%	....

* The name given here is fictitious.

The first fact that becomes obvious from Table 2 is the marked difference between the studies in terms of time, background, and persons. Economic conditions at the time of the Fairbanks and Kennedy studies were somewhat comparable, while Baller's study took place under adverse economic conditions. All three studies differ as to the backgrounds, familial and environmental, of the subjects. Fairbanks' subjects came from an isolated district in a large urban center. Occupational opportunities in this district were largely restricted to ship and railroad yards and shops complementary to those industries. Baller's subjects had a wider range of occupational opportunities because of their location—an urban center in an agricultural state. Kennedy's subjects were centered in an industrial center contiguous with other industrial centers. They, too, had a wider range of occupational opportunities.

In terms of differences between study groups, Fairbanks' and Baller's groups present the least differences, while Kennedy's subjects are somewhat of a diagnostic mystery. Fairbanks' subjects appear to be slightly higher in IQ but might be in the same age range if one is permitted to estimate their ages. Kennedy's subjects appear to have been younger at the time of the study than the other subjects.

Generally, Fairbanks' and Kennedy's studies are in agreement in the picture of the adjustment of subjects, while Baller's appears to have netted different results. The crucial factor effecting differences seems to be the economic conditions at the time of the study. This is borne out by Charles (1953), who followed up on Baller's group of mentally retarded persons some sixteen years later. Charles located 127 of the original 206—77 males and 50 females. Under later economic conditions comparable to those prevailing during the Kennedy study, Charles found that his group and Kennedy's compared favorably in marital status, occupational status, and financial independence as represented by agency assistance. Charles's group had exceeded Kennedy's in home ownership (55 per cent as compared with 9 per cent).

The most striking differences between the Fairbanks, Baller, and Kennedy study groups appear to be as follows: (1) More of the Fairbanks' mentally retarded and control group married than did the group in the other studies. (2) Both of Fairbanks' groups had greater incidence of divorce and separation. (3) Only Baller's control-group families appear to have markedly fewer children than the retarded group. (4) Both of Fairbanks' groups appear to be on more substantial financial ground in terms of home ownership while Kennedy's groups are proportionately greater in self-support. (5) While markedly more of Kennedy's groups are supported by their mates than Fairbanks', the ratio in both studies is very similar—approximately 3 mentally retarded to 2.75 controls. (6) More of Kennedy's two groups are dependent upon family support. (7) Far more of Kennedy's groups received agency assistance than did Fairbanks' or Baller's, even though Baller's sample was in the midst of a serious depression. (8) More of Baller's mentally retarded group had police records, while all three control groups are almost on a par.

These broad differences in key areas led to the conclusion that unqualified comparison of groups of mentally retarded with controls is hardly warranted. The data raise other questions that are difficult to answer from the information in the study. For example:

1. Fewer of both Fairbanks' groups are self-supporting than are Kennedy's, yet the incidence of home-ownership is in favor of Fairbanks' groups. Is this the result of inheritance? Might it be due to lack of rental dwellings? Might it be the result of cultural values related to home-ownership?

2. The differences between Fairbanks'

and Kennedy's subjects in terms of divorce and separation are strikingly in favor of the Kennedy subjects. Is this due to better marital relationships or is there some restriction on divorce imposed by the predominantly Catholic backgrounds of Kennedy's people?

3. Markedly more of Kennedy's groups are in the semiskilled labor classification, while few are in the unskilled classification. Is this due to greater occupational skill, or might it be an outcome of increasing mechanization which has diminished the number of hand jobs and increased machine operation within the range of competence of the mentally retarded workers?

These and other questions arising out of the study raise a serious question concerning the methodology of this type of study. The question might be stated as follows: Is one justified in comparing two obviously different groups of adult persons on elements of social adjustment simply because they have attended schools during a common interval and came from the same neighborhood? In actuality, these are predominantly the bases for matching. While Kennedy did match her groups accurately in terms of family vital statistics, i.e., sex, age, nativity, religion, and nationality, she was unsuccessful in matching in terms of internal family conditions that might have bearing on social adjustment such as divorce rate, commitments to institutions, broken families, remarriages, and the like.

In addition to the above, there are other differences built into the design as it now stands. Kennedy's data show there were no significant differences in the ratings of workers in both groups on the nine factors of accuracy, speed, learning rate, reliability of judgment, learning ability, absenteeism, tardiness, efficiency, and co-worker relations when rated on a four-point scale. It is very obvious, however, that while this is a comparative study, judgments for ratings of retarded

and normal subjects could not have been made on a comparative basis since the list of jobs held by both groups shows similarity in only two cases: "Protective" and "Agricultural" jobs, while the other categories are strikingly dissimilar in the proportion of mentally retarded persons and controls holding the position. Differences in the types of positions held by mentally retarded persons and by the controls are characteristic of the findings of Fairbanks and Baller.

It is in the differences in the types of levels of occupations that one can see the basic methodological flaw. Considering all three studies, the fact that the controls generally hold positions higher in the occupational hierarchy may well be the basis for Fairbanks' statement:

On the whole, one is impressed with the somewhat better living conditions in the control group (and), most of the men and women in the control group are interested in some form of social life—they entertain in their homes, belong to social clubs, and go away on trips during vacations (p. 198).

On the other hand, most of the subnormal group are interested in home and children, in sewing or fixing things up around the house, and their social activity is centered in the church or in the clubs at the school (p. 202).

Briefly, the studies of Fairbanks, Baller, and Kennedy present the following conclusions:

1. The majority of higher grade mentally retarded persons will make an acceptable adjustment in their communities. In this sense, the data corroborate previously reported studies.

2. Higher grade mentally retarded persons in the community are hard hit occupationally in times of economic depression. While they appear to lose out in steady jobs, they get more than their share of part-time jobs.

3. Economic conditions, community facilities, and local practices seem to determine the participation of mentally retarded persons in such affairs as home

ownership, dependency on agency assistance, recreation and leisure-time activities.

4. Occupationally, the mentally retarded persons appear to cluster at the semiskilled and unskilled end of the scale.

Since Kennedy's study, few comparative investigations of the accomplishments of adult mental retardates have been attempted. The most recent was that of Peterson and Smith (1960) who compared forty-five former special-class students in the Cedar Rapids, Iowa public schools with forty-five normal age peers, all of whom came from low economic status families at the time that they attended school.

The age range at the time of the study for both groups was twenty-one years to thirty-one years, eleven months, with the median range approximately twenty-four years. The mean IQ for the retarded was 65; for the comparison group, 103. Both groups showed similar division by sex— fifteen females and thirty males.

The 117-item questionnaire showed that the retarded group left school earlier, changed jobs more often, held lower level jobs (service and unskilled), earned markedly less, lived in poorer quarters, owned fewer homes, had a higher divorce rate, participated less in group activities, had committed more total legal offenses and more serious crimes, and had been confined more often in correctional institutions or given suspended sentences than the comparison group— the usual depressing picture developed by a study of this type.

DISCUSSION OF COMPARATIVE
FOLLOW-UP STUDIES

The major purpose of the comparative follow-up study of mentally retarded adults was to ascertain the nature of their adjustment to community life and compare it with that of normal peers of comparable derivation or educational background. These studies show that the retarded do not generally fare as well as the normal subjects in the large majority of factors considered to be significant of social adjustment or maladjustment. They also suggest that there is a relationship between the status of the retarded, the nature of the community environment (rural or urban), and economic conditions before and during the course of the study. The proportion of the sample employed, the need for social welfare services, engagement in recreational facilities, size of family, home ownership and other indexes of adjustment are all affected to some degree by any or all of these conditions. Further, there is a suggestion, at least in the Fairbanks study, that differences in neighborhood mores rather than retardation, as such, influence differences between comparison groups.

The pervasive influence of mores and customs raises some question as to the efficacy of a design that utilizes retroactive matching of groups on the basis of common attendance at a public school or residence in the same general neighborhood during the school-age years. It is generally accepted that there is a high correlation between amount of education and income. It might therefore be accepted, even without a study, that normal children who generally go farther along the educational path will hold better jobs and earn more than their retarded schoolmates. Further, an increase in income at least permits for mobility, and, as indicated in the Fairbanks study, there is a good chance that the normal sample will scatter to various parts of the community according to their economic status. By the same token, the retarded are economically trapped and comparatively immobilized.

Is there any real information gained, then, from comparing a retarded laborer with a member of the country club set simply because they both had attended the same school? One does not need an elaborate study to discern the differences between such discrepant subjects, not only in their differing standards of living, but also in the ways in which they are influenced by the customs and mores of their adult environment.

Since socio-economic factors appear to play a critical role in the adjustment of the retarded, and since socio-economic status is often an index of standard of living, locale of resident, values, and aesthetics, the researcher might better compare the retarded with a sample of non-retarded drawn from a common and contemporary socio-physical milieu. A study in a common social context will go farther in answering questions that are only partially answered by current studies. For example, the three studies cited indicate that the retarded samples have received more welfare assistance than the normals. Is this a function of retardation? Existing studies do not answer this question. Would these data be the same if the retarded were compared with fellow workers of comparable income living in similar neighborhoods or under similar conditions? The answer to this question might present an interesting and more realistic picture.

VOCATIONAL STATUS OF MENTALLY RETARDED PERSONS

It is obvious that all of the treatment of higher grade mentally retarded persons is predicated upon the notion that self-subsidy is the keystone of adequate community adjustment. In order to arrive at a clearer appraisal of the occupational expectancy of mentally retarded persons, studies have been made to (1) define the areas or categories of employment possibilities and (2) define the characteristics considered requisite to a compatible relationship between the person and the job. At the same time, institutional and public school workers and vocational-guidance workers have been studying the merits of various methods of coping with this problem.

The early studies of Fernald, Foley, Storrs, Thomas, and others illustrated the fact that higher grade mentally retarded persons can and do get jobs in their communities. Fairbanks, Baller, and Kennedy listed a variety of jobs or job categories held by subjects in their studies. Their treatment of the subject of job categories, however, was not occupationally definitive. Fairbanks, for example, listed a large proportion of her subjects as "factory worker" and "in shipyards"; Baller showed a sizable number listed as "labor: odd jobs" and "labor: railway yards, paving, and so on"; Kennedy presented the number of persons in the ten job classifications of the *Dictionary of Occupational Titles* of the U. S. Employment Service.

STUDIES OF THE OCCUPATIONS HELD BY MENTALLY RETARDED PERSONS

Since persons engaged in the occupational placement of mentally retarded persons might receive material assistance from specific information concerning occupations frequently held by such persons, a number of studies were directed at this problem.

Channing (1932) studied the work histories of former special-class students in Newark, New Jersey, Rochester, New York, Detroit, Michigan, Cincinnati, Ohio, and Los Angeles, San Francisco, and Oakland, California. The majority of the 949 boys and girls located for the study had left their classes during the years 1917 to 1920. The 181 subjects in Newark, New Jersey, left school in the period 1916 to 1919.

Ninety-four per cent of the boys and girls had been employed after leaving school, and 168 girls were married. The subjects in this study were employed the greater part of the time after leaving school. At the same time, Channing found that the amount of unemployment of these subjects was greater than what might be expected among workers of unselected mentality. Reasons given for unemployment included slack season, indifference to getting work, seeking a better job, and illness.

First jobs were kept but a short time. This was found true for young workers generally. A majority, however, ultimately found work in which they were regularly employed for long periods. The median length of the longest position held by boys was twenty months; by girls, nineteen months. Some 17 per cent of the boys and 25 per cent of the girls held the same job for more than three years.

TABLE 3

CATEGORIES OF OCCUPATIONS HELD BY
RETARDATES IN CHANNING STUDY

OCCUPATIONAL CLASSIFICATION	PERCENTAGE OF SUBJECTS	
	Boys	Girls
Agriculture............	3	less than 1
Extraction of minerals..	less than 1	less than 1
Manufacturing and mechanical industries....	59	61
Transportation.........	12	less than 1
Trade.................	10	9
Public service..........	2	0
Professional service.....	1	1
Personal and domestic service..............	4	23
Clerical occupations....	7	5

Applying the occupational classification system of the U.S. Census, Channing found that the subjects in the study fell into the following categories shown in Table 3.

The percentages shown in Table 3 are for the total group. By cities, they varied according to the opportunities characteristic of the community. For example, 2 per cent of the Detroit male subjects held jobs in the "Agriculture" classification as compared with 11 per cent of the California subjects. The subjects in this study were employed in factory and other mechanical occupations to a greater extent than children of comparable age of unselected mentality whose occupations were reported in the 1920 census (Channing, 1932).

Employment in other than factory or

laboring positions was confined to boys with IQ's of 60 or better. Boys and girls with IQ's above 60 filled positions in sales, stock work, truck driving, and clerical work, and some operated power machines. Those under 60 IQ held positions of errand boy, laborer, and semiskilled operative in manufacturing and mechanical industries.

In the period of the study, the employed boys held a total of 4,415 jobs, and the girls held a total of 1,729 jobs. Channing originally reclassified these positions according to the five-group Sims (1928) Scale. The data applying to the classification system of the currently more universally employed *Dictionary of Occupational Titles* to list of positions tabulated by Channing appear in Column 1, Table 4.

It is certainly unusual and highly unlikely that none of the subjects in this study held skilled positions. The fact that no person is shown in this category may be a function of the way Channing described the position. She stated, "Only a few boys had been successful in learning a skilled trade; a few others had attempted or were still trying at the time of the study to learn a trade" (p. 67). Some may be in the unclassified group although most of these, if they had to be placed anywhere, might go in the unskilled category. As the distribution stands, however, it is not radically different from those of the Fairbanks, Baller, and Kennedy studies.

In almost 60 per cent of all cases, boys and girls left the job of their own accord. Reasons for leaving included dislike for the work, self-betterment, higher-paying jobs, or, simply, desire for change. Slack season and temporary shutdowns accounted for the loss of approximately one-quarter of the terminations. Some girls were taken on as extra help in stores, and boys as extra help during the holiday seasons. Discharges due to inefficiency, misconduct, and the like were accounted for by approximately 10 per cent of the boys and girls. Six per cent of the boys and 10 per cent of the girls terminated jobs in order to change occupations. In the large majority of cases, such changes represented promotions. There was little relationship between mental status and frequency of discharge.

From this study, Channing concluded

In view of the lack of occupational training and vocational guidance given most of the young persons included in the present study, it is perhaps surprising that by the trial and error method they had succeeded as well as they did in getting and keeping employment (p. 42).

posed by the employer for inefficiency or misconduct. (6) The need for training and occupational placement at the time of this study and, in considerable degree, today is indicated.

In a similar study, Keys and Nathan (1932) collated the data obtained in five separate studies of occupational status of mentally retarded boys and girls by Carpenter (1921), Hanna (1924), Johnson (1928), Lewin (1945), and Thomas (1928). To these data, the authors added the occupational records of 466 boys and girls who had passed through the un-

TABLE 4

OCCUPATIONAL DISTRIBUTION BY SEX

	CHANNING		KEYS AND NATHAN		MARTENS		BOBROFF*	
	% Males	% Females	% Males	% Females	% Males	% Females	% Males	% Females
Professional and managerial.....	0	0	0	0	0	0	1	....
Clerical and sales..	10	10	6.5	9.8	28	12	6	....
Service..........	3	16	0.9	15.7	8	48	4	14
Agriculture.......	3	1	5.9	0	6	0	1	....
Skilled..........	0	0	9.4	1.9	1	7	16	....
Semiskilled	51	58	5.9	2.0	8	0	34	14
Unskilled.........	18	8	60.5	27.0	50	32	27	14
Unclassified......	14	7	10.9	13.6	....	....	....	....
Unemployed......	....	....	....	....	....	....	8	....
Military..........	....	....	....	....	....	....	3	....
Homemaking.....	....	....	....	....	....	....	....	58

* Combined groups.

In general, the following conclusions may be derived from Channing's data: (1) Under ordinary circumstances, the large majority of boys and girls graduating from special classes will become occupationally placed. (2) Like other youngsters just out of school they will tend to change jobs in the early years of employment. (3) Compared with the general population, their record of unemployment might be expected to be slightly higher. (4) They tend to cluster in the semiskilled and unskilled categories of employment. Positions held in other categories are essentially low level for the category. (5) Termination of jobs is, for the most part, voluntary. Only a small proportion of the terminations was im-

graded classes in the San Francisco Public Schools. The total 2,755 positions held by the groups studied were classified according to the five-group Sims Scale.

The data showed that over 80 per cent of the positions held by the subjects in all of the studies were in the unskilled category. In examining the data, however, it becomes obvious that this distortion is due to the inclusion of the data on institutionalized subjects contained in Hanna's study. The data have, therefore, been recalculated here with this sizable group omitted and the results reclassified according to the *Dictionary of Occupational Titles*. The data are shown in Column 2, Table 4.

As in previous studies, Keys and Nathan noted that job opportunities varied in each locale according to the nature of industry and agriculture in operation. From the diverse nature of the occupations held by the subjects, they question the wisdom of training mentally retarded youths for specific jobs.

In 1936, Martens (1937) surveyed the occupational status of former students in special classes in forty-one communities to ascertain how such persons fared in the midst of a serious financial depression. She found that males had been engaged in 217 occupations and females in 157. Martens then classified the occupations by the Sims Scale. For the purpose of this section, the data have been regrouped according to the *Dictionary of Occupational Titles* and listed by percentages in each class as shown in Column 3, Table 4.

The large proportion of boys in clerical positions and girls in service positions may be a sign of the times. As compared with studies made prior to the depression, the number of factory positions listed in this survey is very small. Quite possibly this is a result of the number of plants shutting down during the depression. This may well account for the large number of boys working as messengers and errand boys and the girls working as domestic employees. Under more typical employment conditions, it might be expected that the proportions shown in Column 3, Table 4 would more nearly approach previously listed results.

Recently, Bobroff (1956) studied the economic adjustment of 121 former students in two types of Detroit public school special secondary level classes some twelve years after graduation. One group of 61 had attended self-contained classrooms while the others, 60 in all, had attended special classes where the students participated with regular students in vocational courses. He found that there was no obvious difference in the earning power of both groups. There was no significant difference between the groups in terms of job tenure. Occupa-

tionally, the two groups distributed themselves as shown in Column 4, Table 4.

As compared with previous studies, the numbers in the skilled and semiskilled categories are outstanding. Again, this may be a function of local job opportunities or of job descriptions as observed by the researchers or both. The effect of limitations of job opportunities in the community may best be noted in the jobs held by females. These include packer, spray painter, cab driver, laboratory aid, nurse's aid, and others. While the large number of homemakers reduces the labor pool, it is not known which categories, if any, have been eliminated by their withdrawal.

Part of the difference between Bobroff's group and those in other studies might be accounted for by the limited number of subjects studied and the fact that they are products of a well-organized secondary program which extends into placement and supervision and which exercises selective factors in both. Until other school systems with well-structured programs present comparable data, the basis for judgments of results must be conjecture.

The results of the Channing, Keys and Nathan, Martens, and Bobroff studies are shown in Table 4. From this table, the following may be seen: (1) Mentally retarded workers tend to cluster into positions classified below the skilled category regardless of the community. (2) Females are more frequently found in the services category than males. (3) Almost no females hold jobs in the agricultural category. (4) When factory positions are scarce, females tend to gravitate toward domestic jobs in the service category. Fewer males appear to be affected by factory layoffs; those who are seem to obtain messenger and errand boy jobs in the clerical category.

It is interesting to note the differences in the semiskilled and unskilled categories as shown by Channing when compared with the other studies. This calls attention to one of the major problems in interpreting data of this type—the problem of describing the occupation. In employing the system of classification in the *Dictionary of Occupational Titles,* the category in which a given occupation is placed depends on the degree to which the researcher defines or describes the occupation. Thus, an observer may class a person who mows lawns and spades flower beds as a "gardener," thus placing this position in the agricultural class, while another observer may class this same work as a "gardener's helper," which places the position in the unskilled class. It appears that this may have occurred in Channing's study, in which she labeled jobs involving machine operation, semiskilled jobs, and hand-work jobs as unskilled. The *Dictionary of Occupational Titles* does not make the distinction on this basis but rather on the basis of the amount of technical training and ability involved.

It is also noteworthy that, other than as a descriptive tool, the intelligence of the individual does not have much impact on the occupational picture in these studies. Channing segregated the positions held by males and females by IQ levels. Her tables show that in the IQ range 50 to 70 intelligence does not seem to make very much difference in the type of job held. Baller, Fairbanks, Shimberg and Reichenberg, and others indicated that level of intelligence among the higher grade mentally retarded persons does not have much influence in determining the types of jobs held by this group.

STUDIES OF THE RELATIONSHIP BETWEEN OCCUPATIONS AND INTELLIGENCE

Since the development of Taussig's scale (1921), there have been a number of efforts to establish minimum intellectual levels of operation for occupations. Burr (1931) reported the work of the Vocational Adjustment Bureau of New York City, which studied the minimum demands upon intelligence of certain occupations.

Burr studied 375 girls placed in various trades by placing girls with differing mental ages in jobs of varying levels according to the complexity or difficulty in the work. In the millinery trade, for example, it was possible to identify three different grades of jobs as they related to mental age. Judgment was based on the ability of the girl to hold the job for at least three months and to show satisfactory performance.

It was found that girls with mental ages of seven and one-half years could handle packaging of small unbreakable merchandise. When packaging involved folding of articles and separating the articles from a large quantity, the minimum mental age goes up to nine years, nine months. Stock-keeping, labeling, and checking required a minimum mental age of ten years, five months.

Beckham (1930) reviewed Fryer's (1922), Hanna's (1924), and Raymond's (1926) efforts to establish minimum intelligence levels in occupations and arranged their combined recommendations into categories of jobs for males and females by mental age. Thus, it was established that a boy with a mental age of five years could wash dishes, sandpaper wood, scrub and polish floors, and so on. Girls of the same mental age could follow the pattern in simple sewing, pare vegetables, and the like. The scale progresses one year at a time to mental ages of eleven and twelve years when boys might be expected to work competently as janitors, at labeling, checking, and so on.

Beckham then studied the relationship of intelligence and jobs in a laundry by getting quality of work ratings on twenty workers. He found that there was little difference in the level of intelligence of good, fair, and poor workers but the six workers with excellent ratings had an average mental age of nine years and one month. They ranged in mental age, however, from seven years, two months to eleven years, two months.

Continuing her study of minimum age levels for occupations, Burr (1924) analyzed 41 different forms of occupations encompassing some 2,049 jobs. It was found that girls with mental ages of six years had adequate abilities to hold 19 jobs such as packing and simple factory work. Occupations such as assembling, packing, pasting, cutting, press-machine operating, garment-machine operating, and the like could be filled by girls with mental ages of less than twelve years.

Researchers began to note, however, that establishing minimum mental age levels for occupations was touching on only one facet of a complex situation. Burr noted the following:

It is assumed, in working out these conclusions, that the task to be performed by these girls is not complicated by disturbing factors such as excessive noise, too rapid tempo of machinery, or irritability on the part of the foreman or shop manager. . . . It is also essential that . . . the counsellor should not rely wholly upon the results of the mental tests, but take into account the total situation surrounding each individual child (p. 58).

Beckham wrote, "Apparently factors other than intelligence are of great importance for success in the laundry craft, assuming a seventh or eighth year minimum age level" (p. 313). Durling (1931) found that ". . . persons between 50 and 60 IQ obtain employment about as frequently as the group between 60 and 70 IQ, that they secure positions of the same types at the same salaries, and lose or abandon them no more frequently" (p. 281). Cowdery (1922) concluded that intelligence influences trade success during learning stages of the occupation depending upon the trade and conditions of instruction but that degree or fact of success was not wholly dependent upon intelligence. Wallin (1922a) studied the records of mentally retarded adolescents formerly in special classes in the St. Louis schools and found that they held a wide variety of occupations.

In a subsequent study, Wallin (1922b) grouped these former students by levels of intelligence and economic efficiency to ascertain whether or not this treatment would differentiate the industrially efficient from the inefficient. He found that there was a wide range of intelligence quotients in each group. He concluded:

It is a fact that we cannot adequately diagnose a child's educational or social capacity or prognose his industrial capability by intelligence tests alone, although the intelligence level is probably the most important single determinant of scholastic or industrial success. The danger to be avoided in the educational and industrial classification of children and adults is the tendency to lean too exclusively on intelligence tests and scores and to minimize the importance of comprehensive analysis (pp. 124–25).

The data on the vocational status of the retarded supplement the follow-up and comparative studies of their social adjustment in two ways. First, they indicate the degree of occupational mobility by retarded workers. Second, they show how the retarded are distributed in the range of occupational categories as portrayed by the *Dictionary of Occupational Titles.*

Occupational mobility.—There is little to indicate that the retarded are significantly more transient in their jobs than are their normal counterparts. Of course, the nature of the labor market and the extent to which there is a shortage of workers undoubtedly play a large part in determining the rate of job changes. Since this aspect of conditions was not taken into account by researchers, one can only surmise the impact of these conditions on the changing of jobs.

One of the interesting factors in the picture of occupational mobility is the reason given for leaving positions. Both the retarded and the normal had in common reasons such as boredom, active dislike of the work or of working conditions, and the like. Not unexpectedly, the proportion of changes by the retarded that could be attributed to promotions or more skilled positions was quite small.

Strangely enough, interviews elicit mainly negative features about the work but not about the worker. This is not unexpected when only the worker is the source of information. There are indications, however, that there must be some instances where the characteristics of the worker or his fellow workers acted to stimulate mobility. Channing, for example, found that the retarded were the first to be laid off or discharged during slack seasons, thus suggesting that the retarded were less efficient or productive than others.

Peckham (1951) found that the most frequent reason given for job termination by clients of vocational rehabilitation was that they were the targets of teasing, ridicule, and practical jokes on the part of their fellow workers. In all probability, workers would be more likely to report such occurrences to a counselor with whom rapport had been established than to the casual interviewer.

There is a good possibility that the retarded drew the invective of their fellow workers through their behavior on the job. Peckham reported that the retarded workers demonstrated lack of social and vocational sophistication by disregarding rules for punctuality, dress, and general deportment. They sometimes could not handle the problem of getting to and from work and would show up for work at unusual hours or not at all. They had trouble with the time clock, in the cafeteria, and the like. Their responses to teasing and ridicule were immature. That this conflict between retarded and normal workers is not transitory was shown by Brainerd (1954), who found that it sometimes took as long as two years for retarded workers to be accepted as regular employees by their fellow workers.

While studies indicate, then, that the retarded change jobs for reasons of personal choice based on the nature of the work, they may often be motivated to change by the rejection of their fellow workers.

Occupational categories.—The studies of vocational status of the retarded indicate that the large majority of workers cluster at the lower end of the scale, with most in the unskilled category. In only one study (Martens, 1937) is there a noteworthy number above the skilled group—in clerical and sales occupations, where an unusually large number of retardates, male and female, were employed as messengers and a large proportion of females were in service jobs.

The critical aspect of the status of the retarded in an occupational hierarchy is not so much where they were as why they are where they are. The studies by Burr (1931) and others attempted to relate intelligence to categories of jobs with little success. This may have resulted because of two conditions: (1) the concept of intelligence, in all cases, was global and did not differentiate or relate intellectual factors to job skills, and (2) the jobs proper were generally gross in their description so that it is difficult to determine to what extent jobs with similar titles were similar in elements.

The studies of the vocational status of the retarded indicate that the nature of jobs held by these workers is a function of the technology and the labor market in any given community. As a by-product, these studies show that the availability of certain jobs is as much to be considered as the ability of the retarded worker to fulfil the work requirements. Further, they suggest that there is some hazard in assuming that certain jobs are the property of the retarded. Competition for jobs during recessions and slack seasons has been demonstrated to be keen, and the retarded usually lose out to more skilled and more dependable normal workers.

Finally, studies indicate that counseling and guidance play critical roles in the preparation and placement of retarded workers. In many ways, these services may be contributing to the consistency in the employment picture that the training program played in the social adjustment of former inmates of institutions. Without the benefits of counseling and guidance, the proportion of workers getting and holding jobs might have showed a continuous reduction over the years.

THE OCCUPATIONAL OUTLOOK

With increasing frequency one hears of the impact of mechanization and automation on technology. Reuther (1955) and Diebold (1952) have predicted sweeping changes in the role of labor and suggested that revisions and relocations in occupations and in occupational skills lay ahead.

While mechanization and automation appear to be recent phenomena, there are indications that there is a long history of change in the occupational picture and that these changes have considerable meaning for the vocational and, ultimately, social adjustment of the retarded.

Marten's (1937) study showed an unusually high incidence of workers in the category of Clerical and Sales. As it turned out, the majority of persons holding positions in this category were messengers.

During the decade of Marten's study, the nineteen thirties, messengers comprised 1.8 per cent of all clerical workers. By 1940, 1.3 per cent of clerical workers occupied this position. In 1950, this proportion was further reduced to 0.8 per cent. This trend acquires considerable significance in light of the fact that the proportion of the total work force engaged in jobs in the clerical category increased over the same period (8.9 per cent in 1930, 9.6 per cent in 1940, and 12.3 per cent in 1950). This suggests that despite an increase in clerical workers, communication was carried on through the mechanical means of telephone and intercommunication systems more effectively and less expensively than through messenger.

The trend demonstrated in the employment of messengers is seen in all of the occupational categories traditionally the province of the retarded as seen in Figure 1.

This table indicates that (1) there has been a general decrease in the proportion of the total United States labor force in the categories of jobs most frequently held by the retarded, (2) jobs in industry (A_1 and A_2) show a steady decline that becomes more accelerated in the decade following the close of World War II, (3) household workers (B_1 and B_2) show a rapid decline after World War II (males seem to have figured little in this category), (4) jobs for males and females in farming (C_1 and C_2) also show a sharp decline with females reaching what appears to be a plateau during the decade following World War II.

The decrease in the proportion of jobs usually held by the retarded can be accounted for in terms of the advent of mechanized and automated equipment as well as the pressures of economic conditions. The proportion of females in household positions, for example, declined rapidly in the interval 1900–1920. In the period 1920–40, there was an increase of approximately 3 per cent over the preceding period. This may be explained by the availability of cheap labor during the depression and the need for household workers during the war years while able-bodied housewives went off to work in defense plants and in USO's and to replace males in office positions. It is interesting to note that the trend of female workers to the factory and the office during the war years effected an increase in the white-collar, skilled, and semi-skilled categories but not in the labor and unskilled categories. Note how abruptly the proportion in this category drops in the decade 1940–50 when automatic and automated washing machines, dryers, stoves, dishwashers, and the like became available as standard home equipment. The household worker of today must make many high-level distinctions and discriminations if she is not to destroy the family wardrobe and other assets.

The important message in this table is that the number of jobs usually identified with the retarded is on the decrease and that competition for these jobs will become more keen.

The Research Division of the National Education Association indirectly suggests that much of the competition for jobs in the aforementioned categories may come from high school drop-outs. This report states, "Persons lacking a high school diploma are the first to feel the results of the diminishing demand for unskilled labor ..." (p. 11). It further points out that one in every three ninth graders fails to finish high school. To illustrate the diminishing demand for unskilled labor, the category occupied by a sizable proportion of retarded workers, the *Research Bulletin* presents the following data derived from unpublished data from the U. S. Bureau of Labor Statistics. These are shown in Figure 2.

The data in Figure 2 incorporate the curves seen in Figure 1 and present a composite picture of the labor market as it

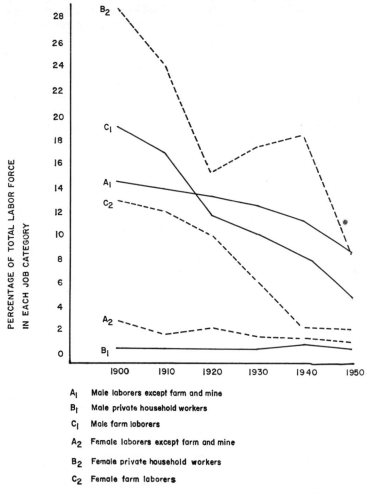

A₁	Male laborers except farm and mine
B₁	Male private household workers
C₁	Male farm laborers
A₂	Female laborers except farm and mine
B₂	Female private household workers
C₂	Female farm laborers

Fig. 1.—Trends in employment in the occupational categories traditionally the province of the retarded.

now exists as well as a prediction of how this market will appear in the decades that follow. Indications are that the decline in the number of unskilled positions will continue, although at a diminished rate. More important, there does not seem to be any condition or influence on the horizon that would indicate that this picture will become more optimistic in the immediate or distant future.

It seems obvious, then, that the conclusions of researchers who followed the social and occupational careers of the retarded, namely those who concluded that the efficacy of training programs and counseling and guidance services play key roles in the adjustment of the adult retarded, merit tnorough consideration. If the retarded are going to have to compete with normal workers for unskilled positions, it will be necessary for them to be well prepared and well advised. The institutional and public school program and the services of agencies such as State-Federal Vocational Rehabilitation must become more efficient and more extensive. If the retarded candidates for occupational placement become overwhelmed in a highly competitive labor market, it may some day become necessary to consider the presently placeable retarded in the same light as present-day trainable mentally handicapped, that is, as candidates for placement in a shel-

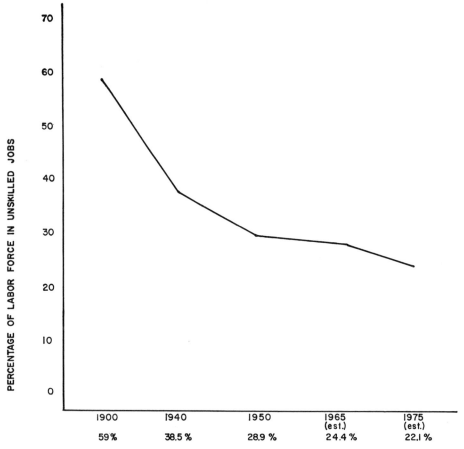

FIG. 2.—Percentage of labor in unskilled jobs, past, present, and predicted future. (From unpublished data of the U.S. Bureau of Labor Statistics.)

tered work setting. Certainly, that proportion of the retarded who currently fail at independent social and occupational adjustment are already in need of such a sheltered work setting.

The geographically spotty nature of the labor market denies the data in Figures 1 and 2 at the present time. Studies in those communities not yet at a high level of mechanization and automation indicate that there is little if any decrease in the categories of positions available to the retarded. Researchers and administrators in such communities would be well advised to consult local industry and commerce, rural and urban, to ascertain changes in technology and current trends.

SUMMARY

It was the intent of the first state schools for the mentally retarded to train and return their inmates to their communities as expeditiously as possible. The static nature of resident populations and the nature of their home environments, however, immobilized institutions and transformed them into custodial centers. Goals were necessarily modified to encompass intramural rather than extramural training.

The institutional movement presaged a growing awareness of mental retardation in society. The attitudes of professional and lay persons were essentially negative. Professional workers in particular maintained that the retarded posed a serious threat to society because of their predisposition to lives of crime, prolific breeding, and the almost entirely inherited nature of their defect. Studies showed that there was comparatively little truth to these concepts but not before the sterilization-segregation movement got under way. The movement was minimally effective, since only those retarded in institutions were reachable for sterilization. At the same time, there was never enough bed space in public institutions to accommodate more than 10 per cent of the total mentally retarded in this country.

The results of follow-up studies of former inmates of institutions for the mentally retarded indicated that the pervading pessimism of professional and lay people was unwarranted. The successful adjustment of the large majority of adult retardates in their communities opened institutional gates and stimulated training programs in state institutions and in public school special classes. Training programs appear to be effective in maintaining the high proportion of successful adjustment in the face of increasing complexity in factors of social adjustment and technology.

The training and placement programs in institutions required that a selection procedure be developed that would differentiate candidates on the basis of their predicted ability to adequately fit into society. Studies of characteristics and psychometric patterns of successful and unsuccessful retarded adults did not produce techniques of selection that were any better than the clinical impressions of institutional and public school personnel.

Comparative studies of the social adjustment of adult retardates and normal peers indicated that the retarded were generally inferior in most criteria including employment, welfare records, police records, and community participation. Since matching of groups was based on common attendance at a public school or residence in the same neighborhood during school years, it is not surprising to find that differences exist. Whether these differences might be accounted for by intellectual differences or by differences in mores and customs is difficult to ascertain in existing studies. For this reason, it is recommended that studies comparing retarded and normal adults be conducted within the lifespace common to both. In this way socio-economic factors and values will be held constant.

Studies of the vocational status of retarded adults indicate that the retarded do not change jobs significantly more frequently than normal workers. However, they appear to be the first laid off or discharged during slack periods. Reasons for changing jobs frequently have to do with dissatisfaction on the part of the retarded. There is some evidence, however, that suggests that retarded workers also have a more difficult time being accepted by their fellow workers.

Occupationally, the retarded cluster in the unskilled category. The next most populated category is that of service occupations. Information concerning other categories such as semiskilled and skilled is a bit unclear because of the judgmental aspects in the description of the jobs. It is likely that adherence to the job descriptions in the *Dictionary of Occupational Titles* might have given a more uniform basis for judgments of job categories and more dependable information.

Attempts to relate occupations to levels of intelligence were inconclusive. For the most part, they indicated that training and counseling in preparation for the job were critical factors.

The occupational picture for the retarded is far from encouraging. Occupational categories once the province of the retarded have been decreasing markedly in the past half-century. Predictions of experts indicate that this trend will persist, but at a reduced pace. Much of the disappearance of jobs for the retarded may be attributed to technological changes wrought by automation and mechanization in industry, on the farm, and in homes. Competition for remaining jobs has become more keen because of the large labor pool available for such work. The spotty nature of this problem has created crisis conditions in a limited number of occupational centers. It is suggested, however, that this problem will become more universal as technological changes take place.

Indications are that training programs as well as counseling and guidance serv-ices for the retarded are already playing a critical role in the social adjustment of these workers. Unless these services maintain an effective level of contribution, it may be necessary to consider the advisability of providing sheltered work settings for these retardates similar to those now typical for the trainable mentally retarded.

REFERENCES

ABEL, T. M. and KINDER, E. F. 1942. *The Subnormal Adolescent Girl.* New York: Columbia University Press.

BALLER, W. R. 1936. A study of the present social status of a group of adults who, when they were in elementary schools, were classified as mentally deficient. *Genet. Psychol. Monogr.,* **18**:165–244.

BANCROFT M. 1901. Classification of the mentally deficient. *In:* I. C. BURROWS (ed.), *Proc. Nat. Conf. Charities Correction.* Boston: Geo. H. Ellis.

BARRON, M. L. 1954. *The Juvenile Delinquent in Society.* New York: Knopf.

BECKHAM, J. J. 1930. Minimum intelligence levels for several occupations *Personnel J.,* **9**:309–13.

BICKNELL, E. 1896. Feeblemindedness as an inheritance. *In:* I. C. BURROWS (ed.), *Proc. Nat. Conf. Charities Correction.* Boston: Geo. H. Ellis.

BIGELOW, E. B. 1921. Experiment to determine the possibilities of subnormal girls in factory work. *Ment. Hyg.,* **5**:302–20.

BOBROFF, A. 1956. Economic adjustment of 121 adults formerly students in classes for mental retardates. *Amer. J. Ment. Defic.,* **60**:525–35.

BRAINERD, B. 1954. Increasing job potentials for the mentally retarded. *J. Rehab.,* **20**: 4–6, 23.

BRILL, M. 1935. Psychometric data as indices of instability. *Proc. Amer. Assoc. Ment. Defic.,* **59**:421–34.

BURGESS, E. W., and COTTRELL, L. S. 1939. *Predicting Success or Failure in Marriage.* New York: Prentice-Hall, Inc.

BURR, E. T. 1924. Minimum intellectual levels of accomplishment in industry. *Personnel J.,* **3**:207–21.

———. 1931. The vocational adjustment of mental defectives. *Psychol. Clinic.,* **20**:55–64.

BURT, C. 1938. *The Young Delinquent.* London: University of London Press.

CARPENTER, M. S. 1921. *A Study of the Occupations of 207 Subnormal Girls after Leaving School.* ("University of Michigan, Dept. Voc. Educ., Special Studies," 2.)

CARR, L. J. 1940. *Delinquent Control.* New York: Harper.

CATE, H., and GEGENHEIMER, R. 1950. The community supervisor looks at parole. *Amer. J. Ment. Defic.,* **55**:275–78.

CHANDLER, C. S., and SHAFTER, A. J. A. 1955. A critique of the group placement concept. *Amer. J. Ment. Defic.,* **59**:517–21.

CHANNING, A. 1932. *Employment of Mentally Deficient Boys and Girls.* ("Children's Bureau, U.S. Dept. of Labor, Bureau Pub." No. 210.) Washington, D.C.: Government Printing Office.

CHARLES, D. C. 1953. Ability and accomplishment of persons earlier judged mentally deficient. *Genet. Psychol. Monogr.,* **47**: 3–71.

COAKLEY, F. 1945. Study of feebleminded wards employed in war industries. *Amer. J. Ment. Defic.,* **50**:301–6.

COLLMAN, R. D., and NEWLYN, D. 1956. Employment success of educationally subnormal expupils in England. *Amer. J. Ment. Defic.,* **60**:733–43.

COWDERY, K. M. 1922. Intelligence and success in trade learning. *J. Appl. Psychol.,* **6**:311–30.

CRAFT, J. H. 1936. The effects of sterilization. *J. Hered.,* **27**:379–87.

CRAFTS, L. W. 1916. Bibliography of feeblemindedness in relation to juvenile delinquency. *J. Juv. Res.,* **1**:195–208.

DAVENPORT, C. G. 1911. *Heredity in Relation to Eugenics.* New York: Henry Holt.

DAVIES, S. P. 1930. *Social Control of the Mentally Deficient.* New York: Crowell.

DEARDON, H. M. 1951. The efforts of residential institutions to meet the problem of job finding and employment. *Amer. J. Ment. Defic.,* **56**:295–307.

DIEBOLD, J. 1952. *The Advent of the Automatic Factory.* New York: Van Nostrand.

DIVISION OF OCCUPATIONAL ANALYSIS, U.S. EMPLOYMENT SERVICE, Federal Security Agency. 1949. *Dictionary of Occupational Titles.* Washington, D.C.: U.S. Govt. Printing Office.

DOLL, E. A. 1929. Community control of the feeble-minded. *Amer. Assoc. Stud. Feebleminded,* **53**:161–75.

———. 1947. Is mental deficiency curable? *Amer. J. Ment. Defic.,* **51**:420–28.

DUGDALE, E. L. 1877. *The Jukes.* New York: Putnam Sons.

DUNCAN, J. 1942. *The Education of the Ordinary Child.* London: Nelson.

DURLING, D. 1931. The low intelligence quotient as economic index. *J. Juv. Res.,* **15**:279–87.

EARL, C. J. C. 1940. A psychograph for morons. *J. Abnorm. Soc. Psychol.,* **34**: 428–48.

EAST, E. M. 1927. *Heredity and Human Affairs.* New York: Scribner's Sons.

ELLIS, W. J. 1941. Training the mentally deficient for community adjustment. *Amer. J. Ment. Defic.,* **46**:255–61.

ENYON, W. A. 1913. Mental measurement of four hundred juvenile delinquents by the Binet-Simon system. *N.Y. Med. J.,* **98**: 175–78.

ESTABROOK, A. H. 1915. *The Jukes in 1915.* ("Carnegie Institution Pub.," 240.) Washington: The Carnegie Institution.

FAIRBANKS, R. F. 1933. The subnormal child —seventeen years later. *Ment. Hyg.,* **17**: 177–208.

FENTON, N., et al. 1935. *The Delinquent Boy and the Correctional School.* Claremont, Calif.: Claremont College Guidance Center.

FERNALD, W. E. 1893. The history of the treatment of the feebleminded. *In:* I. C. BURROWS (ed.), *Proc. Nat. Conf. Charities Correction.* Boston: Geo. H. Ellis.

———. 1919. After-care study of the patients discharged from Waverly for a period of twenty-five years. *Ungraded.,* **5**:25–31.

FOLEY, R. W. 1929. A study of patients discharged from the Rome State School for the twenty year period ending Dec. 31, 1924. *J. Psycho.-Asthen.,* **34**:180–207.

FREEMAN, F. W., HOLSINGER, J., and MITCHELL, B. C. 1928. The influence of environment on the intelligence, school achievement and conduct of foster children. *NSSE, Twenty-seventh Yearbook,* Part II.

FRY, L. M. 1956. A predictive measure of work success of high grade mental defective. *Amer. J. Ment. Defic.,* **61**:402–8.

FRYER, D. 1922. Occupational intelligence standards. *Sch. and Soc.,* **16**:276–313.

GAMBLE, C. J. 1951. The prevention of mental deficiency by sterilization. *Amer. J. Ment. Defic.*, **56**:192–97.

GAMBLE, C. J. 1952. What proportion of mental deficiency is preventable by sterilization? *Amer. J. Ment. Defic.*, **57**:124–26.

GLUECK, S., and GLUECK, E. T. 1934. *One Thousand Juvenile Delinquents*. Cambridge, Mass.: Harvard University Press.

GODDARD, H. H. 1914a. *Feeblemindedness, Its Causes and Consequences*. New York: MacMillan.

———. 1941b. *The Kallikak Family*. New York: Macmillan.

GODDARD, H. H., and HILL, H. 1911. Delinquent girls tested by the Binet scale. *Training Sch. Bull.*, **2**:50–56.

GOSNEY, E. S., and POPENOE, J. 1929. *Sterilization for Human Betterment*. New York: MacMillan.

GRANT, M. 1921. *Passing of the Great Rao*. New York: Scribner's Sons.

GREEN, C. L. 1945. A study of personal adjustment in mentally retarded girls. *Amer. J. Ment. Defic.*, **49**:472–76.

GUNZBURG, H. C. 1959. Earl's moron-battery and social adjustment. *Amer. J. Ment. Defic.*, **64**:92–103.

HAMLIN, R. 1938. Test patterns of high-grade mentally defective girls. *Proc. Amer. Assoc. Ment. Defic.*, **43**:161–65.

HANNA, G. C. 1924. Occupational efficiency of the mentally defective. *University of Minnesota Bull.*, **28**, No. 55; College of Education, Monogr. No. 7.

HARMES, M. 1949. Casework in the social adjustment of adult defectives. *Amer. J. Ment. Defic.*, **48**:67–71.

HASKELL, R. H., and STRAUSS, A. 1943. One hundred institutionalized mental defectives in the armed forces. *Amer. J. Ment. Defic.*, **48**:67–71.

HEALY, W., and BRONNER, A. E. 1926. *Delinquents and Criminals*. New York: Macmillan.

HEGGE, T. G. 1944. The occupational status of higher-grade mental defectives in the present emergency. A study of parolees from the Wayne County Training School at Northville, Michigan. *Amer. J. Ment. Defic.*, **49**:86–98.

HILL, I. B. 1950. Sterilization in Oregon. *Amer. J. Ment. Defic.*, **54**:399–403.

JOHNSON, B. S. 1946. A study of cases discharged from Laconia State School from

July 1, 1924 to July 1, 1934. *Amer. J. Ment. Defic.*, **50**:437–45.

JOHNSON, H. A. 1928. *A Summary of the Case Histories of 447 Atypical Pupils Who Have Left School*. Oakland, Calif.: Public Schools, Bureau of Res., Curr., and Guid.

KENNEDY, R. J. R. 1948. *The Social Adjustment of Morons in a Connecticut City*. Willport, Conn.: Commission To Survey Resources in Connecticut.

KEPHART, N. C. 1939. The effect of a highly specialized program upon the I.Q. in high-grade mentally deficient boys. *Proc. Amer. Assoc. Ment. Defic.*, **44**:216–21.

———. 1940. Influencing the rate of mental growth in retarded children through environmental stimulation. *NSSE, Thirty-ninth Yearbook*. Part II.

KEPHART, N. C., and STRAUSS, A. A. 1940. A clinical factor influencing variations in I.Q. *Amer. J. Orthopsychiat.*, **10**:343–50.

KEYS, N., and NATHAN, J. 1932. Occupations for the mentally handicapped. *J. Appl. Psychol.*, **16**:497–511.

KINDER, E., CHASE, A., and BUCK, E. 1941. Data secured during a follow-up study of girls discharged from supervised parole from Letchworth Village. *Amer. J. Ment. Defic.*, **45**:572–78.

KINDER, E., and HAMLIN, R. 1937. Consistency in test performance patterns of mentally subnormal subjects. *Proc. Amer. Assoc. Ment. Defic.*, **61**:132–37.

KINDER, E., and RUTHERFORD, E. 1927. Social adjustment of retarded children. *Ment. Hyg.*, **11**:811–33.

KIRK, S. A. 1959. *Early Education of the Retarded*. Urbana, Ill.: University of Illinois Press.

KIRK, S. A., and JOHNSON, G. O. 1951. *Educating the Retarded Child*. Boston: Houghton Mifflin.

KNOLLIN, H. E., and TERMAN, L. W. 1918. A partial psychological survey of the prison population of San Quentin, California. *In: Surveys in Mental Deviation*. Sacramento, Calif.: State Printing Office.

KOLSTOE, O. P. 1961. An examination of some characteristics which discriminate between employed and non-employed mentally retarded males. *Amer. J. Ment. Defic.*, **66**:472–82.

KOLSTOE, O. P., and SHAFTER, A. J. 1961. Employability predictions for mentally retarded adults: a methodological note. *Amer. J. Ment. Defic.,* **66**:287–89.

KVARACEUS, W. C. 1945. *Juvenile Delinquency and the School.* Yonkers-on-the-Hudson, N.Y.: World Book Co.

LANDMAN, J. H. 1932. *Human Sterilization.* New York: Macmillan.

LAUGHLIN, H. H. 1922. *Eugenic Sterilization in the U.S.* Psychopathic Lab of the Municipal Court of Chicago.

LEE, J. L., HEGGE, T. G., and VOELKER, P. H. 1959. *A Study of Social Adequacy and of Social Failure of Mentally Retarded Youth in Wayne County, Michigan.* Michigan: Wayne State University.

LEWIN, L. 1945. "The education treatment of the mentally deficient." Unpublished Master's thesis, Dept. of Educ., University of Calif.

LITTLE, A. N., and JOHNSON, B. S. 1932. A study of the social and economic adjustment of 133 discharged parolees from Laconia State School. *Proc Assoc. Stud. Feebleminded,* **56**:233–51.

LURIE, L. A., SCHLAM, L., and FRIEBERG, M. 1932. Critical analysis of the progress of fifty-five feebleminded children over a period of eight years. *Amer. J. Orthopsychiat.,* **2**:58–59.

McKEON, R. M. 1946. Mentally retarded boys in wartime. *Ment. Hyg.,* **30**:47–55.

MARCHAND, J. G., JR. 1956. Changes of psychometric test results in mental defective employment care patients. *Amer. J. Ment. Defic.,* **60**:852–59.

MARTENS, E. H. 1937. Occupational preparation for mentally handicapped children. *J. Psycho.-Asthen.,* **42**:157–65.

MATTHEWS, M. 1922. One hundred institutionally trained male defectives in the community under supervision. *Ment. Hyg.,* **6**:332–42.

MEESE, M. A. 1946. A complete program for training of institutional inmates. *Amer. J. Ment. Defic.,* **50**:464–68.

MERRILL, M. A. 1947. *Problems of Child Delinquency.* Boston: Houghton Mifflin.

MICKELSON, P. 1951. Minnesota's guardianship program as a basis for community supervision. *Amer. J. Ment. Defic.,* **56**:313–25.

MOORE, F. 1911. Mentally defective delinquents. *In:* I. C. BURROWS (ed.), *Proc. Nat. Conf. Charities Correction.* Boston: Geo. H. Ellis.

MORROW, L., and BRIDGEMAN, O. 1912. Delinquent girls tested by the Binet Scale. *Training Sch. Bull.,* **2**:33–36.

OHLIN, L. E. 1951. *Selection for Parole.* New York: Russell Sage Foundation.

PEARSON, K., and JAEDERHOLM, G. A. 1914. *Mendelism and the Problem of Mental Defect. II. On the Continuity of Mental Defect.* London: Dolan.

PECKHAM, R. 1951. Problems in job adjustment of the mentally retarded. *Amer. J. Ment. Defic.,* **56**:448–53.

PERO, J. F. 1955. Social orientation method of social training in an institution. *Amer. J. Ment. Defic.,* **60**:390–96.

PETERSON, L., and SMITH, L. L. 1960. A comparison of the post-school adjustment of educable mentally retarded adults with that of adults of normal intelligence. *Except. Child.,* **26**:404–8.

PHELPS, H. R. 1956. Post-school adjustment of mentally retarded children in selected Ohio cities. *Except. Child.,* **23**:58–62, 91.

PITKIN, A. B. 1928. *Twilight of the American Mind.* New York: Simon & Schuster.

POPENOE, P. 1926. Success in parole after sterilization. *J. Psycho.-Asthen.,* **32**:86–102.

PRITCHARD, W. I. 1949. Sterilization of the mentally deficient in Virginia. *Amer. J. Ment. Defic.,* **53**:542–46.

RAYMOND, C. S. 1926. Industrial possibilities of the feebleminded within an institution. *J. Psycho.-Asthen.,* **31**:28–39.

REUTHER, W. 1955. *Labor's Stake in the Challenge of Automation.* Washington, D.C.: Public Affairs Press.

SARASON, S. 1943. The use of the Thematic Apperception Test with mentally deficient children. II. A study of high-grade boys. *Amer. J. Ment. Defic.,* **48**:169–73.

SHAFTER, A. J. 1957. Criteria for selecting institutionalized mental defectives for vocational placement. *Amer. J. Ment. Defic.,* **61**:599–616.

SHIMBERG, M., and REICHENBERG, W. 1933. The success and failure of subnormal problem children in the community. *Ment. Hyg.,* **17**:451–65.

SIMS, V. M. 1928. *The Measurement of Socio-economic Status.* Bloomington, Ill.: Public School Pub. Co.

SKEELS, H. M. 1936. Mental development of children in foster homes. *J. Genet. Psychol.,* **49**:91–106.

SKEELS, H. M. 1942. A study of the differential stimulation on mentally retarded children. *Amer. J. Ment. Defic.*, **46**:340–50.

SKODAK, M. 1939. *Children in Foster Homes: A Study of Mental Development.* ("University of Iowa Studies in Child Welfare," 16, No. 1.) Pp. 156.

SKODAK, M., and SKEELS, H. M. 1945. A follow-up study of children in adoptive homes. *J. Genet. Psychol.*, **66**:21–58.

SLOAN, W. P. 1948. Prediction of extramural adjustment of mental defectives by use of the Rorschach Test. *J. Consult. Psychol.*, **12**:303–9.

SOUTHWICK, W. E. 1939. Sterilization policy, economic expediency, and fundamental inheritance. *J. Ment. Sci.*, **85**:707–18.

STORRS, H. C. 1924. A report on an investigation made of cases discharged from Letchworth Village. *J. Psycho-Asthen.*, **34**:220–32.

Supreme Court Report, No. 584, 274, U.S. 200 (1927).

SUTHERLAND, E. H. 1931. Mental deficiency and crime. *In:* K. YOUNG (ed.), *Social Attitudes.* New York: Henry Holt.

TAUSSIG, F. W. 1921. *Psychological Examining in the U.S. Army.* ("Memoirs Nat. Acad. Sci.," Part III, Vol. 15.)

THOMAS, B. E. 1943. A study of factors used to make a prognosis of social adjustments. *Amer. J. Ment. Defic.*, **47**:334–36.

THOMAS, H. P. 1928. The employment history of auxiliary pupils between sixteen and twenty-one years of age in Springfield, Mass. *J. Psycho.-Asthen.*, **33**:132–48.

TREDGOLD, A. F. 1948. *Mental Deficiency.* London: Bailliere, Tindall.

VOLD, O. B. 1935. Prediction methods applied to the problems of classification within institutions. *J. Crim. Law Criminol.*, **25**:202–9.

WALLIN, J. E. W. 1922a. An investigation of the sex, relationship, marriage, delinquency and training of children assigned to special public school classes. *J. Abnorm. Soc. Psychol.*, **17**:19–34.

———. 1922b. A study of industrial record of children assigned to public school classes for mental defectives and legislation in the interest of defectives. *Ibid.*, pp. 120–31.

———. 1955. *Education of Mentally Handicapped Children.* New York: Harper.

WARDELL, W. R. 1946. Adjustment of moron males in a group placement. *Amer. J. Ment. Defic.*, **50**:425–33.

WELLMAN, B. G., and PEGRAM, E. L. 1944. Binet I.Q. changes orphanage pre-school children. *J. Genet. Psychol.*, **65**:239–63.

WHITCOMB, M. A. 1945. A comparison of social and intellectual levels of 100 high-grade adult mental defectives. *Amer. J. Ment. Defic.*, **50**:257–62.

WHITNEY, E. A., and SCHICK, M. McC. 1931. Some results of selected sterilization. *Proc. Amer. Assoc. Stud. Feebleminded,* **55**:330–38.

WIGGAM, A. E. 1924. *Fruit of the Family Tree.* Indianapolis: Bobbs-Merrill.

WILLIAMS, H. J. 1919. The intelligence of the delinquent boy. *J. Delinq. Monogr.*, No. 1.

WINDLE, C. D. 1962. Prognosis of mental subnormals. *Monogr. Suppl. Amer. J. Ment. Defic.*, **66**:1–180.

WINDLE, C. D., STEWART, E., and BROWN, S. J. 1961. Reasons for community failure of released patients. *Amer. J. Ment. Defic.*, **66**:213–17.

WOLFSON, N. 1956. Follow-up study of 92 male and 121 female patients who were discharged from Newark State School in 1946. *Amer. J. Ment. Defic.*, **61**:224–38.

ZELENY, L. D. 1931. "A Comparative Study of the Investigations of Intelligence of Criminals: U.S. 1910–1930." Unpublished Ph.D. dissertation, University of Minnesota.

EPIDEMIOLOGY

Ernest M. Gruenberg

Epidemiology is the science which studies "the mass phenomena of disease" (Greenwood, 1935) by determining the distribution of conditions or diseases and the factors which determine these distributions (Lilienfeld, 1957); that is, it is "the study of the distribution and determinants of disease prevalence in man" (MacMahon *et al.*, 1960). The analysis which epidemiology makes of these findings results in a "medical ecology" (Gordon, 1952).

Epidemiology at any given time is more than the total of its established facts. It includes their orderly arrangement into chains of inference which extend more or less beyond the bounds of direct observation. Such of these chains as are well and truly laid, guide investigation to the facts of the future; those that are ill made fetter progress (Frost, 1936).

This chapter reviews a portion of the epidemiological studies which have been made of mental retardation, grouping the studies according to the uses as classified by Morris (1957), to which epidemiological information can be put. The beginner is frequently baffled by the way in which epidemiological discussions frequently seem to shift frames of reference and employ a single table for several different purposes sometimes to estimate how much of a given disorder is present in the population, sometimes to estimate whether the health services are succeeding in doing their business, sometimes to compute the risk of a person's becoming ill, sometimes to change his notion of what the illness is like, and sometimes to produce a suggestion that two clinical illnesses really emanate from a single cause. All of these are proper uses of epidemiology. Its most important use is to develop and track down clues as to the causation of disorders.

This review is an introduction to the epidemiological literature as an aid to those who wish to gain perspective on current research reports, as a help to those planning their own studies, and for anyone else with an interest in understanding more about the social and human problem of mental retardation. It is intended to bring the reader into contact with the various studies which have been done and to help him get some idea of studies which might usefully be done.

OMISSIONS

The use of epidemiology to compute individual risks of illness is illustrated occasionally in the text. Those who study MacMahon's review (1961) will find more examples of this important technique, and the chapter on genetics has copious illustrations of the computation of empirical risk. The use of epidemiology to study the working of health services has been entirely omitted from this review. A discussion of this would include studies on whether special classes lead to more learning, whether sterilization programs have reduced the incidence of anything they were designed to reduce the incidence of, and whether iodizing salt has lowered the incidence of cretinism. (No objective evidence on this question has been found.) It would also include the field of therapeutic trials of various medications and special education devices for raising the level of functioning of groups of retarded individuals. Such matters have been covered adequately in other sections of this book, and the epidemiologist here, as everywhere, is glad to let his colleagues carry the load.

COMMUNITY DIAGNOSIS

Epidemiology makes a contribution to what can be termed "community diagnosis." The purpose of such studies of the cases of disorder in a community is to provide quantitative information to (1) estimate the size, nature, and location of the community's problems, (2) identify the component parts of the problem, (3) locate populations at special risk of being affected, and (4) identify opportunities for preventive work and needs for treatment and special services. Thus, epidemiology serves as the diagnostician for the official or community leader who is practicing community medicine, social medicine, public health, or public welfare. The nature of the community's health problems is approached diagnostically with epidemiological methods.

A community diagnosis is directed at a particular community; it is obvious that the diagnosis which fits one community cannot be expected to fit every other community. This error is the same error made by the sick person who borrows his neighbor's X-ray film or electrocardiogram to save the expense of getting his own. This point is sometimes obscured in practice because those needing a community diagnosis are often in no position to employ the proper procedures and must make the best judgments they can with inadequate information. They tend to look for another community which they have reason to think is like their own and which has been studied diagnostically and then to guess that, if similar studies were made in their own community, the results would be similar. While the conclusions may be either right or wrong, the in-

ference is sensible in that it uses the best data available to the decision-maker; but the nature of the inference should be remembered and community uniqueness should be expected. The specific nature of each community diagnosis is blurred when investigators deliberately select "sample" communities for intensive investigation to study the problems of a large area. This procedure is justified in theory if sufficient information on which to base the sampling is already accumulated. The fact is that one does not have such information in this field. Almost nothing reliable is known about the differences in incidence and prevalence rates in different communities or in different types of communities. The procedure is partially justified in the presence of pressing needs for more precise information and inadequate facilities for examining the whole area of interest. This is what was done deliberately in the Survey of England and Wales (Lewis, 1929) and in the Onondaga County Census discussed below. Another justification of such a procedure at certain stages of development is that such *ad hoc* investigations of "sample" communities develop techniques and help to make more widespread and scattered investigations feasible.

There are dangers in such community-diagnosis surveys. One danger, that of overgeneralization, has already been mentioned. Another is that the motives of those encouraging and financing such studies are not always confined to getting information so as to produce better services more appropriate to the needs of the population. Expensive as surveys are, they are a good bit cheaper than services to sick people, so that this type of research is particularly vulnerable to misuse on the part of those who are opposed to extensions of service and are using the "need for more information" as a delaying tactic in the political arena. When this is done by someone insisting on the necessity of measuring the size and scope of the problem, it is usually possible for the investigator to avoid this role by pointing out that there is often enough information available about unmet service needs to go ahead with service planning without awaiting the results of the new study, since these can be roughly predicted, in broad outline, by anyone acquainted with the field. This cannot be said about judgments regarding the *efficacy* of services when they have not been systematically studied previously.

It is not possible to review comprehensively all attempts at community diagnosis which have ever been made. A few examples of community diagnosis will be summarized, some methodological issues detailed, and examples given of different types of diagnostic questions which can be asked.

One picture of the kinds of cases arising in a population comes from the cases in the network of service institutions. The New York State Department of Mental Hygiene (1958) has been doing this for some time through its highly developed Bureau of Statistics. In its report for fiscal year 1957 it gives the table of diagnoses reproduced on page 262.

From the data (p. 128) of this report, we find that 72 per cent of first admissions occur under the age of fifteen, so that if we wish to relate these numbers to the state's population we should give special attention to the size of that age group. Unfortunately, age-specific first-admission rates for the different diagnoses are not provided, but an over-all first-admission rate to state schools per 100,000 of general population for a thirty-year time span is given. This is shown to have varied between 7.7 and 15.5. This gives some indication of the order of magnitude of the demand for state-school placement. This figure was 9.4 for the year 1957 (p. 132) but varied greatly from one local area to the other. In New York City's Borough of Manhattan it was 15.2, while in the Borough of Richmond (Staten Island) it was 11.4. However, in another borough, Queens, it was even lower—6.7. The range in the upstate counties was even greater. Since part of this variation obviously results from the age composition of the population at risk, it does not help our understanding of the distribution of the cases or of the demands and patterns of use of the state institutions to try to unravel the reasons for these variations. The range gives us a way of making rough approximations of this part of the community diagnosis. A similar use can be made of administrative reports from other jurisdictions and later reports.

Institutional data are not, of course, the whole story. In order to get a more comprehensive picture of mental retardation in their communities, some investigators have made summaries of the experience of particular general hospitals or pediatric clinics. While these are helpful in getting some sense of proportion regarding the problems, they have long since been found unsatisfactory when taken alone. A better picture is obtained from community-wide surveys. The results of some such surveys are shown in Figure 1, which portrays the age-specific prevalence of mental retardation found in these surveys.

These studies are summarized in this way, rather than in rates of mental retardation found per 100,000 general population, because the enormous variation with age which has been found in most surveys makes gross summaries more confusing than helpful. These surveys varied greatly in their methods and criteria as well as in locale, and it is not very surprising to find that at the age of peak prevalence, about fourteen, they vary tenfold, from around 1.0 per cent to around 10 per cent. It is very remarkable, however, to note the large variations from age group to age group. One will have to examine these two types of variations, from survey to survey and from age group to age group, before it is possible to deal with the other internal variations found in these surveys.

METHODS

The survey of England and Wales.[1] —This survey, conducted by Lewis (1929), defined its terms extensively.

"Idiots" were "persons so deeply defective in mind from birth or from an early age as to be unable to guard them-

[1] The points on Figure 1 reflecting the rates observed in this survey are derived from Penrose (1949), where calculations based on Lewis' data plus approximations based on the 1921 census of England and Wales are used.

TABLE 1

NUMBER OF PATIENTS ADMITTED AS FIRST ADMISSIONS BY CLINICAL DIAGNOSIS, SEX, AND
MENTAL STATUS, IN STATE SCHOOLS FOR THE MENTALLY RETARDED,
YEAR ENDED MARCH 31, 1957

CLINICAL DIAGNOSES	TOTAL	MENTAL STATUS			
		Idiot	Imbecile	Moron Including Borderline	All Other
Total...	1,532	381	544	585	22
Familial....................................	358	17	107	233	1
Mongolism...............................	154	38	92	24	0
With developmental cranial anomalies..........	88	42	31	15	0
With congenital cerebral spastic infantile paralyses	66	50	13	3	0
Post-infectional............................	57	26	19	11	1
Post-traumatic.............................	157	70	63	24	0
With epilepsy..............................	51	19	24	8	0
With endocrine disorder.....................	10	5	3	2	0
Familial amaurosis.........................	1	0	0	1	0
With tuberous sclerosis.....................	1	1	0	0	0
With other organic nervous disease............	70	40	24	5	1
Undifferentiated............................	467	71	166	226	4
Other forms...............................	10	2	2	5	1
Not mentally defective......................	42	0	0	28	14
Male..	872	211	304	338	19
Familial....................................	212	12	66	133	1
Mongolism...............................	78	17	46	15	0
With developmental cranial anomalies..........	40	18	16	6	0
With congenital cerebral spastic infantile paralyses	33	23	7	3	0
Post-infectional............................	34	16	13	4	1
Post-traumatic.............................	102	49	39	14	0
With epilepsy..............................	26	13	11	2	0
With endocrine disorder.....................	6	2	2	2	0
Familial amaurosis.........................	1	0	0	1	0
With tuberous sclerosis.....................	1	1	0	0	0
With other organic nervous disease............	29	19	10	0	0
Undifferentiated............................	276	41	94	138	3
Other forms...............................	5	0	0	4	1
Not mentally defective......................	29	0	0	16	13
Female...	660	170	240	247	3
Familial....................................	146	5	41	100	0
Mongolism...............................	76	21	46	9	0
With developmental cranial anomalies..........	48	24	15	9	0
With congenital cerebral spastic infantile paralyses	33	27	6	0	0
Post-infectional............................	23	10	6	7	0
Post-traumatic.............................	55	21	24	10	0
With epilepsy..............................	25	6	13	6	0
With endocrine disorder.....................	4	3	1	0	0
With other organic nervous disease............	41	21	14	5	1
Undifferentiated............................	191	30	72	88	1
Other forms...............................	5	2	2	1	0
Not mentally defective......................	13	0	0	12	1

selves against common physical dangers." "Imbeciles" had "mental defectiveness not amounting to idiocy, yet so pronounced that they are incapable of managing themselves or their affairs, or, in the case of children, of being taught to do so." In adults, social performance was limited to those simple tasks expected of a person with a mental age between five and one-half and six years. The criterion in children was a mental ratio below 45–50 or approximately equivalent test or task performances. The "feeble-minded" had "mental defectiveness not amounting to imbecility yet so pronounced that they require care, super-

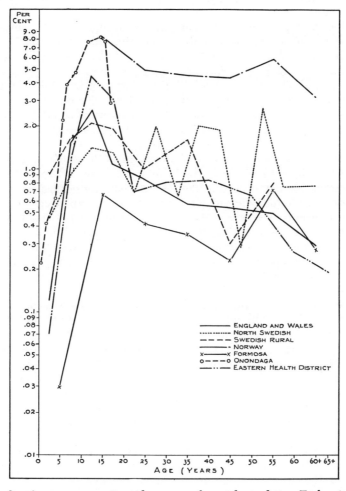

FIG. 1.—Results of seven community-wide surveys of mental retardation. Each point on the graph represents the percentage of people retarded in the corresponding age group; the horizontal position of the point represents the midpoint of the age *group* for which the rate was reported. Hence the lines connecting the points do not represent measured rates at all but are only aids to the reader's eye to help him see the points from each study as a single group. The vertical scale is logarithmic, which means that rises in prevalence and drops in prevalence are reflected by the slopes in the lines connecting points which are proportional to the rate of rise or the rate of fall regardless of whether these changes are in the upper or lower part of the graph. However, the logarithmic scale tends to reduce the differences between the figures found in the different surveys—the numbers on the left-hand margin must be looked at to be appreciated.

vision, and control for their own protection or for the protection of others, or in the case of children, that they by reason of such defectiveness appear to be permanently incapable of receiving proper benefit from the instruction in ordinary schools." Also, children who met the criteria of the Education Act of 1921 for "defective children" . . . "are by reason of mental defect incapable of receiving proper benefit from the instruction in the ordinary public elementary schools, but are not incapable by reason of that defect of receiving benefit from instruction in . . . special classes of schools." In adults, the investigator required "full evidence of . . . lack of social adaptation." The resulting socially defective individuals were classified as "intellectually defective" or "morally defective." It is not possible here to describe this entity in the extensive detail used in the original report, but the following may be viewed as a summary sentence: "Evidence was obtained to show that most of the defective's instincts or emotions, i.e. 'acquisitiveness, submission, sex or anger' were too strong for his control, or so weak and feeble as to render him socially inefficient or morally callous" (p. 51). Some, but not all, who were morally defective were also found to be intellectually defective.

In this study, the areas investigated were half rural and half urban. The names of the areas are not given, but some of their general characteristics are described. That is to say, this was area-sampling for England and Wales. The information given is insufficient to judge the representativeness of the areas or to judge whether the areas sampled have similarities to, or differences from, any other community. Each of the six areas had about 100,000 population.

One was an "extra-metropolitan area," which is what might be described today in this country as a moderately new member of the metropolitan sprawl (of the railway era, not of the superhighway

era). The age distribution is given and indicates a young population. The second area is a "Cotton Town in the North." "It is typical of towns where textile industries predominate." The prevalence of maternal factory workers was believed to have had some effect on the results of the survey, but "in general the community had adapted itself fairly satisfactorily to so fundamental a handicap as the absence of the mother from the home for the greater part of the day." The economic depression in the cotton trade at the time was thought to account for a higher prevalence of reported adult mental retardation. No ethnological peculiarities were noted. The report stated that any observer could notice the predominantly short stature and the rachitic signs in both adults and children. Furthermore, a record from the early nineteenth century confirmed the report that when these towns were being developed as factory towns "poor-law" children were sent from London to the factory owners on contract; under this arrangement it was evidently permissible to include one idiot for twenty "sound" children.

The third area was planned to include a mining community, but this "was not thought practicable on account of the industrial conditions prevailing at the time" in the northern and Welsh mines, so a Midlands district, where the predominant industry was coal mining and the main subsidiary industries steel and engineering, was substituted. It consisted of a town and a rural area where almost the entire population lived in towns and villages and were employed in the mines or in industry.

The fourth was one of the more prosperous farm areas in England with a high stability of population (decreasing in size) and a special "Fen" district in which people seemed to be even slower and duller than the ordinary rustic.

The fifth was "a rural area in the South-West" which consisted in part of what was evidently an agricultural market town of about 60,000 and a surrounding rural area of some 40,000 living on poor farming land sandwiched between two moors. The town had social extremes of wealth and poverty.

The sixth was "a Welsh rural area" of two counties and "probably no better choice of a typically rural bilingual district in Wales could have been made." The children spoke Welsh at home and were taught in Welsh in the younger school years. The tests given here were done in Welsh. The population is described as having high cohesion, a "peasant culture." The aged and females predominated because the husbands and older boys were away in the mines.

It is hard now to imagine a contemporary community which would fit the descriptions given. Few objective indexes of social and demographic characteristics are given. The graphic literary descriptions are hardly a substitute when re-interpretations of data are needed. Unfortunately these areas are not named, and this makes it impossible for later readers to use other sources of data for describing the community. Since the field investigator rarely knows what is going to be relevant in his findings as knowledge progresses, he can assure a better use of his work if he identifies the communities he studies by name. Much more intimate details of communities than are given here have been published by investigators without untoward results; those who are likely to take offense at having "their" community used as a guinea pig are the most likely to search out and identify what has been said. The cult of anonymity for studied communities cannot be recommended as a satisfactory way of dealing with the sensitive community relationships necessary for such a survey.

Lewis used a special device to gauge the "representativeness" of his population with respect to the population of all of England and Wales. He computed the rate of ascertainment per thousand total population of mentally retarded individuals by the local authority. (In England and Wales there is a local Mental Deficiency Authority who has a responsibility spelled out in law for the supervision of reported mental retardates and a responsibility for reporting such cases.) He then computed a "mean incidence" of such reporting for the whole sample. This mean rate is computed simply by adding up each of the area rates and dividing by six. There are two difficulties with this procedure: First, he told us that the age distribution of the different areas was very different, and this means that the reported rates might vary purely on the basis of age distribution. Second, the rate for the whole sample is not, strictly speaking, the mean of the rates for the parts, but each of the six populations is so close to 100,000 that the effect of such weighting would be trivial. However, he compared this mean rate (1.88) with the "mean" rate for England and Wales (1.59). If he used a simple average in getting this rate and failed to apply weightings according to the size of each reporting jurisdiction, this comparison could be deceptive. The mean prevalence of retarded children on the public elementary school registers in the districts for his sample (0.603 per cent) compared to the "mean" for England and Wales (0.638 per cent) deals only with school-age children and so is not open to the same criticism. Similarly, crude calculations of the number per thousand on poor-law relief and the number per thousand of "rate-aided insane" are given, which correspond quite closely to the computations for England and Wales. This is an ingenious way of testing comparability of a sample with the universe, and, although it has certain crudities, it reflects a sensible empirical approach.

The procedure for ascertainment is described in fifteen pages (pp. 21–36). Only a summary can be given here. The ultimate criterion for children was a diagnosis by Dr. E. O. Lewis, the medical investigator. He personally examined every one of the reported retardates. A screening device was used to locate a group of children, which would include all the retarded children; this group was about 15 per cent of all children. For children over nine years of age this screen had two stages: Head teachers were asked to name the two or three "most backward" children of each *age* group (not each grade) in his school; these children were then given a group test by Lewis or his assistant. He personally examined those who scored low on the group test. All children under nine reported in the first stage were examined. Furthermore, the head teachers were asked to name all epileptic or paralyzed children, and these were all examined individually. The group test specially prepared for this inquiry was kept secret to prevent coaching. Individual examinations consisted of intelligence and educational-achievement tests plus a routine physical examination. At times this routine was modified. Special inquiries were made if children old for their grade had not been reported. In some small rural schools the number reported over the age of nine was considered too small to be worth the trouble of group tests, so all were examined individually. "There were however a number of exceptions; some of the small rural schools were reputed to have many backward children, and in these schools we applied the group tests to all pupils over the age of nine."

The standard for selecting children for examination on the basis of group-test performance is not entirely satisfactory. "After we had examined a few hundred pupils we were able, without too much difficulty, to select the children likely to prove to be mentally defective. We invariably included, however, in our list of those to be examined individually one or two of each age group who could be

regarded as borderline cases." This step, justifiable in terms of the Herculean task which Lewis undertook and executed, seriously modifies the purpose of group test as he interpreted it. The object of the group test was to pick all children who, on individual examination, would have been found to be retarded; it was meant as a comprehensive screen with no false negatives but a considerable number of false positives. But when the group test is used to pick children *likely* to be found retarded and an arbitrary two or three borderline cases are added, its function as a technique for assuring that *every* retarded child will fall into the hands of the examiner is weakened. It would have been sounder to pick a quantitative score on the group test as a ground for individual testing and to apply it throughout. In the gross, this deviation from the most desirable procedure probably made little difference, but if there were schools which had a high prevalence of unsuspected mental retardation, picking two or three borderline cases might very well have led to missing some retarded children. Thus, the effect of this procedure is to lower the rates for those locations with unsuspected very high prevalences. This is particularly unfortunate, since special steps were taken to be *inclusive* (as described above) when the school had a reputation for having many retardates. Where the group test was not used as a screen (presumably in children under nine) the head teachers were asked to rank the children in order of "backwardness." The children were then examined individually, the most backward first, until the examinations became non-productive and thus were stopped. (If the teachers' judgments were considered worthwhile as a first screen and suitable for use under the age of nine, it is hard to see why this procedure was not used all the way through without recourse to the group tests. It would have saved a step; it is hard to see how it could have resulted in more examinations to be performed, and it avoids the possible pitfalls of the group test technique.)

For children under school age, reliance was placed upon the local Mental Deficiency Authority, child welfare clinics, health visitor, and district nurses for names. Children out of school were listed by head teachers where they knew them or had the appropriate records. "Naturally it was impossible to investigate these with the same thoroughness as the school children. The defective children ascertained in this investigation who were either below school age or not attending school were generally lower grade children and therefore easily recognized as defective."

Methods for ascertaining adult cases were less systematic and more irregular. "The completeness with which we were able to ascertain the adult mental defectives living in the general community depended largely upon the degree to which the various social services had been organized." This comment relates to the urban areas. Lewis' method was that which is sometimes referred to as the "key informant method." That is, he talked to key people who, by virtue of their occupation or community position, would be likely to know, recognize, and name mentally retarded individuals. These included many types of officials, head teachers, social workers, and so forth. The presence of the local Mental Deficiency Officer in each jurisdiction is an important factor in this process. Poorlaw institutions were visited. Inquiries were made about outdoor poor-law recipients. Jails were visited (but apparently not very successfully). Mental institutions were queried and accounted for about half the ascertained cases. Those in institutions were not always examined. There is an extremely interesting discussion (pp. 114 ff.) on the relationship between juvenile dementia praecox and mental retardation or primary amentia, including some good case

sketches which illustrate the issues involved. In this investigation psychotic episodes in youths who later showed intellectual defects seem to have been regarded as results of previously unrecognized mental retardation. In the case of people living in the general community who were reported by his "key informants" Lewis counted only cases which he had examined personally. He also only considered those who were definitely reported as mentally retarded by members of their social circle.

The North Swedish survey.—During the summers of 1946–49 the parishes of Pajala, Junosuando, and Muonionalusta were studied by Böök (1953*a*, *b*) with a view to ascertaining the cases of schizophrenia and of mental retardation prevalent in the three parishes on September 1, 1949. The purpose was to prepare a genetic statistical analysis, but the data can be used to get a partial picture of community diagnosis. The three parishes are all Finnish-speaking, lie on the Swedish-Finnish border, and had not experienced previous field studies. The investigator's wife, who was his main assistant, came from a local Finnish-speaking family, and through her and her family connections extensive co-operation for conducting the study was obtained. The investigator acted as district physician during part of the investigations and thus gained further access.

Ninety-nine cases alive and residing in the parishes as of September 1, 1949 were located in the indicated numbers through seven sources: (1) the parish registers of mentally diseased, mentally retarded, or epileptics from January 1, 1902 to September 1, 1949 (73 cases), (2) records of admissions to the State Mental Hospital since 1893 (1 additional case), (3) records of all admissions to the Mental Asylum since 1922 (when all prior records had been destroyed in a fire) (1 additional case), (4) a spot check in two special institutions to which patients can be transferred from the Mental Asylum (no additional cases), (5) a welfare organization of the State Mental Hospital which provides psychiatric supervision of registered patients being cared for outside the institutions and has been in operation since 1938, (6) the lists of the district physicians who had these duties prior to 1938 and who, from 1917 to 1937, reported yearly to the Royal Medical Board. These reports and the archives of the physicians' records and of the general hospital out-patient clinic and the lying-in service were all scrutinized for neuropsychiatric diagnoses, and (7) all clergymen, school teachers, other local officials, and district nurses were used as key informants as were certain other leading citizens of long residence [22 cases from sources (5), (6), and (7)].

The diagnosis of oligophrenia was based mainly on a clinical and social evaluation of the case. Thus it means an individual who, due to arrested or incomplete development of mind existing before the age of 18 years, was incapable of normal social adjustment. This latter incapacity was taken in the sense that the individual could not, due to his mental defect, independently earn his own living or, if he was a child, could not reasonably be expected to do so. Furthermore, the oligophrenics had not been able to attend ordinary public schools. It would be more correct to say that under normal conditions they would not have been admitted. Due to rather primitive school conditions in the area up to relatively recent years, a number of the oligophrenics of this study were actually admitted in spite of the fact that they turned out to be completely uneducable. The group comprises idiots with an IQ of approximately 0–35 who are uneducable even in special schools and imbeciles with an IQ of approximately 35–70 who to some extent can be educated in special schools or colonies for the feebleminded. I did not perform any psychometric tests. However, most of the institutionalized oligophrenics had been tested. Apart from the general unreliability of such tests, they would have been of no great value for the present study. What was attempted

was to sort out those individuals who show the sharp clear-cut difference, the pathologic variants. For the purpose of studying whether specific entities could be disclosed among the oligophrenics of this population, the dividing line against the higher-grade defectives who might be considered as constituting the tail of the normal intelligence curve need only be approximately correct. As there is considerable overlapping concerning the IQ's of such entities, psychometric tests would not have made the differentiation easier or more adequate than the combined clinical and social evaluation that was relied upon here (p. 35).

The distribution of IQ levels can be seen from Figure 2 to be bimodal and not to extend much, if at all, beyond a level of about 70.

The Norwegian fishing village survey. —Bremer's study (1951) is a study purely of opportunity. The investigator was stationed in a small fishing village above the Arctic Circle on the Finnmark coast of Norway on January 9, 1939. Because of well-known historical events his tenure as the sole medical officer in this village was protracted until August 12, 1945. He studied the entire population, which numbered 1,325 on March 31, 1944, the day of his prevalence count.

Generally, community diagnostic studies depend on census estimates for measures of the size and characteristics of the population which is not found to be ill, but Bremer studied both the ill and the well at the same time and essentially by the same methods, which is the ideal situation. He writes:

. . . [T]here is an obvious statistical weakness in this investigation; it deals with a small community and restricted numbers—a fact that should call for reserve and caution in the evaluation of its results and conclusions. The advantage of this limited material lies in the fact that the investigation can be characterized as extremely intensive. . . . Most investigations build on information supplied by department and public authorities and institutions of all descriptions, to a lesser degree on personal knowledge and research. . . . As a consequence of the methods they . . . treat only of such mental deviations as are of an obvious nature. . . . In my own investigations on the other hand . . . special weight has been also laid on establishing the frequency of less apparent mental deviations—that is, of mild, transient psychoses and the less serious cases of mental deficiency. . . .

Because the study was carried on during a period of enemy occupation, transportation to other parts of the country was highly restricted. In practice, the village was apparently inaccessible except by

left back scholastically or stopped schooling after seven years. The adults, too, had manifested fairly severe social incapacity as judged by others (except for fourteen who were judged only by Bremer's impressions from conversations). "Considering the length of the period of observation, I think it likely that it was possible to keep the diagnosis of oligophrenia strictly to those cases only of true mental deficiency (i.e. morons, imbeciles and idiots), thereby excluding 'borderline' cases. These I have

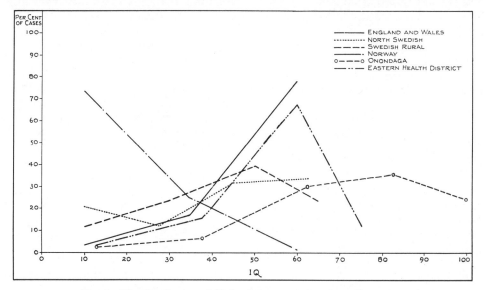

FIG. 2.—The distribution of IQ levels in six community-wide surveys

boat and is perhaps more clearly conceived of as an island, as far as contact with the rest of the world is concerned, rather than as part of the main continental land mass.

In spite of his assertions and evident intent, and in spite of the fact that Bremer found one of the highest prevalences yet observed, his sixty cases are more heavily weighted with severely disabled individuals than any of the other studies summarized in Figures 1 and 2. This is partly accounted for by his casefinding procedures (p. 78 ff.). The younger people enumerated had all been

made no attempt to include in my material." The difficulty of interpreting Bremer's data, because of small numbers, is further complicated by the fact that no less than nineteen of the sixty cases he classed as oligophrenia consisted of four sisters, their progeny, and three spouses! This unusual fact illustrates the point that basically community diagnosis is a problem for each community; transfers of data from one community to another result in only the most approximate type of guesswork.

Eastern Health District.—In 1936 Lemkau, Tietze, and Cooper made a mental health survey of the Eastern Health District of Baltimore. They reviewed all the records of medical agencies and social agencies, re-evaluating diagnoses according to their own standards. The area studied is a residential segment of eastern Baltimore.

They identified cases of mental retardation with and without epilepsy or other personality disorders, classifying cases as "idiots" (IQ less than 25), "imbeciles" (IQ 25–49) and "morons" (IQ 50–69) and "feebleminded" (no tests). The feebleminded were mostly adults. The record search included the public institutions and their waiting lists, voluntary general hospitals and clinics, psychiatric clinics, the social agencies, the school psychological clinic, special classes and attendance divisions, courts, institutions for delinquents, and prisons. "In addition to the necessary identifying data, all information relating to mental status and behavior was copied from the records. Special care was taken to include only cases 'active' in the survey year and only information pertaining or applicable to the period was recorded." Individuals screened as Eastern Health District cases were then checked to show that they were members of households in the rosters of the National Health Survey of 1936 when the District was one of the canvassed units. Cases identified by the National Health Survey as "feebleminded" were also included in the tables. If the agency's case history included a psychiatric diagnosis for 1936, the most recent was accepted at face value; otherwise staff members, or conferences of staff members in ambiguous cases, studied the records and assigned diagnoses. "In doubtful cases we inclined toward understatement of the deviation rather than exaggeration of it."

The Formosa study.—Tsung-yi Lin (1953) conducted a survey of three areas of Formosa.

. . . [T]hree communities were selected as a sample population for the census. These communities are populated by descendants of immigrants from China arriving between 1664 and the beginning of the Japanese era. The culture of these communities is characterized by the extended-family system, ancestor worship, Chinese ideography, and Chinese philosophy as embodied in Confucian and Lao-tse teachings.

None of the aboriginal communities was studied. The investigation was conducted in three stages. The first stage gathered information from town and village registers regarding the sex, age, occupation, living standard, and education of each person in every family. From the same source, information was gathered regarding suspected cases of mental abnormality. The second stage consisted of interviews with family members, elders, and neighbors to further elaborate data on the suspected case and to uncover new suspects. The third stage consisted of interviews with each member of each family. Village elders asked the people to stay home on the day of their survey wherever possible—those who could not were interviewed in the evening. The teams consisted of a physician with at least one year of psychiatric training, assisted by two or three fourth-year medical students accompanied by an elder or village official. The survey included the full range of psychiatric diagnoses; every individual receiving a diagnosis was assigned to only one category, but, unfortunately, Lin does not state by what rule cases of epilepsy with mental retardation were counted, i.e., as cases of epilepsy or as cases of mental retardation. Clearly they were counted only in one category. The same holds true for schizophrenia, alcoholism, psychopathic personality, etc.

The South Swedish study.—Essen-Möller (1956) and his three associates did a comprehensive psychiatric survey of two small parishes in the countryside near Lund, Sweden. The population of 2,550 lived on farms and in one town. The investigators sought to interview every person on the parish registers. This is a special way of defining a population and depends on the particular practices of keeping parish registers. Persons living in the parishes but not registered were not interviewed. Persons registered but living temporarily outside the parish were interviewed and counted. The surveyors tried to measure the occurrence of all types of mental disorders and also the prevalence of each type of personality structure. A classification of personality types developed by Sjöbring, the teacher of all four interviewing psychiatrists, was used for this purpose. In this survey everyone in the population studied received a diagnosis, although, of course, only a small portion received a diagnosis of a disorder. This unusual objective required the interviewers to obtain sufficient contact with each member of the population for classification into one of their personality types. For example, each person was classified as "subvalid" —reserved, cautious, tense, precise, lacking in self-confidence—or "supervalid"— expansive, self-confident, calm, venturesome, enterprising, persevering—or at some point in between. Sjöbring's classification places all varieties of human personality on several different dimensions. The fact that the 98.8 per cent of the registered population individually examined was so thoroughly classified according to personality type makes this survey unique, in that we have unusual assurance that the people not included as cases were really examined thoroughly and were as interesting to the examiners as people as the "cases."

Essen-Möller reports oligophrenics with IQ ratings under 70 (Fig. 2). He regards the findings as in reasonable agreement with Lewis' and emphasizes that the peak in prevalence observed is in the ten- to fourteen-year age group. "The explanation suggested is that many cases, quite similar to those which reveal themselves at school, will earlier as well as later adjust themselves to the require-

ments of the surroundings and therefore not be recognized." He points out that his peak is not as sharp as some others and says that this is "possibly due to the use of a personal method of case finding." Presumably this is meant to suggest that his method will detect young children who will later become notably retarded as well as old adults who in the past have been notably retarded with a higher degree of certainty. However, it is difficult to claim that the personal case-finding method is likely to be more comprehensive in children in any systematic sense than the method used by Lewis. Furthermore, if his "pathologically dull" cases are added, his rates are even more like Lemkau's, and the peak even sharper.

The Onondaga County special census. —A census of suspected referred mentally retarded children under eighteen years of age was conducted by the Mental Health Research Unit of the New York State Department of Mental Hygiene in Onondaga County, New York, as of March 1, 1953 (1955). It sought to enumerate all individuals under the age of eighteen whom any responsible child-caring agency or professional person suspected of being mentally retarded. The investigators made no assumptions about the duration or permanency of the state of functioning. "Total prevalence" was the entire group of children regarded as possibly retarded, whether or not they were reported in the census. "Incomplete reporting" would be due to the failure to communicate to the census-takers the name of an individual who was thought to be possibly retarded. "Over-reporting" would consist of erroneous transmittal of names of children whom the reporting agency did not think possibly retarded. The census was an attempt to get a clearer picture of the size and nature of the population which responsible agencies called retarded and for whom many leaders felt inadequate services were being provided.

The initiative arose from a committee of the state legislature which wanted the information for planning purposes. It complemented other studies done by other agencies which were looking into the various educational and social service techniques appropriate for different subgroups of the population. The Mental Health Research Unit had been placed in Syracuse, at the center of Onondaga County after a review of possible locations made it appear as a good location for the study of a variety of mental health problems. The county is a regional market center in the middle of New York State which has developed a mixed group of industries during the period of New York State's industrialization. It contains, in addition, a number of important cultural institutions, including a large university, one of the state medical schools, a state college of forestry, and one of the older state schools for mentally retarded. Its social agencies are a matter of local pride, and the city's populace is accustomed to co-operating with community studies.

The census procedure was selected after taking into consideration the discussions of Kanner (1949) and Tizard (1953) regarding the variegated criteria relevant to determining the presence or absence of mental retardation. Recognizing that definitions are different in different types of agencies and that different criteria were currently in use, it was thought more valuable to find out about the children to whom these variegated criteria were being applied rather than to apply a set of criteria independent of current practices. Therefore, responsible child-care agencies were requested to report all children under eighteen years of age and residents of Onondaga County on March 1, 1952, identified as definitely mentally retarded or suspected of mental retardation on the basis of developmental history, poor academic performance, IQ score, or social adaptation when contrasted with their age peers. The rates

are obviously higher, and the average IQ rating (when known) is also higher than in any of the other surveys.

DIFFERENCES IN THE SURVEYS

No two of these community surveys are similar in their sample selection, in their case-finding methods, or in their diagnostic criteria. This does not mean that all are wrong or that none of the investigators knew what he was doing. On the contrary, it means that they were all attempting different features of community diagnosis under different circumstances, with different goals in mind and with different tools available to them. Figure 2 emphasizes that the cases found in the different surveys were not similarly distributed according to grade of retardation. Some specific paradoxes may be noted. The Norwegian fishing village survey which has rates so much higher than the Swedish rural or England and Wales surveys had predominantly more seriously handicapped cases. Only the North Swedish survey shows a bimodal distribution of cases. These curves only emphasize the enormous differences between the surveys. Their study reconfirms the impressions gained from the variations in the investigators' descriptions of methods and criteria that the objects of investigation were similar in only the most general sense. It is interesting to note the similarities and differences in the prevalence rates obtained by placing the points on the graph as is done in Figure 1, but it can only serve as a way of summarizing the experience of different surveys not as a way of checking one against the other. The figures can be used to gain a quantitative perspective on the kinds of problems likely to be encountered under the heading of mental retardation in various types of communities and by various types of criteria and case-finding methods. Such numbers can be used in planning services and in planning more detailed studies; they help in making a reasonable advance estimate of what is going to be encountered.

Sometimes the question is asked, "But what is the real prevalence of real mental retardation?" The proper response to this question is that wearisome and irritating counter-question, "Why do you want to know?" Although this phrase is used as an evasive technique under some circumstances, in this circumstance it is the only honest answer. The question itself has no "real" meaning, and it is useless to try to give any answer to it. If the reason for wanting to know is the need to plan services, then it is necessary to specify in detail which kinds of services are thought to be needed for which type of retarded individual of each age. In the course of doing this, the group of "really retarded individuals" becomes redefined in such a way that operational criteria can be used. It was in such a framework that Lewis conducted his survey, and his answers were usable in a rough way in estimating the size of certain types of educational and custodial needs in England and Wales.

If the purpose is to locate cases in order to estimate the frequency with which certain forms of handicapped individuals are being produced so as to estimate their relative importance as public health problems and to gain clues regarding causes, then the *prevalence* (the number of cases alive in a given population at a given point in time) is the wrong measure. To estimate the frequency with which a condition occurs, a measure of *incidence* is needed, that is, the number of new cases occurring in a given population in a given period of time. There are various methods for transforming data on prevalence into estimates of incidence, and a number of the surveyors have done this. A frequently employed technique is one developed by Weinberg (1927) but this formula is valid only when certain assumptions about the population are true. It is unusual for them to be completely

true, and one rarely knows enough to guess how close they come to the truth. In particular, when dealing with conditions which are thought to have their onset before birth it is almost impossible to make the necessary corrections for mortality. The conditions associated with mental retardation are known to have a high association with mortality and, in particular, with prenatal mortality. In many types of conditions this high mortality can be expected to occur during the early life of the fetus, so abortions always represent an unknown proportion of cases in such computations. When one studies the incidence of conditions which arise during extra-uterine life, one has fairly well-established techniques for computing the risks of death to different populations; but, when one deals with conditions which have their onset in intra-uterine life, other techniques are necessary. When one believes the onset is at the time of ovulation or of fertilization one would like to get rates in relationship to the unaffected number of ovulations or fertilizations. But the only clue as to the frequency of affected and unaffected ovulations arises as a result of fertilization and development of the fetus.

From these considerations it should be clear that prevalence rates are of relatively limited value in studying the epidemiology of mental retardation thought to begin before birth.

Age.—Prevalence figures are the product of the incidence of new cases and their average duration. It is conventional in approaching prevalence figures of mental retardation to regard duration as limited only by survival. But it is apparent from a study of the data from the Eastern Health District, from Southern Sweden, from Onondaga County, and from England and Wales that mortality alone cannot account for the fact that after the age of fourteen the prevalence is rarely half as high as at the age of fourteen. These studies, diverse as they are, emphasize and re-emphasize that many types of "retarded" individuals at the age of fourteen simply will not be counted at higher ages. This phenomenon cannot be explained satisfactorily as an artifact of the case-finding methods as is frequently implied. As a matter of fact, the case-finding methods are all designed to perpetuate the diagnosis once reached, because they all depend on informants who are likely to be acquainted with the past history of each individual, and the nature of the questions asked about mentally retarded individuals tend to bring up memories of growth rates. The methods then are biased toward an accumulating prevalence with age. But the findings are of declining prevalence with age, after fourteen. For this to occur, a large group of people regarded as retarded at fourteen must improve in their functioning to the point where people no longer regard them as retarded and also must succeed in escaping their history of earlier unsatisfactory performance.

This is the most important single finding of these surveys. It is an observation which the investigators do not emphasize in their analyses and are inclined to explain away in terms of case-finding mechanisms. However, it appears that the phenomenon cries out for investigation. Either these individuals are continuing to be extremely handicapped in later life and are unknown because the services they need are unavailable to them (in which case society is failing to do its duty toward them and ought to learn how to find and help them), or they have stopped being retarded in any real sense at all and do not need any special protection, help or services, in which case one had better change one's concept of what "real" mental retardation "really" is. The author cannot see any middle ground between these two alternatives, and it appears that a great deal needs to be learned about benign mental retardation, self-limiting retarda-

tion, and neglected mental retardation in adults. Probably all three exist, but almost nothing is known about them at present.

Grades and types.—Figure 2 shows that in each survey there is a wide range of degrees of retardation in the reported cases and that the relative frequency of each degree varies from survey to survey.

The type of care being received was different in preschool and school-age children. The 181 Onondaga County children under five years of age were mostly being cared for at home (78.5 per cent), not in any type of school or institution. Of those not at home, 11.6 per cent were in institutions, 4.4 per cent were in regular public school classes, and 1.1 per cent were in special schools. The 3,603 children between the ages of five and seventeen years were, for the most part, going to regular classes in the public schools (63.9 per cent). The remainder were in parochial schools (8.4 per cent), special classes or special schools (11.7 per cent), or institutions (5.8 per cent); only 4.5 per cent were outside of any school or institution.

There were 442 in the clinical group (those with a medical diagnosis of a chronic brain syndrome). Of these, 138 were in institutions. These 138 are 60 per cent of the total of 231 children who were in institutions, which may be compared with Penrose's 76 per cent in his survey of an institutional population. In Onondaga County less than one-third of the brain-syndrome cases were in institutions.

The whole group of 442 brain-syndrome cases were distributed by age, sex, and diagnosis as shown in Table 2.

These data would be of more value if they reflected systematic medical examination of all members of the census according to explicit criteria. In fact, they reflect the use of medical diagnoses in the care of these children at that time.

Physical handicaps were present in

one-third of the children enumerated. Their distribution is shown in Table 3.

One hundred and twenty-six of the school-age children were not toilet trained. Of these, 70 were in institutions.

Grade placements for the 2,161 reported children in regular schools showed that three quarters (1,641) were one or more years behind their proper grade placement, if six-year-olds are assumed to make up the first grade and to be promoted annually. In a school environment where "automatic promotion" is often assumed to be the order of the

TABLE 2

ORGANIC CASES OF SUSPECTED REFERRED MENTAL RETARDATION BY
DIAGNOSIS, AGE, AND SEX, ONONDAGA COUNTY, MARCH 1, 1953

DIAGNOSIS	TOTAL	MALES		FEMALES	
		Under 5	5-17	Under 5	5-17
Total organic cases............	442	73	171	30	168
Epilepsy.................	104	14	43	3	44
Cretinism................	8	....	3	1	4
Mongolism...............	80	17	29	6	28
Cephalic deformities........	18	4	6	....	8
Cerebral palsy.............	128	15	51	13	49
Amaurotic................	2	....	....	....	2
Post-infectional...........	25	1	10	2	12
Hydrocephalic.............	24	12	6	3	3
Luetic...................	2	....	1	....	1
Other....................	19	4	10	....	5
Unknown etiology.........	70	13	26	4	27
Total organic diagnoses........	480	80	185	32	183

Physical handicaps were present in one-third of the children enumerated. Their distribution is shown in Table 3.

TABLE 3

REPORTED CASES OF SUSPECTED REFERRED MENTAL RETARDATION WITH
PHYSICAL HANDICAPS BY TYPE OF HANDICAP, SEX, AND AGE,
ONONDAGA COUNTY, MARCH 1, 1953

	TOTAL	MALES		FEMALES	
		Under 5	5-17	Under 5	5-17
Total cases with physical handi-					
caps....................	1,242‖	69	710	30	430
Deaf*....................	140	8	77	4	51
Blind†....................	83#	9	37	5	30
Minor visual‡............	559	18	323	4	214
Severe debilitating disease§..	129	7	80	5	37
Orthopedic................	250	45	96	19	90
Speech defect.............	294#	26	121	14	131
Total physical handicaps.......	1,455**	113	734	51	553

* Deaf or gross hearing loss in one or both ears.
† Blind or error of refraction of 20/200 or greater in one or both eyes.
‡ Error of refraction of 20/40 up to 20/200 in one or both eyes or other minor visual defects.
§ Includes cancer, tuberculosis, rheumatic fever, etc.
‖ Includes 3 cases with sex or age unknown.
Includes 2 cases with sex or age unknown.
** Includes 3 cases (4 physical handicaps) with sex or age unknown

day, it is remarkable to find such a large number of children behind in grade placement. Figure 3 shows that the number of reported children in regular school placements rises with age until age ten and then declines, so that by age seventeen very few children are being reported as retarded from regular school placements. Likewise the proportion of these children who are in the proper grade placement declines steadily from age seven onward. It thus appears that the

the community surveys. The sex ratio reported varies considerably in different reports and in different segments of the retarded groups but is consistent in showing a larger prevalence of defect of all types for males as compared to females. This is most marked in the "clinical" or chronic brain-syndrome groups. Figures to illustrate this point are reproduced in Figure 3 and in Table 13.

From the Onondaga County chronic brain-syndrome figures given it can be

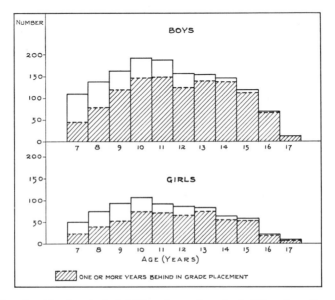

FIG. 3.—Educational lag in retarded children in regular schools (Onondaga County Survey)

regular school classrooms are an increasing source of case identification up until the age of ten and that during these years a larger and larger proportion of the reported children are behind in grade placement. It may be concluded that during the later school years the regular classes exclude increasing numbers of children and continue to carry retarded children only if they are behind in grade placement.

Intersex comparisons.—The two sexes are not equally represented in the surveys, boys being more commonly reported than girls. This is true in all of

seen that males exceed females more in the younger age groups than in the older age groups. It can also be seen that an academic lag is commoner in subnormal boys than in subnormal girls and that this continues throughout the school years.

The higher rates of retardation among males is an important and well-established fact that is relevant to the special services planning and also to educational administration. Its explanation is a problem. Essentially three classes of explanation have been offered. One is that boys are more susceptible to the extrinsic factors or agents which produce a retardation in intellectual development. That is, the male is more vulnerable. Second, the standards for intellectual development in our society are related to communication skills more readily learned by girls (Masland, Sarason, and Gladwin, 1958). The third, which is rarely brought out explicitly and runs counter to some other general biological presuppositions, is that brain-damaged girls die at a higher rate. The first theory, that the male is more vulnerable to agents which damage the central nervous system, is linked with the more general biological problem of explaining sex ratios. The sex ratio of babies born alive is slightly in favor of males, but the proportion of males in most human populations declines from birth onward, until, as the last decades of life approach, there is an excess of females over males. This switching of the sex ratio during the course of postnatal life is due to a differential mortality rate from a large proportion of the major causes of death, males having a higher death rate at every age from accidents, suicides, and a number of infectious illnesses. The tendency for males to die at higher rates than females has been increased in recent decades because many causes of death associated with childbirth have been conquered and because lung cancer and coronary heart disease, both of which affect males much more than females, have become more common. Congenital anomalies are more prevalent in boys as are prematurity, neonatal death, and stillbirth. This complex of facts strengthens the argument for the viewpoint developed by Pasamanick and Knobloch (1960) that there is a "continuum" of grades of fetal damage due to factors which interfere with intra-uterine life, and the fact that more boys are affected by both the congenital anomalies and the forms of intra-uterine and neonatal (or paranatal) deaths may be used to buttress the view that males are more

susceptible to damage. Acceptance of this explanation of the observed sex ratios at different ages after conception requires an assumption that there are many more male conceptions than female, the ratio being somewhere in the neighborhood of 125 per cent.

The second explanation is a cultural one and is based on the obvious fact that girls in elementary school have a more positive approach to most classroom work than boys do, on the whole. This observation is correctly emphasized by Masland *et al.* (1958), but it cannot explain the excess of subnormal boys in the preschool years or among the seriously brain injured.

The third explanation is scarcely mentioned in discussions of this problem, because to suggest a situation that is more likely to produce fetal deaths in damaged girls than in damaged boys simply intensifies the problem of accounting for the falling sex ratio between conception and birth and implies that the sex ratio of males to females at conception may be even higher than 125 per cent. Nonetheless, it is possible that certain conditions such as mongolism and hydrocephaly produce higher fetal and neonatal mortality in girls than in boys, resulting in a larger number of boys surviving. Such an explanation is not incompatible with the fact that later death rates are higher for boys than for girls with these conditions. Indeed, if severely damaged male fetuses have a greater longevity, then their postponed deaths could account for higher death rates in boys than in girls later on. It is also possible that these conditions are particularly damaging to young female and older male children. Such issues cannot be settled by argument but must become further clarified by the accumulation of more precise data.

There is some evidence for this viewpoint as far as mongolism is concerned. Table 2 shows that in Onondaga County there was an excess of males under the age of five but that in the five- to seventeen-year age group there was an approximately equal number of boys and girls. This suggests that in mongoloids over five, males died more frequently than females. But Record and Smith (1955) found that mortality rates of mongoloids from shortly before birth until five years of age (in most periods) were higher for females than for males, as shown in Table 4.

TABLE 4

MORTALITY RATES FOR MALE
AND FEMALE MONGOLS

AGE PERIOD	MORTALITY RATE (%)	
	Males	Females
Shortly before or during birth	0.84	3.06
1 week	5.93	13.68
1 month	6.31	8.54
1 year	26.92	28.00
2 years	5.41	4.04
3 years	1.54	7.06
4 years	1.69	0.00
5 years	0.00	6.35

Judging from these data, it appears that in mongolism young females have a higher mortality rate than young males and older males have a higher mortality rate than older females. It does not follow that other congenital forms of mental retardation follow the same pattern or that the other types of explanation for the greater frequency of male retarded individuals never operate. These data do show that the problem of sex ratios is complicated and is heavily influenced by differential mortality rates.

The cultural argument is at times still further elaborated and entangled with the difference in IQ scores received by groups of boys and girls. Masland et al. (1958) have an excellent discussion of this problem in which they point out that those who construct intelligence tests have made a practice of throwing out questions which "dis-

criminate" between boys and girls, assuming that a difference in average IQ achieved by boys and by girls in standardized tests must represent an error in test construction. This point is certainly correct, but two other issues are not so well dealt with in their discussion. First, it is extraordinary that test-makers have had difficulty finding test items which discriminate between, say, ten-year-old and eleven-year-old performance, which do not simultaneously show ten-year-old girls doing better than ten-year-old boys. With application and ingenuity it is possible to avoid the second discrimination and keep the first, but the difficulties suggest that those tasks which are straightforward indexes of chronological development are done better by girls of a given age than by boys. It would therefore make sense to confine comparisons between populations to intrasex comparisons and to give up the attempt to produce a single scale for the purpose of gauging the rate of development of individual boys or girls or selected groups of boys and girls. It is hard to see what is gained by such single scales, and they undoubtedly lead to great confusion. It is important to make intersex comparisons of development of boys and girls, but it is not necessary to have complete mastery of this problem before establishing useful sex-specific tests which reflect intellectual maturation within single cultural groups.

Second, since certain more or less well-understood causes of low intellectual performance occur at different rates in the two sexes, it is useless to try to make two populations containing different proportions of individuals with such defects show the same distribution of task performance. The typical intelligence tests can be very useful in epidemiological studies of the distribution of poor performers on intellectual tasks. Their usefulness will be increased if comparisons are made within sex and age groups on frequencies of low scorers in different types of tasks without trying to place each individual in terms of a mental ratio or intelligence quotient. These tests are designed well to compare the performance of single age and sex groups in two or more different populations; they are less adequate for measuring the distribution of "intelligence" in populations or for comparing the "intelligence" of two different age-sex groups within one population.

Place of residence.—The survey of England and Wales (Tredgold, 1947), and the Onondaga County census (pp. 93, 102 ff.) reported marked differences in the prevalence of cases by sub-areas. In the Onondaga County census there are differences between the city of Syracuse and the rest of the county.

In both males and females it may be seen that there are slightly higher rates of reporting from the rest of the county in the five- to nine-year age group and markedly higher rates of reporting from the city population in the ten- to seventeen-year age groups. This suggests the possibility that the relationship of the county schools to the mentally retarded is different from that of the city schools. Possibly the outlying-area schools identify a few more cases in the earlier school years but identify fewer in the later years of school life, perhaps because they permit a larger drop-out rate.

The contrast between the city and the county, however, is not due to conditions which prevail throughout the city. A group of four census tracts can be identified readily as producing more than their share of a large variety of health and welfare problems (Census Tracts 32, 33, 34, and 42). These census tracts have large Negro and Jewish populations and a low economic status. Comparisons can then be made between the remainder of the city (excluding these four census tracts) and the county outside of the city limits. It can be seen in Table 6 that the contrast between the

TABLE 5

PREVALENCE OF SUSPECTED REFERRED MENTAL RETARDATION AMONG WHITES BY AGE AND SEX, SYRACUSE CITY AND REST OF COUNTY, MARCH 1, 1953

	MALES		FEMALES	
AGE	Syra-cuse	Rest of County	Syra-cuse	Rest of County
	REPORTED CASES			
Total..........	1,190	885	665	453
Under 1......	3	5	2	......
1–2.........	19	13	14	2
3–4.........	35	21	14	8
5..........	46	40	31	26
6..........	76	74	38	41
7–9.........	249	219	140	108
10–13.......	454	339	259	186
14..........	119	65	75	28
15..........	123	51	66	24
16–17.......	66	56	26	30
Unknown.....	......	2	......	......
	RATE PER 1,000 ESTIMATED POPULATION			
Total..........	38.6	38.9	22.7	20.6
Under 1......	1.2	2.7	0.8	......
1–2.........	4.0	4.0	3.2	0.6
3–4.........	8.0	7.0	3.3	2.7
5..........	20.3	24.6	14.8	16.1
6..........	40.3	48.7	21.0	28.8
7–9.........	51.3	55.4	29.8	28.9
10–13.......	81.9	82.1	50.3	47.1
14..........	102.1	73.5	67.3	34.6
15..........	105.6	57.7	59.2	29.7
16–17.......	28.3	33.1	11.7	18.6
Unknown.....	......	......	......	......

TABLE 6

WHITE CASES PER THOUSAND OF POPULATION REPORTED IN CENSUS

	AGE			
	0–4	5–9	10–14	15–17
County outside of Syracuse........	3.0	37	64	32
Syracuse without four tracts...........	3.1	31	63	39

city and the county beyond the city has been somewhat reduced. The enormously high rates in the deteriorated section of the city obscured the contrast between the ways in which city and county identify retardation in the early elementary school years. The rates in the four census tracts listed above are shown in Table 7.

These data indicate that prevalence rates are a function of age, sex, color, and place of residence. The non-white population is congregated in a crowded undesirable neighborhood, and that neighborhood exhibits the highest rates

TABLE 7

NUMBER OF CASES PER THOUSAND REPORTED IN CENSUS FROM TRACTS NO. 32, 33, 34, 42

| | AGE | | | |
	0–4	5–9	10–14	15–17
White..........	13	60	152	68
Non-white......	5	125	318	265

which were found for school-age children. Its prevalence rate is twice that of the white children from the same general areas.

In addition, the white children in the remainder of the city exhibit rates significantly different from the rates for white children from the rest of the county. In the full report of this census (pp. 102 ff.) a more detailed analysis of only school-referred children confirms the impression that school practices differ in these two areas. A separate analysis by age and sex of only those cases referred by schools showed the rate of case-reporting in the five- to nine-year age group to be definitely higher in the areas outside the city limits than in the city. This was true even when the four deteriorated tracts mentioned above were left in the city data. Had they been removed, the contrast would almost certainly have been even more marked. It

is also true that school referrals in the over ten-year age group were more common for both sexes among white children in the city population.

It is not easy, with the limited information available, to come to a definite conclusion as to the reasons for these variations. It is quite possible that there are significant differences in district-school administration which, on the one hand, precipitate identification of elementary school children as retarded at a higher rate than the city school system does and, on the other hand, precipitate such identification at a lower rate in the junior and senior high school age groups. On the basis of the information now available, however, it is equally plausible to suggest that there are different conditions occurring in the two areas and that their ages of manifestation are different. It is fairly certain that both the white and non-white children in the deteriorated tracts are suffering from multifarious unhealthy circumstances surrounding slum life; there is every reason to believe that both the physical and cultural environments create a higher risk of impaired intellectual development for the children of these areas—more so for the non-white than for the white child. A study of the relative frequency of organic cases in the white and non-white groups would help, but a defect in the data-gathering procedures left 321 protocols unmarked as far as color is concerned. While these 321 cases could not produce great fluctuations in the figures reported for 3,197 cases known to be white, only 269 of the cases were known to be non-white. Therefore, if any large part of the unclassified 321 were non-white, they would have a very large effect on any computations.

Lewis (1929) also found marked geographic variations in prevalence within his survey, but because he does not give age- and sex-specific rates for the different areas it is not possible to make a detailed analysis. His urban areas had lower rates than his rural areas, and he was inclined to attribute this to the tendency of the cities to draw off the intellectually more competent. Mullen and Nee (1952) have an interesting paper which is related to this problem. They contrasted children excused from school with children placed in ungraded classes in Chicago in 1949. They assume that the excused children represent more serious retardation than those placed in ungraded classes. They then showed that neighborhoods with high frequencies of children excused from school had low frequencies of children placed in ungraded classes. They argue that the ungraded-class group is a culturally deprived group which does not arise from the same circumstances as does the excused group. They argue that the neighborhoods with high frequencies of ungraded-class placements do not have high frequencies of excused-from-school. Their neglect of the differences in mortality rates in these neighborhoods weakens their data, however much one wishes to agree with their belief in the usefulness of investing special effort to raise the performance levels of the children who are in ungraded classes. They do show that the highest incidence of placement in ungraded classes occurs in the slum areas, and this is enough to suggest that these areas have an environment conducive to mental retardation.

COMMUNITY DIAGNOSIS OF SPECIFIC CONDITIONS: MONGOLISM

This section has concentrated on the problems of community diagnosis of all forms of mental retardation. Within this broad category a number of specific conditions can be identified. Some of these are the chronic brain syndromes. For each of these a community diagnosis can be made. Some of the relevant data for such a diagnosis have been given but could be pursued in considerably more detail. In addition, one could produce a community diagnostic study for some of the other non-organic types of mental retardation which can be defined and identified systematically in the community. For example, it would be well worth knowing about the distribution of retarded children who have lacked a mothering relationship in early infancy. When one studies such a specific entity within the larger heterogeneous group of mental retardation, one is likely to encounter examples of the disorder which have not produced retardation. This can be expected in examples of maternal deprivation, lead poisoning, post-encephalitic encephalopathy, etc. In these conditions mental retardation is only sometimes the consequence of damage to the central nervous system or to personality development, and the diagnostic study must include both types of cases if it is to help us in understanding the size and nature of the problems we are tackling.

The scope of this review is too limited to go into the available evidence in this type of community diagnosis. Instead of scattering references among a wide variety of studies of many specific entities, mongolism is used as an illustrative example of a specific form of mental retardation. Mongolism has not been reported in the absence of some degree of mental retardation. New knowledge, as will be described later, has brought it to the forefront as an important cause of mental retardation which is ripe for further investigation and ultimate control.

The prevalence of mongolism in the populations of various communities has not been ascertained with any exact precision. Bleyer in 1932 computed the frequency in children attending pediatric clinics. Its frequency has also been estimated among residents of state institutions for mental retardates. Such statistics of service agencies can give figures for their admissions or for their resident populations (See reviews in Penrose [1949, p. 185] and Record and Smith [1955].) Interest has apparently focused on first admissions, although in various administrative reports there are undoubtedly tabulations of the numbers of children with mongolism in residence. In the survey of Onondaga County, eighty of the reported children were reported as mongoloids. This can be expressed as a prevalence of 0.744 per 1,000 children under eighteen years of age, but this is not the same at all ages nor in the two sexes (Table 2). The figures reported undoubtedly result from some under-enumeration in the lower age groups and from a rather high mortality rate. Record and Smith (1955) have gone into these phenomena in much more detail in the city of Birmingham, England. In a carefully conducted study they obtained the mortality rates shown in Table 4. The mortality rates of the two sexes are different and vary with age. In both their data and the reports (1958) of New York State schools for mentally retarded, over one-fourth of the deaths are from infections. Indeed, in the New York State schools over two-thirds of the deaths among mongoloids were attributed to pneumonia.

Because high mortality rates so greatly affect the survival of mongoloid children, measures of prevalence tend to have a large degree of instability from place to place and time to time. These factors make it difficult to obtain reliable information on the incidence of mongolism per birth, which is another index of importance both for community diagnosis and in the search for causes. In terms of the search for causes, the incidence per conception is more relevant and the data quoted above from Record and Smith show that the prevalence just before birth is significantly higher than just after birth. Their data, which are the most reliable available for a large series of births from an entire community gives an incidence of 1.09 mongoloid children per 1,000 births. (As shown in Table 15 this rate varies with maternal age.)

The proportion of the burden of mental retardation caused by mongolism may be estimated in various ways. Of first admissions to New York State schools about 7 per cent have been diagnosed as mongoloids during the last few years (New York State Department of Mental Hygiene, 1958, 1960). In the Onondaga County survey, which included all varieties of school-age children regarded as retarded, the percentage reported as mongoloid was 0.22 per cent.

Whether or not there is any change in the incidence of mongoloid births, the advances of modern medicine have already affected, and will undoubtedly continue to affect, the survival rates of mongoloids. No efforts at quantitative estimates of the extent and nature of this process have been found, but there are no real grounds for doubting that the immediate future will be accompanied by a rising prevalence of this condition due to greater survival. Even if a major discovery led to a radical reduction in the high incidence of mongoloid births, it would take over a decade before its full effect would be felt by the community and government agencies responsible for caring for these children and for helping their families.

HISTORICAL TRENDS

Time trends in the rates at which different illnesses are occurring over the years are of importance in understanding health phenomena. Knowledge of whether an illness is becoming more common or less common is of practical value in planning the use of health resources. A number of diseases have become less common over the centuries and, in particular, during the last half-century—notably leprosy, cholera, typhoid, diphtheria, smallpox, pellagra, tuberculosis, and typhus. In fact, the illnesses to which our grandparents and their cousins succumbed are no longer major causes of death. The disappearance and decline of some of these, such as smallpox, typhoid, and typhus, can be directly connected with social advances or the introduction of particular techniques. The decline of others appears to be intimately linked with general changes in the circumstances of life associated with advancing civilization and rising living standards as much as with any particular technical innovations; this is probably true of tuberculosis, typhus, and pellagra. Why leprosy and some other dying diseases have declined is not known.

The decline of some forms of illness is thus associated with advancing civilization. But civilization also brings on new diseases (Sigerist, 1945), and at the present time there is good reason for believing that lung cancer, coronary heart disease, peptic ulcer, and some other conditions are becoming more common (Morris, 1955). Industrial poisons and allergens which were not part of the environment at all a few decades ago exist today.

We would like to know something about these secular trends, both as an aid in planning the use of our resources and also as an indicator of the efficacy of measures which have been taken to combat a disease. Furthermore, long-term trends in the rate of occurrence of an illness sometimes provide clues as to its cause: if it is declining or increasing in frequency in a changing environment, it is reasonable to link the changes in rates of occurrence to the changes in the environment.

While the evidence regarding details is weak and in most respects inadequate, there can be no doubt that stupidity, dullness, and idiocy have been with mankind as long as he has been able to make written records describing the behavior of his neighbors. Mental retardation is nothing new. Likewise, if mental retardation is becoming less common with the advance of civilization, it is doing so at a rather imperceptible rate, not visible to those overburdened professionals charged with providing the special services these handicapped people desperately need. As a broad category of human disability it is neither a new nor a disappearing condition.

If one looks at that part of the population of mentally retarded which has been institutionalized, one can find some evidence of the volume, in each of the last few generations, of institutionalized subnormal people in those countries which have built facilities. Such a review would provide a panoramic picture of the development of these institutions and their place in our society. Study of their statistics could provide a realistic appraisal of whether such accommodations are being provided for a decreasing or increasing proportion of the general population. This might be of some interest to the planners of services, but such an analysis has not been made. In any case, it would not tell us much about the time trends in the over-all occurrence of mental retardation, since we know that at no time have all cases been institutionalized, and none of our information is adequate for making reliable estimates of changing proportions of uninstitutionalized cases.

The data in the section of this chapter on community diagnosis show that the reliability of techniques for doing community surveys is not sufficiently developed at the present time to make long-range, repeated measurements of the prevalence of all forms of mental retardation. In order to make such measurements one must have some set of criteria which can be used repeatedly over a prolonged period of time. Because knowledge and viewpoints change rapidly in our advancing technology, epidemiological study of time trends rarely can develop the high degree of precision and reliability possible in studying defined populations over a short period of time. The student of long-range trends must locate relevant data from older researches and interpret them in the light of what has been learned since. What we know about the decline of the great killers is known only in broad terms, not in precise or quantitative terms; but for some the change has been so dramatic and the record so clear that there can be no doubt that an enormous change has occurred. Such judgments regarding conditions which do not kill and whose presence is not systematically recorded in some public record are much harder. The definitions of, diagnostic criteria for, and administrative modes of recording cases of mental retardation do not promise to become sufficiently stabilized in the near future to provide us with a clear picture.

REASONING FROM ENVIRON-
MENTAL CHANGES

Judgments regarding the probable true trends in the rate of occurrence of people with any particular degree or type of intellectual handicap will have to be made largely on the basis of present experiences and a few assumptions. These assumptions will tend to be based on the best picture of common causes and whether one believes these common causes are becoming more common or less common.

In particular, if the concept that mental retardation is a type of defect in the functional relationship between an individual and his immediate social environment, the number of individuals with defective functioning will depend both upon individual task performance abilities and on the tasks the environment sets. If the "schologenic" (Stevenson, 1956, pp. 139 ff.) peak of prevalence at about the age of fourteen reflects a tendency of the schools to set tasks for this age group which many cannot perform, then modification of the school environment for this age group could be expected to reduce the number of children judged retarded. At the present time in all of the industrialized countries there appears to be a trend to place more and more rigid demands on this age group, and if this trend continues it can be expected that the proportion of children

judged incompetent will rise. Similarly, in countries which have not yet introduced compulsory universal education through the fourteenth year, we can expect the schools to produce—or weed out, depending on the viewpoint—an ever increasing number of retarded individuals.

On the other hand, if our notions regarding the importance of malnutrition and infection in fetal life are correct, one can reasonably infer that the frequency with which children are born with brain damage attributable to malnutrition or infection has been declining and will continue to decline. If the assumptions regarding the importance of maternal, familial, and cultural stimulation are correct, then one may assume that, with increasing family stability, the spread of literacy and universal education, and the rising living standards referred to earlier, there has been and will continue to be a decline in the frequency with which retardation occurs because of nutritional, social, psychological, and educational deprivation. But if the incidence of cases from prenatal infection or malnutrition declines, the rate of survival of those who are born will rise, and the net result may be either a decline or rise in the number of such individuals alive in a population at a given time, depending on which trend affects more people.

Those concerned with the gene composition of the human population have expressed concern over the consequence of compensating for the phenylketonuric's metabolic defect by the provision of a phenylalanine-free diet. There is good reason to believe that if these children mature and have children they will increase the frequency of the detrimental gene in the next generation. On the other hand, if the increased number of persons with phenylketonuria resulting from this measure are identified early in life (and they will be easy to identify, since the extra cases will be descended from the treated cases) and are given the modified diet, they will not, presumably, be mentally retarded.

The above paragraphs illustrate the only kind of reasoning which is possible today regarding the historical trends. They are sufficient to indicate the kind of data which would help us to make better estimates as to which of these inferences are correct and which are false. Such data is simply not available at present.

THE TREND OF SCOTTISH INTELLIGENCE

Only one serious effort to estimate changes directly has been located. "The Trend of Scottish Intelligence" (1949) was a study instigated by the Population Investigation Committee, which had been influenced by reasoning regarding the relationship between low intelligence and high fertility and was alarmed at the possibility that British intelligence might be falling. The orientation of this group was largely genetic and eugenic. The study was executed in co-operation with the Population Investigation Committee by the Scottish Council for Research in Education, which had done a number of prior studies—notably an important survey of intelligence test performance of all Scottish children born in 1921 during their eleventh year, that is, in 1932. The object of a resurvey in 1947 was to examine by the same method all the Scottish children who had been born in 1936, with the purpose of finding out whether the noted higher fertility of persons wtih lower IQ scores had led to a decline in the national intelligence level. The seriousness of the purpose can be gauged by the fact that some 80,000 eleven-year-old children were, in fact, given the same intelligence test that had been used fifteen years earlier, again, on a single day. The report is recommended reading for anyone contemplating resurveys or field investigations of this type. It is sufficiently detailed to give the reader a rather complete picture of what was done, and the special tabulations are reproduced in sufficient detail for the serious student to manipulate the data to attempt to answer his own questions.

The finding with respect to the feared decline in national intelligence was negative; that is, it was not possible to demonstrate a sufficient change in mean score to prove that there had been any change in national intelligence. But even this finding must remain uncertain because there was so much difficulty in keeping track of the important factors. The author has tried to reinterpret the data to determine whether the frequency of low scorers had changed. But in the first survey children believed to be unable to take the test were not counted, while in the second survey such children were included with the zero scorers (pp. 80 f.); hence, at the bottom end of the scale the criteria for inclusion into the population was modified in such a way as to increase the proportion of low scorers. Parenthetically, this procedure would also tend to lower the average scores found on the second survey. Furthermore, if one examines the relationship between the Terman-Merrill Intelligence Scale, which was given to a random sample individually, and the results of the survey test on this sample, the frequency of major discrepancies is disturbing to anyone contemplating such an analysis (pp. 62 ff.).

However, Dr. Fraser Roberts gives some data (Table 8) which can be looked at from this viewpoint.

These figures show little change in the proportion of the children who scored under 10 out of a possible 76 in this particular test, but they are not very satisfactory because one does not know enough about the difference between the two operations as far as the admission of very handicapped children to the examination is concerned, and one is left too uncertain as to whether Roberts has handled the absentees in a comparable manner.

However, the data provided in this

publication, combined with the more extensive publications of crude tables in the appendix to the 1953 volume, tempt the outsider to introduce his own methods of analysis of this compendious set of figures. Although the procedures used for admitting children to the examination differed as indicated and the second

TABLE 8

VERY LOW SCORES ON THE
GROUP TEST (0–9)

	1932	1947
Boys		
Number.......	608	3,191
Per cent.......	7.63	8.91
Girls		
Number.......	465	1,810
Per cent.......	6.05	5.17

The 1932 numbers are based only on May and June births in 1921, since in this context the comparison to the sample given individual Binet tests is being discussed, and it was found after this sample was drawn that its age distribution was not representative of the whole group but was close to that of the May–June group.

survey obtained more information about children not registered in school and the number of special classes had increased in the interval, when all is said and done, considering the absentees from school on the day of the mass tests, both surveys tested approximately the same proportion of the eleven-year-olds residing in Scotland. (See Table 9.) Figures are not given for the absentees in 1932, but they are for 1947. It will be recalled that children thought to be incapable of taking the test were excluded from the testing in 1947 and were marked "YY," while in 1932 tables were made only on children who could take the test, although some of them scored zero. Presumably, if the 1932 procedure had been followed in 1947 some of the "YY" group would have scored zero, and the remainder would not have been included in the tables at all. One can then make several

different estimates of the proportion of eleven-year-old Scottish children scoring 0–9 on the basis of different figures, as shown in Table 10.

It can be seen from the data in Table 10 that refinements which handle the most handicapped children in the later test procedures in the same way as they were handled in the earlier test, lower the rates obtained for children born in 1936. While none of these adaptations is completely satisfying, they, and other factors, suggest the possibility that in fact the frequency of low performers declined in this population during the fifteen-year period. Much of the whole procedure is subject to doubt because it has failed to take into consideration the changes in mortality rates and migration patterns, and no one can be certain about the changing meaning of a verbal intelligence test in the interval of time which brought the movies to every village and a consciousness of a war-torn

TABLE 9

PROPORTION OF TOTAL ELEVEN-
YEAR-OLDS TESTED ACCORD-
ING TO TWO POPULATION ESTI-
MATES

	ESTIMATE	
	Registrar General	Scottish Dept. of Education
1947......	88.17%	92.76%
1932......	87.23%	91.12%

world during the whole of the second group's school lives. The extent to which this generation, brought up in a country fighting for its existence and dominated by overtime work and ration books was "examination wise," can be a subject of endless speculation. But even if the poorer performers benefited much from these events, the fact that low performers were no more common among the children born in 1936 than among those born in 1921 deserves some attention.

This type of time-trend analysis is superior to attempts to use time trends in IQ. The intelligence scores on an IQ test of a given population provide a comparison of the tested population with the population on which the test was standardized. In a study which undertakes to compare the performance of two different populations (in this case children born in Scotland in 1921 with children born in Scotland in 1936), it is in addition, would have given information about the children who had died, had migrated away from Scotland, or were not included in the Department of Education's registers for various reasons. One is justified in suspecting that in these groups there is a disproportionate amount of pathology. As a matter of constructive criticism it can be pointed out that the data obtained in the more economical procedure used by the Council would have been made even more valuable if a random sample of the children

TABLE 10

ESTIMATES OF PROPORTION OF ELEVEN-YEAR-OLD CHILDREN
SCORING VERY LOW (0–9)

SAMPLE	BORN IN 1921		BORN IN 1936	
	No.	%	No.	%
All boys...........................	44,210	8.07	37,998	8.40
"Thirty-six-day sample"* excluding....				
those absent......................	....	....	3,420	7.48
YY................................	....	....	3,395	6.80
All girls...........................	43,288	6.36	37,213	5.10
"Thirty-six-day sample"* excluding				
those absent......................	....	....	3,437	5.24
YY................................	....	....	3,415	4.63

* The "thirty-six-day sample" consists of children born the first, second, or third of each month in 1936 and was selected for some special studies. Only the tabulations on this sample indicate in detail which children were absent and which were scored "YY."

more appropriate to discard the third population (the population on which the test was originally standardized) entirely and compare the performance of the two populations directly. When one is interested in the retarded individuals, the group of children who were not in school is of particular importance. Additional elegance, both from our point of view and from the point of view of those who asked the original questions, could have been added by starting with the birth registers for 1921 and 1936. If an appraisal of those born in those two years had been attempted, it would have required much additional work but would have given us two populations more relevant to appraising time trends and, born in those years had been searched for as a supplementary study. Most of them would have been found in the roster of children examined, but the fate of the few who did not show up in the roster would have been of great interest and knowledge about them would have helped us to interpret these extensive studies.

NEEDS

While the surveys of Scottish school children represent the only attempt located to study time trends directly by repeating the same measurement at two successive points in time, there is no reason why further investigations of time trends should not be made. It would have been surprising if the first such re-survey would have been satisfactory in all respects. We should not be discouraged, but encouraged, by the limited success achieved to try similar techniques in the future.

The most important and pressing problem calling for time-trend studies is the need to know the incidence of various congenital anomalies whose incidence is expected to increase as a result of radiant energy from artificial sources. For these purposes, attention can be focused on more sharply defined clinical entities, and selected lists of pregnancies in sample populations can be followed. It cannot be said that epidemiological methods have failed to give us any precise information on this problem during the fifteen years since Hiroshima; it can be said that epidemiological skills have not been systematically applied to getting the information.

COMPLETING THE CLINICAL PICTURE

Epidemiology takes the clinician away from the cases for which he has responsibility and exposes him to many other cases, sometimes cases for whom no one has been asked to take responsibility. In the course of this process the clinician sees a wider variety of cases and gains a different perspective on the nature of the illnesses which he is treating. The contrast between the data in the Colchester survey and in the Onondaga County census illustrates the fact that the relative frequency of different conditions in a population of retarded individuals depends upon the breadth of the search for cases. The prognosis of mongolism is clearly different at different ages when the very young cases are taken into account, and the differences described in the course of the disorder in boys and girls depends on the age and place at which the boys and girls are collected.

The extension of our picture of the nature of a disorder can also be enlarged when the preclinical or subclinical cases

are added to the data. The discovery of subclinical forms of phenylketonuria and of phenylketonuric carriers changes our concepts of the nature of phenylketonuria. (See the chapter on genetics in this volume.)

It is difficult to get a picture of subclinical forms of the syndromes one is describing; it is difficult to locate the cases. But if subclinical forms were studied in younger children one might get a better idea of the nature of the syndromes which are labeled mental retardation.

The easiest group of cases to approach are the former cases. Follow-up studies of mentally retarded individuals have been unable to show a uniform prognosis. In fact, they show the most amazing variety of outcomes. For example, Wolfson (1956), after completing a five-year follow-up of boys and girls who had left Newark (N.Y.) State School in 1946, was so impressed with the variety of outcomes, that he was led to assert:

> As one studies these case histories one wonders how the contemporary theory which emphasizes the importance of early parent-child relationships and wholesome family situation on development of personality applies in these cases. Why is it that such a a large proportion of boys and girls with glaringly adverse family background grow up to be stable and responsible people? . . .

It does not appear to be true that limited intellectual endowment is always associated with lesser judgment, lesser imaginative powers, lesser emotional and volitional control. He questions the stability of intelligence as measured by tests and points out that good adjustments are made by those with both higher and lower scores. This illustrates the reaction of an experienced clinician to a series of case records which followed patients beyond the clinical relationship and forced a reappraisal of the clinical pictures regarding prognosis.

The studies by Kennedy (1948) have

similarly shown a remarkable range of adaptation in adults who, as children, had been regarded as retarded. While her data are not adequate, it is unfortunate that more studies based on similar principles of data-gathering have not been done. The Onondaga County census offers an excellent springboard for a follow-up study of the sample of children who were reported in 1953. What is the difference at age fourteen between the half or more who will at age twenty-four be making a good adjustment and the other portion who will continue to be regarded as mentally retarded? What effect does intelligence level have on adult adaptation and clinical signs? What ever happened to the 514 school-age children who were reported as retarded although they had intelligence quotients on record of over 90? Over 180 of them were behind in the school-grade placements; what difference did that make in final outcome? Epidemiologic studies of the later lives of these cases would help to give us a much clearer picture of the nature of the disorders they were experiencing. *There is a remarkable dearth of information on the course of the various forms of mental retardation.*

IDENTIFICATION OF SYNDROMES

In the course of medicine's advance in mastering human illness, it has happened on several occasions that a group of cases which had been seen as examples of a single disorder have been broken into two or more groups because they apparently arose from different population groups or different circumstances. On some occasions this has been the first lead by which new disease entities with particular chains of causation have become identified and ultimately conquered. An outstanding example is the differentiation of typhoid from typhus. On other occasions, two conditions which appear clinically different may become linked to each other by epide-

miological evidence and ultimately be found to be the result of a single causal agent.

An example of the latter, which brought together a benign feverish rash of short duration in young married women and congenital permanent brain damage (and other congenital defects) in their children born some months later, was the observation of Gregg (1941, 1944) on German measles. The original observations were purely epidemiological: a sudden rise in congenital cataracts and a prior epidemic of German measles. It is noteworthy that this epidemiological observation was made by a clinician and was not dependent on quantitative analysis. Sometimes epidemiology is regarded as a purely statistical activity, but this is incorrect. Original epidemiological observations are often made without using statistical techniques by clinicians rather than by those studying statistical tabulations. It is from clinical observation that epidemiology often gets its first leads. The exact investigations come later. Without the subsequent careful statistical studies such as those by Hill *et al.* (1958), Gregg's original observation could not have been accepted as reliable. From these studies the relationship between maternal rubella and congenitally defective brain structure has been well established. Hill *et al.* carefully appraised the fetal syndrome associated with rubella infection in cohort studies, and they conclude that the major fetal defects occur in approximately 50 per cent, 25 per cent, 17 per cent and 0 per cent of the fetuses infected in the first, second, third, and fourth month of pregnancy, respectively. The fetal syndrome resulting is characterized by congenital cataract, deafness, and, inconstantly, by heart anomalies, microcephalus, and a chronic brain syndrome. This type of advance in medical knowledge brings hitherto unrelated units together, and, simultaneously, a proportion of cases of some other entity (in this instance, congenital brain syndrome of unknown cause) is lost. Kirman (1955) reports that of 791 cases of mental retardation studied a maternal history of rubella could be obtained in 7, which gives some idea of the size of this loss.

Epidemiology has played a role in linking congenital brain syndromes to other fetal events (MacMahon and Sowa, 1961).

This role of epidemiology in dissecting clinical groups of mentally retarded individuals has been played in three areas. One series of observations differentiated one group of retarded from the other on the ground that some fall within the Gaussian curve on intelligence tests and others do not. A second series of observations differentiated one group of retardates from another on the basis of their parents' mental level. A third series of studies sought to show that severe and mild cases represent different entities because the severe and mild cases show different rates of occurrence in the two sexes and in different socio-economic groups and are differently related to maternal age at the time of conception. Examples of these studies will be reviewed here because the method can be useful, primarily in providing clues and circumstantial evidence. Inferences from such studies must be drawn with caution, however; the cases of a single illness may have different pictures in people living under different conditions, and there are other possible reasons for such differentiating epidemiological patterns than the presence of two different types of causal mechanism.

CLINICAL AND RESIDUAL CASES

The cases which do not fall under the Gaussian umbrella.—A good exposition of this argument is to be found in Penrose (1949, p. 44 f.). "A fresh approach to the problem of clinical classification was made by Lewis (1929), who suggested the division of defectives into 'pathologi-

cal' and 'subcultural' types. . . ." Cases of mental retardation contain a number with definite diseases or pathological conditions which interfere with the functioning of the brain. Many idiots and imbeciles are "pathological" on the basis of clinical investigation. The diseases may be of hereditary or environmental origin.

There are statistical grounds for Lewis' classification if we assume that the distribution of ability on intelligence tests in a normal human population, should be Gaussian. Far too many individuals exist, whose abilities are more than three or four times the standard deviation below the normal mean, to be fitted under a Gaussian curve. On that assumption, only about 1 idiot among 10,000 and 1 imbecile among 6 could belong to a normal population with a standard deviation of 15 IQ points . . . for the feebleminded, the position is different and, on the basis of intelligence tests alone, the great majority of them might be regarded as members of the normal population. Diminished intellectual capacity of relatively mild degree can be interpreted as failure to meet the demands of local culture. Hence, the term "subcultural" can be applied to most of the feebleminded, though few imbeciles or idiots can be reasonably included in this category.

This line of reasoning is fallacious. It does not recognize the essential characteristics of intelligence tests. Wechsler (1939) describes the construction of his test as follows:

The classification offered . . . , like all others making use of IQ's is based essentially on a statistical concept of intelligence. . . . The important thing about all such classifications (whether one admits it or not) is that they abandon all attempts at an absolute definition of intelligence. An IQ merely tells you how much better or worse, or how much above or below the average any individual is, when compared with persons of his own age . . . mental age is no more an absolute measure of intelligence than any other test score.

Such frank recognition of the arbitrary nature of the intelligence score is becoming more widespread. However,

Wechsler's phrase "how much above or how much below the average an individual scores" has permitted some readers to miss the fact that the "how much" refers to how much of the standard population scored at points in between the individual's score and the average score and not how much intelligence more or less he showed than the average person. If the full implication of this fact is recognized it is obvious that *intelligence tests cannot determine how intelligence is distributed in the population.* The designer of an intelligence test selects, on the basis of accumulated experience, a series of tasks which the subjects are asked to perform. A "good" task is one which some people can perform and others cannot perform. A series of graded tasks are 'good" if, generally speaking, people who can do the harder tasks can do the easier tasks. People are graded according to where they stand in relationship to the others to whom the test has been given. One task is "easier" than another if more people can perform it. There are no units of difficulty, so it is not possible to say that any task is twice as hard as any other task. Values are assigned to task performances in such a way that half the population at any given age will score 100 or more, and half will score 100 or less. Further adjustments to the scoring are made so that half will score between 90 and 110 and so that the remainder will be distributed as nearly as possible in a symmetrical curve. The result, of course, is that the distribution of observed scores falls on a symmetrical continuous normal curve. It is often stated, as though it were a demonstrated fact, that "General intelligence is an uninterrupted continuum . . ." (Wechsler, 1939, p. 37), whereas, in fact, it is not possible to demonstrate anything of the kind.

In order to picture the situation, imagine that you are given a pile of coins and are told to develop a way of measuring any given coin's weight. You have no standard weights, but you have a delicate chemical balance and a beach full of stones from which you may develop a series of standardized weights. You are told that, on theoretical grounds, the distribution of the coins' weights should form a normal curve. Suppose, further, that the balance is very sensitive and the coins are variously worn in such a way that no two coins exactly balance one another and that no two stones exactly balance one another. The appropriate procedure would be to find first a stone which outweighed about half the coins and thus divide them into two groups. Assign this stone the numerical value of 100. Then take the pile of coins and divide it into two piles, the 100+ pile and the 100— pile. Next, work on the 100+ pile; find a stone which weighs more than about half and less than about half. Give this stone the numerical value 110. Now find a stone heavier than half of the 100— pile and assign it the numerical value of 90. You will need several thousand coins to develop the whole scale and about 700 stones selected from many tens of thousands of stones in order to get a nice percentile rank for the coins by weighing them against the numbered stones. But when you are done you will be able to produce a table very much like Wechsler's (on page 43 of his book). One per cent of the coins will weigh less than stone number 59 and the heaviest 1 per cent will weigh more than stone number 130. Forty-five per cent of the coins will weigh less than the stone numbered 99.7 and 45 per cent will weigh more than the stone numbered 101.4. Likewise, the percentile rank of the values assigned to each of our selected stones (IQ's), when determined by the per cent of the coins which weigh less than it, will form an array from 1 to 100 per cent. Having followed the procedure of the intelligence test constructer, the frequency of different weights, when measured by the assigned numbers, will fall on a normal distribution as specified.

If the original pile was made up of several thousand quarters worn to various degrees of thinness, this procedure could be carried out, even though the stones varied from each other only by fractions of a milligram in weight. If the pile were made up of a mixture of dimes and quarters you could still carry the procedure out as outlined. Then some stones would vary around the weight of a quarter and some around the weight of a dime, but the numerical sequence for the whole mixed pile would still be able to meet the criteria outlined. The same would hold for a pile of pennies, nickels, dimes, quarters, half dollars, and silver dollars. If you carry out the instructions, the frequencies of weights as measured by the numbered stones will fall on a normal curve. Obviously, this does not mean that the actual weights of coins form a normal curve. If all that were known was their weights as measured by these selected stones, the frequency of the coins' weights might appear to be distributed on a normal curve if we forgot that our procedure is bound to produce a normal distribution of measured weights regardless of whether or not the coins jump in weight from one weight group to another.

As Wechsler correctly states, his ground-breaking work lays bare the assumptions behind an intelligence test to a greater extent than earlier workers had done. "Our aim was not to produce a set of brand new tests but to select, from whatever source available, such a combination of them as would best meet the requirements of an effective adult scale" (1939, p. 78). His set of stones has smoother properties than some of the earlier ones, but is, as he correctly says, purely arbitrary.

This detailed discussion is necessary because it is often stated, for example, that the prevalence of mental retardation is 2.2 per cent or about 3 per cent. Such measures flow from the assumptions which the testers have built into their scoring systems. It is often also asserted that intelligence is graded and that there are no sharp distinctions.

No breaks, no gaps, mark off the defectives from the normal, or the normal from the genius. Nowhere do we find discrete mental types, or well-marked classes abruptly separated and sharply defined. Subnormality, like abnormality, turns out to be a relative term. Most significant of all, the distribution itself conforms very closely with a well-known statistical law. Like height and weight, and sizes of bones of skulls and, indeed, most anthropometric measurements, intelligence is distributed in accordance with what is termed the "normal curve of error" (Burt, 1955, p. 36).

This is not an observed fact, but an assumption of intelligence scoring methods.[2]

[2] There is only one exact meaning for the concept of continuous distribution, and that is that between any two values there are intermediate values (as with the points on a line, or the real numbers). Intelligence as an observable characteristic of humans cannot be continuous, since only a finite number of people have ever had it, so there must be examples of two individuals who have differed in intelligence in such a way that no other individual has had an intelligence intermediate between the two. It is also meaningless to say that height or weight is distributed continuously in the population—it cannot be because there is a finite number of persons in any population. What is meant is that the *scales* on which height and weight are measured are continuous and that there are no appreciable segments along the scale where no individuals fall. But the *scales* for intelligence are not continuous: each point is measured by the number of people in the standard population who did not score higher, and this is always a whole number. When these scales are divided by the total number in the corresponding standard population, they appear to be continuous, like the rational numbers. For any particular standardization of a test, only a finite, discontinuous series of scores can be computed. This pedantic discussion is intended only to amplify the point that assertions regarding the continuity of intelligence are only assertions regarding the speaker's own notion of the possible levels of intelligence and not statements regarding observed facts. Whether or not Galton's concept of general intelligence, continuously distributed, because of multifactorial causes, sur-

If a test were designed and standardized on a "standard" population of children in a special school for gifted children so that it would produce a normal curve for that "standard" population, the rest of us would all fall off the bottom of the curve and could be described as "outside the normal distribution of intelligence." Similarly, if another test were standardized (as it could be) on the population of a school for mentally retarded persons, most of us would fall off the upper end of the curve as geniuses beyond the "normal" range. What is "normal" is the "normal curve" constructed for a "normal population." The whole line of reasoning quoted above from Penrose depends on the relation between the observed population and the population on which the test was standardized. In practice, most tests are designed to fit a school system's concept of a normal population. As with the Scottish survey test, there are usually some people who cannot answer any questions. It may be assumed that such people do not exist in most standard populations, because unless everyone can do at least something, the test is unable to assign everyone a score. Now there are some human beings who can do very, very few things. In practice, of course, the standard intelligence tests ordinarily used have simply not faced the problems of the person of very low ability; they have been excluded from the standardizing procedure. When such a standardized test is then applied to a general population which includes the least capable, the people who cannot do much of the test at all

will show up as a lump at the bottom of the curve.

Consequently, any study of the distribution of intelligence test scores in a population is a study of the relation between the population being studied and a standard population. Often the characteristics of the standard population are lost in some technical manual never studied by the users of the tests. Wechsler's description (referred to above) of how he decided how many people there ought to be who functioned at the level to be found in an institution for mentally retarded in his standard population is an instructive and refreshing reminder of this fact. These features of intelligence tests are clearly described by Anastasi (1957) in her college textbook but are not universally appreciated.

Many citations of otherwise highly respectable authorities could be given in which it is asserted that "intelligence tests measure . . . in the same way as a measurement of length, breadth, or girth . . ." and which reason that because such measurements of humans do fall into a normal distribution in many populations and intelligence test scores do (necessarily) then it is reasonable to think that there are in nature units of intelligence similar to units of length, breadth, weight, etc. That this is a specious line of reasoning should be obvious.[3]

The cases whose parents are retarded are different from those whose parents are not retarded.—The refutation of "statistical evidence" above does not dispose of the obvious observation that the pop-

---

vives further scientific investigations cannot be stated with confidence. It can be stated that it has never been demonstrated so far and that no evidence for the existence of the reality corresponding to such a concept has ever been advanced. Those who claim to have done so are reasoning in a circular way. It is not expected that publication of this note will terminate such assertions, but it is hoped that it will give some readers the tools to argue against them.

[3] It also follows that such tests cannot measure the standard deviation of intelligence in a population. Nor can they measure differences in distribution of intelligence in two populations of different ages, because each age group has its own standard population, which, by its performance, gave the testers the numerical values. Even such competent workers as Pasamanick, Knobloch, and Allen perpetuate such misuse of the intelligence test type of measurement (*Science*, February 10, 1961).

ulation of any school of subnormal children, any clinic group, or any special class is heterogeneous and that those with the greatest handicaps as a group look more different and move more differently from other children than do those with the milder handicaps. No epidemiological evidence is necessary to

TABLE 11

PENROSE'S (1949) CLASSIFICATION OF RESIDENTS OF INSTITUTION AT COLCHESTER

GRADE	TOTAL	CLINICAL GROUP		RESIDUAL GROUP*
		No.	%	
Borderline..........	179	145	81.0	34
Mild subnormality...	448	284	63.3	164
Moderate subnormality..............	433	340	78.5	93
Severe subnormality.	220	203	92.3	17
Total	1,280	972	76.0	308

* Halperin (1945) in a review of an American institution, using similar criteria, found 45 per cent in the Residual Group.

two categories; that is, they have no obvious physical deformities, and their defect is more than mild.

Because administrative and legal classifications have given attention only to grades of defect of social and personal functioning and prescribe procedures for handling in terms of these grades, observant people try to develop data to prove that there are qualitative differences too. Understanding of the syndromes can also be advanced if one specifies these groups more sharply and uses epidemiological relationships to see if new differentiations are formed.

The most useful such effort is Penrose's survey of 1,280 residents of an institution at Colchester (1949). Those showing physical signs of an underlying pathological condition he called the "Clinical Group"; the remaining 308 he termed the "Residual Group" (see Table 11).

In Penrose's study the social workers rated the home conditions of the population, as shown in Table 12.

TABLE 12

PENROSE'S (1949) RATING OF HOME CONDITIONS

	PER CENT EACH TYPE OF HOME					TOTAL
	Very Good	Above Average	Average	Below Average	Very Bad	
Mild and borderline..........	0.6	10.4	44.2	34.6	10.2	100.0
Moderate and severe..........	4.9	21.7	49.7	18.8	4.9	100.0

These percentages are based on the 482 mild and borderline cases and the 531 moderate and severe cases which had homes; the remainder had none.

prove that in fact there are at least two readily differentiated groups: (1) those with mild defects of performance and no other clinically evident fault and (2) those whose intellectual defects are accompanied by other abnormalities of body structure and function. The latter group includes some very severely handicapped children. In addition, there is another category (3) of retarded children who do not fall in either of the first

In addition, the parental mental grouping was rated for 2,560 parents of 1,280 cases, and this was tabulated against the patient's mental grade and clinical classification.

Parents were rated as retarded three times as frequently in the Residual (15 per cent) as in the Clinical Group (5 per cent). The parents of mongoloids and of children with neurological lesions were most infrequently rated as retarded.

This finding strengthens the impression that these two conditions have a type of natural history different from the other clinical conditions. In all the clinical conditions the percentage with retarded parents is much lower than in the Residual Group, strengthening the impression that the Clinical Group (of retarded patients) derive predominantly from different kinds of parents. This argument is weakened by the source of the sample, so that factors affecting the likelihood of infant survival and institutionalization could contribute to the pattern. Data from a random sample of all children with intellectual handicaps would provide stronger evidence of the difference between these syndromes.

Levels of defect in relationship to other factors.—Penrose's data show that the parents of the children with mild retardation (borderline or mild retardation, "feebleminded") are themselves cases of retardation (profound, "idiots") more frequently (12.1 per cent) than are the parents of patients with moderate retardation (6.5 per cent). The more severe the patient's retardation, the smaller the probability that one or both of his parents will be retarded. This strongly suggests that among the patients of higher grades of retardation familial aggregation of cases is commoner. Familial concentrations of cases can arise in many different ways, particularly through cultural inheritance, common exposure to agents associated with habits and customs, any type of relationship to economic poverty, transmission of deleterious genes, factors related to social structure (even when unrelated to economic level), etc. Since so many kinds of mechanism can produce familial aggregation of cases, the most useful clue respecting causes contained in these data is in their identification of syndromes with very low levels of familial aggregation. These tend to be the most severe cases and are also more common among the clinical cases.

The borderline group may represent a different type of syndrome, rather than just a less severe form of the same condition. These cases evidently had enough defect of functioning to be certified but scored above 70 on a test. Their parents were retarded infrequently (5.0 per cent), as compared to the parents of children in the mildly retarded group, but as frequently as parents of cases in the clinical group (5.2 per cent). There is a natural temptation to regard "borderline" examples of a condition which is being graded according to levels of severity simply as examples less severe than the least severe of the definite cases. However, borders exist not only at the top but along the edges of such a group, and without further investigation it would be premature to judge these borderline cases as only quantitatively doubtful; they may in many instances be qualitatively doubtful.

Data gathered from an entire population would be worth even more detailed analysis in pursuit of these clues regarding different types of syndromes with different natural histories and manifestations. Such a pursuit should be integrated with laboratory and clinical data.

The continuum of reproductive casualty.—It is clear from the foregoing that the epidemiological identification of syndromes is never completely separated from the search for causes. The most sweeping and the most hopeful attempt to redefine syndromic groupings through epidemiological methods has been the effort by a number of investigators in the last few decades to bring together what Pasamanick has called a "continuum of reproductive casualty extending all the way from death to minimum cerebral damage resulting in minor behavioral dysfunction" (Lilienfeld and Parkhurst, 1951; Pasamanick, 1952; Lilienfeld and Pasamanick, 1954; Pasamanick and Lilienfeld, 1955; Pasamanick and Kawi, 1956; Kawi and Pasamanick, 1958; Mac-

TABLE 13

MENTAL STATUS OF PARENTS OF 1,280 PATIENTS (COLCHESTER SURVEY, 1938)

CLASSIFICATION	DESCRIPTION	NUMBER OF PATIENTS	SEXES OF PARENTS	NUMBER OF PARENTS IN EACH MENTAL GRADE						PERCENTAGE OF PARENTS GRADED FEEBLEMINDED OR IMBECILE
				Superior	Normal or Average	Dull or Borderline	Feeble-minded	Imbe-cile	Unascer-tained	
By sex of patient	Male	710	Male	6	580	69	22	0	33	3.1
			Female	2	521	103	65	2	17	9.5
	Female	570	Male	3	427	80	26	1	33	4.7
			Female	0	380	99	78	1	12	13.9
By mental grade of patient	Borderline	179	Both	1	255	63	18	0	21	5.0
	Feebleminded	448	"	3	580	159	106	3	45	12.1
	Imbecile	433	"	4	687	92	55	1	27	6.5
	Idiot	220	"	3	386	37	12	0	2	2.7
By clinical type of patient	Mongolism	63	Both	0	119	5	2	0	0	1.6
	Endocrine disorder	88	"	2	135	24	9	0	6	5.1
	Congenital syphilis	50	"	0	75	9	6	0	10	6.0
	Neurological lesion	128	"	3	230	13	8	0	2	3.1
	Skeletal malformation	142	"	1	227	35	12	1	8	4.6
	Miscellaneous abnormalities	87	"	1	141	20	9	0	3	5.2
	Idiopathic epilepsy	210	"	2	321	52	29	0	16	6.9
	Non-epileptic mental disorder	204	"	1	293	69	26	0	19	6.4
	Clinical group	972	Both	10	1,541	227	101	1	64	5.2
	Residual group	308	"	1	367	124	90	3	31	15.1
Total of each classification	All patients	1,280	Both	11	1,908	351	191	4	95	7.6

Mahon, 1961; MacMahon and Sowa, 1961) summarizes the method used as follows:

The method has been to identify from medical care facilities a group of children affected with a variety of neuropsychiatric abnormalities—cerebral palsy, epilepsy, mental retardation and tics. Information was obtained, either from birth certificates, hospital records, or both as to the frequency of recorded complications of pregnancy or labor. For comparison purposes similar information was abstracted for a group of infants selected from the same series of birth certificates and matched with the patients for race and maternal age and, sometimes, sex and place of

are difficult and time-consuming to gather, but a beginning has been made. Meanwhile, despite the weaknesses of this method, there seems to be ample reason to believe that there is a high relationship between several congenital brain syndromes which are clinically somewhat different and a group of pregnancy complications which are clinically entirely different.

This type of regrouping data can be helpful in the pursuit of causes as well as in the redefinition of syndromes. But it would not be correct to conclude that this type of grouping represents the end

TABLE 14

PREGNANCY COMPLICATIONS AND SELECTED DISORDERS

	Pre-maturity	Toxemias	Late Bleeding	Non-puerperal Complications
Mental retardation..........	+*	—	?	+
Reading disorders..........	+	+	+	+
Speech disorders............	—	+	....	+
Epilepsy...................	+	+	+	+?
Cerebral palsy.............	+	+	+	+
Behavioral disorders........	+	+	+?	+?

* Plus sign (+) indicates complication found more commonly in histories of cases than of controls.

delivery. While some elementary data have been presented for specific complications of pregnancy, much of the analysis deals with comparisons of the cases and comparison groups with respect to the frequency of one, two, or more "complications" including conditions as diverse as "non-puerperal complications" and breech presentations. It is clear that the group has in mind a "continuum" of causative agents as well as of end results.

The results of the studies as abstracted by MacMahon so far are summarized in Table 14.

As Pasamanick has pointed out, the statistical significance of the association but not the increased risk associated with any of these complications can be appraised from the type of data he has been able to collect. The data which would be preferred for this type of study

of a road; it is rather the beginning of a new road, and as future investigations further clarify the picture, the syndromes listed above may be brought closer together or become differentiated more sharply or along entirely new planes. It is well known from studies in experimental teratology that a wide variety of insults can produce similar disorders in the offspring. It can also be shown that the time of the insult is at least as important as its nature. There are, in the findings of this group of studies, important clues and numerous suggestions for specific prospective studies. For some of these it is not necessary to plan a study over many years. Some signs of defective functioning can be picked up early in life. As is pointed out on p. 293, the intelligence test or developmental test may have defects with respect to its original intent, but it is an excellent device for comparing the development of two groups which contrast in some particular way. Hence, with all the weaknesses of early tests it is possible to compare the central nervous system development of groups of children who have had different prior experiences. In addition, many of the limitations of the studies made so far on this "continuum of reproductive casualty" can be overcome by using a different method for selecting the populations to be studied. If live births from single sources of records, such as specific obstetrical services, generated both the study of those with the suspected "cause" and the control populations, many more inferences could be drawn from the data, even if the pregnancies had occurred many years ago. Thus it would be possible to pick a series of well-recorded pregnancies from a population born fourteen years prior to the date of study and find out which children are presently retarded. This method has the advantage of producing evidence regarding all of the suspected syndromes, including neonatal deaths. It has the disadvantage of requiring that the investigators be at least as mobile as the children who are selected. However, if one wishes to study health problems in a mobile population, there is no great virtue in planning investigations which require that the population stay in one place.

IN SEARCH OF CAUSES

GENES

The chapter on genetics discusses the way in which field studies which demonstrate certain patterns of familial aggregation of cases produce evidence that the cause of a given disorder is either a rare recessive or a rare dominant gene. The chapter on genetics also gives the approximate frequency of these genes in the population and the expected fre-

quency of damaged individuals born per thousand by birth. The "empiric risks" are also discussed there.

MONGOLISM

Defects of chromosome development have long been observed in plants and lower animals, but only in the last few years has it been possible to discern such conditions in humans (*Am. Soc. Hum. Genet.*, 1960). Considering the amount of dogmatic literature on genetic transmission of mental disorders and mental retardation, it is startling to realize that only in the last few years has the number of chromosomes in the human cell been determined correctly. Previously it was believed that the normal human cell had forty-eight chromosomes, but it is now known to have forty-six. This is the most important single piece of information we have gained as a result of an astounding new technique involving the cultivation of human cells in tissue cultures and the interruption of the mitotic process through various maneuvers which make it possible to separate the chromosomes visually and see them under the microscope clearly. This adds a new tool for investigating the causes of disease, and its most important single contribution to human pathology has been the discovery that mongolism is due to the presence of an extra chromosome at the number twenty-one position (Rowley, 1962). (This trisomy of chromosome twenty-one will generally produce a total of forty-seven chromosomes, but it is important to recognize that this condition can be combined with a translocation to yield a total count of forty-six chromosomes [Böök, 1959; Breg, 1962].) Careful studies suggest that the extra chromosome is probably always at the number twenty-one position (*Lancet*, 1961). Identical twins are generally concordant for mongolism (Allen and Kallman, 1957). This new knowledge derived from the laboratory brings increased hope of an early discovery of the mechanism by which mongolism is produced. The frequency of mongolism in the population and proportion of mental retardation in a population which is due to mongolism are discussed in the section, "Community Diagnosis," in this chapter.

Studies of familial aggregation of mongolism have been unable to show the high concentration in families which would suggest transmission of defective germ plasm. A few mongoloids have conceived children; some of them have had mongoloid children, and others have not. The fact that some have not had mongoloid children but have had normal children is strong evidence that the chromosome abnormality is not always transmitted. There are also dizygotic twins, including several of different sex, on record who have both been mongoloids (Benda, 1960).[4] The most outstanding piece of epidemiological information we have is that maternal age is closely related to the probability of mongolism developing (see Table 15). On the basis of what we know about the development of chromosomal abnormalities, it is possible that the fault in disjunction, which leads to the extra chromosome, could occur in oögenesis, spermatogenesis, or both. For this reason the relationship to paternal age becomes very important. It is extremely difficult to get data which separate paternal and maternal age.

Penrose (1933) tabulated 150 sibships each containing one or more mongoloids, a correlation of maternal age and the incidence of mongolism (+0.36), and of paternal age and incidence of mongolism (+0.29). The correlation between maternal and paternal age was —0.83. This made it possible to compute a par-

[4] Over a decade ago Tredgold (1947) was able to reason: ". . . Further investigation of cases, particularly of cases of twins, one of whom was a mongol and the other normal, has caused me to think that the abnormality is inherent in the germ and that mongolism is probably the result of some change having been produced in the ovum before its fertilization."

tial correlation between paternal age and the incidence of mongolism for constant maternal age which was —0.01 ± 0.04, ". . . which is as near to zero as could be wished. Hence it may be concluded that paternal age has no real effect."

It is quite clear from the epidemiological evidence that higher parity which had been considered a possible explanation of the mothers' higher ages is not present. Record and Smith (1955) have shown that primogeniture is unusually common among mongoloids born to mothers of each age group.

Experimental non-disjunction of chromosomes has been produced by radiation, colchicine, and other chemicals. Gentry's study (Gentry, Parkhurst, and Bulin, 1959) on congenital malformations shows a number of congenital malformations associated with conditions he presumed to be related to the intensity of background radiation. Mongolism was not among these and does not show geographical variation with some of the other congenital malformations. But the data do not show directly that the different townships had different background radiations, nor was Gentry able to take account of migratory patterns of people who gave birth to children in these towns.

This problem could be approached by studying the frequency of mongolism in children of X-ray specialists and technicians and industrial workers exposed to radiation hazards. This would make it possible to evaluate both the question of whether the error in disjunction can occur in spermatogenesis and the question of whether exposure to radiation in either men or women leads to an increased risk of mongolism in their children. These data have not yet been accumulated.

In interpreting epidemiological data about the causes of non-disjunction leading to mongolism, one must remember that our present knowledge, regarding the time at which ova are formed in the life of the maternal organism is not entirely adequate.

Anatomical and embryological evidence has not been sufficiently precise to decide between two currently held theories. One view is that oögenesis goes on throughout the period of ovulation and that each ovum is formed a short time before ovulation. The other view is that all ova are formed during fetal life or during early infancy and that early in life each female infant has in her ovaries all the ova which will be ovulated (Arey, 1954). If the extra chromosome responsible for mongolism is formed during oögenesis, these two views would lead to two different expectations regarding the distribution of mongoloid children. If the agent responsible acts during the fetal life of the mother, then we would investigate suspected agents in terms of the mother's birthplace and time. If the agent is a factor which acts over a long period of time and is distributed unevenly geographically, we would expect that all of the women born in one area would be equally exposed. On this ground, it would be reasonable to expect a high incidence of mongoloid births among the sisters of the mothers of mongoloids. If, on the other hand, the agent affecting oögenesis is acting a few weeks before ovulation, then we would expect the distribution of mongoloid births to be clustered in certain places and at certain times, and such clustering would yield clues as to the nature of the agent. At present one cannot completely exclude either of these alternatives. While we know from laboratory observations that chromosome tripling can occur as a result of non-disjunction during the meiotic division, this does not prove that no other mechanism for tripling occurs. It is not possible to be sure that tripling does not occur before or after disjunction.

It is possible that the agent may enter the maternal organism some time before it acts on the egg. Thus, if various forms of background radiation are considered, it is possible to imagine that strontium-90, for instance, might be deposited in the bones throughout the life of the maternal organism and that this increasing load of strontium-90 would itself be the source of the radiations which produce non-disjunction at the time of oögenesis. Such an accumulation of the source of the agent throughout the mother's life would fit the facts regarding the rising risk of a mongoloid birth with maternal age. Similarly, hypotheses regarding gradual changes in the structure of the endometrium resulting from repeated exposure to damaging agents (or simply from the repeated changes of the menstrual cycle) would fit the observed epidemiological facts. Another type of agent which could act this way is the accumulation of small doses of toxic substances which are not excreted and which reach higher and higher levels through the life of the organism. Possibly the mother herself produces the agent, and the ability of the maternal organism to produce it may grow with the years. Immune bodies formed in response to some environmental stimulus, if the agent, would have more chance of being formed in older than in younger women.

In addition to the other types of change which can occur and incorporate the agent in the mother's organism, the possibility of low-grade infection with a virus not otherwise actively pathogenic should be considered.[5] Ingalls and Phil-

[5] Studies in Victoria, Australia, published since the preparation of this chapter have advanced evidence that the number of live mongoloid children per thousand live births (adjusted for maternal age) is (1) higher in cities than in rural areas, (2) lower in the winter than in the summer, and (3) rises periodically about every five years (the urban rises preceding rural rises by about one year). (R. D. Collman and A. Stoller, Notes on the Epidemiology of Mongolism in Victoria, Australia, from 1942 to 1957.) These data strongly suggest that variations in the proportion of live births diagnosed as mongoloids are affected by one or more infectious diseases. As the data have not been related to variations in

brook (1957) have reported that rheumatic heart disease is more common in women who have mongoloid children than in other mothers. This is a clue which could readily be pursued by epidemiological methods.

Another type of phenomenon may be involved in the development of mongolism. Smith and Record's (1955) finding of an excess of first-borns among mongoloid children born to mothers under forty and other observations suggesting a period of relative sterility prior to the birth of a mongoloid child suggest that perhaps this is a particular chromosomal abnormality which is produced by the same mechanism as are other chromosomal abnormalities, some of which are lethal to the egg or very young fetus. The fact that some mongoloid individuals have been known to have more than one chromosomal abnormality lends support to this view. Hence we may find that mongolism, Turner's syndrome, Trisomy-17, Trisomy 13–15, Klinefelter's syndrome, and leukemia are related epidemiologically (*Lancet*, 1961; Lubs, Koenig, and Brandt, 1961). This possibility points to the need for studies of fertility in relation to mongolism and studies of mongolism in conjunction with other chromosomal abnormalities.

It has also been suggested (Penrose, 1949) that antibodies might be formed in response to fetal tissue and be directly destructive, but this suggestion is no longer relevant to mongolism, since the time of action must be before the onset of embryonic development.

However, if it is assumed that the trisomy has occurred prior to the mother's birth, different types of mechanisms would be needed to produce the higher

incidence in pregnancies occurring in older women. If this possibility is to be considered at all, it requires that some agent acts during the mother's fetal development and leads to tripling of a chromosome in some of the ova laid down at that time.[6]

Obviously, testing each theory with epidemiological data requires a different kind of data. We now need to know where both the child and the mother were born and about the mother's pregnancy experiences, her use of medicines, exposure to poisons and radiation, and infections. We would like to know whether first-cousin pairs of mongoloids are more frequent through the mothers' being sisters than through a mother and father being siblings. Since half the mothers of mongoloids were born more than thirty years before the birth of their children, the gathering of such data is difficult. But it is not impossible.

The data from which we conclude that maternal age is an important factor were gathered relatively recently within the lifetime of people still living, and all subjects come from technically advanced communities. Perhaps the inference regarding maternal age is false, and the apparent pattern is observed because the older mothers of any series went through their early development in earlier historical decades. It might be due to an

---

[6] The uncertainties regarding the time of mammalian oögenesis are mixed with uncertainties regarding the predecessor cells of mature ova. One view is that they derive from the primordial cells, and the other from the germinal epithelium. There does not appear to be an adequate basis for saying that either is impossible. Non-disjunction could be relatively common in ova derived from primordial cells and never occur in those derived from germinal epithelium. A speculation may be offered that the ova from primordial cells ovulate rarely but do so more commonly as the germinal epithelium becomes less active toward the end of the childbearing period. This speculation is recorded here to show that it is possible to put evidence from epidemiology together with laboratory and clinical evidence and produce new theories: it is not suggested that this theory is well founded.

---

infant mortality rates it is not possible to judge whether infection is increasing the numbers of mongoloids conceived or decreasing the number born live and surviving long enough for diagnosis. The low winter rates suggest that infections are producing the observed variations by causing earlier deaths.

agent which has become less common during the past few decades. This possibility illustrates the use of historical trends in the search for causes. Data on the historical trend in the frequency of mongoloid births would put this theory to the test. But such data are hard to come by because methods of sampling births in a population have changed, and stillbirth and infant-mortality rates have been changing markedly. Mortality rates strongly affect the incidence of identifiable mongoloids. Smith and Record's series give some basis for studying this line

TABLE 15

MONGOLOID BIRTHS PER 1,000 BIRTHS

Maternal Age	Births	Per Thousand Births	(Year of Mothers' Births)
15–19........	3	0.31	(1930)
20–24........	17	0.31	(1925)
25–29........	37	0.52	(1920)
30–34........	44	0.80	(1915)
35–39........	65	2.15	(1910)
40–44........	67	7.27	(1905)
45–49........	8	9.99	(1900)

of reasoning. They studied mongoloid births to women normally resident in Birmingham from 1942 to 1952 and found 241 with sufficient data. So as to be able to study maternal age they obtained detailed information on every 200th birth of the 231,200 births during that period for comparison purposes. This made possible a computation (see Table 15) of the rate of mongoloid births per 1,000 births for each maternal age.

The data draw attention to the marked increase in the incidence of mongoloid births with maternal age. The author has placed in parenthesis the middle year of the fifteen-year period in which the women of each age group were born. So the rates per 1,000 births can be looked at as the rates for women who were born within seven years of the year in the last column. To search for an

agent which had acted during a presumed period of oögenesis during the mother's fetal development is the appropriate way of looking at these data. The inference would be that the incidence of the type of chromosome-tripling which leads to mongolism declined markedly in frequency just before the first World War and had been declining during the decade previously. Such an interpretation assumes that the tripling occurred early in the mother's life and (1) suggests a large number of hitherto unsuspected agents associated in time with the decline of animal power and the introduction of electric lights, (2) suggests that the past causes of mongolism have largely disappeared, and (3) raises the possibility that current cases are remnants of an agent which had largely disappeared by the time of the first World War.

This speculative line of reasoning is spelled out here, not because of the strength of the evidence for pursuing it, but because of the weakness of the evidence for rejecting it.[7] A relationship to age was observed earlier but not examined so thoroughly. Smith and Record's data could be reorganized to test this rather farfetched theory. Earlier clinical literature published before 1850 could be searched to see if this marked syndrome had been described by earlier clinicians.

INFECTIONS, INJURIES, POISONING, AND MALNUTRITION

A detailed consideration of research regarding these causes of mental retardation would require an enormous exten-

---

[7] If solid evidence that mothers of mongoloid children had experienced more radiation than other mothers were available this line of reasoning would be ruled out. The best attempt found to settle this issue is indecisive (Uchida et al., 1961). The presence of other illnesses in the mother (Rundle et al., 1961) can be used as clues to causes acting on the older mother's ovaries or as clues for common causes acting during mother's fetal development (Oster, 1953).

sion of this chapter. No attempt is made to do so because the masterly review by MacMahon and Sowa (1961) covers more ground thoroughly than could have been compressed here and with many useful suggestions. It gives such a wealth of citations of epidemiological evidence regarding the causes of mental retardation and so many examples of well-founded epidemiological reasoning that the best service the author can do the reader of this chapter is to refer him to it.

SUMMARY AND CONCLUSIONS

This brief excursion through the large and scattered literature on the epidemiology of mental retardation has tried to point out some of the major landmarks, to give a detailed description of some of the structures to be encountered, and to provide the reader with a general orientation to the field. Certain areas have been bypassed, but they are described in other chapters of this book and in MacMahon and Sowa's recent review (1961).

While epidemiological data can be put to several different uses, as illustrated in different sections of this chapter, the way in which data are gathered and organized by an investigator depends largely on the use to which he intends to put them. A recurring theme in this chapter has been that data from well-conducted studies can frequently be used to throw light on questions which the investigator did not have in mind, sometimes because his interests were different and sometimes because new knowledge acquired later makes one wish to set different questions for the data. For this reason it is useful to have the basic data of studies published so they can be used for additional purposes. Publishers of technical journals and books need to be apprised of this fact.

It has probably occurred to the reader at several points that investigators could have pursued their data further or could have gathered supplementary data to elucidate the meaning of findings they reported. This is true. But the practicalities of field research rarely leave the investigator in contact with the sources of the data by the time he has finished his analysis and seen the need for more information. One reason for this is that so many studies are conceived of as one-time undertakings rather than as steps in a sequence of investigations. Another is that the financiers of studies rarely allow enough time either for the preparation and planning of an investigation or for its analysis. A third is that when the data-collection phase of a study is over, all sorts of professional pressures and career needs inundate the investigator, and he is rarely able to remain in the position from which he started the investigation unless he is willing to forego promotions for several years. Administrators and financiers of research should be apprised of these facts.

Two approaches to these problems have gained momentum in recent years. One is the development of mental disorder registers on an ongoing basis which seek to produce files of known cases of certain types of disorder in defined populations, usually political jurisdictions. Several such registers in the field of psychiatry have been started in the United States, and if these can begin to include the various forms of mental retardation they can form a stable base from which specific studies of specific problems can be launched in the selected population. The other approach is that of the National Health Survey now being conducted on a continuing basis by the Public Health Service. This survey periodically reviews the health problems of samples of the population of the United States. It has a system for drawing samples of households on a national basis, and waves of interviews are conducted. Before it can be of substantial help in studying mental disorders, however, it will be necessary for it to extend its sampling procedures to include people who do not live in the survey's concept of a human household, in particular those living in hospitals, state schools, and prisons and jails. It will also have to develop techniques for identifying people with intellectual handicaps or some of the disorders which produce mental retardation.

Despite these two new developments in the organization of epidemiological research, the important progress will continue to be made by investigators pursuing problems on an *ad hoc* basis, generally unaware that someone someday will label their work "epidemiological."

REFERENCES

ALLEN, G., and KALLMAN, F. J. 1957. Mongolism in twin sibships. *Acta Genet. (Basel)*, **7**:385–94.

AMERICAN SOCIETY OF HUMAN GENETICS. March, 1960. Symposium on chromosome abnormalities. *Amer. J. Hum. Genet.*

ANASTASI, A. 1957. *Psychological Testing*. 5th ed.; New York: Macmillan.

AREY, L. B. 1954. *Developmental Anatomy*. 6th ed.; Philadelphia: W. B. Saunders.

BENDA, C. 1960. *The Child with Mongolism*. New York: Grune & Stratton.

BÖÖK, J. A. 1953a. A genetic and neuropsychiatric investigation of a North-Swedish population with special regard to schizophrenia and mental deficiency. Part I. *Acta Gent. (Basel)*, **4**:1–100.

———. 1953b. A genetic and neuropsychiatric investigation of a North-Swedish population with special regard to schizophrenia and mental deficiency. Part II. Mental deficiency and convulsive disorders. *Ibid.*, pp. 345–414.

BÖÖK, J. A., FRACCARO, M., and LINDSTEN, J. 1953. Cytogenetical observations in mongolism. *Acta Paediat.*, **48**:453–68.

BÖÖK, J. A., and REED, S. C. 1950. Empiric risk figures in mongolism. (*J.A.M.A.*, **143**: 730–32.

BREG, W. R., MILLER, O. J., and SCHMICKEL, R. D. 1962. Chromosomal translocations in patients with mongolism and in their normal relatives. *New Engl. J. Med.*, **286**: 845.

BREMER, J. 1951. A social psychiatric inves-

tigation of a small community in northern Norway. *Acta Psychiat. Scand.* Suppl. 62. Pp. 163.

BURT, SIR C. 1955. *The Subnormal Mind*. Heath Clark Lectures of 1933. 3d ed.; New York: Oxford University Press.

ESSEN-MÖLLER, E. 1956. Individual traits and morbidity in a Swedish rural population. *Acta Psychiat. Scand.*, Suppl. 100. Pp. 161.

FROST, W. H. 1936. Introduction to "Snow on Cholera." New York: Commonwealth Fund.

GENTRY, J. T., PARKHURST, E., and BULIN, G. V., JR. 1959. An epidemiological study of congenital malformations in New York State. *Amer. J. Pub. Health*, **49**:479.

GORDON, J. 1952. The twentieth century—yesterday, today, and tomorrow (1920——). *In:* F. H. TOP (ed.), *The History of American Epidemiology*, chap. v, pp. 114–67. St. Louis: C. V. Mosby.

GREENWOOD, M. 1935. *Epidemic and Crowd Diseases*. London: Williams & Norgate.

GREGG, N. M. 1941; 1944. *Trans. Opthalmol. Soc. Australia*. **3**:35–46; **4**:119–31.

GROUP FOR THE ADVANCEMENT OF PSYCHIATRY. 1961. *Problems of Estimating Changes in Frequency of Mental Disorders*. New York: Group for the Advancement of Psychiatry.

HALPERIN, S. L. 1945. A clinico-genetic study of mental defect. *Amer. J. Ment. Defic.*, **50**:8–26.

HILL, A. B., DOLL, R., GALLOWAY, T. McL., and HUGHES, J. P. W. 1958. Virus disease in pregnancy and congenital defects. *Brit. J. Prev. Soc. Med.*, **12**:1–7.

INGALLS, T. H., and PHILBROOK, R. 1957. Mothers of mongoloid babies: a retrospective appraisal of their health during pregnancy. *Amer. J. Obstet. Gynec.*, **74**: 572–81.

KANNER, L. 1949. *A Miniature Textbook of Feeblemindedness*. ("Child Care Monograph," No. 1.) New York: Child Care Publications.

KAWI, A. A., and PASAMANICK, B. 1958. Association of factors with reading disorders in childhood. *J.A.M.A.*, **166**:420.

KENNEDY, R. J. R. 1948. *The Social Adjustment of Morons in a Connecticut City*. Hartford, Conn.: Mansfield, Southbury Training Schools.

KIRMAN, B. H. 1955. Rubella as a cause of mental deficiency. *Lancet,* **2:**1113–15.

Lancet Editorial: Complicating the chromosomal abnormalities. *Lancet,* 1961, 31–32.

LEMKAU, P., TIETZE, C., COOPER, M. 1941; 1942. Mental-hygiene problems in an urban district. *Ment. Hyg.,* **25:**624–46; **26:**100–119, 275–88.

LEWIS, E. O. 1929. *Report on an Investigation into the Incidence of Mental Deficiency in Six Areas, 1925–1927.* (Part IV of Report of the Mental Deficiency Committee, being a Joint Committee of the Board of Education and Board of Control.) London: H.M. Stationery Office.

LILIENFELD, A. M. 1957. Epidemiological methods and inferences in studies of non-infectious diseases. *Pub. Health Rep.,* **72:** 51–60.

LILIENFELD, A. M., and PARKHURST, E. 1951. A study of the association of factors of pregnancy and parturition with the development of cerebral palsy: preliminary report. *Amer. J. Hyg.,* **53:**262–82.

LILIENFELD, A. M., and PASAMANICK, B. 1954. Association of maternal and fetal factors with the development of epilepsy: abnormalities in the prenatal and paranatal periods. *J.A.M.A.,* **155:**719–24.

LIN, T. 1953. Study of the incidence of mental disorders in Chinese and other cultures. *Psychiatry,* **16:**313–36.

LUBS, H. A., KOENIG, E. Y., and BRANDT, I. K. 1961. Trisomy 13–15: a clinical syndrome. *Lancet,* 1001.

MACMAHON, B., PUGH, T. F., and IPSEN, J. 1960. *Epidemiologic Methods.* Boston, Mass.: Little, Brown.

MACMAHON, B., and SOWA, J. M. 1961. Physical damage to the fetus. The conference on causes of mental disorders: a review of epidemiological knowledge, 1959. *Milbank Memorial Fund Quarterly,* **39:** 14–73.

MASLAND, R. L., SARASON, S. B., and GLADWIN, T. 1958. *Mental Subnormality.* New York: Basic Books.

MORRIS, J. N. 1955. The uses of epidemiology. *Brit. Med. J.,* **2:**395–401.

———. 1957. *The Uses of Epidemiology.* Baltimore: Williams & Wilkins.

MULLEN, F. A., and NEE, M. M. 1952. Distribution of mental retardation in an urban school population. *Amer. J. Ment. Defic.,* **56:**777–90.

NEW YORK STATE DEPARTMENT OF MENTAL HYGIENE. 1958. *Sixty-ninth Annual Report for the Year Ended March 31, 1957.* (Legislative Document, No. 104.) Albany.

———. 1960. *Seventieth Annual Report for the Year Ended March 31, 1958.* (Legislative Document, No. 118.) Albany.

NEW YORK STATE DEPARTMENT OF MENTAL HYGIENE, MENTAL HEALTH RESEARCH UNIT. 1955. A special census of suspected referred mental retardation, Onondaga County, New York. *In: Technical Report of the Mental Health Research Unit.* Syracuse University Press.

OSTER, J. 1953. *Mongolism.* Copenhagen: Danish Science Press.

PASAMANICK, B. 1952. Patterns of research in mental hygiene. *Psychiat. Quart.,* **26:** 577–89.

PASAMANICK, B., and KAWI, A. A. 1956. Study of the association of prenatal and paranatal factors with the development of tics in children. *J. Pediat.,* **48:**596–601.

PASAMANICK, B., and KNOBLOCH, H. 1960. Brain damage and reproductive casualty. *Am. J. Orthopsychiat.,* **30:**298–305.

PASAMANICK, B., and LILIENFELD, A. M. 1955. Maternal and fetal factors in the development of epilepsy. II: Relationship to some clinical features of epilepsy. *Neurology,* 77–83.

PENROSE, L. S. 1933. The relative effects of paternal age in mongolism. *J. Genet.,* **27:**219.

———. 1949. *The Biology of Mental Defect.* London: Sidgwick & Jackson.

RECORD, R. G., and SMITH, A. 1955. Incidence, mortality, and sex distribution of mongoloid defectives. *Brit. J. Prev. Soc. Med.,* **9:**10–15.

REID, D. D. 1960. Epidemiological methods in the study of mental disorders. Geneva: World Health Organization.

ROWLEY, J. D. 1962. A review of recent studies of chromosomes in mongolism. *Amer. J. Ment. Defic.,* 529–32.

RUNDLE, A., COPPEN, A., and COWIE, V. 1961. Steroid excretion in mothers of mongols. *Lancet,* 846.

SCOTTISH COUNCIL FOR RESEARCH IN EDUCATION. 1949. *The Trend of Scottish Intelligence.* London: University of London Press.

———. 1953. *Social Implications of the 1947*

Scottish Mental Survey. London: University of London Press.

SIGERIST, H. 1945. *Civilization and Disease*. Ithaca: Cornell University Press.

SMITH, A., and RECORD, R. G. 1955. Maternal age and birth rank in the aetiology of mongolism. *Brit. J. Prev. Soc. Med.*, **9**:51–55.

STEVENSON, G. S. 1956. *In: New Directions for Mentally Retarded Children*. New York: The Josiah Macy, Jr., Foundation.

TIZARD, J. 1953. The prevalence of mental subnormality. *Bulletin of the World Health Organization*, **9**:423–39.

TREDGOLD, A. F. 1947. *A Textbook of Mental Deficiency*. 7th ed.; Baltimore: Williams & Wilkins.

UCHIDA, I. A., and CURTIS, E. J. 1961. A possible association between maternal radiation and mongolism. *Lancet*, 848.

WECHSLER, D. 1939. *The Measurement of Adult Intelligence*. Baltimore: Williams & Wilkins.

WEINBERG, W. 1927. Mathematische Grundlage der Probandenmethode. *Z. indukt. Abstamm. u. Vererbgsl*, 48.

WOLFSON, I. N. 1956. Follow-up studies of 92 male and 131 female patients who were discharged from the Newark State School in 1946. *Amer. J. Ment. Defic.*, **61**:224–38.

BIOCHEMICAL AND CLINICAL CORRELATIONS

Harry A. Waisman and Theo Gerritsen

In the last fifteen years of the nineteenth century those scientific reports that were concerned with an understanding of the workings of the brain were necessarily general in nature. The gross abnormalities in brain structure observed from birth or altered by overwhelming infection, hemorrhage, or tumorous growths were the substance of the early descriptive reports. Soon after, however, the investigators dealt not only with the gross anatomy but with changes in specific histology, physiology, and clinical pathology of the brain. The stirrings of biochemistry in the early part of the twentieth century alerted several investigators, first, to analyze parts of the central nervous system for organic substances then, later, to define certain chemical changes due to diseases of the central nervous system. When during the following years biochemical methods and techniques became more elegant, the stage was set for an intensive study of the concepts first proposed in 1908 by Garrod (1909a), which he aptly named "inborn errors of metabolism," i.e., that the brain could be involved or affected by biochemical aberrations. Because diseases of the central nervous system were generally thought to be based on gross congenital structural changes or brought about by external influences, Garrod's suggestion of a metabolic error was accepted with reluctance and not without some skepticism. Similarly, the changes in the brain which caused decreased mental ability were not known, and clinical descriptions of retardation were not adequately classified.

Mental retardation was first thought to be either low-grade "amentia" or high-grade "amentia" and was first carefully described in 1914 by Bolton. The fact that patients with amentia were thought to suffer "from deficient neuronic development" implied an anatomic deficiency or maldevelopment. Knowledge of the significance of chemical influence on normal brain metabolism was to come later. The finding by Folling in 1934 of phenylpyruvic acid excretion in some severely mentally retarded children first focused attention on the probability that a distinct clinical entity could be associated with a biochemical abnormality. Several years later interest in this original observation was re-awakened by Jervis (1937), so that today we have more knowledge of the abnormal biochemistry in this disease as well as more information on its clinical pattern.

It is a truism that we are at present on the threshold of a new phase in biochemical studies of the brain regarding causation of mental retardation. It is likely that within the next few years more and more biochemical knowledge will help explain many of those diseases associated with mental retardation.

The science of genetics also progressed concurrently with the advance of biochemistry, so that a distinct relationship between the two sciences has now been firmly established. Many of the nearly ninety diseases due to inborn errors are transmitted by means of an hereditable trait. This implies a defect in some gene which controls a certain enzyme system necessary for the normal function of a body tissue. Thus, the intimate relationship between genes and enzymes underlines the significance of biochemistry and genetics in those diseases which are associated with mental deficiency.

Investigators of brain chemistry owe a debt to a practitioner of medicine, Thudichum, who, despite his daily efforts in dealing with the sick, found time to pursue what turned out to be the beginnings of brain biochemistry (Page, 1937). Thudichum has today come into his own, since he has now deservedly been hailed as the father of brain chemistry. He pursued his work in his private laboratory during the years 1865–85 (Thudichum, 1884) and with his co-workers isolated complex compounds from brain which we still consider as having formidable chemical structures. These include cephalin, kerasin, phrenosine, sphingomyelin, and other substances. As science progressed and as chemistry and medicine were becoming more closely allied, the observations by Thudichum were furthered by numerous chemists interested in brain metabolism. With the aid of finer techniques of biochemical measurement and using the instrumentation of the present day, nerve cells and their constituent parts are yielding information not known heretofore (Barcroft, 1938). Finer microscopic evaluation by means of better staining procedures has provided increasing information on smaller structures of the cell. The electron microscope has now extended the horizons so that the identification of submicroscopic particles within cells is possible and may further our knowledge of those particles which play an active role in the many biochemical functions of the brain. Lumsden (1959), in an entertaining and concise lecture, pointed out the correlation that can be made between biochem-

ical knowledge and subcellular particles photographed with an electron beam.

Biochemical research in the metabolism of the individual nerve cell has been the basis for much progress, but more effort is still required to delineate the role of nutrients for the nerve cell and their biochemical function in enzymes and their substrates. As a pathologist, Lumsden felt that placing nerve tissue in a Warburg flask was not an appropriate experiment to divulge what was going on within the nerve cell. In the few years since Lumsden made the statement that "biochemistry singularly lacks the precision that we need for many problems at the cell level," the combination of biochemistry and the electron microscope may, indeed, have begun to help in the understanding of brain function as well as of some aspects of mental retardation.

The nerve cell photographed by the electron microscope can give some clues as to the detailed anatomy of the cell, and, by studying the various cell fractions biochemically, it should be possible to obtain important data. The best example of such subcellular structures is the mitochondria obtained from either heart or brain cells. These cigar-like filaments surrounded by membrane and containing a system of ridges or cristae give adequate evidence that some of the enzymes of the cell that take part in oxidative and energy-yielding reactions, such as the dehydrogenases, phosphorylases, succinic oxidases, and cytochrome oxidases, may actually be located in this double-layer canal-like system. From the work by Akert, Hable, Wang, and Waisman (1961) we know that the administration of high amounts of phenylalanine can apparently disturb the metabolism of the cell and its contents sufficiently to make the cristae disappear. What remains to be done now is to determine whether this disappearance can be correlated with changes in the enzyme activity of these cell constituents.

The existence of the so-called "blood-brain barrier" has provided a challenging area of research in the form of efforts to obtain evidence for what has been designated as the "discriminatory activity of the brain." Apparently substances can pass out of the blood into the brain cells by means of active transport, and the properties of the membrane account for the selective activity of the blood-brain barrier. This action is a reflection of specific structural components in the membrane. Today, too, we know that the neuroglial cells have an active and vital function, and the old idea, which assumed that these were simply cement-like structures between cells, is now untenable. It is quite clear from a number of reports that the glial cell is able to transfer the metabolic products in and out of other brain cells, thus influencing the latter's metabolism and function.

An important aspect of the biochemistry of the newborn brain is the sequence of chemical alterations which occur during maturation and which greatly change the brain's composition. This means that some chemical compounds seen in the adult brain do not come to full maturation until the brain is matured. This is, in part, accounted for by the deposition of myelin around nerve sheaths as the brain grows and as the brain function matures. The rather close correlation that has been found in the past between increasing motor accomplishments in the child with increasing myelinization of the nerve fiber is now reasonably well established.

CHEMISTRY AND METABOLIC PATHWAYS IN NORMAL BRAIN

The activity of the central nervous system depends ultimately upon its endogenous energy supply. The brain normally derives its energy from oxidative processes. In the normal adult man, the oxygen consumption of the brain is 3.5 ml/100 gm/min which is among the highest of all tissues in the body.

Reduction in cerebral oxygen consumption occurs in patients with hepatic coma, brain damage and edema, hypoglycemia, and dementia, during Pentothal anesthesia, but not in schizophrenia. The degree of impairment of "consciousness" goes parallel with the decrease in oxygen consumption. In early stages of brain development, glycolysis plays an important role as an energy producing system. After birth, respiration begins and subsequently becomes the major source of energy for the brain.

A. CARBOHYDRATES

Quastel and Wheatly showed in 1932 that of all sugars, glucose, fructose, and mannose were the best substrates for brain respiration; galactose had a small effect, but other sugars, including all pentoses, were inert (see also Quastel, 1961). In vivo, under normal conditions, glucose is almost completely the only substrate for brain respiration (Himwich, 1951). The normal human adult brain uses about 5 mg/100 gm brain/minute (Kety, 1957). Much of this (85 per cent) is fully oxidized, but a small variable fraction is converted into lactate and pyruvate ions and amino acid precursors. There is no evidence that a normally functioning brain removes substances from the blood stream, other than glucose, that contribute to the energy supply. A decrease in blood glucose level below a certain critical concentration causes disturbances in cerebral function and mental behavior. Intravenous injection of glucose can promptly restore mental function in insulin coma of short duration, but after prolonged hypoglycemic coma the damage done to the brain is partly irreversible, and the oxygen consumption will remain lower than normal. Many substances have been tested for their capacities to restore consciousness in hypoglycemic states. The only ones that were found to be effective were glutamate, arginine, glycine, and succinate (Weil-Malherbe and Bone, 1952), but it is most likely that their effectiveness is related to their ability to contribute to the glucose pool via transamination.

1. *Monosaccharides.*—The major energy for the brain is obtained from the oxidation of glucose. This takes place via the formation of pyruvate, which in turn can enter the tricarboxylic acid cycle. Amino acids can transfer their α-amino groups to pyruvate and to α-ketoglutarate in order to form alanine and glutamic acid. These, in turn, may be converted to 3 carbon residues which can be used for energy. The alternative pathway of

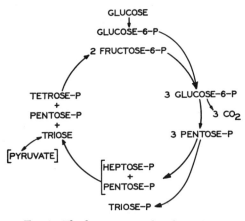

FIG. 1.—The hexose-monophosphate shunt

glucose oxidation is through the so-called "pentose-shunt" or "hexosemonophosphate-shunt" (Scott and Cohen, 1951; Horecker, 1953). This pathway involves a heptose and a series of pentoses and the over-all reaction may be given as:

(e.g., inhibition of glucose oxidation) it may be of great importance.

Brain has a high rate of anaerobic glycolysis, following the Embden-Meyerhof scheme. This process yields considerably less energy than the complete oxidation of one molecule of glucose but is of importance in the brain of the newborn. There is, however, some evidence that it plays a role in the regulation of the pH, and this could have an effect on the efficiency of the blood-brain barrier.

2. *Mucopolysaccharides and mucoids.* —On chemical analysis of these substances the following products are detected: glucosamine and galactosamine, hexuronic acid, galactose, mannose and fucose, sialic acid, hyaluronic acid, and chondroitin sulfate. The hexosamine content of fresh brain is about 0.1 per cent; more than half of this is bound in the mucopolysaccharide and mucoid fraction, which corresponds to a content of 0.2 per cent of this fraction in wet brain. More glucosamine is found than galactosamine. Although very little is known about the actual function of the mucopolysaccharides in the body, it is presumed that they have important functions in the interstitial and interglial spaces, where it is known that compounds are found with cation-exchanging and water-binding properties (Brante, 1958).

B. LIPIDS

The total lipid content of the brain is 10 per cent of wet weight (or 50 per cent

$$\text{Glucose-6-P} + 6\text{TPN}^* \rightarrow \text{triose-P} + 3CO_2 + 6\text{TPNH}_2\dagger$$

* Triphosphonucleotide.   † Reduced triphosphonucleotide.

A simplified scheme (Coxon, 1957) is given in Figure 1. The amount of TPN in the brain is less than 10 per cent of the amount of DPN* (Glock and McLean, 1953). Therefore the "shunt" here described is probably less active in this tissue, but under certain circumstances

* Diphosphonucleotide.

of the dry weight). Gray matter contains 5–6 per cent, and white matter 16–22 per cent lipids. It is now generally accepted that most of the energy required by the brain is derived from carbohydrate, mainly glucose. However, Geiger, Yamasaki, and Lyons (1955) have demonstrated that isolated cat brain can survive and maintain its excitability in the absence of glucose for over an hour by using part of its structural components, lipids and nucleotides.

1. *Cholesterol.*—Kabara and Okita (1961) demonstrated with labeled precursors that active brain cholesterol biogenesis occurs in nine- to sixteen week-old mice injected intraperitoneally with labeled acetate, leucine, glucose, and mevalonate. It is thus possible that during the period of growth cholesterol is formed *in situ* in brain tissue and does not exchange with other parts of the body (Waelsch *et al.*, 1940).

2. *Glycerophosphatides.*—As far as is known up to now, there exist in the brain at least five types of glycerophosphatides: (1) lecithin or phosphatidyl-choline, (2) colamine-cephalin or phosphatidyl-ethanolamine, (3) serine-cephalin or phosphatidyl-serine, (4) phosphoinositides, and (5) the plasmalogens or acetalphosphatides. Phosphatidyl-choline, -ethanolamine and -serine [general formula (I)] have all been isolated in pure form from brain material.

$$CH_2—O—CO—R'$$
$$CH—O—CO—R''$$
$$CH_2—O—PO_2—O"N"$$

R = Fatty acid residue

$$"N" = —CH_2—CH_2—NH_2$$
$$—CH_2—CH_2—N^+(CH_3)_3$$
$$—CH_2—CH(NH_2)—COOH$$

(I)

For a complete survey of the composition of these interesting compounds refer to Klenk (1958).

The occurrence of inositol as a constituent of a phosphatide fraction from cephalin was first demonstrated in 1942 (Folch and Wooley). Although there is some indication that a monophosphoinositide has been obtained from brain lipid extracts, most work has been done on diphosphoinositides [probable formula (II)].

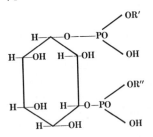

R = Monoglyceride

(II)

Its existence in brain extracts was demonstrated by chromatography on alumina and silicic acid columns (Hanahan *et al.*, 1957). Isolation of triphosphoinositide from ox brain was recently reported and its structure confirmed (Dawson and Dittmer, 1961; Dittmer and Dawson, 1961).

It is well established now that the plasmalogens are phosphoglycerides, containing a fatty acid residue, an aldehydogenic unit (or vinyl ether), and glycerophosphoethanolamine or -choline (Klenk, 1958; Hanahan, 1960). The "classic" hemiacetal formula has been replaced by the following most likely structure (Rapport *et al.*, 1957; Debuch, 1959) [formula (III)].

$$CH_2—O—CH=CH_2—R'$$
$$CH—O—CO—R$$
$$CH_2—O—PO_2—"N"$$

R = Fatty acid residue

$$"N" = —CH_2—CH_2—NH_2$$
$$—CH_2—CH_2—N^+(CH_3)_3$$

(III)

3. *Sphingolipids.*—Sphingolipids are lipids containing the long-chain amino alcohol sphingosine [formula (IV)].

Sulfatides, or cerebroside sulfuric esters, can be isolated from brain. The sulfate is esterified through the primary OH

$$CH_3-(CH_2)_{12}-CH=CH-\overset{(2)}{CH}-\overset{(1)}{CH}-CH_2OH$$

$$\underset{OH}{\mid} \quad \underset{NH_2}{\mid}$$

(IV)

To this complicated group belong the sphingomyelins, cerebrosides, sulfatides, and mucolipids. The importance of these compounds is due to the fact that they often accumulate in various organs in the lipidoses (see page 317).

The general formula for sphingomyelin isolated from brain is

$$R' \, Sph - P - Ch \,,$$

in which R is stearic, lignoceric, or nervonic acid, Sph is sphingosine, and P-Ch is choline phosphate. The fatty acid is connected to the β-NH$_2$ group, while the choline phosphate esterifies the α-OH group of sphingosine.

Cerebrosides contain sphingosine, a long-chain fatty acid, and a sugar [formula (V)]. The fatty acid, substituted on the α-amino group, is generally lignoceric [CH$_3$ $-(CH_2)_{22}-COOH$] or α-hydroxylignoceric acid, but several other acids such as nervonic and cerebronic acid are also found. Cerebrosides usually contain galactose as the sugar component, but in Gaucher's disease glucose is the main sugar constituent.

group attached to C$_6$ of galactose.

4. *Mucolipids.*—These complex high molecular weight substances—including gangliosides, strandin, and similar compounds have chemical structures which are only partly known. They contain fatty acids, sphingosine, galactose, some glucose, galactosamine, chondrosamine, and neuraminic (Bogoch, 1958), and acetylated neuraminic (sialic) acids. Klenk (1935) isolated these substances from tissues of patients with Niemann-Pick and Tay-Sachs diseases.

5. *"Trypsin resistant protein residue."* —This name is given to a group of highly complex substances whose function is still obscure. They consist of fatty acids, sphingosine, about 25 per cent amino acids, 4.5 per cent P, and 10 per cent inositol (Folch and LeBaron, 1958).

C. AMINO ACIDS

In vivo studies of the metabolic activity of the brain have shown that under normal physiological conditions amino acids or other nitrogenous blood constituents are not actively utilized in the brain (Kety, 1957, p. 221). Even under

R′ = fatty acid residue

(V)

conditions of great loss of protein from other body tissues, brain proteins, mainly present in nerve cells and glial cells, remain practically unchanged (Richter, 1958).

The study of the metabolism of free amino acids in the brain has only become possible by the recent development of new methods for their separation and determination. Amino acids in the brain are not only important as building stones for protein molecules but are also necessary for the synthesis of neurohormones. The brain amino acid pool in cat (Tallan *et al.*, 1954) and rat (Schurr *et al.*, 1950) contains practically all essential and nonessential amino acids unlike the cerebrospinal fluid. The essential amino acids have the same concentration in brain and plasma, but threonine and most of the nonessential amino acids have a higher concentration in brain than in plasma.

mate in the brain, since this would involve ammonia formation. Synthesis of glutamine from glutamic acid and ammonia is an endothermic reaction which needs a high energy phosphate such as ATP[*] (Krebs, 1935).

Another source of this amino acid is from the transamination reactions between α-ketoglutarate and an amino acid. Glutamic-oxaloacetic transaminase is very active in the brain, but the equilibrium of the reaction favors the formation of aspartic acid. The unique role of glutamate in brain metabolism is underlined by the finding that it was the only one of thirteen naturally occurring amino acids that could be oxidized in the brain (Weil-Malherbe, 1936). Since no ammonia formation or increase in glutamine could be observed during this oxidation, it was suggested that the reaction starts with a transamination (Strecker, 1957):

$$\frac{\text{glutamate} + \text{oxaloacetate} \rightarrow \text{aspartate} + \alpha\text{-ketoglutarate}}{\alpha\text{-ketoglutarate} + \tfrac{3}{2}\,O_2 \rightarrow \text{oxaloacetate} + CO_2 + H_2O}{\text{glutamate} + \tfrac{3}{2}\,O_2 \rightarrow \text{aspartate} + CO_2 + H_2O} \; .$$

Seventy-five per cent of the free amino acids in the brain are represented by glutamic acid, glutamine, γ-aminobutyric acid and N-acetylaspartic acid, the combined concentration being six times the amount present in plasma.

1. *Glutamine and glutamic acid.*—Wet brain contains 2 per cent total nitrogen, 5 per cent of which is bound in glutamine and glutamic acid (Roberts *et al.*, 1959). The synthesis of cerebral glutamic acid can be increased by glucose via the formation of α-ketoglutarate (Kini and Quastel, 1959). Glutamic dehydrogenase, although relatively ubiquitous in various parts of the brain, does not normally operate in the direction of oxidative deamination but will always favor glutamic acid formation in the presence of ammonia. Since glutamic acid is unable to pass the blood-brain barrier, whereas glutamine does, it seems unlikely that plasma-glutamine is a source of gluta-

In general, the system glutamine-glutamic acid is apparently capable of regulating, directly or indirectly, the levels of ATP and ADP[†] in the brain as well as of several other metabolites such as ammonia, GABA, and the components of the tricarboxylic acid cycle.

2. *Gamma amino butyric acid (GABA).* —Much has been written about GABA and its possible role in synapsis (Elliot *et al.*, 1958). It exists in the interstitial fluids in the brain and depending on its concentration exerts a continuous effect on neuronal activity. Although small amounts are excreted in the urine its highest concentration is found in the brain. It is possible that more significance is attached to GABA because of its high concentration in brain but it may be that other amino acids in much lower

[*] Adenosine triphosphate.

[†] Adenosine diphosphate.

concentrations play an equal or even more important role.

Formation of GABA by decarboxylation of glutamic acid is accomplished by a vitamin B_6 dependent enzyme. Vitamin B_6 deficiency or semicarbazide poisoning can cause a drop of 30 per cent in the GABA concentration of the brain (Roberts and Frankel, 1950). In the ammonia metabolism of the brain GABA plays a role indirectly as shown by (1) its relationship with glutamate, and (2) the transamination reaction

dihydroxyphenylalanine (DOPA.)—These three amino acids are closely related to the synthesis of norepinephrine and epinephrine which takes place mainly in the adrenal medulla and the adrenergic neurones. Phenylalanine and tyrosine are metabolically available in the brain and in many other organs. Decarboxylation of phenylalanine has not been found to take place normally, but formation of tyramine from tyrosine takes place under certain pathological circumstances. Nothing is known, however, about the func-

$$\text{GABA} + \text{arginine} \rightleftarrows \text{ornithine} + \gamma\text{-guanidino-butyrate}$$

(Du Ruisseau *et al.*, 1957; Pisano *et al.*, 1957; Bessman, 1958). The transamination reaction

tion of this amine. Under special circumstances (absence of phenylalanine hydroxylase, as in phenylketonuria),

$$\text{GABA} + a\text{-ketoglutarate} \leftrightarrows \text{glutamate} + \text{succinic semialdehyde}$$

is a shunt in the tricarboxylic acid cycle and makes GABA a substrate in oxidative metabolism (Bessman *et al.*, 1953).

3. *Tryptophan and 5-hydroxytryptophan.*—The concentration of tryptophan in the brain is comparatively high; its decarboxylation product, tryptamine, is present in small amounts, but its function is unknown. Although 5-hydroxytryptamine (serotonin) is present in the brain, the actual presence of 5-hydroxytryptophan has not been established in this organ or in the liver. The brain is unable to hydroxylate tryptophan, but the tryptophan hydroxylation system has been demonstrated recently in rat liver (Freedland *et al.*, 1961a). The concept is that hydroxylation of tryptophan takes place in the liver and that both tryptophan and 5-hydroxytryptophan can pass through the blood-brain barrier into the brain. Decarboxylation of 5-hydroxytryptophan by the decarboxylase takes place in the brain and accounts for the widely distributed quantities of serotonin (see Fig. 4). For a review on tryptophan metabolism, see Udenfriend (1958).

4. *Phenylalanine, tyrosine, and 3, 4-*

phenylalanine can be metabolized to phenylpyruvic acid, p-hydroxyphenylacetic acid, and p-hydroxyphenyllactic acid, which are found in the urine of these patients. This is discussed later.

Excretion of free DOPA in urine was found recently under abnormal conditions (Gerritsen *et al.*, 1961a). DOPA can be oxidized to melanin, while decarboxylation by the L-DOPA decarboxylase forms dopamine. This enzyme is present in high concentration in many tissues as well as in extracts of adrenergic nerves (Holtz and Westermann, 1956). Except for the role of dopamine in the biosynthetic pathway of the catecholamines, it is not known to have a specific role in the brain. Excess DOPA is metabolized to homovanillic and homoprotocatechuic acids, which are normally found to be present in the urine. In view of the different metabolic pathways in which DOPA plays a role, its excretion in urine under any circumstances is difficult to explain.

5. *Glycine.*—This amino acid can be decomposed in rat brain cortex slices to yield CO_2. The manner in which it is me-

tabolized in the brain is uncertain and the amount is small compared with glutamic acid.

6. *Histidine.*—The brain contains free histidine, and nervous tissue contains varying amounts of histamine (Clouet *et al.*, 1957). This is especially stored in the mast cells and may be released by reserpine. It is thought that the function of histamine in the brain is not concerned with conduction but that its release from the mast cells can act as a line of defense against injury (West, 1957).

7. *Valine, leucine, and isoleucine.*—These branched-chain amino acids pass comparatively freely through the blood-brain barrier. The half-life time of free leucine injected intracisternally in the mouse brain was less than one hour (Lajthe, 1959). Decarboxylation and transamination to form the corresponding keto-acids takes place in different tissues, mainly in the liver. (See under "Maple syrup urine disease," this chap., p. 326)

8. *Amino acids of the urea cycle.*—With the exception of transcarbamylase all enzymes necessary for urea formation are present in the brain (Sporn *et al.*, 1959; Ratner *et al.*, 1960). Ornithine, citrulline, and arginine are present in cat brain (Tallan *et al.*, 1954) and since Walker (1958) found argininosuccinase activity in dog brain, it is inevitable that free argininosuccinic acid is present in brain too. However, little is known about the role of these different amino acids, except a suggestion by Sporn *et al.* (1959) that the ornithine-urea cycle in the brain may play a role in the ammonia detoxification mechanism.

METABOLIC ABNORMALITIES CAUSING MENTAL RETARDATION

Those diseases which cause mental retardation on the basis of a biochemical abnormality can be categorized best under the three large classes of chemical substances described previously as the carbohydrates, the lipids, and the amino acids. Under each group a number of dis-

eases can be listed which vary in their symptomatology but have as their common clinical defect a degree of mental retardation which is apparent to the trained observer.

A. CARBOHYDRATES

The carbohydrate disturbances can be grouped in a number of ways. Hsia (1959) has suggested that these diseases are related to abnormalities in (1) five-carbon sugars, (2) six-carbon sugars, (3) glycogen or polysaccharides, and (4) disturbances in carbohydrate metabolism of red blood cells. Regardless of the manner in which the diseases are classified, it seems quite clear that the normal activity of the enzymes involved in the metabolism of any of these sugars is disturbed to the point where the patient shows typical signs and symptoms. Abnormal excretions of rare carbohydrates have been described by others but have not been associated with mental retardation. This chapter will concern itself only with those diseases in which mental retardation is accompanied by abnormal carbohydrate metabolism.

1. *Galactosemia.*—Hereditary galactose disease is characterized by the inability to convert the galactose part of the lactose molecule to glucose in a normal manner so that it can be properly utilized by the body (Kalckar and Maxwell, 1958). The name "hereditary galactose disease" was first given by Von Reuss in 1908, but it was not until 1935 that the first case was reported in this country (Mason and Turner, 1935). The increasing frequency of such reports today indicates that the disease is characterized by multiple manifestations of varying severity, which present challenges to those physicians involved in the over-all care of children with galactosemia.

The main symptoms, which can be explained by the abnormal biochemistry in these patients, appear by the first or second week. The jaundice which persists far beyond the usual period of so-called physiological jaundice is an indication that the child will soon be in jeopardy. Growth failure, feeding problems, and early cataract formation are accepted as early signs and symptoms. Bleeding, probably as a result of liver damage by the deposition of abnormal carbohydrate, together with the rapid onset of spleno-megaly, hepatomegaly, and ascites are indications of progressive difficulties. The condition occasionally develops slowly so that some of these cases are incorrectly diagnosed. The mental retar-dation becomes apparent as the child

consequently, more infants will survive to adulthood to insure perpetuation of the trait.

The defect in the normal conversion of galactose to glucose lies in the absence of the uridyl-diphospho-galactose trans-ferase enzyme which normally changes galactose to glucose. This change in-volves the transfer of an hydroxyl group from one side of the molecule to another, since the body must metabolize glucose rather than galactose for energy pur-poses. The reactions can be listed as fol-lows:

$$\text{Galactose} + \text{ATP} \xrightarrow{\text{Galactokinase}} \text{Galactose-1-PO}_4 + \text{ADP}$$

$$\text{Galactose-1-PO}_4 + \text{uridyl-di-PO}_4 - \text{glucose} \xrightarrow{\text{Transferase}}$$

$$\text{Glucose-1-PO}_4 + \text{uridyl-di-PO}_4 - \text{galactose} .$$

grows older and remains untreated and undiagnosed.

An early diagnosis made by testing the urine of the infant for galactose is a well-accepted laboratory procedure and should be part of the many diagnostic considerations entertained by any physi-cian who has the responsibility for a child who fails to thrive and develop normally. Reducing substances in the urine, such as glucose or galactose, can be tested for by a number of ways, but paper chromatography appears to be the best procedure to differentiate between the various sugars. Galactosemia is inher-ited as an autosomal recessive trait, and, since the defect has been noted among siblings in half the families reported, the report of an abnormal galactose-tolerance test among parents and relatives of galac-tosemic infants (Holzel and Komrower, 1955) was not unexpected. These work-ers thought that the trait was much more common than originally believed and suggested that the disease will become more widespread with improved treat-ment, since removing the milk and its ac-companying milk sugar from the diet will avoid the biochemical abnormality and,

These enzymes are normally found in liver, brain, and erythrocytes, and the ease of testing for the transferase in the red cells makes the diagnostic procedure comparatively simple. The work of Issel-bacher et al. (1956) showed equal con-centrations of galactokinase in normal and galactosemic individuals, but ab-sence of the transferase in the red blood cells of galactosemic individuals.

The diagnostic tests for galactosemia are now well established and can be used in testing high-risk populations. First, the presence of a reducing sugar in the urine should alert the physician to identify the sugar. This can be done easily, since spe-cial commercial filter-paper sticks, name-ly, Tes-tape[*] and Clinistix,[†] can be used to give a positive reaction only in the presence of glucose. A galactose-contain-ing urine would thus give a positive re-ducing sugar test and be negative for Clinistix. A confirmatory test can also be accomplished by the oral or intravenous galactose-tolerance tests, but is undesira-ble, especially in infant patients with galactosemia, because of the hypoglyce-mia that develops.

[*] Eli Lilly Company.   [†] Ames Company.

The observations by Schwarz *et al.* (1956) that circulating erythrocytes in normal patients metabolize galactose, and that galactosemic cells do not, were the basis for a definitive and accurate diagnostic test. This test takes two days, however, and is based on the accumulation of galactose-1-phosphate in galactosemic red cells. The red cells are incubated with galactose, phosphorylated derivatives are isolated as barium salts, and the sugar phosphates are hydrolyzed so that the free sugars can be separated on paper chromatograms. Using known concentrations of galactose as standards, the galactose in the unknown cells can be estimated.

Another test can be done to quantitatively determine the transferase activity of the red cell. This method by Anderson *et al.* (1957) is the best of all tests because of its specificity and lack of false positives. It can be performed on cord blood shortly after birth, thus avoiding the error introduced by the first milk feeding. The duration of the test is two to three hours in contrast to the two to three days needed for the test based on the accumulation of galactose-1-phosphate.

The treatment of galactosemia by rigid exclusion of galactose from the diet by withholding milk or any milk products is easily accomplished by using a soybean milk substitute. It is quite obvious that the diet should be adequate in protein, vitamins, minerals, and fats. With early diagnosis and treatment, it is possible to reverse the severe physical, mental, and metabolic manifestations.

2. *Fructosuria.*—The recognition that fructose can be excreted in some patients without any clinical symptoms was made seventy years ago. Patients with "essential fructosuria" were known to excrete "sweet urine" following ingestion of fruits. This abnormality was recognized as an inborn error of metabolism by Lasker (1941), who discovered that the error was due to the absence of hepatic fructokinase.

Within the recent past, a second anomaly of fructose intolerance has been described by Froesch *et al.* (1957, 1959) in which ingestion of fructose caused a sharp and prolonged fall in the blood-glucose level, accompanied by all the signs and symptoms of hypoglycemia. When the infants consumed fructose in any form, they failed to thrive, developed poorly, and were mentally retarded. The deficiency in this disease is most likely due to lack of fructose-1-phosphate aldolase, the enzyme which converts fructose-1-phosphate to two 3-carbon fragments. In patients with this type of fructosuria, the glucose tolerance curve is normal. Identification of a reducing sugar in the urine may therefore be essential for proper diagnosis and treatment.

3. *Other carbohydrate abnormalities.* —The other carbohydrate abnormalities seen in patients, such as sucrosuria (Montcrieff and Wilkinson, 1954), xylulosuria, pentosuria, glycogen-storage disease in all of its manifestations, hereditary spherocytosis, and hereditary non-spherocytic hemolytic anemia, produce no symptoms of mental retardation as part of the clinical manifestations of the disease. The description of the abnormal excretion of these sugars can be found in textbooks (Hsia, 1959; Stanbury, Wyngaarden, and Fredrickson, 1960) and will not be included here, since the limited space precludes a full description of these hereditary errors of carbohydrate metabolism.

B. LIPIDS

One of the most promising areas in which to seek a *raison d'être* for an understanding of brain damage and resulting mental retardation is in lipid metabolism, not because fatty substances in the brain are unknown or have not been studied, but because more information is desirable on the intracellular function of those compounds, which are related to metabolism of fat precursors.

The lipids are fatty materials which include such compounds as phospholipids, phosphatidyl-cholines, -serines, and -ethanolamines, phosphosphingosides, glycosphingosides, gangliosides, sulfatides, phosphoropeptides, cholesterol, and various hydrocarbons which are precursors of fatty materials. These lipids are difficult to identify and analyze. They play an important part in the developing brain, and it should be stressed that any abnormality of the central nervous system can involve any one of the entire spectrum of the lipids. A particular clinical disease associated with disturbances in lipid metabolism may take a number of forms.

1. *Sphingolipidoses.*—Perhaps the best-known, but not yet chemically defined, disease of this group is that categorized under the general term "amaurotic familial idiocy." This is a general term applied to several diseases all of which may be related but are reflected in a common disturbance in lipid metabolism. The hereditary pattern has altered with time, since Tay-Sachs disease was earlier believed to be found only in children of Hebrew ancestry, but, as more cases were diagnosed, increasing percentages of non-Jewish patients were identified. The disease is in all likelihood transmitted by a rare recessive gene. Four variations of this disease are now known and are best described under the name of the investigator associated with the disease.

a) Early infantile amaurotic idiocy is familial in nature and was first reported in 1881 by Tay. Later, Sachs (1896), a neurologist, described the autopsy findings and gave the condition the name "amaurotic idiocy." The two names are thus intimately associated with the disease at the present time. The clinical features of the disease are predominantly observed in children below the age of four months. The irritability, lack of

development, and increased sensitivity to sound later progress to a loss of motor power and lack of visual acuity, followed by blindness and, of course, mental retardation. Children with this form of disease seldom survive to the third year of age, and the cause of death is usually respiratory in nature. The visual portion of the eye is affected by a degenerative process which gives the typical "cherry-red spot" in the retina of the eye. The increased deposition of lipid in the nerve cells produces a whitish zone around the red spot, and at this stage pathological observations of the brain reveal a hard and leathery consistency. A special histopathological stain is used to demonstrate droplets of lipid in nerve cells from patients with the disease.

b) Late infantile amaurotic idiocy has the name Bielschowsky-Jansky associated with it and is quite rare. As the name indicates it usually appears after three years of age. It develops more slowly than the infantile variety and besides the symptoms described in the infantile type, children affected with it develop cerebellar signs with ataxia as well as optic atrophy and pigmentation in the retina.

c) Juvenile amaurotic familial idiocy has the euphemious name Spielmeyer-Vogt. Originally described by Batten in 1903, it is clinically similar to Tay-Sachs disease but is characterized by an even later onset and a slower progression than the late infantile amaurotic familial idiocy. It was separated out as an entity by Spielmeyer (1929) and by Vogt (1905) earlier in this century. Although the child has developed normally up to the time of the onset of the disease, muscle rigidity, signs of tremor, paralysis, athetosis, tonic and clonic convulsions, personality changes, loss of emotional control, irritability, and regression in mental ability ultimately appear in these adolescent individuals. Unhappily this diagnosis is not made until late in the disease or at the autopsy table, and unless cases are adequately described and carefully evaluated, it is unlikely that all have been identified.

d) Late juvenile amaurotic familial idiocy carries the name Kufs's disease and is an even rarer juvenile form of the disease, beginning past the teen age and progressing very slowly with appropriate symptoms appearing as even more severe manifestations of those described above.

These four classifications of amaurotic familial idiocy demonstrate that this disease is a continuum, and the occurrence of any individual affliction is at a particular place in the spectrum of the sphingolipidoses.

The biochemistry of the amaurotic familial idiocy group of diseases is now more clear than it was fifty years ago, but more data are necessary to categorize the particular lipid involved in a given disease that is part of an entire disease spectrum. The compounds involved are sphingomyelins which contain sphingosine (see p. 312), and it is interesting to note that Thudichum (1884) first chemically separated this compound in 1874 but understandably did not know its structure. Klenk (1959) found that the neuraminic acid content of gray matter was increased ten to twenty times in infantile amaurotic familial idiocy (1939). It is not unexpected that the decrease in cerebroside and sphingomyelin content of these brains results from the demyelinization which takes place.

Svennerholm and Raal (1961) reported on a case of Tay-Sachs disease in which 90 per cent of the brain gangliosides were of an abnormal type. They were monosialogangliosides containing a large amount of an aminoglycolipid lacking sialic acid, which was different from the corresponding neutral aminoglycolipid from normal brains.

2. *Niemann-Pick disease.*—This disease is relatively rare but can be found in any hospital for mentally deficient children. It is due to accumulation of sphingomyelin in reticuloendothelial and nervous tissue. Thus, one can expect signs and symptoms such as hepatosplenomegaly, poor growth, and many neurologic abnormalities. The typical cherry-red spot observed in the retina is a characteristic sign of the lipid abnormality.

The accumulation of lipid in reticuloendothelial cells together with destruction of ganglion cells and demyelinization in cells of the nervous system are two characteristic pathological findings and can be correlated with the clinical complaints of poor feeding habits, abdominal enlargement, slow weight increase, and poor developmental milestones. Microscopic examination of tissue from a patient with this disease shows large, foam-line cells, engorged with material not stained by the usual stains. Supravital stains are superior for detecting these cells.

The biochemistry of this disease shows mainly a sphingomyelin lipidosis. When Crocker and Farber (1958) analyzed white matter and gray matter separately, they found that the total lipid content of the white matter was less than that of the gray, an exact reversal of the usual finding. There is no doubt that the main change is the increase in sphingomyelin. The lipids in the serum apparently increase, although the sphingomyelin concentration in the serum is normal.

Much of the biochemistry of sphingomyelin is now concerned with its synthesis by enzymes found in cell-free preparations from liver, kidney, spleen, and brain. Many studies are being conducted on the synthesis of phospholipids using radioactively labeled phosphorus (Hanahan, 1960).

The diagnosis of this disease must be made mainly on clinical grounds, remembering the combination of hepatomegaly, splenomegaly, and neurologic signs. The disease is strongly suspected when typical cells are found in the bone marrow or tissue biopsies. If it were possible, the best criterion would be a chemical determination of the increase in sphingomyelin in the tissues. Newer methods are becoming available for the determination of this substance, using lipid phosphorus analyses of tissues.

Unhappily, there is no treatment for this condition at the present time despite the suggestions to use desperate means, ranging from chemotherapeutic agents to X-ray and cortisone. Undoubtedly an unraveling of the chemical mediators of the deposition of the sphingomyelin will provide more definitive therapy. Since this is an inheritable condition, the enzyme defect needs to be more clearly understood.

3. *Gaucher's disease.*—This disease was first described more than eighty years ago by Phillipe Gaucher in Paris, who called attention to the symptoms which are now well accepted as classical for the cerebroside lipidosis. The splenomegaly, hepatomegaly, chronic progressive course, and skin pigmentation with recognizable cells in the spleen are characteristic. As interest in the disease progressed over the years, more and more workers became aware of the lipoidal nature of the substance in the spleen cells. Lieb (1924) should receive the credit for isolating the substance kerasin, a cerebroside, first described by Thudichum fifty years before. In the brain, the cerebroside contains galactose, but when it occurs in the abdominal organs, glucose is substituted for the galactose.

For the diagnosis of Gaucher's disease it is necessary to consider the various age groups. In the period of early infancy, the poor feeding pattern, laryngospasm, spasticity, cachexia, and mental retardation are accompanied by enlargement of the spleen and liver with lymphnode enlargement—all resulting from accumulation of cerebroside in these tissues. The deposition of the lipid most often causes destructive lesions in the ganglion cells in the brain, and this is associated with central nervous system dysfunction at a time when the brain is most susceptible. When a child develops the disease after six months of age, mental retardation is the significant sign and death does not occur until several years after onset. In the adult, the increasing number of Gaucher cells deposited in the spleen, liver, lymph nodes, and bone marrow account for the pancytopenia, bone fractures, and poor nutritional state.

The Gaucher cell is biochemically distinctive because of the presence of kerasin, which is chemically identified as N-lignoceryl-O-galactosyl-sphingosine. The molar ratios of sphingosine base, fatty acid, and hexose are 1:1:1. The manner in which the various parts are linked together and the slight variation in the size of the fatty acid provide the different compounds identified with the enlargement of the various tissues. The degradation of the molecule by various processes accounts for some of the hexoses and cerebrosides found as breakdown products. Fredrickson and Hofmann (1960) have summarized numerous reports in which variable cerebroside sugars in a variety of tissues were found by many investigators. One curious fact stands out, namely that brain cerebrosides contain galactose only.

Presumably the abnormal cerebroside metabolism accounts for the clinical symptoms noted in patients with this disease, but it is not yet clear why visceral cerebrosides contain glucose in contrast to those in the brain, which contain galactose. It is also not clear why myelinization is practically undisturbed despite the abnormal metabolism. The role of the phosphatases appears to be important but has not been adequately correlated with all the histological data.

The treatment for this group of diseases remains unsatisfactory, and the removal of the spleen is mostly for mechanical relief of the abdominal discomfort. Other suggestions for treatment have not been successful.

The cerebrosides, proteolipids, and trypsin-resistant protein fractions prepared by some workers can be closely correlated with the morphological development of brain. Much of this work was originally done with mice by Folch and his co-workers (Folch *et al.*, 1959). The cerebrosides are absent in brain prior to myelinization. Apparently the phosphatides, cholesterol, and the lipoproteins, as well as the cerebrosides do gradually increase with age as the mouse matures. There is no reason to suppose that the maturation of the human brain is any different.

In a review on lipid biosynthesis by peripheral and central nervous tissue as a function of age, Karnovsky, Moser, and Majno (1959) investigated the conversion of the glucose carbon to brain lipid carbon and the incorporation of acetate carbon into lipid by the gray matter, the white matter, and peripheral nerve in the mouse and rat, respectively. These workers studied the changes in these animals from birth to maturity and found that the cerebroside galactose is formed from blood glucose without rearrangement of the carbon skeleton. Cerebroside galactose formation from glucose labeled with C^{14} showed a very different pattern with age from that of cholesterol or other lipid components, since there was a great decrease with age in the specific activity achieved by cerebroside galactose. These workers also showed that peripheral nerve can incorporate acetate and form lipid in vitro. A correlation was shown between the growth rates and changes in the incorporation of acetate into lipids of the gray matter and the peripheral nerve. The Schwann cells of the peripheral nerve showed their lowest lipogenic activity at birth, and then this activity gradually increased with maturation. The results cited above are, in all probability, applicable to all mammals including man. The findings of Folch *et al.* (1959) as well as those of Waelsch, Sperry, and Stoyanoff (1941) showed that there was a constant increase in the phosphatide concentration of the brain from the first day of life throughout the period of myelinization, more taking place soon after birth than later.

4. *Hurler's disease.*—Hurler's disease, or gargoylism, is one of the several storage diseases in which a metabolic disturbance accounts for the accumulation of a lipid fraction combined in some manner with a hexosamine. The storage material gives histochemical reactions of a lipid and a high molecular weight polysaccharide (Seitelberger, 1957). The chemistry of this material is not well characterized by present methods, and only the mildest reliance can be placed on staining reactions for certain fat-like compounds. Presumably glycolipid deposition affects all cells and usually involves most of the major organs. Again, the accumulation of intermediate fat-like products is thought to be due to the blockage of an enzyme reaction. These intermediate compounds are part of the transformation of gangliosides first to cerebrosides and then to sphingomyelin. The work of Seitelberger indicated that mainly gangliosides are involved in this disease. This contrasted with the original work of Brante (1952), who found that the storage cells contained, besides or instead of the lipid, a mucopolysaccharide which seemed to be related to the carbohydrate group of the gangliosides. Patients with Hurler's disease excrete chondroitin sulfate B, a polysaccharide-like substance in the urine (Dorfman and Lorincz, 1957), which presumably can be demonstrated with toluidine-blue (see this chapter, under Spot-tests).

5. *Familial leuco-dystrophy* (Degai, 1957).—This pathological entity has now become associated with a slight but significant increase of the values for lipid-hexosamine content of white matter, as compared with the values obtained in normal infants.

C. AMINO ACIDS AND PROTEINS

Some of the most intriguing diseases causing mental retardation are known to be abnormalities in amino acid metabolism. Productive areas for future research in the biochemistry of mental retardation still exist in those diseases related to amino acid metabolism which can be clearly identified. It is commonplace now to point out that many diseases not yet distinguished from the larger group of hereditable causes of mental retardation will be identified with abnormalities of a single amino acid. We are well into the period of increasing interest in the role of amino acids and their metabolites on brain function, and it is not unlikely that the effort to decipher the abnormal enzyme pattern in some retarded individuals will provide information on the nature of biochemical influence on intelligence.

The diseases already identified with abnormalities in amino acid metabolism provide the clues for future research. Only those disorders associated with defects in mental function will be considered here. Others, which can be grouped as inborn errors of metabolism and have no apparent influence on intellectual function, will only be mentioned. Still others, in which the patients have mental retardation apparently unrelated to the metabolic error, will be referred to because of the newness of the information. Also, a number of amino acid abnormalities in mentally retarded patients which thus far have no clear biochemical explanation will be described. These are hypoaminoacidurias and hyperaminoacidurias, and since only relatively few individual cases have been described for each of these diseases, inadequate metabolic information is available. They are included in this discussion for completeness, since many of these may indeed turn out to be important syndromes.

1. *Phenylketonuria.*—The original prediction made by Garrod in his Croonian Lectures (1909*b*) that inborn errors of metabolism could explain many diseases yet unknown found its best support in the work of Folling (1934), whose initial observation in 1934 identified phenylpyruvic oligophrenia as the first metabolic error associated with mental retardation. Garrod (1909*a, b*) later described his ideas in two editions of his book, but it was the subsequent work of Folling (1934) and Jervis (1947) that made phenylpyruvic oligophrenia the fountainhead of these metabolic diseases associated with mental retardation.

By 1960, some twenty-six years after the initial observation on this disease, a whole host of investigators had contributed several hundred manuscripts to that knowledge which provided for satisfactory recognition and adequate treatment of the disease. These accomplishments have been attained in spite of the yet unexplained manner by which the brain is damaged by phenylalanine metabolites.

The orderly manner in which chemical compounds are metabolized in the body is reflected in normal growth and development of all tissues, including the brain. When any one of these chemical reactions is so distorted that an abnormal compound appears in the blood or is excreted into the urine, the accumulation of this substance is evidence for the "error" of metabolism. In phenylketonuria, the error is due to the deficiency of phenylalanine hydroxylase, an enzyme in the liver which normally converts phenylalanine to tyrosine. Because phenylalanine is unable to be carried through its normal pathway, the absence of the enzyme requires that the amino acid be metabolized in an alternative manner, so that it is oxidized to products not usually found in the blood or urine, namely, phenylpyruvic acid, phenylacetic acid, o-hydroxyphenylacetic acid, phenylacetylglutamine, and perhaps other compounds. The chemical reactions are illustrated in the scheme on page 323.

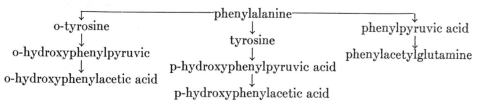

The deficiency of the phenylalanine hydroxylase is genetically determined and is considered to be transmitted as a recessive trait; the hereditary factors of the disease have been worked out. If the husband is a carrier of this autosomal gene, it can be predicted that each time the heterozygous woman is pregnant there is a one-in-four chance that she will give birth to a phenylketonuric child. Some families with phenylketonuric children may, therefore, have as many as seven out of eight or as few as one out of eight children with the disease.

The determination of the carrier state is a firm biochemical procedure based on the work of Hsia, Driscoll, Troll, and Knox (1956), who administered L-phenylalanine by mouth and determined the concentration of phenylalanine in the plasma at intervals over several hours. The heterozygotes had higher and more sustained levels when compared to normal control individuals. The value of determining carriers for this disease lies in the ability to predict whether prospective parents will or will not have phenylketonuric children. A number of modifications of the phenylalanine-tolerance tests have been suggested by Hsia, Price, and Driscoll (1957) and by Wang, Morton, and Waisman (1961). The latter workers have utilized the discrimination-function test to reduce the error in identifying the heterozygotes to about 4 per cent. While the test is easily performed using established methods for plasma phenylalanine, the limits proposed by the mathematical formula may be slightly altered for each laboratory.

Phenylketonuria is now reasonably well known to readers of this book, so great details of the clinical condition are unnecessary. Patients with this disease vary considerably in their signs and symptoms from the original description by Folling, but this is not unexpected because as more cases are discovered biological variability provides a spectrum of the symptomatology. Children with the disease have altered developmental milestones since they do not hold up their heads, sit, walk, or talk in the usual time. They do not grow in height or gain weight at normal rates and have defective muscle tone. Eczema is a striking finding in untreated patients. Abnormal behavior, muscle hypertonicity, and decreased tendon reflexes, hyperkinesis, tremors, and seizures are usually found in these patients. Not all patients with phenylketonuria are blond-haired and blue-eyed, but it is likely that the examiner will find his patient to be lighter in color than the normal siblings or of lighter complexion than the mother or father. The brain damage may sometimes be so severe that spastic diplegia is observed. Phenylketonuria has now been observed occasionally in Jews and in Japanese.

The diagnosis of phenylketonuria can be made by a number of biochemical tests. The first and most reliable is the determination of phenylalanine in the blood plasma by the methods of Udenfriend and Cooper (1953), La Du and Michael (1960), or by column chromatography according to the method of Moore and Stein (1954; Spackman *et al.*, 1958). The diagnosis is most easily made by the addition of $FeCl_3$ to the urine of a suspected patient: a blue-green-black color is distinctive for phenylpyruvic acid. This color results from the chelation of the ferric ion with the enol group of phenylpyruvic acid, and although other enol compounds give colors, they cannot be confused with the green-black color. The enol group can also react with 2,4-dinitrophenylhydrazine so that a fine orange-yellow precipitate forms with phenylpyruvic acid. Paper chromatographic methods are also adequate to determine large amounts of phenylalanine. Microbiologic assay methods can be used to determine smaller amounts with good accuracy. A recent method by Guthrie and Susi (1963), using phenylalanine inhibitors in the bacteriological media, allows for the detection of small amounts of the amino acid.

Some interesting aspects of the disordered biochemistry of phenylketonuria are reflected in the relationship between phenylalanine and tryptophan. The story begins with the observation that the decreased level of serotonin (5-hydroxytryptamine) in phenylketonuric patients is a result of the impaired synthesis of 5-hydroxytryptophan or of the depressed activity of 5-hydroxytryptophan decarboxylase (Pare *et al.*, 1958). The hydroxylation of tryptophan was not clearly understood until Freedland *et al.* (1961*b*) demonstrated that phenylalanine hydroxylase could also function to hydroxylate tryptophan. This observation was confirmed by Renson *et al.* (1961). With this fundamental observation established, it was necessary to investigate the influence of various concentrations of both amino acids on the serotonin content of brain and liver. The work of Wang *et al.* (1962) showed that high concentrations of tryptophan encouraged preferential hydroxylation of this amino acid. However, when significant concentrations of phenylalanine were added, with tryptophan, to the diet, the hydroxylation of tryptophan was suppressed. Whether the high circulating phenylalanine in patients with phenylketonuria helps to inhibit the hydroxylation of tryptophan is not known at

present. Perhaps the purification of the hydroxylase enzyme will enable definitive experiments to be done so that the relationship of serotonin to normal intellectual performance can be clarified.

The most gratifying aspect of the biochemical understanding of phenylketonuria lies in the successful treatment of these patients with a low phenylalanine diet. Since the use of a protein hydrolysate low in phenylalanine initially prepared by Woolf of England and later by Bickel *et al.* (1954) and by Armstrong and Tyler (1955), numerous reports on improved intellectual performance and reversed biochemical abnormalities have been published. These are too numerous to mention in this review. The decrease in excretion of all phenylalanine metabolites is paralleled by increased 5-hydroxyindoleacetic acid excretion, improved skin condition, increasing pigmentation of the skin, decreased seizures, and improved neurologic signs. The most heartening improvement was in the scores on intelligence tests. Knox (1960) has summarized the improved intelligence of his patients treated with low phenylalanine diets. A carefully controlled summary of the treatment of seven patients for various lengths of time over a four-year period was described by Berman *et al.* (1961). These workers, using specialized developmental intelligence tests designed for brain-injured children, found that treated phenylketonuric children had superior performance over their untreated phenylketonuric siblings. Other siblings who were unaffected by the disease were also used as controls. The careful biochemical and dietary control contributed to the good results, and an asymptotic curve was obtained which statistically validates the concept that the earlier the phenylketonuric patient is diagnosed and placed on a low phenylalanine diet treatment, the better the outcome will be (Fig. 2).

In the three years since the publication by Berman *et al.* (1961), nearly twenty-five patients with phenylketonuria have been seen at monthly intervals for complete examination, proper dietary instruction, determination of the plasma phenylalanine level, and counseling. There is no question that proper identification of these patients by early diagnosis, followed by treatment with low-phenylalanine diet (Lofenalac) and low-protein foods can provide significant increases in intellectual attainment far beyond that observed in non-treated phenylketonuric siblings (Waisman, unpublished data).

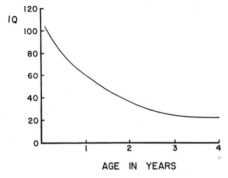

FIG. 2.—Idealized curve of relationship of intelligence quotient with the age when phenylalanine-low diet in phenylketonuria patients was started.

2. *Tryptophan abnormalities.*—Hartnup disease received its name from the index case first studied in 1951 by Baron *et al.* (1956), who saw a twelve-year-old boy with symptoms of mild cerebellar ataxia, red scaly rash over the face, arms, and legs, mental deficiency, and urinary excretion of free amino acids. This was apparently a familial condition, as hyperaminoaciduria also occurred in other members of the family. The variations in symptomatology became apparent after seven other cases of the disease were studied. It is interesting that the neuropsychiatric manifestations varied in different patients from mild emotional instability to complete delirium. These signs and symptoms are also observed in cases of pellagra seen as a result of dietary nicotinic acid insufficiency. Here,

then was the first biochemical relationship realized between the observations on the Hartnup disease patients and what is observed in true pellagra.

In order to explain the pellagra-like skin rash in these patients, it has been suggested that the tryptophan is diverted from its normal metabolic pathway into the wasteful pathway of indican formation (Knight and McIllwain, 1955). In other words, rather than allowing tryptophan to assume its role in protein formation or to be used for conversion to nicotinic acid, much of it is wasted in the indican pathway.

Pellagra had earlier been shown to be a disease in which inadequate tryptophan intake prevents the conversion of this amino acid to nicotinic acid. It is interesting that the normal metabolic pathway of tryptophan proceeds through formylkynurenine and kynurenine, through the action of the tryptophan pyrrolase enzyme. The reaction then proceeds directly to 3-hydroxykynurenine before it is converted to 3-hydroxyanthranilic acid which can be converted to nicotinic acid. Normally very little tryptophan is converted to nicotinic acid, since the equivalent of 1 mgm. nicotinic acid or niacin is approximately 60 mgm. of dietary tryptophan (Goldsmith, 1958). Tryptophan, besides following the formylkynurenine-niacin pathway, is also converted to serotonin and 5-hydroxyindoleacetic acid as previously described. This must be considered a minor pathway, as is the conversion of tryptophan to indolic acid.

The aminoaciduria in Hartnup disease has an altered pattern compared to other aminoacidurias. Alanine, serine, threonine, asparagine, glutamine, valine, leucine, isoleucine, phenylalanine, tryptophan, histidine, and citrulline are excreted in amounts five to ten times normal. It has been stated that the most striking difference between the Hartnup pattern and those of other generalized aminoacidurias such as the Fanconi syndrome, Wilson's disease, and galactosemia is the lack of any abnormality in proline excretion (Jepson and Spiro, 1960). The reabsorption mechanism is not functioning efficiently. The aminoaciduria is of renal origin, which means that the kidney cannot properly retain and "clear" the amino acids in the blood presented to the renal tubule. Apparently the inborn error of metabolism in this disease controls those enzymes that are concerned with renal tubular re-absorption. An apparent anomaly is that the amino acid concentration in the plasma is 30 per cent lower than normal as shown by ion-exchange chromatography (Evered, 1956). The free tryptophan in the plasma in three of the Hartnup family males ranged from 6.2 to 10 μg/ml of plasma.

It should be pointed out that the specific aminoaciduria and increased production of indoleacetic acid together with the retarded absorption of tryptophan from the intestine always accompanies the small conversion of nicotinic acid from tryptophan. The intestinal bacteria evidently play a large role in the conversion of tryptophan to a number of products which are in fact, not metabolic products due to errors in the patient himself, but rather reflections of the metabolism of the micro-organism living within the intestine.

When Hartnup-disease patients are given an oral loading test of tryptophan, great amounts of indolic acids are excreted. Indoleacetic acid is excreted in small quantities. Most of the D-tryptophan is recovered from the feces, and the defect of absorption of the L-tryptophan prolongs its oxidative metabolism to indoleacetic acid. Not all of the indolic acids have been completely studied in this disease.

The best way to make a diagnosis of Hartnup disease is from the specific excretion pattern of free amino acids mentioned above. Whenever a patient has skin lesions which look like pellagra but this diagnosis is unacceptable because of an adequate nutritional status, Hartnup

disease should be suspected. Any patient with skin disease, photosensitive rash accompanied by neurological changes, and high indican or high indoleacetic acid excretion should have his urine examined for total free amino acids.

While the Hartnup family itself did show mental deterioration, studies on other patients demonstrated that mental retardation was not significant (Jepson and Spiro, 1960).

3. *Branched-chain ketoaciduria* (or *maple syrup urine disease*).—In the several years since 1954 when Menkes, Hirsch, and Craig described the first patient with this disease, some thirty-eight additional cases have been reported. Apparently all the children are mentally retarded and most die early in infancy. The reason for death is not yet adequately explained, nor has the biochemistry of the disease been completely elucidated. It was apparent that the branched-chain amino acids, valine, isoleucine, and leucine were involved since these amino acids were elevated in the blood and their appropriate keto acids were found in the urine. The branched-chain amino acids are thus named because each of these contains a methyl group branching out from a central carbon atom which is not part of the longest carbon chain. Like all other essential amino acids, these are used for protein structure or are metabolized for energy. The catabolism of these branched-chain amino acids may take place by transamination or oxidative deamination. This is illustrated in the chemical reactions listed below.

valine———→α-ketoisovaleric acid
leucine———→α-ketoisocaproic acid
isoleucine→α-keto-β-methylvaleric acid

In the patients so far studied the up to tenfold increase in urine concentration of the branched-chain amino acids was accompanied by an apparently high methionine and a low cystine level in the plasma. A review of maple syrup urine disease has been offered by Dancis and Levitz (1960). Later studies by Norton *et al.* (1962) showed that the amino acid previously identified as methionine was probably alloisoleucine and that methionine levels were normal.

Transamination takes place in most animal tissues and does not involve the transfer of free ammonia, but oxidative deamination does, in fact, allow for liberation of free ammonia. Since α-ketoglutaric acid is a prime acceptor of α-amino groups in enzymatic transamination, it can efficiently couple with valine, leucine, and isoleucine and thus convert them to their appropriate ketoacids as shown above. It is important to point out that for these transaminase reactions vitamin B_6 is a most important co-factor. Therefore, in vitamin B_6 deficiency, the transamination reactions do not proceed properly and oxidative deamination takes place instead.

Another reaction that would involve the α-ketoacids is associated with the decarboxylase enzyme. The appropriate reactions are described by Dancis and Levitz (1960). It is not quite clear whether the cases described by Westall, Dancis, and Miller (1957) and by Mackenzie and Woolf (1959) are similar to the original cases described by Menkes, Hurst, and Craig (1954).

The branched-chain amino acids may be involved in tryptophan metabolism, since both Mackenzie and Woolf (1959) and Dancis *et al.* (1960) found that indoleacetic and indolelactic acid play a part in this disease. Again, the relationship between branched-chain amino acids and tryptophan finds a parallel in the phenylketonuric patient who had disturbed tryptophan metabolism.

Diagnosis of branched-chain ketoaciduria disease in infants is usually made by the observation of the symptoms of vomiting, muscular hypotonicity, failure to feed, and a maple syrup odor to the urine. This last might not be an adequate criterion because of the failure of the individual investigator to detect appropri-ately by olfactory means a dubious odor derived from various products of the maple tree sap. The mental retardation is clearly evident, and early death in most cases is a clue that certain families should be carefully observed. The diagnosis is, of course, more reliable when amino acid analysis of the urine or the plasma can be performed, together with appropriate ketoacid analyses on the urine.

4. *Histidinemia.*—Ghadimi, Partington, and Hunter (1961, 1962) were the first to report on two mentally retarded children who excreted an excess of histidine in the urine and had increased histidine plasma levels. These workers suggested, and this was confirmed about the same time by Auerbach *et al.* (1962), that patients with histidinemia represent a genetic defect in histidine metabolism, which is a result of a deficiency in the enzyme histidase. Normally histidase will catalyze the formation of urocanic acid from histidine, but when this pathway is blocked, histidine is metabolized in a manner similar to phenylalanine in phenylketonuria, namely to imidazole pyruvic, -lactic, and -acetic acids. These products were identified in the urine of patients with histidinemia, by spraying a two-dimensional paper chromatogram of the urine with Pauly's reagent to demonstrate presence of imidazole compounds. The enzymatic defect in histidinemia was further investigated by La Du *et al.* (1962, 1963) on two siblings and their nearest relatives. The interesting observation was made that the epidermis of the patients had no histidase activity while in the normal sister and in the parents activity was strongly reduced as compared with thirty control children and adults.

Urine from a patient with histidinemia, collected after a normal or high-protein meal, will give a positive Phenistix reaction, a bluish-green precipitate with 7½ per cent $FeCl_3$ solution, but no precipitate with dinitro-phenylhydrazine solution. One should be aware of this abnormality when testing a urine sample for phenylketonuria. Although mental retardation was found generally not to be associated with histidinemia, it was, however, part of the clinical picture in three patients with this disease seen by Waisman (unpublished data). Clinically, the major finding is a speech defect and there is difficulty in the pronunciation of certain words and in sentence construction.

Although it is possible to decrease the histidine level of the blood of a patient with histidinemia by feeding a diet low in histidine (Waisman and Gerritsen, unpublished data), no adequate trial has been made to prevent the consequences of this disease.

5. *Gylcinuria.*—Idiopathic hyperglycinemia and hyperglycinuria have been described by Childs *et al.* (1961). The child under study was a three-year-old white male who was apparently in difficulty from birth because of episodes of vomiting, lethargy, ketosis, neutropenia, periodic thrombocytopenia, hypogammaglobulinemia, and retarded development. The significant findings of eleven times the normal amount of glycine in plasma and nearly thirty times the normal amount of glycine in the urine indicate marked deviations from the norm. This particular patient's intolerance to adequate protein intake of any kind and to glycine itself is an unusual circumstance, considering the nonessential nature of glycine. Since the body normally can produce as much glycine as is necessary, the amount provided by the diet would ordinarily be dealt with adequately. However, in the patient under study intolerance existed, not only to glycine, but also to several branched-chain amino acids.

6. *Cystathioninuria.*—Harris (1959) has commented on an unusual case in which an elderly imbecile excreted as much as 500 mgm. of cystathionine daily. Since this compound is an intermediate in the formation of cysteine and homoserine from methionine, it normally is found in almost undetectable amounts in urine. This patient appeared to have unusual amounts of cystathionine in the extracts of liver and kidney, which indicates that intracellular accumulation was occurring and that the cystathioninuria was not renal in origin but was of the so-called overflow type. Cystathionine was also found in the brain. The disease was presumed to represent a genetically determined enzyme defect.

7. *Argininosuccinic aciduria, citrullinuria, and hyperammonemia.*—These syndromes are mentioned together because each compound takes part in the Krebs-Henseleit urea cycle. This cycle starts with the formation of carbamylphosphate from CO_2, NH_3, and ATP. Ornithine reacts under the influence of ornithine-transcarbamylase with carbamylphosphate to form citrulline. The condensation of citrulline with aspartate to argininosuccinic acid is catalyzed by a magnesium-activated condensing enzyme. A cleavage enzyme splits argininosuccinic acid into arginine and fumarate. The enzyme arginase hydrolyzes arginine to ornithine and urea. Citrullinuria was described by McMurray *et al.* (1963) in only one severely mentally retarded patient, who frequently vomited after the age of nine months. Citrulline was excreted in the urine in amounts of 2 to 3 grams per day, while blood plasma and cerebrospinal fluid levels were increased twenty to fifty fold. On feeding a high protein diet, citrulline excretion increased, and in the post-absorptive state blood ammonia levels were found to rise extremely high.

Argininosuccinic aciduria was described by Allen *et al.* (1958) and later by Levin *et al.* (1961) in three seriously retarded children, two of whom were siblings from a family of four. The patients excreted large amounts of an unknown compound, which Westall (1960) identified as argininosuccinic acid. This compound occurs only transiently under normal conditions, but in the patients under study an increased output of argininosuccinic acid occurred after oral intake of ornithine and citrulline.

In citrillinuria it is very probable that the reaction activated by the condensing enzyme is blocked, while in argininosuccinic aciduria the same applies for the cleavage enzyme. However, in both syndromes urea formation seems to be normal. From this one may conclude that the liver-urea cycle enzyme system is functioning adequately to maintain normal blood urea and arginine concentrations, so that both conditions are possibly due to extrahepatic enzyme defects. Westall (1960) suggests that in argininosuccinic aciduria, this enzyme defect is situated in the brain, which would explain the high concentration of the amino acid in the cerebrospinal fluid. The capacity of brain tissue to synthesize citrulline, however, is unknown.

Hyperammonemia, the third metabolic defect involving a compound taking part in the urea cycle, was described by Russell *et al.* (1962) in two first cousins, in whom high blood and cerebrospinal fluid ammonia levels were found, exceeding even the toxic levels usually found in hepatic coma. The patients were both mentally retarded, vomited frequently, and had cerebral degeneration. Enzyme determinations in a liver biopsy from one case showed strongly decreased ornithine transcarbamylase activity. The level of activity of the carbamylphosphate synthetase, however, was within normal limits. On drastic reduction of the protein intake, the blood and cerebrospinal fluid ammonia levels fell to within normal levels.

No ammonia determinations were done on the plasma of any one of the argininosuccinic aciduria patients. However, the suggestion that there is a correlation between the high ammonia levels in the brain, the brain damage, and the mental retardation in citrullinuria and hyperammonemia is obvious.

8. *DOPA-uria.*—The identification of L-DOPA in the urine of two mentally retarded youngsters (aged five) with understature as a prominent sign of undernutrition was first made at the University of Wisconsin by Gerritsen, Copps, and Waisman (1961). Copps, Gerritsen, Smith, and Waisman (1963) described the clinical and biochemical findings associated with these cases of mental retardation. The two boys were remarkably alike in that they had a bone age of two and one-half years in contrast to their chronological age of five years. Their mental ability was shown by psychological tests to be in the range of 60 to 70. A number of tolerance tests with phenylalanine and tyrosine demonstrated that these boys excreted DOPA in remarkably high amounts when stressed with DOPA precursors. No explanation for this circumstance is known, and additional cases are desirable to confirm these findings.

9. *Lowe's syndrome.*—The clinical condition of physical and mental retardation, cataracts, glaucoma, renal tubular acidosis, osteomalacia, and rickets was observed for the first time in 1952 by Lowe, Terrey, and MacLachlan. These patients excreted most of the amino acids except cystine. The administration of calcium lactate and sodium citrate resulted in improvement of the rickets; the question of whether this simply represents an imbalance of amino acid metabolism in some way or whether the amino acids are not utilized simultaneously to form protein provides the basis for future research.

10. *Homocystinuria.*—A new inborn error of sulfur amino acid metabolism was discovered by Gerritsen, Vaughn, and Waisman (1962) and described by Carson *et al.* (1963) and Gerritsen and Waisman (1964). Patients with this disease have seizures, ectopia lentis, failure to thrive, thinning of the hair, poor developmental milestones, abnormal neuro-

logical signs, and mental retardation. One patient who died was found to have microgyria, myelin degeneration, spongy degeneration of the subcortical layers, and thrombo-embolic phenomena (Chou and Waisman, unpublished). Small amounts of homocystine (7 to 70 mg. per 24 hrs.) were excreted by the patients. The amino acid was identified by paper chromatography but was also identified more accurately, according to the method by Gerritsen, Vaughn, and Waisman, on the automatic amino acid analyzer before and after oxidation to homocysteic acid. Excessive excretion of amino acids

inability to convert methionine to cysteine. Carson et al. (1963) could not demonstrate a difference in plasma methionine levels between control adults and the parents of a patient when a methionine loading dose was given. Although the first patient described by Gerritsen and Waisman may be different from other homocystinurics, all of the reactions leading from methionine to cysteine (Fig. 3) appear to be intact. The excretion defect may reside partly in the kidney, but the enzyme defect, the inborn error of metabolism, is probably located in the liver.

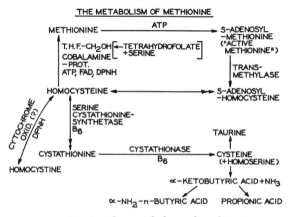

FIG. 3.—The metabolism of methionine

containing sulfhydryl groups can easily be detected by use of the nitroprusside reaction.

In the first homocystinuric described by Gerritsen and Waisman (1964) the methionine plasma level was markedly elevated, but other patients have not shown this. Administration of methionine to a homocystinuric patient causes increased excretion of homocystine, while a loading dose of homocystine results in increased excretion of cystathionine. This observation does not lend credence to the notion that an enzymic dysfunction exists between homocysteine and cystathionine. Cystine deficiency is also not an acceptable hypothesis, since there is no apparent lack of this amino acid as a result of

As additional cases are discovered, the clinical as well as the biochemical variations along a "spectrum of disease" will be sorted out. These variations as demonstrated in a particular patient can be illustrated by the case reported by Komrower and Wilson (1963).

11. *Other aminoacidurias.*—Generalized aminoaciduria is found in other patients with mental retardation, but these are not adequately characterized as yet. For example, a patient with microcephaly, mental retardation, spastic diplegia, and cerebellar hypoplasia was described by Paine (1960). The significance of such cases would be vastly improved by additional reports.

COMMENTS ON AMINOACIDURIAS

It should be remembered that the excretion of amino acids in the urine may be due to a specific defect in some liver or kidney enzyme which prevents the incorporation of the amino acids into a specific protein. The result is that other amino acids which are due to be incorporated into that protein are also not utilized, and the amino acids are, therefore, all excreted. Whether or not this is an acceptable explanation must be determined by future research. However, the generalized aminoaciduria or the variation in pattern of excretion of the amino acids is not easily explained by the information now at hand. Individual aminoaciduria can exist on the basis of the deficiency of a specific transaminase or oxidative enzyme which does not allow normal metabolic pathways to be followed. The role of kidney function is also unexplained. The identification of new patterns of amino acid excretion would, in all likelihood, provide regrouping of those diseases which are now troubling investigators because of inadequate information derived from isolated reports.

OTHER ASPECTS OF MENTAL RETARDATION

A. DISTURBANCES IN ENDOCRINE METABOLISM

The only well-established hormonal abnormality known today that has mental retardation as part of its symptomatology is cretinism. Mental retardation has been linked with calcification of cerebral vessels in cases of hypoparathyroidism (sometimes called Fahr's disease), but this relationship must still be considered a tenuous one (Bowman, 1954). This is not to say that in the future some other causes for mental retardation might not be elucidated, but at present the various forms of cretinism remain striking examples of hormonally related disturbances associated with brain damage during pregnancy.

There are three types of cretinism and their biochemical etiology is well known.

1. *Cretinism due to failure of organic iodine to form.*—This defect is the simple inability to transfer inorganic iodide to the organic molecule. Since this is an essential first step for the formation of thyroid hormone, the fetus is affected from before birth. This defect produces hyperplasia of the gland in the fetus and ultimately causes coarse skin, thick hair, and the mental and physical retardation that is typical of all cretins.

In order to identify the cretinism resulting from the inability to form organic iodide, radioactive I^{131} is administered and its uptake by the thyroid gland is determined. Following this, potassium thiocyanate is given to the patient with a resulting rapid disappearance of the uncombined labeled iodine from the gland, indicating that it is not part of an organic molecule.

Simple thyroid hormone substitution would rationally be the best treatment.

2. *Cretinism due to inability of iodotyrosines to couple.*—There are relatively few of these cases, and the pathogenesis of the biochemical defect is the inability to combine two iodonated tyrosine rings together to form the thyroxin or tetraiodothyronine. This primary failure to couple the iodotyrosines is, in all likelihood, an enzymatic defect which results in the clinical deficiency of thyroid hormone with resulting thyroid hyperplasia and all the signs and symptoms of the disease.

The diagnosis of this type of cretinism is by means of I^{131} administration and observation of its uptake by the thyroid gland. Following the administration of potassium thiocyanate the glands fail to discharge any of the retained but labeled iodine. Previous studies on direct analysis of blood from these patients have demonstrated the presence of labeled thyroxin and tri-iodothyronine, but very little was found in the gland. The gland did have great quantities of mono- and di-iodotyrosine. Through the use of this knowledge of iodine metabolism the diagnosis is not difficult to make.

The treatment with thyroid hormone is also of unproved value, but it seems likely that any substitution with thyroid hormones should help these patients.

3. *Cretinism due to decreased activity of iodotyrosine de-iodinase.*—During the sixty or more years since the original clinical condition was first described by Sir William Osler, much effort has been expended to understand the biochemistry of iodine metabolism. This type of cretinism can be considered the most common congenital defect, and the patients are markedly retarded in both mental ability and physical development. The patients are unable to show normal developmental milestones from infancy. They walk and talk late, are seldom toilet trained, and have the coarse hair and edematous rough skin typical of all cretins. These signs, together with the large thick tongue, doltish faces, and the enlargement of the thyroid gland make the diagnosis a simple one.

Once elemental or inorganic iodine is taken up in the body and converted to organic iodide in order to form either mono- or di-iodotyrosine, the next step involves coupling of these two molecules to give either thyroxin with four iodine atoms or tri-iodothyronine with three iodine atoms divided between the two benzene rings. Stanbury *et al.* (1956) demonstrated that intravenously administered mono- and di-iodotyrosine are excreted unchanged in the urine, thus providing indirect evidence that iodotyrosine de-iodinase (a deshalogenase) was absent in thyroid tissues of these familial goitrous cretins. When this enzyme is absent, mono- and di-iodotyrosine accumulate in the blood or are excreted through the urine, thus accounting for great losses of iodide.

This type of congenital hypothyroidism is easily diagnosed by the presence of labeled mono- and di-iodotyrosine in the blood following the administration of I^{131}.

The therapy for this type of patient is, again, thyroid hormone. This will relieve most of the clinical signs and symptoms if the drug is started early, but even then the mental ability is not completely restored.

One of the challenges that remains in thyroid gland physiology is to explain why these individuals are mentally retarded despite adequate therapy over a long period of time and fail to reach normal levels of intelligence. Whether the effect on the brain is direct or indirect or whether the hormone has any relationship to an appropriate enzyme action in the brain is far from clear.

B. CHROMOSOMAL RELATIONSHIPS TO MENTAL RETARDATION

Undoubtedly the increasing interest in chromosomal pattern and number will bring to the fore a number of diseases that have mental retardation as one of their primary findings.

1. *Mongolism.*—This entity is the first mental defect disease in which abnormal chromosomal numbers were demonstrated (Lejeune, Gautier, and Turpin, 1959). It is now an accepted fact that mongoloids have an extra chromosome in addition to the normal forty-six chromosomes. It should be pointed out that some of these patients have been found to have forty-six chromosomes, but the genotype demonstrated that these particular patients derive from families that normally have forty-five chromosomes, so that the extra chromosome idea is still extant. Lejeune and Turpin (1960) reported a decrease in the urinary excretion of 5-hydroxyindoleacetic acid, indoleacetic acid, and xanthurenic acid in fifteen mongoloids. The enzymatic disorder causing this abnormality may be related to the trisomy, and these authors suggest a deficit in the serotonin pathway. Whether the extra chromosome is a reduplication of a known chromosome

or whether the genes on a particular chromosome are actually altered in order to give a biochemical difference remains to be studied.

2. *Autosomal trisomy.*—There are other human syndromes associated with increased numbers of chromosomes. The reports of a new syndrome associated with autosomal trisomy were published in 1960 by a group in England (Edwards *et al.*) and by a group in the United States (Patau *et al.*). The first report described a patient with an odd-shaped head, narrow frontal and wide occipital and parietal diameters, small triangular mouth, a receding chin, low-set ears, and hypermobility of the shoulders. The fingers were held in a tightly clenched position and mental development was obviously retarded. Patau and his group and Smith *et al.* (1960) described two cases of congenital trisomy syndrome apparently unrelated to mongolism. In one of these there was anophthalmia, no response to sound, cleft palate, hare-lip, creases across the palm of the hand, flexion of the thumbs, capillary hemangioma, and congenital heart disease. In the other syndrome the child had a small mandible, low-set malformed ears, mental defects, spasticity, flexion of the fingers, and also another kind of associated heart defect. The syndrome concurrently described by Edwards *et al.* (1960) and by Patau *et al.* (1960) is now known as the trisomy of the number 17 chromosome pair.

Whether the trisomy can be associated with any biochemical abnormality is unknown at the present time. Amino acid analyses performed on the urine of the trisomy patients by Gerritsen, Waisman, and Smith (unpublished data) have failed to turn up any distinctive amino acid differences. No abnormality in excretion of sugars was detected. Further work is certainly necessary to decide whether an abnormal chromosome can contain an abnormal gene or whether it

is simply a replication of part of a well known chromosome.

Many causes for mental retardation are known which have up to now not been recognized as chromosomal abnormalities. Among these can be listed the following, with full recognition that mental retardation is simply part of the general syndrome:

> Anencephaly
> Achondroplasia
> Neurofibromatosis
> Acrocephalosyndactaly
> Chondrodystrophy
> Crouzon's disease
> Epiloia
> Gargoylism
> Gaucher's disease
> Hypopituitary dwarfism
> Juvenile amaurotic idiocy
> Lawrence-Moon Biedl syndrome
> Little's disease
> Osteogenesis imperfecta
> Phenylketonuria
> Hydatidiform mole
> Ovarian teratoma

This list is not as foreboding as it appears, since several of the above have already been carefully described in this chapter, thus demonstrating that a good start has been made in elucidating the biochemical abnormalities of some of these diseases.

C. MISCELLANEOUS

1. *T-substance.*—Coles, Priestman, and Wilkinson (1960) first demonstrated by paper chromatography a substance in the urine of a mentally retarded child and some of his normal relatives. The child had poor growth, lack of mental development, and cyanosis that was probably the result of a congenital heart lesion. Urinalysis revealed that large amounts of glycine, alanine, taurine, glutamine, and histidine were excreted together with serine and γ-aminobutyric acid, β-aminoisobutyric acid, threonine, valine, arginine, and aspartic acid. Interestingly, a more normal pattern of excretion was observed

as the child became older. However, a reddish-purplish spot which had the mobility of taurine appeared on all the chromatograms. When a purine-free diet was given to the child the spot disappeared from the urine chromatogram. In a subsequent report, Coles (1961) described a case of a child who excreted the *T*-substance in association with a demonstrable horseshoe kidney. There is apparently no relationship between the kidney anomaly and the *T*-substance. Wilkinson and Sidle in a personal communication to Coles demonstrated that the *T*-substance may be a quinone or a quinolone type of material. Obviously, additional chemical and clinical information needs to be gathered on this particular disease.

2. *α-Hydroxybutyric acid.*—The patient described by Smith and Strang (1958) was first seen at nine days of age, unresponsive to stimuli and accompanied by flaccid paralysis. She died at ten months of age, and prior to this, urinary studies had shown excess α-hydroxybutyric acid, phenylpyruvic acid, phenylalanine, methionine, and tyrosine. Interestingly, no α-aminobutyric acid was found in the urine, although this could be suspected as one source of the α-hydroxybutyric acid. The report of an odor and positive ferric chloride test may indicate that phenylalanine and perhaps other amino acids were involved. Whether this represented an absence of some enzyme system or hyperactivity of a transaminating enzyme was not determined.

3. *Hyperbilirubinemia.*—Nearly half of all newborn infants become visibly jaundiced by the second or third day of life with gradual decrease of the cutaneous pigmentation by the seventh day. Apparently the excess bilirubin responsible for the physiological icterus has not been properly metabolized by the hepatic cells. In those infants in which the bilirubin circulates at a high level as the result of immature liver function or because of other factors not yet understood, the pig-

ment can damage the brain by being deposited in specific areas. This occurrence is most likely in premature infants whose total body function is not yet completely developed. The deposition of the bilirubin pigment in the basal ganglia makes these children, who are often mentally retarded, subject to convulsions and to generalized choreoathetoid movements as seen in cerebral-palsied individuals. The exact biochemical reason for the deposition of the pigment in this selected area has not yet been discovered.

BIOCHEMICAL TECHNIQUES AND CLINICAL DIAGNOSIS

Apart from the normal chemical techniques in the routine clinical chemical laboratory, the biochemist active in the field of mental retardation makes use of other methods to assist in, or complete the information needed for a diagnosis. While biochemists are well informed about the qualitative and quantitative methods, the following elementary procedures are described to acquaint those interested readers who are less familiar with biochemistry. Five of these methods —paper chromatography, column chromatography, gas chromatography, thin-layer chromatography, and color tests on urine-impregnated filter-paper strips— will be discussed here, although for specific technical details of these methods the reader is referred to the original literature and to textbooks (Block and Weiss, 1956; Block *et al.*, 1958; Smith, 1960; Heftman, 1961; Stahl, 1962).

A. PAPER CHROMATOGRAPHY

Paper chromatography is a simple technique used to separate small amounts of closely related substances, usually for qualitative analyses but sometimes also for preparative purposes.

When a body fluid such as urine, plasma, or cerebrospinal fluid contains a number of chemically related compounds, a small amount (5–100 μl) is brought onto a small spot on one end of a strip of filter paper, dried, and subsequently developed. This means that the strip is placed so that a few millimeters of the paper dip into a solvent mixture but the spot itself does not. The solvent now starts to migrate along the paper strip, over the spot, and toward the other end of the paper. This can take several hours or a whole day, after which the paper is dried. To prevent evaporation of the solvent from the paper, the developing is performed in a chromatography jar with an airtight cover. To obtain a steady flow rate, the jar is placed in a constant-temperature room. The solvent can ascend or descend, and this may have different effects on the separation of the compounds. A substance on a chromatogram is usually specified by its *Rf*-value, which is the ratio between the distance this substance has traveled along the paper and the distance the solvent has migrated during the same time. If, as occasionally happens, the separated substances are colored, the chromatograms can be read directly. Most compounds such as amino acids and sugars are colorless, and a color is developed on the paper by spraying with, or dipping in, a proper reagent. In the case of indole compounds, some can be seen to fluoresce in ultraviolet light.

1. *Carbohydrates.*—For the detection of sugars in urine, the urine has to be desalted with a mixed resin (Rexyn IRG 501*) and concentrated in a Flash-evaporator to one-tenth the original volume. Ten to 20 μl. of this concentrate is applied onto the paper. Usually the ascending technique is used, although good results are obtained with the descending procedure. The solvent mixtures used are isopropanol water, 160:40, which gives good separation but is not very sensitive to small changes in temperature, or ethylacetate/pyridine/water, 120:50:40. The latter is especially useful for the difficult separation of galactose and glu-

* Fisher Scientific Company.

cose but is rather temperature-sensitive and can only be used in a well-ventilated room or fume hood. Aniline-diphenylamine reagent (Smith, 1960) produces different colors with different sugars, but has the disadvantage that the paper gets dark after a few days and thus cannot be kept for further reference. In paper chromatography of sugars *Rg* values are used instead of *Rf* values. The *Rg* value is the ratio between the distance the sugar has traveled along the paper and the distance glucose has migrated in the same time. Therefore, the *Rg* value of glucose is 100.

Normal urine from a healthy person should not contain any mono- or disaccharides. In cases of mellituria a number of sugars have been found in urine (Table 1), but not all have been implicated in mental retardation.

a) Glucose alone or in combination, if excreted in amounts of less than 100 mg. per day can be considered as non-significant. It may also be of renal origin, in which case it is usually accompanied by aminoaciduria.

b) Galactose is present in the blood and urine of patients with galactosemia, an inborn error of metabolism which was discussed above. The galactose is derived from the lactose in milk. It is advisable to examine the urine of a suspected galactosemia patient, first when receiving a milk diet, and then on a lactose-free diet, because separation of galactose and glucose on the chromatogram is difficult to perform. The presence of galactose in the urine of lactating women can be considered to be physiological.

c) Fructose is found in the urine of a patient with a benign congenital error of metabolism called essential fructosuria. In infants fructosuria has little or no meaning.

d) Lactose is easily recognized on the chromatogram. For further identification it can be demonstrated that the spot disappears after dilute-acid hydrolysis of the urine, but this produces glucose and galactose. Lactose excretion in infants up to fourteen days of age is normal (Bickel, 1961) but beyond that age it is a sign of an intestinal lactase deficiency. Two cases were found by Gerritsen *et al.* (1963) to excrete lactose often in combination with lactulose, which has a slightly higher *Rg*-value and gives a brown color with aniline-diphenylamine reagent. It was found that the lactulose, a disaccharide composed of fructose and galactose, originated in the diet, a liquid canned modified milk product.

to be L-xylulose. L-arabinose and d-xylose are sometimes found in urine but are mainly of dietary origin (fruits, ice cream). Ribosuria is associated with progressive muscular dystrophy, the ribose presumably originating from endogenous nucleoprotein metabolism.

2. *Amino acids.*—The technique of amino acid paper chromatography differs from that of the sugars in that one-dimensional separation usually does not produce interpretable results, and therefore, a two-way or two-dimensional chro-

TABLE 1

Rg-VALUES AND COLOR REACTIONS OF SUGARS WHICH
HAVE BEEN FOUND IN URINE

Sugar	IPrAq*	EtAcPy†	BuEtAm‡	Color§
Xylulose........	155	200	....	y
Ribose..........	135	185	155	gb
Xylose..........	130	155	140	gb
Arabinose.......	115	130	120	gb
Fructose........	105	115	115	br
Glucose.........	100	100	100	b
Galactose.......	95	85	90	b
Sucrose.........	80	75	65	br
Lactose.........	35	40	45	b
Glucuronic acid....	20	15	....	br

   * Isopropanol/water = 160:40.

   † Ethylacetate/pyridine/water = 120:50:40.

   ‡ n-butanol/ethanol/water/1% ammonia = 60:16.5:40:1.

   § Colors with aniline–diphenylamine reagent: b = blue; br = brown; y = yellow;
gb = gray-brown.

e) Sucrose easily missed in the clinical chemical laboratory is often excreted in the urine of very young children. Adults with benign sucrosuria excrete sucrose only and no other sugars.

In cases of disacchariduria (lactose or sucrose) mental retardation can be expected. Usually these patients excrete sugar mixtures including sucrose, galactose, fructose, and some pentoses (Montcrieff and Wilkinson, 1954).

f) Pentoses have been excreted in cases designated as essential pentosuria, a benign inborn condition (Flynn, 1955). The metabolic disturbance is linked with glucuronic acid metabolism, and the pentose excreted in large amounts is claimed

matogram is necessary. A spot is placed in the corner of a square paper about one inch from the sides. The paper is first developed in one direction in the first solvent, dried, and subsequently developed in the second direction with the other solvent. An often used solvent pair is n-butanol/acetic acid/water, 120:30:50 followed by phenol/water/ammonia (38 per cent), 160:40:1, but many other combinations are possible. The most frequently used color-reagent for detection of amino acids which can be used for spraying or dipping is ninhydrin (0.2 per cent in acetone). With this reagent a number of amino acids become purple-red within fifteen minutes at room temperature, while for others the color has to be developed for a few minutes at 100° C. Several other sprays for specific purposes are used, and their compositions can be found in the textbooks.

The desalting of urine prior to chromatography of the amino acids can be done in an electrolytic desalter or with an ion-exchange column. Both methods have advantages and disadvantages and are about equally effective, but the column procedure is easier.

In a normal adult "map" of 50 μl. of desalted urine, containing 10 to 25 mg. α-amino nitrogen per 100 ml., will show about five or six ninhydrin positive compounds excreted in amounts of more than 15 mg. per day. These are glutamine, glycine, alanine, histidine, 3-methyl-histidine, and, when present, β-aminoiso-butyric acid. In a chromatogram of 200 μl. one will find cystine (partly oxidized to cysteic acid), serine, threonine, valine, lysine, tyrosine, and a spot of leucine, iso-leucine, and phenylalanine which is not well separated. In infants and young children one may find proline and homo-citrulline.

a) Aminoaciduria of the renal-overflow type in which no renal tubular defect is present is recognized by a raised plasma level of a specific amino acid.

In phenylketonuria a two-dimensional paper chromatogram of 50–100 μl. urine using the solvent system outlined above reveals a dark spot in the upper left quadrant of the paper (phenylalanine).

In maple syrup urine disease valine, leucine, and isoleucine are accumulated in all body fluids and can easily be demonstrated in the urine.

Other metabolic abnormalities which can be detected with paper chromatography and belong to this group are ar-gininosuccinic aciduria, cystathioninuria, glycinuria, histidinuria, and perhaps other high concentrations of one or several amino acids, resulting from overflow of the compound from the plasma into the urine. Dihydroxyphenylalanine could not

be detected in the paper chromatograms of two cases described by Gerritsen *et al.* (1961) since the concentrations were too low. However, by using the column technique as in the automatic amino acid analyzer, levels of 2 to 17 mgm. per twenty-four hours were found.

b) Aminoaciduria with renal tubular defect and normal plasma concentrations can be found in almost all cases with renal tubular injury to such a degree that re-absorption is insufficient. In most diseases in this group the aminoaciduria is of the general type and is part of the toxic symptomatology. Examples are poisoning by heavy metals or phenol, endogenous factors such as the free plasma copper in Wilson's disease, and the galactose-1-phosphate in galactosemia. This same type of aminoaciduria is found in some vitamin deficiencies (rickets, scurvy), in nephrotic syndrome, and kwashiorkor. A number of congenital abnormalities such as Fanconi syndrome, Hartnup disease, and cystine-lysinuria (Rowley *et al.*, 1960) belong under this group. They cause a generalized aminoaciduria, although sometimes some amino acids tend to produce more intense spots on the chromatogram than others.

c) Aminoaciduria with renal tubular defect and raised plasma levels is understandably a rare condition, in which exceptionally high amino acid excretions can be found. Examples are coeliac disease and phosphorus poisoning.

3. *Indole compounds.*—Paper chromatography of indole compounds in urine requires filtered but not necessarily desalted urine. Fifty to 200 μl. is applied to a square paper, and good separations are obtained by performing a two-dimensional chromatogram—first, in one direction, isopropanol/ammonia (38 per cent)/water, 200:15:20, followed by n-butanol/acetic acid/water, 120:30:50 in the other direction. Some indole compounds can be distinguished by their fluorescence in ultraviolet light, but the color reagent of choice is Ehrlich reagent (one volume of

10 per cent p-dimethylaminobenzalde-
hyde in concentrated HCl, four volumes
acetone), which gives different shades of
purple-blue colors with indole derivatives
like tryptophan and any of its 5 and 6
position substitutes. Other compounds,
such as indoxyl-sulfate, urea, kynurenine,
etc., give yellow, orange, and brown
shades, which make them easily recognizable. Fifty to 100 μl. of normal human
urine usually shows only a few Ehrlich
positive substances, namely urea (a yellow landmark in every chromatogram),
indoxyl-sulfate, sometimes tryptophan,
and traces of indoleacetic acid and 5-hy-
droxyindoleacetic acid. Oral administration of large doses of L-tryptophan to
normal humans increases the urinary excretion of kynurenine and kynurenic acid
and produces a spectrum of spots all over
the paper. If D-tryptophan is fed, the
tryptophan spot is very dark, and some
indolelactic acid is excreted.

The chromatogram of the urine from
a phenylketonuric child will show increased amounts of indoleacetic acid and
indolelactic acid. In monkeys, made
phenylketonuric by feeding large amounts
of phenylalanine, decreased excretion of
5-hydroxyindolyl acetic acid was found.
Removal of the phenylalanine from the
diet was followed by an appropriate increase in excretion of the acid. Interestingly, there was no significant difference
in excretion of the 3-indolyl acids (in-
dolyl-3-acetic, -lactic, and -pyruvic acid)
between normal control and phenylketonuric monkeys. No correlation was
noted between the twenty-four hours excretion of the indolyl acids and the
weight of the monkey, or the length of
time the monkey was on high-phenylal-
anine diet (Boggs et al., 1963). In Hartnup disease there is, apart from general
aminoaciduria, a highly increased excretion of tryptophan, indoxyl-sulfate, and
to a lesser extent, indoleacetic acid and
indolyl-acetyl-l-glutamine.

4. *Phenolic acids.*—The technique for
paper chromatography of phenolic acids
was described by Armstrong, Shaw, and
Wall (1956). Paper chromatography of
phenylketonuric urine will demonstrate
o-hydroxyphenylacetic acid as the outstanding hydroxymetabolite of phenylalanine. It can even be detected on a one-
dimensional paper chromatogram in iso-
propanol/ammonia/water, 8:1:1, the col-
or being developed with 2,6-dichloroqui-
none chlorimide. This procedure can be
considered as one of the accurate tests
for phenylketonuric metabolites in the
urine.

In a case of untreated galactosemia, a
greatly increased excretion of p-hydroxy-
phenylpyruvic acid and p-hydroxyphenyllactic acid was found (Tashian,
1961).

One must bear in mind that the phenolic acid chromatograms can be easily
misinterpreted because of the excretion
of metabolites of phenobarbiturate and
its hydroxylated derivatives.

B. QUANTITATIVE DETERMINATION OF AMINO ACIDS BY COLUMN CHROMATOGRAPHY

Quantitative amino acid analysis of
urine and plasma is not only of value in
all the cases mentioned above in the discussion of paper chromatography of
amino acids, but also in those circumstances where only a statistical comparison of results can determine if a hyper-
or hypo-aminoaciduria is present or
where a single amino acid not found in
normals is present in small amounts.
Chromatography of amino acids on columns of sulfonated polystyrene resins according to Moore and Stein (1954) or
the method of Spackman et al. (1958),
using an automatic apparatus, can, in the
hands of an experienced technician, give
reliable and reproducible results.

1. *Urine.*—A twenty-four-hour urine
sample is collected under ice and preserved with a few crystals of thymol.
The urine is filtered, acidified to pH2,
and if necessary filtered again. The protein from high protein-containing urine
is removed by an alcohol precipitation
method. Two ml. or some suitable aliquot

can now be placed directly on the 150-cm. column. Before the basic amino acids can be analyzed, ammonia has to be removed from the urine. In order to detect homocitrulline in the urine of infants and young children, it is advisable to use the modification by Gerritsen *et al.* (1961*b*) of the standard procedure of Spackman (1960) for the 150-cm. column.

2. *Plasma.*—The sample must be free of protein and obtained from non-hemolyzed blood, since iron will be strongly adsorbed on the resin, thus resulting in decreased resolution capacity of the column. There are several techniques for the removal of protein from plasma. The one normally used is the picric acid method described by Spackman (1960), but higher recoveries are obtained by mixing 1 ml. of plasma with 5 ml. of 3 per cent sulfosalicylic acid and placing the filtrate directly on the column.

C. GAS CHROMATOGRAPHY

This technique, also called vapor-phase chromatography or gas-liquid chromatography (Desty and Harbaum, 1957), is undoubtedly a promising and still rapidly expanding method of separation and analysis. It involves the use of a column containing a liquid phase, which is stationary and usually attached to celite, and a gas phase, which is mobile. Generally speaking, the technique can be applied to the separation of any mixture of compounds, as long as these or their derivatives can be brought into the gas phase. Methyl esters of fatty acids, aldehydes formed from amino acids, free hydrocarbons, and many other compounds are separated by pumping the sample in the vapor state through the column at an increased temperature using a steady stream of an inert gas, nitrogen or argon, as a carrier. Originally developed by James and Martin (1954) for the separation of fatty acids on a column of stearic acid and silicone oil, the technique has now found widespread use in the biochemical research laboratory.

D. THIN-LAYER CHROMATOGRAPHY

In this microchromatographic technique, sheets of glass covered with a very thin, uniformly spread layer of adsorptive material (silica or cellulose powder) are used instead of paper (Stahl, 1956). The sheets are dried and activated by heating. One or two dimensional separations of mixtures of the same type of compounds are performed on eight-inch square sheets exactly as in paper chromatography. The advantages of the thin-layer method are (1) the short time necessary for separations (only one to three hours), (2) its wide quantitative range with small samples, (3) its high sensitivity and sharp separations, and (4) the fact that corrosive spray reagents may be safely applied. Although first used mainly for the separation of lipids and fatty acids (Fontell *et al.*, 1960), the method is now adapted to separation of amino acids (Brenner and Niederwieser, 1960) and other materials (see also Stahl, 1962).

E. DETECTION OF METABOLIC DISORDERS BY PAPER SPOT TESTS

In several metabolic abnormalities associated with mental retardation, characteristic substances are excreted in the urine. Berry (1959) described methods for the detection of a number of these compounds, and the following is based partly on her work. Infant-urine specimens are obtained by placing a two-inch square of filter paper in the diaper. The paper moistened with urine is dried and stored. Most urinary compounds are stable in the cold, so various direct spot tests can be done at a later date. If the urine is to be used for paper chromatography, the material can be eluted with water.

1. *Phenylpyruvic acid.*—Specimens containing this compound turn black-green when a drop of a 7.5 per cent aqueous $FeCl_3$ solution is added to the paper. A positive test is an indication that phenylketonuria is suspected.

2. *Proline.*—The presence of this amino acid in the urine can be demonstrated with isatine reagent (Block *et al.*, 1956). It is excreted with other amino acids by patients with Wilson's disease (Stein *et al.*, 1954) and infants with osteogenesis imperfecta.

3. *Tyrosine.*—When tyrosine or other p-hydroxyphenyl acids are present in the urine, a brown ring develops around a drop of Millon's reagent on the paper (Feigl, 1960). Tyrosine may be found in large amounts in a number of liver diseases, heavy-metal poisoning, and galactosemia.

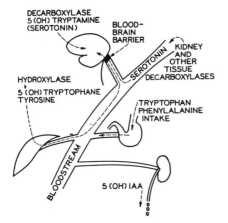

FIG. 4.—Conversion of tryptophan to serotonin, and phenylalanine to tyrosine in the normal organism.

4. *Chondroitin sulfate B.*—It has been proposed that this muco-polysaccharide metabolite in the urine of patients with Hurler's disease (gargoylism) can be demonstrated with toluidine blue (Berry, 1959).

5. *Other amino acids.*—In order to test for the presence of the branched-chain amino acids (valine, leucine, and isoleucine) and for amino acids like histidine, argininosuccinic acid, cystine, lysine, etc., the urine is eluted from the paper according to the technique described by Berry (1959), and two-dimensional paper chromatograms are prepared.

6. *Sugars.*—A positive reaction with aniline-phthalate reagent (Berry, 1959), brown for most of the hexoses and disaccharides and pink for the pentoses, should be followed up with a paper chromatogram.

7. *Copper.*—An almost too sensitive test for this element (Feigl, 1958) is with o-toluidine-ammonium thiocyanate reagent. Highly positive tests may indicate Wilson's disease.

THE FUTURE OF BIOCHEMICAL RESEARCH IN MENTAL RETARDATION

It is now becoming increasingly manifest that for a better understanding of normal brain function, tissues other than the brain must also be studied. The role which the enzymes of the liver and the kidney play in brain metabolism must be clarified. Knowledge of the enzyme functions in these tissues is increasing continuously, and it is now apparent that certain reactions carried out by these enzymes provide necessary substances which the brain can use to advantage. Understandably, favorable substrates for the enzymes present in the brain are those compounds which can easily cross the blood-brain barrier. Certain reactions taking place in brain tissue can also be carried out in other tissues, but the products of these reactions cannot always enter the brain. An example of such a situation is the formation of serotonin. Although this important neurohormone can be formed in the kidneys and in the gastrointestinal tract, the serotonin necessary for normal brain function must be formed *in situ* by decarboxylation of 5-hydroxytryptophan. This substrate, which can cross the blood-brain barrier, must be provided by hydroxylation of tryptophan, which presumably takes place only in the liver (Fig. 4).

Other reactions, both simple and complex, will undoubtedly be found which will confirm the thesis that "the brain cannot survive by itself," but is interdependent on other tissues for maximum function.

Continued research in many of the disciplines that are concerned with the mentally retarded child will definitely provide better care and treatment for these patients. The improvements now being made in day-care centers, slow-learning classes, and community services are all important. However, if mental retardation is to be prevented rather than treated, then one must look to the biochemical investigations to provide the necessary information. While this statement is made with understandable prejudice, there is no question but that the diligent application of new biochemical techniques and methods for the study of brain and other tissues will provide productive information.

The biochemical approach must take at least three directions. The first is that basic work on the role of lipids, carbohydrates, and amino acids in the brain needs to be examined. The isolation of brain mitochondria and other cellular fractions can provide information on the enzymes concerned with the metabolism of these three major classes of compounds.

The second approach is the biochemical investigation of the mentally retarded child. This evaluation will provide the best clues for discovering new diseases. While the clinical grouping and categorization of retarded children is desirable, more than this is necessary: once a homogeneous group is identified, a complete biochemical evaluation must be made according to the analytical methods described in this chapter.

A third need in mental-retardation research for the future is expansion of the idea first successfully followed in this laboratory (Waisman *et al.*, 1959, 1960), that mental retardation can be produced in experimental animals. Signs of specific diseases as phenylketonuria, branched-chain ketoaciduria, and galactosemia have already been produced in rats and/or monkeys. By pursuing these animal experiments additional valuable data could be obtained, not only by drawing blood and collecting urine from

these animals, but also by obtaining liver and brain biopsies for biochemical-research purposes. By performing the latter procedures in animals the biochemist avoids those moral considerations that restrain him from removing parts of the brain and liver from human patients.

Now that we are well into the second half of the twentieth century, we find ourselves on the threshold of a new era in research on mental retardation. In the pursuit of new knowledge, the findings will, in all probability, enable the use of pure enzyme preparations which can replace the deficits in the body. A whole group of enzyme inhibitors and psychopharmacological drugs will be available for clinical trials. The use of electronic devices and many new and improved products of modern instrumentation will create exciting opportunities for the laboratory investigator in the field of mental retardation.

The goals are unlimited and there is light on the horizon.

REFERENCES

AKERT, K., HABLE, K., WANG, H. L., and WAISMAN, H. A. 1961. Ultra structural cerebral changes in experimental phenylketonuria. *Exerpta Medica*, No. 39, p. 6, International Congress Series.

ALLEN, J. D., CUSWORTH, D. C., DENT, C. E., and WILSON, V. K. 1958. Disease, probably hereditary, characterized by severe mental deficiency and constant gross abnormality of amino acid metabolism. *Lancet*, 1:182.

ANDERSON, E. P., KALCKAR, H. M., KURAHASHI, K. and ISSELBACHER, K. J. 1957. A specific enzymatic assay for the diagnosis of congenital galactosemia. *J. Lab. Clin. Med.*, 50:569.

ARMSTRONG, M. D., SHAW, K. N. F., and WALL, P. E. 1956. The phenolic acids of human urine. Paper chromatography of phenolic acids. *J. Biol. Chem.*, 218:293.

ARMSTRONG, M. D., and TYLER, F. H. 1955. Studies on phenylketonuria. I. Restricted phenylalanine intake in phenylketonuria. *J. Clin. Invest.*, 34:565.

AUERBACH, V. H., DiGEORGE, A. M., BALDRIDGE, R. C., TOURTELLOTTE, C. D., and

BRIGHAM, M. P. 1962. Histidinemia. *J. Pediat.*, **60**:487.

BARCROFT, J. 1938. *The Brain and Its Environment.* Yale University Press, New Haven, Conn.

BARON, D. N., DENT, C. E., HARRIS, H., HART, E. W., and JEPSON, J. B., 1956. Hereditary pellagra skin rash with temporary cerebellar ataxia, constant renal aminoaciduria, and other bizarre biochemical features. *Lancet*, **2**:421.

BERMAN, P. W., GRAHAM, F. K., EICHMAN, P. L., and WAISMAN, H. A. 1961. Psychologic and neurologic status of diet-treated phenylketonuric children and their siblings. *Pediatrics*, **28**:924.

BERRY, H. K. 1959. Procedures for testing urine specimens dried on filter paper. *Clin. Chem.*, **5**:603.

BESSMAN, S. P. 1958. Ammoniagenic coma: the chemistry of an endogenous intoxication. *In:* F. BRÜCKE (ed.), *Biochemistry of the Central Nervous System*, p. 141. *Proc. IV Int. Cong. Biochem.*, Vienna.

BESSMAN, S. P., ROSSEN, J., and LAINE, E. C. 1953. Transamination of γ-aminobutyric acid and β-alanine in brain and liver. *J. Biol. Chem.*, **201**:385.

BICKEL, H. 1961. Mellituria: a paper chromatographic study. *J. Pediat.*, **59**:641.

BICKEL, H., GERRARD, J., and HICKMANS, E. M. 1954. Influence of phenylalanine intake on the biochemistry and behavior of a phenylketonuric child. *Acta Paediat.*, **43**:64.

BLOCK, R. J., DURRUM, E. L., and ZWEIG, G. 1958. *A Manual of Paper Chromatography and Paper Electrophoresis.* New York: Academic Press.

BLOCK, R. J., and WEISS, K. W. 1956. *Amino Acid Handbook.* Springfield, Ill.: C. C Thomas.

BOGGS, D. A., McLAY, D., KAPPY, M. and WAISMAN, H. A. 1963. Excretion of indolyl acids in phenylketonuric monkeys. *Nature*, **200**:76.

BOGOCH, S. 1958. Brain gangliosides and neuraminic acid in the central nervous system. *In:* F. BRÜCKE (ed.), *Biochemistry of the Central Nervous System*, p. 196. *Proc. IV Int. Cong. Biochem.*, Vienna.

BOLTON, J. S. 1914. *The Brain in Health and Disease.* London: Edward Arnold.

BOWMAN, M. S. 1954. Familial occurrence

of "idiopathic" calcification of cerebral capillaries. *Amer. J. Path.*, **30**:87.

BRANTE, G. 1952. Gargoylism, a mucopolysaccharidosis. *Scand. J. Clin. Lab. Invest.*, **4**:43.

———. 1958. Mucopolysaccharides and mucoids of the nervous system. *In:* F. BRÜCKE (ed.), *Biochemistry of the Central Nervous System*, p. 291. *Proc. IV Int. Cong. Biochem.*, Vienna.

BRENNER, M., and NIEDERWIESER, A. 1960. Dünnschicht-Chromotographie von Aminosäuren. *Experentia*, **16**:378.

CARSON, N. A. J., CUSWORTH, D. C., DENT, C. E., FIELD, C. M. B., NEILL, D. W., and WESTALL, R. G. 1963. Homocystinuria: a new inborn error of metabolism associated with mental deficiency. *Arch. Dis. Child.*, **38**:425.

CHILDS, B., NYHAN, W. L., BORDEN, M., BARD, L., and COOKE, R. E. 1961. Idiopathic hyperglycinemia and hyperglycinuria: a new disorder of amino acid metabolism. *Pediatrics*, **27**:522, 539.

CLOUET, D. H., GAITONDE, M. K., and RICHTER, D. 1957. The free histidine, histamine and arginine content of the rat brain. *J. Neurochem.*, **1**:228.

COLES, H. M. T. 1961. T-substance anomaly with horseshoe kidney. *Proc. Roy. Soc. Med.*, **54**:330.

COLES, H. M. T., PRIESTMAN, A., and WILKINSON, J. H. 1960. T-substance anomaly. An inborn error of purine metabolism. *Lancet*, **2**:1220.

COPPS, S. C., GERRITSEN, T., SMITH, D. W., and WAISMAN, H. A. 1963. Urinary excretion of 3, 4-dihydroxyphenylalanine in two malnourished short-statured children. *J. Pediat.*, **62**:208.

COXON, R. V. 1957. Carbohydrate metabolism in relation to the nervous system. *In:* D. RICHTER (ed.), *Metabolism of the Nervous System*, p. 303. New York: Pergamon Press.

CROCKER, A. C., and FARBER, S. 1958. Niemann-Pick disease: a review of 18 patients. *Medicine*, **37**:1.

DANCIS, J., and LEVITZ, M. 1960. Maple syrup urine disease. *In:* J. B. STANBURY, J. B. WYNGAARDEN, and D. S. FREDRICKSON (eds.), *The Metabolic Basis of Inherited Diseases*, p. 473. New York: McGraw-Hill.

DANCIS, J., LEVITZ, M., and WESTALL, R. G.

1960. Maple syrup urine disease: branched-chain keto-aciduria. *Pediatrics*, 25:72.

DAWSON, R. M. C., and DITTMER, J. C. 1961. Evidence for the structure of brain triphosphoinositide from hydrolytic degradation studies. *Biochem. J.*, 81:540.

DEBUCH, H., 1959. Über die Stellung des Aldehydes im Colamin-plasmalogen aus Gehirn: *Hoppe Seyler Z. Physiol. Chem.*, 314:49.

DEGAR, G. W. F. 1957. Leuco-dystrophy as an "inborn metabolic error," comparable to lipidosis. *In:* J. N. CUMINGS and A. LOWENTHAL (eds.), *Cerebral Lipidoses*, p. 186. Oxford: Blackwell Scientific Publications.

DESTY, D. H., and HARBAUM, C. L. A., 1957. *Vapor Phase Chromatography*. New York: Academic Press.

DITTMER, J. C., and DAWSON, R. M. C., 1961. The isolation of a new lipid, triphosphoinositide, and monophosphoinositide from ox brain. *Biochem. J.*, 81:535.

DORFMAN, A., and LORINCZ, A. E. 1957. Occurrence of urinary acid mucopolysaccharides in the Hurler's syndrome. *Proc. Nat. Acad. Sci.*, 43:443.

DU RUISSEAU, J. P., GREENSTEIN, J. P., WINITZ, M., and BIRNBAUM, S. M., 1957. Free amino acid levels in the tissues of rats protected against ammonia toxicity. *Arch. Biochem. Biophys.*, 68:161.

EDWARDS, J. H., HARNDEW, D. G., CAMERON, A. H., CROSSE, V. M., and WOLFF, O. H., 1960. A new trisomic syndrome. *Lancet*, 1:790.

ELLIOT, K. A. C., ROBERTS, E., and BAXTER, C. F. 1958. γ-aminobutyric acid: an inhibitory factor in brain. *In:* E. BRÜCKE (ed.), *Biochemistry of the Central Nervous System*, p. 251. *Proc. IV Int. Cong. Biochem.*, Vienna.

EVERED, D. F. 1956. The excretion of aminoacids by the human: a quantitative study with ion exchange chromatography. *Biochem. J.*, 62:416.

FEIGL, F. 1958. *Spot Tests in Inorganic Analysis*, p. 84. New York: Elsevier.

——. 1960. *Spot Tests in Organic Analysis*, pp. 196 and 242. New York: Elsevier.

FLYNN, F. V. 1955. Pentosuria. *Brit. Med. J.*, 1:391.

FOLCH, J., CASALS, J., POPE, A., MEATH, J. A., LE BARON, F. M., and LESS, M. 1959. Chemistry of myelin development. *In:*

S. R. KOREY (ed.), *The Biology of Myelin*, p. 122. New York: Hoeber-Harper.

FOLCH, J., and LE BARON, F. M. 1958. Biochemistry of inositol lipids of the central nervous system. *In:* F. BRÜCKE (ed.), *Biochemistry of the Central Nervous System*, p. 157. *Proc. IV Int. Cong. Biochem.*, Vienna.

FOLCH, J., and WOOLEY, D. W. 1942. Inositol, a constituent of a brain phosphatide. *J. Biol. Chem.*, 142:963.

FOLLING, A. 1934. Über Ausscheidung von Phenylbrenzträubensäure in den Harn als Stoffwechselanomalie in Verbindung mit Imbezillität. *Hoppe Seyler Z. Physiol. Chem.*, 227:169.

FONTELL, K., HOLMAN, R. T., and LOMBERTSEN, G. 1960. Some new methods for separation and analysis of fatty acids and other lipids (Review). *J. Lipid Res.* 1:391.

FREDRICKSON, D. S., and HOFMANN, A. F. 1960. Gaucher's disease. *In:* J. B. STANBURY, J. B. WYNGAARDEN, and D. S. FREDRICKSON (eds.), The Metabolic Basis of Inherited Disease, p. 603. New York: McGraw-Hill.

FREEDLAND, R. A., WADZINSKI, I. M., and WAISMAN, H. A. 1961a. The enzymatic hydroxylation of tryptophan. *Biochem. Biophys. Res. Commun.*, 5:94.

——. 1961b. The effect of aromatic amino acids on the hydroxylation of tryptophan. *Biochem. Biophys. Res. Commun.*, 6:227.

FROESCH, E. R., PRADER, A., LABHART, A., STUBER, W. H., and WOLF, H. P. 1957. Die hereditäre Fructoseintoleranz, eine bisher nicht bekannte kongenitale Stoffwechselstörung. *Schweiz. Med. Wehnschr.*, 87:1168.

FROESCH, E. R., PRADER, A., WOLF, H. P., and LABHART, A. 1959. Die hereditäre Fructoseintoleranz. *Helvet. Paediat. Acta.*, 14:99.

GARROD, A. E. 1909a. Inborn Errors of Metabolism. 1st ed.; London: Harry Frowde. (2d ed.; London: H. Frowde and Hodder & Stoughton, 1923.)

——. 1909b. Inborn Errors of Metabolism: The Croonian Lectures Delivered before the Royal College of Physicians of London in June, 1908. London: Oxford Medical Publications.

GEIGER, A., YAMASAKI, S., and LYONS, R. 1955. Changes in nitrogenous components of brain, produced by stimulation of short duration. *Amer. J. Physiol.*, **184**:239.

GERRITSEN, T., COPPS, S. C., and WAISMAN, H. A. 1961a. Excretion of 3, 4-dihydroxyphenylalanine in urine. *Biochem. Biophys. Acta*, **53**:603.

GERRITSEN, T., LEMLI, L., PTACEK, L. J., and WAISMAN, H. A. 1963. The presence of lactulose in the urine of children with lactosuria. *Pediatrics*, **32**:1033.

GERRITSEN, T., LIPTON, S. H., STRONG, F. M., and WAISMAN, H. A. 1961b. On the isolation and identification of homocitrulline from urine. *Biochem. Biophys. Res. Commun.*, **4**:379.

GERRITSEN, T., VAUGHN, J. G., and WAISMAN, H. A. 1962. The identification of homocystine in the urine. *Biochem. Biophys. Res. Commun.*, **9**:493.

GERRITSEN, T., and WAISMAN, H. A. 1964. Homocystinuria, an error in the metabolism of methionine. *Pediatrics*, **33**:413.

GHADIMI, H., PARTINGTON, M. W., and HUNTER, A. 1961. A familial disturbance of histidine metabolism. *New Engl. J. Med.*, **265**:221.

———. 1962. Inborn error of histidine metabolism. *Pediatrics*, **29**:714.

GLOCK, G. E., and McLEAN, P. 1953. Further studies on the properties and assay of glucose-6-phosphate dehydrogenase and 6-phosphogluconate dehydrogenase of rat liver. *Biochem. J.*, **55**:400.

GOLDSMITH, G. A. 1958. Niacin-tryptophan relationships in man, and niacin requirement. *Amer. J. Clin. Nutrition*, **6**:479.

GUTHRIE, R., and SUSI, A., 1963. A simple phenylalanine method for detecting phenylketonuria in large populations of newborn infants. *Pediatrics*, **32**:338.

HANAHAN, D. J. 1960. *Lipid Chemistry*, p. 94. New York: Wiley.

HANAHAN, D. J., DITTMER, J. C., and WARASHINA, E. 1957. A column chromatographic separation of classes of phospholipids. *J. Biol. Chem.*, **228**:685.

HARRIS, H., PENROSE, L. S., and THOMAS, D. H. H. 1959. Cystathioninuria. *Ann. Human Genet.*, **23**:442.

HEFTMANN, E. 1961. *Chromatography*. New York: Reinhold.

HIMWICH, H. E. 1951. *Brain Metabolism and Cerebral Disorders*. Baltimore: Williams & Wilkins.

HOLTZ, P., and WESTERMANN, E. 1956. Über

die Dopadecarboxylase and Histidinedecarboxylase des Nervengewebes. *Arch. exper. Path. Pharmakol.*, **227**:538.

HOLZEL, A., and KOMROWER, G. M. 1955. A study of the genetics of galactosemia. *Arch. Dis. Child.*, **30**:155.

HORECKER, B. L. 1953. A new pathway for the oxidation of carbohydrate. *Brewer's Digest*, **28**:214.

HSIA, D. Y. 1959. *Inborn Errors of Metabolism*. Chicago: Yearbook Publishers.

HSIA, D. Y., DRISCOLL, K. W., TROLL, W., and KNOX, W. E. 1956. Detection of the heterozygous carrier for phenylketonuria by phenylalanine tolerance tests. *Nature*, **178**:1235.

HSIA, D. Y., PRICE, R. S., and DRISCOLL, K. W. 1957. Phenylketonuria: detection of the heterozygous carrier. *J. Ment. Defic. Res.*, **1**:53.

ISSELBACHER, K. J., ANDERSON, E. P., KURAHASHI, K., and KALCKAR, H. M. 1956. Congenital galactosemia, a single enzymatic block in galactose metabolism. *Science*, **123**:635.

JAMES, A. T., and MARTIN, A. J. P. 1954. Gas-liquid chromatography: a technique for the analysis and identification of volatile materials. *Brit. Med. Bull.*, **10**:170.

JEPSON, J. B., and SPIRO, M. J. 1960. *In:* J. B. STANBURY, J. B. WYNGAARDEN, and D. S. FREDRICKSON (eds.). *Hartnup Disease, The Metabolic Basis of Inherited Disease*, p. 1338. New York: McGraw-Hill.

JERVIS, G. A. 1937. Phenylpyruvic oligophrenia: introductory study of 50 cases of mental deficiency associated with excretion of phenylpyruvic acid. *Arch. Neurol. Psychiat.*, **38**:944.

———. 1947. Studies of phenylpyruvic oligophrenia: the position of the metabolic error. *J. Biol. Chem.*, **169**:651.

KABARA, J. J., and OKITA, G. T. 1961. Brain cholesterol: biosynthesis with selected precursors *in vivo. J. Neurochem.*, **7**:298.

KALCKAR, H. M., and MAXWELL, E. S. 1958. Biosynthesis and metabolic function of uridyldiphospho-glucose in mammalian organisms, and its relevance to certain inborn errors. *Physiol. Rev.*, **38**:77.

KARNOVSKY, M. L., MOSER, H., and MAJNO, G. 1959. Lipid biosynthesis by peripheral and central nervous tissue as function of age. *In:* S. R. KOREY (ed.), *The Biology of Myelin*. New York: Hoeber-Harper.

KETY, S. S. 1957. The general metabolism of the brain in vivo. *In:* D. RICHTER (ed.), *Metabolism of the Nervous System,* p. 221. New York: Pergamon Press.

KINI, M. M., and QUASTEL, J. H. 1959. Carbohydrate-amino acid interrelationships in brain cortex *in vivo.* Nature, **184**:252.

KLENK, E. 1935. Über die Natur der Phosphatide und anderer Lipoide des Gehirns und der Leber bei der Niemann-Pickschen Krankheit. *Hoppe Seyler Z. Physiol. Chem.,* **235**:24.

———. 1939. Beitrage zur Chemie der Lipiodosen. Niemann-Picksche Krankheit und amaurotische Idiotie. *Hoppe Seyler Z. Physiol. Chem.,* **262**:128.

———. 1958. Die Glycerinphosphatide des Gehirns. *In:* F. BRÜCKE (ed.), *Biochemistry of the Central Nervous System,* p. 146. *Proc. IV Int. Cong. Biochem.,* Vienna.

———. 1959. On gangliosides. *A.M.A. J. Dis. Child.,* **97**:711.

KNIGHT, R., and McILLWAIN, H. 1955. Indicanuria in the psychosis of a pellagrant. *J. Ment. Sci.,* **101**:884.

KNOX, W. E. 1960. An evaluation of the treatment of phenylketonuria with diets low in phenylalanine. *Pediatrics,* **26**:1.

KOMROWER, G. M., and WILSON, V. K. 1963. Homocystinuria. *Proc. Roy. Soc. Med.,* **56**:996.

KREBS, H. A. 1935. The synthesis of glutamine from glutamic acid and ammonia and the enzymatic hydrolysis of glutamine in animal tissues. *Biochem. J.,* **29**:1951.

LA DU, B. N., HOWELL, R. R., JACOBY, G. A., SEEGMILLER, J. E., SOBER, E. K., ZANNONI, V. G., and CANBY, J. P. 1963. Clinical and biochemical studies on two cases of histidinemia. *Pediatrics,* **32**:216.

LA DU, B. N., HOWELL, R. R., JACOBY, G. A., SEEGMILLER, J. E., and ZANNONI, V. G. 1962. The enzymatic defect in histidinemia. *Biochem. Biophys. Res. Commun.,* **7**:398.

LA DU, B. N., and MICHAEL, P. J. 1960. An enzymatic spectrophotometric method for the determination of phenylalanine in blood. *J. Lab. Clin. Med.,* **55**:491.

LAJTHA, A. 1959. Turnover of leucine in mouse tissues. *J. Neurochem.,* **3**:358.

LASKER, M. 1941. Essential fructosuria. *Human Biol.,* **13**:51.

LE JEUNE, J., GAUTIER, M., and TURPIN, R.

1959. Les chromosomes humaines en culture de tissus. *C. R. Hebdom. Séances Acad. Sci.,* **248**:602.

LE JEUNE, J., and TURPIN, R. 1960. Study of the urinary excretion of some tryptophan metabolites in mongoloid children. (Fr.) *C. R. Hebdom. Séances Acad. Sci.,* **251**:474.

LEVIN, B., MACKAY, H. M. M., and OBERHOLZER, V. G. 1961. Argininosuccinicaciduria. *Arch. Dis. Child.,* **36**:622.

LIEB, H. 1924. Cerebrosidespeicherung bei Morbus Gaucher. *Hoppe Seyler Z. Physiol. Chem.,* **140**:305.

LOWE, C. U., TERREY, M., and MACLACHLAN, E. A. 1952. Organic aciduria, decreased renal ammonia production, hydrophthalmos, and mental retardation: a clinical entity. *A.M.A. J. Dis. Child.,* **83**:164.

LUMSDEN, C. E. 1959. *Nourishing Brain Cells.* Cambridge: Leeds University Press.

MACKENZIE, D. Y., and WOOLF, L. I. 1959. Maple syrup urine disease, an inborn error of the metabolism of valine, leucine and isoleucine associated with gross mental deficiency. *Brit. Med. J.,* **1**:90.

McMURRAY, W. C., RATHBUN, J. C., MOHYUDDIN, F., and KOEGLER, S. J. 1963. Citrullinuria. *Pediatrics,* **32**:347.

MASON, H. H., and TURNER, M. D. 1935. Chronic galactaemia. *A.M.A. J. Dis. Child.,* **50**:359.

MENKES, J. H., HURST, P. L., and CRAIG, J. M. 1954. New syndrome: progressive familial infantile cerebral dysfunction associated with unusual urinary substance. *Pediatrics,* **14**:462.

MONTCRIEFF, A. A., and WILKINSON, R. H. 1954. Sucrosuria with mental defect and hiatus hernia. *Acta Paediat.,* **43** (Suppl. 100):495.

MOORE, S., and STEIN, W. H. 1954. Procedures for the chromatographic determination of amino acids on four percent cross-linked sulfonated polysterene resins. *J. Biol. Chem.,* **211**:893.

PAGE, I. H. 1937. *Chemistry of the Brain,* p. 6. Springfield, Ill.: C. C Thomas.

PAINE, R. S. 1960. Evaluation of familial biochemically determined mental retardation in children with special reference to aminoaciduria. *New Engl. J. Med.,* **262**:658.

PARE, C. M. B., SANDLER, M., and STACEY,

R. S. 1958. Decreased 5-hydroxytryptophan decarboxylase activity in phenylketonuria. *Lancet,* **2**:1099.

PATAU, K., SMITH, D. W., THERMAN, E., INHORN, S. L. and WAGNER, H. P. 1960. Multiple congenital anomaly caused by an extra autosome. *Lancet,* **1**:790.

PISANO, J. J., MITOMA, C., and UDENFRIEND, S. 1957. Biosynthesis of γ-guanidinobutyric acid from γ-aminobutyric acid and arginine. *Nature,* **180**:1125.

QUASTEL, J. H. 1961. *The Chemistry of Brain Metabolism in Health and Disease.* Springfield, Ill.: C. C Thomas.

QUASTEL, J. H., and WHEATLY, A. H. M. 1932. Oxidations by the brain. *Biochem. J.* **26**:725.

RAPPORT, M. M., LERNER, B., ALONZO, N., and FRANZL, R. E. 1957. The structure of plasmalogens. *J. Biol. Chem.,* **225**:859.

RATNER, S., MORELL, H., and CARVELLO, E. 1960. Enzymes of arginine metabolism in the brain. *Arch. Biochem. Biophys.,* **91**:280.

RENSON, J., GOODWIN, F., WEISSBACH, H., and UDENFRIEND, S. 1961. Conversion of tryptophan to 5-hydroxytryptophan by phenylalanine hydroxylase. *Biochem. Biophys. Res. Commun.,* **6**:20.

RICHTER, D. 1958. Protein metabolism in the brain. *In:* F. BRÜCKE (ed.), *Biochemistry of the Central Nervous System,* p. 173. *Proc. IV Int. Cong. Biochem.,* Vienna.

ROBERTS, E., and FRANKEL, S. 1950. γ-aminobutyric acid in brain: its formation from glutamic acid. *J. Biol. Chem.,* **187**:55.

ROBERTS, R. B., FLEXNER, J. B., and FLEXNER, L. B. 1959. Further observations relating to the synthesis in amino acids and proteins by the cerebral cortex and liver of the mouse. *J. Neurochem.,* **4**:78.

ROWLEY, P. T., MUELLEN, P. S., WATKIN, D. M. and ROSENBERG, L. E. 1960. Familial growth retardation, renal aminoaciduria and Cor Pulmonale: I. Description of a new syndrome; II. Investigation of renal function, amino acid metabolism and genetic transmission. *Amer. J. Med.,* **31**:187, 205.

RUSSELL, A., LEVIN, B., OBERHOLZER, V. G., and SINCLAIR, L. 1962. Hyperammoniaemia. *Lancet,* **2**:699.

SACHS, B. 1896. A familial form of idiocy, generally fatal, associated with early blindness. *J. Nerv. Ment. Dis.,* **21**:475.

SCHURR, P. E., THOMPSON, H. T., HENDERSON, L. M., WILLIAMS, J. N., and ELVEHJEM, C. A. 1950. The determination of free amino acids in rat tissues. *J. Biol. Chem.,* **182**:39.

SCHWARZ, V., GOLDBERG, L., KOMROWER, G. M., and HOLZEL, A. Some disturbances of erythrocyte metabolism in galactosemia. *Biochem. J.,* **62**:34.

SCOTT, D. B. M., and COHEN, S. S. 1951. Enzymatic formation of pentose-phosphate from 6-P-gluconate. *J. Biol. Chem.,* **188**:509.

SEITELBERGER, F. 1957. The position of gargoylism amongst the sphingolipidoses on the basis of the histochemistry of cellular storage substances. *In:* J. N. CUMINGS and A. LOWENTHAL (eds.), *Cerebral Lipidoses,* p. 77. Oxford: Blackwell Scientific Publications.

SMITH, A. J., and STRANG, L. B. 1958. Inborn error of metabolism with the urinary excretion of α-hydroxybutyric acid and phenylpyruvic acid. *Arch. Dis. Child.,* **33**:109.

SMITH, D. W., PATAU, K., THERMAN, E., and INHORN, S. L. 1960. A new autosomal trisomy syndrome: multiple congenital anomalies caused by an extra chromosome. *J. Pediat.,* **57**:338.

SMITH, I. 1960. *Chromatographic and Electrophoretic Techniques.* Vol. 1: *Chromatography.* London: Heineman Med. Books; New York: Interscience Publishers.

SPACKMAN, D. H. 1960. *Instruction Manual and Handbook* (Beckman/Spinco Model 120 Amino Acid Analyzer). Beckman Instruments, Inc.

SPACKMAN, D. H., STEIN, W. H., and MOORE, S. 1958. Automatic recording apparatus for use in the chromatography of amino acids. *Anal. Chem.,* **30**:1190.

SPIELMEYER, W. 1929. Vom Wesen des anatomischen Prozesses bei der familiaren amaurotische Idiotie. *J. Psychol. Neurol.,* **38**:120.

SPORN, M. B., DINGMAN, W., DEFALCO, A., and DAVIES, R. K. 1959. The synthesis of urea in the living rat brain. *J. Neurochem.,* **5**:62.

STAHL, E. 1956. Thin layer chromatography: the method, affecting factors and a few examples of application (Ger.). *Pharmazie,* **11**:633.

———. 1962. Dunnschicht-Chromatographie.

Ein Laboratoriumshandbuch. Berlin: Springer-Verlag.

STANBURY, J. B., KASSENAAR, A. A. H., and MEIJER, J. W. A. 1956. The metabolism of iodotyrosines. I. The fate of mono- and di-iodotyrosines in normal subjects and in patients with various diseases. *J. Clin. Endocrinol.*, 16:735.

STANBURY, J. B., WYNGAARDEN, J. B., and FREDRICKSON, D. S. 1960. *The Metabolic Basis of Inherited Disease.* New York: McGraw-Hill.

STEIN, W. H., BEARN, A. G., and MOORE, S. 1954. The amino acid content of the blood and urine in Wilson's disease. *J. Clin. Invest.*, 33:410.

STRECKER, H. J. 1957. Glutamic acid and glutamine. *In:* D. RICHTER (ed.), *Metabolism of the Nervous System*, p. 459. New York: Pergamon Press.

SVENNERHOLM, L., and RAAL, A. 1961. Composition of brain gangliosides. *Biochim. Biophys. Acta*, 53:422.

TALLAN, H. H., MOORE, S., and STEIN, W. H. 1954. Studies on the free amino acids and related compounds in the tissues of the cat. *J. Biol. Chem.*, 211:927.

TASHIAN, R. E. 1961. Problems of the chemical diagnosis of some hereditary metabolic diseases. *Clin. Chem.*, 7:441.

TAY, W. 1881. Symmetrical changes in the region of the yellow spot in each eye of an infant. *Trans. Ophthalmol. Soc. U. K.*, 1:155.

THUDICHUM, J. L. W. 1884. *A Treatise on the Chemical Constitution of the Brain.* London: Bailere, Tindall & Cox.

UDENFRIEND, S. 1958. Serotonin metabolism and the central nervous system. *In:* F. BRÜCKE (ed.), *Biochemistry of the Central Nervous System*, p. 301. *Proc. IV Int. Cong. of Biochem.*, Vienna.

UDENFRIEND, S., and COOPER, J. R. 1953. Assay of L-phenylalanine as phenylethylamine after enzymatic decarboxylation: application of isotopic studies. *J. Biol. Chem.*, 203:953.

VOGT, H. 1905. Uber familiare amaurotische Idiotie und verwandte Krankheitsbilder. *Monatschrifte Psychiat. Neurol.*, 18:161, 310.

VON REUSS, A. 1908. Zucker Ausscheidung in Säuglingsalter. *Wiener med. Wochenschrift*, 58:799.

WAELSCH, H., SPERRY, W. M., and STOYANOFF, V. A. 1940. A study of the synthesis and deposition of lipids in brain and other tissues with deuterium as indicator. *J. Biol. Chem.*, 135:291.

––––. 1941. Influence of growth and myelinization on the deposition and metabolism of lipids in the brain. *J. Biol. Chem.*, 140:885.

WAISMAN, H. A., WANG, H. L., HARLOW, H. F., and SPONHOLZ, R. R. 1959. Experimental phenylketonuria in the monkey. *Proc. Soc. Exper. Biol. Med.*, 101:864.

WAISMAN, H. A., WANG, H. L., PALMER, G., and HARLOW, H. F. 1960. Phenylketonuria in infant monkeys. *Nature*, 188:1124.

WALKER, J. B. 1958. Role for pancreas in biosynthesis of creatinine. *Proc. Soc. Exp. Biol.*, 98:7.

WANG, H. L., HARWALKAR, V. H., and WAISMAN, H. A. 1962. Effect of dietary phenylalanine and tryptophan on brain serotonin. *Arch. Biochem. Biophys.*, 96:181.

WANG, H. L., MORTON, N. E., and WAISMAN, H. A. 1961. Increased reliability for the determination of the carrier state in phenylketonuria. *Amer. J. Human Genet.*, 13:255.

WEIL-MALHERBE, H. 1936. Studies on brain metabolism. I. The metabolism of glutamic acid in brain. *Biochem. J.*, 30:665.

WEIL-MALHERBE, H., and BONE, A. D. 1952. The concentrations of adrenaline-like substances in blood during insulin hypoglycaemia. *J. Ment. Sci.*, 98:565.

WEST, G. B. 1957. Histamine in nervous tissue. *In:* D. RICHTER (ed.), *Metabolism of the Nervous Tissue*, p. 578. New York: Pergamon Press.

WESTALL, R. G. 1960. Argininosuccinic aciduria: identification and reactions of the abnormal metabolite in a newly described form of mental disease. *Biochem. J.*, 77:135.

WESTALL, R. G., DANCIS, J., and MILLER, S. 1957. Maple syrup urine disease. *A.M.A. J. Dis. Child.*, 94:571.

GENETICS IN MENTAL
RETARDATION

V. Elving Anderson

The past decade has witnessed a vigorous growth and expansion in the study of genetics. From a position of relative unimportance, genetics has moved into the role of one of the central integrating disciplines within biology. One of the reasons for this central position is the scope of the field, ranging from the study of molecular phenomena within cells to the investigation of population dynamics on a world-wide scale.

Whether it be in micro-organisms or in man, the careful study of "inborn errors of metabolism" has become an essential tool for analyzing the intricate biochemical pathways. Information obtained about these deviations leads to an understanding of the more usual mechanisms. As is common in research, further complexities have developed. Some conditions, such as cystinuria, were thought to be caused by a simple metabolic block resulting from the absence of an enzyme. More careful study has shown that this problem is rather one of faulty transport of materials across the wall of the kidney tubule. In other instances, the effect of the gene is shown to be an altered and less effective enzyme rather than the complete absence of the enzyme.

In human genetics, important advances have been made possible by new techniques. The use of computers has facilitated more sophisticated statistical analysis of large masses of data. New methods for tissue culture have made possible the study of human chromosomes. New methods for the analysis of proteins have led to an understanding of the genetic loci controlling the formation of human hemoglobin and this understanding is as comprehensive as that for any other locus in any other organism.

"Behavior genetics" is emerging as an experimental approach to the neural basis of behavior. As general principles emerge from such comparative studies, we should have more appropriate models and hypotheses for analyzing differences in human behavior. It is interesting to observe that psychology, sociology, anthropology, and genetics all agree upon the importance of the family in the development of behavior patterns. All of these disciplines together face the difficult problem of trying to disentangle the many variables affecting behavior.

It is possible to conclude that the field of genetics offers some powerful tools for the analysis of a number of important problems. At the same time, geneticists have become keenly aware of the limited scope of some of these methods. The purpose of this chapter, then, is to review some types of genetic methodology for the study of mental retardation and some of the tentative conclusions derived from such studies. It seems appropriate, moreover, to outline areas of ignorance and make some tentative suggestions for new avenues of approach. In general, the emphasis is more upon questions and tools than upon answers. The selection of details from the voluminous literature was based on a desire to stimulate more effective interdisciplinary research, even though the choices are inevitably somewhat arbitrary and personal.

Genetic Aspects of Mental Retardation

As a starting point for discussion, it may be interesting to go back to a report by Roberts at the 1950 International Congress of Psychiatry for an excellent summary of the interpretation of the genetics of "oligophrenia" current at that time. In order to illustrate the problems encountered in the study of mental retardation he used an analogy between blindness and retardation:

If the eye were not an external organ, if the ophthalmoscope had not been invented and if the pathology of the eye were as complicated as that of the brain, a conference somewhat like this one would no doubt be discussing the genetics of "poor vision." It would be easily recognized that blindness or near-blindness undoubtedly constituted poor vision, but there would be endless discussion about where poor vision ended and normal vision began. We should perceive exasperating glimpses of causation; a dominant gene here, a recessive or sex-linked gene there; its association on occasion with other malformations and defects; the pointers to much of it being due to a combination of genetic and environmental causes; the clear nongenetic instances due to infection or trauma. There would be those who would wish to define and classify poor vision on the basis of measurement and those who would prefer to use the criterion of social adaptation—the capacity of the individual to succeed in his work and in his life in the community. Some would hold that given a certain measured amount of poor vision, the success or otherwise of this social adaptation depended on additional emotional, educational and social factors. Others would maintain with heat that given two individuals with identical errors of refraction, one had a certain inborn something about him which definitely and infallibly made him a person of poor vision, whereas the other lacking those qualities must equally definitely be classified as normal (Roberts, 1950, p. 56).

Roberts then pointed out that the population distribution of IQ scores tends to form a normal curve, with the exception that there is an excess of individuals at the very low end of the scale. From a variety of forms of evidence he postulated that the majority of cases with *severe* retardation result from pathological processes. The majority of cases of *mild* retardation, on the other hand, were thought to represent the lower end of the distribution of "normal" measured intelligence. (For purposes of discussion the line between mild and severe retardation might be set approximately at IQ 50.) This general concept has received further experimental support and general acceptance (Roberts, 1952; Dingman and Tarjan, 1960).

Implicit in this argument is a classification of cases with retardation on two different dimensions: (1) the severity of retardation, and (2) the probable etiology. If this approach to the problem is restated in the form of Table 1, it becomes apparent that four categories are theoretically involved in Roberts' concept. Among cases with mild retardation, those with multiple etiology (class C) can be assumed to be more frequent than those with one major cause (class A). In severe retardation, however, class B (single cause) is much more common than class D (multiple etiology).

This formulation does not make a distinction between genetic and non-genetic factors. The research methods for making such a distinction, in fact, are quite different for the different categories. A positive laboratory test for phenylketonuria, a photomicrograph showing forty-seven chromosomes, or a clinical history of hyperbilirubinemia with signs of kernicterus can be assumed to provide sufficient evidence for the most important "cause" of the mental retardation in a given case of class B. On the other hand, the experimental design for the analysis of class C would involve complex statistical methods; the number of variables and the nature of the inter-actions between them makes the identi-fication of separate factors extremely dif-ficult.

Single major factors do not always lead to retardation so severe as to appear discontinuous on an IQ scale. The single-locus genetic causes of mental retarda-tion produce a basic discontinuity for those traits which are the direct result of gene action but not necessarily for the more complex patterning of traits meas-ured by IQ tests. The distribution of phenylalanine blood levels in phenylke-tonurics, for example, does not at all

sent the lower end of a continuous IQ distribution for the general population and would thus fall into class C. If this be true, it would be difficult to reduce noticeably the frequency of such cases until we understand more about the nature of "normal" behavior. At the same time, any advances in the understanding of mild retardation may have some im-plications for the entire IQ range.

With these general considerations in mind, we can proceed to a review of what is presently known about genetic factors in mental retardation. This re-view is not intended to be comprehen-

TABLE 1

CLASSIFICATION OF MENTAL RETARDATION
BY ETIOLOGY AND SEVERITY

	Mild Retardation	Severe Retardation
Single major cause	A. Some cases with meta-bolic defect or birth trauma	B. Metabolic defect Chromosomal anomaly Birth trauma Low birth weight
Many factors involved	C. Polygenic traits inter-acting with environmen-tal factors	D. Assumed to be infre-quent Severe environmental deprivation

overlap the distribution in persons who have a normal supply of the enzyme phenylalanine hydroxylase. When phen-ylketonurics are tested for IQ, how-ever, the distribution overlaps that for non-affected persons. In terms of Table 1, most phenylketonurics would fall into class B, but some would be found in class A. In a similar manner, major en-vironmental factors can lead to different degrees of retardation. Knobloch and Pasamanick (1961) have reviewed the evidence indicating that mild retardation may result from prematurity or other perinatal problems. We can expect that further research will reveal other single major causes for mild retardation.

A majority of the cases of mild retar-dation, however, are assumed to repre-

sive. The purposes are: (1) to indicate the variety of mechanisms which can lead to mental retardation, (2) to dem-onstrate the implications of genetic de-fects for an understanding of normal function, and (3) to illustrate some of the genetic questions involved. Further details are available in the book by Pen-rose (1963), the survey by Masland (1958), and the shorter reviews by Goodman and Herndon (1959) and by Zellweger (1963). Biochemical aspects are treated in the books by Hsia (1959) and Stanbury et al. (1960) and in the general reviews by Wright et al. (1958), Moncrieff (1960), Paine (1960), Slack et al. (1960), Zellweger (1961), and Scriver (1962).

AMINO ACID AND HORMONE METABOLISM

The classic example of an inborn error of metabolism as a cause of mental retardation is phenylketonuria (PKU), (Knox, 1960; Lyman, 1963). The first step was the discovery in 1934 among inmates in a Norwegian mental institution of several persons with an unusual urinary constituent. Shortly thereafter, biochemical analysis showed that the urinary findings resulted from an enzyme deficiency which led to a high plasma level of phenylalanine and a subsequent overflow through the kidney. It was not until family studies were made, however, that it was possible to conclude that the condition resulted from homozygosity for a rare recessive gene. The sequence of these findings illustrates the fact that three types of data are required for the analysis of such a disorder: clinical, biochemical, and genetic.

From the clinical point of view the most striking finding is a mental retardation of such severity that most affected persons (in the absence of dietary treatment) have an IQ of 30 or less. Some behavioral changes are observed, including a decreased attention span and decreased responsiveness to the environment. Neurological findings include seizures, spasticity, hyperactive reflexes, and tremors (Jervis, 1963). An abnormal EEG pattern is also reported. Physical findings may include a slight reduction in stature and head size, a lighter color of hair, eyes and skin, and a tendency to develop dermatitis. There is considerable variability, however, so that a single person seldom exhibits all of these signs.

In spite of very intensive research, the basic biochemical lesion within the central nervous system has not yet been clearly defined. In a few cases, it has been possible to obtain autopsy examination on persons with PKU (Knox, 1960). The pathological reports showed defective myelination with an excessive number of oligodendrocytes and astrocytes. These findings are quite non-specific and would not have been recognized as a distinctive syndrome without the prior clinical history and biochemical tests. These findings, however, suggest the value of neuropathological examination in any of the other biochemical defects known to lead to mental retardation. Documentation of this kind may help to close the gaps in our knowledge and be profitable to all of the disciplines involved—pathology, neurology, pediatrics, genetics, biochemistry, and psychology.

Another puzzle is the failure to find any correlation between the measured intelligence (IQ) and the quantity of urinary amino acids. Part of the problem has arisen from difficulties in correcting for age or for other variables such as diet. One possible approach would be through studies of pairs of same-sexed twins in which both are affected with PKU. If modifying genes or variant alleles are involved, monozygotic twin pairs should show a greater similarity than dizygotic twin pairs with respect to measured intelligence and pattern of urinary amino acids. Tashian (1959) demonstrated individual variability in the metabolism of D-phenylalanine and suggested that a part of such variability may be genetic in origin.

The deficiency in the enzyme phenylalanine hydroxylase results not only in an accumulation of phenylalanine and a deficiency of tyrosine but also in other readjustments to this distorted pattern of amino acid metabolism. Knox (1960) reports changes in epinephrine tolerance and the finding of abnormal beta-lipoproteins. It may be of interest that abnormalities in epinephrine tolerance have also been suspected in schizophrenic patients.

PKU has provided a very valuable illustration of the effect of treatment in a genetic biochemical defect. If started early enough, a diet low in phenylalanine is apparently effective in eliminating most of the gross harmful effects of the disease. Knox and Hsia (1957) report that when the special diet is given to older patients the IQ is observed to increase slightly, possibly only because of improved testability resulting from increased attention span and other psychological changes. Careful psychometric examination of such patients before and after dietary treatment might provide interesting evidence about the effect of attention span and other variables upon measured IQ.

The genetic studies of phenylketonuria illustrate the basic genetic questions which may arise in the study of any single-locus genetic defect.

1. *Gene frequency.*—The estimation of gene frequency is one of the basic problems of human genetics. If the gene frequency should vary in different populations, further study may reveal differences in the direction and strength of natural selection (Haldane, 1961). Estimates of gene frequency, together with information about reproductive fitness, will permit estimates of mutation rates (Crow, 1961; Neel, 1962). PKU was first identified in Norway, and reports suggest that the frequency of the disease may be higher in the Scandinavian countries and other parts of northern Europe than elsewhere. The incidence is reported to be very low among Jewish people (Knox, 1960, 1963). Better data from other geographic areas are required, however, before any valid conclusions can be drawn.

2. *Heterozygote detection.*—With an estimated frequency of PKU at birth of 4 per 100,000, about 1.3 per cent of the general population would be expected to be carriers or heterozygotes (having only one gene for PKU). Carriers would be 300 times more numerous than those actually affected with the disease. If the frequency of PKU is 10 per 100,000, about 2 per cent of the population would be carriers. Recent refinements in loading tests and in the analysis of the data

have permitted the distinction of carriers from the rest of the normal population with a minimum of overlap (Wang, Morton, and Waisman, 1961). This information is important to the geneticist as an aid in obtaining more accurate estimates of gene frequency. Furthermore, there is a theoretical possibility that heterozygotes may show some slight deviation from the "normal" phenotype. Penrose (1935) suggested that carriers for phenylketonuria might show psychotic symptoms at a greater frequency than persons in the general population, but the data do not yet permit a final conclusion (Knox, 1960). Nevertheless, the possibility of some heterozygote effect should be checked in other recessive biochemical defects.

3. *Linkage.*—One of the basic facts of genetics is that genes are on chromosomes. In man there are twenty-three pairs of chromosomes. A specific location on one of these pairs of chromosomes is designated a *locus*, and the different genes which may be found at a specific locus are termed *alleles*. (A single chromosome, of course, will carry only one allele at the locus.) Thus, the dominant gene for the normal enzyme, phenylalanine hydroxylase, and the recessive gene leading to phenylketonuria are alleles at a single locus on one of the pairs of chromosomes. It is obvious that on this same pair of chromosomes there are a number of other loci which control other characteristics. All of these loci are said to be linked since they are carried on the same chromosome pair. Renwick, Lawler, and Cowie (1960) analyzed the data from seventy-four families and concluded that the phenylketonuria locus and the ABO blood-group locus may be on the same chromosome pair, although the evidence is still weak. Linkage studies provide an important research tool as a test of genetic heterogeneity (Renwick, 1961).

The term *linkage* must not be confused with *association*. The signs of phenylketonuria include phenylpyruvic acid in the urine, seizures, spasticity, and mental retardation. The association of these traits in the syndrome must result in some manner from the single enzyme defect, but this association has nothing to do with linkage. Similarly, the finding of an association between duodenal ulcer and blood group O tells us nothing about the linkage of any genetic loci involved.

4. *Heterogeneity.*—Frequently in microbial genetics the careful study of what appeared to be a single mutation has revealed that several different mutations were involved, either at the same locus or at different loci. What originally appeared to be the absence of an enzyme turned out to be an altered (and less effective) enzyme. Or a normal enzyme was produced in normal quantity, but its effect was inhibited by another enzyme controlled by a different set of genes. Sutton (1961) has described some of the different types of "metabolic blocks" observed in man. Kalow (1959) reviewed the evidence which led to the identification of two different types of cholinesterase, the result of two different genes at the same locus. There is no indication as yet that the cases presently diagnosed as phenylketonuria include several types of metabolic defects, but the possibility must be kept open.

Some of the other genetic conditions involving amino acid or hormone metabolism and leading to mental retardation are listed in Table 2. The list is clear evidence of the fact that mental retardation is quite heterogeneous genetically. The existence of normal mental function in an individual is evidence that these and other genetic mechanisms are all operating in a normal manner. The list also gives some idea of the different combinations of clinical signs which have been observed (but is not intended as a complete summary of all diagnostic criteria). Many of the amino acid disorders lead to seizures and motor problems (such as spasticity), but few of them involve eye changes or congenital malformations.

There have been several attempts to develop biochemical screening procedures (tests of urine or blood) which can be applied to large populations. Tashian (1961), however, has pointed out the need for caution. The effect of diet and drugs must always be kept in mind, since these may produce misleading results. Furthermore, biochemical or symptomatic similarities in different conditions tend to make accurate diagnosis difficult.

A recent illustration of possible misdiagnosis is seen in the discovery of a familial disturbance in the metabolism of histidine. Ghadimi *et al.* (1961) observed high levels of histidine in the plasma and urine of two siblings. There was also a substance in the urine which gave a positive test with ferric chloride similar to the reaction with phenylpyruvic acid. Auerbach *et al.* (1962) identified the unusual urinary constituent as imidazolepyruvic acid. La Du *et al.* (1962) have shown the absence of the enzyme histidase. Histidine-tolerance tests showed that both parents of the affected children showed an abnormal response, supporting the view that histidinemia is inherited as a recessive trait. Of particular interest is the observation that these children have a normal IQ but show speech defects (in articulation) and short auditory memory. Careful clinical examination of affected children by specialists in speech pathology may help to identify the nature of the defect. Additional families must be studied to rule out the possibility of a chance association of the enzyme deficiency and speech defects in the few children already examined.

The fact that a supposed entity becomes subdivided with further investigation is illustrated by recent data concerning mental retardation in cretinism with goiter. Stanbury (1960) reviewed

TABLE 2

SOME CONDITIONS INVOLVING DISTURBANCES IN AMINO ACID OR HORMONE
METABOLISM AND LEADING TO MENTAL RETARDATION

Condition and Mode of Inheritance*	Biochemical and Pathological Findings	Intellectual, Behavioral, and Emotional Signs	Motor Signs	Other Clinical Signs
Arginosuccinic-aciduria (probably AR)	Arginosuccinic acid in urine	Early development normal but severely retarded by about five years of age. Periods of apathy and fretfulness	Motor retardation, convulsions	Dry and brittle hair (fluorescing red), liver enlargement
Citrullinuria [one child, parents first cousins (McMurray et al., 1963)]	High level of citrulline in serum, spinal fluid and urine. Elevated blood ammonia	Developmental regression, IQ under 20	Parkinsonian tremor of head and hands	Severe vomiting episodes beginning at nine months of age
Cystathioninuria [two adults: (a) female and (b) male (Frimpter et al., 1963)]	Abnormal excretion of cystathionine	(a) IQ 42. (b) Low normal intelligence, difficulty in concentrating, impaired judgment		(a) Small pituitary and thyroid, clubfoot. (b) Acromegaly, enlarged thyroid
Familial goiter (four types, probably AR)	Defects in the synthesis, storage, or secretion of thyroid hormone	Gross mental retardation in many cases		Dwarfism, thyroid enlargement, dry skin and hair
Familial hormonal disorder (Richards and Rundle, 1959: probably AR)	Gross reduction of urinary estrogen, pregnandiol, and total 17-neutral ketosteroids	Mental retardation	Ataxia, some peripheral muscle wasting	Deaf-mutism, underdevelopment of secondary sex characteristics
Hartnup disease (AR)	Generalized aminoaciduria. Probably defect in tryptophane transport in gut, liver, and kidney	Emotional instability. Mild mental retardation in some. Some with confusional psychosis, depression, and anxiety state	Reversible cerebellar ataxia, nystagmus	Pellagra-like rash
Homocystinuria (Carson et al., 1963: probably AR)	Homocystine in urine, increased methionine in plasma and urine	Severe mental retardation	Convulsions, progressive paraplegia	Dislocation of lenses, fine hair, red cheeks, short fingers and toes

* AR indicates autosomal recessive. XR indicates X-linked recessive.

References not listed here will be found in the text of this chapter, in Paine (1960), Stanbury et al. (1960), or Merritt (1963).

354

TABLE 2—*Continued*

Condition and Mode of Inheritance*	Biochemical and Pathological Findings	Intellectual, Behavioral, and Emotional Signs	Motor Signs	Other Clinical Signs
Lowe's oculocerebro-renal syndrome (probably XR)	Aminoaciduria, albuminuria, reduced ability of kidneys to form ammonia	Mental retardation	Hypotonia, diminished or absent reflexes	Cataracts, glaucoma, hypophosphatemic rickets
Maple syrup urine disease (probably AR)	Keto acids of leucine, isoleucine and valine in urine (defect in oxidative decarboxylation)	Severe mental retardation	Convulsions, muscular hypertonicity, decerebrate rigidity	Physical retardation, vomiting, poor feeding, maple syrup odor to urine
Microcephaly with spastic diplegia (Paine, 1960: XR)	Mild generalized aminoaciduria	Severe mental retardation	Spastic diplegia, myoclonic seizures	Microcephaly
Nephrogenic diabetes insipidus (XR, with some expression in carrier females)	Persistently hypotonic urine. No response to antidiuretic hormone	Mental retardation in some, perhaps secondary to repeated severe dehydration	Convulsions in infants	Excessive thirst and urine production
Oasthouse urine disease (one case)	Urinary excretion of alpha-hydroxy-butyric acid and phenylpyruvic acid	Severely retarded, unresponsive to stimuli	Hypotonicity, muscular flaccidity	Episodes of fever, rapid breathing, and generalized pitting edema, , unusual smell to urine
Phenylketonuria (AR)	Elevated serum phenylalanine, phenylpyruvic acid in urine. Deficiency of phenylalanine hydroxylase	Mental retardation usually severe in untreated; IQ rarely up to 100. Hyperkinesis, irritability, digital mannerisms. Some destructiveness, unpredictable behavior	Increased muscle tone. Some with seizures, tremors, or spasticity	Eczema, often blond with blue eyes
Pseudohypoparathyroidism (possibly AR)	High serum phosphorus, low serum and urinary calcium. No response to parathyroid extract	Frequently mentally retarded. Face expressionless, masklike. Said to be friendly, docile	Tetanic and epileptic convulsions	Short stature, short round face, short digits, cataracts
Wilson's disease (AR)	Abnormal pattern of amino acid excretion, deficiency of serum ceruloplasmin in almost all cases, deposition of copper in tissues	Usually normal as child, then mental deterioration. Restless, excitable, affective instability. May present with symptoms suggesting schizophrenia	Dyskinesia (tremor, dystonia, or choreoathetotic movements). Rigidity and spasms of muscles	Pigmented (Kayser-Fleischer) ring in cornea, cirrhosis of liver

the evidence showing that subtypes of familial goiter can be identified as biochemical defects at several different stages in the manufacture and release of the thyroid hormone. The affected persons show gross mental retardation, with the exception of certain families in which the persons with congenital goiter show deaf-mutism instead of mental retardation.

The observation of mental retardation in cases of vasopressin-resistant diabetes insipidus presents an unsolved puzzle (Orloff and Burg, 1960). The retardation has sometimes been described as a secondary result of problems of water balance. Pathological and histochemical studies of brains from affected persons may provide interesting clues to the normal control of brain water balance.

LIPID METABOLISM

Lipids are a significant component of brain tissue accounting for about one-half of the total solids. These lipids in the central nervous system are highly complex and are considerably different from lipids in the rest of the body. Studies with deuterium-labeled fatty acids suggest that lipids are synthesized within the central nervous system from simpler components rather than being transported from other parts of the body (Tower, 1958).

It is not surprising, then, to find a number of different genetically determined metabolic defects involving the cerebral lipids and resulting in mental retardation. Recent developments in histochemical techniques have made possible a clearer differentiation of the various types, and genetic studies have helped to define entities by showing the range of variability within a family (and thus presumably resulting from the same defect). The two major classes involve (1) abnormal storage within neurons and (2) defects in myelination. (See Table 3.)

The neuronal storage diseases are clas-sified on the basis of the age at onset (infantile, juvenile, or adult), the type of compound stored, and the organs involved (whether limited to the brain or not). In Tay-Sachs disease, for example, the affected children appear normal at birth, but the neurological signs are usually well defined by one year of age. The abnormal storage involves a ganglioside and is limited to the brain. In Spielmeyer-Vogt disease the storage compound is also a ganglioside, but the age at onset ranges from five to ten years, and cases are not found together with Tay-Sachs disease in the same family (Fredrickson, 1960). In Niemann-Pick disease (involving sphingomyelin) and Gaucher's disease (involving cerebrosides) the biochemical lesions are often found in the liver, spleen, and other parts of the body as well as in the brain. Each of the latter two diseases may include three genetically distinct conditions (Hsia et al., 1962; Knudson and Kaplan, 1962). The variability observed among these diseases is a cogent reminder of the need for a combined evaluation of biochemical, genetic, and clinical information in the definition of syndromes.

A feature of special interest in Tay-Sachs disease is the fact that it is more common among Ashkenazic Jews than among other Jewish or non-Jewish populations. Myrianthopoulos (1962) studied death records in the entire United States for the years 1954 to 1957 and found that in two-thirds of the cases one or both parents were Jewish. The frequency of carriers (heterozygotes) was estimated at one in 40 for Jews and one in 380 for non-Jews. Myrianthopoulos discussed differentials in breeding pattern, mutation rate, and fertility of heterozygotes as possible explanations for the higher rate among Jews. The factors responsible for the difference may have been active several centuries ago and may not be observable now.

A progressive loss of myelin may

TABLE 3

SOME CONDITIONS INVOLVING DISTURBANCES IN CARBOHYDRATE OR LIPID
METABOLISM AND LEADING TO MENTAL RETARDATION

Condition and Mode of Inheritance*	Biochemical and Patho-logical Findings	Intellectual, Behavioral, and Emotional Signs	Motor Signs	Other Clinical Signs
Crigler-Najjar syndrome (AR)	Elevation of unconjugated bilirubin in serum, reduced excretion of bilirubin by liver, kernicterus	Severe mental retardation in most cases	Ataxia, dysarthric speech, intention tremor, muscular rigidity	Severe persistent jaundice
Fructosemia [AR (Levin *et al.*, 1963)]	Fructosuria, hypoglycemia. Liver biopsy showed marked reduction of aldolase activity to fructose-1-phosphate and fructose-1,6-diphosphate	Mild mental retardation in some cases		Cane sugar intolerance, attacks of vomiting and anorexia, liver enlargement
Galactosemia (AR)	Galactosuria, aminoaciduria, albuminuria. Deficiency of galactose-1-phosphate uridyl transferase	Mental retardation of varying degree in untreated cases. Lethargy	Hypotonia	Cataracts, enlargement of liver and spleen, jaundice, vomiting
Gaucher's disease, infantile type (AR)	Accumulation of glucocerebrosides (kerasin) in ganglion cells and other tissues	Severe mental retardation	Spasticity, paralysis	Enlarged liver and spleen
Generalized glycogenosis (Pompe's disease: AR)	Excessive accumulation of glycogen in all muscles	Severe mental retardation	Hypotonia of muscles, some with seizures	Cardiac enlargement and failure. Death usually within one year of life
Hurler's disease (AR and XR forms)	Abnormal urinary excretion of chondroitin sulfate B and heparitin sulfate	Severe mental retardation. Irritability, fits of anger, aggressive behavior		Dwarfism, enlarged liver and spleen. Deafness in XR form; corneal clouding in AR form
Hypoglycemia, type described by Lewis *et al.*, 1963 (probably AR)	Hypoglycemia following 12-hour fast. Liver biopsy showed absence of glycogen synthetase activity	Of three affected sibs, one normal, one mildly retarded, one severely retarded. Retardation probably secondary to hypoglycemic episodes	Convulsions	Apnea and cyanosis in first 48 hours of life

* AR indicates autosomal recessive. XR indicates X-linked recessive.
References not listed here will be found in the text of this chapter, in Stanbury *et al.* (1960), in Merritt (1963), or in Penrose (1963).

TABLE 3—*Continued*

Condition and Mode of Inheritance*	Biochemical and Pathological Findings	Intellectual, Behavioral, and Emotional Signs	Motor Signs	Other Clinical Signs
Krabbe's disease (globoid cell sclerosis: AR)	Demyelination and gliosis, globoid cells in brain	Mental deterioration, irritability	Progressive weakness, tremors, spastic quadriplegia. Some with convulsions	Some with deafness, visual impairment
Metachromatic leukodystrophy, infantile (AR)	Sulfatides in urine, elevated cerebrospinal fluid protein. Diffuse demyelination	Mental deterioration, become dull and apathetic	Weakness and spasticity, ataxia, nystagmus. Some with convulsions	Some with optic atrophy
Myoclonus epilepsy (AR)	Intracellular bodies (Lafora bodies, presumably amyloid) in brain, heart, and liver	Mental retardation in some	Convulsive seizures, myoclonic jerks (especially in extremities). Signs of cerebellar ataxia late in disease	*Café au lait* pigmentation on skin
Niemann-Pick disease (AR)	Accumulation of lipid (mainly sphingomyelin) in reticuloendothelial and other cells	Mental retardation, progressively severe. Late-onset cases may present with behavior and personality problems (hyperactivity, emotional instability)	Athetosis, tremors, muscular rigidity. Some with seizures	Enlarged liver and spleen, retarded physical growth, pigmented areas on skin. Deafness common. Some with cherry-red spot in retina
Pelizaeus-Merzbacher disease (XR)	Diffuse demyelination of cerebral white matter and basal ganglia	Mild or moderate intellectual deterioration	Spasticity, ataxia, nystagmus, intention tremor, dysarthric speech	Slowly progressive, may survive to middle age
Spielmeyer-Vogt disease (AR)	Biopsy of brain or rectum shows nerve cells with lipid (sphingolipid)	Intellectual deterioration starting at age 5–10 years. Some with psychotic reactions, delusions, hallucinations	Disturbance of balance and co-ordination, seizures, paralysis	Rapid deterioration of vision (cerebromacular degeneration)
Tay-Sachs disease (AR)	Increased neuraminic acid in white matter, diffuse severe demyelination. Deficiency of fructose-1-phosphate aldolase reported (Aronson *et al.*, 1962)	Severe mental retardation, apathy	Muscular weakness, seizures	Cherry-red spot in retina, optic atrophy, blindness. Death often in second or third year of life

occur as a secondary process in the neuronal storage diseases, but there are at least four conditions (the leucodystrophies) in which a myelin defect appears to be a primary feature of the disease. The signs involve different combinations of deafness, blindness, nystagmus, ataxia, rigidity, or seizures. In metachromatic leucodystrophy an accumulation of sulfatides has been demonstrated, and the staining material characteristic of the disease can be found in the urine as well as in various body tissues. It is not yet clear whether these conditions represent the breakdown of normal myelin or whether they result from the production of a faulty myelin which is more susceptible to destruction than normal myelin (Poser, 1962).

CARBOHYDRATE METABOLISM

Carbohydrates are important for the nervous system as an energy source (mainly in the form of glucose) and as components in some of the structural compounds. One of the disturbances in carbohydrate metabolism is galactosemia, an enzyme deficiency which may lead to cataract formation, enlargement of the liver and spleen, and mental retardation. Ingested lactose (the main carbohydrate of milk) is normally split into its two components, glucose and galactose, which differ from each other only in structural arrangement. The galactose is then converted into glucose or glucose derivatives by a series of enzyme reactions.

In galactosemics, however, the deficiency of a specific enzyme results in the accumulation of an intermediate compound, galactose 1-phosphate. This intermediate is known to accumulate in the lens of the eye and other tissues, but it also can inhibit the activity of several enzymes required for normal metabolism. The precise reason for the mental retardation is not yet established, however. All of the symptoms and signs may regress and even disappear if a galac-

tose-free diet is instituted early enough in life. Recessive inheritance is established by a relatively high frequency of consanguineous matings, by the frequency of the defect among siblings, and by the fact that parents are free from the disease but show a reduced enzyme activity compatible with heterozygosity (Kalckar, 1959; Isselbacher, 1960; Holzel, 1961).

The enzyme involved can be found in tissues of normal individuals but cannot be demonstrated in corresponding tissues of galactosemic patients. With this fact in mind, Krooth and Weinberg (1961) developed cell lines by means of tissue culture. It was possible to distinguish a galactosemic, a non-galactosemic, and a heterozygous cell line by observing their relative growth in glucose and galactose. This type of approach has implications, not only for the understanding of galactosemia itself, but also for more theoretical genetic problems such as transformation and somatic recombination.

Some of the changes in interpretation brought about by new findings are illustrated by Hurler's syndrome (gargoylism). The affected persons are mentally retarded and have multiple deformities of bone and cartilage as well as enlargement of liver and spleen. Earlier studies of the brain revealed a storage of gangliosides in the cells, leading to the description of the disease as a lipochondrodystrophy. More recent biochemical analysis indicated that the primary defect involves the metabolism of acid mucopolysaccharides, which are constituents of connective tissue and of brain lipoprotein. The genetic analysis of families demonstrated an autosomal recessive type affecting both males and females and showing increased consanguinity among parents. Those affected with this type often have a clouding of the cornea, a feature not seen in the sex-linked recessive variety (Herndon, 1954). A similar defect in mucopolysaccharide metabolism has been observed in snorter dwarf cattle (Lorincz, 1961).

A point of possible future genetic interest in the biochemical disorders concerns the "blood-brain barrier." The presence of such a barrier infers a selective membrane as well as transfer systems for materials which are carried across the barrier. It seems reasonable to assume that the blood-brain barrier must involve specific enzyme systems. There are already several instances of renal defects of a genetic nature in which the kidney tubules are apparently unable to carry out the normal transfer processes. Recent work suggests that similar enzymatic defects are found in the gut, leading to difficulties in absorption (Milne *et al.*, 1961). If enzymatic transfer systems are involved in the blood-brain barrier, we might expect to find genetic transfer defects which could result in damage to the brain.

A different type of genotype-phenotype pathway has been observed in agammaglobulinemia (Good *et al.*, 1960). The abnormal genotype apparently blocks the differentiation of plasma cells which are the source of gamma globulin. It is possible that a similar type of genetic defeat may lead to an abnormality in the oligodendrocytes (which are involved in myelin formation) or in some other type of cell significant for brain structure or function.

CHROMOSOMAL ANOMALIES

Many of the problems associated with the etiology of mongolism were essentially resolved by the discovery of an additional chromosome in affected persons. (It should be observed that the term "Down's syndrome" is replacing "mongolism.") The specific mechanism whereby the extra chromosome leads to the multiple defects is not yet clear, however. The findings may result in part from the triple dose of alleles at specific loci and in part from a more gen-

eralized disturbance of the developmental processes.

The chromosomal studies were made possible by the development of techniques for the tissue culture of human cells (leucocytes, skin, or bone marrow) and for the preparation of slides which are suitable for the microscopic examination of chromosome morphology. Individual chromosomes can then be identified by differences in total length and by the relative position of the centromere (in the middle of the chromosome or toward one end). The normal chromosome complement includes two sex chromosomes (XX for females and XY for males) and forty-four others, designated as autosomes. The X chromosome is medium sized, while the Y is one of the smallest. Among the autosomes, the longest pair is identified as number 1, and the shortest pairs are numbers 21 and 22. Further details may be found in the excellent reviews by Sohval (1963) and Hirschhorn and Cooper (1961).

The most common chromosomal mechanism leading to Down's syndrome involves non-disjunction in the formation of germ cells, with the result that one of the gametes contains two of the number 21 chromosomes. As a result the child has a total of forty-seven chromosomes. In these cases of "trisomy-21" the mean age of the mother at the birth of the child is significantly older than for control populations, but the mean age for fathers is not increased. This leads to the inference that the non-disjunction usually has taken place in the formation of the ovum rather than the sperm (Penrose, 1961*b*).

The other major mechanism leading to Down's syndrome involves a translocation of the major part of chromosome 21 to another chromosome. Most commonly chromosome number 15 appears to be involved, resulting in a 15/21 type of translocation. In almost all the cases where such a translocation is found in the affected child, the mother is shown to have forty-five chromosomes, one of which is the combination of 15 and 21. A second type of translocation involves chromosome 22, leading to a 21/22 type of translocation. In this type the translocation chromosome is frequently found in the father. Furthermore, Penrose (1962) has pointed out that the paternal age at birth of children with a 21/22 type of translocation is significantly older than the control population. Penrose summarized the observations in the different types by suggesting that there appears to be strong selection against: (1) sperm with an extra chromosome 21, (2) chromosomally unbalanced sperm with 15/21 fusion, and (3) unbalanced ova with 21/22 fusion.

The question of the upper limit of the intelligence range in Down's syndrome was explored by Dunsdon, Carter, and Huntley (1960). Among fifty-two children given the Terman-Merrill Test, the highest IQ was 68. They concluded that the upper limit appears to be an IQ of approximately 70. If a patient with a higher measured IQ is thought to have Down's syndrome, a chromosome count should be obtained. Two major possible explanations for a relatively high IQ are mosaicism (in which some cells have forty-seven chromosomes while the others have the normal forty-six), or the presence in triplicate of only a part of chromosome 21. Clarke *et al.* (1961) described a girl who, at two years and three months of age, was of normal intelligence but showed some mongoloid characteristics. Forty-three per cent of the cells studied had forty-seven chromosomes.

Since the discovery of the chromosomal basis for Down's syndrome, two other well-defined autosomal trisomies have been identified. The first of these involves an extra chromosome in the group numbered 13-15, the D group (Smith *et al.*, 1963). The signs include mental retardation, seizures, deafness, eye defects, hyperconvex fingernails, and cleft palate. The other syndrome is characterized by mental retardation, spasticity, failure to thrive, a flexion of finger two over finger three, small mandible, and low-set, malformed ears. There is still disagreement as to whether the latter syndrome should be called trisomy-18 or trisomy-17 (Gottlieb *et al.*, 1962; Uchida *et al.*, 1962).

When these three trisomies are compared it is clear that all involve mental retardation, other neurological problems, and multiple malformations (especially of the heart). Within a given trisomy syndrome there is some variability in signs from individual to individual, but enough constancy in the pattern so that the diagnosis often can be made from clinical findings. The complexity of the clinical findings is a reminder of the need for detailed reporting of all the defects rather than a simple statement of "multiple malformation."

There are several isolated reports of interest. An extra chromosome, possibly number 22, was described in each of twin girls reported to be dizygotic (Biesele, Schmid, and Lawlis, 1962). One had an IQ of 70, whereas the other had an IQ of 38. They did not show any mongoloid characteristics, but both displayed mannerisms which were described as schizoid. Moorhead *et al.* (1961), described a family in which four siblings bore a translocation (possibly a fusion of chromosomes 13 and 22). All four children showed mental retardation (the highest IQ was 70) and severe speech problems, with three failing to develop intelligible speech. The family also included one normal sibling and a sixth child who was a mongol with forty-seven chromosomes. Of considerable interest was the finding that the mother also carried the translocation but showed only a mild speech hesitation.

Another class of chromosomal anomalies with implications for the study of mental retardation involves differences in the number of sex chromosomes

(Harnden and Jacobs, 1961). The initial discovery was made in a retarded male with Klinefelter's syndrome who was shown to have two X chromosomes plus a Y chromosome. In the few years since that initial discovery, the following general principles have emerged:

1. Individuals with one or more Y chromosomes appear male regardless of the number of X chromosomes present, while those individuals with no Y chromosomes appear female. (There are certain exceptions in the case of hermaphrodites or errors in sex differentiation.)

2. Those who have a sex-chromosome constitution other than XX or XY usually show some type of morphological abnormality. Many of these persons are infertile.

3. The simplest population-screening procedure involves the microscopic examination of cells taken from the lining of the mouth. A single staining body (sex chromatin or Barr body) near the nuclear membrane is found in many cells from normal females, while such a body is usually absent from normal male cells. Some problems may be encountered in interpreting the slides, however (Hamerton, 1961).

4. Among those with abnormalities of the sex chromosomes, males are more severely retarded than females. Maclean et al. (1962) summarized the data for 2,607 males and 1,907 females from fifteen institutions for the mentally retarded. The frequency of abnormal males (mostly XXY) in the institutionalized population was 10.7 per thousand, while the rate for XXX females was 4.2 per thousand and for XO females was 0.5 per thousand. The degree of retardation is probably more severe as one progresses from XXY males to XXXXY males. An XYY male reported by Hauschka et al. (1962), however, was found to have average intelligence.

New syndromes may be described. Theoretically there could be twenty-two different trisomy syndromes involving the autosomes, one for each of the twenty-two pairs. It is likely, however, that a number of these combinations are lethal for the embryo and could be observed only in an abortus.

The range of possibilities is extended by the concept of partial trisomy, which involves the addition of only part of an extra chromosome to the usual set (Patau et al., 1961). The cytological study of this phenomenon is complicated by the fact that the extra chromosome portion may be attached to a different chromosome in different families. Furthermore, variations in the size of the extra piece will produce variation in the number of different abnormal signs observed in different individuals. Partial trisomy for a small segment may be indistinguishable from a dominant mutation.

The type of mental retardation involved in each of the identifiable syndromes should be documented carefully, including psychometric and psychiatric evaluation whenever appropriate. It appears that the mental retardation in D- and 18-trisomics is vastly more severe than that found in mongoloids (Patau, 1962; Smith et al., 1963). An explanation for such differences will require neurological examinations and anatomical and histochemical studies of the brains.

OTHER GENETIC CAUSES OF RETARDATION

In some disorders described up to this point the biochemical defect has been well defined in terms of the metabolic pathways involved. In other cases a disturbance has been observed in the storage of materials within nerve cells or in the process of forming the myelin sheath, even though the primary biochemical defect has not been identified. There remain syndromes, however, which involve defects in the cranium or other parts of the body with little information available about the brain pathology or the biochemical sequences involved (see Table 4).

TABLE 4

SOME CHROMOSOMAL ANOMALIES AND OTHER SYNDROMES OF GENETIC ORIGIN LEADING TO MENTAL RETARDATION

Condition and Mode of Inheritance*	Biochemical and Pathological Findings	Intellectual, Behavioral, and Emotional Signs	Motor Signs	Other Clinical Signs
Alpers' diffuse cerebral degeneration (Blackwood et al., 1963: probably AR)	Progressive myelin degeneration	Initially normal, progressing to severe retardation. Inattentive to surroundings	Spasticity, myoclonic jerks, frequent convulsions. Occasional choreo-athetosis and tremor	Occasional blindness
Böök's genetic spastic oligophrenia (AR)		All of low mentality	Spasticity and muscular atrophy of legs	Congenital deformities of feet
Börjeson et al. syndrome (1962: XR with some expression in carrier females)			Epilepsy	Hypogonadism, marked obesity, dwarfism, grotesque face with large ears
Crouzon's cranio-facial dysostosis (AD)				Skull deformity, exophthalmos, prognathism, parrotnose. Some with visual impairment
Dystrophia myotonica (Caughey and Myrianthopoulos, 1963: AD)	Abnormal contractility and hyperexcitability of muscle fibers, reduction in urinary creatinine	Abnormally few ganglion cells in cortex, gliosis in cortex and white matter. Severe mental retardation. Hyperactive, aggressive. Mental retardation in some. More or less pronounced intellectual deterioration. Reduced initiative, carefree temperament	Delayed relaxation of skeletal muscle, muscle weakness and wasting	Cataracts, frontal baldness, testicular atrophy, cardiac anomalies, endocrine and skeletal changes
Friedreich's ataxia (AR)	Degeneration of spinocerebellar tracts, dorsal columns, pyramidal tracts	Progressive mental retardation or psychotic manifestations in small proportion of cases	Ataxia, nystagmus, dysarthric speech. Diminished reflexes. Muscle weakness and atrophy	Scoliosis, clubfoot. Impairment of position and vibratory senses. Some with optic atrophy or involvement of heart muscle
Hallervorden and Spatz disease (AR)	Brown discoloration (positive for iron stains) of the globus pallidus and substantia nigra	Mental deterioration in some. Emotional disorders of the pseudobulbar type	Dysarthric speech, progressive rigidity. Some with athetosis, epilepsy	Clubfoot. Some with optic atrophy, retinitis pigmentosa
Hallgren's syndrome (1959: AR)		Mental deficiency in about one-fourth of the cases, schizophrenia-like psychosis in about one-fourth	Vestibulo-cerebellar ataxia	Retinitis pigmentosa, congenital deafness, cataract by age 40 in most
Huntington's chorea (AD)	Degeneration of cortex, thalamus, corpus striatum	Progressive impairment of memory and intellectual ability, usually after age 30. Irritability, anxiety, impulsive behavior, psychotic episodes	Choreiform movements, abrupt and jerky. Seizures in some	

* AD indicates autosomal dominant. AR indicates autosomal recessive. XR indicates X-linked recessive. References not listed here will be found in the text of this chapter, in Goodman and Herndon (1959), in Merritt (1963), or in Penrose (1963).

363

TABLE 4—*Continued*

Condition and Mode of Inheritance*	Biochemical and Pathological Findings	Intellectual, Behavioral, and Emotional Signs	Motor Signs	Other Clinical Signs
Hydrocephalus (XR form)	Stenosis of aqueduct	Severe mental retardation	Spasticity of legs, with wasting and contractures	Mild hydrocephalus, thumbs flexed
Kjellin's familial spastic paraplegia (1959: possibly AR)		Non-progressive mental retardation	Spastic paraplegia with onset about age 25 and slowly progressive. Amyotrophy in hand muscles by age 35	Central retinal degeneration
Klinefelter's syndrome (XXY karyotype)		Often retarded, sometimes severely. Apathy, hypokinesia, poor socialization		Long legs, atrophic testes, sterility. Some with gynecomastia, eunuchoid proportions
Laurence-Moon-Bardet-Biedl syndrome (probably AR)		Mental deficiency in most cases, occasionally severe. Defects in visual perception and organization reported	Some with spasticity, nystagmus	Retinitis pigmentosa, polydactyly, obesity, hypogenitalism
Marinesco-Sjögren syndrome (Alter et al., 1962: AR)	Cystic degeneration of cerebral gray and white matter, atrophy of cerebellar granular layer. Possible increase in serum glutamic acid level	All mentally retarded, most of them severely. Speech poorly developed	Cerebellar ataxia from early childhood, nystagmus, intention tremor, muscle wasting in lower extremities	Congenital cataracts, short stature, deformities of feet and spine
Menkes et al. syndrome (1962: XR)		Severe early mental retardation	Spasticity, focal or generalized seizures	Stubby white hair showing variable diameter, twisting, and breaks at regular intervals
Moynahan's alopecia-epilepsy-oligophrenia syndrome (1962: possibly AR)		Mental retardation	Grand mal convulsions	Congenital alopecia, unusual EEG pattern
Multiple neurofibromatosis (AD)	Neurofibromas, usually multiple, pedunculated, involving skin, nerve trunks, and central nervous system. Gliomas of optic nerve, acoustic neuromas	About half of the cases are retarded to a varying degree	Cerebellar and motor signs variable depending on part of nervous system involved	*Café au lait* pigmentation on skin, short stature, bony lesions

TABLE 4—Continued

Condition and Mode of Inheritance*	Biochemical and Pathological Findings	Intellectual, Behavioral, and Emotional Signs	Motor Signs	Other Clinical Signs
Orodigitofacial dysostosis (families with affected females)		About half show mild retardation	Occasional trembling	Cleft palate and tongue, hyperplasia of frenula, hand anomalies, dryness of scalp or alopecia
Pseudoglioma (Forssman, 1960: XR)		Mental retardation from infancy, becoming more severe		Congenital blindness (from pseudoglioma), cataract, atrophy of iris
Sjögren's syndrome (Sjögren and Larsson, 1957: AR)		Severe mental retardation	Congenital spasticity of extremities, especially legs. Muscular atrophy and contractures	Congenital ichthyosis
Sturge-Weber syndrome (partial trisomy postulated)	Localized atrophy and calcification of cerebral cortex	Mental retardation in most cases, varying in severity	Hemiplegia (transient or permanent). Seizures, usually focal	Port-wine colored facial nevus, often following distribution of trigeminal nerve
Trisomy-D	Arhinencephaly	Severe mental retardation	Seizures	Microcephaly, eye defects, harelip, cleft palate, polydactyly, hemangiomata, cataracts, deafness
Trisomy-E (17 or 18)		Severe mental retardation	Hypertonicity	Small mandible, low-set malformed ears, clubfoot, corneal opacity, fingers flexed
Trisomy-21 (Down's syndrome or mongolism)	Reduction in myelination and cortical differentiation	Retardation usually severe; IQ rarely up to 70. Emotional instability, aggressive behavior, or catatonia may occur	Hypotonicity	Characteristic eyes and face, short stature, short fingers, congenital heart defects, cataracts, sexual immaturity
Tuberous sclerosis (AD)	Calcified cerebral nodules	Mental impairment of varying degree, stereotyped motor activity, a few with auditory hallucinations, delusions	Recurrent convulsive seizures, generalized or focal. Some with paralysis	Facial fibroangiomatous nevi. Tumors in retina, kidney, and other organs
Turner's syndrome (XO karyotype)		Mild retardation in some		Short stature, webbed neck, small mandible, coarctation of aorta, ovarian dysgenesis, amenorrhea, often sterile

Sjögren and Larsson (1957) analyzed the data for thirty-three individuals (from seventeen families) who showed a syndrome including low-grade oligophrenia, congenital ichthyosis, and spastic disorders of the type found in Little's disease, with macular degeneration of the eye in some of the cases. The mode of inheritance was autosomal recessive. These authors reviewed a number of other reported cases in which ichthyosis was associated with mental retardation but without spastic symptoms. A third type of variation is seen in the syndrome of "genetic spastic oligophrenia" (without ichthyosis) studied by Böök (1953). A larger series of cases and more detailed pathological and histochemical data might provide an explanation for the different combinations of signs found in these syndromes.

Some types of mental retardation are associated with cranial anomalies, and certain of these can be shown to be genetic in origin. Myrianthopoulos and Kurland (1961) reviewed the variety of mechanisms producing interference in the circulation of the cerebrospinal fluid and leading to hydrocephalus. Family studies show an increased risk of this problem among siblings of affected children. One specific type of hydrocephalus is inherited as a sex-linked recessive trait and involves a narrowing or stenosis of an internal brain passageway, the aqueduct (Edwards, 1961). The head is slightly enlarged and there is spasticity of the legs, a curious facial appearance, a deformity of the thumbs, and a flexor plantar reflex together with mental deficiency.

Evidence for a genetic variety of microcephaly inherited as an autosomal recessive was reviewed by Böök, Schut, and Reed (1953) and by Komai et al. (1955). Mental retardation was observed in eight out of sixteen cases of orodigitofacial dysostosis (Gorlin and Psaume, 1962). A greater than normal interpupillary distance (hypertelorism) is found in a variety of malformations associated with retardation (Penrose, 1963; MacGillivray, 1957).

Mental retardation may also be observed in association with eye defects. Sjögren and Larsson (1949) studied fifty-eight cases of microphthalmos or anophthalmos combined with oligophrenia. Epilepsy was observed in 28 per cent of the cases, and skeletal anomalies (feet and spine) in 71 per cent. The consanguinity rate among parents was somewhat increased over that for the general population, indicating recessive inheritance for at least some of the cases. Hallgren (1959) described a syndrome involving retinitis pigmentosa, congenital deafness and ataxia, with mental retardation in one-fourth of the cases and a schizophrenia-like psychosis in one-fourth. Retinitis pigmentosa, optic atrophy, cataracts, or glaucoma have been observed in other genetic syndromes leading to retardation.

A further category includes tumors of genetic origin. In tuberous sclerosis (epiloia) skin tumors characteristically form a rash on the face with a "butterfly" distribution, and gliomata develop in the brain. The clinical signs may include paralysis, severe mental retardation, or psychosis. Neurofibromatosis involves nerve-sheath tumors which may be numerous on the skin and may form in different internal organs. About 10 per cent of the cases are reported to be mentally retarded as the result of brain involvement. Both of these disorders are inherited as autosomal dominants (Kurland et al., 1962). In the ataxia-telangiectasia syndrome a vascular dilatation develops on the face, other skin areas, the conjunctiva of the eye, and the cerebellum (Sedgwick and Boder, 1960). Vascular nevi on the face and meninges characterize the Sturge-Weber syndrome; clear evidence for genetic origin has not been obtained, although a partial trisomy has been postulated (Patau et al., 1961).

With further research, disorders once thought to be non-genetic will turn out to have a genetic basis, and the converse will also be true. An illustration of the latter is provided by McKusick's (1960) discussion of the Marfan syndrome, which is inherited as a simple Mendelian dominant. This syndrome includes long, thin digits (arachnodactyly) and defects in other parts of the skeleton, the lens of the eye, and the aorta. Arachnodactyly has been described as a genetic defect associated with mental retardation, but, in McKusick's opinion, mental retardation is not a component of Marfan's syndrome. The probable reason for the confusion is that a clinical picture including arachnodactyly and resembling the Marfan syndrome may result from circumstances such as maternal rubella, maternal exposure to X-ray, and Rh incompatibility. The persons affected with arachnodactyly of this type do show mental retardation in a number of cases.

The difficulty in distinguishing between genetic and non-genetic causes of a condition (such as arachnodactyly) is a fundamental problem in genetic research. Some of the other conditions listed in Table 4 are also known to arise from non-genetic causes. Cataract, microphthalmos, chorioretinitis, hydrocephalus, syndactylism, and deafness have been observed in children born to women with a history of rubella during pregnancy (Lundström, 1962). Fetal irradiation is clearly established as a cause of microcephaly. Induced defects such as these, which resemble genetic defects, are known as *phenocopies*.

A continuing effort must be made to obtain more complete data about the defects mentioned in this section. A systematic psychometric evaluation has not been made for many of the disorders. Further work probably will show that some of the presently identified syndromes include several separate entities and may reveal the biochemical pathways for some of the conditions now identified only by the familial aggregation of cases.

PRENATAL CAUSES OF RETARDATION

There is no doubt that circumstances in the prenatal environment (such as fetal irradiation or maternal rubella) and events during the birth process (such as anoxia) can injure the fetus severely enough to produce mental retardation (Graham *et al.*, 1962; MacMahon, 1962). Efforts to reduce the frequency of such problems and to alleviate their effects are a significant part of the attack upon mental retardation. Within the scope of the present chapter it is appropriate only to comment upon possible genetic components which may interact with these prenatal events. The significance of the genotype in response to teratogenic agents is fully discussed by Fraser elsewhere in this volume. Davies' (1960) review of research in problems of gestation may also be helpful.

Prematurity.—The association of low birth weight with mental retardation has been noted frequently (Rosanoff and Inman-Kane, 1934). More recently Illingworth and Woods (1960) concluded that the high incidence of twins among the mentally retarded may result merely from the higher rate of prematurity in twins. It must be kept in mind, however, that the causes of prematurity itself (aside from twinning) are not fully understood. Warkany, Monroe, and Sutherland (1961) have pointed out that if certain factors (possibly including genetic ones) lead to retarded development and mental retardation, the low birth weight cannot be said to be a cause of the retardation. Other genetic aspects of growth and development of the fetus have been reviewed by Penrose (1961*a*).

Birth injury.—Penrose (1949) listed three criteria which must be met in order to prove that birth injury is a cause of mental deficiency: (1) The signs and symptoms must be reasonably attributable to the injury. (2) There must be a history of traumatic events at birth. (3) The effect of any injury on intellectual level must be assessed. Unless such precautions are taken, cases of mental retardation from a variety of causes may be ascribed improperly to birth injury.

Kernicterus.—One of the results of Rh incompatibility between mother and fetus is the destruction of fetal red blood cells and the release of the pigment bilirubin into the fetal circulation. The presence of bilirubin may lead to the clinical diagnosis of jaundice, and the pigment may also stain and damage brain cells. The brain damage (kernicterus) can cause mental retardation or cerebral palsy, but early exchange transfusions usually prevent such an outcome (Zuelzer, 1960; Diamond, 1963). The general genetic principles governing these and other types of maternal-fetal incompatibility were discussed by Penrose (1946). Neonatal jaundice with kernicterus can also result from ABO hemolytic disease, from an enzyme-system defect in the Crigler-Najjar syndrome (Schmid, 1960), or from a deficiency of the enzyme glucose-6-phosphate dehydrogenase (Doxiadis *et al.*, 1961).

MILD RETARDATION—SINGLE MAJOR CAUSE

Most descriptions of a newly identified syndrome are based upon cases with severe and more easily discernible defects. As experience with a new clinical entity accumulates, individuals with a less severe expression of the trait can be detected.

An interesting discovery in phenylketonuria has been the identification of individuals with positive biochemical findings but with measured intelligence in the normal range (Sutherland *et al.*, 1960; Allen and Gibson, 1961; McLean, 1961). Very few of these persons, however, would be considered normal. Of fourteen cases reported by these authors, only three had IQ estimates over 100. A number showed hyperactivity, short attention span, fearfulness, and minor neurological changes.

Knox (1960) reviewed four possible explanations for mild retardation in phenylketonuria: (1) alternate biochemical pathways (there was no evidence, however, of a milder biochemical defect), (2) a variant allele (a different mutation at the same genetic locus—this is not a likely explanation, since at least half of the cases had sibs with severe phenylketonuria), (3) heterozygosity (the action of a single unpaired gene—the pedigrees, however, were typical of regular recessive inheritance), and (4) a physiological difference (no evidence of kidney alteration or changes in carbohydrate metabolism was found, however). Knox concluded that the effect of environment or modifying genes is the most likely explanation.

All of the possible explanations mentioned by Knox should be considered for the other metabolic defects. The significance of heterozygosity, in particular, was discussed in an earlier section of this chapter and by Lippman (1958). There is also the possibility that the general population may contain some unidentified phenylketonurics, but Larson (1955) failed to find any by urine tests of 8,220 individuals.

The study of mild retardation with an identifiable major cause may contribute to our understanding of "normal" intelligence. It is a common procedure in microbial genetics and human biochemical genetics to explore "normal" enzyme pathways through the analysis of genetic enzyme defects. As part of a similar research strategy one might select samples of children with untreated cases of different biochemical defects known to cause retardation. In order to permit the use of standard psychometric examinations, it may be desirable to select those with mild retardation (for example, with an IQ of 50 or more), and administer a careful psychometric and psychiatric examination. The test data could then be evaluated to look for patterns of behavior specific for diseases X and Y, and not observed in diseases Z and W. By this inductive process it may be possible to make a different approach toward the difficult, but important, task of trying to define the components involved in intelligence.

MILD RETARDATION—MULTIPLE CAUSES

In mild retardation with multiple causes, a different type of evidence and a new set of problems are involved. It is here that the most vigorous controversies over the relative roles of heredity and environment are found. For the most part these disagreements reflect a misunderstanding of the genetic theory of quantitative inheritance.

After a discussion of heredity and environment in mental subnormality, Sarason and Gladwin (1958, p. 211) conclude

... that the IQ is unstable over time, cannot be reliably measured by any agreed-upon single instrument and has strong environmental determinants, and that its genetic determinants are sufficiently multifactorial that they do not lend themselves to existing techniques of genetic research. Therefore, genetic studies based upon the test IQ, or upon the even vaguer concepts of mental deficiency or retardation, do not present a very promising avenue for research.

It is true that those traits which are influenced genetically by polygenes are more subject to environmental modification than are those characteristics controlled by a single genetic locus (Falconer, 1960; Lush, 1945). A breeding program for the improvement of plants or animals will be ineffective if environmental variations are assumed by mistake to be genetic in origin.

Sarason and Gladwin's dismissal of research based upon the IQ is less defensible. Surely any serious investigator in this field recognizes the limitations of a single score for a complex behavior pattern and wishes for more suitable means of evaluation. It should be obvious, however, that such a limitation affects the analysis of environmental components, just as well as the genetic factors. Furthermore, the development of more suitable tests may be more successful if the investigator has a reasonable theoretical model of the interactions between heredity and environment. A statement by Heber may be helpful at this point.

The paradox is that those who are ready to renounce the IQ, on the basis that it is essentially useless for the predictions they wish to make, find themselves in the predicament of having to fall back on the IQ when communicating with their colleagues for lack of having any other descriptive terminology at their disposal. If we are to relegate the IQ to its proper role it will be necessary for research to isolate the major dimensions of behavior which relate to the ultimate socio-cultural adequacy we are interested in predicting. Once we have these dimensions we will be faced with the added task of developing those tools and techniques that will permit a reliable and valid assessment of an individual's behavior on each of the important parameters (Heber, 1959, p. 1018).

A more serious problem is introduced, however, when Sarason and Gladwin state that "it will be our thesis that a hereditary determinant of mental capacity must not be assumed to exist unless proven." This point of view is surprisingly arbitrary, and it unnecessarily restricts the design of future research. A most appropriate comment is one by Mather as he discussed a paper by Woolf which had presented similar ideas:

The antithesis here is a false one, of use only as a possible means of separating "environmentalists" from "heredicists" and both from impartial students of variation. The first principle of genetics is that the phenotype is the joint outcome of genotype and environment. ... Our primary task in investigating the nature of variation must surely be to make our observations, and conduct our analyses, in such a way that the effects of *both* environmental and genetic differences are assessed. If we are left in doubt about the causation of any part of the variation, we must accept the uncertainty and seek to design future experiments, or amass further observations, in such a way as to permit the doubt to be resolved. . . . Our business is to see that environmental variation is not ascribed to the genotype, that genetic variation is not ascribed to the environment, and that due to the interaction of the two is not ascribed to either alone (Mather, 1952, pp. 105–6).

Pasamanick (1959) listed the following results from several studies of variables affecting mental retardation: (1) Complications of pregnancy and prematurity are related to neuropsychiatric disorders. (2) Neuropsychiatric disorders are more common in the lowest socio-economic strata. (3) Of 1,000 infants only 2 per cent had developmental quotients under 85, while among school-age children 14 per cent had quotients under that level.

He went on to state the following:

We have interpreted these findings, which are supported by a series of further investigations, to mean that, except for a few hereditary clinical deficiencies and for exogenous injury to neural integration, behavior variation does not seem to be the result of genetically determined structural origin. It is now possible to entertain a new *tabula rasa* theory hypothecating that at conception individuals are quite alike in intellectual endowment except for these quite rare hereditary neurologic defects. It appears to us that it is life experience and the sociocultural milieu influencing biological and psychological function which, in the absence of organic brain damage, makes human beings significantly different from each other (Pasamanick, 1959, p. 318).

Pasamanick's work has made valuable contributions to our understanding of environmental factors affecting behavior. The evidence, however, does not permit the complete negation of a significant effect of genetic variables. The fact that the range of variability (and the proportion classified as retarded) increased between infancy and school age must reflect the net result of several different factors. Bayley (1955) pointed out that IQ scores may be altered by (1) the emotional climate, the cultural milieu, and environmental deprivation or (2) developmental changes in the nature and composition of the behaviors tested. It is the latter component which Pasamanick appears to have neglected. The complex patterning of traits involved in a school-age intelligence test cannot be measured in an infant developomental examination. Furthermore, the influence of the genotype upon a trait cannot be measured adequately until the trait is fully developed. Genetic variability in certain reflexes could be evaluated either at six months of age or at six years, but Hallgren's (1950) study of specific dyslexia (congenital word-blindness) obviously required school-age children as subjects. Finally, a critical test for the role of genetic factors always requires the analysis of data by family units and cannot be based upon a comparison of two different populations.

One of the classic studies assessing the relative importance of heredity and environment was carried out by Wright (1920) on the spotting pattern of guinea pigs. For some years twenty-three families had been maintained by brother-sister matings. A control outbred stock was maintained without mating even second cousins.

These inbred lines very early showed conspicuous differences in the average amount of white, thus indicating the existence of hereditary differences. But it was observed that no type of pattern became well fixed. Within each line, variations could be found almost from solid color to solid white. The distribution of white for several of the families is shown in Figure 1. *Family 39*, for example, had 20 per cent white on the average and *Family 13* had 85 per cent white, while *Family 35* had a mean of 50 per cent white.

The outbred line (*Experiment B*) had a distribution somewhat like that of *Family 35*. Wright chose these two lines to illustrate the use of path coefficients in partitioning the observed variance into three components: heredity, the environment common to the litter mates before birth, and the residue—largely irregularity in development. The results are shown in Table 5.

It must be remembered that it would have been difficult to distinguish individual animals from these two lines by looking at them. Both lines showed animals with almost solid white, and others with almost solid color; yet, the causes of variability were quite different in the

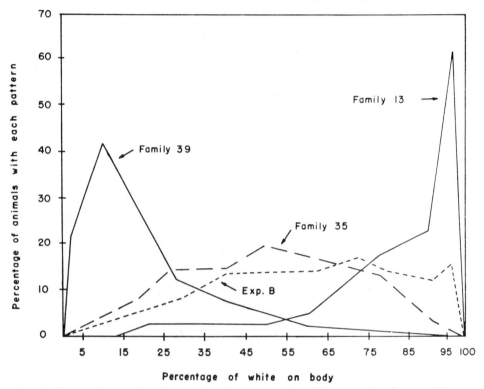

Fig. 1.—The percentage distribution of guinea pigs from certain inbred and outbred lines by relative proportion of white on body surface. After Wright (1920).

TABLE 5

THE PROPORTION OF VARIANCE IN SPOTTING PATTERN ASCRIBED TO DIFFERENT CAUSAL COMPONENTS IN TWO GUINEA-PIG LINES*

COMPONENT	RANDOM-BRED LINE (EXPERIMENT B)		INBRED LINE (FAMILY 35)	
	Variance	% of Total	Variance	% of Total
Heredity	0.271	42.2	0.010	2.8
Environment common to litter mates	.002	0.3	.020	5.5
Irregularities in development	.370	57.5	.334	91.7
Total	0.643	100.0	0.364	100.0

*From Wright, 1920.

two lines. In the inbred line (*Family 35*) the genotypes of the parents and offspring were very much alike. Therefore, the variability observed must have resulted from differences in environmental factors. On the other hand, in the random-bred line (*Experiment B*) almost half of the variability could be ascribed to differences in genotype.

It is extremely easy to lose sight of this important principle. Heritability (the proportion of variance that can be ascribed to heredity) is not a property of a trait, but rather of a specific

TABLE 6

APPROXIMATE RELATIVE EFFECT OF CAUSES OF
VARIATION IN HUMAN BIRTH WEIGHT*

Component	Per Cent of Variance
Maternal hereditary constitution...	20
Fetal hereditary: sex..............	2
Fetal hereditary: remaining constitution........................	16
Maternal health and nutrition......	16
Maternal health during each pregnancy........................	8
Maternal parity..................	7
Maternal age....................	1
Unidentified intra-uterine influence, posture, etc....................	30
Total.....................	100

* From Penrose (1961*a*).

population under specific environmental conditions (Dexter, 1956). This limitation, of course, makes it very difficult to assess the hereditary or environmental component as far as intelligence is concerned. Certain general principles may be listed, however: (1) It is impossible to judge the relative importance of genetic factors without breeding experiments (in animals) or without data within families (for human populations). (2) When environment has to be taken into account, a much larger number of families is required than where environment can be neglected (Penrose, 1932). (3) The nature of the data needed for the analysis can be determined only after a theoretical model is prepared showing the vari-

ables which are assumed to operate and the most likely direction of influence. Wright (1954) prepared such a model for Burks's data on foster children. The sophistication of model-building, of course, must be tempered by limitations in the availability of data. (4) Progress on this most complex problem will be made possible only through the co-operative effort of investigators from several disciplines. Psychologists may have to develop new measurement techniques. Geneticists would have to provide new methods of analysis for quantitative traits. It is neither certain nor impossible that significant progress can take place in the near future.

An interesting illustration of the analysis of a complex trait can be seen in the study of birth weight by Penrose (1961*a*). An approximate partition of the causes of variation of birth weight is shown in Table 6. Roughly one-third of the total variation is the result of differences in maternal and fetal genotypes, another third from variations in maternal health, parity, and age, with the remaining third unidentified. The type of data used for some of these estimates reveals the different kinds of information that can be utilized. The estimate of maternal hereditary constitution came from comparing the correlation in birth weight of children born to sisters with the correlation for children born to brothers. The estimate for fetal genotype came from comparing monozygotic with dizygotic twin pairs. Further discussion of problems of quantitative inheritance in man will be seen in the volume by Osborne and DeGeorge (1959) and in the papers by Edwards (1960), Roberts (1961), Crittenden (1961), Kempthorne and Osborne (1961), and Spuhler (1962).

Now what meaning does this have for an *individual person?* The concept of a "reaction norm" as proposed by Allen (1958) may be helpful. Allen pointed out that advances in the study of quantitative variation have come more from the assimilation of concepts from theoretical genetics than by a direct attack on the medical problem itself. He then introduced a concept from physiological genetics. Let us assume, for purposes of discussion, that an individual's genotype establishes a probability distribution of potential for IQ. As a first approximation we may assume that this curve is bell-shaped. Under an "average" environment, the person's measured IQ would turn out to be near the middle of this curve. With poor environment and training the measured IQ would be lower. If the median of this curve were 100, it is possible that severe environmental deprivation may lead to an IQ as low as 50 or 60, but the probability that this will happen is extremely small. If the environment is unusually satisfactory, the measured IQ will be higher than the median for the curve.

In a discussion of this paper, Baroff suggested that the shape of such a curve may not be symmetrical, but rather skewed. Allen agreed to this possibility and suggested that an individual's distribution of potentialities may be skewed to the left (perhaps like the spotting-pattern distribution for *Family 13* in Figure 1). Among mentally retarded the distribution of potential may be more nearly symmetrical or skewed to the right.

This general idea is a theoretical one, but it appears to provide a reasonable correlation of genetic theory with the empirical data. It is clear that we should not expect the genotype to rigidly fix the IQ (Hunt, 1961). At the same time we should not expect an infinite plasticity in response to differences in environment. It is more reasonable to expect a distribution of probabilities as suggested by Allen.

Another item from genetic theory with possible application to mental retardation is the concept of genetic homeostasis as proposed by Lerner (1954). In a polygenic system, individuals toward the center of the phenotypic scale would be exected to be heterozygous at a number of the genetic loci involved. It is assumed that the heterozygous genotype has a higher "buffering" capacity, thus reducing the sensitivity to the environment. At either end of the phenotypic scale the organisms are more susceptible to environmental influence. If this concept has any relevance for the polygenic system probably involved in intelligence, it is possible that persons with unusually high or unusually low genetic potential may be more susceptible to the effects of experience than other persons.

A final point of genetic interest is the topic of differential reproduction. Higgins, Reed, and Reed (1962) considered the long history of concern about the apparently negative correlation between family size and IQ. To the extent that genetic factors are involved as causes of variability in intelligence, this differential reproduction might be expected to lead to a gradual decline in the mean intelligence of the population as measured by IQ tests. Such a decline, however, has not been observed (Scottish Council, 1961).

Higgins *et al.* analyzed IQ scores which were made available as a result of a state-wide testing program which has been carried on for a number of years. All persons were tested while they were of school age. Figure 2 presents the results for 1,016 families in which IQ scores were available for both parents and at least one child. The solid line (limited to those persons who were married and produced children) demonstrates the frequently observed negative corelation between IQ score and family size. The broken line shows the results when the unmarried and non-reproducing sibs of the parents are included. The differential reproduction is no longer apparent.

If this finding is confirmed in other studies it will become clear that the impression of differential reproduction may be a statistical artifact. The fact that a person with a low IQ score is a member of a large sibship does not mean that he will necessarily produce a large family. Furthermore, persons who reproduce are a biased sample of the entire population with regard to IQ. These observations suggest that a decline in IQ score over time need not be expected. Instead, the factors responsible for differences in IQ score may interact to

line the following basic requirements for a genetic approach to research in mental retardation:

1. An adequate definition of the condition under study.

2. An appropriate source of probands.

3. Clear understanding of basic genetic principles.

4. Knowledge of the biological and cultural variables significant in the development of adaptive behavior.

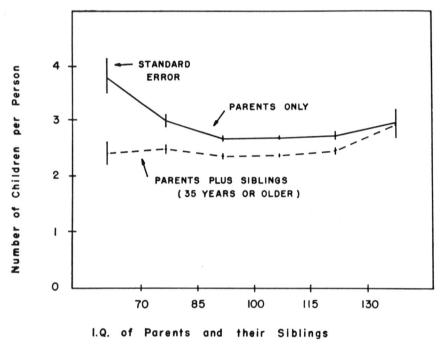

FIG. 2.—Mean number of children born to persons in different IQ groups. Based on data from Higgins, Reed, and Reed (1962).

form a balanced system, with the population in equilibrium. It is even possible that there could be a gradual increase in measured intelligence.

GENETIC METHODS FOR ANALYSIS

It may be desirable now to turn to the methods which are available for research in the field and point out the types of information which should be collected routinely if data are to be used for genetic analysis. The discussion will out-

Fortunately, a number of literature sources have become available in the last few years. There is an excellent short review of medical genetics by Motulsky and Gartler (1962), a book for clinicians by Clarke (1962), as well as the comprehensive texts by Stern (1960) and Lenz (1963). Shorter reviews of methodology are provided by Penrose (1959), Schull (1959), Steinberg (1959), Morton (1959) and Smith (1961). For a detailed discussion of methods and problems, the reader is referred to Neel and Schull (1954), Li (1961), Steinberg (1961) and Burdette (1962). A very helpful set of mathematical tables has been prepared by Maynard-Smith *et al.* (1961). For an application of some of these methods to behavior genetics, the best source is Fuller and Thompson (1960).

PROBLEMS IN DEFINITION AND CLASSIFICATION

The system used for classifying cases of mental retardation has significant effects upon the conduct of research. A research study based upon a single institution is obviously limited to the patients placed therein and cannot include persons who may have been assigned elsewhere on the basis of a diagnostic label. Furthermore, the grouping of patients into wards or the classification of medical records by diagnosis may be adopted by a research worker as separate categories for study, even when a different set of categories might be more suitable for the problem under investigation.

Kurland (1957) pointed out that definitions which are useful for patient care and treatment may be very misleading if adopted for research in etiology. One of the problems is that for research purposes the definitions should be stated in terms as limited and narrow as possible. The word "familial," as applied to mental retardation, may become a wastebasket term for what is left after known or supposed organic causes are removed. Even when more carefully defined, cases with "familial" retardation may be heterogeneous in etiology and may vary in composition from one study to another. As a result it would be surprising to find consistent results when different studies are compared. Benoit (1959) has already suggested that the dichotomy of "organic" versus "familial" be discarded.

If a psychological study of *organic* retardation is desired, one might use as a test panel several of the types of re-

tardation known to result from genetic biochemical defects. This approach would provide a defined sample, the results of which could be more readily compared with other sets of data. Another advantage is that biochemical diagnoses can be made in any country and in any culture.

Another fundamental problem in classification arises from the difficulty in making a distinction between mental retardation and mental disorder, especially in young children (Cassel, 1957; Kirman, 1958). The decision may depend in part upon the orientation of the person who makes the diagnosis (Pollack, 1958). Furthermore, if both retardation and disorder occur in the same individual, there apears to be a tendency to regard the mental disorder as secondary to the retardation, an assumption which may not be justified (Craft, 1960). The alternative assumption, that an emotional block has caused the apparent retardation, may be just as unfounded in specific instances (Eisenberg, 1958).

It seems reasonable to assume that neurological damage can result in both emotional and intellectual problems in the same individual. In fact, the data in Tables 2–4 indicate that behavioral disorders have been observed in several genetic syndromes usually described as producing only mental retardation. Some cases with Hurler's syndrome, for example, show severe emotional disturbance during the earlier stages of the disease but become more tractable as retardation progresses. Severe retardation appears to mask the effect of the disorder upon behavior.

Scheinberg (1958) studied the emotional disturbance in several adolescents with relatively mild cases of Wilson's disease. The behavioral changes had been interpreted as a secondary result of the adolescents' knowledge of the nature and severity of the disease, but Scheinberg points out that it is equally plausible to assume that the biochemical lesion in the brain has produced a primary disturbance of behavior in addition to mental retardation.

It should be clear, then, that the description of genetic syndromes such as these should include reference to the behavioral disorder as well as the type of mental retardation involved. Furthermore, the careful study of such conditions may yield insights into the biological control of "normal" behavior. This point of view has been stated forcefully by Lippman, Perry, and Wright (1958, p. 279):

> The distinction between amentia and dysmentia is arbitrary and may have little significance. It is important to recognize that the problems are closely related. The behavior of certain subjects with mental deficiency mimics the behavior of psychotic subjects. For example, patients with phenylketonuria sometimes resemble very closely, in their behavior, patients with schizophrenia in severe deterioration (catatonic and hebephrenic types). Abnormalities of indole metabolism, which have been reported in schizophrenia, are also present in phenylketonuria. Although psychiatrists have claimed that the patient with phenylketonuria is easily distinguished from the schizophrenic by detailed consideration of the behavior, we question this assertion and prefer to emphasize the similarities, which are great. We strongly suspect that the distinction between schizophrenia and phenylketonuria, in an adult subject, could be made only by biochemical laboratory studies, by the specific odor of phenyl acetic acid in the urine, or by the use of information from exogenous sources.

> In addition, every institution for mental defectives has a large group of young patients in whom the diagnosis is uncertain and in whom careful study often fails to resolve the distinction between amentia and dysmentia. From these observations, we suggest that improved knowledge concerning the biochemical basis of amentia will probably lead to discoveries concerning the biochemical basis of dysmentia as well.

A final suggestion is that in studies of etiology the primary classification of cases must not include any decision as to apparent cause. If the presence of similarly affected cases in the family is part of the diagnosis, it becomes impossible to make an unbiased genetic study of the disease. For genetic purposes, then, the primary classification of cases with mental retardation should be based upon objective criteria such as the following: (1) psychometric examination, yielding both a general estimate of IQ as well as scores on any separate "factors" deemed appropriate for the problem under investigation, (2) psychiatric evaluation for behavioral disorders, (3) neurological examination, (4) physical examination, with a detailed record of the physical signs, (5) pertinent laboratory data, and (6) information concerning the age at onset of specific symptoms. Information about possible etiological factors would be reserved for use in the analysis of the data on (7) the home environmental setting, (8) medical history, with particular reference to trauma and infection, and (9) family history, including the presence or absence of defect among parents and siblings and a pedigree showing the precise pattern of any consanguinity involved.

Most of these items are included in a classification scheme designed by Heber (1961). Each individual is scored for the presence or absence of cranial anomaly, impairment of special senses, convulsive disorder, psychiatric impairment, and motor dysfunction. A number of behavioral observations are also recorded. A few comments about the genetic aspects of Heber's classification may be in order. Since the mode of inheritance (sex-linked or autosomal, dominant or recessive) cannot always be determined by inspection of a pedigree, it would be more objective to indicate the presence or absence of retardation in specified categories of relatives (primarily parents and sibs). It is doubtful that "multiple gene transmission" can be identified at present. Finally, it is not clear how the new laboratory tests for the growing list of genetic disorders will be accommodated.

Genetic investigation requires information about families. There are different ways in which the families may be identified for study, however, and each type of research strategy has its unique advantages.

One procedure is to study an entire population and then organize the data into family units. Roberts (1940) investigated all children living in Bath, England, who were born during a specified four-year period—a total of 3,400. Careful studies of Scandinavian populations have been carried out by Sjögren (1948), Böök (1953) and Åkesson (1961). Such population surveys permit an unbiased ascertainment of all persons with neurological disease and psychiatric disorder, with or without mental retardation. The prevalence of psychosis and mental retardation in the general population can be compared directly with the expectation among relatives of affected persons, all on an age-corrected basis. The frequency of consanguinity can be determined in the population as well as among parents of affected persons.

A large-scale study currently under way is based upon comprehensive medical records for British Columbia (Newcombe, 1962). Information from birth and marriage records is recorded on magnetic tape, and computer programs have been written to link these records into family units. From a number of other sources information is obtained about medical problems, including causes of death. Of particular interest for this discussion is the availability of records from the British Columbia Register of Handicapped Children. Twenty-one per cent of the cases in this registry involve mental defects and personality disorders. Thus, it will eventually be possible to do family studies on the entire population of British Columbia. A number of by-products are expected in the form of twin studies, child-spacing studies in relation to stillbirth and infant death, and studies of fertility in relation to social characteristics.

The study of individual pedigrees is still a basic dimension of genetic analysis. This approach has been held in disrepute, in part because of the problems in interpreting selected pedigrees like that of the Kallikak family. The Dight Institute is collecting a large number of pedigrees to yield a more representative sampling of families (Higgins, Reed, and Reed, 1962). IQ scores are available for many of the persons, and this will permit a more meaningful analysis than would be possible with subjective evaluation of individual intelligence.

Many studies involve the selection of a systematic sample of probands (index cases) and their relatives. In mental retardation some preliminary information about the patterns of institutional admission is essential (Kramer, 1959; Tarjan *et al.*, 1958; Reid, 1960). The method of ascertainment of probands must be specified clearly, and potential sources of bias should be explored (Anderson, 1961). Several different types of proband studies are discussed in later sections of this chapter.

Although representative sampling is usually essential, there are some very real advantages which may come from biased samples of families. The selection of families in which two or more siblings have been hospitalized for mental retardation should yield a sample in which a higher proportion of the cases have a simple genetic etiology. (The possibility that some of these "familial" cases may result from severe environmental deprivation or non-genetic perinatal events must be kept in mind, however.) Wright *et al.* (1959) studied sixty-one families selected in this way. Priest *et al.* (1961) analyzed data from eighty-three families, and Karlsson *et al.* (1961) from fifty families.

Wright *et al.* (1961) made careful examinations of urine, blood and buccal smears on 110 siblings in their 61 families in a search for previously unidentified biochemical or chromosomal anomalies, but failed to find any. They suggested that the sampling procedure would have been improved by using only cases with severe retardation (IQ under 50) and without report of significant environmental factors. Furthermore, some biochemical defects might cause death at young age, with the result that such diseases will be under-represented in an institutional population. The study of cerebrospinal fluid might be more revealing than the analysis of blood or urine.

Such studies of multiple-affected families would be improved further by some of the procedures utilized by Morton (1962) and by Allen *et al.* (1962). Specifically, details of ascertainment within families should be described carefully, and the effect of such ascertainment upon analysis should be examined. Information about other possible causes of retardation such as birth trauma, birth weight, and family cultural setting should be recorded.

A different type of selected sample might be based upon families in which both parents are retarded. Dekaban (1958) studied a family in which both parents and all three of their children had IQ's below 60. He interpreted this as evidence of recessive inheritance, although other possibilities were considered. It should be clear, however, that recessive inheritance is not demonstrated by such a single pedigree in the absence of other kinds of data. The basic approach, nevertheless, might be suitable for a larger-scale study.

Biased samples of one of these types might be used for investigation by psychologists. Pearson and Kley (1957) pointed out the value of genetic infor-

mation in selecting populations for the study of human behavior disorders. The efficiency of a longitudinal study of the development of retardation in young children would be increased if a population with a high risk of such retardation were selected.

CONSANGUINITY

One of the most powerful genetic tools is the analysis of the effects of inbreeding, or consanguinity. The reason is that inbreeding increases homozygosity to an extent that is predictable from the degree of inbreeding. Consanguineous matings thus have a higher risk than the general population of producing children affected with rare, recessive traits. Furthermore, in the study of rare diseases with uncertain inheritance an increase in parental consanguinity is evidence for a recessive genetic factor (Morton, 1961; Neel and Schull, 1954).

The relative effect of inbreeding is greater for rare traits than for common ones and is greater in populations with a higher average rate of inbreeding. The best quantitative measure of inbreeding is the coefficient of inbreeding, designated as F. This is defined as "both the genetic correlation between uniting gametes and the probability that two genes in the offspring are identical by descent from a common ancestor" (Morton, 1961). The value of F ranges from 0.0 for completely unrelated parents to 0.06 for parents who are first cousins and 0.25 for a brother-sister mating. The principal types of consanguineous matings, together with the coefficient of inbreeding for each, are shown in Figure 3.

In one Brazilian population, where the frequency of first-cousin marriages has been estimated at 3.5 per cent, about 21 per cent of deaf-mute children were born to first-cousin marriages. Some cases of deaf-mutism undoubtedly arose from non-genetic factors. Thus, the frequency of consanguinity in cases of genetically determined deaf-mutism would even be higher (Freire-Maia, 1957).

In a large-scale Japanese study it was possible to identify a group of 4,598 children born to parents who were related and who did not receive appreciable radiation from the atomic bombs. A comparison group of 4,784 children was selected from those born to unrelated parents. Extensive examinations of these children (including neurological examinations and measurements of IQ) have been concluded, but the data are not yet available (Schull and Neel, 1962).

A matter of special interest is the effect of consanguinity upon quantitative traits, such as birth weight or IQ score. Morton (1958) analyzed data from three Japanese cities to test the effect of inbreeding upon birth weight, gestation time, and certain measurements of infants at the age of eight to ten months. There was no effect of inbreeding upon length of gestation and head girth. There

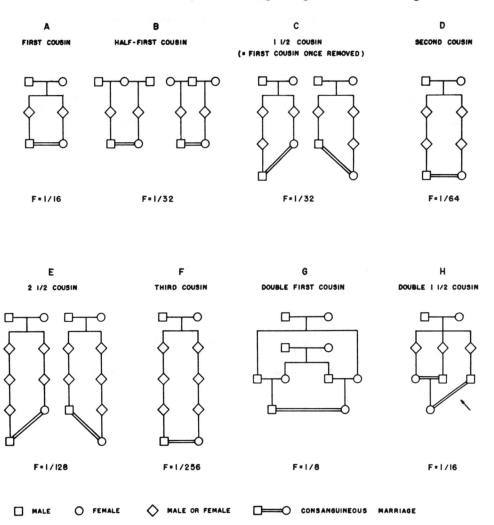

FIG. 3.—Pedigrees from some of the possible types of consanguinity, with the inbreeding coefficient for each. After Morton (1961).

was a small but significant decrease in weight at birth and in weight, height, and chest girth at eight to ten months. Inbreeding had no significant effect upon the variances of any of these measurements.

Schull (1961) employed a multivariate technique of analysis to re-examine these data. This permitted the evaluation of interactions among the three factors: sex of child, age at examination, and coefficient of inbreeding. One resulting observation was that "one month's additional growth would appear to offset roughly the disadvantage of being the offspring of first cousins."

Slatis and Hoene (1961) analyzed intelligence scores for eighty-seven children from consanguineous matings and for seventy-two control children. The mean IQ score for the consanguineous group was 101.5 and for the control group was 104.1, a difference which is not statistically significant. The standard deviation for the consanguinity group was 14.1 and that for the control group was 11.1, a difference which is significant at 0.05 level. The greater variability in IQ score with consanguinity may reflect homozygosity for genes with a major effect upon intelligence score.

The basic requirement for further advances in this field is the accumulation of accurate data on selected populations of suitable size, such as the geographical isolates in north Sweden studied by Böök (1957). With respect to intelligence two factors appeared to be operating: (1) In the cousin families there were relatively more parents with intelligence below normal (that is, having an estimated IQ below 85 or having severe school difficulty). This would imply that persons with below normal intelligence may more frequently marry a cousin. (2) When the analysis was limited to matings between parents with normal intelligence, 33 of 125 children from cousin marriages were considered below normal, while 13 of 88 control children

were considered below normal. In the same families, the number of gifted children was three for the cousin marriages, as compared with ten for the control marriages. The "morbid risk" for mental deficiency of unknown cause was estimated at 4.6 per cent for the cousin marriages, as compared with 1.3 per cent for the control marriages. In addition, there were three cases of genetic spastic oligophrenia in the cousin families.

TWINS

A discussion of the value of twins for research in mental retardation might well start with a review of what was known about twins in mongolism before the chromosomal basis of mongolism was discovered (Allen and Baroff, 1955). Among dizygotic twin pairs, both twins were affected in only about 3 per cent of the pairs. This was strong suggestive evidence that temporary conditions in the uterine environment were not of significant importance. Among monozygotic pairs, the concordance was almost 100 per cent. This was strong evidence for the importance of the genotype, either as a direct cause of the defect or in making the fetus susceptible to deleterious factors in the uterine environment.

At the same time the limitations of twin analysis are made clear by this illustration. Although the concordance data for mongolism provided strong evidence for the importance of genetic factors, they did not give any clues to the nature of these factors (Stern, 1960). It was not until new laboratory techniques were developed that it was possible to proceed any further.

Another way to state this limitation is to say that twin studies may demonstrate the importance of genetic factors, but they cannot exclude the possibility that significant environmental components are also present. If monozygotic twins are concordant for a trait, we know that both twins must have been genetically susceptible, but we may not have evidence concerning the relative importance of environmental agents (Penrose, 1961*a*).

The twin method has been used extensively to study IQ differences in the normal range (Fuller and Thompson, 1960). Earlier in this chapter it was indicated that in this range there must be a complex interaction of many genetic and environmental factors. Critics have argued that twin comparisons are usually made with co-twins from fairly similar environmental circumstances, thus yielding an underestimate of the amount of potential variability. (On the other hand, Price, 1950, concluded that the net effect of the twin-study method is biased toward an underestimation of the genetic component of the trait involved.) Such arguments may lead to the impression that twin studies in general are not valid methods for the analysis of psychological variables. This line of reasoning fails to grasp the fact that the present need is not so much for better methods of analysis as it is for a clearer definition of traits for genetic study. With better defined traits and more appropriate tests and measurements, the full range of genetic methods (proband studies, segregation analysis, and consanguinity studies) would become more applicable. In this task of defining traits and screening available test batteries twin studies may be a valuable tool, however.

Kempthorne and Osborne (1961) reexamined the basic statistical problems encountered with paired data and listed the forces acting upon monozygotic and dizygotic pairs of twins. On this basis they evaluated several statistical models and found that use of the Holzinger heritability formula may give a misleading picture of the role of genes and environment because certain assumptions are seldom fulfilled. They concluded that twins provide an effective method for studying heredity-environment interactions in quantitative attributes, but

that additional data about parents, siblings, and other relatives would extend the range of interpretation.

Vandenberg (1962) studied 117 psychological variables in forty-five monozygotic and thirty-seven dizygotic pairs of twins. For 24 variables (20.5 per cent of the total) the differences between the two groups were significant at the 1 per cent level, and these variables represented a wide variety of distinct attributes. Vandenberg made the interesting observation that those psychological tests which work well as predictors of social criteria, such as success in academic studies or in different occupations, may not be the most promising for the study of hereditary components. Tests based upon identifiable differences in infant personality are more likely to be useful. Co-operative efforts by psychologists and geneticists to define traits and to design tests should be encouraged.

It seems rather surprising, moreover, that twin data have not been used more widely for the study of causes of severe retardation. Part of the difficulty may be that twins have been used in an inefficient manner to answer questions for which other methods would be more appropriate. A most urgent need, then, is to restate questions in such a form that twin studies can provide answers. Allen pointed out one such approach when he stated:

It is likely that for many medical conditions the same clinical picture may be produced either by heredity or by environment. In such a case, a sample of single-born probands will contain a proportion of the environmental cases, or phenocopies, and a family study has to start out by lumping the relatives of both types of case. If, however, one starts with monozygotic twins as probands, a separation of the concordant and discordant pairs will in general segregate the genetic cases from the phenocopies. This permits from the outset a separate analysis of two groups of relatives practically without reference to familial incidence, so that the latter can be studied as an independent variable in the cases presumed to be genetic. Even with a very incomplete separation of genetic from nongenetic cases, the method may bring to light important statistical differences between the two groups of relatives. At the very least, this method of analysis provides another type of internal control in twin studies (Allen, 1954, p. 163).

Rosenthal (1959) adopted this approach in re-evaluating some of the twin data concerning schizophrenia. He limited his attention to the monozygotic twins and divided these into the concordant and discordant pairs. In each such pair of twins both individuals can be assumed to have the same genotype. If only one of the twins develops schizophrenia, we may assume that environmental factors have played an important role. Rosenthal found that in the families of the discordant twin pairs there was almost a total absence of schizophrenia, but the illness occurred in about 60 per cent of the families of the concordant twin pairs. The affected, discordant male co-twins tended to have a later age at onset and more favorable outcome than the concordant male twin pairs.

In a later paper, Rosenthal (1961) showed that the hospital population for schizophrenia yields a biased sample of twins with respect to chronicity; that is, a chronic case with long stay in the hospital is more likely to be sampled. The simplest way to eliminate this bias is to restrict the sample to consecutive first admissions. When Rosenthal made an appropriate correction, the concordance between monozygotic co-twins with respect to severity of illness was much less than in the uncorrected data.

This type of bias is a special case of the general problem of ascertainment mentioned earlier. Allen (1955b) has pointed out the need for care in reporting details concerning ascertainment of twins. Morton (1962) has further suggested that the data should not be reported in terms of concordant pairs, but rather as twin individuals, with each

affected individual being identified as a proband if ascertained independently or as a secondary case if discovered only by being the co-twin of a proband. Rosenthal's (1962) summary of problems of sampling and diagnosis in twin studies in schizophrenia has many implications for research in mental retardation.

The diagnosis of zygosity in twin pairs has been the subject of considerable discussion. Adequate laboratory and statistical methods are now available (Maynard-Smith, Penrose, and Smith, 1961). Reliance is usually placed upon similarity for a number of different blood-group antigens, with a definite exclusion of monozygosity if differences are observed. Several possible problems should be noted, however. Inaccuracies in determining ABO and MN types have been observed within one month after a blood transfusion (Clarke et al., 1962). The presence of vascular anastomosis in some placentae and the principle of immunological tolerance may occasionally lead to the apparent similarity of blood types in dizygotic twins with genotypic differences for one or more blood-group systems (Benirschke, 1961). Benirschke also points out that placental evidence, if properly recorded, can be of great value in establishing zygosity.

Allen et al. (1962) have completed the study of a series of mentally retarded twins, for which several preliminary reports were published earlier (Allen and Kallman, 1955; Allen, 1955a). A total of 177 multiple birth sets was included. The twin individuals formed 3.1 per cent of the mentally retarded institutionalized population, as compared with 2 per cent in the general population. The twinning rate was highest in the cases with reported birth trauma, reflecting the higher rate of birth trauma in twins because of their prematurity and the complications of delivery. The next highest twinning rate was found in the mentally retarded with cerebral palsy.

There was still some excess of twinning (over the general population rate) in the cases of undifferentiated mental retardation. Further examination of the data revealed an interesting possible source of bias. Among the dizygotic twin pairs in which both twins were institutionalized, there were sixteen pairs of same-sex twins and five pairs of opposite-sex twins. (Among all dizygotic twin pairs in the population, half would be expected to be same-sex and half opposite-sex.) Allen *et al.* felt that this discrepancy could result if parents were more likely to institutionalize both twins if they were of the same sex but to keep one at home if they were of opposite sex.

A particularly important part of the analysis concerned the birth weight in discordant twins (in which one twin had low-grade retardation while the other had only mild retardation or was normal). Among the discordant monozygotic twins (twelve pairs) the mean birth weight for the affected twin was 4.2 pounds, while the mean for the normal twin was 5.1 pounds (a difference of 0.9 pound). For the dizygotic twins (forty pairs) the mean weight for the affected twin was 4.7 pounds, as compared with 5.0 for the normal twin (a difference of 0.3 pound). Thus, among monozygotic twins who were discordant for severe mental defect, factors associated with low birth weight were probably the cause of the defect in a majority of cases. Among the dizygotic discordant twins, however, low birth weight was not as important, and the causes of the retardation in the affected twin were more likely to be genetic in nature. This type of study of discordance in twin pairs is a very useful approach and is not subject to some of the sources of bias which cause difficulty in other twin methods.

SEGREGATION ANALYSIS

Many of the important genetic principles can be illustrated by a discussion of segregation analysis as developed by Morton (1962). This approach is based upon the assumption that genes segregate in a predictable manner, thus permitting a rigorous statistical test.

Such a genetic analysis cannot be done upon groups of single individuals, but only through the study of families. A family with two or more cases of the condition under study is called *multiplex*, whereas a family with an isolated case is called *simplex*. (The terms "hereditary" and "familial" are frequently used in clinical descriptions in a vague manner, without the precise definition required for research purposes.)

In principle, these families may be divided into high-risk and low-risk families. In the high-risk families the probability of an affected child can be predicted from genetic theory. For example, the segregation frequency for an autosomal dominant is one-half, and that for an autosomal recessive is one-fourth. A low-risk family, on the other hand, includes what is termed a *sporadic* case. A sporadic case, in this terminology, is not the result of simple genetic mechanisms, but has arisen from such causes as mutations, phenocopies, extra-marital conceptions, chromosomal non-disjunction, and polygenic complexes.

Two points need emphasis: (1) Sporadic cases may occur in any type of condition, even in those which are assumed to result almost always from simple genetic factors. (2) The isolated case in a simplex family can be either sporadic (and hence a member of a low-risk family) or isolated by chance (a member of a high-risk family in which by chance only one person is affected).

Segregation analysis requires careful attention to the manner in which the affected persons are discovered. If, for example, a family with two affected children is included in the study, it is important to note whether both children were discovered independently through medical records or whether one child was found to be affected only because it was a sibling of the other child. All affected persons ascertained independently are termed *probands,* in contrast to *secondary cases* discovered by investigating relatives. If details concerning the mode of ascertainment are carefully recorded, an appropriate method of analysis can be employed.

Another important variable is information concerning consanguinity. It is not enough to inquire merely about the presence or absence of blood relationship. The manner of relationship should be stated as precisely as possible, preferably including a pedigree.

Dewey, Barrai, and Morton (unpublished) applied these methods of segregation analysis to the Colchester data on mental deficiency (Penrose, 1938). (It is of interest to note that data which are collected with care and reported adequately can often be used for analysis later as new techniques are developed.) Cases due to trauma, infection, neoplasm, mongolism, and hydrocephalus were excluded, as were those with an IQ of 50 or more. In order to avoid cultural defectives or those resulting from polygenic or dominant inheritance, the analysis was further limited to those cases in which both parents had an IQ greater than 85. This left a sample of low-grade cases from normal parents.

A second sample was obtained through a survey of the state of Wisconsin which yielded fifty-two families with two or more low-grade retardates (IQ below 50). In these multiplex families there were 86 probands, 31 secondary cases, and 129 normals. Post-infectional and post-traumatic cases were excluded, as in the first sample.

The analysis then showed that 88 per cent of the cases could be considered sporadic, and the remaining 12 per cent due to highly penetrant recessive genes. (It should be remembered that the sporadic cases are not necessarily all non-genetic, since those resulting from complex genetic mechanisms cannot be distinguished from other sporadic cases by

this method.) This conclusion was confirmed by the fact that the mean inbreeding coefficient of the isolated probands ($F = 0.001018$) was considerably less than that for the multiplex families ($F = 0.011574$).

The number of loci involved in recessive low-grade mental defect was estimated to be at least 126 ± 88. The total frequency of such genes per gamete was 0.234 ± 0.082. The authors pointed out that Böök's (1957) data for recessive genes in *all types* of mental defect indicated a total frequency per gamete of 0.694 ± 0.341. The difference between these two estimates suggests that many recessive genes may be involved in high-grade defect.

Both samples showed a highly significant excess of affected males among the probands. The simplest hypothesis is a greater tendency to institutionalize affected males because they are more difficult to take care of at home than are affected females. An inherently greater susceptibility of males to low-grade mental defect cannot be excluded, however, particularly when the possibility of sex-linked syndromes is considered.

Further analysis of larger samples will no doubt change these specific estimates quoted above; nevertheless, there are two general implications: (1) Among low-grade defectives, a sizable fraction of cases (here estimated at 12 per cent) results from segregation for simple recessive genes. In view of the restrictions in selecting cases and in the method of analysis, however, this figure is not comparable with other estimates of the proportion of mental retardation due to genetic causes. (2) A number of simple recessive types of retardation still remain to be identified. There is overwhelming evidence for great heterogeneity (genetic and non-genetic) in mental retardation.

GENETIC LOAD

A significant theoretical advance in the study of populations was made by Morton, Crow, and Muller (1956) in their definitions of the concept of genetic load (see also Fraser, 1962). Genetic variability is both desirable and inevitable; yet part of the price for maintaining this variability is the presence of a load of defect which cannot be eliminated entirely.

The major components of this genetic load have been identified by Crow (1962): (1) the mutation load, the extent to which the population is impaired by recurrent mutation, (2) the segregation load, the result of the recombination (by sexual reproduction) of the genes already in the population, and (3) the incompatibility load, resulting from the fact that some genotypes have a reduced fitness with certain parents.

One of the important implications of this total concept is the realization that we cannot expect to eliminate all genetic causes of a problem such as mental retardation. In Fraser's words,

. . . [B]oth mutation and segregation are regarded, whether viewed at single loci in isolation or in any form of synthesis . . . as necessary evils. While it is not denied that individuals, families and sometimes entire nations have to pay a very heavy socio-economic price, a genetical load is something which no species, least of all man, will ever be without. We can only strive to keep it to the minimum; the ideal homozygote will never be found (Fraser, 1962, p. 410).

BEHAVIOR GENETICS

Mental retardation is, of course, only one aspect of behavior, and some reference to the broader context may be appropriate. Behavior involves a response to the environment, and it is clear that the repertoire of response depends upon the type of nervous system available—the receptors, the central nervous integration, and the response mechanisms.

Human behavior is made unusually complex by the presence of culture, based upon man's ability to communicate, to receive, and to store information and ideas. Dobzhansky (1962) has emphasized the idea that human culture is made possible by man's genotype, although the genotype cannot specify the content of the culture. He further states that "the quality most consistently favored in man by natural selection has been educability. Capacity to profit by experience, to adjust one's behavior to the requirements and expectations of one's surroundings, trainability for whatever occupations or professions the society has available—educability, in short, confers the highest Darwinian fitness on human genotypes" (Dobzhansky, 1962, p. 251). A selection for educability, however, does not result in genetic uniformity. A population with much genetic variability would be more able to cope with the complex of environments by which it is confronted.

It has proved to be difficult, however, to define human behavioral traits in a manner entirely suitable for genetic analysis. It is reasonable to turn to other organisms in the hope that the analysis of their behavior will lead to principles which then can be used in designing further studies in man. Furthermore, the study of behavior is important for the understanding of these organisms themselves, particularly as related to ecology and evolution.

Some genetic aspects of behavior have been studied as part of research directed primarily toward other questions (Roe and Simpson, 1958). The analysis of reproductive behavior, for example, is important in the identification of mechanisms for reproductive isolation between closely related species. In general, those traits which are essential for the maintenance of species would be expected to show a strong dependence upon genetic factors. It is also known that major genes affecting morphological traits [such as eye color in *Drosophila* (Scott, 1943)] may have some effect upon behavior. Recently the field of behavior genetics has emerged as part of a more systematic effort to explore the biological bases of behavior (Ginsburg, 1958; Hirsch, 1958; Scott and Fuller, 1963). The volume by Fuller and Thompson (1960) provides a valuable synthesis and interpretation of the major sources of data.

Research in this area depends not only upon the definition of traits but also upon the selection of organisms most suitable for study. Genetic analysis always involves the study of differences, but this can be carried out at several levels (Scott, 1949): (1) The description of behavioral patterns in separate species is a first step. Genetic factors are probably involved in any differences that are observed, but the nature of these factors cannot be determined from species comparisons. (2) More explicit information can be obtained from a comparison of breeds or strains within a single species, such as the study of dogs by Scott and Charles (1953). A fair amount of genetic variability remains within each breed, however. (3) Genetic variability can be reduced by the development of closely inbred lines. Unfortunately, rats and mice are the only mammals for which such lines are presently available. It is important to remember that a number of inbred lines must be studied and the results compared before general principles can be established. (4) Crosses between two different inbred lines offer several advantages. The first-generation hybrids may be more stable and more uniform in response to the environment than either parental inbred line. By means of appropriate crosses the mode of inheritance of the trait can be determined.

Observations made on a number of different organisms indicate that behavior patterns may be conditioned and modified by early experience. Scott (1962) has summarized the evidence for the existence in young animals of critical periods for the formation of basic social relationships. Outside of these periods social attachments may be formed, but at a slower rate. Similarly, it appears that "the critical period for any specific sort of learning is that time when maxi-mum capacities—sensory, motor, and motivational, as well as psychological ones—are first present" (Scott, 1962, p. 955). The effects of early environment clearly must be taken into account in genetic studies, but genetic differences in response are not thereby ruled out. Lindzey *et al.* (1960), for example, showed that mice exposed to a noxious auditory stimulus at four to eight days of life showed strain differences in response as measured by emotionality, timidity, and motility in adults.

The general approach in behavior genetics (exclusive of man) appears quite different from that used for human mental retardation. The selection of bright and dull strains of rats must involve the sorting out of multiple genetic factors, thus resembling category C in Table 1 (mild retardation with multiple causation). Most of the successes in human mental retardation, on the other hand, come from the identification of single major causes. Further creative interplay between these two lines of research seems highly desirable.

CONCLUSIONS

Cases of mental retardation represent a large number of different entities. The etiology of some types is relatively simple, involving a single major process, genetic or non-genetic. Many cases, however, probably arise from the interaction of multiple genetic and environmental factors. The existence of this diversity provides an insight into the complex requirements for normal function of the human nervous system.

Adequate methods for genetic analysis are now available for the study of single-locus traits, but further development in methods for polygenic traits would be desirable. Even more urgent is the need for better definition of mental and behavioral traits in a manner suitable for genetic study.

Our knowledge of the different types of mental retardation dependent upon genetic factors is still incomplete. A more complete documentation of each syndrome would eventually include the following details: (1) exploration of the biochemical sequence involved, including the primary enzyme block and subsequent metabolic changes in the body fluids, especially those in contact with the nervous system, (2) histochemical and anatomical studies of the brain whenever possible, (3) careful description of the morphological changes in all parts of the body, (4) evaluation of measured intelligence, adaptive behavior, and psychiatric impairment, as well as neurological tests, to ascertain the complete range of effect upon brain function, and (5) genetic data concerning twinning, consanguinity, and segregation of the trait within families.

Acknowledgments.—The author wishes to acknowledge helpful comments and suggestions from Dr. Sheldon C. Reed, Dr. Harold O. Goodman, Dr. Ntinos C. Myrianthopoulos, and Dr. Milton A. Alter.

REFERENCES

ÅKESSON, H. O. 1961. *Epidemiology and Genetics of Mental Deficiency in a Southern Swedish Population.* Uppsala, Sweden: The Institute for Medical Genetics of the University of Uppsala.

ALLEN, G. 1954. Discussion on twin data. *Amer. J. Hum. Genet.,* **6**:162–64.

———. 1955a. Cases of cerebral palsy in a series of mentally defective twins. *Amer. J. Ment. Defic.,* **59**:629–39.

———. 1955b. Comments on the analysis of twin samples. *Acta Genet. Med. Gemell.,* **4**:143–60.

———. 1958. Patterns of discovery in the genetics of mental deficiency. *Dis. Nerv. Syst.* (Suppl.), **19**:31–39.

ALLEN, G., and BAROFF, G. S. 1955. Mongoloid twins and their siblings. *Acta Genet.,* **5**:294–326.

ALLEN, G., and KALLMANN, F. J. 1955. Frequency and types of mental retardation in twins. *Amer. J. Hum. Genet.,* **7**:15–20.

ALLEN, G., KALLMANN, F. J., BAROFF, G. S., and SANK, D. 1962. Etiology of mental subnormality in twins. *In:* F. J. KALLMANN (ed.), *Expanding Goals of Genetics in Psychiatry,* pp. 174–211. New York: Grune & Stratton.

ALLEN, R. J., and GIBSON, R. M. 1961. Phenylketonuria with normal intelligence. *Amer. J. Dis. Child.,* **102**:115–22.

ALTER, M. A., TALBERT, O. R., and CROFFEAD, G. 1962. Cerebellar ataxia, congenital cataracts, and retarded somatic and mental maturation. Report of cases of Marinesco-Sjögren syndrome. *Neurology,* **12**:836–47.

ANDERSON, V. E. 1961. Statistical studies of probands and their relatives. *Ann. N.Y. Acad. Sci.,* **91**:781–96.

ARONSON, S. M., PERLE, G., SAIFER, A., and VOLK, B. W. 1962. Biochemical identification of the carrier state in Tay-Sachs' disease. *Proc. Soc. Exp. Biol. Med.,* **111**:664–67.

AUERBACH, V. H., DiGEORGE, A. M., BALDRIDGE, R. C., TOURTELLOTTE, C. D., and BRIGHAM, M. P. 1962. Histidinemia. A deficiency in histidase resulting in the urinary excretion of histidine and of imidazolepyruvic acid. *J. Pediat.,* **60**:487–97.

BAYLEY, N. 1955. On the growth of intelligence. *Amer. Psychologist,* **10**:805–18.

BENIRSCHKE, K. 1961. Accurate recording of twin placentation. *Obstet. Gynec.,* **18**:334–47.

BENOIT, E. P. 1959. Toward a new definition of mental retardation. *Amer. J. Ment. Defic.,* **63**:559–65.

BIESELE, J. J., SCHMID, W., and LAWLIS, M. G. 1962. Mentally retarded schizoid twin girls with 47 chromosomes. *Lancet,* **1**:403–5.

BLACKWOOD, W., BUXTON, P. H., CUMINGS, J. N., ROBERTSON, D. J., and TUCKER, S. M. 1963. Diffuse cerebral degeneration in infancy (Alpers' disease). *Arch. Dis. Child.,* **38**:193–204.

Böök, J. A. 1953. A genetic and neuropsychiatric investigation of a north Swedish population with special regard to schizophrenia and mental deficiency. *Acta Genet.,* **4**:1–100, 345–414.

———. 1957. Genetical investigations in a north Swedish population. The offspring of first-cousin marriages. *Ann. Hum. Genet. (London),* **21**:191–223.

Böök, J. A., Schut, J. W., and Reed, S. C. 1953. A clinical and genetical study of microcephaly. *Amer. J. Ment. Defic.*, **57**: 637–60.

Börjeson, M., Forssman, H., and Lehmann, O. 1962. An X-linked, recessively inherited syndrome characterized by grave mental deficiency, epilepsy, and endocrine disorder. *Acta Med. Scand.*, **171**:13–21.

Burdette, W. J. (ed.). 1962. *Methodology in Human Genetics.* San Francisco: Holden-Day.

Carson, N. A. J., Cusworth, D. C., Dent, C. E., Field, C. M. B., Neill, D. W., and Westall, R. G. 1963. Homocystinuria: a new inborn error of metabolism associated with mental deficiency. *Arch. Dis. Child.*, **38**:425–36.

Cassel, R. H. 1957. Differentiation between the mental defective with psychosis and the childhood schizophrenic functioning as a mental defective. *Amer. J. Ment. Defic.*, **62**:103–7.

Caughey, J. E., and Myrianthopoulos, N. C. 1963. *Dystrophia Myotonica and Related Disorders.* Springfield, Ill.: C. C Thomas.

Clarke, C. A. 1962. *Genetics for the Clinician.* Philadelphia: F. A. Davis.

Clarke, C. A., Donohoe, W. T. A., McConnell, R. B., Martindale, J. H., and Sheppard, P. M. 1962. Blood groups and disease; previous transfusion as a potential source of error in blood typing. *Brit. Med. J.*, **1**:1734–36.

Clarke, C. M., Edwards, J. H., and Small-piece, V. 1961. 21 trisomy/normal mosaicism in an intelligent child with some mongoloid characteristics. *Lancet*, **1**:1028–30.

Craft, M. 1960. Mental disorder in a series of English out-patient defectives. *Amer. J. Ment. Defic.*, **64**:718–24.

Crittenden, L. B. 1961. An interpretation of familial aggregation based on multiple genetic and environmental factors. *Ann. N.Y. Acad. Sci.*, **91**:769–80.

Crow, J. F. 1961. Mutation in man. *Progr. Med. Genet.*, **1**:1–26.

———. 1962. Population genetics: selection. *In:* W. J. Burdette (ed.), *Methodology in Human Genetics*, pp. 53–75. San Francisco: Holden-Day.

Davies, J. 1960. *Survey of Research in Gestation and the Developmental Sciences.* Baltimore: Williams & Wilkins.

Dekaban, A. S. 1958. Mental deficiency. Recessive transmission to all children by parents similarly affected. *Arch. Neurol. Psychiat. (Chicago)*, **79**:123–31.

Dewey, W. J., Barrai, I., and Morton, N. E. Recessive genes in low-grade mental defect. Unpublished.

Dexter, L. A. 1956. Heredity and environment re-explored: specification of environments and genetic transmission. *Eugen. Quart.*, **3**:88–93.

Diamond, L. K. 1963. Erythroblastosis. *In:* M. Fishbein (ed.), *Birth Defects*, pp. 219–27. Philadelphia: J. B. Lippincott.

Dingman, H. F., and Tarjan, G. 1960. Mental retardation and the normal distribution curve. *Amer. J. Ment. Defic.*, **64**: 991–94.

Dobzhansky, T. 1962. *Mankind Evolving: The Evolution of the Human Species.* New Haven: Yale University Press.

Doxiadis, S. A., Fessas, P., Valaes, T., and Mastrokalos, N. 1961. Glucose-6-phosphate dehydrogenase deficiency. A new aetiological factor of severe neonatal jaundice. *Lancet*, **1**:297–301.

Dunsdon, M. I., Carter, C. O., and Huntley, R. M. C. 1960. Upper end of range of intelligence in mongolism. *Lancet*, **2**: 565–68.

Edwards, J. H. 1960. The simulation of Mendelism. *Acta Genet.*, **10**:63–70.

———. 1961. The syndrome of sex-linked hydrocephalus. *Arch. Dis. Child.*, **36**:486–93.

Eisenberg, L. 1958. Emotional determinants of mental deficiency. *Arch. Neurol. Psychiat.*, Chicago, **80**:114–21.

Falconer, D. S. 1960. *Introduction to Quantitative Genetics.* New York: Ronald Press.

Forssman, H. 1960. Mental deficiency and pseudoglioma, a syndrome inherited as an X-linked recessive. *Amer. J. Ment. Defic.*, **64**:984–87.

Fraser, G. R. 1962. Our genetical "load." A review of some aspects of genetical variation. *Ann. Hum. Genet. (London)*, **25**: 387–415.

Fredrickson, D. S. 1960. Infantile amaurotic family idiocy. *In:* J. B. Stanbury, J. B. Wyngaarden, and D. S. Fredrickson (eds.), *The Metabolic Basis of Inherited Disease*, pp. 553–79. New York: McGraw-Hill.

Freire-Maia, N. 1957. Effect of inbreeding

levels of population on incidence of hereditary traits due to induced recessive mutations. *In:* WORLD HEALTH ORGANIZATION: *Effect of Radiation on Human Heredity*, pp. 151–56.

FRIMPTER, G. W., HAYMOVITZ, A., and HORWITH, M. 1963. Cystathioninuria. *New Engl. J. Med.*, **268**:333–39.

FULLER, J. L., and THOMPSON, W. R. 1960. *Behavior Genetics.* New York: Wiley.

GHADIMI, H., PARTINGTON, M. W., and HUNTER, A. 1961. A familial disturbance of histidine metabolism. *New Engl. J. Med.*, **265**:221–24.

GINSBURG, B. E. 1958. Genetics as a tool in the study of behavior. *Perspect. Biol. Med.*, **1**:397–424.

GOOD, R. A., ZAK, S. J., CONDIE, R. M., and BRIDGES, R. A. 1960. Clinical investigation of patients with agammaglobulinemia and hypogammaglobulinemia. *Pediat. Clin. No. Amer.*, **7**:397–433.

GOODMAN, H. O., and HERNDON, C. N. 1959. Genetic factors in the etiology of mental retardation. *Int. Rec. Med.*, **172**:61–74.

GORLIN, R. J., and PSAUME, J. 1962. Orodigitofacial syndrome—a new syndrome. A study of 22 cases. *J. Pediat.*, **61**:520–30.

GOTTLIEB, M. I., HIRSCHHORN, K., COOPER, H. L., LUSSKIN, N., MOLOSHOK, R. E., and HODES, H. L. 1962. Trisomy-17 syndrome. Report of three cases and review of the literature. *Amer. J. Med.*, **33**:763–73.

GRAHAM, F. K., ERNHART, C. B., THURSTON, D., and CRAFT, M. 1962. Development three years after perinatal anoxia and other potentially damaging newborn experiences. *Psychol. Monogr.*, **76**:1–53.

HALDANE, J. B. S. 1961. Natural selection in man. *Progr. Med. Genet.*, **1**:27–37.

HALLGREN, B. M. 1950. Specific dyslexia ("congenital word-blindness"). A clinical and genetic study. *Acta Psych. (Kbn.),* Suppl., **65**:1–287.

———. 1959. Retinitis pigmentosa combined with congenital deafness; with vestibulo-cerebellar ataxia and mental abnormality in a proportion of cases. *Acta Psychiat. Scand.*, Suppl. 34, **138**:1–101.

HAMERTON, J. L. 1961. Sex chromatin and human chromosomes. *Int. Rev. Cytol.*, **12**:1–68.

HARNDEN, D. G., and JACOBS, P. A. 1961. Cytogenetics of abnormal sexual development in man. *Brit. Med. Bull.*, **17**:206–12.

HAUSCHKA, T. S., HASSON, J. E., GOLDSTEIN, M. N., KOEPF, G. F., and SANDBERG, A. A. 1962. An XYY man with progeny indicating familial tendency to nondisjunction. *Amer. J. Hum. Genet.*, **14**:22–30.

HEBER, R. 1959. Promising areas for psychological research in mental retardation. *Amer. J. Ment. Defic.*, **63**:1014–19.

———. 1961. Manual on terminology and classification in mental retardation. *Monogr. Suppl. Amer. J. Ment. Defic.*, **64**:1–111.

HERNDON, C. N. 1954. Genetics of the lipidoses. *Res. Pub. Assoc. Nerv. Ment. Dis.*, **33**:239–58.

HIGGINS, J. V., REED, E. W., and REED, S. C. 1962. Intelligence and family size: a paradox resolved. *Eugen. Quart.*, **9**:84–90.

HIRSCH, J. 1958. Recent developments in behavior genetics and differential psychology. *Dis. Nerv. Syst., Monogr. Suppl.*, **19**:17–24.

HIRSCHHORN, K., and COOPER, H. L. 1961. Chromosomal aberrations in human disease. A review of the status of cytogenetics in medicine. *Amer. J. Med.*, **31**:442–70.

HOLZEL, A. 1961. Galactosaemia. *Brit. Med. Bull.*, **17**:213–16.

HSIA, D. Y.-Y. 1959. *Inborn Errors of Metabolism.* Chicago: Year Book Publishers.

HSIA, D. Y.-Y., NAYLOR, J., and BIGLER, J. A. 1962. The genetic mechanism of Gaucher's disease. *In:* S. M. ARONSON and B. W. VOLK (eds.), *Cerebral Sphingolipidoses,* pp. 327–42. New York: Academic Press.

HUNT, J. McV. 1961. *Intelligence and Experience.* New York: Ronald Press.

ILLINGWORTH, R. S., and WOODS, G. E. 1960. The incidence of twins in cerebral palsy and mental retardation. *Arch. Dis. Child.*, **35**:333–35.

ISSELBACHER, K. J. 1960. Galactosemia. *In:* J. B. STANBURY, J. B. WYNGAARDEN, and D. S. FREDRICKSON (eds.), *The Metabolic Basis of Inherited Disease*, pp. 208–25. New York: McGraw-Hill.

JERVIS, G. A. 1963. The clinical picture. *In:* F. L. LYMAN (ed.), *Phenylketonuria*, pp. 52–61. Springfield, Ill.: C. C Thomas.

KALCKAR, H. M. 1959. Biochemical genetics as illustrated by hereditary galactosaemia. *In:* G. E. W. WOLSTENHOLME and C. M. O'CONNOR (eds.), *Biochemistry of Human Genetics*, pp. 23–38. Boston: Little, Brown, & Co.

Kalow, W. 1959. Cholinesterase types. *In:* G. E. W. Wolstenholme and C. M. O'Connor (eds.), *Biochemistry of Human Genetics,* pp. 39–59. Boston: Little, Brown, & Co.

Karlsson, J. L., Kihara, H., Grant, J., and Nelson, T. L. 1961. Metabolic disorders leading to mental deficiency. I. Screening for excessive urinary excretion of nitrogenous compounds. *J. Ment. Defic. Res.,* 5:17–29.

Kempthorne, O., and Osborne, R. H. 1961. The interpretation of twin data. *Amer. J. Hum. Genet.,* 13:320–39.

Kirman, B. H. 1958. Early disturbance of behaviour in relation to mental defect. *Brit. Med. J.,* 2:1215–19.

Kjellin, K. 1959. Familial spastic paraplegia with amyotrophy, oligophrenia, and central retinal degeneration. *A.M.A. Arch. Neurol.,* 1:133–40.

Knobloch, H., and Pasamanick, B. 1961. Genetics of mental disease. 2. Some thoughts on the inheritance of intelligence. *Amer. J. Orthopsychiat.,* 31:454–73.

Knox, W. E. 1960. Phenylketonuria. *In:* J. B. Stanbury, J. B. Wyngaarden, and D. S. Fredrickson (eds.), *The Metabolic Basis of Inherited Disease,* pp. 321–82. New York: McGraw-Hill.

———. 1963. Incidence and inheritance. *In:* F. L. Lyman (ed.), *Phenylketonuria,* pp. 11–51. Springfield, Ill.: C. C Thomas.

Knox, W. E., and Hsia, D. Y.-Y. 1957. Pathogenetic problems in phenylketonuria. *Amer. J. Med.,* 22:687–702.

Knudson, A. G., Jr., and Kaplan, W. D. 1962. Genetics of the sphingolipidoses. *In:* S. M. Aronson and B. W. Volk (eds.), *Cerebral Sphingolipidoses,* pp. 395–411. New York: Academic Press.

Komai, T., Kishimoto, K., and Ozaki, Y. 1955. Genetic study of microcephaly based on Japanese material. *Amer. J. Hum. Genet.,* 7:51–65.

Kramer, M. 1959. Measurement of patient flow in institutions for the mentally retarded. *Amer. J. Ment. Defic.,* 64:278–90.

Krooth, R. S., and Weinberg, A. N. 1961. Studies on cell lines developed from the tissues of patients with galactosemia. *J. Exper. Med.,* 113:1155–72.

Kurland, L. T. 1957. Definitions of cerebral palsy and their role in epidemiologic research. *Neurology,* 7:641–54.

Kurland, L. T., Myrianthopoulos, N. C., and Lessell, S. 1962. Epidemiologic and genetic considerations of intracranial neoplasms. *In:* W. S. Fields and P. C. Sharkey (eds.), *The Biology and Treatment of Intracranial Tumors,* pp. 5–48. Springfield, Ill.: C. C Thomas.

La Du, B. N., Howell, R. R., Jacoby, C. A., Seegmiller, S. E., and Zannoni, V. G. 1962. The enzymatic defect in histidinemia. *Biochem. Biophys. Res. Commun.,* 7:398–402.

Larson, C. A. 1955. The absence of phenylketonuria in 8,220 individuals not known to be mental defectives. *In:* L. Gedda (ed.), *Novant' anni delle leggi Mendeliane,* pp. 311–12. Rome: Istituto Gregorio Mendel.

Lenz, W. 1963. *Medical Genetics.* Chicago: University of Chicago Press.

Lerner, I. M. 1954. *Genetic Homeostasis.* New York: Wiley.

Levin, B., Oberholzer, V. G., Snodgrass, G. J. A. I., Stimmler, L., and Wilmers, M. J. 1963. Fructosaemia. An inborn error of fructose metabolism. *Arch. Dis. Child.,* 38:220–30.

Lewis, G. M., Spencer-Peet, J., and Stewart, K. M. 1963. Infantile hypoglycemia due to inherited deficiency of glycogen synthetase in liver. *Arch. Dis. Child.,* 38:40–48.

Li, C. C. 1961. *Human Genetics: Principles and Methods.* New York: McGraw-Hill.

Lindzey, G., Lykken, D. T., and Winston, H. D. 1960. Infantile trauma, genetic factors, and adult temperament. *J. Abnorm. Soc. Psychol.,* 61:7–14.

Lippman, R. W. 1958. The significance of heterozygosity for hereditary metabolic errors related to mental deficiency (oligomentia). *Amer. J. Ment. Defic.,* 63:320–24.

Lippman, R. W., Perry, T. L., and Wright, S. W. 1958. The biochemical basis of mental dysfunction. II. Mental deficiency (amentia). *Metabolism,* 7:274–80.

Lorincz, A. E. 1961. Heritable disorders of acid mucopolysaccharide metabolism in humans and snorter dwarf cattle. *Ann. N.Y. Acad. Sci.,* 91:644–58.

Lundström, R. 1962. Rubella during pregnancy. A follow-up study of children born after an epidemic of rubella in Sweden, 1951, with additional investigations on prophylaxis and treatment of maternal rubella. *Acta Paediat. (Stockh.)*, **51** (Suppl. 133): 1–110.

LUSH, J. L. 1945. *Animal Breeding Plans.* Ames, Iowa: Iowa State College Press.

LYMAN, F. L. (ed.). 1963. *Phenylketonuria.* Springfield, Ill.: C. C Thomas.

MACGILLIVRAY, R. C. 1957. Hypertelorism with unusual associated anomalies. *Amer. J. Ment. Defic.*, **62**:288–91.

McKUSICK, V. A. 1960. *Heritable Disorders of Connective Tissue.* 2d ed.; St. Louis: C. V. Mosby.

MACLEAN, N., MITCHELL, J. M., HARNDEN, D. G., JACOBS, P. A., BAIKIE, A. G., WILLIAMS, J., BUCKTON, K. A., COURT BROWN, W. M., McBRIDE, J. A., STRONG, J. A., CLOSE, H. G., and JONES, D. C. 1962. Sex-chromosome abnormalities among 4,514 mental defectives. *Lancet*, **1**:293–96.

McLEAN, W. T. 1961. Phenylketonuria with borderline and normal intelligence. *N. C. Med. J.*, **22**:528–30.

MACMAHON, B. 1962. Epidemiologic studies of the prenatal environment. *Res. Pub. Assoc. Nerv. Ment. Dis.*, **39**:141–49.

McMURRAY, W. C., RATHBUN, J. C., MOH-YUDDIN, F., and KOEGLER, S. J. 1963. Citrullinuria. *Pediat.*, **32**:347–57.

MASLAND, R. L. 1958. The prevention of mental subnormality. *In:* R. L. MASLAND, S. B. SARASON, and T. GLADWIN, *Mental Subnormality. Biological, Psychological, and Cultural Factors*, pp. 11–141. New York: Basic Books.

MATHER, K. 1952. Comment on Dr. B. Woolf's paper. *In:* E. C. R. REEVE and C. H. WADDINGTON (eds.), *Quantitative Inheritance*, pp. 103–11. London: Agricultural Research Council, H.M. Stationery Office.

MAYNARD-SMITH, S., PENROSE, L. S., and SMITH, C. A. B. 1961. *Mathematical Tables for Research Workers in Human Genetics.* Boston: Little, Brown, & Co.

MENKES, J. H., ALTER, M., STEIGLEDER, G. K., WEAKLEY, D. R., and SUNG, J. H. 1962. A sex-linked recessive disorder with retardation of growth, peculiar hair, and focal cerebral and cerebellar degeneration. *Pediatrics*, **29**:764–79.

MERRITT, H. H. 1963. *A Textbook of Neurology.* 3d ed.; Philadelphia: Lea & Febiger.

MILNE, M. O., ASATOOR, A., and LOUGH-

BRIDGE, L. W. 1961. Hartnup disease and cystinuria. *Lancet*, **1**:51–52.

MONCRIEFF, A. 1960. Biochemistry of mental defect. *Lancet*, **2**:273–78.

MOORHEAD, P. S., MELLMAN, W. J., and WENAR, C. 1961. A familial chromosome translocation associated with speech and mental retardation. *Amer. J. Hum. Genet.*, **13**:32–46.

MORTON, N. E. 1958. Empirical risks in consanguineous marriages: birth weight, gestation time, and measurements of infants. *Amer. J. Hum. Genet.*, **10**:344–49.

———. 1959. Methods of study in human genetics. *In: Genetics and Cancer* (Symposium on fundamental cancer research, 13th, Houston, Tex.), pp. 391–407. Austin: University of Texas.

———. 1961. Morbidity of children from consanguineous marriages. *Progr. Med. Genet.*, **1**:261–91.

———. 1962. Segregation and linkage. *In:* W. J. BURDETTE (ed.), *Methodology in Human Genetics*, pp. 17–52. San Francisco: Holden-Day.

MORTON, N. E., CROW, J. F., and MULLER, H. J. 1956. An estimate of the mutational damage in man from data on consanguineous marriages. *Proc. Nat. Acad. Sci. (Washington, D.C.)*, **42**:855–63.

MOTULSKY, A. G., and GARTLER, S. M. January, 1962. General principles of medical genetics. *Disease-a-Month*, pp. 1–77.

MOYNAHAN, E. J. 1962. Familial congenital alopecia, epilepsy, mental retardation with unusual electroencephalograms. *Proc. Roy. Soc. Med.*, **55**:411–12.

MYRIANTHOPOULOS, N. C. 1962. Some epidemiologic and genetic aspects of Tay-Sachs' disease. *In:* S. M. ARONSON and B. W. VOLK (eds.), *Cerebral Sphingolipidoses*, pp. 359–74. New York: Academic Press.

MYRIANTHOPOULOS, N. C., and KURLAND, L. T. 1961. Present concepts of the epidemiology and genetics of hydrocephalus. *In:* W. S. FIELDS and M. M. DESMOND (eds.), *Disorders of the Developing Nervous System*, pp. 187–202. Springfield, Ill.: C. C Thomas.

NEEL, J. V. 1962. Mutations in the human population. *In:* W. J. BURDETTE (ed.), *Methodology in Human Genetics.* San Francisco: Holden-Day.

Neel, J. V., and Schull, W. J. 1954. *Human Heredity.* Chicago: University of Chicago Press.

Newcombe, H. B. 1962. Population genetics: Population records. *In:* W. J. Burdette (ed.), *Methodology in Human Genetics,* pp. 92–113. San Francisco: Holden-Day.

Orloff, J., and Burg, M. B. 1960. Vasopressin-resistant diabetes insipidus. *In:* J. B. Stanbury, J. B. Wyngaarden, and D. S. Fredrickson (eds.), *The Metabolic Basis of Inherited Disease,* pp. 1274–94. New York: McGraw-Hill.

Osborne, R. H., and DeGeorge, F. V. 1959. *Genetic Basis of Morphological Variation. An Evaluation and Application of the Twin Study Method.* Cambridge: Harvard University Press.

Paine, R. S. 1960. Evaluation of familial biochemically determined mental retardation in children, with special reference to aminoaciduria. *New Engl. J. Med.,* **262:** 658–65.

Pasamanick, B. 1959. Research on the influence of sociocultural variables upon organic factors in mental retardation. *Amer. J. Ment. Defic.,* **64:**316–20.

Patau, K. 1962. Personal communication.

Patau, K., Therman, E., Smith, D. W., Inhorn, S. L., and Picken, B. F. 1961. Partial-trisomy syndromes. I. Sturge-Weber's disease. *Amer. J. Hum. Genet.,* **13:**287–98.

Pearson, J. S., and Kley, I. B. 1957. On the application of genetic expectancies as age-specific base rates in the study of human behavior disorders. *Psychol. Bull.,* **54:**406–20.

Penrose, L. S. 1932. On the interaction of heredity and environment in the study of human genetics (with special reference to mongolian imbecility). *J. Genet.,* **25:**407.

———. 1935. Inheritance of phenylpyruvic amentia (phenylketonuria). *Lancet,* **2:** 192–94.

———. 1938. *A Clinical and Genetic Study of 1,280 Cases of Mental Defect.* (Special report No. 229.) London: H.M. Stationery Office.

———. 1946. On the familial appearances of maternal and foetal incompatibility. *Ann. Eugen. (Lond.),* **13:**141–45.

———. 1949. Birth injury as a cause of mental deficiency. The statistical problem. *J. Ment. Sci.,* **95:**373–79.

———. 1959. Genetical analysis in man. *In:*

G. E. W. Wolstenholme and C. M. O'Connor (eds.), *Biochemistry of Human Genetics,* pp. 9–20. Boston: Little, Brown, & Co.

———. 1961a. Genetics of growth and development of the foetus. *In:* L. S. Penrose (ed.), *Recent Advances in Human Genetics,* pp. 56–75. Boston: Little, Brown, & Co.

———. 1961b. Mongolism. *Brit. Med. Bull.,* **17:**184–89.

———. 1962. Paternal age in mongolism. *Lancet,* **2:**1101.

———. 1963. *The Biology of Mental Defect.* 2d ed. rev.; New York: Grune & Stratton.

Pollack, M. 1958. Brain damage, mental retardation and childhood schizophrenia. *Amer. J. Psychiat.,* **115:**422–28.

Poser, C. M. 1962. Concepts of dysmyelination. *In:* S. M. Aronson and B. W. Volk (eds.), *Cerebral Sphingolipidoses,* pp. 141–64. New York: Academic Press.

Price, B. 1950. Primary biases in twin studies: A review of prenatal and natal difference-producing factors in monozygotic pairs. *Amer. J. Hum. Genet.,* **2:**293–352.

Priest, J. H., Thuline, H. C., Laveck, G. D., and Jarvis, D. B. 1961. An approach to genetic factors in mental retardation. Studies of families containing at least two siblings admitted to a state institution for the retarded. *Amer. J. Ment. Defic.,* **66:**42–50.

Reid, D. D. 1960. *Epidemiological Methods in the Study of Mental Disorders.* (World Health Organization, "Geneva Public Health Papers," No. 2.) New York: Columbia University Press International Documents Service.

Renwick, J. H. 1961. Elucidation of gene order. *In:* L. S. Penrose (ed.), *Recent Advances in Human Genetics,* pp. 120–38. Boston: Little, Brown, & Co.

Renwick, J. H., Lawler, S. D., and Cowie, V. A. 1960. Phenylketonuria: A genetical linkage study using phenylalanine tolerance tests. *Amer. J. Hum. Genet.,* **12:**287–322.

Richards, B. W., and Rundle, A. T. 1959. A familial hormonal disorder associated with mental deficiency, deaf-mutism and ataxia. *J. Ment. Defic. Res.,* **3:**33–55.

Roberts, J. A. F. 1940. Studies on a child population. V. The resemblance in intelligence between sibs. *Ann. Eugen. (Lond.)*, 10:293–312.

———. 1950. The genetics of oligophrenia. *Cong. Int. Psychiat. (Paris), VI. Psychiat. Soc.*, 6:55–117.

———. 1952. The genetics of mental deficiency. *Eugen. Rev.*, 44:71–83.

———. 1961. Multifactorial inheritance in relation to human traits. *Brit. Med. Bull.*, 17:241–46.

ROE, A., and SIMPSON, G. G. (eds.). 1958. *Behavior and Evolution.* New Haven: Yale University Press.

ROSANOFF, A. J., and INMAN-KANE, C. V. 1934. Relation of premature birth and underweight condition at birth to mental deficiency. *Amer. J. Psychiat.*, 13:829.

ROSENTHAL, D. 1959. Some factors associated with concordance and discordance with respect to schizophrenia in monozygotic twins. *J. Nerv. Ment. Dis.*, 129:1–10.

———. 1961. Sex distribution and the severity of illness among samples of schizophrenic twins. *J. Psychiat. Res.*, 1:26–36.

———. 1962. Problems of sampling and diagnosis in the major twin studies of schizophrenia. *J. Psychiat. Res.*, 1:116–34.

SARASON, S. B., and GLADWIN, T. 1958. Psychological and cultural problems in mental subnormality. *In:* R. L. MASLAND, S. B. SARASON, and T. GLADWIN, *Mental Subnormality. Biological, Psychological and Cultural Factors*, pp. 145–400. New York: Basic Books.

SCHEINBERG, I. H. 1958. Hereditary defects in protein synthesis as related to psychiatry. *Dis. Nerv. Syst.*, Suppl., 19:25–30.

SCHMID, R. 1960. Hyperbilirubinemia. *In:* J. B. STANBURY, J. B. WYNGAARDEN, and D. S. FREDRICKSON (eds.), *The Metabolic Basis of Inherited Disease*, pp. 226–70. New York: McGraw-Hill.

SCHULL, W. J. 1959. Genetics of man: Some of the developments of the last decade. *In: Genetics and Cancer* (Symposium on fundamental cancer research, 13th, Houston, Tex.), pp. 377–90. Austin: University of Texas.

———. 1961. Some considerations on the statistical and mathematical problems in consanguinity studies. *Jap. J. Hum. Genet.*, 6:12–20.

SCHULL, W. J., and NEEL, J. V. 1962. The child health survey: A genetic study in Japan. *In: Seminar on the Use of Vital and Health Statistics for Genetic and Radiation Studies*, pp. 171–93. New York: United Nations.

SCOTT, J. P. 1943. Effects of single genes on the behavior of Drosophila. *Amer. Naturalist*, 77:184–90.

———. 1949. Genetics as a tool in experimental psychological research. *Amer. Psychologist*, 4:526–30.

———. 1962. Critical periods in behavioral development. *Science*, 138:949–58.

SCOTT, J. P., and CHARLES, M. S. 1953. Some problems of heredity and social behavior. *J. Genet. Psychol.*, 48:209–30.

SCOTT, J. P., and FULLER, J. L. 1963. Behavioral differences. *In:* W. J. BURDETTE (ed.), *Methodology in Mammalian Genetics*, pp. 283–96. San Francisco: Holden-Day.

SCOTTISH COUNCIL FOR RESEARCH IN EDUCATION. 1961. *The Level and Trend of National Intelligence: The Contribution of the Scottish Mental Surveys by James Maxwell.* London: University of London Press.

SCRIVER, C. 1962. Hereditary aminoaciduria. *Progr. Med. Genet.*, 2:83–186.

SEDGWICK, R. P., and BODER, E. 1960. Progressive ataxia in childhood with particular reference to ataxia-telangiectasia. *Neurology*, 10:705–15.

SJÖGREN, T. 1948. Genetic-statistical and psychiatric investigations of a west Swedish population. *Acta Psychiat. (Kbh.)*, Suppl., 52:1–102.

SJÖGREN, T., and LARSSON, T. 1949. Microphthalmos and anophthalmos with or without coincident oligophrenia. *Acta Psychiat. (Kbh.)*, Suppl., 56:1–103.

———. 1957. Oligophrenia in combination with congenital ichthyosis and spastic disorders. A clinical and genetic study. *Acta Psychiat. (Kbh.)*, Suppl., 113:1–113.

SLACK, J., SIMPSON, K., and HSIA, D. Y.-Y. 1960. Hereditary metabolic disorders involving the nervous system. *Pediat. Clin. No. Amer.*, 7:627–63.

SLATIS, H. M., and HOENE, R. E. 1961. The effect of consanguinity on the distribution of continuously variable characteristics. *Amer. J. Hum. Genet.*, 13:28–31.

SMITH, C. A. B. 1961. Methodology in human genetics. *Amer. J. Hum. Genet.*, 13:128–36.

SMITH, D. W., PATAU, K., THERMAN, E., INHORN, S. L., and DeMARS, R. I. 1963.

The D₁ trisomy syndrome. *J. Pediat.* **62:** 326–41.

SOHVAL, A. R. 1963. Chromosomes and sex chromatin in normal and anomalous sexual development. *Physiol. Rev.* **43:**306–56.

SPUHLER, J. N. 1962. Empirical studies in quantitative human genetics. *In: Seminar on the Use of Vital and Health Statistics for Genetic and Radiation Studies,* pp. 241–52. New York: United Nations.

STANBURY, J. B. 1960. Familial goiter. *In:* J. B. STANBURY, J. B. WYNGAARDEN, and D. S. FREDRICKSON (eds.), *The Metabolic Basis of Inherited Disease,* pp. 273–320. New York: McGraw-Hill.

STANBURY, J. B., WYNGAARDEN, J. B., and FREDRICKSON, D. S. (eds.). 1960. *The Metabolic Basis of Inherited Disease.* New York: McGraw-Hill.

STEINBERG, A. G. 1959. Methodology in human genetics. *J. Med. Education,* **34:** 315–34.

———. 1961. *Progress in Medical Genetics,* Vol. 1. New York: Grune & Stratton.

STERN, C. 1960. *Principles of Human Genetics.* 2d ed.; San Francisco: W. H. Freeman.

SUTHERLAND, B. S., BERRY, H. K., and SHIRKEY, H. C. 1960. A syndrome of phenylketonuria with normal intelligence and behavior disturbances. *J. Pediat.,* **57:** 521–25.

SUTTON, H. E. 1961. *Genes, Enzymes, and Inherited Diseases.* New York: Holt, Rinehart & Winston.

TARJAN, G., WRIGHT, S. W., KRAMER, K., PERSON, P. H., JR., and MORGAN, R. 1958. The natural history of mental deficiency in a state hospital. I. Probabilities of release and death by age, intelligence quotient, and diagnosis. *Amer. J. Dis. Child.,* **96:**64–70.

TASHIAN, R. E. 1959. Individual variability in the metabolism of D-phenylalanine in human subjects. *Acta Genet.,* **9:**226–35.

———. 1961. Problems in the chemical diagnosis of some hereditary metabolic diseases. *Clin. Chem.,* **7:**441–56.

TOWER, D. B. 1958. The neurochemical substrates of cerebral function and activity. *In:* H. F. HARLOW and C. N. WOOLSEY (eds.), *Biological and Biochemical Bases*

of Behavior, pp. 285–366. Madison: University of Wisconsin.

UCHIDA, I. A., BOWMAN, J. M., and WANG, H. C. 1962. The 18-trisomy syndrome. *New Engl. J. Med.,* **266:**1198–1201.

VANDENBERG, S. G. 1962. The hereditary abilities study: Hereditary components in a psychological test battery. *Amer. J. Hum. Genet.,* **14:**220–37.

WANG, H. L., MORTON, N. E., and WAISMAN, H. A. 1961. Increased reliability for the determination of the carrier state in phenylketonuria. *Amer. J. Hum. Genet.,* **13:**255–61.

WARKANY, J., MONROE, B. B., and SUTHERLAND, B. S. 1961. Intra-uterine growth retardation. *Amer. J. Dis. Child.,* **102:**249–79.

WRIGHT, S. 1920. The relative importance of heredity and environment in determining the piebald pattern of guinea pigs. *Proc. Nat. Acad. Sci. (Washington, D.C.),* **6:**320–32.

———. 1954. The interpretation of multivariate systems. *In:* O. KEMPTHORNE, T. A. BANCROFT, J. W. GOWEN, and J. L. LUSH (eds.), *Statistics and Mathematics in Biology,* pp. 11–33. Ames, Iowa: Iowa State College Press.

WRIGHT, S. W., TARJAN, G., LIPPMAN, R. W., and PERRY, T. L. 1958. Etiologic factors in mental deficiency; errors of metabolism that may lead to mental deficiency. *Amer. J. Dis. Child.,* **95:**541–62.

WRIGHT, S. W., TARJAN, G., and EYER, L. 1959. Investigation of families with two or more mentally defective siblings: clinical observations. *Amer. J. Dis. Child.,* **97:** 445–63.

WRIGHT, S. W., SHAW, K. N. F., ROTH, P., TRAUB, J., and JOHNSON, A. 1961. Families with two or more mentally defective sibs. II. Biochemical studies. *Amer. J. Dis. Child.,* **102:**302–7.

ZELLWEGER, H. 1961. Amino-aciduria and mental retardation. *Clin. Chem.,* **7:**315–27.

———. 1963. Genetic aspects of mental retardation. *Arch. Int. Med.,* **111:**165–77.

ZUELZER, W. W. 1960. Neonatal jaundice and mental retardation. *A.M.A. Arch. Neurol.,* **3:**127–35.

TERATOGENESIS OF THE CENTRAL NERVOUS SYSTEM

F. Clarke Fraser

Gross malformations of the central nervous system are not usually considered in discussions of mental retardation. Anencephalics, for instance, are certainly mentally defective, but anencephaly is not customarily included as a cause of mental deficiency. Perhaps the justification for a chapter on central nervous system malformations in a book on mental retardation is supplied by the story of the inebriated man looking under a street lamp for a lost quarter, who, when asked why he was looking for it there rather than farther down the street where he had lost it, replied "The light's better over here." Perhaps the concepts and principles being formulated in studies of central nervous system morphogenesis and its errors may throw some light on problems of central nervous system function and *its* errors.

The author has recently reviewed the causes of malformations in human beings (Fraser, 1959, 1961a), and this paper will deal mainly with experimental work relevant to the causes of malformations. To begin with, it may be helpful to consider briefly some of the recent progress in fundamental embryology and genetics which may have important applications to the problems of abnormal development in mammals including, eventually, human beings.

RECENT ADVANCES IN EMBRYOLOGY AND GENETICS

GENE STRUCTURE AND FUNCTION

It seems generally accepted that all stages of mammalian development are guided by genes, and rapid advances are being made in our understanding of how the genetic information is stored in the chromosome and how it directs the development and function of the organism.

The carrier of the genetic information appears to be the chromosomal deoxyribosenucleic acid (DNA). The DNA molecule, according to the model proposed by Watson and Crick (1953a), is made up of two helical strands of nucleotides (consisting of deoxyribose, phosphate, and a purine or pyrimidine base which may be adenine, guanine, cytosine, or thymine) held together by hydrogen bonds between the base pairs. The physico-chemical requirements are such that the strands will only fit together if adenine on one strand pairs with thymine on the other, and guanine on one strand with cytosine on the other. When the strands separate, each can synthesize a chain complementary to itself, and the result is two pairs of chains, each with the same sequences of bases as the original pair (Watson and Crick, 1953b). Other models are possible (Penrose, 1960; Dounce, 1962), but a great deal of evidence now supports this concept of DNA structure (Fresco and Straus, 1962).

The recent spectacular advances in understanding of how the genetic information is coded in the DNA and conveyed to the developing organism represent one of mankind's major scientific achievements. These advances have been well reviewed elsewhere (Fresco and Straus, 1962; Hurwitz and Furth, 1962) and can only be mentioned briefly here. Only a few selected references are cited.

Essentially the concept is this: Proteins and the polypeptides from which they are constituted are chains of amino acids. The amino acids are assembled into polypeptide chains on cytoplasmic particles, the ribosomes. Each kind of protein has a specific sequence of amino acids, different from any other kind, which gives it its individuality. The sequence of amino acids in a particular kind of protein polypeptide is determined by the sequence of nucleotide base pairs in the DNA of a particular region of a chromosome. It appears that a sequence of (probably) three base pairs in the chromosomal DNA specifies one amino acid in the protein (Crick et al., 1961). For instance, a sequence, or "triplet," of three adenines at a particular place on the DNA chain may specify a phenylalanine at a particular place in the corresponding protein. Thus, a gene, at least from one point of view, can be thought of as a sequence of base pairs in a region of chromosomal DNA which specifies the amino acid sequence of a particular polypeptide (Sager and Ryan, 1961).

The DNA appears to exert its control of protein synthesis by means of a special type of ribosenucleic acid (RNA) called "messenger RNA," which is synthesized in the nucleus in such a way that its sequence of nucleotide base pairs corresponds to the sequence in the chromosomal DNA. A recent major breakthrough has been the experimental demonstration of which nucleotide triplets specify which amino acids (Matthaei et al., 1962). Thus, the DNA code for a particular protein is transmitted to the messenger RNA, which then migrates into the cytoplasm and attaches itself to a ribosome, where its sequence of nucleotide triplets determines the order in which the amino acids are lined up to form the corresponding polypeptide. For details of this elegant mechanism, including the role of transfer RNA, the reader is referred to the reviews mentioned above and a series of papers rapidly appearing in the current literature (e.g., Helinski and Yanofsky, 1962; Matthaei et al., 1962; Smith, 1962).

This knowledge has provided a remarkable insight into how genes produce their effects, including, of course, the unfavorable effects known as inherited diseases. In fact, studies of certain human diseases, the hemoglobinopathies, have played a major role in developing the one gene–one polypeptide hypothesis (Rucknagel and Neel, 1961). For instance, a disease, sickle-cell anemia, shown by family studies to be associated with a change at a single genetic locus (and presumably, therefore, a change in a single triplet in the chromosomal DNA), is caused by the production of an abnormal hemoglobin. The sickle-cell hemoglobin differs from normal hemoglobin only in the fact that one particular amino acid in its beta-chains is a valine instead of a glutamic acid, i.e., the mutant gene causes the disease by the alteration of one specific amino acid in the polypeptide it controls.

Much of the knowledge of the genetic code has come from bacteria and bacteriophage, where the relative simplicity of the system has made the analysis easier. In higher organisms, on the other hand, the DNA is intimately involved with protein and incorporated into a multi-stranded and coiled chromosome; much remains to be found out about the mechanical aspects of DNA replication and RNA synthesis in this relatively complicated structure (Ris, 1961) and the role of the chromosomal protein which may activate or inhibit certain areas of chromosome at certain stages of development (Markert, 1961). The role of the messenger RNA and ribosomes may also differ from that in bacteria (Bishop et al., 1961). Nevertheless, the point has been reached when the possibility of controlled alteration of the genetic code, either at the level of DNA or RNA, can be considered a real one, with all its implications for the control of hereditary disease.

Differentiation.—If all the cells of the body are derived from the fertilized egg by mitosis, which insures that they all have the same chromosomal constitutions (except for some cells that are normally polyploid), and if synthesis of cytoplasmic large molecules is under nuclear control, how is it that the cells of a developing organism become increasingly different from other cells in such a beautifully regular way? The probable answer is that the genes are not entirely autonomous; the results of their actions depend upon what they are acting on. The cytoplasm of the fertilized egg is not homogeneous (Brachet, 1957). Cleavage separates the spatially differentiated cytoplasm of the egg into a number of unequal daughter cells, so that each nucleus is acting on a somewhat different substrate. The same chromosomal message sent to different cytoplasmic receivers may produce different results. Furthermore, different cytoplasms may evoke different messages from the chromosomes. There is cytological evidence that chromosomes may show visible modifications of particular areas at particular stages of development (Beerman, 1956; Kroeger, 1960). Genetic evidence also supports the view that some genes act only at certain stages of development or in certain types of cells (Markert, 1961). It may be that genes are activated and, perhaps, inhibited by the DNA combining with specific proteins, so that which genes will act at any one time will depend on what proteins are available at that time (Markert, 1961). Eventually the nuclei themselves may become different in different cells, as demonstrated by studies on *Paramecium* (Sonneborn, 1960) and by the nuclear transplantation experiments of King and Briggs (1956) in frogs. When this happens, maintenance of the cyto-

plasmic differences between tissues is stabilized, and the cell can be said to be differentiated.

In some cases differentiation is associated with polyploidy, although there is some question as to whether polyploidy is a result of differentiation or vice versa. Walker and Prud'homme (1960) present evidence that in mouse-bladder epithelium, the appearance of polyploidy precedes cellular differentiation. However, such a mechanism could account for only a limited number of differentiations, since polyploidy is not a constant concomitant of differentiation.

Another possible mechanism by which differentiation might occur is suggested by the demonstration of self-reproducing cytoplasmic particles such as those determining antigenic type in *Paramecium aurelia*. In this case the evidence suggests that a number of different types of particle (determined by the genotype) exist in the cytoplasm, but that some sort of competition exists such that one type gains the ascendancy and determines the antigenic quality of the cell. The conditions of culture determine which type predominates (Beale, 1958). Thus, genetically identical descendants of one *Paramecium* may differ antigenically, depending on their environments. Possibly differentiation in a multicellular organism could occur in a similar way. Further discussion of the role of the cytoplasm and of other interesting aspects of differentiation will be found in reviews by Stern (1958), Sonneborn (1960), and Fischberg and Blackler (1961).

A new insight into the problem of differentiation has recently been provided by the discovery of "operator" and "regulator" genes. The genes which specify the amino acid sequences of proteins are called "structural" genes. In a number of micro-organisms it is now known that the activity of a structural gene (or a group of genes with closely related functions) is controlled by a closely adjacent, or contiguous, "operator" gene. The activity of this operator gene is controlled by a "regulator" gene elsewhere on the chromosomes, which appears to act through the cytoplasm in some way. This mechanism can induce, or inhibit, formation of the enzyme(s) controlled by the structural gene(s) in response to specific environmental alterations, such as addition of a particular substrate (Jacob and Monod, 1961). This, then, is another mechanism by which cells with the same genotype in different environments would have different phenotypes, and it is possible to construct theoretical models to account for differentiation in higher organisms (Monod and Jacob, 1961). Similar systems have been identified, though not in such precise biochemical terms, in higher organisms (McClintock, 1961), and it has been suggested that the system determining the switch from production of fetal to adult type hemoglobin may be of this type.

Thus differentiation appears to be a progressively more specific set of interactions between nucleus and cytoplasm which are just beginning to be analyzed in biochemical terms. Rapid progress is hoped for, since many gross malformations and other lesions of the developing nervous system involve errors in differentiation. However, developmental mechanisms cannot be fully understood in terms of individual cells. Tissues and organs have properties that transcend the properties of the individual cells of which they are constituted. What are the factors that guide the migration of cells and groups of cells, their adhesions, the co-ordinated movements and changes of shape of tissues, and the interactions of tissues that occur during morphogenesis?

Induction.—Induction consists of the initiation, by one region of an embryo, of morphogenetic processes in another. For instance, transplantation experiments show that the tissues in front of the blastopore will cause the overlying tissue to form neural tube, and the optic cup, as it grows out from the brain, initiates lens formation in the adjacent ectoderm. For a long time workers have attempted to identify the biochemical nature of the inducing agent, or organizer, and recent progress has been encouraging (Brachet, 1960). Undifferentiated embryonic ectoderm placed in culture with bits of adult tissues will differentiate according to the nature of the adult tissue. The inducing principle in some cases is claimed to be a ribonucleoprotein fraction, and in other cases a protein not associated with nucleic acid. The qualitative activity varies with concentration (suggesting gradient effects in the embryo) and can be altered by heat or chemical treatment.

On the other hand, Niu (1959) has shown that RNA seems to be the active principle that influences gastrula ectodermal cells grown in cultures with extracts of adult organs, such as kidney, liver, or thymus, to develop characteristics of the organ from which the extract came. It remains to be seen whether these substances are representative of those that actually cause induction in the embryo, but in any case it seems likely that inductors from different areas and developmental stages may represent quite different classes of compounds and that their biochemical identification is not far off. Once this has been achieved it will be possible to attack the problem of inductive errors and their resulting malformations in biochemical terms.

Inductive relationships appear to be more complicated than was originally thought (Zwilling, 1961). For instance, experiments with chicken limbs have shown that there is a reciprocal inductive relationship between mesoderm and ectoderm in feather formation. Mesoderm is able, for a limited period of time, to induce feather formation in the ectoderm and determines the regional specificity of the feathers formed, but the ectoderm also induces the formation of dermal papillae in the mesoderm and determines genetically controlled features such as color and texture of the feathers (Fell, 1960).

Another example of such a reciprocal relationship has been beautifully demonstrated by the experiments of Zwilling (1956) on limb formation in chicks. By grafting ectoderm of one limb on mesoderm of another, and utilizing a number of genetically determined limb abnormalities, he was able to show that the ectoderm (specifically the apical ectodermal ridge) promotes continued outgrowth of the underlying mesoderm but also receives from the mesoderm a stimulus necessary for its maintenance.

It is now possible to observe inductive processes in tissue culture, which provides a useful approach to the analysis of inductive mechanisms. For instance, Grobstein and Parker (1958) have shown that embryonic mouse spinal cord will induce tubule formation in kidney mesenchyme without cytoplasmic contact. This technique has been ingeniously put to use by Bennett (1958) in the analysis of the effects of mutant genes that alter inductive relationships (see p. 403).

Further analysis of these relationships in biochemical terms will be important, since inductive errors may be involved in many types of malformation.

CELL MIGRATION AND MORPHOGENESIS

Morphogenesis involves migration of cells, migration of tissues, and co-ordinated movements of groups or layers of cells. The subject has been thoughtfully discussed in a review by DeHaan (1958). Many aspects of the problem are now being investigated, and it can be anticipated that the present rather motley array of facts will eventually be co-ordinated into a more comprehensive view—a conceptual morphogenesis.

Migrating cells may be guided by mechanical directional features of the substrate—termed "selective contact guidance" by Weiss (1947)—and may also depend on chemotactic attractions and repulsions. Abercrombie (1958) has drawn attention to the phenomenon of contact inhibition: when a migrating fibroblast meets another the membranes fuse at the point of contact and movement is inhibited. Later, a new leading membrane may form and migration begins in another direction. This seems to be entirely a surface effect, probably not involving transfer of substances from one cell to the other. There is also evidence for selective cell surface compatibilities that may determine the final location of cells once they reach the general area of their destination.

Mass cell movements may occur by mitotic division, which could cause a tissue to spread, and, if its spread were mechanically limited, to buckle, warp, or thicken. Tissues may also change shape through the formation and subsequent contraction of intercellular cytoplasmic connections. In some cases masses of cells move by amoeboid activity of their individual cells. When tissues were excised from amphibian embryos during neurulation and separated into single cell suspensions, the different cell types of the randomly dispersed mixture sorted out into distinct, homogeneous layers corresponding to the normal germ layers. From these and other examples DeHaan (1958) concludes that "those movements of gastrulation, neurulation and organ formation which involve active amoeboid behavior are to a large extent controlled by the characteristics of the cell surfaces. . . ." Physico-chemical studies of such problems should be rewarding.

Morphogenetic movements may also consist of movements of entire layers of cells. Mitosis does not seem to be a major causal factor in such movements, but rather changes in cell shape, either by sol-gel transformations similar to those occurring in amoeboid movements, the formation of fibrous structures in the internal cytoplasm, or changes in cell adhesiveness (Waddington, 1956). Again the importance of cell membranes is emphasized. DeHaan (1958) has reviewed the evidence concerning the nature of cell adhesiveness and emphasizes the importance of calcium in this regard. He concludes that "it should be possible, by means of limited removal of calcium from a developing embryo, to produce disturbances of inter-cellular or substrate adhesion of just sufficient severity to cause abnormal morphogenetic movements" and supports his conclusions by demonstrating that cardia bifida and other malformations could be produced in chick embryos by agents that would be expected to remove calcium.

Not only cell membranes but also the inter-cellular matrix have long been thought to play important roles in morphogenesis. Edds (1958a) has reviewed the recent advances in knowledge of the microscopic and ultramicroscopic structure of intercellular substances (particularly mucopolysaccharide and collagen molecules). The importance of intercellular substances in directing the organization of cells into tissues is emphasized by Moscona (1960) in a review of in vitro studies on disassociated cells. For instance, a mixture of disaggregated embryonic kidney and cartilage cells will sort themselves out and form recognizable kidney and cartilage tissues. The factors guiding these aggregation and grouping maneuvers appear to be tissue-specific but not necessarily species-specific, since disaggregated embryonic mouse-liver cells will combine with chick-liver cells to form "heterospecific" liver tissue. It is postulated that these movements are guided by an exudate from the embryonic cells, probably mucoprotein in nature, with an organized interdigitating lamellar structure, which may carry the "cues" that allow cells of similar histogenetic nature to find one another and organize themselves into tissues. Further evidence that intercellular substances are important in embryogeny is presented by Walker (1961),

who suggests that acid mucopolysaccharides are intimately concerned with morphogenetic movements such as palate closure in the mouse. Future investigations along these lines should be productive.

IMMUNOLOGICAL ASPECTS OF DEVELOPMENT

The progressive appearance of protein specificities in the developing embryo and the relevance of these specificities to differentiation and growth are now being investigated by immunological methods with encouraging results. For instance, Ebert (1958a) has demonstrated the appearance of cardiac myosin in that part of the embryo that has the capacity to form heart and its subsequent localization to the area that actually does become heart. New lens proteins appear successively in the embryonic chick lens, each preceding or coinciding with the appearance of a new morphological structure (Langman and Maisel, 1962).

A number of intriguing facts about the immunological characteristics of embryos are known, which, although they cannot yet be fully related to the problem of normal development, will surely find a significant place in the understanding of embryological mechanisms eventually. Embryos do not seem able to produce circulating antibodies. When young rabbits are injected before they acquire the capacity to make antibody with nucleoprotein from adult rabbits immunized against S. parathyphi, they begin making antibody against this organism within two days (Sterzl and Hrubesova, 1957, cited by Ebert, 1958b). The nucleoprotein apparently conveys information that initiates the formation of a very specific protein in the developing rabbit.

Ebert (1958b) has shown that grafts of adult spleen placed on the chorioallantoic membrane of a chick embryo will cause hypertrophy of the embryonic spleen. Such a stimulated embryonic spleen used as a graft will, in turn, have a growth-stimulating effect, although an untreated embryonic spleen will not. If the graft is left in place for some time it may cause degenerative changes in the host spleen, and in the chorioallantoic membrane around the graft, as if it were making antibodies against host antigens. This and other graft-host interactions suggest that circulating antigens may be present in the embryo and play a role in the control of normal differentiation and growth. If so, fetal cells would have to be selective in their handling of antigenic molecules, and this has now been clearly demonstrated experimentally (Hemmings, 1961).

Another immunological phenomenon attracting interest recently is that very young animals may be rendered tolerant to antigens against which, later in life, they would normally develop antibodies (Medawar, 1961). This may account for the fact that embryos do not normally develop antibodies against their own differentiating tissues and the fact that materials, such as lens, which are physiologically separated from the host reticuloendothelial systems, may be auto-antigenic (Billingham, 1958). The possible significance of this to the problem of malformations will be referred to later.

Thus it seems that the embryo is capable of responding in specific ways to specific large molecules. However, as Edds (1958b) points out, "the evidence favoring a significant role of antigens as developmental regulators, though both tantalizing and suggestive, is inconclusive and difficult to evaluate. A large area has been opened for exploration, but as yet only the crude boundaries of the problem have been established."

In summary, the genetic information appears to be carried from generation to generation by DNA. Within the organism it is carried from nucleus to cytoplasm by RNA, and determines the specificity of the proteins being synthesized there. Because of cytoplasmic gradients in the original egg, cleavage divides the early embryo into a number of cells which differ in their cytoplasms, thus providing a variety of substrates upon which the chromosomes can act. Differences in the cytoplasm may result in different responses to the same chromosomal messages and may also evoke different chromosomal messages from similar nuclei. This dynamic and progressive nucleocytoplasmic interaction may lead eventually to changes in chromosomal structure, thus insuring the relative permanence of cellular differentiation.

As this process proceeds, cells in certain areas of the embryo acquire the capacity to influence the developmental fate of others, and a series of progressively more specialized inductions occur. The mechanisms of information-transfer are much less well understood at this level but appear to involve increasingly specialized cell-membrane properties, diffusion of biochemical substances, and feed-back mechanisms—some of which may be of an immunological nature. Finally there are the complicated movements and shape changes involved in organogenesis, the biochemical nature of which is still largely unknown.

Limitations of space and of the author's competence allow no more than this inadequate review of a large and rapidly developing subject (see reviews by Glass, 1958; Weiss, 1959; Brachet, 1960). It is hoped that at least some idea has been given of the great strides that have been made in the understanding of developmental processes and the promising prospects for progress in their characterization in physico-chemical terms.

MUTANT GENES AND ABNORMAL CENTRAL NERVOUS SYSTEM DEVELOPMENT

There are a large number of mutant genes which cause developmental abnormalities of the mammalian central nervous system, and virtually all stage' of its embryogenesis can be altered by one or more of these. Study of the effects of mutant genes can help to clarify both the pathogenesis of malformations and the nature of normal developmental mechanisms. As we have seen, genes appear to have very specific biochemical effects, and abnormal genes must therefore cause very specific biochemical abnormalities. It should be possible, with sufficiently precise methods, to identify the primary biochemical error that underlies any malformation resulting from a change at a single gene locus. So far, little progress has been made in this direction, but with the rapid advances in biochemical techniques now occurring the opportunity is ripe.

Furthermore, the use of a genetically determined malformation can provide virtually unlimited numbers of embryos, at any desired stages, in which the primary developmental error is constant, so that the train of events can be traced back from the malformation seen at birth, through successively earlier stages, to the point where the first detectable deviation from normal development occurs. This is the stage at or before which the underlying biochemical abnormality must occur. Conversely, analysis of the embryological results of a highly specific alteration of development (much more specific than one could obtain by experimental manipulation) allows, by inference from the abnormal results of this alteration, conclusions as to what the normal developmental relationships may be. Only a few of the many available examples (Gruneberg, 1960) can be presented here.

THE "T" LOCUS

One of the most intriguing, and intensively studied, series of mutants causing malformations of the central nervous system is the "T" locus in the mouse. This locus has many features of extraordinary interest from the point of view of fundamental and population genetics. It appears to be a unique example in mammals of a complex locus, i.e., a locus in which the main genetic unit contains sub-units which influence different aspects of its function (Dunn, 1956). The locus also influences the function of the gametes in ways that can lead to abnormally high proportions of mutant offspring (Braden, 1960), which provides an interesting example of a mechanism that can maintain the frequency of a deleterious gene in a population in spite of strong selection against it (Dunn, 1960). However, it is the embryological aspect that will be considered here.

The recessive lethal t^{12} acts earlier in development than any other mutant known in mammals. In homozygous embryos mitosis stops just prior to blastocyst formation, at about the thirty-cell stage, when the separation of trophoblast from the inner cell mass normally occurs. RNA synthesis is reduced, the embryos never progress beyond the morula stage, and the entire cell mass disintegrates before the time of implantation (Smith, 1956). In t^0/t^0 homozygotes no mesoderm forms, and death occurs before gastrulation (five to six days), while t^4/t^4 embryos show abnormalities of the archenteron and die at seven to eight days. In t^9/t^9 embryos which die at about nine days there are duplications of the embryonic axis (Glueckson-Waelsch, 1954).

The T mutant was the first of the series to be described. Heterozygous $(T/+)$ animals are born with short tails. The notochord in the tail region and often in the cloacal region becomes incorporated into the neural tube, and the distal tail is subsequently resorbed. In homozygous (T/T) embryos the notochord is incorporated more or less completely in the roof of the gut or in the neural tube, perhaps as a result of changes in its surface properties. The widespread changes in the posterior half of the body suggest that the notochordal disturbances may result from a more general disturbance of the primitive streak (Gruneberg, 1958*b*).

Another group of t alleles (t^{w5}/t^{w5}) cause pycnosis of the embryonic ectoderm and failure of the endoderm to differentiate (Bennett and Dunn, 1958). Mesoderm formation is retarded but does occur in the less severely affected embryos, which may also form notochord before they die at eight to ten days. The extra-embryonic tissues are unaffected and form chorion, yolk sac, and allantois, showing that the formation of these structures does not depend on the presence of an embryo.

Finally, there is a group of t alleles that act relatively late in embryonic development and result in reduced size, edema, hydrocephaly, microcephaly, and death anywhere between nine days and birth (Bennett *et al.*, 1959). The first histological abnormality in homozygotes is pycnosis in the floor of the hind brain, primarily in the mantle layer, beginning at about nine days. Pycnosis in older embryos appears in the spinal cord and is sharply limited to the ventral portion. There is reduction in size and retardation in time of appearance of all cartilaginous structures, followed by foreshortening of the anterior skull, cleft palate, and other bony abnormalities.

Thus we have a situation where a group of mutant genes appear, on genetic grounds, to occur within the same genetic locus but vary in their developmental effects from failure of blastocyst formation to ectoderm deterioration in early egg-cylinder stages, to disturbances of the chorda-mesoderm inductive relationships resulting in varying degrees of failure in development of, or duplication of, the neural axis (with only secondary effects on ectodermal derivatives), to later degenerative changes in specific parts of the central nervous system and axial cartilaginous system. Analysis of such systems should provide new understanding of the development and function of the central nervous system.

Bennett (1958) has begun an experimental analysis of the inductive relationships in T/T embryos. Neural tube from T/T embryos that is already visibly abnormal will, when cultured in vitro with somites from a normal embryo, induce cartilage in them. T/T somites, however, will not form cartilage when cultured with normal neural tube, although they have no visible signs of abnormality. It is suggested that this may result from a lack of a pre-inductive stimulus, perhaps from the notochord, which the somites require before they can respond to induction by the neural tube. Obviously the inductive relationships are not simple, and the use of mutant genes as analytical tools in this way appears to be a promising approach to their clarification.

The t series has been discussed to demonstrate how analysis of the developmental effects of mutant genes may aid in the understanding of both normal and pathological development. Other examples in the mouse where this approach could be equally rewarding have been cited by Gruneberg (1960) and Gluecksohn-Waelsch (1961). The mutant gene "Kink" causes an excessive formation of neural tissue and, in homozygotes, duplications of the entire embryonic axis, indicating disturbance of the normal organizer process. The genes for "Looptail" and "Splotch" interfere with normal closure of the neural tube and lead to overgrowth of the neural tissue which (at least in Splotch) appears to follow the failure of normal tube closure, as it does in craniorachischisis produced by environmental teratogens (Warkany *et al.* 1958; Giroud *et al.*, 1959; see this chapter, section on "pathogenetic studies of experimentally produced CNS malfunctions"). The gene for Danforth's short tail provides a striking example of widespread developmental effects which can be interpreted as all stemming from a single root cause, though the necessary interactions have not been experimentally proven. The most fundamental anomaly may reside in the primitive streak and give rise to structural abnormalities of the notochord and its eventual disintegration, which results in a series of secondary inductive disturbances leading to malformation of the vertebrae and vertebral disks, loss of the tail, and reduction of the cloaca and tail gut. Shrinkage of the cloaca is thought to result in absence of bladder, urethra, and genital papilla and may interfere with growth of the ureter buds, leading to absence of the metanephros. In vitro experiments have shown that the mutant metanephric anlage can respond to the inductive stimulus of a ureteral bud, and a mutant ureter can provide the necessary stimulus. Here the developmental error is one only of timing—the ureter does not reach its proper position soon enough to induce formation of the metanephros (Gluecksohn-Waelsch, 1961).

A number of examples of inherited hydrocephalus are known in the mouse and other animals, involving a variety of pathogenetic mechanisms. In one case the basic cause appears to be abnormal fluid circulation in the embryo (Bonnevie and Brodal, 1946). In another, abnormalities of the precartilaginous mesenchymal condensations lead to malformation of the chondrocranium with abnormal pressures on the developing brain, and this causes mechanical interference with cerebrospinal fluid circulation (Gruneberg, 1943). This emphasizes that the same pathological end result can have different genetic causes and developmental mechanisms.

A striking example of the extraordinarily widespread and variable effects a gene can have on development is that of the "disorganization" gene in the mouse (Hummel, 1958). In the heterozygote the gene may either have no apparent effect (i.e., it shows reduced penetrance) or one or more of a wide variety of defects including exencephaly, rachischisis, small ectopic or missing eyes, absence or

hypoplasia of mandible and maxillae, cleft lip or palate, branchiogenic cysts, accessory tongues, rib malformations, missing or extra limbs, gastroschisis, bladder exstrophy, and duplications of large intestine and rectum. Penetrance varies with both the genetic background and the intra-uterine environment, but the type of malformation does not. The large number of organogenetic processes interfered with by this mutant suggests that it must alter some biochemical process common to a number of different inductive systems. Identification of the biochemical defect would therefore be a most valuable contribution to our knowledge of inductive mechanisms and might have important implications with respect to some of the bizarre multiple malformations that occur in human beings.

Many other examples of central nervous system abnormalities caused by mutant genes in experimental animals can be cited, including deafness, labyrinthine defects, chorea, anophthalmia, and convulsions (Gruneberg, 1947, 1952). Many of them resemble abnormalities that occur in human beings. Their further exploitation by studying their embryological origins and inductive relationships and by identification of the gene-determined biochemical errors involved should greatly increase our knowledge of normal and abnormal embryological mechanisms and guide us to a better understanding of central nervous system malformations in human beings.

Environmental Teratogens and Central Nervous System Malformations

As we have seen, mutant genes may alter development in very specific ways, but almost nothing is yet known about the basic biochemical errors involved. Another approach, now beginning to be exploited, is the use of environmental agents to interfere with mammalian embryonic development. With some of these, the biochemical error is better known, but the developmental alterations are often not so specific. A combination of the two approaches should be productive (see Russell, 1956, for further discussion of the relation of induced malformations to mutants).

GENERAL PRINCIPLES OF EXPERIMENTAL TERATOLOGY

The field of experimental mammalian teratology has rapidly expanded; emerging principles, which have recently been stated by Wilson (1961), are recapitulated with minor modifications here.

The stage of development at which an agent acts determines which embryonic parts are susceptible to maldevelopment. —This principle was stated by Stockard as far back as 1921 (cited by Wilson, 1961) when he produced a variety of malformations by treating sea minnow eggs with a number of physical and chemical agents. The idea is a reasonable one, since one would not expect to interfere with morphogenetic processes after they are complete, and one might intuitively expect that a developing system would be most easily interfered with at the time when differentiation is most rapidly occurring. However, it would be a mistake to oversimplify the principle (as some have done) to the point of saying that no matter what the noxious agent, if it is applied at a given developmental stage, the same type of malformation will be produced. A morphogenetic process must be preceded by a number of interacting biochemical processes occurring at various times before visible differentiation begins, and one teratogenic agent may affect a different biochemical precursor than another. Thus a two-hour inhibition of nicotinamide activity by 6-aminonicotinamide in the mouse is most effective in producing cleft palate when the analogue is given thirteen days after con-

ception, about a day before palate closure begins (Goldstein *et al.*, 1963), whereas X-radiation interferes with palate closure most effectively between ten and twelve days after conception, and there is another period of sensitivity at about the eighth day, before there is any visible primordium of the palate (Russell and Russell, 1954).

Most workers agree that malformations are not usually produced by teratogens applied prior to commencement of differentiation in the embryo (Wilson, 1961). However, the Russells (1954) have observed a low but significant frequency of vertebral and rib anomalies in mouse embryos from mothers X-irradiated between one-half and five and one-half days after conception; Rugh and Grupp (1959a) have produced exencephaly, again with a low frequency, by irradiation during the same period. One wonders if these could have resulted from radiation damage to the maternal endometrium or even from chromosomal anomalies induced by the radiation.

Each teratogen has specific metabolic effects on the embryo, which may produce characteristic patterns of malformations.—This principle would be difficult to substantiate experimentally for agents, such as X-rays, which may act by killing cells by (non-specific) chromosomal damage or in other ways. However, it may be a useful working hypothesis for agents, such as vitamin antagonists, for which the primary biochemical effect is known. Even under these circumstances, though, the picture may not be entirely clear. For instance, 6-aminonicotinamide is known to form a DPN analogue inactive in several DPN-dependent enzymatic systems, though not in others (Dietrich *et al.*, 1958). Thus it cannot be assumed that all 6-aminonicotinamide-induced malformations result from blocking the same enzyme system.

Similarly, Landauer (1954) has shown

that rumplessness, produced in chick embryos by insulin, could be prevented by simultaneous treatment with pyruvic acid. Micromelia caused by insulin treatment at a later stage was not prevented by pyruvic acid but was by nicotinamide. Clearly a teratogen may have different specific biochemical effects on different developmental pathways.

Nevertheless, the principle serves to emphasize that the type of malformation produced is not merely a matter of the developmental stage at which the agent is applied. Each agent, when applied to a given species at a given time, tends to produce a characteristic array of malformations different from those produced by agents acting in other ways. When two agents produce the same array of defects, it can be inferred that they probably affect the same biochemical pathways in the embryo. For instance, Landauer (1954) has shown that boric acid and riboflavin deficiency produced the same types of malformation in the chick embryo. Boric acid–treated embryos were found to be riboflavin deficient, so a common metabolic pathway existed to account for the teratogenic similarity.

Whether or not an embryo exposed to a teratogen develops a malformation is determined, in part, by its genetic constitution.—Numerous examples now exist of genetic differences in response to teratogens, and the principle should be virtually self-evident to those who are aware that the pattern of development is the result of constantly interacting genetic and environmental factors. The existence of such genetic differences is not merely of academic interest—their value in analyzing developmental mechanisms will be discussed later (pp. 410–12).

Intra-uterine mortality tends to vary directly with the rate of malformations. —This principle seems to be valid for many teratogens and emphasizes that the severity of effect necessary to alter de-

velopment is often close to the degree that will inhibit it completely. The frequency of malformation and the mortality rate usually increase in roughly parallel fashion (Wilson, 1954a), and mortality (usually embryonic resorption) decreases with advancing embryonic age (Fraser *et al.*, 1954; Nelson *et al.*, 1955). However, some intriguing exceptions occur. The frequency of resorptions induced in the A/Jax mouse strain by a two-hour inhibition of nicotinamide activity by 6-aminonicotinamide is not increased when treatment is given on certain days, although a high frequency of malformations may result from treatment on these days. Furthermore, the resorption frequency is much higher following treatment at ten days after conception than at nine or eleven days (Goldstein *et al.*, 1963). Perhaps the teratogen in this case is interfering with some process, such as placentation, vital to the whole embryo.

The converse principle, that agents causing embryonic death will, in lower concentrations, cause malformations, does not always hold. There are a number of agents that will kill the embryo but have not been demonstrably teratogenic—e.g., hemorrhagic anemia in the rat (Wilson, 1954b) and mouse (Clark, 1956) and certain chemicals in the rat (Thiersch, 1958). It remains to be seen (1) whether this can be accounted for by failure to test the proper dose at the proper stage, or (2) whether some features of the embryonic system are so fundamental to its integrity that they cannot be disturbed, even slightly, without killing the embryo, or (3) whether the processes of morphogenesis are so resistant to some noxious agents that the teratogenic dose is higher than the dose that kills the embryo by its systemic toxic effects.

A teratogenic agent need not be deleterious to the maternal organism.—This is well demonstrated by the production of severe malformations in human embryos by the rubella virus, which may produce the mildest of symptoms in the mother. It is also true of some experimental teratogens (Nelson *et al.*, 1955; Murphy, 1959; Pinsky and Fraser, 1960), though by no means all of them. Teratogens such as hypoxia, trypan blue, and maternal fasting and other dietary deficiencies do have obvious deleterious effects on the mother, although recovery may be rapid after treatment is stopped. Certainly, as Wilson (1961) points out, it is time to discard the time-honored belief that the embryo lives as a favored parasite upon the mother, able to obtain scarce materials at her expense.

PATHOGENETIC STUDIES OF EXPERIMENTALLY PRODUCED CENTRAL NERVOUS SYSTEM MALFORMATIONS

A great many environmental teratogens are now known which will cause malformations of the central nervous system in the offspring of mothers treated during pregnancy. These include *vitamin A* deficiency (retinal anomalies, hydrocephalus), *riboflavin* deficiency (hydrocephalus, microphthalmia, encephalic malformations), *folic acid* deficiency (hydrochepalus, spina bifida, cranium bifidun, anophthalmia, exencephaly, microcephaly), *pantothenic acid* deficiency (exencephaly, anophthalmia), *vitamin E* deficiency, (exencephaly, hydrocephalus), *thiamin* deficiency (exencephaly), *nicotinamide* deficiency (exencephaly), maternal *fasting* (exencephaly), *nucleic acid* antagonists (anophthalmia, hydrocephalus), *insulin* (microcephaly, spina bifida), *thyroid deficiency* (retinal abnormalities, anophthalmia), *hypervitaminosis A* (exencephaly, hydrocephalus, eye defects, spina bifida), *trypan blue* (hydrocephalus, cranioschisis, meningocoele, spina bifida, anophthalmia, exencephaly), *hypoxia* (cranioschisis, exencephaly, abnormal foldings of brain and cord), *hypothermia* (hydrocephalus, exencephaly, spina bifida, anophthalmia), *nitrogen mustard* (exencephaly, hydrocephalus), *X-radiation* (anencephaly,

anophthalmia, encephalocoele, hydrocephalus, microcephaly, cranio-spinal anomalies, cerebellar defects), and *salicylates* (craniorachischisis)—see review by Kalter and Warkany (1959).

Hydrocephalus has been produced in the offspring of pregnant rabbits fed excessive amounts of sugar (Sumi, 1960), and central nervous system abnormalities have been produced by maternal immunization of mice with brain extracts (Gluecksohn-Waelsch, 1957) and by injecting anti-kidney sera in pregnant rats (Brent, 1961). Clamping of the uterine vessels for several hours produced anencephaly and anophthalmia in rats (Brent and Franklin, 1960). As mentioned above, these teratogens are not specific to the central nervous system but cause various malformations of other parts of the body as well. For only two of these agents is there convincing evidence of teratogenicity in human beings. These are radiation (Murphy, 1929; Yamazaki *et al.*, 1954) and folic acid deficiency (Warkany *et al.*, 1959), but convincing evidence is so hard to collect that it cannot be concluded that the others are entirely harmless to the human fetus.

The use of experimentally produced malformations to illuminate the pathogenesis of a congenital defect is well demonstrated by the work of Warkany *et al.* (1958) on the embryology of myeloschisis and myelomeningocoele produced by injecting pregnant rats with trypan blue on the eighth, ninth, and tenth days of pregnancy. Embryos were removed at various ages after this for study of stages leading to the congenital defect. On the twelfth day (when the neural tube normally completes closure), there was overgrowth of the neural plate and irregularity in formation of the tube. On the fourteenth day the tube was everted, and further overgrowth of neural tissue had occurred. By the seventeenth day the subarachnoid space, now lying between the open neural plate and the vertebral column, was enlarged and filled with a loose network of meningeal tissue and capillaries. During the next few days there was progressive enlargement of this space, with degeneration and shedding of the neural plate tissue and epithelization and vascularization of the supporting meninges. This succession of observations demonstrates the transformation of the open neural plate (myeloschisis) to a denuded, heavily vascularized meningeal sac enclosing a large, fluid-filled subarachnoid space (myelomeningocoele). Thus it has been possible to demonstrate the succession of degenerative and regenerative changes (some of them postulated but not seen in humans) leading from myeloschisis to myelomeningocoele, and to provide experimental support for the group of human embryologists who maintain that this is the way myelomeningocoele develops in human beings. Of course this does not rule out the possibility that in some cases other mechanisms may exist that will bring about the same end result. Gardner (1960), for instance, suggests that the original myeloschisis results from rupture of a hydrocephalic neural tube rather than failure to close.

Giroud and Martinet (1954) have used vitamin A–induced anencephaly in the rat to study the pathogenesis of this malformation. The first deviation from normal development is failure of the encephalic tube to close. Organogenesis and histogenesis proceed relatively normally, however, so that all the major structures of the brain can be distinguished, but the brain is, so to speak, turned inside out. Later, degeneration sets in, and soon only necrotic debris and some nerves remain. Anencephaly thus appears, in this case, to result from regressive changes in an exencephalic brain, rather than from inhibition of brain formation.

The use of X-rays in producing central nervous system and other malformations has been exploited by a number of workers (reviewed by Russell, 1956),

but many of them have limited their observations to embryos near term and have not studied progressive stages in development of the malformations observed. However, Hicks et al. (1961) have made extensive observations on the embryonic changes occurring after irradiation in rats by removing embryos for observation from periods of a few hours after exposure until after birth. Specific groups of cells could be followed by radioisotope labeling. Exposure to 200 R of X-irradiation causes extensive and rapid necrosis, mainly of two cells types —those in early prophase and postmitotic primitive cells just beginning to differentiate. (Even doses as low as 30–40 R will cause some necrosis, and doses as low as 15 R are harmful to very early mouse embryos—Rugh and Grupp, 1959b.) Primitive mitotic cells and differentiated ones are spared. In animals irradiated eleven days after conception one-third to one-half of the cells of the embryo were damaged, and yet recovery could occur more or less completely, since some treated embryos had no malformations, which demonstrates the astonishing recuperative powers of the developing organism. Hicks concluded that in some cases cell destruction by itself is not enough to explain the abnormal development and that there must have been interference with inductive processes, e.g., in the prechordal mesoderm, leading to anencephaly, and in the optic cup-ectoderm relationships, leading to anophthalmia. On the other hand, anophthalmia caused by irradiation at later stages (eleventh day) appears to be due to destruction of early lens and retina. Again, the same end effect appears to arise by different mechanisms (Hicks and D'Amato 1961).

It is hoped that the above examples will emphasize the great need for further studies in which a teratogen is used to produce a high proportion of malformations of a given type, and the pathogenesis of the malformation can be followed by observing embryos at successive stages after treatment. Much could be learned about pathogenetic mechanisms by this approach.

Biochemical studies in teratology.— Little has been done in the way of directly identifying the biochemical effects of teratogens on embryos, perhaps because knowledge of normal embryonic biochemistry has only recently begun to advance (Kretchmer, 1959; Brachet, 1960). In fact, evidence is lacking for many teratogens that they even get into the embryo. Trypan blue is teratogenic when injected directly into chick embryos, and Wilson *et al.* (1959*a*) present indirect evidence that it acts directly on the embryo in the rat, its limited span of teratogenic activity being attributed to the protective action of the developing yolk-sac placenta. However, it has not yet been reported in the tissues of the embryo itself. Giroud *et al.* (1950) have shown that maternal riboflavin deficiency in rats is accompanied by an even greater decrease in riboflavin concentration in the embryo and (1957) that a maternal excess of vitamin A is accompanied by an increase (though not a large one) in vitamin A in the embryonic liver. Radiation has been shown to be teratogenic to embryos radiated *in utero* with the mother shielded (Wilson 1954*a*), but for most teratogens there is no proof that the agent does not act by producing metabolic aberrations in the mother, with secondary consequences to the embryo. An ingenious method which could be used for investigating this question has been developed by Brent and Franklin (1960). If one horn of the uterus is clamped while the teratogen is injected into the mother, and if the embryos in the unclamped horn are malformed, while those of the clamped horn are not, it is likely that the teratogen is acting directly, rather than by producing secondary systemic effects in the mother (unless these were very rapid and transient).

*Specific antimetabolites.—*The use of analogues with specific antimetabolic effects is a useful way to produce known metabolic deficiencies during limited periods of development, and this approach is being increasingly utilized in teratology (Kalter and Warkany, 1959; Dagg, 1960; Murphy, 1960; Nelson, 1960; Fraser, 1962). Injection of the nicotinamide antagonist 6-aminonicotinamide is teratogenic in mice even when its effects are terminated by giving nicotinamide two hours later (Pinsky and Fraser, 1960). There is evidence to suggest that it takes more nicotinamide to correct the deficiency at some stages than at others, and the pattern of malformations varies widely depending on the gestational stage at which the treatment is given. This sort of approach should provide useful information about the enzymatic requirements of the embryo and the roles of specific enzymes in various morphogenetic processes.

Information about the mechanism of action of a teratogen may be gained indirectly by studying its teratogenicity in combination with other compounds. For instance, Runner and Dagg (1960) have shown that maternal treatment with hypoxia and trypan blue act additively with fasting (in terms of frequencies of vertebral malformations produced in the offspring of treated mothers), whereas iodoacetate, 9-methyl folic acid, and X-radiation show non-additive effects. From this he makes some ingenious deductions about the metabolic requirements of the somites and neural tube during differentiation, and how they are altered by the teratogens. A great deal might be learned about the biochemistry of teratogenesis by studying the potentiating and inhibiting effects of pharmacological agents on teratogens. This type of analysis has been exploited effectively in chickens by Landauer (1954), and there are many opportunities for its useful application in mammalian teratology (Woollam and Millen, 1960).

Another indirect approach to the nature of the mechanisms by which teratogens act utilizes the varying responses of inbred strains. For instance, galactoflavin produces more cleft palates in the C57BL/6 than in the A/Jax mouse strain (Kalter and Warkany, 1957), whereas cortisone produces more cleft palates in the A/Jax than in the C57BL strain (Kalter, 1954). This shows that galactoflavin and cortisone must interfere with palate closure in different ways. On the other hand, the relative frequencies of cleft palate induced by cortisone and by 6-aminonicotinamide, respectively, correspond in the two strains and in the offspring of reciprocal crosses between them (Goldstein, Pinsky, and Fraser, 1963). This suggests that cortisone may act through the same metabolic pathway as 6-aminonicotinamide, though comparisons between other strains will be needed before firm conclusions can be drawn. This example is given to illustrate how comparisons of the effects of different teratogens on a variety of inbred strains can provide information about the biochemical pathways involved (Fraser, 1963).

Immunological studies.—The possibility that embryonic development may be interfered with by maternally-produced antibodies has been investigated by a number of workers. Gluecksohn-Waelsch (1957) injected brain extracts (with Freund's adjuvant) into female mice of the DBA strain over a two-week period and then mated them with DBA males. About 9 per cent of the offspring had abnormalities of the central nervous system. Similar treatment using heart extracts produced no central nervous system abnormalities. No antibodies were demonstrated in the maternal serum. Brent *et al.* (1961) produced a variety of severe malformations in rats by injecting anti-kidney serum during pregnancy. Langman *et al.* (1962) and others have shown that lens antiserum produced a variety of eye defects in chick embryos.

Similar effects of lens antiserum have been produced in rabbit embryos (Wood, 1957). Langman's anti-lens sera also produced defects in the optic vesicles, retina, and brain, which contained lens antigens at the time of treatment (Langman *et al.*, 1962).

Further study by this intriguing approach should be rewarding, although it is far from clear what significance such findings may have with respect to the problem of malformations in human beings. It is possible that certain tissues such as lens, brain, or thyroid that are normally separated physiologically from the rest of the organism may be antigenic if, through some untoward event, a portion of such tissue does get into the maternal blood stream and that the resulting antibodies may inhibit development of that particular tissue (Billingham, 1958). Little has been done to investigate this possibility, but some evidence for such a mechanism does exist. Blizzard *et al.* (1960) have found antibodies to thyroglobulin in the sera of some mothers of babies with athyrotic cretinism and in some children with this malformation. Two maternal sera contained a factor cytotoxic for thyroid tissue in culture. It is suggested that placental transfer of maternal antibodies to thyroglobulin and subsequent destruction of the fetal thyroid may account for at least some cases of athyrotic cretinism. A search for other examples of maternal-fetal immunological reactions in cases of other types of malformations (anophthalmia, anencephaly?) might be rewarding.

GENETIC DIFFERENCES IN RESPONSE TO ENVIRONMENTAL TERATOGENS

Differences between strains in the frequencies of malformations produced by environmental teratogens have been reported by a number of workers. These include diaphragmatic hernia produced by maternal vitamin-A deficiency in rats (Andersen, 1949), malformations resulting from maternal hypoxia in mice (Ingalls *et al.*, 1953), cortisone-induced cleft palate in mice (Fraser *et al.*, 1954), eye defects caused by thyroxine (Giroud and Martinet, 1954), X-ray induced vertebral defects in mice (Russell and Russell, 1954), a variety of malformations resulting from a transitory riboflavin inactivation in mice (Kalter and Warkany, 1957), vertebral and rib defects caused by maternal fasting in mice (Miller, 1959), cleft palate and limb defects induced in mice by 5-fluorouracil (Dagg, 1960), and cleft palate produced by a transitory inhibition of nicotinamide activity in mice (Goldstein *et al.* 1963). There are also marked species differences in response to teratogens. Maternal treatment with cortisone causes cleft palate in mice (Fraser *et al.*, 1954) and rabbits (Fainstat, 1954) but not in a number of rat strains (Sobin, 1954; Gunberg, 1957; Curry and Beaton, 1958). These genetic differences are not surprising, at least not to a geneticist, but their value as an aid to the study of teratological mechanisms needs to be exploited (Fraser, 1963).

In tracing back through embryogenesis the sequence of changes leading to a congenital defect, it is useful to know that a high proportion of the embryos studied would have had the malformation at birth. If only a low frequency of malformations is produced by the treatment, it is difficult to be sure whether abnormalities observed in embryos studied shortly after treatment are, in fact, those leading to the defect observed in (necessarily not the same) embryos at term. Choice of a suitable strain can insure a high frequency of the malformation concerned. For instance, maternal treatment with cortisone (at an appropriate dosage and stage) produces cleft palate in virtually 100 per cent of the offspring in the A/Jax strain of mice, but in only 17 per cent of the offspring in the C57BL/6 strain. Observation of treated C57BL/6 embryos shortly after the time of normal palate closure

showed that in a majority of embryos the palates were closed, though there was some delay in the process. These observations by themselves did not demonstrate whether the cleft palates observed at birth resulted from failure to close, from failure of the palatal shelves to fuse once they had closed, or from regressive changes leading to re-opening of the palate. However, in the A/Jax strain no treated embryos were ever observed with the shelves touching (Walker and Fraser, 1957), showing that failure to close, rather than failure to fuse or post-closure re-opening was the correct explanation for the cleft palates observed at birth. Thus interstrain comparisons and, particularly, the use of a strain in which a high frequency of the defect could be produced contributed greatly to our understanding of the pathogenesis of cortisone-induced cleft palate.

Further insight was provided by a comparison of cortisone-induced cleft palate frequency and time of normal palate closure in various crosses involving the two strains. These showed that the frequency of cortisone-induced cleft palate was determined by an interaction of fetal and maternal genes (Kalter, 1954). Furthermore, there was a close correspondence between cortisone-induced cleft palate frequency and the time of palate closure in untreated embryos—the earlier the normal palate begins to close, the lower the frequency of cleft palate in cortisone-treated litters (Trasler and Fraser, 1958; Fraser, 1961*b*). This (and other evidence) suggests that the force that builds up in the palate shelves and eventually allows them to push their way above the tongue and close is genetically controlled. The more rapidly it builds up, the earlier the palate closes and the more resistant the embryo is to the cleft palate-producing effects of cortisone.

Thus a genetic analysis of strain differences has shown that the response of an embryo to a teratogen may be determined by genetically controlled variations in a normal developmental pattern. It is easy to see why little progress has been made in defining the genetic and environmental factors determining similar kinds of malformations in man.

THE EMBRYONIC GENOTYPE AND THE
INTRA-UTERINE ENVIRONMENT

As we have seen, the development of the embryo depends both on its genes and on its environment, which, in turn, depend on the mother's genes and her environment.

A most puzzling aspect of the interaction between the embryo and its uterine environment is the fact that when genetically similar embryos in the same uterus are exposed to the same teratogen some may become malformed and others may not. The same question applies to the "spontaneous" occurrence of malformations in certain inbred lines in the absence of any experimentally applied teratogen. For instance, about 9 per cent of the animals in the highly inbred C57BL/Fr mouse strain are born with microphthalmia or anophthalmia. Only a few animals in any one litter are affected. Why not all of them? The frequency of microphthalmia in the offspring of microphthalmic mothers is no higher than that in the offspring of their non-microphthalmic sisters, suggesting that genetic segregation is not involved (Fraser and Glick, unpublished data). In the A/Jax strain Trasler (1960) found that embryos with "spontaneous" cleft lip occur more frequently at the uterine site next to the ovary than at other sites but could not find why the embryo develops differently at this site in spite of intensive efforts to identify the predisposing factor. It is clear that the occurrence of microphthalmia in the C57BL strain and of cleft lip in the A/Jax strain are genetically determined, since they are strain-specific, but the occurrence of malformed and non-malformed animals

in the same uterus is not genetically determined; it must depend on some environmental difference that so far eludes identification. It is concluded that the action of the A/Jax genotype must be to make the lip closure process more variable, presumably by making it more sensitive to relatively small environmental disturbances. Similarly the C57BL genotype must make the eye anlage developmentally unstable. It would seem that even when no major gene determinants can be demonstrated the genotype may be vital in determining whether a given embryo is malformed. If so, it might be more profitable to attempt to identify the biochemical properties of the A/Jax embryonic lip or the C57BL eye primordium that make them developmentally unstable rather than to try to identify minor and probably heterogeneous intra-uterine factors involved.

Although this conclusion may be unwelcome to those workers (including the writer) who have attempted to identify environmental prenatal factors in human malformations, the same situation may well apply to many of the congenital defects that show some familial tendency in human beings, but no demonstrable major genetic or environmental causes.

POSTNATAL EFFECTS OF PRENATAL EN-
VIRONMENTAL TERATOGENS ON THE
CENTRAL NERVOUS SYSTEM

The effect of prenatal insults on postnatal cerebral function would seem to be a fertile field which is just beginning to be actively explored. Thompson and Sontag (1956) found that the offspring of rats subjected to audiogenic seizures during pregnancy were slower in water-maze learning than control animals, though the differences were significant only at the 5 per cent level. Thompson (1957) has reported the effects of procedures designed to produce anxiety in pregnant rats on their offspring and tentatively concluded that there was an increase in emotionality (as measured by behavioral tests) in the offspring of the treated mothers. Maternal electric shock or adrenalin administration during pregnancy also produced definite changes in behavior of the offspring (Thompson, 1960). These experiments were well controlled, with cross-fostering to insure that the observed behavioral differences did not arise postnatally, as a result of differences in maternal behavior between treated and control females. Interestingly enough the same maternal stress could produce opposite effects in the young, probably depending on the amount of stress and stage of pregnancy and on the genotype of the animals involved (Thompson and Olian, 1961).

Werboff *et al.* (1961 *c, d*) gave pregnant rats a number of psychopharmacologic agents and showed a variety of postnatal effects on the offspring. All offspring of mothers treated with iproniazid were born dead or died within thirty days. There was some indication that maternal treatment with the benzyl analogue of serotonin (BAS) and 5-hydroxytryptophan (5-HTP) increased activity and emotionality in the offspring. Lower doses of iproniazid reduced the frequency and duration of audiogenic seizures in the offspring, whereas reserpine and 5-HTP increased them (Werboff *et al.*, 1961c). Prenatal irradiation appeared to lower the audiogenic seizure response when given early and to raise it when given late in pregnancy (Werboff *et al.*, 1961a) as well as to produce detrimental effects on motor performance (Werboff *et al.*, 1961b). However, cross-fostering was not used, and it is difficult to rule out postnatal maternal effects in these cases.

Maternal deficiencies in thiamine and in iron, instituted on the first day of pregnancy, did not impair maze learning of the offspring in rats. The iron deficiency was great enough to cause anemia in the newborn animals, but the stage at which the embryos became depleted is not known (Scarpelli, 1959). Windle and his collaborators have shown that asphyxia of full-term embryos for periods ranging from ten to twenty minutes caused cytolysis of neurons and neuroglia, principally in the thalamic and brain-stem nuclei, in guinea pigs (Bailey and Windle, 1959), and monkeys (Ranck and Windle, 1959), with consequent neurologic deficits including (in the guinea pigs at least) learning defects. Obviously, the effects of prenatal insults on postnatal mental efficiency is a field worthy of intensive study and has important clinical implications. Direct clinical studies are also sorely needed but are much more difficult to accomplish.

In a study on the effects of vitamin supplementation of pregnant and lactating mothers on the intelligence quotients of their children (Harrell *et al.*, 1956), intelligence quotient tests were done on children whose mothers received vitamins or placebos during and after pregnancy. The vitamin-supplemented group had children with higher intelligence quotients than the control group when the sample was drawn from a largely Negro population in relatively poor environmental circumstances, but there was no difference between treated and control groups when the sample was drawn from a white population with a better basic diet. Since the vitamin supplementation was continued during lactation it is not clear whether the benefit was conferred pre- or postnatally.

Clinical studies on the effects of prenatal factors on postnatal cerebral function have been done by a number of workers, using the retrospective method. Because of the biases of retrospective studies (Fraser, 1959), because many of the differences reported were not highly significant (especially since, when large numbers of comparisons are made some will be "statistically significant" by chance alone), and because some results conflict with other evidence, the results are difficult to interpret. For instance, Stott (1958) found from data obtained retrospectively (partly by interview and partly by questionnaire) that maternal emotional trauma was reported more often in the prenatal histories of mongoloid children than in those of non-mongol mental defectives, which, in turn, had a higher frequency than the controls. It now appears, however, that mongolism usually results from a chromosomal aberration probably occurring before fertilization (Warkany, 1960a). In a subsequent study, also by questionnaire, Stott (1961) again found an increased incidence of "emotional shock" in pregnancies leading to mongoloid babies (18 per cent) as compared with those leading to non-mongoloid mental defectives (8 per cent) and speculatively suggested that the "emotional shock," rather than causing mongolism, interferes with the maternal mechanism that normally causes abortion of imperfect embryos. If so, one ought to find a decreased incidence of "emotional shock" preceding spontaneous abortions, but I do not know of any data on this point.

The difference observed by Stott might also result from "maternal memory bias," i.e., the tendency of a mother to recall more frequently those abnormal events that occurred in a pregnancy resulting in an abnormal child than in a pregnancy resulting in a normal child (Fraser, 1959). This is a bias most difficult to avoid or allow for. For example, in a study on cleft lip and palate, upsetting experiences occurring in the first trimester were reported in 18 per cent of 187 pregnancies resulting in an affected child and in only 5 per cent of 340 other pregnancies of the same mothers. This might be taken as evidence of a causal role for maternal "stress" and indeed was taken as such in another study (Strean and Peer, 1956). The memory bias was revealed by study of a control series of children with diseases caused by mutant

genes (e.g., albinism, hemophilia, fibrocystic disease of the pancreas) and clearly not caused by prenatal "stress." The histories were classified without reference to whether they involved affected children, their sibs, control children, or their sibs. In the control series the mother reported upsetting events in 14 per cent of 90 patients, and in 4 per cent of 141 other pregnancies of the same mothers (Fraser and Warburton, 1964). Clearly, the higher frequencies of reported emotional stress in the prenatal histories of affected babies as compared to their sibs is a result of bias, not of any causal relation. The results of the control series also suggest that for studies of this sort a control consisting of normal children or those admitted to hospital for a clearly environmental cause (e.g., fractures, tonsillitis) would be inadequate. This sort of bias will have to be recognized in any retrospective studies of factors affecting the unborn child.

These remarks should not be interpreted as a condemnation of retrospective studies, which can certainly be valuable if properly controlled. Prospective studies involve studying tremendous numbers of pregnancies to obtain adequate data on abnormal offspring—one would need to observe 250,000 pregnancies to obtain 100 cases of cleft palate to analyze, for instance. Furthermore, prospective studies, to be successful, must ask the right questions under the right circumstances. None of the prospective studies on malformations reported to date would have detected the teratogenic effects of rubella or of thalidomide, for instance, and both these human teratogens were first identified by retrospective studies.

Rogers et al. (1956) found a higher frequency of prenatal (and paranatal) abnormalities in the histories of children with behavior disorders than in controls (39 per cent versus 31 per cent for 363 white cases), but when those born prematurely were excluded, the difference disappeared, suggesting that perhaps the prenatal factors (toxemia and bleeding) were associated with prematurity, and the prematurity with behavior disorders. Similar trends were found in children with reading disorders and other psychoneurological abnormalities (Kawi and Pasamanick, 1958). Again, the question of memory bias arises, and the authors themselves point out the need for prospective studies.

ENVIRONMENTAL TERATOGENS IN
HUMAN BEINGS

When an agent is found to be teratogenic in experimental animals it is natural to ask whether it may be a cause of human malformations. Unfortunately, it is usually difficult to obtain an answer to this question. Sporadic reports of malformations in babies resulting from pregnancies during which the mother was exposed to the agent in question are not enough. To establish the teratogenicity of an environmental agent, it is necessary either to show that the malformed children have a history of prenatal exposure to the agent more often than nonmalformed children (the retrospective approach) or that pregnancies during which exposure to the agent occurred give rise to malformed children more often than other pregnancies (the prospective approach). Only a few specific environmental teratogens have so far been identified in human beings. Discussion of some of these follows.

Radiation.—That radiation can be damaging to the human embryo has been demonstrated both by retrospective (Murphy, 1929) and prospective (Yamazaki, 1954) studies. Russell and Russell (1952) point out that radiation can be teratogenic in the mouse at levels possibly reached during diagnostic radiological procedures and recommend that, if possible, pelvic irradiation in women of child-bearing age should be done only in the two weeks following the menstrual period.

Rubella.—The biases inherent in the retrospective nature of the early studies led to an overestimate of the risk that a child, born of a mother exposed to rubella in the first trimester, would be malformed (Warkany and Kalter, 1961). Prospective studies are so difficult that there is still a dearth of relevant data. Following maternal infections with rubella in the first trimester, malformations have been observed in about 17 per cent of the offspring (Warkany and Kalter, 1961). Data from seven prospective, well-controlled series (Michaels and Mellin, 1960; Lock *et al.*, 1961) estimate the risk of malformation in live-born infants born of mothers infected with rubella as 48 per cent if the infection occurred in the first four weeks after the first day of the last menstrual period. However, this represents only eleven of twenty-three cases and cannot, therefore, be regarded as a reliable figure. The risk was found to be about 24 per cent (twelve of fifty cases) following infection in the fifth through eighth weeks, and 12 per cent (seven of fifty-nine cases) if infection was in the ninth through twelfth weeks. Beyond this, the malformation frequency does not appear to be significantly elevated. Cataract, with or without microphthalmos, congenital heart disease (usually patent ductus arteriosus), and deafness are the most frequent defects. There is also an increase in prematurity (25 per cent), and in fetal death (50 per cent) following infection in the first eight weeks (Siegel and Greenberg, 1960). It is not clear whether other defects, such as cleft lip, that occur occasionally following maternal infection with rubella are caused by the virus, but 2 cases of cleft lip of 202 pregnancies exposed to rubella (Michaels and Mellin, 1960; Lock *et al.*, 1961) may be more than a coincidence, considering that the population frequency is about 1 per 1,000 births. Whether exposure, without infection of the mother, can be teratogenic is also an unsettled question.

Asian influenza.—Coffey and Jessop (1959) have reported an increased frequency of malformations, particularly anencephaly, following maternal infection with Asian influenza. However, in many cases the infection occurred after the neural tube would normally have closed (Warkany, 1960*b*). Since anencephaly occurs more frequently in the lower social classes (Edwards, 1958) it is possible that there may also be an increased attack rate of influenza in these classes, so that more mothers of anencephalic children would have had a history of influenza during pregnancy than control mothers, without there being any causal connection between the influenza and the malformation. Other workers (Walker and McKee, 1959; Wilson *et al.*, 1959*b*; Saxen, 1960) have noted slight increases in the malformation rate following maternal influenza, but the differences were not statistically significant. The question, therefore, remains open. In any case, if there is a teratogenic effect of influenza it must be rather small (Doll and Hill, 1960).

Other viruses.—There is some suggestion that cytomegalic inclusion disease may cause microcephaly and other abnormalities (Weller *et al.*, 1960), and further studies in this field will be followed with interest. As far as I know, there is no convincing evidence for human teratogenicity of any other virus, including Echo 9 (Rantasalo *et al.*, 1960), mumps, and chicken pox (Hill *et al.*, 1958). Although there are a number of isolated cases reported of malformations following maternal viral infections, these of course do not establish a relationship. The claim of Hyatt (1961) that maternal mumps can cause congenital defects is unjustified, since several of the cases cited in his review were reported *because* the child had a malformation, and the mother was later found to have had mumps. However,

some viruses, particularly mumps and poliomyelitis, may increase the fetal death rate (Siegel and Greenberg, 1960).

Dumont (1960), in a prospective study of 224 women who were exposed to rubella, measles, chicken pox, or mumps during pregnancy but had no clinical signs of infection, found malformations in 8.4 per cent of the babies, the highest frequency following infection with rubella or measles. However, the numbers are small, and no explanation is offered for the fact that malformations were just as frequent following exposure in the second or third trimester as after first-trimester exposure. Further investigations are needed to establish whether viruses can be teratogenic to the fetus without visibly affecting the mother.

Toxoplasmosis.—Infection of the mother during pregnancy with the protozoan *Toxoplasma gondii* can produce a variety of defects in the baby, including hydrocephaly, microcephaly, microphthalmos, chorioretinitis, convulsions, and mental retardation. Because most maternal infections with these organisms go unrecognized, no figures are available on the risk that a child will be affected following infection of the mother (Feldman, 1958).

Antimetabolites.—The use of specific antimetabolites to interrupt pregnancy in experimental animals was followed by attempts to use a folic acid antagonist, 4-amino-pteroylglutamic acid (Aminopterin), as an abortifacient in human beings (Thiersch, 1955). Four cases in which the baby was not aborted by the treatment were malformed. Regrettably, this drug has been used unsuccessfully to attempt illegal abortion, and in at least two cases the resulting baby was seriously malformed (Warkany *et al.*, 1959). It should be noted, however, that antimetabolites may be used during pregnancy in anti-leukemic doses without necessarily harming the embryo (Murphy, 1960*b*).

Progestins and androgens.—It appears

that the use of synthetic progestins, usually in the prophylactic treatment of abortion, occasionally results in masculinization of the genitalia in female embryos (Wilkins, 1960). Testosterone and its analogues (Grumbach and Ducharme, 1960) and perhaps also estrogens (Bongiovanni *et al.*, 1960) may have similar effects. The frequency with which treatment results in such effects is not known but must be fairly low, though some of the synthetic progestins (e.g., Norlutin) may be particularly dangerous (Wilkins, 1960).

Thalidomide.—One of the most tragic examples of a human environmental teratogen was revealed by the discovery that thalidomide, a relatively new drug widely used as a sleeping pill and antinauseant, when taken in the early stages of pregnancy, could cause a characteristic syndrome of malformations in the offspring. These include absence or gross deformities of the long bones, intestinal atresias, cardiac anomalies, and hemangioma of the nose and upper lip. It is instructive to review the course of events. A remarkable increase in frequency of children born with this unusual syndrome in West Germany led Lenz (1962) to review the prenatal histories of the affected children, and he noted that many of the mothers reported having taken thalidomide in early pregnancy. His first report was greeted with some skepticism, since thalidomides were widely used in Germany, a number of cases were known where thalidomide had been taken and the baby was unaffected, and in some cases where the baby had the syndrome there was no history of having taken the drug. A flurry of case reports then began to appear in the literature from Germany and from other countries where the thalidomides had been more recently released to the public. Speirs (1962) reported several affected children where neither the physician nor mother concerned could remember any exposure to the drug, but examination of the drug-

gist's records showed that it had indeed been prescribed (again demonstrating the difficulties of retrospective studies). Production of similar defects in offspring of pregnant rabbits given thalidomide removed almost all doubts about the causal association (Somers, 1962). There is still no accurate measure of the frequency with which malformations occur as a result of taking the drug, but the probability is roughly estimated at about 20 per cent (McBride, 1961). Nothing is known of why the other embryos escape, but a search for genetic differences in metabolism of the drug might be rewarding.

It is noteworthy that the teratogenic effects of thalidomide were discovered only because it produced malformations of a very unusual kind, and before the drug was withdrawn from the market several thousand babies had been severely malformed. Who knows how many malformations of more common types are being produced by the numerous new drugs now appearing on the market? Antibiotics, for instance, are often anti-mitotic agents, and at least one of them (actinomycin D) has been shown experimentally to be teratogenic at doses lower than those used clinically (Tuchmann-Duplessis and Mercier-Parot, 1960). The warning of Lucey (1961) that ". . . many new drugs . . . are being given during pregnancy, and there is no adequate evidence that these are completely non-toxic to the fetus" was indeed prophetic.

CHROMOSOMAL ABERRATIONS

The recent discovery that some congenital abnormalities are caused by chromosomal imbalance, i.e., excesses or deficiencies of whole chromosome or parts of them, has important implications for the problem of mental retardation. This advance was made possible by the development of improved techniques for the examination of human chromosomes in tissue culture (Hsu and Pomerat,

1953), which led to the discovery that the normal number of chromosomes in human somatic cells is forty-six (Ford and Hamerton, 1956; Tjio and Levan, 1956) instead of forty-eight as previously supposed. Techniques are now available for studying human chromosome morphology from fibroblasts (Lejeune et al., 1959a), bone marrow (Ford et al., 1958), skin (Puck et al., 1958), and peripheral leucocytes (Moorhead et al., 1960).

The first demonstration that a human defect could be caused by a chromosomal imbalance was the discovery that children with mongolism have forty-seven chromosomes, first reported by Lejeune et al. (1959a, b) and almost simultaneously by Jacobs et al. (1959). One of the small chromosomes with a subterminal centromere, number 21 according to the accepted classification (Lancet, 1960), was represented three times instead of twice (trisomy).

Five days after Lejeune's publication of his first three cases of aneuploidy in mongolism (1959a), Jacobs and Strong (1959) reported a patient with Klinefelter's syndrome (testicular dysgenesis, sometimes with mental retardation) who had forty-seven chromosomes. The extra chromosome was considered likely to be an X, and this was confirmed by subsequent studies. This syndrome accounts for about 1 per cent of mentally defective children (MacLean et al., 1962). The use of the Barr technique for examining the sex chromatin in the nuclei of somatic cells has permitted rapid screening of populations for sex-chromosome anomalies, since, in general, the number of sex-chromatin bodies is one less than the number of X chromosomes (Barr and Carr, 1962). This may account, at least partly, for the fact that many of the chromosomal aberrations reported so far involve the sex chromosomes.

In addition to Klinefelter's syndrome, the sex-chromosome anomalies include XXYY in normal or mentally retarded males, XXXY in mentally retarded males with microorchidism, an XXXXY male with microorchidism, malformed external genitalia, mental retardation, congenital heart disease, and a peculiar facies, Turner's syndrome (ovarian dysgenesis with variable combinations of short stature, neck webbing, cubitus valgus, coarctation of the aorta and sometimes mild mental retardation) in females with only one X chromosome (Polani, 1961), XXX in females who are usually physically normal but often mentally retarded (with a frequency of 0.4 per cent in a mental retardation hospital [MacLean et al., 1962]), and XXXX in physically normal females with mental retardation. These are well reviewed by Harnden and Jacobs (1961). It should be emphasized that many of the cases of sex-chromosome anomalies were found in surveys of patients in institutions for the mentally retarded who were of necessity mentally defective. Except for Turner's syndrome, there is little data on the proportion of persons with a given sex-chromosome anomaly that are mentally retarded.

The discovery that mongolism was a result of trisomy for chromosome 21 added a new facet to our knowledge of the causes of mental retardation (Penrose, 1961). For one thing, it throws into disrepute most of the numerous theories that attributed mongolism to an extrinsic factor acting in the second month of pregnancy, since the chromosomal aberration must occur during gametogenesis or, at the latest, in the very early stages of cleavage of the ovum (Warkany, 1960a). It accounts (1) for the fact that mongolism rarely occurs in more than one offspring of the same parents, (2) for the fact that when it occurs in twins it almost always affects both members of the pair if they are monozygotic but only one if they are dizygotic, and (3) for the fact that about half of the few reported offspring of mongoloids are themselves mongoloid. The long-recognized tendency for mongoloids to occur more frequently in the offspring of old than of young mothers presumably means that the probability of error in separation of the number 21 chromosomes at meiosis (non-disjunction) that leads to the presence of an extra chromosome 21 in the egg is increased by some characteristic of an aging cytoplasm (though what this is remains a mystery).

A puzzling feature pointed out some years ago by Penrose—that in some families mongolism may occur in several members, and that in these families there is no relation with increasing maternal age—is clarified by the discovery that in some cases a 21 chromosome may become attached to some other chromosome (usually of the 13–15 group) by a process known as reciprocal translocation. In such a case the unattached chromosome 21 may segregate in the same gamete as the translocated one, and a third chromosome 21 is added by the other gamete at fertilization. A person carrying the translocated chromosome but not the extra 21 is clinically normal but has a high probability of having mongoloid offspring (Hamerton *et al.*, 1961). This has important practical applications in genetic counseling, since examination of the chromosomes of the parents of a mongoloid child can distinguish those cases where the child's trisomy is associated with a translocation, and has a high risk of recurring, from those where it is due to primary non-disjunction, usually with a negligible risk of recurrence.

A further complication is added by the discovery of chromosomal mosaicism. In this case the non-disjunction occurs after fertilization, during mitosis in the developing ovum, and some cells of the resulting individual will have a different chromosomal constitution than others. Most frequently mosaicism seems to involve the sex chromosomes (Miller, 1962), but a number of cases have been described where some cells of a person are trisomic for chromosome 21 and others are not (Richards and Stewart, 1962). This may be found in fairly characteristic mongoloids, in children with some mental retardation and relatively minor mongoloid stigmata (the "borderline" mongoloids), and in mentally normal individuals with virtually no mongoloid stigmata. The latter type represent another group that may be predisposed to have mongoloid offspring. Chromosomal mosaicism makes it difficult to rule out a chromosomal abnormality in a given patient, since it may be detected in skin cultures but not in blood cultures or vice versa and then perhaps only after repeated attempts.

At least two other syndromes including mental retardation have been described as resulting from autosomal trisomy. Anophthalmia or microphthalmia, with cleft palate and mental retardation, is associated with trisomy of one member of the 13-15 group—the D syndrome (Patau *et al.*, 1961*b*). A syndrome including small mandible, low-set malformed ears, flexion deformities of the fingers, interventricular septal defect, hypertonicity, and probable mental retardation is associated with trisomy of number 17 or 18—the E syndrome (Patau *et al.*, 1961*a*), and a case of an E syndrome resulting from translocation of a chromosome from the E group to one of the D group has recently been observed in this laboratory (L. Dallaire, personal communication). Further information about these and other chromosomal aberrations (deletions, inversions, triploidy) will be found in the excellent review by Hirschhorn and Cooper (1961).

Needless to say, a great many fascinating possibilities are provided by this advance. It has already clarified several problems concerning sexual differentiation. For instance, contrary to previous opinion, the Y chromosome must carry male sex-determinants. It may be possible, by studying the segregation of known genetic markers in families of aneuploid individuals or demonstrating quantitative differences in genetic traits such as blood groups in aneuploid individuals, to associate specific gene loci with particular chromosomes. The existence of mosaics—individuals with cells of different chromosome constitutions—may contribute to our understanding of developmental problems (e.g., what proportion of cells trisomic for chromosome 21 are necessary to make an individual mongoloid?). Finally, we need to seek out the causes of non-disjunction and other sources of chromosomal anomalies, since this would be a first step toward preventing an appreciable number of cases of mental retardation.

CONCLUSIONS

In this discussion, which may appear to have very little to do with mental retardation, a number of recent advances in genetics, embryology, and experimental teratology have been reviewed (albeit briefly and inadequately) in the hope that some of them will eventually lead to better understanding, and perhaps control, of prenatal factors that influence postnatal mental function.

The combination of genetic and biochemical studies leading to the identification of gene effects, in enzymatic terms, has had important applications in the field of mental retardation (Harris, 1959) which are dealt with elsewhere in this volume. We have discussed the transfer of information from generation to generation by the gene and from nucleus to cytoplasm by RNA, knowledge of which has advanced to the point where it is not inconceivable that directed changes may be brought about in DNA, thus making it possible to "cure" abnormal genes in the egg or gametes. This possibility (which is still very far indeed from realization) might make it feasible to reduce greatly the frequency of diseases due to single dominant gene

changes, but unfortunately (from this point of view) these represent a great minority of all diseases. Genes for recessively inherited diseases would be less easily transformed, since the great majority of recessive deleterious genes are carried in the heterozygous condition, undetected. (But, an increasing number of "recessive" mutant genes, including those for phenylketonuria, galactosemia, and juvenile amaurotic idiocy, can now be detected in the clinically normal heterozygote—Hsia, 1959.) Conditions such as non-specific mental retardation and many of the common malformations which are probably due to the interaction of many genes with a variety of environmental factors could presumably not be controlled by altering DNA structure.

However, if it were possible to cause DNA transformations in somatic cells, this would have great practical benefits. One might, for instance, transform the genes in enough of the liver cells of a child with phenylketonuria so that he would be able to make enough phenylalanine hydroxylase to handle his phenylalanine metabolism successfully.

Knowledge of the chemical and physical factors involved in normal embryogenesis is being advanced by observations on normal embryos, by the use of mutants that produce specific alterations in developmental processes, and by observing the developmental errors produced by teratogens with known biochemical effects.

The use of mutants and of teratogens that regularly produce specific types of malformations provides opportunities for studying the underlying pathogenetic mechanisms and has already contributed significantly to our understanding of the origins of malformations such as anencephaly, myelomeningocoele, and cleft palate.

Many of the teratogenic agents used experimentally are effective only in non-physiological doses and probably do not account for a significant number of human malformations. However, the effects of very short periods of inhibition of specific vitamins at least raises the possibility that transient nutritional deficiencies at critical periods of development might be teratogenic in human beings, and some drugs are teratogenic in experimental animals at dosage levels comparable to those used therapeutically. Unfortunately, the possible harmful effects of transient metabolic disturbances would be very hard to demonstrate clinically. The retrospective studies published to date have been open to criticism because of the biases that are inevitably involved in this approach, and prospective studies present the problem of the tremendous number of cases that must be studied in order to include sufficient numbers of a particular type of malformation for adequate statistical analysis.

The role of immunogenetic mechanisms in the control of development is not at all clear as yet, but the production of specific developmental anomalies by specific antibodies suggests that this is a possible teratogenic mechanism in human beings, and one abnormality (athyrotic cretinism) has been tentatively attributed to such a cause.

The production of postnatal psychological effects by prenatal disturbances has been demonstrated experimentally, and it is possible that such effects may occur in human beings. There is great need for further studies along these lines.

Analyses of the interaction of genetic constitution and the environment have shown how intimately and intricately the two are related. The fact that environmental teratogens are particularly effective in producing a specific malformation when acting on a genetic constitution which is already predisposed to produce such a malformation emphasizes that genetic factors cannot be neglected even when a known environmental factor is involved. Consideration of "spontaneous" malformations in inbred mouse lines and of monozygotic human twins indicates that the genotype may make a particular embryonic process susceptible to what would otherwise be unimportant environmental factors. This suggests that it might be more profitable to search for the biochemical difference that makes an organogenetic process so easily disturbed rather than the subtle, environmental factors that disturb it.

The search for a better understanding of the factors controlling development has led to many fascinating discoveries and to the promise of many more. It is only a matter of time, effort, and inspiration before their practical application to the problem of mental retardation will be achieved.

REFERENCES

ABERCROMBIE, M. 1958. Exchanges between cells. *In:* W. D. McELROY and B. GLASS (eds.), *Symposium on the Chemical Basis of Development,* pp. 318–20. Baltimore: Johns Hopkins Press.

ANDERSEN, D. H. 1949. Effect of diet during pregnancy upon the incidence of congenital diaphragmatic hernia in the rat. *Amer. J. Path.,* **25**:163–85.

BAILEY, C. J., and WINDLE, W. F. 1959. Neurological, psychological, and neurohistological defects following asphyxia neonatorum in the guinea pig. *Exper. Neurol.,* **1**:467–82.

BARR, M. L., and CARR, D. H. 1962. Correlations between sex chromatin and sex chromosomes. *Acta Cytol.* **6**:34–45.

BEALE, G. H. 1958. The role of the cytoplasm in antigen determination in paramecium aurelia. *Proc. Roy. Soc., B.,* **148**:308–14.

BEERMAN, W. 1956. Nuclear differentiation and functional morphology of chromosomes. *Cold Spring Harbor Symposia on Quantitative Biology,* **21**:217–32.

BENNETT, D. 1958. In vitro study of cartilage induction in T/T mice. *Nature,* **181**:1286.

BENNETT, D., BADENHAUSEN, S., and DUNN, L. C. 1959. The embryological effects of four late-lethal t-alleles in the mouse, which affect the neural tube and skeleton. *J. Morphol.,* **105**:105–43.

BENNETT, D., and DUNN, L. C. 1958. Effects on embryonic development of a group of genetically similar lethal alleles derived from different populations of wild house mice. *J. Morphol.*, **103**:135–57.

BILLINGHAM, R. E. 1958. Actively acquired tolerance and its role in development. *In:* W. D. McELROY and B GLASS (eds.), *Symposium on the Chemical Basis of Development*, p. 575. Baltimore: Johns Hopkins Press.

BISHOP, J., FAVELUKES, G., SCHWEET, R., and RUSSELL, E. 1961. Control of specificity in haemoglobin synthesis. *Nature*, **191**:1365–68.

BLIZZARD, R. M., CHANDLER, R. W., LANDING, B. H., PETTIT, M. D., and WEST, C. D. 1960. Maternal autoimmunization to thyroid as a probable cause of athyrotic cretinism. *New Engl. J. Med.*, **263**:327–36.

BONGIOVANNI, A. M., and McPADDEN, A. J. 1960. Steroids during pregnancy and possible fetal consequences. *Fertility and Sterility*, **11**:181–86.

BONNEVIE, K., and BRODAL, A. 1946. Hereditary hydrocephalus in the house mouse. IV. The development of the cerebellar anomalies during foetal life with notes on the normal development of the mouse cerebellum. *Skrifter utgitt av Det Norske Videnskaps-Akademi, Oslo. Matematisknaturvidenskapelig klasse*, No. 4, pp. 5–60.

BRACHET, J. 1957. *Biochemical Cytology*. New York: Academic Press.

——. 1960. *The Biochemistry of Development*. New York: Pergamon Press.

BRADEN, A. W. H. 1960. Genetic influence on the morphology and function of the gametes. *J. Cell. Comp. Physiol.*, **56**: Suppl. 1, 17–29.

BRENT, R. L., AVERICH, E. and DRAPIEWSKI, V. A. 1961. Production of congenital malformations using tissue antibodies. I. Kidney antisera. *Proc. Soc. Exper. Biol. Med.*, **106**:523–26.

BRENT, R. L., and FRANKLIN, J. B. 1960. Uterine vascular clamping: new procedure for the study of congenital malformations. *Science*, **132**:89–91.

CLARK, K. H. 1956. Factors in the experimental production of congenital cleft palate in mice by cortisone and other agents. Master's thesis, McGill University.

COFFEY, V. P., and JESSOP, W. J. 1959. Rubella and incidence of congenital abnormalities. *Irish J. Med. Sci.*, **397**:1–11.

CRICK, F. H. C., BARNETT, L., BRENNER, S., and WATTS-TOBIN, R. J. 1961. General nature of the genetic code for proteins. *Nature*, **192**:1227–32.

CURRY, D. M., and BEATON, G. H. 1958. Cortisone resistance in pregnant rats. *Endocrinology*, **63**:155–61.

DAGG, C. P. 1960. Sensitive stages for the production of developmental abnormalities in mice with 5-fluorouracil. *Amer. J. Anat.*, **106**:89–96.

DeHAAN, R. L. 1958. Cell migration and morphogenetic movements. *In:* W. D. McELROY and B. GLASS (eds.), *Symposium on the Chemical Basis of Development*, pp. 339–41. Baltimore: Johns Hopkins Press.

DIETRICH, L. S., FRIEDLAND, I. M., and KAPLAN, L. A. 1958. Pyridine nucleotide metabolism: mechanism of action of the niacin antagonist, 6-aminonicotinamide. *J. Biol. Chem.*, **233**:964–68.

DOLL, R., and HILL, A. B. 1960. Asian influenza in pregnancy and congenital defects. *Brit. J. Prev. Soc. Med.*, **14**:167–72.

DOUNCE, A. L. 1962. A new hypothesis for nucleic acid replication. *J. Theoret. Biol.* **2**:152–58.

DUMONT, M. 1960. Viroses inapparentes et malformations foetales. Paris: Presse Medicale, **68**:1087–89.

DUNN, L. C. 1956. Analysis of a complex gene in the house mouse. *Cold Spring Harbor Symposia on Quantitative Biology*, **21**: 187–95.

——. 1960. Variations in the transmission ratios of alleles through egg and sperm in *mus musculus. Amer. Naturalist*, **94**:385–93.

EBERT, J. D. 1958*a*. Antigens as tracers of embryonic synthesis. *In:* D. RUDNICK (ed.), *Embryonic Nutrition*, pp. 54–109. Chicago: University of Chicago Press.

——. 1958*b*. Immunochemical analysis of development. *In:* W. D. McELROY and B. GLASS (eds.), *Symposium on the Chemical Basis of Development*. Baltimore: Johns Hopkins Press.

EDDS, MAC V., JR. 1958*a*. "Origin and Structure of Intercellular Matrix." *In:* W. D. McELROY and B. GLASS (eds.), *Symposium on the Chemical Basis of Development*, pp. 157–70. Baltimore: Johns Hopkins Press.

——. (ed.). 1958*b*. *Immunology and Development*. Chicago: University of Chicago Press.

EDWARDS, J. H. 1958. Congenital malformations of the central nervous system in Scotland. *Brit. J. Prev. Soc. Med.*, **12**:115–30.

FAINSTAT, T. 1954. Cortisone-induced congenital cleft palate in rabbits. *Endocrinology*, **55**:502–8.

FELDMAN, H. A. 1958. Toxoplasmosis. *Pediatrics*, **22**: 559–74.

FELL, H. B. 1960. Experimental Transformation of Cells. *Nature*, **185**:882–84.

FISCHBERG, M., and BLACKLER, A. W. 1961. How cells specialize. *Sci. Amer.*, **205**:124–40.

FORD, C. E., and HAMERTON, J. L. 1956. The chromosome of man. *Acta Genet. Stat. Med.*, **6**:264–66.

FORD, C. E., JACOBS, P. A. and LAJTHA, L. G. 1958. Human somatic chromosomes. *Nature*, **181**:1565–68.

FRASER, F. C. 1959. Causes of congenital malformations in human beings. *J. Chronic Dis.*, **10**:97–110.

———. 1960. Some experimental and clinical studies on the causes of congenital clefts of the palate and of the lip. *Arch. Pediat.*, **77**:151–56.

———. 1961a. Genetics and congenital malformations. *In:* A. G. STEINBERG (ed.), *Progress in Medical Genetics*, pp. 38–80. New York: Grune & Stratton.

———. 1961b. The use of teratogens in the analysis of abnormal developmental mechanisms. *First International Conference on Congenital Malformations*, pp. 179–86. Philadelphia: J. B. Lippincott.

———. 1962. Methodology of experimental mammalian teratology. *In:* W. J. BURDETTE (ed.), *Methodology in Mammalian Genetics*, pp. 233–246. San Francisco: Holden-Day.

FRASER, F. C., KALTER, H., WALKER, B. E., and FAINSTAT, T. 1954. The experimental production of cleft palate with cortisone and other hormones. *J. Cell. Comp. Physiol.*, **43** (Suppl. 1): 237–59.

FRASER, F. C., and WARBURTON, D. 1964. No association of emotional stress or vitamin supplement during pregnancy to cleft lip or palate in man. *Plast. Reconstr. Surg.*, **33**:395–99.

FRESCO, J. R., and STRAUS, D. B. 1962. Biosynthetic polynucleotides: models of biological templates. *Amer. Sci.*, **50**:158–79.

GARDNER, W. J. 1960. Myelomeningocele, the result of rupture of the embryonic neural tube. *Clev. Clin. Quart.*, **27**:88–100.

GIROUD, A., DELMAS, A., and MARTINET, M. 1959. Étude morphogénétique sur des embryons anencéphales. *Arch. Anat., Histol. Embryol. Norm. Exper.*, **43**:203–30.

GIROUD, A., GOUNELLE, H., and MARTINET, M. 1957. Données quantitatives sur le taux de la vitamine A chez le rat lors d'expériences de tératogenèse par hypervitaminose A. *Bull. Soc. Chim. Biol.*, **39**:331–36.

GIROUD, A., LEVY, G., and BOISSELOT, J. 1950. Taux de la riboflavine chez le foetus de rat présentant des malformations due à la déficience B$_2$. *Rev. Int. Vitamin.*, **22**: 308–12.

GIROUD, A., and MARTINET, M. 1954. Influence de la souche de rats sur l'apparition des cataractes thyroxiniennes. *Arch. Fr. Pédiat.*, **11**:1–4.

GLASS, B. 1958. *In:* W. D. McELROY and B. GLASS (eds.), *A Summary of the McCollum-Pratt Symposium on the Chemical Basis of Development.* Baltimore: Johns Hopkins Press.

GLUECKSOHN-WAELSCH, S. 1954. Some genetic aspects of development. *Cold Spring Harbor Symposium of Quantitative Biology*, **19**:41–49.

———. 1957. The effect of maternal immunization against organ tissues on embryonic differentiation in the mouse. *J. Embryol. Exper. Morphol.*, **5**:83–92.

———. 1961. Developmental genetics of mammals. *Amer. J. Hum. Genet.*, **13**: Part 2, 113–21.

GOLDSTEIN, M., PINSKY, M., and FRASER, F. C. 1963. Genetically determined organ specific responses to the teratogenic action of 6-aminonicotinamide in the mouse. *Genet. Res.* **4**:258–65.

GROBSTEIN, C., and PARKER, G. 1958. Epithelial tubule formation by mouse metanephrogenic mesenchyme transplanted in vivo. *J. Nat. Cancer Inst.*, **20**:107–19.

GROLLMAN, A., and GROLLMAN, E. F. 1962. The teratogenic induction of hypertension. *J. Clin. Invest.*, **41**:710–14.

GRUMBACH, M. M., and DUCHARME, J. R. 1960. The effects of androgens on fetal sexual development: androgen-induced female pseudohermaphroditism. *Fertility and Sterility*, **11**:157–80.

GRUNEBERG, H. 1943. Congenital hydrocephalus in the mouse, a case of spurious pleiotropism. *J. Genet.*, **45**:1–21.

———. 1947. *Animal Genetics and Medicine.* London: Hamish Hamilton.

Gruneberg, H. 1952. *The Genetics of the Mouse.* 2d ed.; The Hague: Martinus Nijhoff.

——. 1958a. Genetical studies on the skeleton of the mouse. XXII. The development of Danforth's short-tail. *J. Embryol. Exper. Morphol.,* **6**:124–48.

——.1958b. Genetical studies on the skeleton of the mouse. XXIII. The development of brachyury and anury. *Ibid.,* pp. 424–43.

——. 1960. Developmental genetics in the mouse. *J. Cell. Comp. Physiol.,* **56** (Suppl. 1): 49–60.

Gunberg, D. L. 1957. Some effects of exogenous hydrocortisone on pregnancy. *Anat. Rec.,* **129**:133–54.

——. 1958. Variations in the teratogenic effects of trypan blue administered to pregnant rats of different strain and substrain origin. *Ibid.,* **130**:310.

Hamerton, J. L., Cowie, V. A., Giannelli, F., Briggs, S. M., and Polani, P. E. 1961. Differential transmission of Down's syndrome (mongolism) through male and female translocation carriers. *Lancet,* **2:** 956–58.

Harnden, D. G., and Jacobs, P. A. 1961. Cytogenetics of abnormal sexual development in man. *Brit. Med. Bull.,* **17**:206–12.

Harrell, R. F., Woodyard, E. R., and Gates, A. I. 1956. The influence of vitamin supplementation of the diets of pregnant and lactating women on the intelligence of their offspring. *Metabolism,* **5**:555–62.

Harris, H. 1959. *Human Biochemical Genetics.* Cambridge: Cambridge University Press.

Helinski, D. R., and Yanofsky, C. 1962. Correspondence between genetic data and the position of aminoacid alteration in a protein. *Proc. Nat. Acad. Sci.,* **48**:173–83.

Hemmings, W. A. 1961. Protein transfer and selection. *First International Conference on Congenital Malformations.* Philadelphia: J. B. Lippincott.

Hicks, S. P., and D'Amato, C. J. 1961. How to design and build abnormal brains using radiation during development. *In: Disorders of the Developing Nervous System,* pp. 60–93. Springfield, Ill.: C. C Thomas.

Hicks, S. P., D'Amato, C. J., Coy, M. A., O'Brien, E. D., Thurston, J. M., and Joffes, D. L. 1961. Migrating cells in the developing nervous system studied by their radiosensitivity and tritiated thymidine uptake. *Brookhaven Symposia in Biology,* **14**:246–59.

Hill, A. B., Doll, R., Galloway, T. Mc L., and Hughes, J. P. W. 1958. Virus diseases in pregnancy and congenital defects. *Brit. J. Prev. Soc. Med.,* **12**:1–7.

Hirschhorn, K., and Cooper, K. L. 1961. Chromosomal aberrations in human disease. *Amer. J. Med.,* **31**:442–70.

Hsia, D. Y.-Y. 1959. *Inborn Errors of Metabolism.* Chicago: Year Book Publishers.

Hsu, T. C., and Pomerat, C. M. 1953. Mammalian chromosomes in vitro. II. A method for spreading the chromosomes of cells in tissue culture. *J. Hered.,* **44**:23–29.

Hummel, K. P. 1958. The inheritance and expression of disorganization, an unusual mutation in the mouse. *J. Exper. Zool.,* **137**:389–423.

Hurwitz, J., and Furth, J. J. 1962. Messenger RNA. *Sci. Amer.,* **203**:41–49.

Hyatt, H. W., Sr. 1961. Relationship of maternal mumps to congenital defects and fetal deaths, and to maternal morbidity and mortality. *Amer. Prac. Dig. Treat.,* **12**:359–63.

Ingalls, T. H., Avis, F. R., Curley, F. J., and Temin, H. M. 1953. Genetic determinants of hypoxia-induced congenital anomalies. *J. Hered.,* **44**:185–94.

Jacob, F., and Monod, J. 1961. On the regulation of gene activity. *Cold Spring Harbor Symposia on Quantitative Biology,* **26:** 193–209.

Jacobs, P. A., Baikie, A. G., Brown, W. M. C. and Strong, J. A. 1959. The somatic chromosomes in mongolism. *Lancet,* **1:**710.

Jacobs, P. A., and Strong, J. A. 1959. A case of human intersexuality having a possible XXY sex-determining mechanism. *Nature,* **183**:302–3.

Kalter, H. 1954. The inheritance of susceptibility to the teratogenic action of cortisone in mice. *Genetics,* **39**:185–96.

Kalter, H., and Warkany, J. 1957. Congenital malformations in inbred strains of mice induced by riboflavin-deficient, galactoflavin-containing diets. *J. Exper. Zool.,* **136**:531–66.

——. 1959. Experimental production of congenital malformations in mammals by metabolic procedures. *Physiol. Rev.,* **39:** 69–115.

KAWI, A. A., and PASAMANICK, B. 1958. Association of factors of pregnancy with reading disorders in childhood. *J.A.M.A.,* **166**:1420–23.

KING, T. J., and BRIGGS, R. 1956. Serial transplantation of embryonic nuclei. *Cold Spring Harbor Symposia on Quantitative Biology,* **21**:271–90.

KRETCHMER, N. 1959. Enzymatic patterns during development: an approach to a biochemical definition of immaturity. *Pediatrics,* **23**:606–17.

KROEGER, H. 1960. The induction of new puffing patterns by transplantation of salivary gland nuclei into egg cytoplasm of drosophila. *Chromosoma,* **11**:129–45.

LANCET EDITORS. 1960. A proposed standard system of nomenclature of human mitotic chromosomes. *Lancet,* **1**:1063–65.

LANDAUER, W. 1954. On the chemical production of developmental abnormalities and of phenocopies in chicken embryos. *J. Cell. Comp. Physiol.,* **43**:361–65.

LANGMAN, J., and MAISEL, H. 1962. Formation and distribution of chick lens proteins. *Invest. Ophthalmol.,* **1**:86–94.

LANGMAN, J., MAISEL, H., and SQUIRE, J. 1962. The influence of lens antibodies on the development of lens antigen-containing tissue in the chick embryo. *J. Embryol. Exper. Morphol.* **10** (Pt. 2):178–90.

LEJEUNE, J., GAUTIER, M., and TURPIN, R. 1959a. Les chromosomes humains en culture de tissus. *C. R. Séances Acad. Sci.,* **248**:602–3.

———. 1959b. Études des chromosomes somatiques de neuf enfants mongoliens. *Ibid.,* pp. 1721–22.

LENZ, W. 1962. Thalidomide and congenital abnormalities. *Lancet,* **1**:45.

LOCK, F. R., GATLING, H. B., MAUZY, C. H., and WELLS, H. B. 1961. Incidence of anomalous development following maternal rubella. Effect of clinical infection or exposure and treatment with gamma globulin. *Amer. J. Obstet. Gynec.,* **81**:451–64.

LUCEY, J. F. 1961. Hazards to the newborn infant from drugs administered to the mother. *Pediat. Clin. No. Amer.,* **8**: No. 2, 413–19.

McBRIDE, W. G. 1961. Thalidomide and congenital abnormalities. *Lancet,* **2**:1358.

McCLINTOCK, B. 1961. Some parallels between gene control systems in maize and in bacteria. *Amer. Naturalist,* **95**:265–77.

MACLEAN, N., MITCHELL, J. M., HARNDEN, D. G., WILLIAMS, J., JACOBS, P. A., BUCKTON, K. A., BAIKIE, A. G., COURT-BROWN, W. M., McBRIDE, J. A., STRONG, J. A., CLOSE, H. G., and JONES, D. C. 1962. A survey of sex chromosome abnormalities among 4514 mental defectives. *Lancet,* **1**:293–96.

MARKERT, C. L. 1958. Chemical concepts of cellular differentiation. *In:* W. D. McELROY and B. GLASS (eds.), *Symposium on the Chemical Basis of Development.* Baltimore: Johns Hopkins Press.

———. 1961. Nucleocytoplasmic interactions during development. *First International Conference on Congenital Malformations,* pp. 158–65. Philadelphia: J. B. Lippincott.

MATTHAEI, J. H., JONES, O. W., MARTIN, R. G., and NIRENBERG, N. W. 1962. characteristics and composition of RNA coding units. *Proc. Nat. Acad. Sci.,* **48**: 666–77.

MEDAWAR, P. B. 1961. Immunological tolerance. *Science,* **133**:303–6.

MICHAELS, R. H., and MELLIN, G. W. 1960. Prospective experience with maternal rubella and the associated congenital malformations. *Pediatrics,* **26**:200–209.

MILLER, J. R. 1959. Clinical and experimental studies on the etiology of skull, vertebra, rib, and palate malformations. Ph.D. thesis, McGill University.

MILLER, O. J. 1962. Sex determination: the sex chromosomes and the sex chromatin pattern. *Fertility and Sterility,* **13**:93–104.

MONOD, J., and JACOB, F. 1961. General conclusions: teleonomic mechanisms in cellular metabolism, growth, and differentiation. *Cold Spring Harbor Symposia on Quantitative Biology,* **26**:193–209.

MOSCONA, A. A. 1960. Patterns and mechanisms of tissue reconstruction from dissociated cells. *In:* Developing cell systems and their control. *Society for the Study of Development and Growth, Eighteenth Growth Symposium,* pp. 45–70.

MURPHY, D. P. 1929. Ovarian irradiation and the health of the subsequent child. *Surg. Gynec. Obstet.* **48**:766–79.

MURPHY, M. L. 1959. A comparison of the teratogenic effects of five polyfunctional alkylating agents on the rat fetus. *Pediatrics,* **23**: Part II, 231–44.

———. 1960a. Teratogenic effects of tumour-inhibiting chemicals in the foetal rat. *Ciba Foundation Symposium on Congenital*

Malformations, pp. 78–107. London: Churchill.

MURPHY, M. L. 1960*b*. Discussion. *In: Ciba Foundation Symposium on Congenital Malformations*, pp. 290–91. London: Churchill.

NELSON, M. M. 1960. Teratogenic effects of pteroylglutamic acid deficiency in the rat. *Ciba Foundation Symposium on Congenital Malformations*, pp. 134–51. London: Churchill.

NELSON, M. M., WRIGHT, H. V., ASLING, C. W., and EVANS, H. M. 1955. Multiple congenital abnormalities resulting from transitory deficiency of pteroylglutamic acid during gestation in the rat. *J. Nutrition*, **56**:349–69.

NIU, M. C. 1959. Current evidence concerning chemical inducers: *In: Evolution of Nervous Control*, pp. 7–30. Washington: American Association for the Advancement of Science.

PATAU, K., THERMAN, E., SMITH, D. W., and DEMARS, R. I. 1961*a*. Trisomy for chromosome no. 18 in man. *Chromosoma*, **12**: 280–85.

PATAU, K., THERMAN, E., SMITH, D. W., and INHORN, S. L. 1961*b*. Two new cases of D_1 trisomy in man. *Hereditas*, **47**:238–42.

PENROSE, L. S. 1960. A theory of DNA replication. *Ann. Hum. Genet.*, **24**:359–66.

———. 1961. Mongolism. *Brit. Med. Bull.*, **17**:184–89.

PINSKY, L., and FRASER, F. C. 1960. Congenital malformations following a two-hour inactivation of nicotinamide by its analogue, 6-aminonicotinamide in pregnant mice. *Brit. Med. J.*, **2**:195–97.

POLANI, P. E. 1961. Turner's syndrome and allied conditions. *Brit. Med. Bull.*, **17**: 200–205.

PUCK, T. T., CIECIRUA, S. J., and ROBINSON, A. 1958. Genetics of somatic mammalian cells. III. Long-term cultivation of euploid cells from human and animal subjects. *J. Exper. Med.*, **108**:945–56.

RANCK, J. B., and WINDLE, W. F. 1959. Brain damage in the monkey, *Macaca mulatta*, by asphyxia neonatorum. *Exper. Neurol.*, **1**:130–54.

RANTASALO, I., PENTTINEN, K., SAXEN, L., and OJALA, A. 1960. Echo 9 virus antibody status after an epidemic period and the possible teratogenic effect of the infection. *Ann. Paediat. Fenn.*, **6**:175–84.

RICHARDS, B. W., and STEWART, A. 1962. Mosaicism in a mongol. *Lancet*, **1**:275.

RIS, H. 1961. Ultrastructure and molecular organization of genetic systems. *Canad. J. Genet. Cytol.*, **3**:95–120.

ROGERS, M. E., LILIENFELD, A. M., and PASAMANICK, B. 1956. *Prenatal and Paranatal Factors in the Development of Childhood Behavior Disorders*, p. 157. Baltimore: Johns Hopkins University School of Hygiene and Public Health.

RUCKNAGEL, D. L., and NEEL, J. V. 1961. The hemoglobinopathies. *Prog. Med. Genet.*, **1**:158–260.

RUGH, R., and GRUPP, E. 1959*a*. Exencephalia following X-irradiation of the pre-implantation mammalian embryo. *J. Neuropath. Exper. Neurol.*, **18**:468–81.

———. 1959*b*. Response of the very early mouse embryo to low levels of ionizing radiations. *J. Exper. Zool.*, **141**:571–87.

RUNNER, M. N., and DAGG, C. P. 1960. Metabolic mechanisms of teratogenic agents during morphogenesis. *In: Symposium on Normal and Abnormal Differentiation and Development. Nat. Cancer Inst. Monogr.* No. 2, 41–54.

RUSSELL, L. B. 1956. X-ray-induced developmental abnormalities in the mouse and their use in the analysis of embryological patterns. II. Abnormalities of the vertebral column and thorax. *J. Exper. Zool.*, **131**: 329–95.

RUSSELL, L. B., and RUSSELL, W. L. 1952. Radiation hazards to the embryo and fetus. *Radiology*, **58**:369–76.

———. 1954. An analysis of the changing radiation response of the developing mouse embryo. *J. Cell. Comp. Physiol.*, **43**:103–49.

SAGER, R., and RYAN, F. J. 1961. *Cell Heredity*. New York: Wiley.

SAXEN, L., SJOSTEDT, L. E., HOKOSALO, J., and HOKOSALO, H. 1960. Asian influenza during pregnancy and congenital malformations. *Acta Path. Microbiol. Scand.*, **49**: 114–26.

SCARPELLI, E. M. 1959. Maternal nutritional deficiency and intelligence of the offspring. *J. Comp. Physiol. Psychol.*, **52**:536–39.

SIEGEL, M., and GREENBERG, M. 1960. Fetal death, malformations and prematurity after maternal rubella: results of a prospective study. *New Engl. J. Med.*, **262**:269–93.

SMITH, E. L. 1962. Nucleotide base coding

and amino acid replacements in proteins. *Proc. Nat. Acad. Sci.*, **48**:677–84.

SMITH, L. J. 1956. A morphological and histochemical investigation of a preimplantation lethal (t¹²) in the house mouse. *J. Exper. Zool.*, **132**:51–84.

SOBIN, S. 1954. Experimental creation of cardiac defects. *Proceedings of the Fourteenth M and R Pediatric Research Conference*, pp. 13–16.

SOMERS, G. F. 1962. Thalidomide and congenital abnormalities. *Lancet*, **1**:912–13.

SONNEBORN, R. M. 1960. The gene and cell differentiation. *Proc. Nat. Acad. Sci.*, **46**: 149–65.

SPEIRS, A. L. 1962. Thalidomide and congenital abnormalities. *Lancet*, **1**:303–5.

STERN, C. 1958. The nucleus and somatic cell variation. *J. Cell. Comp. Physiol.*, **52**: (Suppl. 1): 1–27.

STERZL, J., *and* HRUBESOV, M. 1957. *J. Microb. Epidemiol. Immunobiol.* (U.S.S.R.), **28**:305.

STOTT, D. H. 1958. Some psychosomatic aspects of casualty in reproduction. *J. Psychosom. Res.*, **3**:42–55.

———. 1961. Mongolism related to emotional shock in early pregnancy. *Vita Humana*, **4**:57–76.

STREAN, L. P., and PEER, L. A. 1956. Stress as an etiologic factor in the development of cleft palate. *Plastic Reconst. Surg.*, **18**: 1–8.

SUMI, T. 1960. Experimental studies in the congenital hydrocephalus due to excessive sugar. *J. Osaka City Med. Ctr.*, **9**:351–59.

THIERSCH, J. B. 1955. The control of reproduction in rats with the aid of antimetabolites and early experiences with antimetabolites as abortifacient agents in man. *Proceedings of the Fifth International Conference on Planned Parenthood*, pp. 187–93. Tokyo.

———. 1958. Effect of N-desacetylthiocolchicine (TC) N-desacetyl methylcolchicine (MC) on rat fetus and litter *in utero*. *Proceedings of the Society for Experimental Biology and Medicine*, **98**:479–85.

THOMPSON, W. D., and SONTAG, L. W. 1956. Behavioural effects in the offspring of rats subjected to audiogenic seizure during the gestational period. *J. Comp. Physiol. Psychol.*, **49**:454–56.

THOMPSON, W. R. 1957. Influence of pre-natal maternal anxiety on emotionality in young rats. *Science*, **125**:698–99.

———. 1960. Early environmental influences on behavioral development. *Amer. J. Orthopsychiat.*, **30**:306–14.

THOMPSON, W. R., and OLIAN, S. 1961. Some effects on offspring behaviour of maternal adrenalin injection during pregnancy in three inbred mouse strains. *Psychol. Rep.*, **8**:87–90.

TJIO, J. H., and LEVAN, A. 1956. The chromosome number of man. *Hereditas*, **42**: 1–6.

TRASLER, D. G. 1960. Influence of uterine site on occurrence of spontaneous cleft lip in mice. *Science*, **132**:420–21.

TRASLER, D. G., and FRASER, F. C. 1958. Factors underlying strain reciprocal cross, and maternal weight differences in embryo susceptibility to cortisone-induced cleft palate in mice. *Proc. Tenth Int. Cong. Genet.*, **2**:296–97.

TUCHMANN-DUPLESSIS, H., and MERCIER-PAROT, L. 1960. The teratogenic action of the antibiotic actinomycin D. *Ciba Foundation Symposium on Congenital Malformations*, pp. 115–28. Boston: Little, Brown, & Co.

WADDINGTON, C. H. 1956. *Principles of Embryology*. London: Allen and Unwin.

WALKER, B. E. 1961. The association of mucopolysaccharides with morphogenesis of the palate and other structures in mouse embryos. *J. Embryol. Exper. Morphol.*, **9**: 22–31.

WALKER, B. E., and FRASER, F. C. 1956. Closure of the secondary palate in three strains of mice. *J. Embryol. Exper. Morphol.*, **4**:176–89.

———. 1957. The embryology of cortisone-induced cleft palate. *Ibid.*, **5**:201–9.

WALKER, B. E., and PRUD'HOMME, J. L. 1960. Effects of transplantation on the histogenesis of transitional epithelium. *Tex. Rep. Biol. Med.*, **18**:318–30.

WALKER, W. M., and McKEE, A. P. 1959. Asian influenza in pregnancy. *Obstet. Gynec.*, **13**:394–98.

WARKANY, J. (ed.). 1960a. Etiology of mongolism. *J. Pediat.*, **56**:412–19.

———. 1960b. Discussion. *In: Ciba Foundation Symposium on Congenital Malformations*, p. 72. London: Churchill.

WARKANY, J., BEAUDRY, P. H., and HORNSTEIN, S. 1959. Attempted abortion with aminopterin (4-amino-pteroylglutamic acid): malformations of the child. *Amer. J. Dis. Child.*, **97**:274–81.

WARKANY, J., and KALTER, H. 1961. Congenital malformations. *New Engl. J. Med.*, **265**:993–1001, 1046–52.

WARKANY, J., WILSON, J. G., and GEIGER, J. F. 1958. Myeloschisis and myelomeningocele produced experimentally in the rat. *J. Comp. Neurol.*, **109**:35–64.

WATSON, J. D., and CRICK, F. H. C. 1953a. A structure for deoxyribose nucleic acid. *Nature* (London), **171**:737–38.

———. 1953b. Genetical implications of the structure of deoxyribonucleic acid. *Ibid.*, pp. 964–67.

WEISS, P. 1947. The problem of specificity in growth and development. *Yale J. Biol. Med.*, **19**:235–78.

———. 1959. The cell in development. *Lab. Invest.*, **8**:415–30.

WELLER, T. H., HANSHAW, J. B., and SCOTT, D. E. 1960. Virologic and clinical investigations on cytomegalic inclusion disease. *Proc. Soc. Pediat. Res.*, 8–9.

WERBOFF, J., DEN BROEDER, J., HAVLENA, J., and SIKOV, M. R. 1961a. Effects of prenatal X-ray irradiation on audiogenic seizures in the rat. *Exper. Neurol.* **4**:189–96.

WERBOFF, J., GOODMAN, I., HAVLENA, J., and SIKOV, M. R. 1961b. Effects of prenatal X-irradiation on motor performance in the rat. *Amer. J. Physiol.*, **201**:703–6.

WERBOFF, J., GOTTLIEB, J. S., DEMBICKI, E. L., and HAVLENA, J. 1961c. Postnatal effect of antidepressant drugs administered during gestation. *Exper. Neurol.*, **3**:542–55.

WERBOFF, J., GOTTLIEB, J. S., HAVLENA, J., and WORD, T. J. 1961d. Behavioral effects of prenatal drug administration in the white rat. *Pediatrics*, **27**:318–24.

WILKINS, L. 1960. Masculinization of female fetus due to use of orally given progestins. *J.A.M.A.*, **172**:1028–32.

WILSON, J. G. 1954a. Differentiation and the reaction of rat embryos to radiation. *J.*

Cell. Comp. Physiol., **43**: Suppl. 1, 11–26.

———. 1954b. Influence on the offspring of altered physiologic states during pregnancy in the rat. *Ann. N.Y. Acad. Sci.*, **57**:517–25.

———. 1961. General principles in experimental teratology. *First International Conference on Congenital Malformations*, pp. 187–94. Philadelphia: J. B. Lippincott.

WILSON, J. G., BEAUDOIN, A. R., and FREE, H. J. 1959a. Studies on the mechanisms of teratogenic action of trypan blue. *Anat. Rec.*, **133**:115–28.

WILSON, M. G., HEINS, H. L., IMAGAWA, D. T., and ADAMS, J. M. 1959b. Teratogenic effects of Asian influenza. *J. Amer. Med. Assoc.*, **171**:638–41.

WOOD, D. C. 1957. A preliminary study of some effects of antibody on eye differentiation *in utero*. *In*: S. J. ONESTI (ed.), *Twenty-third Ross Pediatric Conference*, pp. 77–81.

WOOLLAM, D. H. M., and MILLEN, J. W. 1960. The modification of the activity of certain agents exerting a deleterious effect on the development of the mammalian embryo. *Ciba Foundation Symposium on Congenital Malformations*, pp. 158–72. Boston: Little, Brown, & Co.

WOOLLAM, D. H. M., PRATT, C. W. M., and FOZZARD, J. A. F. 1957. Influence of vitamins upon some teratogenic effects of radiation." *Brit. Med. J.*, **1**:1219–21.

YAMAZAKI, J. N., WRIGHT, S. W., and WRIGHT, P. M. 1954. Outcome of pregnancy in women exposed to the atomic bomb in Nagasaki. *A.M.A. J. Dis. Child.*, **87**:448–63.

ZWILLING, E. 1956. Genetic mechanism in limb development. *Cold Spring Harbor Symposia on Quantitative Biology*, **21**:349–54.

———. 1961. Inductive mechanisms. *First International Conference on Congenital Malformations*, pp. 133–39. Philadelphia: J. B. Lippincott.

NEUROPATHOLOGY

N. Malamud

The neuropathology of mental retardation has been, until recent times, essentially a descriptive morphologic science. Current investigations along experimental, genetic, and biochemical lines have exerted their influence in bringing about a more dynamic approach. As a result, a better understanding of the pathogenesis and etiology of the changes in the central nervous system is gradually evolving. It is reflected in the appearance of more extensive contributions to the literature on this topic in the past decade than at any time previously.

In general, the literature attempts to deal with the following three fundamental questions:

1. What are the kinds of pathology encountered in the various conditions included under the term "mental retardation"?

2. Is there a patho-anatomic substrate in all cases, or are there some in which there is no demonstrable pathology?

3. Can the pathologic findings be correlated with specific etiologic factors and pathogenetic mechanisms?

The first question revolves around the problem of *classification* of the patho-anatomic findings. It is a truism that mental retardation is not an entity but a clinical syndrome, underlying which are many different disorders. It must be admitted that, to date, classification remains inexact to the extent that our knowledge of etiology and pathogenesis is incomplete. In the past, disorders were labeled either "primary" or "secondary," "endogenous" or "exogenous," often on the basis of unproven assumptions that they were either hereditary or acquired con-

ditions. In more recent years two main trends have become apparent. The first has been to treat a large number of pathologic observations statistically (Benda, 1952; Malamud, 1954; Hallervorden and Meyer, 1956). In this way, a more objective presentation of the grouping and incidence of types of disorder has emerged. A second trend has been an attempt to classify each condition on the basis of the time of its occurrence, viz., prenatal, perinatal, and postnatal. This, in part, is based on the assumption that, irrespective of etiology, the brain reacts differently during the early embryonic period of development than during later fetal stages or following birth. Four main types of disorder have been classified: malformations, destructive processes, metabolic conditions, and neoplastic conditions. On the basis of information derived from embryology and experimental teratology, a timetable of malformations has been constructed (Ingalls *et al.*, 1950; Hicks, 1953). The destructive processes have been classified in accordance with varying interpretations of their morphology and time of occurrence. Relying in part on biochemical and genetic data, two smaller groups have been separated under the designations of metabolic and neoplastic disorders. Although such a classification is in some ways useful, it leaves much to be desired. Experimental data are not always applicable to human conditions. Furthermore, in a great many of the malformations and in some of the destructive processes, it is not possible to establish the time of onset of the disorder either on pathologic or on clinical grounds.

The second question is concerned with whether or not neuropathologic changes can be demonstrated in all cases of mental retardation. At the beginning of the Waverley researches in feeblemindedness (1918–39) the authors were of the opinion that "there is a definite correlation between measurable brain and tractable mind." However, at the end of their survey the final conclusions were to the effect that "there was no relationship of value in the differential diagnosis between the degree of histopathological evidence of malformation and the level of mental age." Yet, in every one of the fifty cases examined, there were definite developmental stigmata. Tredgold (1952), while maintaining that all mental retardation is abnormal and accompanied by defective development of the brain, admitted that in higher grade defectives changes in the brain may not be demonstrable. In more recent years Jacob (1956a) and Hallervorden and Meyer (1956) distinguished a category of "mental defect without anatomic substrate." Lewis (1948) differentiated between a pathological and subcultural group, reserving the latter designation for the higher grade defectives whom he considered as merely showing variations of the Gaussian curve of the normal distribution of intelligence. On the other hand, Benda (1952a) described a form of mental retardation under the term "oligoencephaly," which he considered to be a genetic disorder. This condition, which he found to prevail in the higher grade defectives, Benda characterized as a pathologic stunting of brain development although not to the severe degree observed in low-grade defectives. Masland (1958) has aptly stated the problem as follows:

I consider it likely that the factor of brain injury can operate throughout the whole range of intelligence and, in fact, that minor degrees of injury are far more common than are the severe and grossly evident ones. . . . There has been a remarkable paucity of work reported regarding the careful study of persons suffering from minor degrees of mental retardation or specific organic impairment. At the present time, attempts to differentiate the subcultural or familial retardate from the organically damaged person have depended primarily upon the use of psychological testing techniques, and there has been little opportunity for pathological examination for evaluation or control of the conclusions of such studies.

The third question concerns the contributions of pathology to an understanding of etiology and pathogenesis. In the majority of cases, the patho-anatomic change can be regarded as an end stage of a process that occurred either prenatally, perinatally or postnatally. As such, it is a static condition. In these circumstances the pathologic findings indicate either malformations or destructive processes. The clinical diagnosis is often arbitrary, since it depends largely on historic data, the reliability of which is often open to question. As an initial step, therefore, in the understanding of any given case, the pathologic diagnosis establishes the fundamental type of disorder.

The malformations, as discussed previously, can, in many instances, be classified in terms of stages of arrested development at a given time. But whether this points to the operation of the etiologic factor at or before that specific period of time remains an open question. Furthermore, it is a matter of speculation as to whether such factors are genetic or intra-uterine, and whether the pathologic findings offer any helpful clues in this regard. As is well known, attention has been directed recently toward the possible etiologic role of various intra-uterine factors. This interest has been stimulated largely by the observations of Gregg (1941) and Swan (1949) on fetal anomalies in cases of maternal rubella and by Zappert (1927) and Murphy et al. (1942) on effects of pelvic X-irradiation during pregnancy. It remains to be seen, however, how significant this development will be for the general problem of malformations.

In the case of the destructive processes there are somewhat more reliable criteria of correlating pathologic changes with specific causes and mechanisms. Here, the pattern of a lesion affords a means whereby etiology and pathogenesis may be evaluated with a certain degree of assurance. If a large enough series of cases is investigated, it might be shown that certain stereotyped patterns of brain damage recur under similar conditions. Here belong the perinatal disorders of birth trauma, asphyxia, and kernicterus, and the specific prenatal and postnatal types of encephalitis and encephalomyelitis. Even in these conditions, there is as yet no unanimity of opinion concerning either the specific etiology of the lesion or the interpretation of its pathogenesis. Moreover, there are a number of disorders in this general category in which the etiology remains entirely obscure.

In the smaller groups of metabolic or degenerative and neoplastic disorders the pathologic findings are, generally speaking, sufficiently specific to offer no diagnostic difficulties. Their further understanding depends on histochemical, biochemical, and genetic data.

The questions raised above emphasize the need for an objective reappraisal of the pathologic findings. The intention here, therefore, is to analyze the data in a series of unselected cases and compare them with those reported in the literature. It is hoped that through presentation of a larger amount of material than has hitherto been reported some answers to the questions raised previously might be found.

NEUROPATHOLOGIC DATA

The material was derived largely from consecutive autopsies performed in three hospitals for the mentally retarded in the state of California, over a period of approximately fourteen years and personally examined by the author.[1]

A classification of the neuropathologic findings is given in Table 1. It can best be compared with the one proposed by Benda (1952*b*). The latter found, in a series of 258 cases, an incidence of 50 per cent malformations, 38 per cent destructive processes, and 7 per cent and 5 per cent, respectively, of metabolic and neoplastic disorders. The discrepancies between the two sets of figures may in part be expected from the differences in size

TABLE 1

GENERAL CLASSIFICATION OF
NEUROPATHOLOGIC DATA

Type of Pathology	No. of Cases	%
I. Malformations	864	61.0
II. Malformations plus destructive processes	56	4.0
III. Destructive processes	359	25.5
IV. Metabolic and degenerative disorders	66	5.0
V. Neoplastic disorders	29	2.0
VI. No definite pathology	36	2.5
Total	1410	100.0

and possibly in selection of the material. The classification of a series of 385 cases by Hallervorden and Meyer (1956) cannot be compared very well with either of the two other series. These authors, after excluding cases of mongolism and cretinism, proposed the following classification: (1) mental deficiency without gross anatomic findings (31 per cent), (2) developmental disorders (13 per cent), (3) developmental plus circulatory disorders (3 per cent), (4) circulatory disorders (40 per cent), (5) postmeningitic disorders (3 per cent), and (6) miscellaneous disorders (10 per cent). Such a classification is based on a somewhat different in-

[1] Acknowledgment is made to the staffs of Sonoma, Pacific, and Porterville State Hospitals (California) for furnishing the material and making this study possible.

terpretation of the findings than the author would subscribe to for reasons to be elaborated below.

I. Malformations

Malformations are generally regarded as arrests or disturbances in development. Although they are primarily congenital, it is conceivable that some may be arrested at an early postnatal period of life, since the development of the central nervous system still proceeds during

TABLE 2

CLASSIFICATION OF MALFORMATIONS

Types of Pathology	No. of Cases	%
A. Specific.................	162	19
1. Agyria-pachygyria......	14	
2. Micropolygyria.........	29	
3. Cyclopia..............	4	
4. Hydranencephaly.......	3	
5. Porencephaly...........	7	
6. Cranium bifidum.......	3	
7. Hydrocephalus.........	69	
8. Multiple anomalies......	33	
B. Non-specific.............	702	81
1. With mongolism........	251	
2. With phenylketonuria...	5	
3. With other physical stigmata.................	28	
4. Without physical stigmata.................	418	
Total...............	864	100

the first four years of life. Such inhibitions of development are in general characterized pathologically by deviations from the normal size and structure of the brain and spinal cord but, for the most part, lack any signs of lesions or effects of destructive processes.

Table 2 contains a classification of the various types of malformation as observed in this series of cases, which coincides in the main with those described in the literature (Norman, 1958). In the opinion of the writer, it seemed advisable to distinguish between specific and non-

specific forms. The former are such as are readily recognized by their striking macroscopic features, whereas the latter represent less conspicuous structural abnormalities, either gross or microscopic. Such a subdivision may be further justified on the basis of assuming that arrests in development are stage-specific. For the various types included in the category of specific malformations might be regarded as inhibitions of development during the first five or six months of pregnancy. On the other hand, the nonspecific malformations cannot be adequately timed as they may either represent arrests at later stages or milder and subtler effects of retardation at an earlier stage. It is this latter group which is particularly controversial, since the anatomic substrate is accepted by some and rejected by other authors.

A. SPECIFIC MALFORMATIONS

1. *Agyria-pachygyria* (Plate I).—The brain is characterized by a reduction in the number of gyri and sulci. This ranges from virtually complete lack of gyration (lissencephaly), with only a rudimentary Sylvian fissure, to a brain composed of simple broad gyri in which the primary fissures are developed but the secondary and tertiary sulci are absent. The cut sections in the agyric brain are characterized by an increased depth of gray matter that may extend almost to the wall of the ventricle, leaving only an intervening narrow strip of white matter. Microscopically, beneath the superficial molecular layer, a diffuse mass of immature small and spindle-shaped neurons that lack any arrangement in layers occupies almost the entire section. In the pachygyric brain, the increased width of the gray matter is less pronounced and a vague columnar lamination makes its appearance. In either case the size of the brain may vary from extreme microcephaly to only a mild reduction. The lateral ventricles are at all times enlarged, but in varying degrees.

The agyric brain may be regarded as an example of a simple arrest in development at a three- to four-month embryonic stage, with which it can be compared. The pachygyric brain may correspond to a five- to six-month stage of fetal development. At these early stages the neuroblasts pass from the periventricular matrix through an intermediate zone to reach their ultimate destination in the mantle layer to form the cortex. A failure in this migration accounts for the thick mass of heterotopic gray matter and absence of lamination, associated with a lack of maturation of many of the neurons.

2. *Micropolygyria* (Plate II).—By contrast with the simple pattern of pachygyria, the appearance of this condition is one of a complex wealth of miniature convolutions. These may be observed externally if they are slightly raised from the surface of the brain or may be completely submerged in the form of internal microgyria. They may be symmetrically located, generalized, or focal, and, in rare instances, entirely unilateral. In spite of the increased number of gyri, the impression is that the change is superimposed over a fundamental pachygyria, and the two conditions may, in fact, coexist. Sections exhibit varying degrees of increased width of the cortex and hypoplasia of the white matter, with corresponding dilatation of the ventricles, in the walls of which small nodules of heterotopic cortex are frequently imbedded. Microscopically, the gray matter exhibits complex patterns varying from "finger-like" to "glandular" formations. The lamination is undeveloped and may, in fact, be interpreted as not unlike the agyric state. Thus, beneath a branching molecular layer, a single zone of undifferentiated neurons overlies an acellular strip of white matter, beneath which there is a mass of heterotopic cells. Here, too, the brain may vary in size from extreme reduction to low-average range.

While micropolygyria, in common with agyria and pachygyria, may be regarded as a failure of migration and differentiation of neuroblasts, it is more difficult to explain the abnormally complex pattern of the former condition. Fundamentally, however, it, too, appears to be a disturbance in development during the first half of intra-uterine fetal development.

In both agyria and micropolygyria, the pyramidal tracts are often underdeveloped or completely absent, depending on the location of the convolutional anomalies. Clinically, diplegia and, rarely, hemiplegia are noted.

3. *Cyclopia.*—The cyclopic monster, with the centrally placed single eyeball, can only be considered in cases of mental retardation, when it occurs in a milder form. The characteristic findings then are microphthalmia and absent or rudimentary optic nerves. The condition may be associated with absence of olfactory tracts (arhinencephaly) and lack of separation of the cerebral hemispheres with the consequent absence of corpus callosum and septum pellucidum and the presence of a single ventricle.

4. *Hydranencephaly* (Plate III).—In this condition, the cerebral hemispheres are virtually absent with the exception of what appear to be basal parts of the temporal and occipital lobes that lie in the floor of a membranous sac; the ventricles are enlarged and wide open, while the basal ganglia, brain stem, and cerebellum are well developed. Although in some ways it resembles the condition of porencephaly, the question has been raised as to whether hydranencephaly may result from a prenatal destructive process. As evidence, it has been pointed out that the affected areas correspond to the territories of vascular supply by the internal carotid arteries, although the mechanism is unclear.

5. *Porencephaly* (Plate III).—This is a type of malformation characterized by symmetrically placed clefts or cavities in the cerebral cortex that extend through the entire width of the cerebral wall from the ventricle to the subarachnoid space.

The clefts lie in the line of primary fissures, their walls being fused together, forming a pia-ependymal seam and are lined by malformed tissue resembling that of micropolygyria. In many cases the clefts open up, forming funnel-shaped cavities that are continuous with the ventricles and are covered on the surface by a thin roofing membrane while the pia-ependymal seams are found in the margins of the defects. Yakovlev and Wadsworth (1946) considered these to be true malformations, which they designated "schizencephaly," and distinguished them from cavities due to destructive lesions. They were of the opinion that the clefts arise in the cerebral wall before the end of the second month of embryonic development.

The presence or absence of mental retardation depends on the extent of the porencephaly and on associated cerebral anomalies.

6. *Cranium bifidum (cranioschisis).*—Cranium bifidum is a midline defect, usually located in the posterior part of the skull, resulting in the formation of either meningeal (meningocele) or cerebral (encephalocele) hernias, covered by normal scalp. Like spina bifida (rachischisis), it represents a failure of the neural groove to unite in forming the neural tube.

7. *Hydrocephalus.*—This is a common disorder in the mentally retarded and refers to a progressive enlargement of the ventricles, which is to be distinguished from dilatation of ventricles due to brain atrophy or hypoplasia (hydrocephalus *ex vacuo*). Although it may be caused, under rare conditions, by either excessive formation or defective absorption of cerebrospinal fluid, it usually results from an obstruction in some part of the cerebrospinal fluid channels, whether occurring pre- or postnatally. As a malformation, it is associated with a number of anomalies. The most common are spina bifida with an Arnold-Chiari deformity, stenosis of the aqueduct of Sylvius and

atresia of the foramina of Magendie and Luschka. In the present series of sixty-nine cases of hydrocephalus, there were thirty-one instances of Arnold-Chiari deformity associated with spina bifida, fourteen of stenosis of the aqueduct, six of atresia of the foramina, and eighteen cases of undetermined cause.

Arnold-Chiari deformity (Plate IV), which is constantly present in cases of meningomyelocele, is characterized by a protrusion through the foramen magnum of the lower part of the pons, the medulla, and tonsils or lower part of the vermis of the cerebellum. Additional features are elongation, rotation, and dorsal swelling of the brain stem, narrowing of the aqueduct of Sylvius, and elongation of the lower cranial nerves (Greenfield, 1958a). The pathogenesis of the deformity has been variously interpreted. The two prevalent theories are that it is either a mechanical deformity due to a downward traction by the fixed lower end of the cord in the region of the meningomyelocele (Lichtenstein, 1940) or that it is a primary developmental anomaly occurring at about the third week of embryonic life (Russell and Donald, 1935). The almost invariably accompanying hydrocephalus has been generally interpreted as secondary to the downward displacement of the fourth ventricle, so that its foramina open into the spinal canal, and/or to narrowing of the aqueduct of Sylvius.

Stenosis of the aqueduct (Plate V), as a primary malformation, occurs either in the form of a simple narrowing or a septum or forking of the aqueduct in the absence of abnormal gliosis.

Atresia of the foramina of Magendie or Luschka is seen in a condition that is referred to in the literature as the Dandy-Walker syndrome (Plate VI). It is characterized by agenesis of the posterior vermis, progressive formation of a large cyst in the posterior fossa that appears to represent an enlargement of the fourth ventricle secondary to the atresia of the foramina, and a consequent hydrocephalus (Taggart and Walker, 1942). It is believed that the failure of the foramina to open at about the beginning of the fourth month interferes with the subsequent development of the posterior part of the cerebellar vermis.

In any form of obstructive hydrocephalus, progressive cerebral atrophy through pressure develops, which accounts for the increasing mental retardation.

8. *Multiple anomalies.*—Any combination of the previously described anomalies may occur. Pachygyria and micropolygyria frequently coexist, sometimes with porencephaly and/or hydrocephalus. Malformation of the cerebellum in the form of focal micropolygyria, bilateral or unilateral hypoplasia, may be associated with the cerebral anomalies.

One of the most common malformations is an *agenesis of the corpus callosum* (Plate VII), complete or partial. Such an anomaly may occur as an isolated phenomenon, when it is virtually asymptomatic. In the mentally retarded, however, it is invariably associated with other signs of malformation, as was the case in 60 per cent of the group with multiple anomalies. The agenesis of the corpus callosum is usually accompanied by distortion of the cingulate gyrus, absence of the septum pellucidum, lateral displacement of the ventricles, and an ectopic callosal bundle on the dorsomedial walls of the ventricles. The anomaly is generally attributed to an arrested development occurring at or before the second month of embryonic development, at a time when the corpus callosum and related structures begin to develop from the lamina terminalis. The associated anomalies vary widely from micropolygyria to non-specific convolutional disturbances.

B. NON-SPECIFIC MALFORMATIONS

By contrast with the previous group, these forms do not lend themselves to further subdivision from the standpoint of the changes in the central nervous system. Rather, their breakdown, as given in Table 2, is based on the presence or absence of extracerebral physical (or biochemical) stigmata.

The cerebral changes that characterize the entire group are distinct yet comparatively "mild" or subtle deviations from the normal appearance (Plate VIII). Macroscopically, there is usually a moderate reduction in the size and weight of the brain, although occasionally there are extremes of microcephaly or megalencephaly. The shape, as a rule, is rounded as it is determined by foreshortened frontal, small and flattened occipital, and relatively prominent temporal lobes. There may be slight asymmetry of the hemispheres. The convolutional and sulcal pattern varies from a broad simplified type with few secondary sulci to complex though mild micropolygyria. The sulci are shallow and irregular. The superior temporal gyrus is often narrow and short by contrast to bulky and cauliflower-shaped middle and inferior temporal convolutions. The inferior frontal gyrus may be underdeveloped, and the insula is thus exposed to the surface. The recto-orbital region may be thickened in the midline and protrude in the form of a "rostrum orbitale." In some instances the brain stem and cerebellum are small; in others, the cerebellum may be relatively large and protrude behind the short occipital lobes. In section the cortex appears disproportionately thick and massive compared to a reduced white matter. The cortical pattern may be either abnormally simple or complex, often penetrating deeply into the white substance. Abnormal connections link contiguous or more distant gyri. The reduction in white matter involves all of its components, including the corpus callosum and the descending projection tracts through the brain stem. The basal ganglia are often increased in size. The lateral ventricles are usually dilated in proportion to the degree of hypoplasia of the white matter. The cerebellum may also show disproportion between an increased gray mass and reduced white substance.

Microscopically the changes are less definable than the gross features, probably because the subtle abnormalities require a more careful and painstaking analysis. On the whole, various anomalies in cytoarchitecture can be detected. These are characterized by indistinct lamination, alternating crowded and empty cell layers, and heterotopias of neurons in the molecular layer and in the white matter. Nerve cells are more widely dispersed through the thick cortex. Immature nerve cells of a fetal type, characterized by spindle shape, scant cytoplasm, and relatively prominent nucleus, are commonly encountered. Abnormally large neurons are rare. Persistence of embryonic glia may be present. Disturbances in myeloarchitecture and incomplete myelination of the white matter may occur, although more difficult to evaluate. Asymmetry in distribution of neurons in the Purkinje layer of the cerebellum, inferior olives, and abnormalities in other areas have been reported. Benda emphasized associated anomalies in the spinal cord under the designation of spinal dysraphism.

The above findings closely resemble those reported by Benda under the designation "oligoencephaly," which he distinguished from other malformations as a specific genetic form of mental retardation. It would probably correspond to the group of non-specific malformations without physical stigmata in the present series. In the opinion of the writer, however, there is insufficient evidence that, on purely morphologic grounds, this type can be distinguished from other disorders such as mongolism and phenylketonuria. Nevertheless, the latter conditions deserve separate discussion because of their unusual interest and because of certain concomitant neuropathologic features.

1. *Mongolism.*—The neuropathologic changes of this common disorder, which has perhaps aroused more interest than any other form of mental retardation, have been summed up by Jacob (1956*b*) as follows:

Signs of malformation: Gross features of brachymicrocephaly characterized by a brain of small size and rounded shape with flattened poles, open insula, narrow superior temporal gyrus, simple and plump convolutions, reduced angle of brain stem, and small optic nerves, hypothalamus, pons, medulla and cerebellum, associated with changes in the skull, such as acrocephaly, scaphocephaly or acromicria; microscopic findings of reduction of and lack of differentiation of cortical neurons, disturbances in myeloarchitecture, and signs of myelodysplasia of the spinal cord.

Signs of postnatal pathologic processes: (a) Vascular, in the form of focal lesions, either associated with congenital heart disease or, possibly, hypoplasia of blood vessels, and (b) "precocious senility," characterized by senile plaques and neurofibrillary lesions of Alzheimer.

It may be inferred from the above description that the signs of malformation in the mongol brain (Plate IX) do not differ essentially from those previously outlined for the entire group of non-specific malformations, whether occurring in mongolism, oligoencephaly, etc. In the opinion of some investigators (Penrose, 1949; Minkowski, 1952; Jacob, 1956*b*) mongolism is simply a form of "fetal dysplasia." Jacob finds the same "inner disharmonies" in the mongol as in the non-mongol defective brain. Benda (1946), on the other hand, regards mongolism as a specific disorder, characterized by a congenital acromicria that is determined by arrested development at a stage between the sixth and twelfth week of embryonic life. In line with recent theories, he (Benda, 1960) attributes the deceleration of growth to "a disorder of cellular cleavage and chromosomal dysjunction." The neuropathologic findings, in his opinion, are the result of a combination of stunted growth and chronic anoxia, caused, in part, by local compression of the brain by the anomalous skull and, in part, by general disturbances of growth. As evidence of anoxia, Benda finds regressive changes in the neurons. Jacob disagrees with the latter contention and interprets the small neurons as immature forms or neuroblasts. He also points out that the theory advanced by Benda fails to explain why a deceleration of growth at such an early period of embryonic development does not produce more severe anomalies such as pachymicrogyria.

In regard to the postnatal pathologic changes in the brain, the vascular lesions on the basis of congenital heart disease have been emphasized by Meyer and Jones (1939). In the present series of cases, there was evidence of congenital heart disease in approximately one-third of the 251 cases, but cerebrovascular lesions were present in only a few, usually in association with a tetralogy of Fallot. The most consistent findings in the brains of older mongols were signs of so-called precocious senility in the form of senile plaques and neurofibrillary changes (Plate IX). Twenty of the 251 cases ranged in age, at the time of death, from thirty-seven to sixty-six years, and in all of them there were neuropathologic changes characteristic of Alzheimer's disease or presenile dementia. Such findings were previously noted by Jervis (1948) and others. Also of interest was the frequent occurrence of calcification of the basal ganglia in the mongol brain, irrespective of age. This was found in seventeen cases, or 7 per cent of the total number in this series, which is a higher incidence than in other types of malformation, although calcification is not an uncommon finding in the latter. The significance of all these presumably metabolic changes in mongolism remains unknown.

2. *Phenylketonuria.*—In phenylpyruvic oligophrenia, a specific disorder of protein metabolism takes place, consisting of an inability to hydroxylate phenylalanine to tyrosine so that the former accumulates in the blood and its ketone in the urine. As such, the disorder can be included with the metabolic diseases (Jervis, 1947). However, the neuropathologic findings have not been sufficiently characteristic to permit its precise classification. Alvord *et al.* (1950) reported evidence of both defective myelinization and demyelinization in their cases. Benda (1952) emphasized demyelinization as a persistent feature and noted macromolecular substances, composed of myelin and amyloid, in the spinal cord. Corsellis (1953) also observed in one case an area of demyelinization and gliosis limited to the occipital lobe, which he did not consider as the substrate of the disorder. Crome and Pare (1960) described microencephaly and gliosis in the centrum semiovale, without appreciable loss of myelin, in their cases. A report by Poser and van Bogaert (1959) stressed altered myelination associated with fibrillary gliosis as evidence of a fundamental error in myelin metabolism, similar to the leucodystrophies. In the five cases included in this series, there were gross stigmata of retarded development of the brain, not unlike those of the other forms of nonspecific malformation (Plate X). In one case there was, in addition, an extensive subcortical area of demyelination and gliosis (Plate X) and in the four others there were similar, though microscopic, changes. More recently, on the basis of additional material, I found consistent changes in myelin, varying from spongy foci in the white matter of young patients to demyelinating lesions in more adult cases of PKU. The significance of these findings still remains obscure. It may be that chemical analysis of brain tissue will ultimately clarify the problem.

3. *Malformation with other physical stigmata.*—In a miscellaneous group of other malformations there were the following associated features: cretinism, Rud's syndrome, Marfan's disease, Crouzon's disease, microcephalia vera, megalencephaly, Morquio's disease, Laurence-Moon-Biedl syndrome, polysyndactyly, sickle-cell anemia, and progressive muscular dystrophy. In all these conditions, whether the specific physical stigmata were coincidental or causally related, the brain changes showed the same non-specific anomalies as characterized the entire group. The term microcephaly cannot be considered as a specific disorder since the small size of the brain occurs under a variety of conditions, whether of the specific or non-specific types of developmental anomaly. Included here, however, are several cases in which the pathologic changes were relatively mild, the brain being a miniature of the normal —so-called microcephalia vera. The term megalencephaly is also non-specific, since the large size of the brain is often associated with other stigmata of malformation. To be excluded are such specific conditions as Tay-Sachs disease, tuberous sclerosis, and diffuse gliomatosis in which hyperplasia of glial tissue accounts for the large size of the brain.

4. *Malformations without physical stigmata.*—This, by far the largest subgroup of the malformations in the series, can be regarded as identical with the condition of oligoencephaly reported by Benda. It does not require further elaboration since it presents the same features of maldevelopment as the previous types but without concomitant specific physical disturbances.

II. Malformations Plus Destructive Processes

There were fifty-six cases in this series, in which there was a combination of developmental anomalies and destructive lesions. In fourteen of these, both the history and patho-anatomic changes pointed to complicating birth trauma, and in two, to superimposed postnatal infection. In ten of the cases a history of maternal infectious illness occurring in the first trimester of pregnancy was obtained, while in the remaining thirty cases the history was uninformative.

Of especial interest were the cases in which maternal infection appeared to play a role. A history of maternal rubella was elicited in seven. Of these, the malformation in one case consisted of pachy-micropolygyria, in another of agenesis of the corpus callosum, and in the remaining five, of a non-specific type (Plate XI). In each of these cases, there were in addition varying degrees of perivenous and diffuse gliosis of the cerebral and cerebellar white matter (Plate XI), resembling the chronic changes observed in cases of perivenous encephalomyelitis following measles occurring in postnatal life. In two cases with histories of maternal mumps and "flu" respectively, micropolygyria was likewise associated with gliosis of the white matter. In the tenth case, congenitally acquired skin lesions of herpes simplex were associated with a combination of bilateral porencephaly and extensive gliosis of the brain (Plate XII).

Such findings in cases with a history of maternal rubella have been reported by Mutrux *et al.* (1949) and Friedman and Cohen (1947). In this connection is the case reported by Diezel (1954) of cytomegalic inclusion body disease, apparently acquired in the fourth month of pregnancy, in which the infant's brain showed both micropolygyria and the destructive lesions caused by the salivary gland virus. Of similar interest is the case reported by Hallervorden (1949) in which maternal carbon monoxide poisoning during the fifth month of pregnancy led to changes in the infant's brain, consisting of a combination of micropolygyria and the characteristic softening of the basal ganglia as seen in carbon monoxide poisoning. Relevant to this problem may be the cases of hydranencephaly in which the cerebral agenesis may be associated with destructive lesions. These relatively rare but significant cases may shed some light on the role of intra-uterine factors in the causation of malformations, a problem which will be discussed later.

III. DESTRUCTIVE PROCESSES

This group of disorders is characterized morphologically by chronic lesions in the form of atrophy, glial scars, cysts, or old hemorrhages. By contrast to the malformations, there is no definite evidence of anomalous development of the central nervous system.

The classification of the lesions in Table 3 is based primarily on morphologic

TABLE 3

CLASSIFICATION OF DESTRUCTIVE PROCESSES

Types of Pathology	No. of Cases	%
A. Cerebral atrophy and/or cystic degeneration........	267	75
B. Hydrocephalus............	46	13
C. Kernicterus..............	18	5
D. Neurosyphilis.............	12	3
E. Encephalitis (specific viral).	12	3
F. Encephalomyelitis........	4	1
Total.................	359	100

considerations with the exception of the last four categories, in which a specific etiology is well established. It is apparent that the great majority of destructive lesions present difficulties in classification. For atrophy, scar formation, cystic degeneration, or hydrocephalus can have a similar appearance irrespective of etiology. It is in this area that many opposing theories of pathogenesis have been advanced. Traumatic, circulatory, anoxic, toxi-infectious factors have been variously emphasized. As in the malformations,

attempts have been made to classify the disorders in relation to their time of occurrence. Thus prenatal, perinatal, and postnatal conditions have been distinguished, based largely on clinical information. It is well known, however, that exclusive reliance on the clinical history can lead to many errors, since such data may be either too meager or too complex to be useful. The aim of the patho-anatomic analysis would, therefore, be to establish fundamental patterns of lesions that can be correlated with reliable clinical information.

TABLE 4

CLASSIFICATION OF CEREBRAL ATROPHIES

Types of Pathology	No. of Cases	%
1. Primary subcortical........	133	50
2. Primary cortical..........	53	20
3. Unclassified..............	74	27
4. Infarcts..................	5	2
5. Contusions (postnatal trauma)......................	2	1
Total.................	267	100

A. CEREBRAL ATROPHY AND/OR CYSTIC DEGENERATION

In an attempt to determine whether the lesions, characterized descriptively by atrophy, gliosis, and cyst formation, possess more fundamental diagnostic patterns, the writer proposed in a previous communication (Malamud, 1959*b*), the following classification (see Table 4): (1) a group with primary subcortical pathology and (2) a group with primary cortical pathology.

1. *Primary subcortical pathology.*—This group is characterized by sclerosis or cystic degeneration of the white matter, status marmoratus of the basal ganglia, and ulegyria of the cerebral cortex (Plate XIII). These lesions frequently coexist, but whereas the changes in the white matter and basal ganglia are fairly

constant, they may not involve the cortex at all; when they do, the cortical lesion appears to be either a local extension of or concomitant with the subcortical disturbance. The changes in the white matter (Plate XIV) vary from sclerosis to cystic degeneration, may be diffuse or focal, unilateral or bilateral, and can occur in central or gyral white substance. Status marmoratus (Plate XV) is a characteristic lesion primarily of the corpus striatum and thalamus, usually bilateral, and consisting grossly of an arrangement of fibers in networks that ramify through the basal ganglia. Microscopically, the abnormal networks show fibrillary gliosis, hypermyelination, increase in glial nuclei, and loss of or calcification of the surviving neurons. Ulegyria or sclerotic microgyria is characterized by focal atrophy of gyri that present a peculiar appearance of crowding because the intervening sulci are narrowed and because the basal portions are more sclerotic than the crowns of the convolutions. They are frequently bilateral and symmetrical and may involve any lobe or portion thereof, more commonly the parieto-occipital than the fronto-central regions. Microscopically (Plate XVI), they are characterized by patchy loss of neurons in the deep layers of the cortex, gliosis, and hypermyelination, which exhibit patterns of radial scars, status marmoratus, and mushroom formation. They are invariably connected with a dense subcortical gliosis of the white matter. In some instances, an accompanying independent gliosis is also found on the surface of the cortex.

A survey of a large series of cases with primary subcortical pathology showed that in the majority a history of birth trauma was obtained. The birth injury occurred under a variety of circumstances, such as prolonged labor, precipitate delivery, malposition or abnormal presentation, placenta previa, strangulation of the cord, traumatizing obstetrical manipulation, and Caesarean section.

The significant features in such a history were signs of brain damage, namely, convulsions, paralysis, fetal distress, etc., that developed immediately following birth.

The role of birth trauma in the causation of mental retardation and cerebral palsy has been debated ever since Little (1862) first recognized its importance a century ago. Penrose estimates that about 1 per cent of cases of all types of mental retardation are caused by birth trauma. In Benda's series an incidence of 24 per cent is given, and in the present series an incidence of approximately 10 per cent. In evaluating its significance, birth trauma must be considered in a broad sense to include all types of disturbances occurring during parturition: mechanical trauma, anoxia, interruption of circulation, etc.

The lesions described previously such as ulegyria, status marmoratus, and sclerosis or cavitation of the central white matter are recognized by many as sequelae of birth trauma. Differences of opinion, however, exist as to their pathogenesis. It is conceded by most investigators that mechanical trauma per se, such as is associated with obstetrical manipulation, plays a relatively minor role in the sequelae. Such injuries usually produce tentorial and falx tears, resulting in fatal subdural hemorrhages. Chronic subdural hematoma is, therefore, rarely observed in cases of mental retardation. The major factors held responsible for the cerebral lesions are generally considered to be neonatal asphyxia and circulatory disturbances.

Asphyxia has been held responsible by some for the intraventricular, subependymal, and subarachnoid hemorrhages observed in neonatal deaths (Gruenwald, 1951; Corner and Anderson, 1958; and others). Neuronal degeneration, either diffuse or focal, in regions susceptible to oxygen lack have been emphasized by others, partly based on the experimental observations of Windle et al. (1944). The latter induced anoxia in animals by occluding the uterine-umbilical circulation, allowing them to survive for varying periods of time. The cerebral lesions varied from subdural and intraventricular small hemorrhages to neuronal changes, the latter involving especially the thalamus and brain stem. Courville (1953) is of the opinion that anoxia is the principal mechanism in the etiology of the chronic lesions of cerebral palsy. According to his view, the lesions are caused by fetal respiratory and circulatory disturbances resulting from primary asphyxial anoxia and secondary vascular factors. Hallervorden and Meyer (1956) attribute the lesions to the hypoxia brought about by either functional disturbances of cerebral circulation or by thrombosis of meningeal arteries.

Venous disturbances have been emphasized by Schwartz (1927, 1956) as the chief mechanism in the production of the acute lesions in stillbirths and neonatal deaths, as well as in their chronic sequelae. According to this author, differences between environmental and intra-uterine pressures lead to intracerebral lesions because blood is drawn or sucked into the presenting head. The lesions, whether hemorrhages or softenings, are distributed in the venous territories of either the superior longitudinal sinus and/or the vein of Galen. The latter is particularly vulnerable because of its relatively weak structure at birth, especially in the premature, and because of its intracranial position, arising at a sharp right angle to the rigid straight sinus. The lesions tend to occur in the territory drained by the terminal tributaries of the vein of Galen, such as the anterior and posterior terminal and the lateral ventricular veins that drain the cerebral white matter in frontal, parietal, and occipital regions, and the basal ganglia. In their anatomic location and pattern, such lesions differ from those observed under conditions of asphyxia.

Schwartz, therefore, rejects the hypothesis of an anoxic mechanism in favor of a mechanical circulatory one. He is of the opinion that the suction mechanism operates also in other than head presentations, as well as in Caesarean sections. Marburg and Casamajor (1944) were of the same opinion, emphasizing the effects of the tensions of parturition in inducing phlebostasis in the Galenic system. The present writer believes that the lesions he classified under the category of primary subcortical pathology owe their origin primarily to a disturbance in the Galenic venous system. This seems most likely, since the chronic lesions are usually located in dorsal rather than ventral parts of the brain, whether in the white matter of the superior fronto-parieto-occipital regions, the adjacent cortex, or the dorsal parts of the caudate nucleus, putamen, and thalamus. They coincide, therefore, with the location of the acute lesions as outlined by Schwartz. In like manner, disturbances in the external veins that drain the superior longitudinal sinus can account for the accompanying, though less common, superficial cortical lesions. Furthermore, the pattern of status marmoratus, which is practically pathognomonic of sequelae of birth trauma, appears to be fundamentally a perivenous lesion. The rare occurrence of a similar change under other conditions, such as infection, may owe its origin to complicating venous disturbances.

Arterial disturbances in the course of birth trauma have been emphasized by others. According to Rydberg (1932), extreme pressure on the fetal skull leads to increased intracranial pressure and to a fall in arterial blood pressure. Norman *et al.* (1957) find confirmation of this in the location of some lesions in boundary zones between the main arterial territories, and also in territories of arteries compressed by uncal herniation as a result of raised intracranial pressure. The latter phenomenon of inciscural sclerosis has been especially emphasized by Earle *et al.* (1953).

Hallervorden and Meyer also stress the

circulatory nature of many of the lesions but attribute a greater role to the factor of edema.

2. *Primary cortical pathology.*—This group differs essentially from the previous one. For although cerebral atrophy and cystic degeneration are equally present in these cases, the pattern is different. Grossly (Plate XVII), the atrophy, whether diffuse, focal, unilateral, or bilateral, is primary in the gray matter, causing uniform shrinkage of gyri and widening of sulci similar to that seen in atrophic disorders of adult life. By contrast with the previous group, the location of the atrophy is equally and often predominantly in ventral parts of the brain, especially in the temporal lobes. Microscopically, the cortex exhibits diffuse or laminar loss of neurons with reactive gliosis, with or without cystic degeneration (Plate XVIII). Involvement of the white matter closely parallels that of the gray matter. Primary degeneration of neurons may also occur in the hippocampus, thalamus, and cerebellum, but rarely in basal ganglia. The thalamus and long tracts may show secondary retrograde and prograde degeneration.

A clinical survey of this group showed that in 90 per cent of the cases birth and early development were normal but were followed by an acute illness at some time during infancy or early childhood. The nature of the disorder varied widely. The most common history was that of a febrile illness accompanied by convulsions, often associated with a systemic infection but without evidence of a primary infection of the nervous system. Less frequently, bacterial meningitis and encephalitis were recorded as the cause of the mental retardation.

It has been pointed out by several observers (Wolf and Cowen, 1954; Hallervorden and Meyer, 1956; Norman, 1958) that the common febrile convulsions of childhood that accompany banal infections, such as acute intestinal disturbances, may be responsible for destructive lesions in the central nervous system.

These are thought to be due to hypoxia accompanying the seizures. Under such circumstances the changes predominate in the gray matter, especially in such vulnerable areas as the hippocampus, cerebellum, certain layers of the cerebral cortex, thalamus, dentate nucleus, and inferior olives. The anoxic changes may lead eventually to gross cerebral atrophies. According to Norman, it is possible that some obscure conditions like cerebral hemiatrophy or progressive lobar sclerosis of Schob (1930) and so-called Alpers' disease (1931) or progressive cortical degeneration may actually be a postepileptic encephalopathy. It is obvious, however, that in this group it is difficult to distinguish between toxi-infectious effects of the precipitating illness and the secondary anoxic effects of seizures. In this connection, attention must be drawn to the common findings of Ammon's horn sclerosis and/or cerebellar atrophy in any case in which epilepsy is a symptom, whether the fundamental disorder is a developmental anomaly or a destructive lesion.

3. *Unclassified.*—It is to be expected that among the cerebral atrophies some cases will be found that are neither clinically informative nor pathologically specific. It may be that some of these are caused by interaction of several of the previously mentioned factors. In a few cases the cerebral atrophy was of such severe degree, falling much below the birth weight of the brain, that it suggested a prenatal etiology. In such instances toxoplasmosis and cytomegalic inclusion encephalitis were considered. However, because of chronicity of the lesions, massive destruction and extensive calcification, a demonstration of specific organisms or inclusion bodies was no longer possible.

4. *Infarcts.*—In a small number of cases there was evidence of sequelae of occlusive vascular disease in the form of old infarcts, either in arterial or venous territories. Included were several cases with congenital heart disease and also a

case of sinus-venous thrombosis, similar to those reported by Norman (1936) and by Bailey and Hass (1937). In a few, there was a history of meningitis, apparently complicated by an arterial thrombosis and infarction. Hallervorden and Meyer (1956) described cerebral infarcts caused by emboli in the course of such infections as scarlet fever and diphtheria.

5. *Contusions due to postnatal trauma.* —Cerebral contusion and subdural hematoma occurring as results of a head injury in infancy and childhood are rare causes of mental retardation, and there were two such cases in the series. The pattern of these lesions is essentially similar to that observed in adult life.

B. HYDROCEPHALUS

Obstructive forms of hydrocephalus in this group are such as result from inflammatory or traumatic meningeal lesions that block the cerebrospinal fluid channels. In many such instances a basal arachnoiditis (Plate XIX) is responsible, or an associated ependymitis, resulting in gliosis, may be severe enough to cause stenosis of the aqueduct of Sylvius (Plate XIX). Here, too, determination of etiology depends on precise clinical information. Bacterial meningitis is a common cause, and in some of the cases in this series *E. coli meningitis*, which developed soon after birth, was responsible. In a few the pattern suggested congenital toxoplasmosis. In most the cause remained unknown because of insufficient historical information.

C. KERNICTERUS

This condition, which is so designated because of the yellow or bile staining of the basal nuclei, is best known as a complication of icterus gravis neonatorum associated with erythroblastosis fetalis. It is the result of maternal iso-immunization developing during pregnancy, principally by the Rh factor. However, the disorder is known to occur with septic states, prematurity, and any condition which is associated with hemolytic jaundice. Although its pathogenesis remains controversial, the pathology is well established (Zimmerman and Yannet, 1935; Fitzgerald *et al.*, 1939). The sequelae of kernicterus are, in the majority of cases, characterized by symmetrical atrophy, demyelinization, and gliosis of the globus pallidus, subthalamic body, and hippocampal region (Plate XX). Less commonly, lesions may be found in the putamen, thalamus, dentate nucleus, inferior olives, flocculus of the cerebellum, optic nerves, and nuclei of the eighth nerve. The clinical manifestations of an extrapyramidal syndrome can be related to the lesions in the basal ganglia. Deafness has been attributed by some to degeneration of the cochlear nuclei. There is no definite correlation between the mental retardation and the pathologic changes. The pathogenesis of the condition has been variously interpreted. It is known that glucoronide synthesis is impaired, since the enzyme systems in the liver necessary to convert indirect to direct bilirubin are defective. Indirect bilirubin, which is highly toxic, thus accumulates in the tissues. Some regard kernicterus, therefore, as a bilirubin encephalopathy (Waters *et al.*, 1954). Others maintain that the pigmentation is merely a biliary imbibition of previously damaged nervous tissue through hypoxia (Pentschew, 1948) or the direct effect of the hemolytic anemia (Yannet and Liebermann, 1946). Its unique pathology, however, would argue against the assumption that such generalized pathologic states as anoxia or anemia are the primary factors. In this connection it is significant that in most cases of kernicterus where the hippocampal formation is affected, it is precisely the areas that are usually resistant to anoxia such as the dentate fascia and the dorsal cell band that are most apt to be involved. It has been suggested that anoxia may act as a subsidiary mechanism by increasing the permeability of the blood-brain barrier to the toxic effects of indirect bilirubin.

Yannet and Liebermann (1944) are of

the opinion that Rh incompatibility may also play a role in some cases of undifferentiated mental retardation. Gilmour (1950) disputes this contention and emphasizes that "Rh incompatibility, apart from when it causes erythroblastosis fetalis and kernicterus, plays no part in the etiology of mental defect."

D. NEUROSYPHILIS

Congenital syphilis as a cause of mental retardation is only firmly established in the form of neurosyphilis, namely, juvenile paresis and meningovascular lues. As such, it does not differ essentially from the acquired adult forms. There is, however, a greater tendency in juvenile paresis for an atypical distribution of the lesions, such as involvement of the cerebellum, in which many binucleate ganglion cells are intermingled with the degenerating Purkinje cells.

E. ENCEPHALITIS

Various forms of viral encephalitis may be associated with mental retardation when they have their onset at an early period of life.

Among the twelve cases here included, there were seven of the lethargic or Von Economo's form, one of western equine encephalitis, one of toxoplasmosis, and three of inclusion encephalitis of Dawson.

The pathology of lethargic encephalitis is well established with its characteristic lesions in the brain stem, in particular the substantia nigra (Plate XXI) and periaqueductal area. The mental retardation in such cases is usually relatively mild, and behavior disorders and neurologic signs predominate.

The chronic sequelae of western equine encephalitis (and other related viral forms) are hardly known. The one case of proven western equine encephalitis showed widespread chronic inflammatory lesions (Plate XXII) in the cortex, white matter, basal ganglia, and brain stem, and one of its prominent features was focal calcification (reported from this laboratory by Herzon et al., 1957). There is some reason to believe that three other cases in the series were of this type but, not having been verified bacteriologically, were included in the unclassified group.

Toxoplasmosis, which was first described by Wolf and Cowen (1937), usually occurs in a congenital form; the infection of the fetus is transmitted by the mother who, however, does not show signs of the disease. Its incidence among the mentally retarded is undetermined, and its chronic sequelae are hardly known. In the one case reported here, toxoplasmosis infection was proven by the dye test, both during the acute and chronic phases. The gross pathology was one of focal areas of cerebral atrophy, particularly in the vicinity of the meninges and ventricles (Plate XXIII). Microscopically, chronic areas of tissue disintegration, cyst formation, and reactive gliosis were associated with dense calcification and low-grade inflammatory reaction (Plate XXIII). Here, too, several cases that exhibited similar pathologic changes but in which the specific infection was never established were included among the unclassified forms.

The three cases of inclusion encephalitis included in the series are rare forms of a disease that was first described by Dawson (1933). Because of its tendency to occur in childhood, the disease may give rise to a picture of mental retardation along with various neurologic signs. The pathology (Plate XXIV) is that of widespread subacute and chronic inflammatory lesions that are disseminated throughout the central nervous system (Malamud et al., 1950). Its pathognomonic feature is the occurrence of acidophilic intranuclear inclusion bodies in neurons and oligodendroglia. The specific viral etiology of the disease has hitherto not been proven, although it is suspected to be caused by the herpes simplex virus.

Cytomegalic inclusion encephalitis is a rare disease occurring congenitally or in early childhood. Its systemic lesions resemble those caused by salivary gland viruses. The neuropathology is little known, but Haymaker *et al.* (1954) described hydrocephalus, periventricular calcification and gliosis, and acidophilic intranuclear inclusions in astrocytes and endothelium of small blood vessels.

F. ENCEPHALOMYELITIS

Encephalomyelitis comprises a group of disorders, generally referred to as perivenous or postinfectious encephalomyelitis, in which the pathologic picture suggests a hyperergic antigen-antibody reaction. It may complicate vaccination or occur in the course of various exanthematous diseases of childhood. The pathology is similar, irrespective of the precipitating condition, and consists of perivenous demyelinating necrotic foci that are largely restricted to the white matter. In its chronic form (Plate XXV) perivascular and diffuse demyelinization and gliosis of the white matter predominate (Malamud, 1939). In this series there were four cases of encephalomyelitis following measles, which is the most common cause of such a complication among the exanthemata.

IV. METABOLIC AND DEGENERATIVE DISORDERS

The metabolic and degenerative disorders constitute a heterogeneous group of rare diseases in which the clinical and pathologic features are specific and in which hereditary transmission is common, probably by rare recessive genes (Penrose, 1949). In the past such disorders have been regarded as obscure heredodegenerative states. Recently, however, some, if not all, of them have come to be known as inborn errors of metabolism, since biochemical studies indicate specific enzymatic disturbances in the metabolism of fats, proteins, or carbohydrates (Jervis, 1952).

The sixty-six cases classified in this category are listed in Table 5.

A. LIPIDOSES

The best known of the metabolic disorders in which mental retardation is a prominent feature is the group in which a defect in lipid metabolism is involved. This comprises amaurotic family idiocy, Niemann-Pick's disease, gargoylism, and, occasionally, Gaucher's disease and other rare forms.

Amaurotic family idiocy has been classified into a variety of subtypes, depending on age of onset of the disorder and specific clinical features. Of these, the

TABLE 5

CLASSIFICATION OF METABOLIC AND
DEGENERATIVE DISORDERS

Type of Pathology	No. of Cases
A. Lipidoses {Amaurotic idiocy (17)... {Gargoylism (13)...	30
B. Hallervorden-Spatz disease........	7
C. Fahr's disease....................	2
D. Demyelinating disorders..........	14
E. Cerebellar and extrapyramidal degenerative disorders..............	13
Total.......................	66

best known are the infantile form or Tay-Sachs disease, with its specific retinal cherry red spot, and the juvenile or Batten-Spielmeyer-Vogt form, with a characteristic retinitis pigmentosa. Not so well recognized is a late infantile or Bielschowsky-Jansky form. In the latter the average age of onset is the second to third year, and the clinical manifestations are not characteristic, since amaurosis and retinal changes are usually absent. It is in such cases of "amaurotic idiocy without amaurosis" that the correct clinical diagnosis is rarely made and may vary from Heller's disease or childhood schizophrenia (Malamud, 1959*a*) to Schilder's disease and cerebral palsy. In the present series, there were three instances of Tay-Sachs disease, nine of the

Bielschowsky-Jansky form and five of the juvenile type. The neuropathology, with minor variations, is similar in all types (Plate XXVI). It is a disease in which the neurons of every part of the central nervous system may become distended with lipid material, eventually succumb, and lead to cerebral atrophy. The involved lipids are still under investigation. Histochemically, the material is weakly sudanophilic but frequently stains for "prelipids" with a variety of other methods. Biochemically, the lipid involved in the various types of amaurotic idiocy is considered to be a ganglioside that may or may not be combined with neuraminic acid. In Niemann-Pick's disease the lipid is sphingomyelin, and in Gaucher's disease it is kerasin. It has not been established, however, in each instance whether one is dealing with normal metabolites which are not utilized because of a faulty biochemical mechanism or with abnormal metabolites (Jervis, 1952).

Gargoylism is a disorder characterized by mental retardation associated with dystrophic changes in bones, hepatosplenomegaly, and other extraneural lesions. Neuropathologically, it is virtually indistinguishable from amaurotic idiocy. Biochemically, however, it is believed to be a glycolipoidosis or sphingolipoidosis, connected with an abnormal content of polysaccharides (Seitelberger, 1957).

Disorders of carbohydrate metabolism such as galactosemia and glycogenosis in which mental retardation may be present have not as yet been investigated neuropathologically.

Disorders of amino-acid metabolism include phenylpyruvic oligophrenia (previously discussed) and maple syrup urine disease. Pathologically, the latter condition is believed to be similar to phenylketonuria, since it is characterized by both retarded myelination and demyelination (Silberman *et al.*, 1961).

B. HALLERVORDEN-SPATZ DISEASE

This is a slowly progressive extrapyramidal disorder commonly associated with mental retardation that occurs predominantly in early childhood (Hallervorden and Spatz, 1922). It exhibits a characteristic gross brownish pigmentation of the globus pallidus and of the ventral non-pigmented part of the substantia nigra (Plate XXVII). Microscopically (Plate XXVII), the accumulated pigments that are scavenged by microglia are usually associated with progressive degeneration of the nervous tissue. Although some of the pigments show a positive reaction for iron, the chemical composition of others remains unknown. As a result, the nature of the condition is obscure but, because of its frequent familial occurrence, suggests a specific metabolic disorder.

C. FAHR'S DISEASE

Intracranial calcification associated with mental retardation may be encountered in a great variety of developmental and acquired disorders. However, it may also exist as an "idiopathic" condition (Fahr's disease) in which there is a primary deposition of calcium salts in the small blood vessels of the brain (Plate XXVIII). The particular areas of predilection are the globus pallidus, striatum, thalamus, dentate nucleus, and, less consistently, cerebral and cerebellar gray and white matter. Although in recent years some of these cases have been linked to parathyroid dysfunction, there are others of unknown origin in which a local metabolic defect may be at fault. In the present series, the cases of two siblings are included (reported from this laboratory by Bowman, 1954).

D. DEMYELINATING DISORDERS

These constitute a group of diffuse demyelinating diseases that commonly occur in childhood and often have a heredofamilial basis. Neuropathologically, they have been currently subdivided into (1) sudanophilic form, (2) metachromatic form, (3) Krabbe's disease, and (4) Pelizaeus-Merzbacher's disease. In each of these types, the fundamental change is one of diffuse demyelinization and sclerosis (Plate XXIX). In the first two forms the characteristic features are the conversion of the lipid material in the myelin sheaths respectively into sudan and metachromatic staining products (Plate XXIX). In Krabbe's disease characteristic giant multinucleated forms known as globoid cells form in the demyelinating regions (Plate XXIX). In Pelizaeus-Merzbacher's disease the demyelination is associated with islands of preserved myelin sheaths. In the present series there were nine cases of the sudanophilic, two of the metachromatic form, and three of Krabbe's disease. But whether the morphologic changes are fundamental differentiating criteria or not remains to be determined. Their precise histo- and biochemistry are still under investigation. It has been suggested that, whereas the sudanophilic form may be exogenously determined, the metachromatic form and Krabbe's disease are due to an inborn error of the metabolism of myelin or leucodystrophy (Diezel, 1957; Greenfield, 1958b; Cumings, 1960). Recent studies indicate that the metachromatic form is a sulfatide lipidosis Austin, 1962).

E. CEREBELLAR AND EXTRAPYRAMIDAL DEGENERATIVE DISORDERS

A heterogeneous group of heredofamilial and sporadic cases of mental retardation occurring in childhood is associated with progressive degeneration of the cerebellum and its connections (Plate XXX). As in later forms of cerebellar ataxia, additional lesions in higher centers, such as the basal ganglia and thalamus, may coexist, perhaps accounting for the abnormal mental state (Malamud and Cohen, 1958). In others some of the nuclei of the extrapyramidal system may be chiefly involved, as in the cases of two siblings, children, in whom a clinical picture of bibalismus and mental retardation was related to symmetrical degeneration of the subthalamic and mammillary bodies (Malamud and Demmy, 1960).

V. NEOPLASTIC DISORDERS

The group of neoplastic disorders here considered is also known as neuroectodermal dysplasia or congenital ectodermosis (Yakovlev and Guthrie, 1931). In these cases developmental disturbances at an early blastomatous stage are associated with hyperplasia or neoplasia of various tissues, generally inherited as dominant defects (Penrose, 1949).

The three principal sub-types are tuberous sclerosis, neurofibromatosis, and angiomatosis. In this series there were nineteen cases of tuberous sclerosis, two of neurofibromatosis, and eight of angiomatosis.

Tuberus sclerosis is a complex developmental disorder, presumably of all three primary germinal layers, resulting in lesions of brain, retina, skin, kidneys, heart, and other viscera. Neuropathologically, focal cortical and subependymal nodules of hyperplastic gliosis are intermingled with giant neurons and glial elements (Plate XXXI). Signs of malformation in the form of microscopic disturbances in cytoarchitecture and of heterotopias and, sometimes, of more gross anomalies, such as micropolygyria and hydrocephalus, may coexist. The exuberant subependymal gliosis not infrequently undergoes a neoplastic change, resulting in gliomas of varying grades of malignancy. Calcification, demonstrated by X-rays, is commonly present in the heterotopic and subependymal lesions. Similar glial nodules are found in the retina. The extraneural lesions are adenoma sebaceum of the face and other skin changes, hamartoma of kidneys, rhabdomyoma of the heart and, occasionally, similar changes in adrenal glands, lungs, and other viscera. Opinions differ as to whether the fundamental disorder is one of defective histogenesis or of a spongioblastic overgrowth.

Neurofibromatosis of von Recklinghausen is much less commonly associated with mental retardation than tuberous sclerosis. The lesions are predominantly peripheral in the form of peripheral neurofibromatosis, associated with *café au lait* spots and other skin lesions. Frequently, however, lesions near or in the central nervous system are observed in the form of acoustic neuroma, multiple meningioma, glioma, and scattered microscopic foci of glial hyperplasia. Here, too, the assumption is made that a fundamental developmental disturbance is associated with hyperplasia of neuro-ectodermal tissues.

Angiomatosis is a hyperplasia of malformed blood vessels in the meninges with or without accompanying similar changes in the skin. The best-known example is Sturge-Weber's syndrome or encephalofacial angiomatosis. In this condition, a facial nevus in the distribution of one or more divisions of the trigeminal nerve is associated with excessive vascularity of the pia-arachnoid in the parieto-occipital region of the same side. The proliferated meningeal vessels are of the capillo-venous type (Plate XXXII). The underlying cortex contains massive calcification as a result of diminished blood supply, forming a characteristic pattern in the X-rays of the skull. Angiomatosis of the meningeal and central veins may, however, occur independently of the skin lesions and may be associated with stunted development of the brain, either uni- or bilaterally. The condition may be regarded as a malformation of the primitive embryonic vascular plexus.

GENERAL COMMENT

The previous review of the neuropathologic data in cases of mental retardation may aid in furnishing some answers to the questions raised in the introduction.

A classification based on patho-anatomic findings seems to be justified in our present state of knowledge even though, it must be acknowledged, an etiologic classification should be the ultimate goal. A breakdown of otherwise nondescript clinical types on the basis of their pathologic substrate may lead toward better understanding of their etiology and pathogenesis.

A subdivision of the malformations into various stages of arrested development offers a means of exploring the operation of genetic or intra-uterine factors acting at certain definite periods of time in fetal development. Experimental teratology has provided some information concerning the effects of environmental factors. In human malformations, however, only a relatively small number of cases show a correlation with some maternal disorder occurring during pregnancy. It has been suggested that the effects of such environmental factors will differ depending on the time of their operation. Thus, an infection such as maternal rubella occurring early in pregnancy will result in a pure malformation, while another such as toxoplasmosis acting late in pregnancy would produce destructive lesions. However, some of the cases previously reported indicate that when maternal rubella and other infections or carbon monoxide poisoning occurred early in pregnancy, the effect was not a simple anomaly but a complex of stage-specific malformations and lesions. The latter appeared to be characteristic of the specific etiology, such as a perivenous encephalomyelitis in the case of maternal rubella, an inflammatory gliosis in cases of herpes simplex or cytomegalic inclusion disease, and necrosis of the basal ganglia in the case of carbon monoxide poisoning. These observations would tend to distinguish malformations associated with intra-uterine disorders from pure developmental disorders in which such factors are not known to have been operating. Further studies of such material are indicated.

The separation of the destructive processes from the malformations on patho-anatomic grounds appears to be a necessary initial step toward clarifying many clinical misconceptions of diagnosis and etiology. As is well known, the role of birth trauma has been both de- and overemphasized since Little first drew attention to it. Recent studies on the role of asphyxia neonatorum and circulatory disturbances at the time of birth call for a re-assessment of the importance of perinatal disorders. In the opinion of this writer, the pathologic lesions under conditions of birth trauma appear to be specific not only in their acute but also in their chronic stages. These should be separated radically from such other conditions with which they have been confused, namely, those following toxi-infectious states, kernicterus, convulsive disorders, etc.

The various disorders that are classified in the metabolic, degenerative, and neoplastic categories offer no difficulties in classification. This becomes increasingly clear as their genetic and biochemical bases are more firmly established.

A clinical separation of the low- from the high-grade mentally retarded on the basis of an assumed difference existing, respectively, between pathologic and physiologic or subcultural forms does not seem warranted. To test this, a survey of the different grades of mental retardation has been made, wherever possible, in the series of cases here presented, as shown in Table 6.

The statistical summary reveals that 89 per cent of patients in the series who were tested were low-grade, and 11 per cent high-grade defectives. The high incidence of low-grade defectives is, at least in part, to be expected in any series of autopsied cases on the basis of the shorter life span of such patients. It is true that there is a significantly higher ratio of low- to high-grade defectives in the group with gross lesions (11.5 to 1) versus the group with "milder" lesions (6.5 to 1). Furthermore, in a group with no definite pathology (see Table 1) the ratio of low- to high-grade defectives was 2.5 to 1. Nevertheless, it may be seen that brain injury operates "throughout the whole range of defective intelligence," as stated by Masland. It would seem that

many cases that are considered by other investigators as mental retardation "without anatomic substrate" are found equally among idiots and morons. They are, in fact, the same cases that Benda has classified as oligoencephaly, and this writer as non-specific malformations. For, if anatomic substrate is denied the latter group, the same would have to be applied to the morphologically similar cases of mongolism and phenylketonuria in which the organic basis is not doubted. Perhaps, the

TABLE 6

DISTRIBUTION OF TYPES OF PATHOLOGY IN DIFFERENT GRADES OF MENTAL RETARDATION

TYPE OF PATHOLOGY	No. OF CASES			
	Idiot	Imbecile	Moron	Borderline
Specific malformations............	89	26	5	2
Malformations with mongolism........	58	124	17	6
Other non-specific malformations....	217	155	53	9
Destructive lesions...	205	68	22	5
Total..........	569	373	97	22

experience with such a condition as phenylpyruvic oligophrenia might indicate that a large number of cases under discussion here are related to some unknown biochemical abnormalities. This is not to deny, however, that there exists a minority of cases in whom no definite pathologic changes can be demonstrated. But whether these are very subtle anomalies or deviations in the curve of normal intelligence cannot be decided on the basis of available neuropathologic criteria.

From what has already been stated, the pathologic findings can yield information toward a better understanding of etiology and pathogenesis. For, in spite of the fact that the findings in most cases of mental retardation and cerebral palsy are end stages, the pathologic patterns can be, in many instances, specific. This is particularly true in the group of destructive disorders. The patterns of the sequelae of birth trauma, kernicterus, and viral and parasitic forms of encephalitis can be clearly established. Not so well understood are a number of less clear-cut destructive lesions following various toxi-infectious conditions, post-epileptic encephalopathy, etc. However, further investigation, particularly in correlating acute and chronic phases of such disorders, can be expected to clarify their etiology. It seems obvious, nonetheless, that a number of disorders, particularly the malformations, offer no patho-ana-tomic clues as to their etiology. Any light on this subject will have to be shed through other methods of investigation.

REFERENCES

ALPERS, B. J. 1931. Diffuse progressive degeneration of the gray matter of the cerebrum. *Arch. Neurol. Psychiat.*, **25**:469.

ALVORD, E. C., STEVENSON, L., VOGEL, F. S., and ENGEL, R. L. 1950. Neuropathological findings in phenylpyruvic oligophrenia. *J. Neuropath. Exper. Neurol.* **9**:298.

AUSTIN, J. H. 1962. Recent studies in the metachromatic and globoid forms of diffuse sclerosis. *Ultrastructure and Metabolism of the Nervous System.* Research Publications, A.R.N.M.D., **XL**:189.

BAILEY, O. T., and HASS, G. M. 1937. Dural sinus thrombosis in early life. *Brain*, **60**:293.

BENDA, C. E. 1946. *Mongolism and Cretinism.* New York: Grune & Stratton.

———. 1952a. *Developmental Disorders of Mentation and Cerebral Palsies.* New York: Grune & Stratton.

———. 1952b. Structural cerebral histopathology of mental deficiencies. *Proceedings of First International Congress of Neuropathology, Rome*, **2**:7. Torino: Rosenberg and Sellier.

———. 1960. Mongolism: clinical manifestations, pathology and etiology. *First International Medical Conference on Mental Retardation.* New York: Grune & Stratton.

BOWMAN, M. S. 1954. Familial occurrence of "idiopathic" calcification of cerebral capillaries. *Amer. J. Path.*, **30**:87.

CORNER, G. W., and ANDERSON, J. W. 1958. Asphyxia of the human fetus in relation to *brain damage. In: Conference on Neurological and Psychological Deficits of Asphyxia Neonatorum.* Springfield, Ill.: C. C Thomas.

CORSELLIS, J. A. N. 1953. The pathological report of a case of phenylpyruvic oligophrenia. *J. Neurol. Neurosurg. Psychiat.*, **16**:139.

COURVILLE, C. B. 1953. *Cerebral Anoxia.* Los Angeles: San Lucas Press.

CROME, L., and PARE, C. M. B. 1960. Phenylketonuria. *J. Ment. Sci.*, **106**:862.

CUMINGS, J. N. 1960. Abnormalities of lipid chemistry in cerebral lipidoses and demyelinating conditions. *In: Modern Scientific Aspects of Neurology*, London: Edward Arnold.

DAWSON, J. R., JR. 1933. Cellular inclusions in cerebral lesions of lethargic encephalitis. *Amer. J. Path.*, **9**:7.

DIEZEL, P. B. 1954. Mikrogyrie infolge cerebraler speicheldrüsen-virusinfektion in Rahmen einer generalisierten Cytomegalie bei einem Säugling. *Virchow Arch.*, **325**:109.

———. 1957. Histochemical investigations of degenerative diffuse sclerosis. *In: Cerebral Lipoidosis.* Oxford: Blackwell Scientific Publications.

EARLE, K. M., BALDWIN, M., and PENFIELD, W. 1953. Incisural sclerosis and temporal lobe seizures produced by hippocampal herniation at birth. *Arch. Neurol. Psychiat.*, **69**:27.

FITZGERALD, G. M., GREENFIELD, J. G., and KOUNINE, B. 1939. Neurological sequelae of kernicterus. *Brain*, **62**:292.

FRIEDMAN, M., and COHEN, P. 1947. Agensis of corpus callosum as a possible sequel to maternal rubella during pregnancy. *Amer. J. Dis. Child.*, **73**:178.

GILMOUR, D. J. 1950. The Rh factor: its role in human disease with particular reference to mental deficiency. *J. Ment. Sci.*, **96**:359.

GREENFIELD, J. G. 1958a. Arnold-Chiari malformations. *In: Neuropathology*, chap. v, p. 312. London: Edward Arnold.

———. 1958b. Diffuse cerebral sclerosis. *In: Neuropathology*, chap. vii, p. 459. London: Edward Arnold.

GREGG, N. McA. 1941. Congenital cataract following German measles in the mother. *Trans. Opthalmol. Soc. Australia*, **3**:35.

GRUENWALD, P. 1951. Subependymal cerebral hemorrhage in premature infants and its relation to various injurious influences at birth. *Amer. J. Obstet. Gynec.*, **61**:1285.

HALLERVORDEN, J. 1949. Über eine Kohlenoxydvergiftung im Fetalleben mit Entwicklungstörungen der Hirnrinde. *Allgemeine Z. Psychiat.*, **124**:289.

HALLERVORDEN, J., and MEYER, J. E. 1956. Cerebrale Kinderlähmung. *In: Handbuch der speziellen pathologischen Anatomie and Histologie (Lubarsch-Henke-Rössle)*, **13** (Part IV): 194. Berlin: Springer Verlag.

HALLERVORDEN, J., and SPATZ, H. 1922. Eigenartige Erkrankung im extrapyramidalen system mit besonderer Beteiligung des Globus Pallidus und der substantia nigra. *Zbl. Ges. Neurol. Psychiat.*, **79**:254.

HAYMAKER, W., GIRDANY, B. R., STEPHENS, J., LILLIE, R. D., and FETTERMAN, G. H. 1954. Cerebral involvement with advanced periventricular calcification in generalized cytomegalic inclusion disease in the newborn. *J. Neuropath. Exper. Neurol.*, **13**: 562.

HERZON, H., SHELTON, J. T., and BRUYN, H. B. 1957. Sequelae of western equine and other arthropod-borne encephalitides. *Neurology*, **7**:535.

HICKS, S. P. 1953. Developmental malformations produced by radiation: a timetable of their development. *Amer. J. Roentgenol.*, **69**:272.

INGALLS, T. H., CURLEY, F. J., and PRINDLE, R. A. 1950. Anoxia as a cause of fetal death and congenital defect in the mouse. *Amer. J. Dis. Child.*, **80**:34.

JACOB, H. 1956a. Angeborener erblicher Schwachsinn. *In: Handbuch der speziellen pathologischen Anatomie und Histologie (Lubarsch-Henke-Rössle)*, **13** (Part IV): 58. Berlin: Springer Verlag.

———. 1956b. Mongolismus. *In: Handbuch der speziellen pathologischen Anatomie und Histologie (Lubarsch-Henke-Rössle)*, **13**:82. Berlin: Springer Verlag.

JERVIS, G. A. 1947. Studies on phenylpyruvic oligophrenia. *J. Biol. Chem.*, **160**: 651.

———. 1948. Early senile dementia in mongoloid idiocy. *Amer. J. Psychiat.*, **105**: 102.

———. 1952. Metabolic disorders: general and cellular pathochemistry of mental deficiencies. *Proceedings of First International Congress of Neuropathology, Rome*, **2**: 199. Torino: Rosenberg and Sellier.

LEWIS, E. O. 1948. Mental deficiency and social medicine. *J. Men. Sci.*, **94**:258.

LICHTENSTEIN, B. W. 1940. "Spinal dysraphism," spina bifida and myelodysplasia. *Arch. Neurol. Psychiat.*, **44**:792.

LITTLE, W. J. 1862. On the influence of abnormal parturition, difficult labor, premature birth and asphyxia neonatorum on the mental and physical condition of the child especially in relation to deformities. *Trans. Obstet. Soc. (London)*, **3**:293.

MALAMUD, N. 1939. Sequelae of postmeasles encephalomyelitis. *Arch. Neurol. Psychiat.*, **41**:943.

———. 1954. Recent trends in classification of neuropathological findings in mental deficiency. *Amer. J. Ment. Defic.*, **58**:438.

———. 1959a. Heller's disease and childhood schizophrenia. *Amer. J. Psychiat.*, **116**: 215.

———. 1959b. Sequelae of perinata trauma. *J. Neuropath. Exper. Neurol.*, **18**:141.

MALAMUD, N., and COHEN, P. 1958. Unusual form of cerebellar ataxia with sex-linked inheritance. *Neurology*, **8**:261.

MALAMUD, N., and DEMMY, N. 1960. Degenerative diseases of the subthalamic bodies. *J. Neuropath. Exper. Neurol.*, **19**: 96.

MALAMUD, N., HAYMAKER, W., and PINKERTON, H. 1950. Inclusion encephalitis. *Amer. J. Path.*, **26**:133.

MARBURG, O., and CASAMAJOR, L. 1944. Phlebostasis and phlebothrombosis of the brain in the newborn and in early childhood. *Arch. Neurol. Psychiat.*, **52**:170.

MASLAND, R. L. 1958. *Mental Subnormality.* New York: Basic Books.

MEYER, A., and JONES, J. B. 1939. Histological changes in the brain in mongolism. *J. Men. Sci.*, **85**:206.

MINKOWSKI, M. 1952. Prenatal neuropathologic changes leading to neurologic or mental disorders. *Proceedings of First International Congress of Neuropathology, Rome*, **2**:51. Torino: Rosenberg and Sellier.

Murphy, D. P., Shirlock, M. E., and Doll, E. A. 1942. Microcephaly following maternal pelvic irradiation for the interruption of pregnancy. *Amer. J. Roentgenol.*, **48:**356.

Mutrux, S., Wildi, I. E., and Bourquin, J. 1949. Contribution a l'étude clinique et anatomo-pathologique des troubles cérébraux de l'embryopathie rubéoleuse. *Schweiz. Arch. Neurol. Psychiat.*, **64:**369.

Norman, R. M., 1936. Bilateral atrophic lobar sclerosis following thrombosis of the superior longitudinal sinus. *J. Neurol. Psychopath*, **17:**135.

———. 1958. Malformations of the nervous system, birth injury and diseases of early life. *In: Neuropathology*, chap. v, p. 300. London: Edward Arnold.

Norman, R. M., Urich, H., and McMenemey, W. H. 1957. *Vascular mechanisms of birth injury. Brain,* **80:**49.

Penrose, L. S. 1949. *Biology of Mental Defect.* New York: Grune & Stratton.

Pentschew, A. 1948. Encephalopathia posticterica infantum. *Arch. Psychiat.* **180:**118.

Poser, C. M., and Bogaert, L. van. 1959. Neuropathologic observations in phenylketonuria. *Brain,* **82:**1.

Russell, D. S., and Donald C. 1935. The mechanism of internal hydrocephalus in spina bifida. *Brain,* **58:**203.

Rydberg, E. 1932. Cerebral injury in the newborn. *Acta Path. Microbiol., Scand., Suppl.,* **10:**247.

Schob, F. 1930. Pathologische anatomie der idiotie. *In: Bumkes Handbuch der Geisteskrankheiten,* **12:**779. Berlin: Springer Verlag.

Schwartz, P. 1927. Die Traumatischen Schadigungen des Zentralnervensystems durch die Geburt. *Ergebn. Inn. Med. Kinderheilk.,* **31:**165.

———. 1956. Injuries of the newborn. *Arch. Pediat.,* **73:**429.

Seitelberger, F. 1957. Cerebral Lipoidosis. Oxford: Blackwell Scientific Publications.

Silberman, J., Dancis, J., and Feigin, I. 1961. Neuropathological observations in maple syrup urine disease. *Arch. Neurol.,* **5:**351.

Swan, C. 1949. Rubella in pregnancy as an etiologic factor in congenital malformation, stillbirth, miscarriage and abortion. *J. Obstet. Gynaec.* (British Empire), **56:**341 and 591.

Taggart, J. K., and Walker, A. E. 1942. Congenital atresia of the foramina of Luschka and Magendie. *Arch. Neurol. Psychiat.,* **48:**538.

Tredgold, A. F. 1952. *A Textbook of Mental Deficiency.* Baltimore: Williams & Wilkins.

Waters, W. J., Richert, D. A., and Rawson, H. H. 1954. Bilirubin encephalopathy. *Pediatrics,* **13:**319.

Waverley Researches in the Pathology of the Feebleminded. ("Memoirs of the American Academy of Arts and Sciences," Boston 1918–39.)

Windle, W. F., Becker, R. F., and Weil, A. 1944. Alterations in brain structure after asphyxiation at birth. *J. Neuropath.,* **3:**224.

Wolf, A., and Cowen, D. 1937. Granulomatous encephalomyelitis due to encephalitozoon, new protozoan diseases of man. *Bull. N.Y. Neurol. Inst.,* **6:**306.

———. 1954. The cerebral atrophies and encephalomalacias of infancy and childhood. *Assoc. Res. Nerv. Ment. Dis.,* **34:**199.

Yakovlev, P. I., and Guthrie, R. H. 1931. Congenital ectodermoses (neurocutaneous syndromes) in epileptic patients. *Arch. Neurol. Psychiat.,* **26:**1145.

Yakovlev, P. I., and Wadsworth, R. C. 1946. Schizencephalies: a study of the congenital clefts in the cerebral mantle. *J. Neuropath. Exper. Neurol.,* **5:**116, 169.

Yannet, H., and Liebermann, R. 1944. The Rh factor in the etiology of mental deficiency. *Amer. J. Ment. Defic.,* **45:**207.

———. 1946. Complications associated with kernicterus. *J. A. M. A.,* **130:**355.

Zappert, J. 1927. Über röntgenogene fetale mikrocephalie. *Arch. Kinderheilk.,* **80:**34.

Zimmerman, H. M., and Yannet, H. 1935. Cerebral sequelae of icterus gravis neonatorum and their relation to kernicterus. *Amer. J. Dis. Child.,* **49:**418.

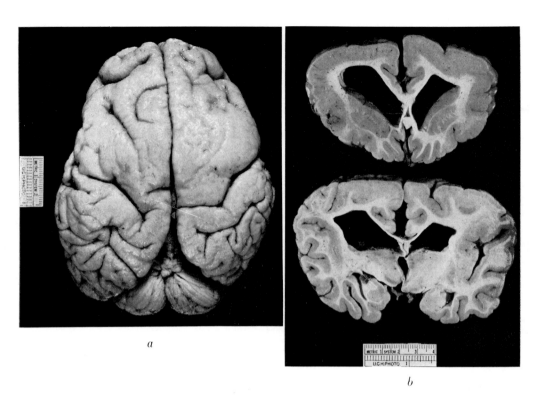

a

b

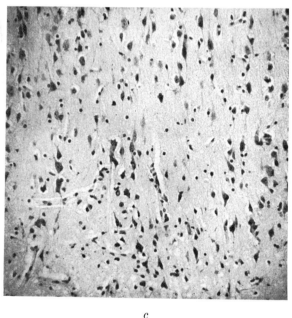

c

PLATE I.—Agyria-pachygyria: (a) external appearance, (b) coronal sections, and (c) cytoarchitecture of cortex, Nissl method × 150

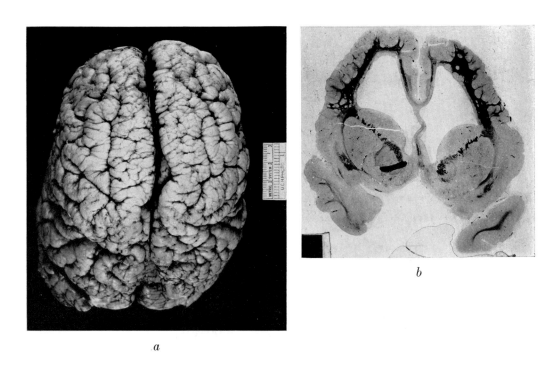

a

b

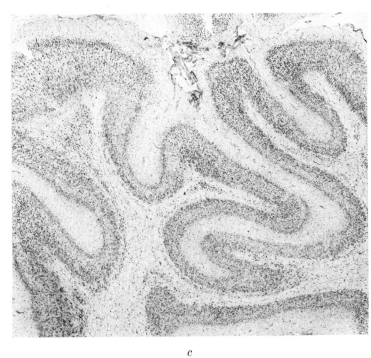

c

PLATE II.—Micropolygyria: (*a*) external appearance, (*b*) section (showing submerged microgyria and heterotopia) Weigert myelin method, and (*c*) cytoarchitecture of cortex, Nissl method × 22

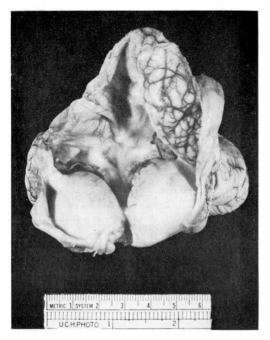

a

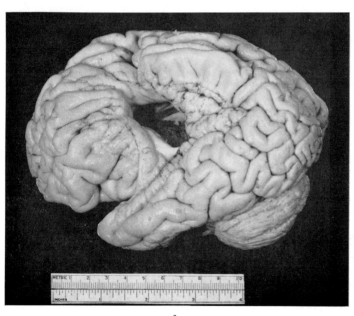

b

PLATE III.—(*a*) Hydranencephaly and (*b*) Porencephaly

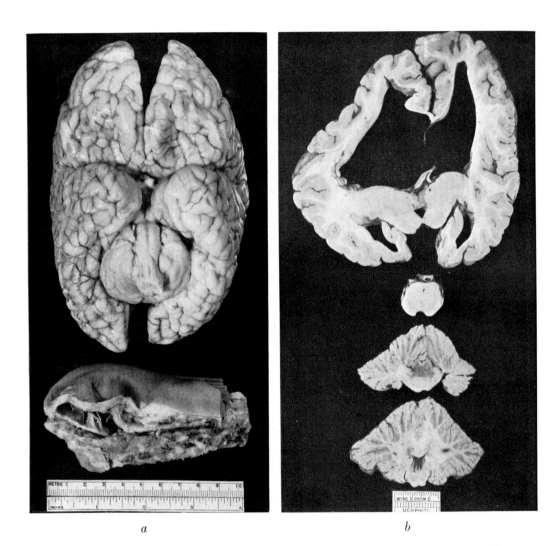

a   b

PLATE IV.—(a) Hydrocephalus with Arnold-Chiari deformity and myelomeningocele, external appearance, and (b) coronal sections of brain showing hydrocephalus and Arnold-Chiari deformity

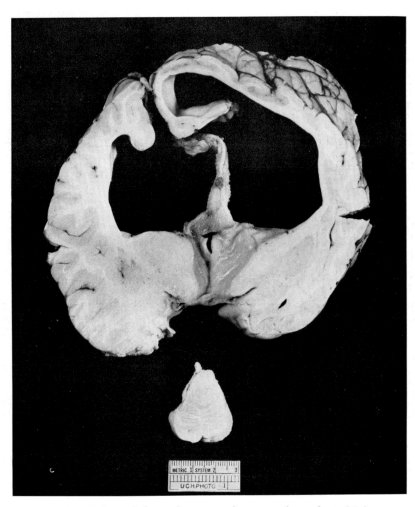

PLATE V.—Hydrocephalus with congenital stenosis of aqueduct of Sylvius

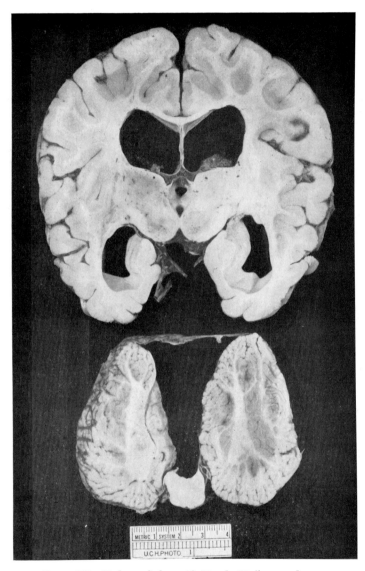

PLATE VI.—Hydrocephalus with Dandy-Walker syndrome

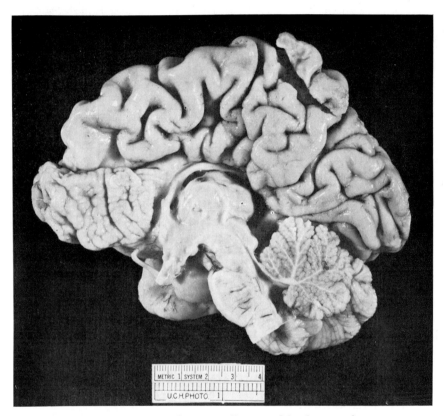

PLATE VII.—Agenesis of corpus callosum and focal micropolygyria

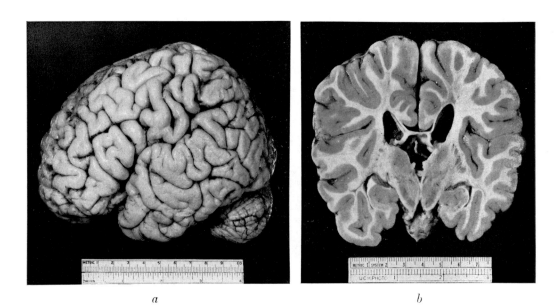

a

b

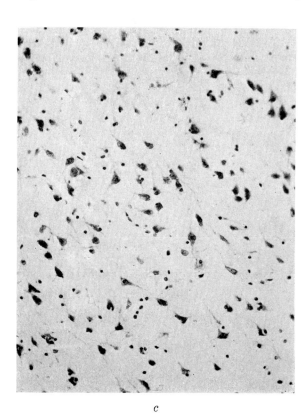

c

PLATE VIII.—Malformation, non-specific: (a) external appearance, (b) coronal section, and (c) cytoarchitecture of cortex, Nissl method × 164

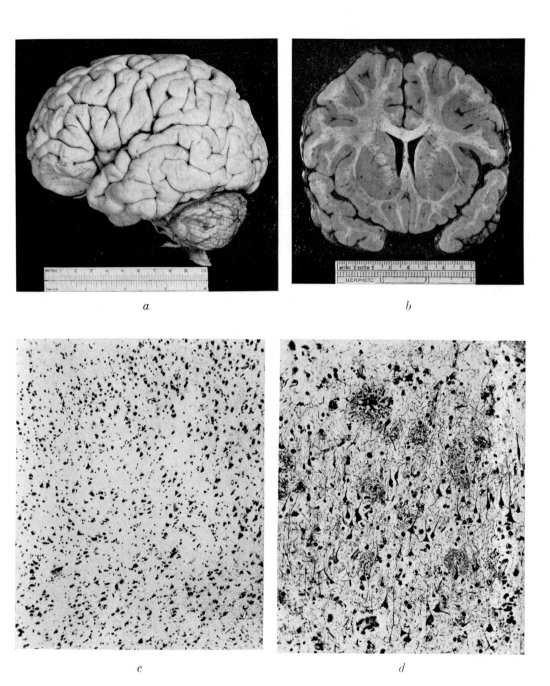

PLATE IX.—Mongolism: (*a*) external appearance, (*b*) coronal section, (*c*) cytoarchitecture of cortex, Nissl method × 71, and (*d*) senile plaques and neurofibrillary changes of cortex, von Braunmuhl silver nitrate method × 142

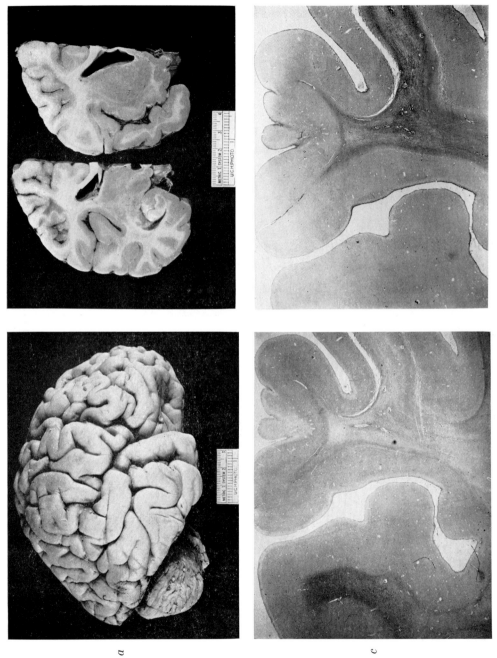

PLATE X.—Phenylketonuria: (a) external appearance, (b) coronal sections (showing subcortical areas of demyelination), (c) focal demyelination, Weil myelin method, and (d) corresponding focal gliosis, Holzer method

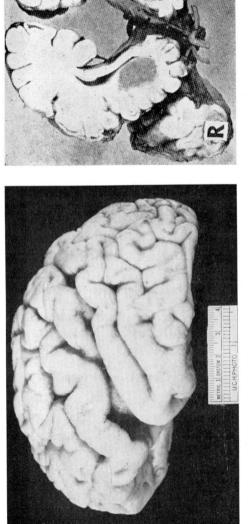

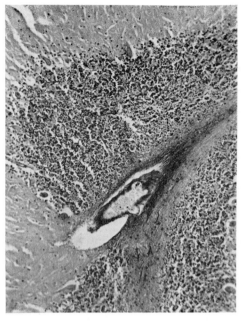

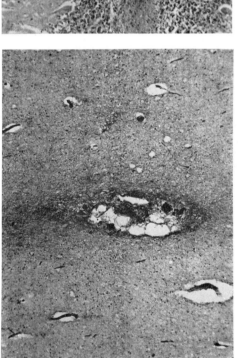

PLATE XI.—Malformation in cases with history of maternal rubella: (*a*) pachymicropolygyria, (*b*) agenesis of corpus callosum, (*c*) perivascular gliosis in cerebral white matter, Holzer method × 73, and (*d*) perivascular gliosis in cerebellar white matter, Holzer method × 73

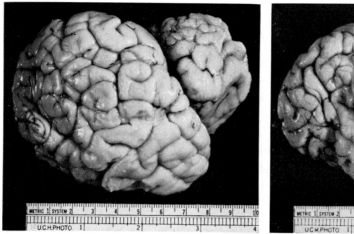
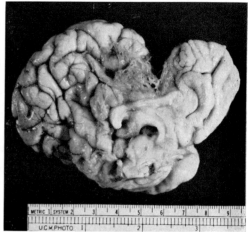

a

b

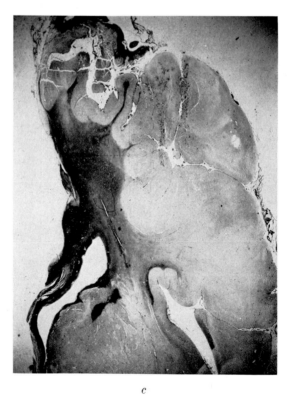

c

PLATE XII.—Malformation in case with congenitally acquired herpes simplex infection: (a) porencephaly, (b) destructive lesion at porencephalic site, and (c) mixed picture of micropolygyria and gliosis, Holzer method

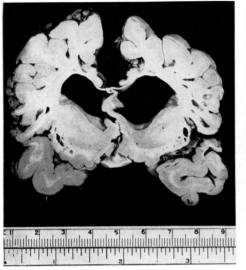

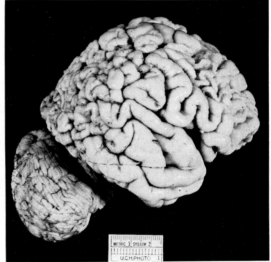

a

b

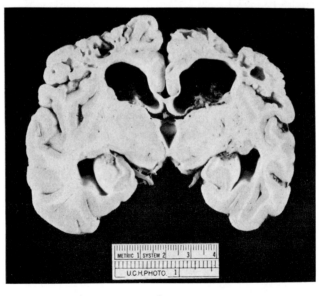

c

PLATE XIII.—Cases with primary subcortical pathology—gross features: (*a*) diffuse sclerosis of white matter and status marmoratus of corpus striatum, (*b*) sclerotic microgyria, external appearance, and (*c*) same in cross section. (Same types of cases in Plates XIV, XV, and XVI as in Plate XIII, microscopic features.)

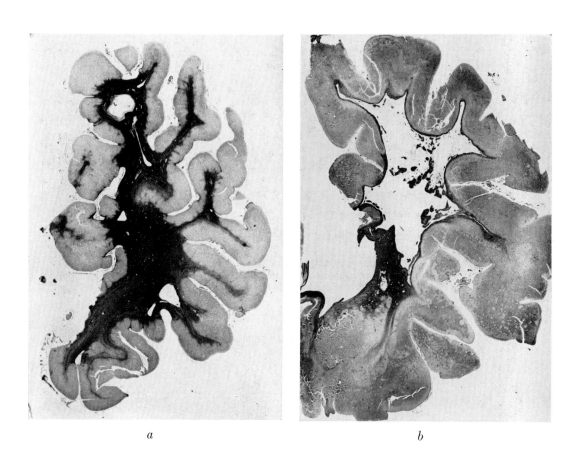

a   *b*

PLATE XIV.—(*a*) diffuse sclerosis of white matter, Holzer method, and (*b*) diffuse cystic degeneration of white matter, Holzer method

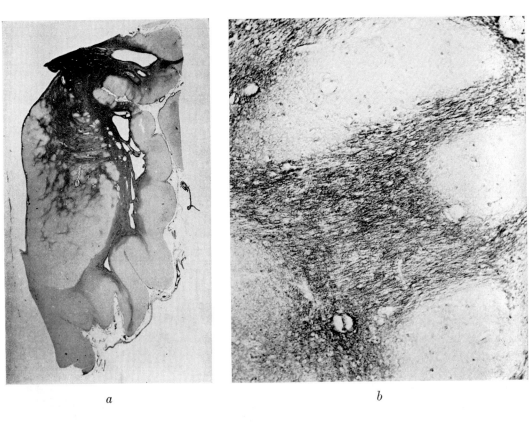

a b

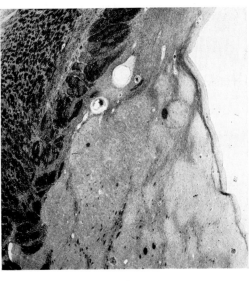

c

PLATE XV.—Status marmoratus of basal ganglia: (a) and (b) Holzer method × 4 and 116, and (c) Weigert myelin method × 15

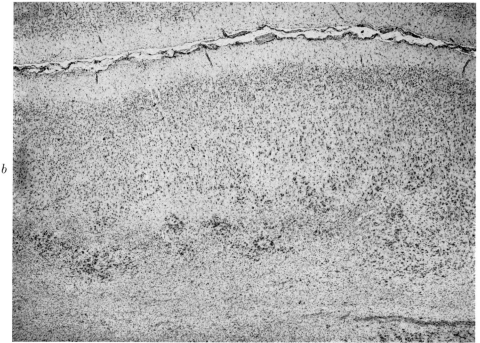

PLATE XVI.—Status marmoratus of cortex: (a) Holzer method × 15 and (b) Nissl method × 40

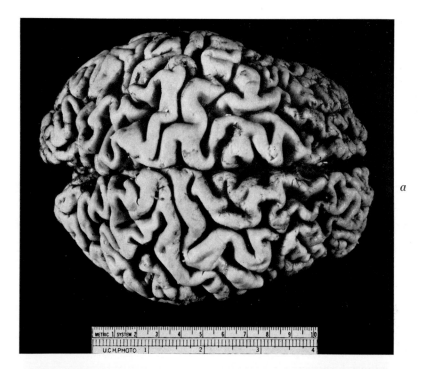

a

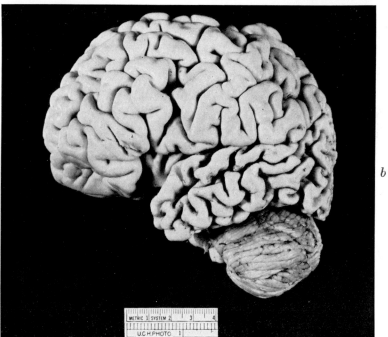

b

PLATE XVII.—Cases with primary cortical pathology—gross features: (*a*) diffuse atrophy and (*b*) focal atrophy temporo-occipital region

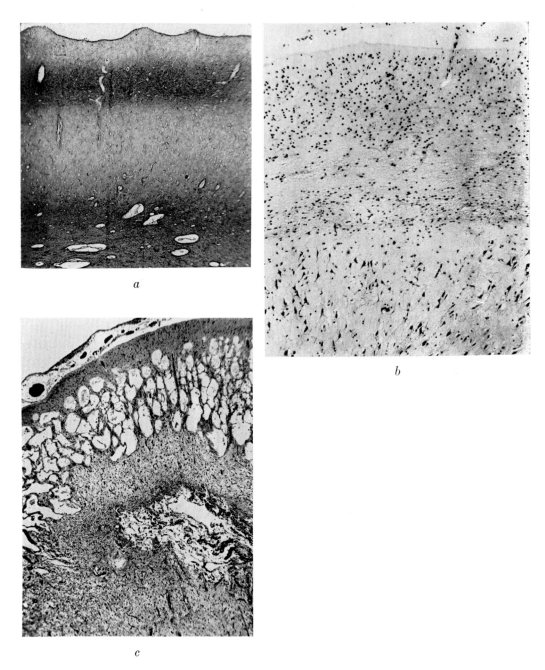

a

b

c

PLATE XVIII.—Same types of cases as in Plate XVII—microscopic features: (*a*) laminar sclerosis of cortex, Holzer method × 23 and (*b*) Nissl method × 81, (*c*) cystic degeneration of cortex, hematoxylin and eosin method × 23

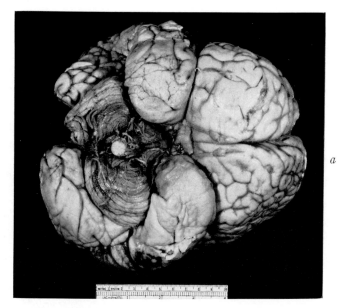

a

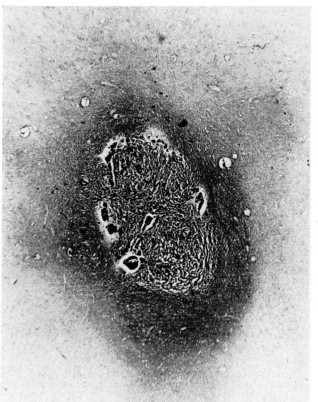

b

PLATE XIX.—Hydrocephalus secondary to (*a*) basal arachnoiditis and (*b*) gliosis of aqueduct of Sylvius

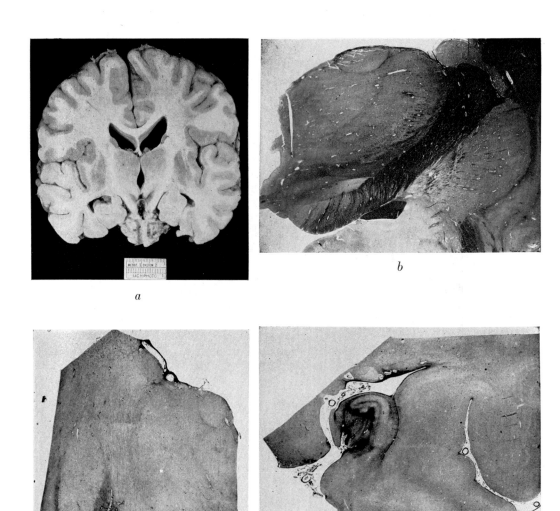

PLATE XX.—Sequelae of kernicterus: (*a*) gross appearance, showing symmetrical atrophy of globus pallidus, subthalamic bodies, and Ammon's horn, (*b*) demyelination of globus pallidus and subthalamic body, Weil myelin method, (*c*) gliosis of globus pallidus and subthalamic body, Holzer method, and (*d*) gliosis of Ammon's horn, Holzer method

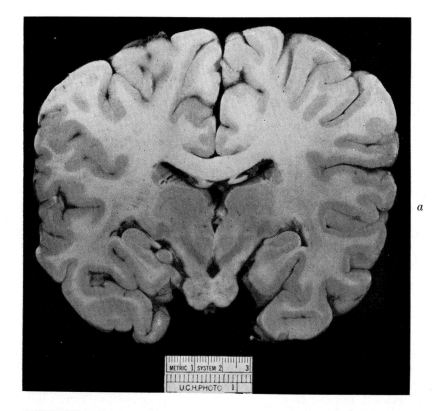

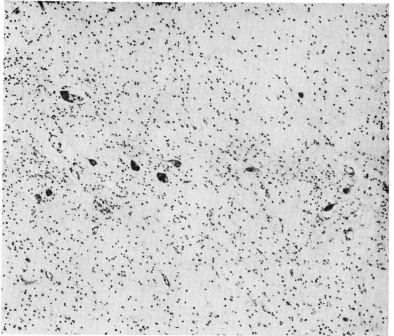

PLATE XXI.—Chronic lethargic encephalitis: (*a*) gross appearance, showing depigmentation of substantia nigra, and (*b*) degeneration of substantia nigra, Nissl method × 100

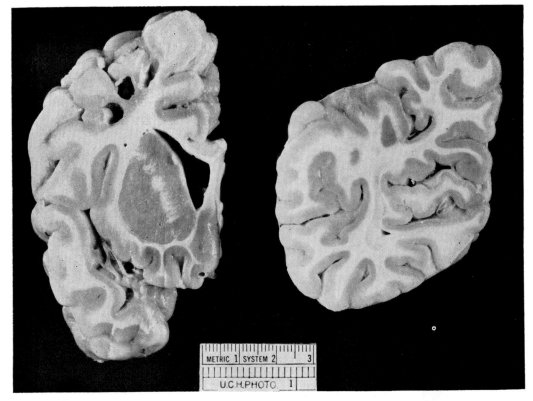

a

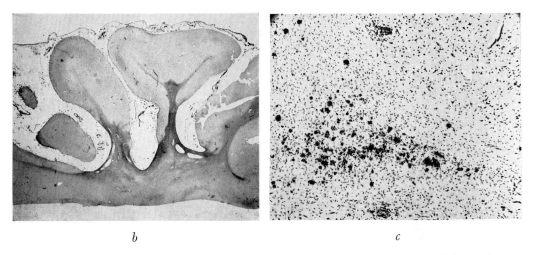

b   *c*

PLATE XXII.—Chronic Western equine encephalitis: (*a*) gross appearance, (*b*) focal gliosis of cortex and white matter, Holzer method, and (*c*) focal calcification and inflammatory lesions, Nissl method × 33

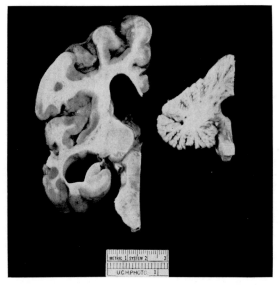

a

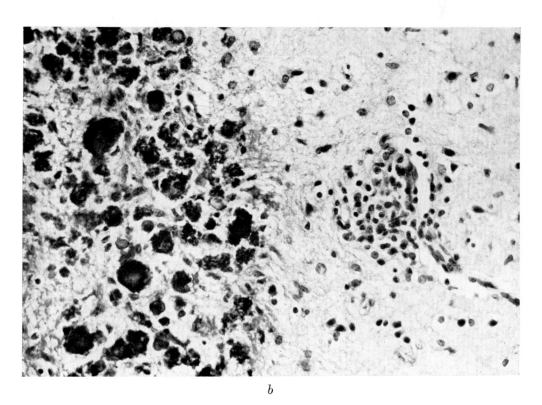

b

PLATE XXIII.—Chronic toxoplasmosis: (*a*) gross appearance; (*b*) focal calcification and inflammatory lesions, Nissl method × 400

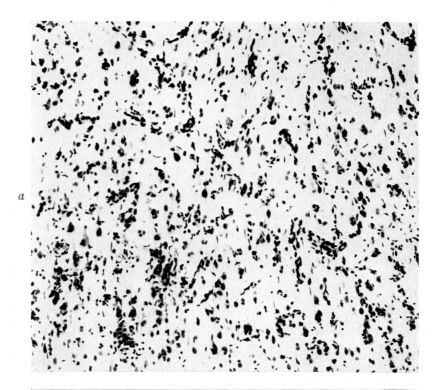

a

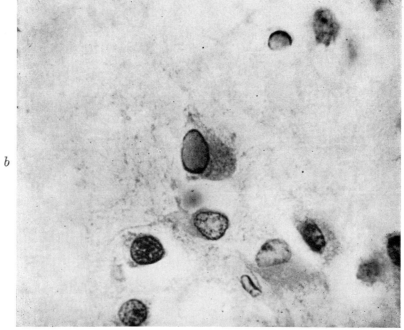

b

PLATE XXIV.—Inclusion encephalitis: (a) subacute inflammation of cortex, Nissl method × 170, and (b) intranuclear inclusion bodies, hematoxylin and eosin method × 850

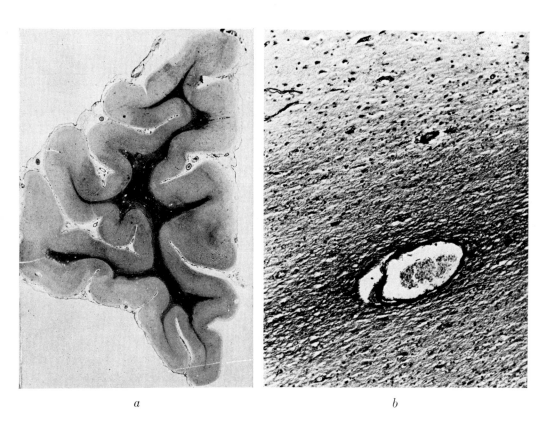

a   b

PLATE XXV.—Post-measles chronic encephalomyelitis: (a) diffuse gliosis of cerebral white matter, Holzer method × 3.3, and (b) perivenous gliosis, Holzer method × 121

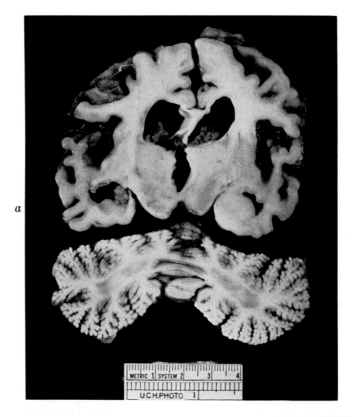

a

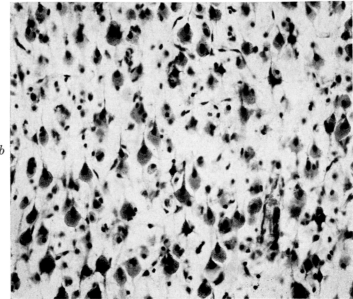

b

PLATE XXVI.—Amaurotic family idiocy: (*a*) gross appearance, showing cerebral and cerebellar atrophy, and (*b*) accumulation of lipids in
neurons of cortex, Nissl method × 225

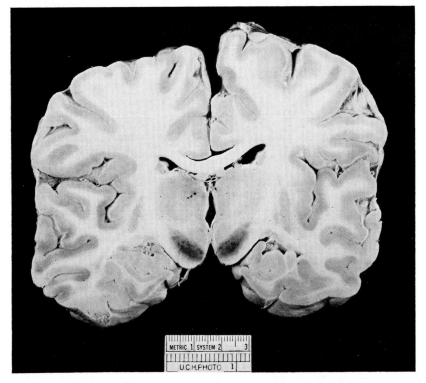

a

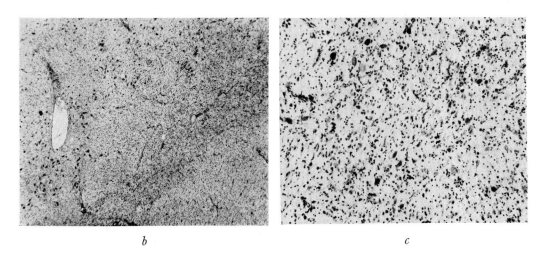

b   *c*

PLATE XXVII.—Hallervorden-Spatz disease: (*a*) pigmentation of substantia nigra, (*b*) deposits of pigment in zona rubra, Nissl method × 19, and (*c*) same, Nissl method × 80

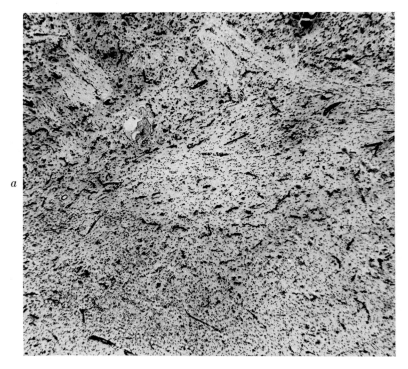

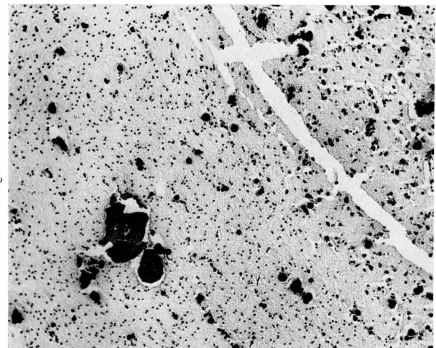

PLATE XXVIII.—Fahr's disease: (*a*) deposition of calcium in basal ganglia, Nissl method × 75, and (*b*) in cerebral cortex and white matter, Nissl method × 100

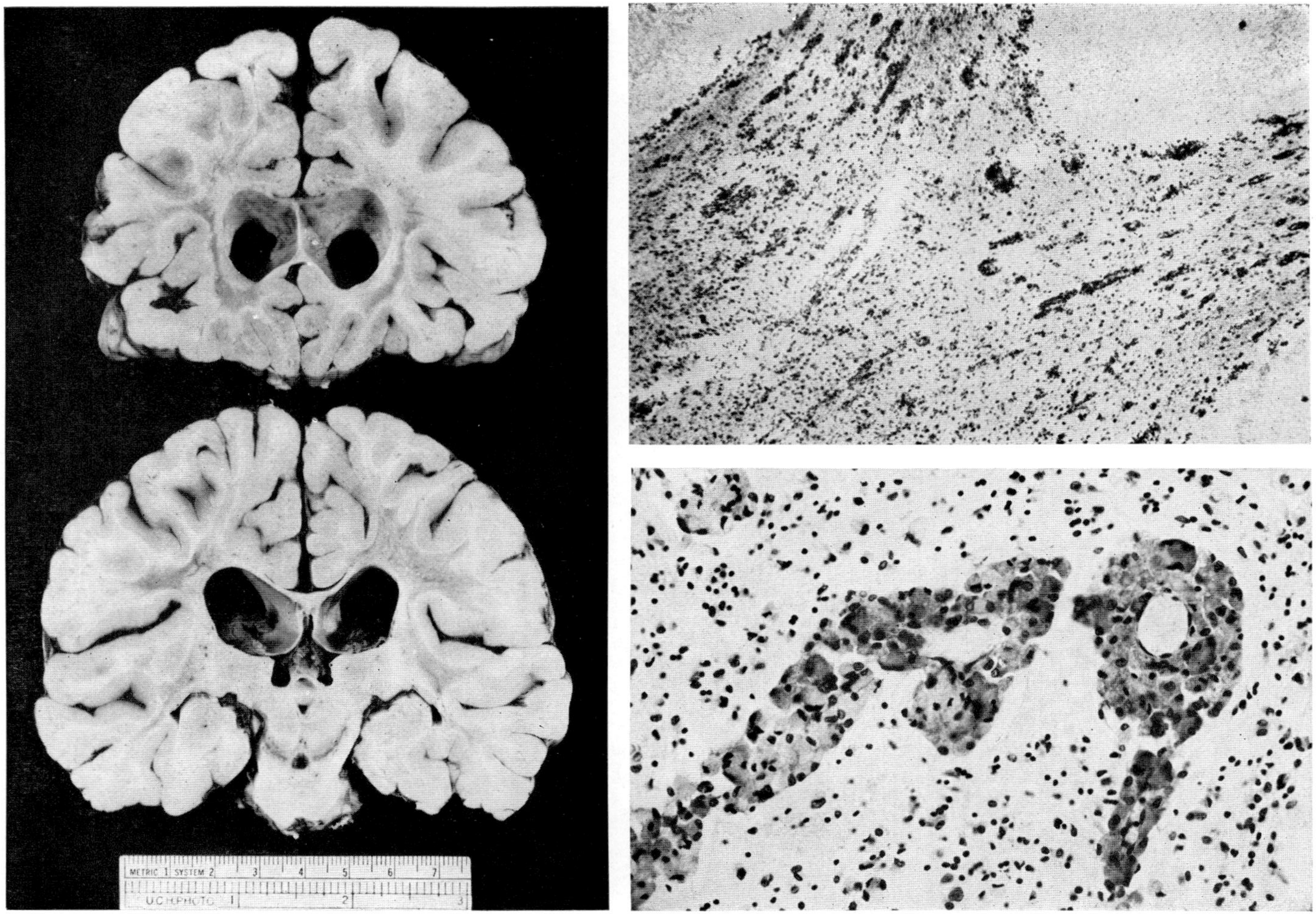

PLATE XXIX.—Diffuse demyelinating diseases: (a) gross appearance, (b) sudanophilic form with lipid deposits in white matter, scarlet red method × 87, and (c) Krabbe's form with perivascular globoid cells × 182

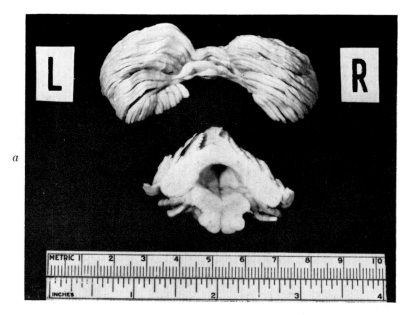

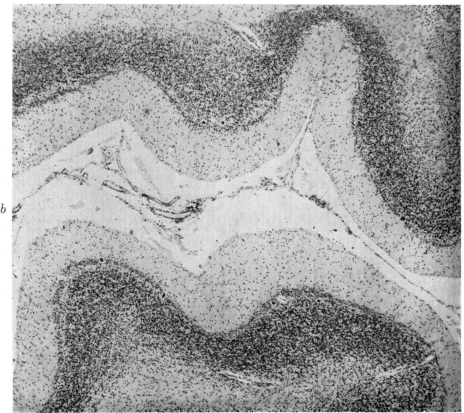

PLATE XXX.—Primary cerebellar degeneration: (*a*) gross appearance and (*b*) diffuse loss of Purkinje cells, Nissl method × 34.

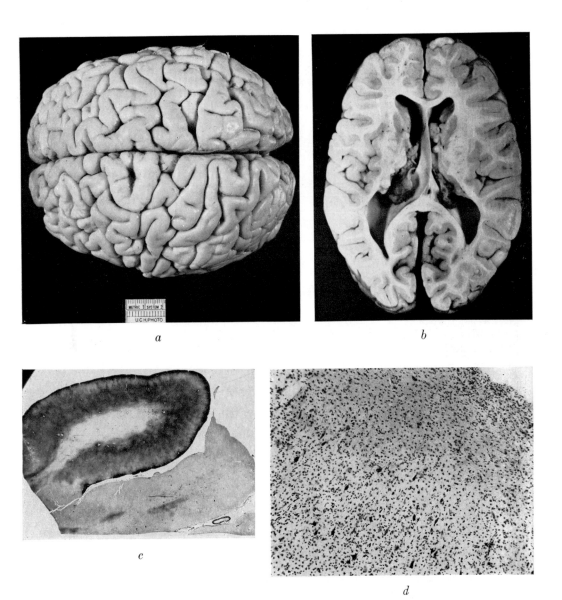

a   *b*

c   *d*

PLATE XXXI.—Tuberous sclerosis: (*a*) external appearance of brain, showing cortical nodules, (*b*) horizontal section, showing periventricular nodules, (*c*) cortical nodule, characterized by hyperplastic gliosis, Holzer method, and (*d*) cortical nodule, showing proliferation of glial cells and giant neurons, Nissl method × 60

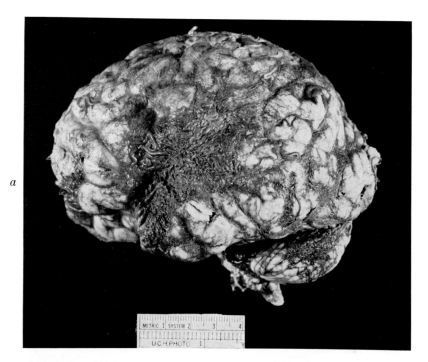

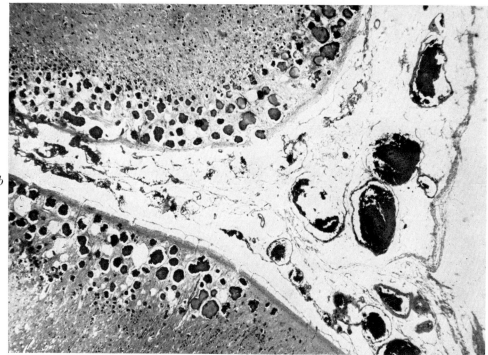

PLATE XXXII.—Angiomatosis (Sturge-Weber syndrome): (a) external appearance and (b) proliferation of meningeal vessels and calcification of underlying cortex, hematoxylin and eosin method × 28

BEHAVIORAL DISTURBANCES IN THE MENTALLY RETARDED

Delton C. Beier

I. Introduction

The purpose of this chapter is to review and evaluate the writings and research on behavioral disturbances in the mentally retarded. No attempt will be made to provide an index to the entire literature related to the field. The general goal is to present a picture of the major considerations, trends, and points of view that might be essential for an understanding of the past and present status of this area of study and to suggest future directions that research might take.

The association of mental retardation and behavioral disturbances has a long history; in fact, primitive notions of psychopathology did not differentiate between them. Despite their many similarities and the fact that they had been equated they eventually did become separated in the thinking of observers of human behavior. Students of psychopathology in the late eighteenth and early nineteenth centuries, stimulated by significant advances in the fields of anatomy and physiology as well as by humanitarian advances in the care and treatment of the psychotic and mentally retarded, became specifically concerned with the association of mental retardation and behavioral disturbances. Early writers on this topic were primarily concerned with the nature and frequency of the coexistence of these two conditions and about matters of differential diagnosis. Generally speaking, their study of this problem was not systematic, and many of their conclusions were based on relatively casual observations and speculation rather than on data. Nevertheless, they stimulated interest in the subject and presented many of the essential problems related to the association of mental retardation and behavioral disturbances.

II. Basic Problems and Issues

Behavioral disturbances among the mentally retarded are of interest for the same reasons that such disorders are of interest when they occur in the general population. Basically, behavioral disturbances are studied (1) in order to understand them as natural phenomena, (2) in order to develop or determine explanatory systems that best fit the data (although such behavioral patterns may seem chaotic and bizarre, they must be explicable by principles already discovered or still unknown), (3) for the light they may shed on normal behavior when viewed as exaggerations, deficiencies, or distortions of such behavior, and (4) in order that the probability of halting or reversing these processes becomes significantly increased through knowledge of how individuals become emotionally disturbed. In addition to these general reasons for studying psychopathology in any population, its occurrence in the mentally retarded raise special problems in matters of etiology, differential diagnosis, prognosis, and treatment.

One of the major problems of any research or review of the literature in the areas of mental retardation or behavioral disturbances is one of defining the populations under consideration. Generally useful and meaningful definitions of mental retardation are given by Beier (1959) and Heber (1961). As Bijou (1963) observes, however, the substitution of "psychological," "developmental," or "behavioral" for the term "mental" would make definitions more meaningful. It should also be pointed out that mental retardation is not a single disease entity but a set of symptoms developing from many different etiologic factors.

A generally acceptable description of the behaviorally disturbed might read as follows: The behaviorally disturbed are those whose adjustment patterns are such that they are in serious conflict with themselves, their families, or their community. Although not necessarily mentally retarded, they are persons whose effectiveness and efficiency are so impaired that they have varying degrees of difficulty dealing with emotional or stress situations, and they display various degrees of peculiarity in adaptive behavior. Furthermore, they are usually unhappy or uncomfortable with themselves and others and show perceptual, thinking, and communication difficulties and distortions.

It is generally agreed that mental retardates as a group have a higher incidence of behavioral disturbance than is found in the general population. This association between retardation and behavior disturbances has been of continuing and increasing interest, and their coexistence in the same individuals raises several basic questions regarding this relationship. The major hypotheses regarding this association are as follows: (1) Behavioral disturbances occur among the mentally retarded for the same reasons that they occur in persons of normal intelligence. (2) Both behavioral disturbances and mental retardation are the results of basic pathological states or dysfunctions of an anatomical, neurological, endocrinological, or biochemical nature. (3) The mentally retarded, because of their deficiencies and inadequa-cies, are subject to more stresses, frustrations, and conflicts and are consequently more liable to develop behavioral disorders. (4) Many cases labeled "mentally retarded" are primarily, and often profoundly, emotionally disturbed, and the intellectual deficiencies are essentially the result of such disturbances. (5) The mentally retarded, because of their maturational lag, are slower to incorporate notions of right and wrong into personal value systems and are deficient in internal controls; they are consequently apt to exhibit peculiar, inappropriate, or antisocial patterns of behavior such as delinquency or sociopathy.

III. Historical Perspectives

As indicated, mental retardation and behavioral disturbances were regarded as a single disorder in the primitive views of psychopathology. The equating of these deviations was, without doubt, a consequence of the many observable similarities between psychotic reactions and the behavior of the more profoundly retarded. Gradually, psychotic behavior was differentiated from mental retardation, and they were classified separately in the relatively crude nosological systems existing up to and through the eighteenth century. This separation continued until the period of Itard and Seguin, when the latter noted that some cases of idiocy might be complicated by psychoses. He also classified the dominant psychotic reaction patterns found in the mental retardates as being of the over-reactive, aggressive, acting-out variety and the withdrawn, under-reactive type. Following these observations came a period of speculation, reports of clinical observations, as well as more or less systematic census-taking of the simultaneous occurrence of behavioral disturbances and mental retardation in the same individuals. This was a period of crude data-gathering, and hypotheses were developed which led to the alarmist studies typified by the surveys of Dugdale in

1900, Davenport and Danielson in 1912, and Goddard in 1912. These and similar studies resulted in views of mental retardation as a stream of malevolency from which flowed delinquency and crime, illegitimacy and degeneracy, pauperism and disharmony, as the source of problems and burdens in every phase of human existence.

After the publication of these surveys and their "startling revelations," social and legislative action took the form of eugenic measures for the prevention of the basic condition of retardation and its sequelae, which had been so ominously portrayed. Enchanted with the rediscovery of Mendel's experiments on heredity, the general assumption was made that at least 50 per cent of the cases of mental retardation were the result of genetic inheritance. These beliefs and attitudes eventuated in the intensification of preventative control through segregation and sterilization techniques. The development and expansion of segregation facilities were, in a sense, the last enthusiastic stand of the "custodial period" in the management of mental retardation. Sterilization was a significant transitional point in the movement to maintain the mentally retarded in, or return them to, the social environments from which they came.

General institutionalization as a panacea had long been suspect, and although it is still a very real necessity, the institutions themselves have lost much of their custodial character and have become more oriented to treatment, training, and research. Sterilization, though probably not making a great deal of difference in the prevention of mental retardation, did foster the development and more general acceptance of local responsibility for the management and education of the mentally retarded.

Along with these items of general background, several other advances should be mentioned to clarify the historical perspectives. The development of taxonomic devices for the classification of plants and animals provided models for the classification of abnormal behavior patterns. The nosological contributions of Kraepelin and his modifiers provided students of psychopathology with a frame of reference and related hypotheses to be proven or rejected through research. Advances in anatomy, physiology, bacteriology, and biochemistry established important relationships between function and structure as well as new techniques for testing various hypotheses about behavior and related biological activities. New concepts and advances in the field of general pathology were reflected in psychopathology and in the development of the somatogenic and psychogenic points of view. These extensions of knowledge and the development of new research techniques, along with the dynamic and poetic theoretical formulations of psychoanalysis by Freud, have all had important and stimulating effects on the study of retardation. Along with these developments, the evolution of psychophysical and statistical methods and the subsequent construction of psychometric tools made possible, in the second decade of the twentieth century, a broader scientific and professional evaluation of the complexities of the association of behavioral disturbances and mental retardation.

IV. Literature Relevant to the Problem

Assumptions about the relationship between mental retardation and the behavioral disturbances have been many and varied. The earliest were based mainly on naturalistic observation, and the later on brief or extended custodial and clinical contacts. It must be remembered that only years after the hospital reforms of Pinel were the records of institutions of value and use in systematic research. Reviews of the earlier literature have been made by Butler (1937), Goddard (1912), Greene (1930, 1933), Hayman (1939), Herskovitz and Plesset (1941), O'Gorman (1954), Pollock (1944, 1945), Potter (1927c), Vanuxem (1935), and Whitten (1938).

Tredgold in 1908 summarized the general views of preceding periods and added his own observations and studies. In this text he estimates that 8 per cent of all mentally retarded in England were certifiable as "insane." In the same volume he emphasizes the "proneness to insanity" of the mentally retarded and estimates the predisposition of the mentally retarded to insanity as "twenty six times the ordinary population." The principal psychoses he discusses are, in his own terms, mania, melancholia, stupor, alternating insanity, delusional insanity, general paralysis, and epileptic insanity; he also makes special reference to insanity in imbeciles and idiots. He considered alcohol and severe fright among the most significant precipitating causes of attacks of insanity in mental retardates. His handling of moral deficiency and criminal aments was a fading reflection of the "moralistic psychiatry" which typified the nineteenth century.

In the seventh edition of his textbook on mental retardation, Tredgold (1947) discusses mental disturbances among the mentally retarded under the headings of psychoneurosis, psychosis, and dementia. He regards hysterical manifestations as the most frequently seen neurotic pattern, followed by anxiety states and obsessive-compulsive reactions. Of the psychoses, mania is most frequently associated with mental retardation, then anxiety, depression, and melancholia. Tredgold reports delusions "fairly common"; however, in the mentally retarded they rarely appeared as well systematized as in paranoia. He concludes that at least 1 per cent of all defectives are schizophrenic aments. Dementia, as indicated, is discussed separately; he suggests that dementia or mental deterioration usually occurs earlier in mental retardates than in the general population,

and the eventual picture is that of the deteriorated schizophrenic. At this period he relates "moral deficiency" to deficiencies of control of the "compelling power of instincts and innate tendencies" and abnormalities of impulse; nevertheless, he concludes that only a small number are genuine psychopaths.

Considerable space has been devoted to a summarization of the views of Tredgold because his views typify the attitude generally prevailing toward, and facts and fictions about, and the behavioral disturbances in the mentally retarded. Of course, many other opinions have been expressed about this association, as suggested by the number of reviews noted above, and the more important will be discussed under headings related to specific psychopathological categories. In addition, several other studies and opinions must be cited to illustrate some of the more general considerations and research attacks on the problem.

Potter in 1927 (1927a) refers to mental retardation as "a condition of social pathology" and suggests that the social pathology is dependent on an abnormality of intelligence which, in turn, is based on structural defects. Herskovitz and Plesset (1941) report a study of eighteen cases of mental retardation with behavioral disorders among which were psychotic episodes, rage reactions and hyperactivity with aggresiveness, apprehensiveness, and gradual deterioration of habit patterns. They also report psychoses due to the effects of degenerative processes occurring during the normal senium. Observing that any psychosis which occurs in persons of normal intelligence can occur in the mentally retarded, they report manic-depressive and schizophrenic psychoses occurring in those with IQ's of less than 80, but none below IQ 50. They conclude that mental illness results from a failure to maintain equilibrium among the dynamic tendencies of personality and, "From the writers' studies, it appears that before such failure can result in a "functional" psychosis the individuals' intelligence quotient should be at least 50."

Penrose (1938), in a clinical and genetic study of 1,280 cases of mental retardation, reports 132 with psychoneuroses and perversions, 24 with affective psychosis, and 48 with schizophrenia. According to his evaluation, only one person showed depressive trends. In his 1954 volume he concludes that mental illness is one of the most important contributory factors in the selection of mental retardates for institutionalization. Interestingly enough, a recent study directed by Saenger (1960) reports that: "With the exception of the degree of retardation itself, the behavior problems of the retarded person taking place out of the home is the single most important factor determining institutionalization. This was particularly noticeable among the retarded whose intelligence quotients exceeded 50." Penrose also arrives at conclusions similar to those of Tredgold in regard to the psychoses. He further notes that, of the major psychoses, schizophrenia is the one most intimately associated with retardation and that the personal history of the individual is vital for differential diagnosis. Regarding the affective psychoses he points out that although they do occur in the retarded, they are milder than with individuals of average ability and that it is difficult to distinguish mild manic attacks in retardates from hysterical reactions. He also observes that since the manic depressive psychoses generally occur late in life they are rarely a contributing factor in commitments.

Pollock (1944), analyzing 444 admissions of the "dull" to hospitals, reports that 39.6 per cent had transient psychotic episodes of excitement, 18.4 per cent schizophrenia, 9.9 per cent epileptic psychoses, and 1.6 per cent were diagnosed as having manic depressive psychoses. Weaver (1946), analyzing a considerably

different population of 8,000 wartime soldiers with IQ's of less than 75, reports on the incidence of maladjustment in this group from a military environment. His results indicate that 44 per cent of the males had to be discharged on psychiatric grounds and 38 per cent of the women were discharged for psychosomatic or disciplinary reasons. He states: "A majority of these dischargees had personality deficiencies, being emotionally unstable, aggressive, antisocial or schizoid and developing anxiety or hysteria or malingering under stress."

In a study of the relationships between behavior disorders in children and mental retardation, Neuer (1947) evaluated 300 new or readmitted patients in a state institution and found 7 cases of manic depressive psychosis and 39 classifiable as neurotic, characterized by restlessness, anxiety, enuresis, and compulsions. He distinguishes between various types and reports that 39 per cent of the admissions were organic, 28 per cent neuropsychotic (having a history of major or minor psychoses), and the remainder were of the simple type with no history of neuroses, psychoses, or other pathologies. The latter were the variety designated by Penrose as the subcultural type. Examination of the social, economic, and familial histories of these admissions led to the conclusion that approximately 70 per cent of the organic type, 74 per cent of the neuropsychotic, and 92 per cent of the simple variety were derived from substandard economic conditions. Furthermore, he found that 49 per cent of organic idiots came from average or higher homes, about 77 per cent of those classified as morons came from substandard economic conditions, and 45 per cent of the latter group had parents who were divorced or separated, or were reared by step-parents, in foster homes, or in residential institutions. He also points out that the earlier in the life history of the individual the behavioral disturbances begin and the longer they last, the more serious will be the consequences on the final intellectual level. A 1951 report of the New York State Department of Mental Hygiene shows that from a total of 84,672 patients classified in this census, 3,072 were mentally retarded with behavior disorders.

In connection with these and similar studies, it should be pointed out that no projections can be made for any general populations, since the subjects of these surveys had already been selected or segregated by special psychological, legal, social, or economic factors and are, therefore, not representative of more general populations.

An article by Goldstein (1948) and texts by Clarke and Clarke (1958), Kugelmass (1954) and Michal-Smith (1957) present the various types of mental retardation, associated behavioral disorders, and problems of differential diagnosis, treatment, and other aspects of specialized services required for their management. These works are important because they discuss the major hypotheses and assumptions regarding mental retardation and associated disorders as well as what might be considered the most important bases for decision-making related to the management and treatment of the various types of retardates.

Robertson and Wibberly (1952), in a study of differences between dementia and mental defect in middle-aged housewives, suggest the need for the development of tests to distinguish dull demented women from the depressed but undeteriorated mental defective. O'Gorman (1954) concludes that some "idiocy results from a psychotic process which also produces catatonia." He suggests that this syndrome should be designated "idiocy due to catatonic psychosis" and argues that the condition has a psychogenic etiology because of the absence of signs of diseases of the central nervous system, the lack of congenital stigmata, their normal appearance, and negative family histories. He speculates, along with others, that one should consider

juvenile schizophrenia as a possible cause of some mental retardation rather than as a sequela. In a study of rearing practices and "mental dwarfism," Bourne (1955) found that 10 per cent of the severely retarded aments in Fountain Hospital, England, seemed to be protophrenics whose deficiency resulted, at least partially, from psychologically unhealthy backgrounds. His group also had no organic pathologies, and he defines protophrenia as a psychogenic failure of ego-formation.

MacGillivray (1956) evaluated the cases of 209 male and female idiots for psychoses and agrees with Hayman (1939) and others that, as we go up the intellectual scale, the various psychoses tend to separate out and become more clearly defined. In addition, he states a preference for the original classifications of psychoses in the mentally retarded proposed by Seguin—hyperkinetic and hypokinetic. The clinical picture of the hyperkinetic is dominated by excitement, ecstasy, impulsiveness, destructiveness, echolalia, and stereotypies. In the hypokinetic one finds autism, waxy flexibility, causeless weeping, a fetal attitude, negativism, slow response to pain, somnolence, and, rarely, stupor. MacGillivray observes that in a few cases these forms may alternate from time to time, and in either condition the idiot "gradually manifests features of deterioration, becomes degraded, destructive, inaccessible, loses whatever speech he may possess, and crude, bizarre rhythmic movements become prominent." He did not find that characteristics of catatonia dominated the clinical picture and consequently preferred the term "Larval Psychosis of Idiocy" to Earl's designation of "Primitive Catatonic Psychosis of Idiocy" (Earl, 1934), which will be discussed under the heading of schizophrenia.

In 1950, Wortis reviewed Soviet psychiatry and referred to mental retardation mainly in terms of educational approaches. Wollen reviewed the status of mental retardation in Poland and the Soviet Union in 1958. He reports that mental retardation is not considered a single nosological entity but a group of symptoms. In Poland and the Soviet Union, "There is firm belief that mental defect predisposes to other organic and functional disorders because it is quite common to find among mental deficients, chronic alcoholics, epileptics, schizophrenics, or even affective psychotics." The belief is also held that "Hysteria, hypochondriasis and other neurotic symptoms may cover mental defect, which may become manifest when symptoms are removed by treatment."

A recent survey conducted among inpatients on the incidence of mental disorders of mental retardates is reported by Craft (1959*a*). His results are similar to those of the 1938 study by Penrose. In this study of mental retardates in the age range sixteen to sixty, 22, or 7 per cent, were characterized as having mental illnesses, and 104, or 33 per cent, were classified as having personality disorders. The total population studied included 324 cases. In his conclusions Craft notes that personality disturbances are common and that true depressive illnesses among the mentally retarded are rare.

It would appear from these general studies and observations that in the mentally retarded populations studied there is a higher incidence of behavioral disturbances than would be found in the general population. There also appears to be general agreement that of the major psychoses, schizophrenia is most frequently associated with mental retardation and depressive psychoses only infrequently.

V. Special Behavioral Disturbances Associated with Mental Retardation and the Effectiveness of Therapy

schizophrenia

1. *General.*—From almost any point of view, schizophrenia is the psychosis most intimately associated with retardation. Probably more has been written about this association than about any other; it is also true that speculation and confusion has surrounded etiological, diagnostic, prognostic, and treatment considerations of this association. In addition to the general reviews of the relationships between mental retardation and behavioral disturbances, extensive reviews of the association of schizophrenia and mental retardation have been made by Bergman, Waller, and Marchand (1951), Bromberg (1934), James (1939), and Kallmann *et al.* (1940–41).

In 1896, Kraepelin coined the term "pfropfhebephrenia" to designate the condition in which dementia praecox was engrafted on mental retardation. After Bleuler's introduction of the term schizophrenia, the same condition was referred to as pfropfschizophrenia. Although the basic concept is a useful one, the term itself, probably because of its almost insurmountable orthographic challenges, has never received much use. A. L. Beier, writing in 1919, agreed with the general views of Kraepelin and the early opinions of Tredgold, that although any kind of psychosis can occur with retardation, schizophrenia has the highest incidence of association because of "common cerebral inferiority." In this view, he has been supported by Greene (1933), James (1939), and others. Other views have their enthusiastic supporters and Kallmann *et al.* (1940–41) indicated that they had "no real objection to the classification of a genuine schizophrenic psychosis occurring coincidently in a basically feebleminded person as pfropfschizophrenia. However, this diagnosis should not be taken as an indication that the two conditions are causally related."

LeVann (1950) presented some interesting speculations and reported that among idiots and lower grade imbeciles one sees a wide range of schizophrenic symptomatology. He stated that the "picture is not regressive" and that in schizophrenia the mind acquires "an archaic form of thinking which in the adult is admixed with cultural experiences and in the idiot shows itself uncomplicated with little distortion." He speculated that low-grade idiots may be "a remote proto-type of *homo sapiens*" and that "this prototype not being adaptable to its environment ultimately died out" but is still carried in our germ plasm as a recessive characteristic. He concluded that the similarities between idiots and schizophrenics is so startling in many cases that a new bit of nomenclature might be devised for such idiots and until that time suggests referring to them as "congenital schizophrenics."

The distinctions between mental retardation and the mentally ill as well as the definitions of psychosis as legally used in adult psychiatry are not meaningful in child psychiatric administration according to Benda, Farrell, and Chipman (1951). Furthermore, they believe that "cerebral defect or dysfunction present at birth is more likely to produce a picture of retarded development while the same process superimposed later, after a period of normal development is more likely to induce a picture of disorganization that is called psychotic."

A general review of the syndrome of schizophrenia was made by Bellak in 1958; the pathological anatomy of the schizophrenias was reviewed by David in 1957; and the biochemical aspects were reviewed by Richter in 1957. Kety (1959*a*, *b*) in a recent two-part review of biochemical theories of schizophrenia, suggested sources of error which exist in much of the research on schizophrenia. Some of the sources he listed are (1) the chronicity of the disease and the relatively long periods of institutionalization during which the schizophrenic will not only pass from age group to age group but will also be subjected to a variety of diets in terms of quality and quantity, (2) the many different kinds of therapies to which they may have been exposed including biochemical, physical, and psychological,

(3) the assumption of homogeneity among schizophrenics in terms of either common etiology or pathogenesis ("Errors involved in sampling from heterogeneous populations may help to explain the high frequency with which findings of one group fail to be confirmed by those of another."), (4) physiological and biochemical changes which may be secondary to the psychological states of patients (emotional stresses and their effects on the organism should be recognized sometimes as playing a primary or etiological role), and (5) the subjective biases of investigators and their hypotheses, which may affect the design of experiments and contaminate the data as well as the interpretation of the results. He observed: "It is both interesting and important to note that even if the conclusions of both the genetic and the environmental approaches to the etiology of schizophrenic psychoses are accepted uncritically, they are not mutually exclusive." Meehl's speculations (1962) are compatible with this view. Investigations in the field of mental retardation are subject to errors similar to those noted by Kety. In research on the relationship between schizophrenia and mental retardation, the sources of error and the methodological difficulties are compounded, and findings may be distorted by either diagnostic or prognostic errors or by both.

2. *Childhood schizophrenia and related disturbances.*—Although behavioral disturbances in children have been observed from ancient times, there has been considerable reluctance to accept the existence of psychoses in children. Seguin, of course, wrote on the association of behavioral disorders and mental retardation; however, the generally prevailing view has been much nearer to one expressed by Rush in 1812. He believed that psychoses rarely affected children under puberty because the effects of their experiences and impressions were too transient to result in per-

manent behavioral pathology. Toward the end of the nineteenth century there seemed to be a rather general acceptance that major psychological disorders can and do occur in children; Browne (1859–60), for example, presented cases from various age groups and concluded that any of the forms and degrees of behavioral disturbances that affect adults could be observed in infants and children. Krafft-Ebing in 1904 stated that psychotic disorders in children were generally the result of organic or somatic factors. Sachs (1895) was of the opinion that the differences between psychotic manifestations in adults and children were due to the incompleteness of development in children and special and unusual sensitivities and irritabilities. Mills (1898) also agreed with Browne but noted that some forms such as paranoia and melancholia occurred only infrequently. In a review of the literature on childhood mental diseases in America before 1900, Rubenstein (1948) observed that although there was considerable speculation in the field, original research was rare, and significant theoretical contributions minimal. In fact, he concluded that child psychiatry was really non-existent in America before the twentieth century.

Kraepelin (1919) concluded that certain cases diagnosed as idiots were probably very early cases of dementia praecox because of the similarity in symptomatology. Richmond in 1932 suggested that many children who are thought of as mentally retarded often display a deterioration comparable to that found in the organic psychoses.

As a generally acceptable diagnostic category, childhood schizophrenia has a relatively short history—probably less than forty years. Of course, there were early observations such as those of A. L. Beier (1919–20), Greene (1930), and Potter (1933b). Potter, for example, noted that: "A careful study from a psychodynamic approach of patients in institutions for mental deficiency might demonstrate that schizophrenia in children is not as rare as now generally believed." Bellak (1948), in a review of the literature on schizophrenia from 1936 to 1946, listed only 54 articles on childhood schizophrenia while Ekstein, Bryant, and Friedman (1958), in their review of the following decade, listed 542 articles. They also point out that the number of articles related to therapy has increased considerably.

The extensive investigations and writings of such workers as Benda, Bender, Kallmann, Kanner, Kasanin, and Mahler have certainly established the concept of childhood schizophrenia; however, a review of the literature certainly gives the impression of considerable conceptual imperialism and partisanship regarding its nosology and etiology. Evidence and speculations about etiologic factors range all the way from the belief of Kallmann and Roth (1956) in a genetic basis for pre-adolescent schizophrenia to the emphasis of many different environmental variables considered to be important in the development of childhood schizophrenia.

Bender (1941–42) from her studies believes that the schizophrenic child shows evidence of pathology at every level and in every area of integration within the functioning of the central nervous system. In another article (1947) she observed that, "this behavior pathology disturbs the pattern of every functioning field in a characteristic way. The pathology cannot therefore be thought of as focal in the architecture of the central nervous system, but rather as striking at the substratum of integrative functioning or biologically patterned behavior." She stated that the age at which the child develops schizophrenia has differential effects on the child's behavior, especially in the area of speech patterning. Psychological problems typically found among schizophrenic children, according to Bender, are related to "identity, body image and body function, object relationships and interpersonal relationships both in the family and the larger social world, orientation in time and space, meaning of language and anxiety." In the same article she concluded that "anxiety is the nucleus of the schizophrenic problem in the earlier stages." Bender subsequently developed the view that childhood schizophrenia involves a maturational lag characterized by a primitive plasticity at an embryonic level; it is genetically determined and precipitated by some physiological crisis such as birth, and the general reaction to the situation is anxiety which calls forth defense mechanisms (1953, 1954, and other works by Bender listed at the end of the chapter).

In 1943 Kanner (1944) introduced his concept of "early infantile autism" which he referred to as "a unique syndrome recognizable as early as in the first or second year of life." He described children with this syndrome as being unable "to relate themselves in the ordinary way to people and to situations from the beginning of life," characterized by extreme aloneness, and failing to develop language or to use language for the purpose of communication (see also Rank [1949]). Other distinctive features described by Kanner include "an anxiously obsessive desire for the maintenance of sameness" and a stereotyped preoccupation with certain inanimate objects. He also states that these children had "good cognitive potentialities," although they were functioning at an extremely low level. In subsequent reports (1944, 1949, 1952), he described these autistic children as showing no anticipatory postures to being picked up and found in their family background a good deal of obsessiveness. He also stated that this disorder bears no resemblance to Heller's disease or any organic condition and that early infantile autism should probably be regarded as the earliest possible manifestation of childhood schizo-

phrenia. In studies of some of the original children described by Kanner, Eisenberg (1958) reported that of sixty-three children they were able to follow to an average age of fifteen, seventy-three per cent were characterized by mental retardation and/or psychotic behavior.

Bender (1959), in a review of the concept of early childhood autism, suggested that although the concept is a valuable one for describing children who have not developed appropriately in intellectual, social, and ego functions, "it is not a clinical or etiological entity." She concluded: "Autism is not synonymous with psychosis nor does it indicate a specific mental illness," and the concept of autism "may say something about the way of life the child adopted at the time the term had been applied, but little about the cause or ultimate outcome."

Mahler (1952) has described a "symbiotic psychosis," which she differentiates from Kanner's early infantile autism. The central pattern of this syndrome seems to be an overwhelming need for support from, and a clinging attachment to, the mother. In 1930, Heller described a number of cases which had attracted his special attention in a large population of mental retardates. To this group of children he gave the name "dementia infantilis." His original paper has been translated by Hulse (1954), and this disorder, which is also referred to as Heller's syndrome, has been described by various authors. The course of the disturbance involves normal development during the earliest years of life with the beginning of the illness usually occurring during the third and fourth years, characterized and followed by general behavioral deterioration, overactivity, irritability, and apprehensiveness. Difficulties in speech occur early and continue throughout the course of the disturbance, and deterioration continues until the final stage when it would be considered profound. In his original article, Heller stated that the pleasant and intelligent expressions of the face and eyes were retained throughout the life of the individual. He took especial precautions to rule out the possibility that these were cases of encephalitis lethargica and also concluded that they were not childhood schizophrenics.

Yakovlev, Weinberger, and Chipman (1948) have reviewed several cases of Heller's syndrome and concluded that "in Heller's syndrome and in childhood schizophrenia in general, one deals with the dissociation of the evolved and derived phases of behavior." Benda and Melchior (1959), in a review of childhood schizophrenia, childhood autism, and Heller's syndrome, emphasized the difficult problem of differentiating between these cases and cases of mental retardation. They indicate that there are four main theories about dementia infantilis and these are: "(1) Heller's syndrome is a clinical syndrome not due to one etiological factor; (2) Heller's syndrome is symptomatic of a post-encephalitic condition; (3) Heller's syndrome is related to childhood schizophrenia; (4) Heller's syndrome represents a form of progressive deterioration due to a metabolic disorder, possibly related to amaurotic idiocy but without amaurosis."

Other psychotic manifestations related to both childhood schizophrenia and mental retardation include Earl's (1934) "primary psychogenic acathexis," which he differentiates from childhood schizophrenia, and MacGillivray's "larval psychosis of idiocy," which has been previously referred to in this review. In a study based on the concept of pfropfschizophrenia, Lanzkron (1957) found that out of 423 cases of male schizophrenic patients examined, 20, or 4.7 per cent, were suffering from pfropfschizophrenia which had been defined by Kraepelin and Bleuler as schizophrenia engrafted on mental retardation. In terms of their prognosis, 25 per cent of the 20 recovered but still retained schizoid features and mental retardation, 25 per cent remained mildly psychotic but able to work, and 20 per cent were unable to work, and their psychosis terminated in dull apathetic deterioration. Lanzkron concluded that the prognosis for pfropfschizophrenics is "not too favorable" and, for release, "very limited in our cultural setting."

Earl's concept of the "primitive catatonic psychosis of idiocy" developed from his intensive study of 135 male idiots. From this group he was able to separate a subgroup of 38 whose outstanding symptomatology was deterioration, catatonia, and emotional dissociation. Of these cases, he classified 20 as mainly cataleptic and 18 as primarily hyperkinetic and concluded that the primitive catatonic psychosis of idiocy is a form of schizophrenia, played out at the psychomotor rather than at the symbolic level. He also reported that the age of onset of this disturbance was early in life, usually before puberty, and that "even on the purely neurological level these people often show a degree of coordination and control complexity of movement quite beyond the pure profound idiot." From his statement, that "no case of congenital profound idiocy occurred," one can infer that the original intellectual level of his cases was above that of the severely retarded.

Almost all observers agree that the incidence of behavioral disturbances among the mentally retarded is much higher than among persons of normal intelligence; they also agree that schizophrenic reactions occur in mental retardates with considerable frequency. Angus (1948) examined 150 cases applying for admission to a special school and found that 43, or 28 per cent, could be "diagnosed as schizophrenic varying in degree from unquestionable psychoses to less well defined cases, which, while not actually mentally ill, showed so many characteristics of the condition that they unmistakably belonged to the borderline group." In the older group of children (thirteen years or more) the symptoms present the classical picture of the simple and paranoid schizophrenic. Angus believes that the active catatonic and hebephrenic types would probably be sent directly to mental hospitals and, therefore, would not be seen in application for a special school. Bergman, Waller, and Marchand (1951)—from a review of the literature and a study of 346 children, ages two to four, admitted to a state school—observed that schizophrenic reactions in children are not infrequently mistaken for signs of mental defect. They conclude that in many cases, regressive processes have been at work since childhood, "a process which is often dismissed through such identifying evasive nomenclature as feeblemindedness and psychopathic personality."

Pollock (1958), in a review of the literature on brain damage, mental retardation, and childhood schizophrenia, reported that estimates of the coexistence of schizophrenic symptomatology and subnormal intelligence range from 18 to 40 per cent. He also pointed out that the findings indicate the level of intellectual functioning in the schizophrenic child is an important prognostic index; an intelligence quotient of 70 and above was considered a favorable sign, while an intelligence quotient of less than 70 indicated that the chances for improvement were apt to be significantly less. Another general belief, he stated, is that the lower the intelligence quotient, the stronger the suspicion that there are disorders of the central nervous system. He found that there is a "marked overlap in intellectual functioning between schizophrenic children and those diagnosed as mentally retarded" and concluded that neither mental retardation nor childhood schizophrenia "is a distinct clinical entity encompassing homogeneous groups." He believes that "Which aspect is stressed—the retardation or the behavior disorder—is, in part a function of the observer's orientation rather than the child's behavior."

Drawing on his general experience and reporting on thirty-one cases of mental retardation in which schizophrenic features were encountered, Wortis (1958) found that of the retarded children seen in his clinic, 80 per cent have some associated psychiatric problem; 5 per cent could be diagnosed as primary schizophrenia, and 13 per cent display a significant degree of withdrawal, self-absorption, or autism. Most present secondary problems related to frustrations, rejection, or isolation, and 24 per cent showed excessive fearfulness. Wortis did not find that schizophrenia was the behavioral disorder most commonly associated with mental retardation, but, rather, he found a combination of hyperactivity and distractability. He believes that it is probably reasonable to expect that some common etiologic factors may induce both mental retardation and schizophrenia; however, he feels that "it would not be surprising to find that the hard core of schizophrenic and the hard core of retarded cases, tend to have different types of etiology with ganglion cell destruction and cerebral defect dominant in retardation and toxic inhibitory factors dominant in schizophrenia."

One of the most interesting investigations of childhood disturbances is that of Bergman and Escalona (1949) who reported that "Some very young children possessed unusual sensitivities manifesting themselves in several, if not in all, sensory modalities (visual, auditory, tactile, etc.)," and that "They were 'sensitive' in both meanings of the word: easily hurt and easily stimulated to enjoyment." These children displayed unusual sensitivities in terms of quality as well as intensity of stimuli. They also observe:

The first impression which some of their reactions and abilities gave was that of unusual giftedness such as might be observed in the budding of a genius. Further observation, however, suggested comparison with individuals suffering from a traumatic neurosis, or a psychosis and even with feebleminded children. Closer study and follow-up then made it appear that childhood psychosis was the fate of these children.

The authors, at the time of their report, were not able to state that psychotic reactions were the ultimate fate of all of the children studied.

These findings of Bergman and Escalona recall the earlier speculations on the etiological significance of unusual sensitivities and irritabilities in the development of childhood psychoses, as well as some of the observations of Morris (1953) on cases of "elective mutism." In the latter report the author described children who displayed fully developed speech in the presence of some people and mutism in the presence of others. Morris further characterized these children as being "unduly timid and sensitive" but concluded that they did not display other symptoms that would justify a diagnosis of childhood schizophrenia.

Taking an overview of general studies of the incidence of psychoses in mental retardates, schizophrenia and psychotic episodes of excitement are most frequently associated with mental retardation, at least in the literature. Most of the observers also concluded that, although any of the psychoses may occur with mental retardation, it appears that true depressive psychoses among the mentally retarded are rare. It seems evident, too, that all psychoses become better differentiated or more clearly defined among the mentally retarded as the intellectual level increases and as the retardate becomes older. There is, however, a paucity of literature on the association of the non-schizophrenic psychoses and retardation, and a majority of the articles are case studies from which few general inferences could be drawn.

The literature on child and adult schizophernia, on the other hand, is copious. Almost all workers in the field recognize the difficulties encountered in making differential diagnoses between retardation and childhood schizophrenia and related disorders. There have been at least partially successful attempts to distinguish among several different types of schizophrenia at the childhood level, and disturbances such as Heller's syndrome appear likely to be assigned status as separate disorders.

Inconsistencies appear in the data gathered about the association of schizophrenia and mental retardation, and many of the inconsistencies are due to differences in the populations studied. The statistics from such varied groups cannot be accepted as having any absolute value, nor is it possible to make inferences from the characteristics of institutionalized populations about the general population of retardates. Errors in sampling, as well as errors in methodology, partially account for the frequency with which contradictory results or failures to find similar results are reported. Other factors which contribute to these discrepancies are related to the nosological confusion in both schizophrenia and mental retardation and the unwarranted assumptions of homogeneity of either group. In the opinion of many, one of the greatest advances is the general recognition that both terms only broadly categorize and that neither implies homogeneity of etiology or pathenogenesis. It is necessary to consider the heterogeneity of both groups in the design of research, since, whether in the search for etiological factors or behavioral characteristics, important differences or similarities between and within sub-groups may be obscured in measures of central tendency within the larger and undifferentiated sample. At the present time it seems safest to conclude that accurate estimates of the co-incidence of psychoses with mental re-tardation cannot be made; see, for ex-ample, the discrepant figures presented by O'Connor (1951) in his review.

PSEUDO MENTAL RETARDATION

The concept of pseudofeebleminded-ness or pseudo mental retardation has been in use for at least thirty years. As a descriptive term it has been used to characterize intellectual subnormality as-sociated with special disabilities, physi-cal, and behavioral disturbances. As an explanatory principle it has been used to account for so-called psychogenic re-tardation as well as errors in diagnosis and prognosis. In 1950, Guertin sum-marized the differential etiological fac-tors underlying pseudofeeblemindedness; these included special intellectual dis-abilities (segmental organization), speech retardation, personality disorders, edu-cational deficits, sensory handicaps, and delayed maturation. Benton (1956) pointed out that there are two principal usages of this concept: (1) Pseudo-feeblemindedness "represents a mistaken diagnosis, that is from the data at hand a child is judged to be mentally retarded when in fact he is not." (2) It is used to represent mental retardation of atypical etiology. The determinants include sen-sory deprivation, motor deficiency, cul-tural deprivation, emotional disturb-ances, etc. Cutts (1957) stressed the im-portance of a thorough clinical study for purposes of differential diagnosis, but observed that such diagnostic differen-tiations are "usually made in retrospect."

Kanner (1948) used three categories to classify mental retardates: (1) the absolute feebleminded, in whom he sees the retardation as irreversible and who are so "markedly deficient in their cog-nitive, affective, and constructively cona-tive potentialities that they would stand out as defectives in any existing civiliza-tion," (2) the relative feebleminded, whose "deficiency" is an "ethnologically determined phenomenon relative to the local standards," and (3) the apparent or pseudofeebleminded, in which group he would include the autistic and schizo-phrenic child.

Almost every behavioral disturbance results in a reduction of the efficiency and effectiveness of the individual and the generality or specificity of this re-duction of capacity should be a part of any description or diagnostic evaluation. Considering the lack of specificity and the varieties of meaning assigned to the concept of pseudo mental retardation, its use would not seem to add anything to either diagnostic or etiological under-standing of mental retardation, and it would seem advisable, therefore, to dis-card the concept as suggested by Cantor (1955) and Benton (1956).

JUVENILE DELINQUENCY AND CRIMINALITY

The early reports on the association of mental retardation, delinquency, and criminality were indeed cause for alarm. The estimates of subnormal intelligence among delinquents and criminals ranged from 0.5 to 55 per cent with the greatest number of early studies reporting esti-mates at the upper end. Crafts made a survey in 1916 of the number of articles concerned with mental retardation and juvenile delinquency and lists a bibliog-raphy of 211 items. Among these were general and case studies, and in 52 of these the Binet and other tests of intelli-gence were used.

Bronner in 1914 questioned the valid-ity of the earlier proportions reported on the incidence of mental retardation and juvenile delinquency. In 1917 Crafts and Doll suggested that natural factors such as isolation, artificial factors such as court attitudes and probation failures, and combined factors of nationality, age, sex, etc., had not been controlled in pre-vious studies and had therefore contam-inated and biased the results. Burt (1923) reported: "We are in absolute harmony upon the central issue of the discussion; namely, that the proportion of intellectually defective cases among the delinquent population is far lower than earlier investigations maintained. The true proportion is in the neighborhood of 5 percent, not 50."

Mateer (1924) concluded that "Mental age is one of the determiners of delinquency, but this determination is not limited to the cases in which mental age is inferior to the point of feeblemindedness." Palmer (1927) observed:

It is clearly established that the defective delinquent presents not only subnormality of intelligence, but that he suffers from personality disorder and shows conduct deviation—that he occurs in the proportion of at least 35 in every 100 inmates of our correctional institutions and that because he is abnormal he is not susceptible to training intended for the normal.

Having pointed out that many mental retardates are maladjusted, Wallace (1929) concluded that they must contribute a considerable number of criminals, since the maladjusted group in our society furnish the largest number of criminals. In these two conclusions we see a changing point of view regarding criminality in general. These statements are among the last of the exaggerated estimates of the incidence of mental retardation and also represent the establishment of the view that many criminals are perhaps mentally ill. In a review of the literature up to 1930, Davies (1930) concluded that the mentally retarded "have no innate propensities toward evil doing" and that how they behave, "generally depends on what good or bad influences society provides."

In 1931, Sutherland surveyed all the available psychometric studies on delinquency made in the United States between 1910 and 1928; he concluded that the 350 studies evaluated had not demonstrated that mental retardation was a generally important cause of delinquency. Following Sutherland's observations,

Zeleny (1933), in a review of 200 articles, reported such divergent statements as: "(a) the criminal population possesses a larger proportion of feebleminded than the non-criminal population; (b) criminals and non-criminals possess similar proportions of feebleminded persons and (c) the criminal population possesses a smaller proportion of feebleminded persons than the non-criminal population." He stated that "it seems reasonable to conclude that feeblemindedness is associated with delinquency and criminality to a slight extent"; however, "About 96 percent of criminals have the ability to care for their affairs with ordinary prudence."

Glueck (1935) suggested, from an examination of her data, that "mental deficiency though not a direct cause of delinquency, is a complicating factor of great potency, the presence of which, in addition to other causative influences, severely breaks down the individual's resistance to antisocial behavior." Mann and Mann (1939) studied 1,731 delinquents referred to a Juvenile Court; these cases had a mean chronological age of 17.47 and a mean intelligence quotient of 84.45. Two-thirds of the cases examined were boys. Penrose (1939), in a comparative study of European statistics on mental disease and crime, recommended that greater attention be paid to general mental health, since this would help prevent the occurrence of serious crimes. In the statistics he surveyed he found that mental retardates were included in the general statistics on mental disease.

A return to the older and more pessimistic point of view was registered by Lurie, Levy, and Rosenthal in 1944. They concluded that defective delinquents constitute a distinct clinical entity and stated that

because of a combination of poor mental heredity and vicious home influences and conditioning the defective delinquent is an intellectually retarded, emotionally immature, and socially inadequate individual. The fundamental basis for this defective personality is the pathologic constitutional endowment on which has been engrafted pathologically conditioned traits which render the individual unable to adjust to his environment. The prognosis with regard to cure of his behavior is uniformly poor. At present, commitment for life to a custodial institution especially equipped to treat this type of child offers the only solution from the standpoint of society.

During the same year Bijou and Mc-Candless (1944) reported, in their study of mentally retarded delinquent boys, that the "mentally retarded pre-delinquents were a heterogeneous group." They indicated that 13 per cent of their group had lowered functional intelligence, accompanied by low behavioral efficiency and high verbal-learning interference.

In a study of frustration types among mentally retarded juvenile delinquents, Foulds (1945) reported that

87 per cent of the extrapunitive subjects have a marked feeling of rejection, either because their parents reject them or treat them harshly. Sixty-seven per cent of the intropunitives overcompensate in their conscious attachment to their parents for an unconscious feeling of neglect, while 46 per cent of impunitives are over attached to their parents, usually because they have been spoiled.

Only 13 per cent of the total group had balanced relationships with their parents. Ehrenwald (1945) interpreted delinquent behavior in retardates mainly as a compensatory reaction for their shortcomings. In a comprehensive study of mentally retarded individuals in New York City, Saenger (1960) reported that behavioral maladjustments were the second most frequent reason for the institutionalization of mental retardates and "Sexual offenses almost invariably lead to institutionalization"—about 17 per cent of a representative sample of high-grade retardates, most of them girls, were institutionalized because of sexual transgres-

sions. In the same study it is also reported that 44 per cent of mental retardates in institutions come from broken homes, while only 7 per cent of retardates who remained in the general community were from broken homes.

At the present time, only one conclusion regarding the association of mental retardation with delinquency and criminality seems justifiable. The mentally retarded are capable of delinquent and criminal acts as are their intellectually normal brethren; however, factors other than intellectual ones appear to be more important in the etiology of such behavior, and these factors are those commonly cited as important to the development of delinquent and criminal behavior in the general population. Though not a direct cause of delinquency or criminality, mental retardation is a complicating factor especially in terms of treatment, in the same way that "heart trouble" may be a complicating factor in the treatment or management of other, though not necessarily related, physical diseases. Smith (1962) pointed out that rather than having any propensities toward crime, the mentally retarded may be involved in delinquent and criminalistic actions as a result of lack of insight, misunderstandings, or lack of appropriate supervision. He also emphasized that society must become concerned with "*life* rather than just *school* planning for the mentally retarded individual." In relation to the types of crimes committed by the retarded, there appear to be some trends emerging from the literature, and it is quite safe to conclude that the mentally retarded would have very few representatives among the "white collar" criminals.

SOCIOPATHIC PERSONALITY

The source of this concept lies principally in "moralistic psychiatry," which reached its height in the nineteenth century. Some of the earliest forms of the term were prominent in the writings of Prichard and Skae, who discussed "moral insanity" and "moral idiocy." The general fascination of the period with such concepts is also mirrored in the writings of many who were principally students of mental retardation. Barr, for example, devotes only a page and a half in his 1904 text, to a discussion of "insanity" among the mentally retarded and eight pages to cases illustrative of "moral imbecility." The cases themselves, in this and similar publications, suggest that very few would now be classified as mentally retarded, but rather as psychopathic deviates or under the more recently adopted name of sociopaths.

The general picture of the sociopath has been presented by Cleckley (1941) along with a variety of case illustrations. Humphreys (1940) stated that the problem of psychopathic personality among the mentally retarded is a part of the general problem of psychopathy. He believes that "The psychopathic defective is suffering from severe mental aberrations similar to those found in the superior psychopaths for whose problems society has not yet made adequate provision." Tarjan (1948) has evaluated concepts of psychopathic personality and recommended the classification of the sociopath on the basis of "dynamic patterns instead of on descriptive lines." Thorne in 1959 reviewed the literature and presented a hypothetical model of sociopathy. He pointed out that, although the condition is considered irreversible, it is not; he outlined the characteristics of a therapeutic regimen that would be required for reversing sociopathic patterns. Thorne, in agreement with many others, concluded that the writings on sociopathy contain many misconceptions and half truths which are widely accepted and stated that "To date, the literature contains few convincing formulations of the etiology and personality dynamics of the large group of character disorders variously known as sociopathic reaction, character neuroses, or psychopathic personality."

Reviewing the literature on the association of mental retardation and the sociopathic reaction, one is led to the conclusion that inept and predominantly antisocial sociopathy is only rarely associated with mental retardation. However, the inadequate pattern of sociopathy which includes the weak, passive, and non-aggressive types is more likely to occur among the mentally retarded. The differentiation between the inadequate and inept manifestations of sociopathy are very well described by Cameron and Magaret (1951). It should also be emphasized that the cases of moral imbecility and idiocy, which appeared so prominently in earlier writings on mental retardation, were so much in evidence because, unlike the docile well-behaved majority of retardates, they were rather exciting, interesting, and spectacular standouts in institutional populations.

The search for special traumatic events or experiences in the life history of the sociopath will probably not prove very fruitful in clarifying etiology. It seems apparent from most case studies of the inept sociopath that the central problem is one which can be explained in terms of learning theory and that what the sociopath learns are a series of social roles, "stage productions," or misrepresentational "acts" which have helped him avoid frustrations and conflicts in the past and have thus been reinforced and overlearned. The dominant family constellations of the sociopath seem designed to prevent his experiencing the ordinary frustrations, conflicts, and social pressures which are necessary for learning acceptable value systems and the incorporation of ordinary notions of right and wrong. Also prominent in the inept sociopath's picture is a history of protection of the sociopath by his family from punishing consequences appropriate to his actions. The relative absence of these experiences, which are common ones for most humans, would explain the sociopath's impulsiveness and his inability to postpone immediate satisfactions for more important gains or goals which might accrue in the future. The inept sociopath is immature in that he always wants what he wants when he wants it, and he always wants it right now! Such immaturities are recognizable in the mentally retarded; however, they also appear appropriately in young children who are intellectually normal. As with delinquency and criminality, sociopathy can and does occur in mental retardates, but though one condition may complicate the other there would seem to be no causal relationship in either direction.

PSYCHONEUROSES AND OTHER
BEHAVIORAL DISORDERS

The vagueness and generality of the title of this section is probably an accurate reflection of both the research and the literature related to the association of these disorders and mental retardation. The surveys and other studies in this area have only rarely avoided the usual errors which have been criticized in similar research with the intellectually normal. There is an obvious lack of standardized criteria in terms of diagnosis, a lack of operationally useful definitions, and a considerable amount of investigator bias which enters into the designs of the studies and the interpretations of results. In this area we have the alarmist approach which, in regard to maladjustments in the mentally retarded, finds maladjustment, not under every tree and bush, but under every leaf of every tree and bush. There are also the conceptually imperialistic approaches, which, at least at the present, do not seem to be as productive as in the field of schizophrenia. At the other extreme there are many studies which do not seem to be related to broader conceptualization of either mental retardation or psychopathology. Feldman in 1946 reviewed the literature on psychoneuroses in the mentally retarded

and pronounced it very sparse. He stated that the "IQ alone cannot express or explain the complex deportment of any individual with social adequacy of some degree."

Much of the research that has been done on the incidence of the psychoneuroses and other so-called minor maladjustments in the mentally retarded is more specifically related to problems in psychological evaluation, differential diagnosis, and research on the personality development and social-vocational adjustment of the mentally retarded. These and other areas of research, such as the relation of environmental factors to intellectual functioning, are more appropriately discussed in other chapters of this review. Information relevant to the topic of this section is also contained in research on, and considerations of, therapeutic approaches to mental retardation, and some of this material will be discussed subsequently in this chapter.

A great amount of attention has been given the adjustmental problems related to the development of the mentally retarded. It seems to be agreed that the mentally retarded child, because of his intellectual deficiency, is subject to more stresses than the ordinary child. The most frequently mentioned problems or experiences of the retardate appear to be rejection and overprotection. The retardate may experience serious frustrations from consistent failures or deprivations and strong feelings of shame, guilt, and hopelessness because of his deficiencies. Beier (1959) pointed out that the mental retardate, because of his slower maturational development, is slower to incorporate notions of right and wrong, or good and bad, into a personal value system, which should be a reflection of the rules and regulations and codes of society. Internalization of controls or development of self-control proceeds at a slower rate with the mentally retarded, and its development may require closer supervision and longer training than with the retardate's normal peers. In this connection, it is interesting to note that the results of a recent survey of emotionally disturbed children in the state of Indiana (Beier, Binder, and Robbins, 1961) showed that an emotionally disturbed child, if he is mentally retarded, is more likely to be retained in school than the non-retarded emotionally disturbed child. It seems probable that the explanation for this is related to the development and maintenance of special classes for the mentally retarded in many school systems.

Kiefer (1949) has stressed the need for research on behavioral disturbances among the mentally retarded and suggested several areas of life that may be particularly stressful. He indicated that among the mild retardates, there may be many feelings of insecurity brought about by attempts to work out "a delayed oedipal complex." He observed that the retardate is necessarily treated differently from his siblings in the matter of privileges, etc., thereby increasing the likelihood of sibling rivalry among retardates. He stated that "the play for affection and attention occurs in the defective child as it does in the normal child." The illegitimate retardate has an especially serious problem, and the frustration of his needs in this area may lead to antisocial acts. Rejection may also lead to similar acts, generally of a compulsive nature. Finally, Kiefer stressed that many retardates "react fearfully in ordinary circumstances," suffer from isolation in both institutional and home settings, and have feelings of not being a part of society.

Anderson (1925), reporting on an investigation of all 125 pupils in a school for retarded children, classified 62 as emotionally stable and 58 as unstable, with no decisions being made in 5 cases. Although for the whole group there were no significant intellectual differences between the stable and the unstable, the 9 children rated as most markedly unstable showed slightly higher intelligence quotients and reading ability as well as higher manual training ability when compared to the 9 pupils rated as most stable. Trippe *et al.* (1959), in a study of 83 school-excluded mentally retarded children, reported that "in six instances mental retardation was adjudged to be secondary to other conditions, most of which were primary behavior disorders." They indicated that "A large proportion of the remaining 77 children, however, also presented multiple problems." Among the latter were secondary emotional problems, hyperactivity, difficult behavior, speech defects, and other sensory and motor handicaps. They conclude that "Only those children, however, whose impairment of mental functioning was secondary to primary emotional disorders were adjudged to have a good capacity for improvement in mental functioning." Gibson in 1953 surveyed the special types of cases encountered in mental retardation clinics, and, of 104 who were certifiable mental retardates, there were 89 other subnormal types. Seven had miscellaneous defects, and 50 had behavioral disturbances of various degrees.

The home and family situations of retardates have received considerable attention in relation to their emotional disturbances and adjustmental problems. Kinder and Rutherford (1927), after evaluating the results of a longitudinal study of 68 mentally retarded children, stressed the home environment as a very important factor in the social adustment of the retarded child. They also reported that 47 of the children studied came from emotionally unhealthy homes and that after five years, "none of those without improved environments were making satisfactory adjustments and only five were making fairly satisfactory adjustments." Walker (1950) observed that "One cannot but wonder as one studies the parents of mentally deficient children that the disturbances of development are not greater," and Davis (1951) stated that "From the psychological standpoint, the parent is as much a casualty as is the child."

The adaptive significance of commonly described behavioral patterns of the mentally retarded are viewed by Hirsch (1959) as the child's attempt to cope with his environment and its various demands. Hirsch emphasized that such behavioral patterns have economic and dynamic meaning in terms of ego-functioning. He considers the major difference between the mental retardate and his normal peer a matter of the retardate's ego limitations. Because of his limitations the retardate must be more dependent on others and submit to more external controls. Hirsch stated that the retardate "reacts with intense effort to maintain his integrity," and the struggle to maintain control of his external situation opposed by the necessity to relinquish control may produce in the retardate hyperactivity, destructive behavior, rapid shifts of focus, or question bombardment. Tendencies to oversubmit to external control may eventuate in passivity or withdrawal. He cited other adaptive mechanisms used by retardates which are interpreted in a straightforward dynamic and analytic fashion. Potter (1927a) uses classical psychoanalytic theory to interpret the domination of infantile or narcissistic erotic behavior in his study of the severely retarded. Walker (1948) also uses an analytic framework in his view of psychosexual behavior in institutionalized retardates and believes that, in addition to other maturational lags, retardates of various intellectual capacities demonstrate typical fixations in their psychosexual development. In the idiot, for example, such patterns as food dyscrasias, finger-sucking, putting everything in his mouth, and other oral symptoms lead Walker to declare that he "cannot accept these symptoms as indicative of other than unresolved oral development." He considered the smearing of feces as similarly indic-

ative of arrest in anal development. Masturbation among the severely retarded is frequently on a skin-sensitivity basis and unaccompanied by erection. The imbecile is at the autoerotic level in terms of psychosexual development, and "masturbation with phantasy seldom occurs with less than the middle imbecile mentality." Walker believes that "Full heterosexual feeling apparently develops about the beginning of moron intelligence," although "Feelings of heterosexual possession are usually weaker in the male than in the female."

In addition to the individual surveys of maladjustment in the mentally retarded conducted by Neuer, Pollock, Weaver, and Wortis which have been previously described in this chapter, three studies require specific mention. Eysenck reported in 1943 on the results of an analysis of some 3,000 male and female neurotic patients in the military services. An evaluation of this English population, for whom intelligence test ratings were available, led Eysenck to the conclusion that, considering all 3,000 cases, there were "far fewer cases of average intelligence and more cases of above average and below average intelligence than would be found in a comparable sample of the normal population." However, the neurotic group tested was on the average neither more nor less intelligent than comparable non-neurotic groups. The results also indicate that conversion hysterics, were, on the average, less intelligent than other neurotics, while the dysmnesic hysteric were, on the whole, of average intelligence. Dewan (1948), in a study of 30,000 male recruits at a reception center, found that "the evidence suggests that the rate of incidence of psychoneurosis and other patterns of emotional instability declines as the degree of intelligence advances, although this becomes less evident in the upper ranges of intelligence." Craft (1959), in a previously mentioned survey, found that of a population of 324 in-patient retardates, 22, or 7 per cent, were suffering from psychoses and neuroses and over half of this group were schizophrenic. Among this population the schizoid and emotionally unstable personality disorders were observed most frequently. A diagnosis of schizoid personality was assigned to 30 cases, and 24 were regarded as emotionally disturbed personalities. The cases in these two categories constituted only slightly less than half of all cases diagnosed as personality disorders.

The problem of mental retardation as a symptom of emotional disturbance has been a topic of considerable interest to writers in the field of mental retardation and psychopathology. In a very real sense, research in this area is about ready to begin. Very few answers are available, but many of the significant questions and problems have been raised by Eisenberg (1958), Harris (1928), Kanner (1952), Sloan (1947), and others. The statements of Eisenberg in 1958 seem to be an accurate reflection of the general attitudes toward emotional determinants of mental retardation:

The interdependence of emotion and intelligence is a fundamental fact of human behavior, at the psychological and biological levels of integration. We should no longer wonder at the evidence of dysfunction in either in the presence of disorder in the other, but rather ask: By what mechanism has it occurred in the particular case and by what means may it be remedied?

Some of the research in psychotherapy is particularly relevant to this problem and will be discussed under that heading.

One of the most persistent beliefs in the field of mental retardation is related to the personality of the mongoloid. He is usually portrayed as a pleasant, affectionate, and generally happy person. Ellis and Beechley (1950) have made a comparison of the emotional adjustments of matched groups of mongoloid and non-mongoloid children. Forty children in each group were equated for intelligence, age, and sex and were given diagnostic evaluations at a mental hygiene clinic. They reported, "The Mongoloid feebleminded children were distinctly less emotionally disturbed than were the non-Mongoloid feebleminded patients and the differences between the two groups are significant at the .01 level of confidence." They also reported that the mongoloid children came from homes which were considered better in terms of social, psychological, and cultural characteristics. They considered that their results supported the notion that mongolism is a "special form of feeblemindedness which has different causes and effects from other types of mental deficiency" and speculate on the possibility that the brain areas affected in the mongoloid are not those related to the emotions.

Other studies of the personality and emotional characteristics of the mongoloid have failed to support the idea that they are generally freer of emotional disturbances than other types of mental retardates. Rollin (1946), for example, cited impressive evidence that there is a high incidence of catatonic psychosis in cases of mongolism. Mongols are probably no more homogeneous in terms of adjustment patterns or problems than any other unselected groups of normals or retardates.

Although the literature on the association between the psychoneuroses and other behavioral disorders with mental retardation is extensive, and some of the research and speculation rich in ideas and stimulating hypotheses, there are relatively few conclusions that can be reported with any degree of confidence. As in so many other areas of research related to adjustment disturbances in the mentally retarded, we still seem to be in a period of hypothesis-construction rather than hypothesis-testing. With the wealth of new knowledge in many fields of science and the many new advances in methodological approaches and tools, many of the worthwhile hypotheses should be submitted to rigorous scientific testing. In terms of the psychoneuroses and other behavioral disorders, many relationships with mental retardation have been hypothesized and a few have been demonstrated; however, the demonstration of relationships, although suggestive, does not establish causal or etiologic connections. The implications of the reports by Scott on critical periods in behavioral development (1962, 1963) would seem to be extremely important to the study and understanding of the development of behavioral disorders in the mentally retarded.

THERAPEUTIC APPROACHES TO THE MENTALLY RETARDED

Behavioral disturbances in the mentally retarded are important because they reduce the retardate's effectiveness and efficiency and make him generally uncomfortable with himself and with others. The training and rehabilitation of the retarded can be interfered with or prevented as much by behavioral disorder as by intellectual deficit. In addition to these effects, behavioral disorders in the mentally retarded may (1) have profound and deleterious effects on the retardate's family and others who surround him, (2) result in the fixation of unnecessarily infantile patterns of behavior, and (3) eventuate in the development of more severe problems of adjustment, behavioral disturbances, or antisocial behavior patterns requiring more extensive care and control in the future.

The history of therapeutic as well as educational approaches for the mentally retarded had its real beginning in the pioneer work of Itard (1932) with the "Wild Boy of Aveyron." Although the educational aspects of his work had relatively immediate influence, there was considerable lag in both interest and application of many of the therapeutic im-

plications inherent in his procedures. One can readily agree with Burton who stated in 1954 that psychotherapy with the mentally retarded was "an uncharted field" and that much systematic research was needed. Cowen (1955), Grunzburg (1958), Sarason (1953), and Masland, Sarason, and Gladwin (1958) have made comprehensive reviews of the literature; in this section, only some of the highlights and the major trends and results will be presented. The therapeutic work of Witmer in the 1920's probably marks the reawakening of interest in therapeutic work with retardates. The lag between the period of Itard and the work of Witmer is not surprising, since relatively little self-conscious psychotherapy was done with patients of any description, until the extensive formulations of Charcot, Janet, and Freud. Nevertheless, there have existed attitudes and beliefs about the incurability and unmodifiability of the retarded which have led to the conclusion that psychotherapy with them could only be disappointing and improvements in their status unlikely. One must recognize, however, that procedures of environmental manipulation and institutionalization were used for the social and psychological rehabilitation of the mentally retarded.

The early writers in the field include Clark (1932, 1933a, b), who, using a psychoanalytic approach, concluded that "Psychoanalysis as a therapy would not claim to remove the fundamental causes of amentia. It would attempt rather, to reduce the amount and depth of fixation so that the excessiveness of retardation may be avoided even though the innate defect is not curable." Potter (1933a) has pointed out a fundamental criticism of many therapeutic efforts with the mentally retarded; he writes: "I am firmly convinced that treatment and training methods will be more effective when they are arranged so as to fit the clinical condition rather than as they now are arranged mainly to fit the mental age level without regard as to what the other clinical factors may be."

Chidester and Menninger (1936) described the treatment of a supposedly mentally retarded boy whose "psychosexual development was almost completely arrested at the anal stage" and reported that his intelligence quotient increased from 62 in 1931 to 90 in 1935 during the course of therapy. They concluded that learning or intellectual development seem to be dependent upon emotional development. In 1944, Kriegman and Hilgard reviewed the literature on the relationship between intelligence level and psychotherapy and concluded that "In general, the results of these studies are contradictory and inconclusive. All may be criticized because of an insufficient number of cases." They also criticized specific studies for inadequate data, frequency of testing, duration of therapy, selection of cases, and inadequate analysis of results. In their own study with borderline to above average cases, they reported that psychotherapy may increase intelligence ratings in particular cases and that they achieved the best results with the anxious, guilty child.

Heiser (1951, 1954) discussed the results of psychotherapy in a residential school for the mentally retarded, and in his first article reported that three out of four cases were definitely helped by psychotherapy and collaborative therapy with cottage parents, teachers, etc. In the second report he indicated that through psychotherapy ten out of fourteen children were able to return to their homes. He concluded that therapy is definitely a benefit in an institution for mental retardates. Wortis (1950) reported that in the Soviet Union and Poland, although the prognosis of retardation is considered uniformly unfavorable, psychotherapeutic approaches of the symptomatic and educative varieties are proving very successful in making the retardate's defect less handicapping.

Medical treatment of the mentally retarded is used "only in cases of known aetiology," and they are institutionalized only in exceptional circumstances.

Group psychotherapy with adults developed after the First World War, and group therapy with children is largely a product of the thirties. The techniques and methods of group psychotherapy were drawn from psychology and psychiatry, recreation, group work, and progressive education. Varying degrees of success have been reported fairly recently with groups of mental retardates. Mehlman (1953) investigated the effects of group psychotherapy on retarded children who had been institutionalized. Using a non-directive approach in this controlled study, Mehlman conservatively suggested that, although there were no remarkable changes in personality and intelligence test scores, one cannot conclude that there were no therapeutic changes. Fisher and Wolfson (1953) reported on group therapy with twelve mildly retarded females who displayed either submissive and withdrawn or aggressive and hyperactive behavior. They noted that the two groups passed through phases similar to those reported in other groups, e.g., testing the limits, regression, transition from ego-centeredness to group-centeredness, positive sibling transference, and finally out-group-centeredness as they developed interest and concern with "outside" values and events. Although there were no changes in IQ ratings, they conclude from before- and after-therapy interviews with staff members that the aggressive tended to become less so and the withdrawn more outgoing. In this study, two groups divided on the basis of chronological age and mental age participated in thirty-six activity group therapy sessions of one and one-half hours per week.

O'Connor and Yonge (1955) worked with twenty-one institutionalized male retardates, aged sixteen to twenty-one, with IQ's ranging from 52 to 89, who were considered behavior problems and manifested sociopathic traits. These subjects were equally divided into three groups—an experimental group which received two sessions of increasingly non-directive therapy per week over a six-month period, a workshop control group which received no treatment but worked with the members of the experimental group in an institutional setting, and a basic control group which received no treatment and did general work around the institution. Evaluations of progress were made quarterly from recordings of discussion sessions and observations on the ward and in the workshop. A checklist of defined "attitudes" was used in making the ratings, and the authors concluded that, although a conclusive evaluation could be made only after the subjects had been followed for several years, there did occur changes in the treatment group in the direction of more positive attitudes toward self and others, more co-operative participation in group discussions, and positive changes in workshop behavior and performance. Similar changes were not recorded for the control group. O'Connor and Yonge also interpreted the results of this experiment as strong evidence that suggested discarding the generally accepted notion that no improvement can be expected in attitudes or behavior through group therapy with cases that combine mental retardation and psychopathic traits.

A majority of studies in the literature on the use of psychotherapy with the retarded have used a non-directive or mixed approach. Snyder and Sechrist (1959) have made a well-designed experimental study of directive group therapy with retarded delinquents. They reported: "At the end of 13 weeks of treatment the inmates receiving therapy were superior to both placebo and no-treatment subjects in their institutional adjustment as represented by significantly more positive comments on routine housing reports and fewer appearances in

behavior courts for more serious violations." These writers believe "that the results are attributable to the more structured directive nature of therapy and to the nature of the measurements, which were definitely and closely related to the institutional program as a whole."

A majority of articles in the literature report successful results in the use of individual and group psychotherapy with mental retardates (quite likely the failures remain unreported). The degree of success is moderate and frequently ill defined. Most often the "improvements" in "adjustment" are subjectively determined and not explicitly explained. Most of the improvements noted in the literature refer to personality variables; increases in intellectual levels are still generally suspect. It appears that either directive or non-directive or combinations of these methods account for successes; however, it seems to be equally clear that the more directive and structured approaches are probably more effective with the aggressively acting-out, impulsive sociopathic, and delinquent varieties of retardates, and the non-directive techniques with the withdrawn, shy, and anxious types. In psychotherapy with retardates the goals must frequently be modified to fit the retardates' potentials, and it is reasonable to predict that new techniques must be developed and combinations of psychotherapy and techniques of chemical management more thoroughly investigated. The use of now existing psychometric devices as instruments for evaluating the effects of psychotherapy suggests only cautious optimism for definitive results. A majority of such devices are either too insensitive or too subject to interpreter biases, within their current systems of scoring, to permit conclusions being made from their use with any reassuring degree of confidence.

Parallel to the psychotherapeutic attempts to assist the emotionally disturbed mental retardate have been the applications of surgical, convulsive, and chemical therapies in the management of the disturbed retardate. Although "cures" are reported for almost every type of medical management approach, there is little enthusiasm recorded for traditional varieties of surgical and convulsive manipulations. Glutamic acid, once the "wonder drug" in the field, has had a relatively short but spectacular history in that role. Currently, it is regarded as a stimulant sometimes useful with the mild and moderately retarded. With unselected groups it may produce both biological and behavioral side effects that are deleterious. Craft and Kugelmass have reviewed the literature on chemical therapies with the mentally retarded. These reviews, which appeared in 1959, obviate the necessity of repeating an examination of the individual studies on which they report. Stimulant therapy as well as ataractic therapy with various chemical agents have proven useful in the management of both the hypokinetic and hyperkinetic mentally retarded, according to Kugelmass. However, he pointed out that both are primarily control techniques having little effect on underlying psychopathology. Either or both may have serious disturbing effects on the psychological level and minor or major toxic effects on the biological level. In the same article Kugelmass reported the results of his study of sixty mental retardates, three to eighteen years of age, with an intelligence quotient range of 30 to 75. All were characterized by unmanageable behavior. "Half the group were offered phenaglycodol after meals and at bedtime and the other half the identical placebos." After a two-month period on this regimen the treatment of the groups was reversed. The amounts of the drug administered were determined individually on the basis of the severity of the behavioral disturbance. The results of this study indicated varying degrees of improvement or worsening in ten fundamental areas of behavior, e.g., feeding, dressing, compulsion, control, activity, attacks, training, toileting, bathing, and sleeping. No significant changes in intelligence test scores were observed in the phenaglycodol-treated children, and the positive results obtained were dependent on the continuation of the drug and disappeared with its discontinuance. Kugelmass concluded:

Clinical assessment of 60 mentally retarded children who were adequately controlled on phenaglycodol therapy revealed statistically significant improvement in 10 fundamental areas of behavior according to the chi-square test. . . . Phenaglycodol enables the available but limited capacities of the mentally retarded child to function more effectively, without side effects, throughout the period of administration.

Craft (1959*b*), in his review of the literature, criticized the experimental designs of many previous studies on the use of tranquilizers with mentally retardates who are emotionally disturbed. He pointed out that very few of the investigations have used the double-blind technique in their investigations and reported his own double-blind studies on the effects of tranquilizers with varying numbers of subjects. Generally, his subjects were divided into two major samples from which his sub-groups were drawn: the first group included cases of moderate and severe retardation with intelligence quotients below 38 and problems of hyperactivity, destructiveness, and aggressiveness; the second group was composed of retardates with intelligence quotients above 39 who had personality disorders or frank mental illnesses. With the sub-groups of lower grade subjects, the effects of hydroxyzine, chlorpromazine, meprobamate, amphetamine sulphate, promethazine hydrochloride, acetyl promazine, prochlorperazine, and promazine hydrochloride were studied. Benactyzine, meprobamate, and acetyl promazine were administered to the high-grade groups. The author concluded on the basis of these well-controlled double-blind studies: "It is felt that pro-chlorperazine is at present date the treatment of choice for the hyperactive syndromes in low grade defectives and reasons for this are given. Benactyzine has been found to be effective in decreasing the activity of high grade defectives with emotionally unstable personalities."

Studies with stimulant therapies and ataractic drugs rather clearly suggest that, barring side effects, these management techniques can be very useful for the control of various behavioral disturbances in the mentally retarded. There are no implications that the basic psychopathology is modified, but there are many that, when combined with other therapeutic and rehabilitative techniques, permanent behavioral modifications may result. Most of the studies on chemical therapies can be criticized on the basis of design and the use of heterogeneous populations; a majority of them are inconclusive, but with the increased use of double-blind and other control techniques, the possibility of generalizing from them should improve.

VI. Summary and Conclusions

The purpose of this chapter has been to review the literature on behavioral disturbances in the mentally retarded. The general goal has been to present a picture of the major considerations, trends, and points of view that are essential for an understanding of the past and present status of this area of study.

The first major problem that becomes apparent in a review of the literature on the association of behavioral disturbances and mental retardation is the matter of defining the populations under consideration. A majority of definitions of mental retardation as well as those of many of the behavioral disorders carry the implication of homogeneity and have involved researchers in apparently endless equivocation and unwarranted assumptions. A majority of definitions of both conditions are descriptive and all

too frequently appear to be projections of their authors' biases, rather than a reflection of the etiologic or behavioral characteristics of the case or groups under consideration. Problems related to the definition of mental retardation and the various categories of psychopathology have been the subject of many publications (see, for example, Zigler and Phillips [1961] and Kramish [1963]) and, although fundamental to the problem of their association, could not be considered extensively in this review. There are, however, many encouraging signs that different and more clearly homogeneous subgroups will be identified in terms of their common etiology or pathogenesis. The successful differentiation of phenylketonuria from the greater mass of mental retardation and the possibility of similar differentiation of Heller's syndrome are examples of both the achievements and other efforts that are being made in this direction. Similar work is progressing in the field of psychopathology, especially with the schizophrenias. Research on the causation and differentiation of both conditions will proceed at a suitable pace only when they become a matter of joint attacks by scientists from many different disciplines who realize that, as Kety (1959b) and Meehl (1962) suggest, many of the different notions of their etiology or pathogenesis are not mutually incompatible or exclusive.

Over the years, interest in the association of behavioral disturbances and mental retardation has continued; research productiveness, however, has been characterized by lags and spurts. Despite this uneven pace, the very real complexity of research in this field, and the combined intangibles of the behavioral disorders and mental retardation, there do appear to be a number of fairly well substantiated conclusions that can be reported:

1. Any of the major or minor behavioral disturbances can and do occur in association with mental retardation.

2. There is a higher incidence of behavioral disturbances among the mentally retarded than would be found in the general population. The specific reasons for this higher incidence have not been established; however, it has been suggested that the retardate, because of his deficiencies and inadequacies, is probably subject to more frustrations, conflict, and pressures than the intellectually normal. Experiences of rejection, overprotection, and isolation are considered of especial importance in this connection.

3. Behavioral disturbance, after the degree of intellectual deficiency itself, is the single most important cause of institutionalization of the mentally retarded.

4. As the age and intelligence levels increase, there is also an increase in the clarity of definition of the behavioral disturbances. This is especially true of the psychoses.

5. Of the major psychoses, the schizophrenias are most often associated with mental retardation, and depressive psychoses only infrequently. There is some evidence that episodes of psychotic excitement or combinations of extreme hyperactivity and distractability occur in the mentally retarded with equal or even greater frequency than do schizophrenic reactions. Accurate estimates of the incidence of various types of behavioral disturbances in mental retardates can not be given because of the differences between the populations sampled. Similarly, no frequency projections of behavioral disturbances in retardates can be made from a majority of studies reported, since the populations surveyed had already been selected or segregated by special psychological, medical, legal, or socio-economic factors and consequently would not be representative of the general population of retardates.

6. There is a paucity of literature on the association of the non-schizophrenic psychoses and retardation, and a majority of the articles are case studies from which no general inferences could be drawn.

7. The coincidence of the various forms of childhood schizophrenia with mental retardation appears high. However, one may expect that as nosological problems are resolved and diagnostic devices become more precise, a considerable number of currently undifferentiated cases will have their primary classification in one or the other group.

8. Regarding the concept of pseudo mental retardation or pseudofeeblemindedness, the lack of specificity and the various meanings assigned to the concept suggest that its use would not seem to add anything to either diagnostic or etiologic understanding of mental retardation, and it would seem advisable, therefore, to discard the concept.

9. At the present time, only one conclusion concerning the association of mental retardation with delinquency and criminality seems justifiable. The mentally retarded are capable of delinquent and criminal acts as are the intellectually normal; however, factors other than intellectual ones appear to be more important in the etiology of such behavior, and these factors are those commonly cited as important to the development of delinquent and criminal behavior in the general population.

10. Concerning the presence of sociopathic patterns in the mentally retarded, one is led to the conclusion that inept and predominantly antisocial sociopathy is only rarely associated with mental retardation and that the inadequate pattern of sociopathy which includes the weak, passive, and non-agressive types is more likely to occur among the mentally retarded. As with delinquency and criminality, sociopathy can and does occur in mental retardates, but though one condition may complicate the other, there would seem to be no causal relationship in either direction.

11. In terms of the psychoneuroses and the so-called minor behavioral dis-

orders, the research does not demonstrate any causal or etiologic connections. The three disturbances most frequently associated with mental retardation appear to be the conversion hysterical reaction, anxiety reactions, and obsessive-compulsive patterns.

12. A majority of articles in the literature report successful results in the use of individual and group psychotherapy with mental retardates. The degree of success is moderate and frequently ill-defined. The behavioral improvements reported in the literature mostly refer to emotional aspects; increases in intellectual measures through psychotherapy are still generally suspect.

13. There is some indication that the more directive and structured psychotherapeutic approaches are more effective with the aggressively acting-out, sociopathic, and delinquent varieties of retardates, and the more non-directive techniques with the withdrawn, shy, and anxious types. There also appears to be little justification for the use with retardates of individual therapeutic techniques based on indiscriminate accepting warmth and the development of relatively intense transferences. Group therapy with the goals of group identifications and interactions combined with some of the newer educative procedures and environmental manipulation would appear to hold more promise than approaches based on watered-down techniques useful with the intellectually normal.

14. In therapeutic work with the mentally retarded, there appears to be little enthusiasm for or use of the traditional varieties of surgical and convulsive techniques.

15. Studies with stimulant therapies and ataractic drugs rather clearly suggest that, barring side effects, these management techniques can be very useful for the control of various behavioral disturbances in the mentally retarded.

There are no implications that the basic pathology is modified.

16. A considerable number of cases labeled retarded are primarily cases of profound emotional disturbance, and the intellectual deficiencies are essentially the result of such disturbances. The non-normality of distribution curves of intelligence at the lower limits has been discussed by Dingman and Tarjan (1960) and others. It appears likely that the "excess" instances in the lower frequencies can, at least in part, be accounted for in terms of severe cases of child schizophrenia, dementia infantilis or Heller's disease, childhood autism, and other differentiated and undifferentiated conditions of behavioral pathology.

Looking backward at the literature and research in this field, a hasty observer might conclude that little is known. However, with reflection, it would appear that we now know many of the questions that we need to ask. The global nature of behavioral disturbances and mental retardation, separately or in association, is such that one could only expect etiologic and nosologic confusion in earlier periods. In addition, of all aspects of behavioral research, mental retardation has probably received less attention and support than any other area. Recent support of research on problems of mental health and retardation encourages the conclusion that many questions that need to be asked through research approaches may now lead to some crucial answers.

From the perspectives of the past, the current state of our knowledge and the availability of improved methodological techniques, one might speculate on some of these questions and possible approaches to the problems of the occurrence of behavioral disturbances in the mentally retarded. Goldstein (1939), Bice (1948), Angus (1949), Jastak (1949), Kanner (1952), Humphreys

(1956), Masland (1958), Masland, Sarason, and Gladwin (1958), Lorge (1959), and many others have suggested areas of needed research regarding adjustment problems of the mentally retarded. It is obvious that any and all possible etiological factors must be investigated; it is equally obvious, however, that unless other causal factors are demonstrated we are left with the necessity of assuming that maladjustive behavior is learned in the same sense that adjustive behavior is learned.

The research and reports on critical periods in behavioral development, such as those of Scott (1962, 1963) emphasize the importance of such periods in determining not only the rate but the direction of sensory, motor, social, intellectual, and emotional development. Scott has stated (1962) that "It is equally possible, however, to 'learn not to learn' and such a negative learning set may act to bring the critical period to a close." The implications of such findings for the concept of, and research on, mental retardation would seem clear and almost limitless. As Bijou (1963) has put it, "Instead of viewing the cause of psychological retardation as a theoretical construct such as mentality, or as a biological phenomenon such as impairment of the brain, it is suggested that it be conceived of as generated by adverse histories or simply as failures of coordinations of stimulus and response functions." Bijou also presents methodological approaches for research to determine the "specific conditions of which limited repertoires may be a function." Related to critical periods, the work of Harlow (e.g., 1958, 1962) also offers many stimulating ideas and possibilities for research extensions in the field of retardation.

Although learning is implicit in many systematic views of behavior pathology, its role and its importance have not been made explicit. Many of the so-called dynamic theoretical systems such as psychoanalysis seem to have already made their maximal contribution to the understanding of abnormal behavior and mental retardation. Such systems cannot be expected to provide much guidance or new leads for research-planning and design in the future. Learning theories, on the other hand, such as those of Hull, Mowrer, and Skinner provide not only ideas about the development of behavior pathology but also methodological techniques suitable for research in this area. Fortunately, the day is rapidly passing when a majority of learning theorists are naïve about psychopathology.

The views expressed by Cameron (1947) and Cameron and Magaret (1951), who consider anxiety the core problem in behavior pathology, are rich in likely hypotheses. Regarding anxiety, a major problem is one of definition. Is it or is it not a component of drive? Is the behavior of the manic or the hyperkinetic produced by a high drive level? Are they behaving with such rapidity to escape or try to keep up with their high drive level? Is anxiety an intense and chronic type of tension which is maintained because of continuing frustrations, conflicts, or stresses that are difficult or impossible to avoid? We need to demonstrate whether it is the characteristics of the individual or the stimulus that seem to elicit differential reactions to different types of stress.

We are in need of developmental models for the mentally retarded and for the behaviorally disturbed. We need to know why different children and adults, normal or retarded, learn certain security operations or defense techniques and not others. What is the connection between the types of defense reactions adopted and parental or social approval or reinforcement? If the mentally retarded are apt to experience rejection, overprotection, and isolation more frequently than the intellectually normal, are there any reactions that typically result from one or the other experience?

The questions reviewed by Zigler and Phillips (1961) and the inadequacies of conventional psychiatric diagnosis which they discuss require concerted attention as does the whole concept of "mental illness" as suggested by Szasz (1961) and others. These problems and other questions need definitive answers and solutions, and although theorizing must probably come first, the hypotheses developed must be tested through research.

It seems likely that in the future we shall see much research with teaching machines, a growing emphasis on problems of aging among the retarded, as well as increased use of therapy as a research tool. Combinations of dietary, chemical, environmental, and psychotherapeutic attacks on behavioral disturbances of the mentally retarded must be tried and extensive evaluations made. Well-controlled therapeutic studies should tell us *why* some children did not respond to a particular kind of therapy instead of just how many did and did not. Such studies could give us important etiological hints for further examination.

The review of Windle (1962) and its emphasis on methodology is rich with suggestions for research especially related to problems of prognosis with the mentally retarded. The fact that the "institution is a relatively depriving environment" as pointed out by Zigler and Williams (1963) and others serves as a reminder that training for life within an institution may be very inappropriate training for life outside the institution.

Looking backward at the research on the existence of behavioral disturbances in the mentally retarded, it seems safe to conclude that, although there is little of which to be sure and many new facts need to be collected, there are many indications, both scientific and practical, to make a reviewer optimistic about future developments.

REFERENCES

ANDERSON, M. L. 1925. An investigation of all pupils of a defective school in regard to their stability or instability. *Training Sch. Bull.*, 21:129–37.

ANGUS, L. R. 1948. Schizophrenia and schizoid conditions in students in a special school. *Amer. J. Ment. Defic.*, 53:227–38.

———. 1949. Psychiatry in the field of mental deficiency. *Ibid.*, 54:198–203.

BARR, M. W. 1904. *Mental Defectives.* Philadelphia: P. Blakiston's Son & Co.

BEIER, A. L. 1919–20. The incidence of dementia praecox among the feebleminded. *J. Psycho-Asthen.*, 24:89–98.

BEIER, D. C. 1959. Factors in the management of mental retardation. *Int. Rec. Med.*, 172:155–61.

BEIER, D. C., BINDER, A., and ROBBINS, C. D. 1961. "Indiana Survey of Emotionally Disturbed Children." Unpublished report to the Indiana Division of Mental Health.

BELLAK, L. 1948. *Dementia Praecox. The Past Decades Work and Present Status: A Review and Evaluation.* New York: Grune & Stratton.

———. (ed.). 1958. *The Schizophrenic Syndrome.* New York: Logos Press.

BENDA, C. E., FARRELL, M. J., and CHIPMAN, C. E. 1951. The inadequacy of present day concepts of mental deficiency and mental illness in child psychiatry. *Amer. J. Psychiat.*, 107:721–29.

BENDA, C. E., and MELCHIOR, J. C. 1959. Childhood schizophrenia, childhood autism and Heller's disease. *Int. Rec. Med.*, 172:137–54.

BENDER, L. 1941–42. Childhood schizophrenia. *Nerv. Child*, 1:138–40.

———. 1947. Childhood schizophrenia: Clinical study of one hundred schizophrenic children. *Amer. J. Orthopsychiat.*, 17:40–56.

———. 1953. Childhood schizophrenia. *Psychiat. Quart.*, 27:663–81.

———. 1954. Current research in childhood schizophrenia. *Amer. J. Psychiat.*, 110:855–56.

———. 1959. Autism in children with mental deficiency. *Amer. J. Ment. Defic.*, 64:81–86.

BENTON, A. L. 1956. The concept of pseudofeeblemindedness. *A.M.A., Arch. Neurol. Psychiat.*, 75:379–88.

BERGMAN, M., WALLER, H., and MARCHAND, J. 1951. Schizophrenic reactions during childhood in mental defectives. *Psychiat. Quart.*, 25:294–333.

BERGMAN, P., and ESCALONA, S. B. 1949. Unusual sensitivities in very young children. *In: The Psychoanalytic Study of the Child.* New York: International Universities Press.

BICE, H. V. 1948. A decade of psychology: a review based on reports in the American Journal of Mental Deficiency. *Amer. J. Ment. Defic.*, 53:57–66.

BIJOU, S. W. 1963. Theory and research in mental (developmental) retardation. *Psychol. Rec.*, 13:95–110.

BIJOU, S. W., and McCANDLESS, B. R. 1944. An approach to a more comprehensive analysis of mentally retarded delinquent boys. *J. Genet. Psychol.*, 65:147–60.

BOURNE, H. 1955. Protophrenia, a study of perverted rearing and mental dwarfism. *Lancet*, 2:1156–63.

BROMBERG, W. 1934. Schizophrenic-like psychoses in defective children. *Proc. Amer. Assoc. Ment. Defic.*, 39:226–57.

BRONNER, A. F. 1914. A research on the proportion of mental defectives among delinquents. *J. Crim. Law Criminol.*, 4:561–68.

BROWNE, J. C. 1859–60. Psychical diseases of early life. *J. Ment. Sci.*, 6:284–320.

BURT, C. 1923. Delinquency and mental defect. *Brit. J. Med. Pyschol.*, 3:168–78.

BURTON, A. 1954. Psychotherapy with the mentally retarded. *Amer. J. Ment. Defic.*, 58:486–89.

BUTLER, F. O. 1937. Psychosis in the mentally defective. *Calif. West. Med.*, 46:84–89.

CAMERON, N. A. 1947. *The Psychology of Behavior Disorders, a Biosocial Interpretation.* Boston: Houghton Mifflin.

CAMERON, N. A., and MAGARET, A. 1951. *Behavior Pathology.* Boston: Houghton Mifflin.

CANTOR, G. N. 1955. On the incurability of mental deficiency. *Amer. J. Ment. Defic.*, 60:362–65.

CHIDESTER, L., and MENNINGER, K. A. 1936. The application of psychoanalytic methods to the study of mental retardation. *Amer. J. Orthopsychiat.*, 6:616–25.

CLARK, L. P. 1932. Psychoanalysis and mental arrest. *Proc. Amer. Assoc. Stud. Feeble-minded*, 37:316–25.

——. 1933a. *The Nature and Treatment of Amentia.* London: Balliere, Tindall & Cox.

——. 1933b. The present and the future outlook in the treatment of amentia. *Psychiat. Quart.*, 7:50–71.

CLARKE, A. M., and CLARKE, A. D. B. 1958. *Mental Deficiency.* Glencoe: Free Press.

CLECKLEY, H. 1941. *The Mask of Sanity.* St. Louis: C. V. Mosby.

COWEN, E. L. 1955. Psychotherapy and play techniques with the exceptional child and youth. *In:* W. M. CRUICKSHANK (ed.), *Psychology of Exceptional Children and Youth.* Englewood Cliffs, N.J.: Prentice-Hall.

CRAFT, M. 1959a. Mental disorder in the defective: a psychiatric survey among inpatients. *Amer. J. Ment. Defic.*, 63:829–34.

——. 1959b. Mental disorder in the defective: the use of tranquillizers, *Amer. J. Ment. Defic.*, 64:63–71.

CRAFTS, L. W. 1916. Bibliography of feeble-mindedness in relation to juvenile delinquency. *J. Delinq.*, 1:195–208.

CRAFTS, L. W., and DOLL, E. A. 1917. The proportion of mental defectives among juvenile delinquents. *J. Delinq.*, 2:119–43.

CUTTS, R. A. 1957. Differentiation between pseudo-mental defectives with emotional disorders and mental defectives with emotional disturbances. *Amer. J. Ment. Defic.*, 61:761–72.

DAVENPORT, C. B., and DANIELSON, M. 1912. *The Hill Folk.* ("Eugenics Record Office Memoir," No. 1.)

DAVID, G. B. 1957. The pathological anatomy of the schizophrenias. *In: Schizophrenia: Somatic Aspects.* London: Pergamon Press.

DAVIES, S. P. 1930. *Social Control of the Mentally Deficient.* New York: Crowell.

DAVIS, P. 1951. Emotional problems of the retarded child. *Training Sch. Bull.*, 48:50–56.

DEWAN, J. G. 1948. Intelligence and emotional stability. *Amer. J. Psychiat.*, 104:548–54.

DINGMAN, H. F., and TARJAN, G. 1960. Mental retardation and the normal curve. *Amer. J. Ment. Defic.*, 64:991–94.

DUGDALE, R. L. 1900. *The Jukes: A Study*

in Crime, Pauperism, Disease and Heredity. New York: G. P. Putnam's Sons.

EARL, C. J. C. 1934. The primitive catatonic psychosis of idiocy. *Brit. J. Med. Psychol.,* **14**:230–53.

EHRENWALD, H. J. 1945. Delinquent defectives. *J. Ment. Sci.,* **91**:113–18.

EISENBERG, L. 1957. The course of childhood schizophrenia. *A.M.A. Arch. Neurol. Psychiat.,* **78**:69–83.

———. 1958. Emotional determinants of mental deficiency. *Ibid.,* **80**:114–21.

EKSTEIN, R., BRYANT, K., and FRIEDMAN, S. W. 1958. Childhood schizophrenia and allied conditions. *In:* L. BELLAK (ed.), *Schizophrenia: A Review of the Syndrome,* pp. 555–693. New York: Logos Press.

ELLIS, A., and BEECHLEY, R. M. 1950. A comparison of matched groups of mongoloid and non-mongoloid feebleminded children. *Amer. J. Ment. Defic.,* **54**:464–68.

EYSENCK, H. J. 1943. Neurosis and intelligence. *Lancet,* **245**:363.

FELDMAN, F. 1946. Psychoneuroses in the mentally retarded. *Amer. J. Ment. Defic.,* **51**:247–54.

FISHER, L., and WOLFSON, I. N. 1953. Group therapy of mental defectives. *Amer. J. Ment. Defic.,* **57**:463–76.

FOULDS, G. 1945. The child family relationship and the frustration types among mental defective juvenile delinquents. *Brit. J. Med. Psychol.,* **20**:255–60.

GIBSON, R. 1953. A survey of special types encountered in mental deficiency clinics. *Amer. J. Ment. Defic.,* **58**:141–42.

GLUECK, E. T. 1935. Mental retardation and juvenile delinquency. *Ment. Hyg.,* **19**:549–72.

GODDARD, H. 1912. *The Kallikak Family.* New York: Macmillan.

GOLDSTEIN, I. 1948. Implications of mental deficiency. *Occup. Educ.,* **5**:149–72.

GOLDSTEIN, K. 1939. *The Organism.* New York: American Book.

GREENE, R. A. 1930. Psychoses and mental deficiencies, comparisons and relationship. *Proc. Amer. Assoc. Stud. Feebleminded,* **35**:128–47.

———. 1933. Conflicts in diagnosis between mental deficiency and certain psychoses. *Ibid.,* **38**:127–43.

GRUNZBURGH, H. C. 1958. Psychotherapy with the feebleminded. *In:* A. M. CLARKE

and A. D. B. CLARKE (eds.), *Mental Deficiency, the Changing Outlook.* Glencoe: Free Press.

GUERTIN, W. H. 1950. Differential characteristics of the pseudo-feebleminded. *Amer. J. Ment. Defic.,* **54**:394–98.

HARLOW, H. F. 1958. The nature of love. *Amer. Psychologist,* **13**:673–85.

———. 1962. The heterosexual affectional system in monkeys. *Ibid.,* **17**:1–9.

HARRIS, H. 1928. Mental deficiency and maladjustment. *Brit. J. Med. Psychol.,* **8**:285–315.

HAYMAN, M. 1939. The interrelations of mental defect and mental disorder. *J. Ment. Sci.,* **85**:1183–93.

HEBER, R. 1961. A manual on terminology and classification in mental retardation. *Monogr. Suppl. Amer. J. Ment. Defic.,* 2d ed.

HEISER, K. F. 1951. Psychotherapy for the mentally retarded child. *Training Sch. Bull.,* **48**:111–19.

———. 1954. Psychotherapy in a residential school for mentally retarded children. *Ibid.,* **50**:211–18.

HERSKOVITZ, H. H., and PLESSET, M. R. 1941. Psychosis in adult mental defectives. *Psychiat. Quart.,* **15**:574–88.

HIRSCH, E. A. 1959. The adaptive significance of commonly described behavior of the mentally retarded. *Amer. J. Ment. Defic.,* **63**:639–46.

HULSE, W. C. 1954. Dementia infantilis. *J. Nerv. Ment. Dis.,* **119**:471–77.

HUMPHREYS, E. J. 1940. Psychopathic personality among the mental defectives. *Psychiat. Quart.,* **14**:231–47.

———. 1956. Widening psychiatric horizons in the field of mental retardation. *Amer. J. Ment. Defic.,* **61**:390–98.

ITARD, J. M. G. 1932. *The Wild Boy of Aveyron.* Translated by G. HUMPHREY and M. HUMPHREY. New York: Appleton-Century-Crofts.

JAMES, S. G. 1939. The relationship of dementia praecox to mental deficiency. *J. Ment. Sci.,* **85**:1194–1211.

JASTAK, J. 1949. A rigorous criterion of feeblemindedness. *J. Abnorm. Soc. Psychol.,* **44**:367–78.

KALLMANN, F. J., BARRERA, S. E., HOCH, P. H., and KELLEY, D. M. 1940–41. The role of mental deficiency in the incidence of schizophrenia. *Amer. J. Ment. Defic.*, **45**:514–39.

KALLMANN, F. J., and ROTH, B. 1956. Genetic aspects of preadolescent schizophrenia. *Amer. J. Psychiat.*, **112**:599–606.

KANNER, L. 1942–43. Autistic disturbance in affective contact. *Nerv. Child*, **2**:217–50.

———. 1944. Early infantile autism, *J. Pediat.*, **25**:211–17.

———. 1948. Feeblemindedness: absolute, relative and apparent. *Nerv. Child*, **7**: 365–97.

———. 1949. Problems of nosology and psychodynamics of early infantile autism. *Amer. J. Orthopsychiat.*, **19**:16–26.

———. 1952. Emotional interference with intellectual functioning. *Amer. J. Ment. Defic.*, **56**:701–7.

KETY, S. S. 1959*a*. Biochemical theories of schizophrenia: Part I. *Science*, **129**:1528–32.

———. 1959*b*. Biochemical theories of schizophrenia: Part II. *Ibid.*, pp. 1590–96.

KIEFER, R. H. 1949. Psychiatric approach to mental deficiency. *Amer. J. Ment. Defic.*, **53**:601–5.

KINDER, E. F., and RUTHERFORD, E. J. 1927. Social adjustment of retarded children. *Ment. Hyg.*, **11**:811–33.

KRAEPELIN, E. 1919. *Dementia Praecox and Paraphrenia*. Translated by R. MARY BARCLAY. Edinburgh: Livingstone.

KRAFFT-EBING, R. VON. 1904. *Textbook of Insanity*. Translated by C. G. CHADDOCK. Philadelphia: F. A. Davis.

KRAMISH, A. A. 1963. Examining for mental deficiency at an induction center (W.W. II). *Ment. Retard.*, **1**:95–96, 124.

KRIEGMAN, G., and HILGARD, J. R. 1944. Intelligence level and psychotherapy with problem children. *Amer. J. Ment. Defic.*, **14**:251–65.

KUGELMASS, I. N. 1954. *The Management of Mental Deficiency in Children*. New York: Grune & Stratton.

———. 1959. Chemical therapy of mentally retarded children. *Int. Rec. Med.*, **172**: 119–36.

LANZKRON, J. 1957. The concept of pfropf-schizophrenia and its prognosis. *Amer. J. Ment. Defic.*, **61**:544–47.

LEVANN, L. J. 1950. A concept of schizophrenia in the lower grade mental defective. *Amer. J. Ment. Defic.*, **54**:469–72.

LORGE, I. 1959. Planning cooperative utilization of data on the mentally retarded. *Amer. J. Ment. Defic.*, **64**:269–77.

LURIE, L. A., LEVY, S., and ROSENTHAL, F. M. 1944. The defective delinquent. *Amer. J. Orthopsychiat.*, **14**:95–103.

MACGILLIVRAY, R. C. 1956. The larval psychosis of idiocy. *Amer. J. Ment. Defic.*, **60**:570–74.

MAHLER, M .S. 1952. On child psychosis and schizophrenia, autistic and symbiotic infantile psychoses. *In: The Psychoanalytic Study of the Child*, Vol. 7. New York: International Universities Press.

MANN, C. W., and MANN, H. P. 1939. Age and intelligence of a group of juvenile delinquents. *J. Abnorm. Soc. Psychol.*, **34**: 351–60.

MASLAND, R. L. 1958. The prevention of mental retardation: a survey of research. *Amer. J. Ment. Defic.*, **62**:991–1114.

MASLAND, R. L., SARASON, S. B., and GLADWIN, T. 1958. *Mental Subnormality: Biological, Psychological and Cultural Factors*. New York: Basic Books.

MATEER, F. 1924. *The Unstable Child*. New York: D. Appleton.

MEEHL, P. E. 1962. Schizotaxia, schizotypy, schizophrenia. *Amer. Psychologist*, **17**: 827–38.

MEHLMAN, B. 1953. Group play therapy with mental retarded children. *J. Abnorm. Soc. Psychol.*, **48**:53–60.

MICHAL-SMITH, H. (ed.). 1957. *Management of the Handicapped: Diagnosis, Treatment and Rehabilitation*. New York: Grune & Stratton.

MILLS, C. K. 1898. Insanity in children. *In: L. STARR (ed.), An American Text-Book of the Diseases of Children*, 2d ed.; Philadelphia: Saunders.

MORRIS, J. V. 1953. Cases of elective mutism. *Amer. J. Ment. Defic.*, **57**:661–68.

NEUER, H. 1947. The relationship between behavior disorders in children and the syndrome of mental deficiency. *Amer. J. Ment. Defic.*, **552**:143–47.

O'CONNOR, N. 1951. Neuroticism and emotional instability in high-grade defectives. *J. Neurol., Neurosurg. Psychiat.*, **14**:226–30.

O'CONNOR, N., and YONGE, K. A. 1955. Methods of evaluating the group psychotherapy of unstable defective delinquents. *J. Genet. Psychol.*, **87**:89–101.

O'GORMAN, G. 1954. Psychosis as a cause of mental defect. *J. Ment. Sci.*, **100**:934–43.

PALMER, L. J. 1927. The defective delinquent as a state problem. *Psychiat. Quart.*, **1**:91–95.

PENROSE, L. S. 1938. *A Clinical and Genetic Study of 1,280 Cases of Mental Defect.* London: Medical Research Council Special Report, No. 229.

———. 1939. Mental disease and crime: outline of a comparative study of European statistics. *Brit. J. Med. Psychol.*, **18**:1–15.

———. 1954. *The Biology of Mental Defect.* Rev. ed.; London: Sidgwick and Jackson.

POLLOCK, H. M. 1944. Mental disease among mental defectives. *Amer. J. Psychiat.*, **101**:361–63.

———. 1945. Mental disease among mental defectives. *Amer. J. Ment. Defic.*, **49**:477–80.

———. 1958. Brain damage, mental retardation and childhood schizophrenia. *Amer. J. Psychiat.*, **115**:422–27.

POTTER, H. W. 1927*a*. An introductory study of the erotic behavior of idiots. *J. Nerv. Ment. Dis.*, **65**:497–507.

———. 1927*b*. Mental deficiency and the psychiatrist. *Amer. J. Psychiat.*, **6**:691–700.

———. 1927*c*. The pathological nature of mental defect. *Ment. Hyg.*, **11**:148–55.

———. 1933*a*. A clinical consideration of mental deficiency. *Psychiat. Quart.*, **7**:195–202.

———. 1933*b*. Schizophrenia in children. *Amer. J. Psychiat.*, **89**:1253–70.

RANK, B. 1949. Adaptation of the psychoanalytic technique for the treatment of young children with atypical development. *Amer. J. Orthopsychiat.*, **19**:130–39.

RICHMOND, W. 1932. The dementia praecox child. *Amer. J. Psychiat.*, **11**:1153–59.

RICHTER, D. 1957. Biochemical aspects of schizophrenia. In: *Schizophrenia: Somatic Aspects.* London: Pergamon Press.

ROBERTSON, J. P. S., and WIBBERLY, H. 1952. Dementia versus mental defect in middle aged housewives. *J. Consult. Psychol.*, **16**:313–15.

ROLLIN, H. R. 1946. Personality in mongolism with special reference to incidence of catatonic psychosis. *Amer. J. Ment. Defic.*, **51**:219–37.

RUBENSTEIN, E. A. 1948. Childhood mental disease in America: a review of the literature before 1900. *Amer. J. Orthopsychiat.*, **18**:314–21.

RUSH, B. 1812. *Medical Inquiries and Observations upon the Diseases of the Mind.* Philadelphia: Kimber & Richardson.

SACHS, B. 1895. *A Treatise on the Nervous Diseases of Children for Physicians and Students.* New York: Wood.

SAENGER, G. 1960. Factors influencing the institutionalization of mentally retarded individuals in New York City. *A Report to New York State Interdepartmental Health Resources Board.*

SARASON, S. B. 1953. *Psychological Problems in Mental Deficiency.* 2d ed.; New York: Harper.

SCOTT, J. P. 1962. Critical periods in behavioral development. *Science*, **138**:949–58.

———. 1963. The process of primary socialization in canine and human infants. *Monographs of the Society for Research in Child Development*, **28**:1–47.

SLOAN, W. 1947. Mental deficiency as a symptom of personality disturbance. *Amer. J. Ment. Defic.*, **52**:31–36.

SMITH, J. O. 1962. Criminality and mental retardation. *Training Sch. Bull.*, **59**:74–80.

SNYDER, R., and SECHRIST, L. 1959. An experimental study of directive group therapy with defective delinquents. *Amer. J. Ment. Defic.*, **64**:117–23.

SUTHERLAND, E. H. 1931. Mental deficiency and crime. In: K. YOUNG (ed.), *Social Attitudes.* New York: Henry Holt.

SZASZ, T. S. 1961. *The Myth of Mental Illness.* New York: Harper.

TARJAN, G. 1948. Current thinking regarding psychopaths. *Amer. J. Ment. Defic.*, **53**:302–12.

THORNE, F. C. 1959. The etiology of sociopathic reactions. *Amer. J. Psychother.*, **13**:319–30.

TREDGOLD, A. F. 1908. *Mental Deficiency.* London: Balliere, Tindall & Cox.

———. 1947. *A Textbook of Mental Deficiency.* 7th ed.; Baltimore: Williams & Wilkins.

TRIPPE, J., McCAFFREY, I., DEMPSEY, P., and DOWNING, J. J. 1959. The school-excluded mentally retarded child. *Amer. J. Ment. Defic.*, **63**:1005–9.

VANUXEM, M. 1935. The prevalence of mental disease among mental defectives. *Proc. Amer. Assoc. Ment. Defic.*, **40**:242–49.

WALKER, G. H. 1948. Some psycho-sexual considerations of institutionalized mental defectives. *Amer. J. Ment. Defic.*, **53**:312–17.

———. 1950. Social and emotional problems of the mentally retarded child. *Ibid.*, **55**:132–37.

WALLACE, G. L. 1929. Are the feeble-minded criminals? *Ment. Hyg.*, **13**:93–98.

WEAVER, T. R. 1946. The incidence of maladjustment among mental defectives in a military environment. *Amer. J. Ment. Defic.*, **51**:238–46.

WHITTEN, B. O. 1938. Psychotic manifestations of mental defectives. *Proc. Amer. Assoc. Ment. Defic.*, **43**:72–79.

WINDLE, C. 1962. Prognosis of mental subnormals. *Monogr. Suppl. Amer. J. Ment. Defic.*, **66**:180.

WOLLEN, W. 1958. Mental deficiency in Poland and U.S.S.R., *Amer. J. Ment. Defic.*, **63**:205–13.

WORTIS, J. 1950. *Soviet Psychiatry*. Baltimore: Williams & Wilkins.

———. 1958. Schizophrenic symptomatology in mentally retarded children. *Amer. J. Psychiat.*, **115**:429–31.

YAKOVLEV, P. I., WEINBERGER, M., and CHIPMAN, C. C. 1948. Heller's syndrome as a pattern of schizophrenic behavior disturbance in early childhood. *Amer. J. Ment. Defic.*, **53**:318–37.

ZELENY, L. D. 1933. Feeblemindedness and criminal conduct. *Amer. J. Sociol.*, **38**:564–76.

ZIGLER, E., and PHILLIPS, L. 1961. Psychiatric diagnosis: a critique. *J. Abnorm. Soc. Pyschol.*, **63**:607–18.

ZIGLER, E., and WILLIAMS, J. 1963. Institutionalization and the effectiveness of social reinforcement: a three-year follow-up study. *J. Abnorm. Soc. Psychol.*, **66**:197–205.

AUTHOR INDEX

Abel, T. M., 31, 32, 42, 234
Abercrombie, M., 399
Adis-Castrow, G., 101
Ainsworth, S. H., 59
Akert, K., 308
Åkesson, H. O., 377
Akutagawa, D., 121
Alderdice, T. T., 34
Aldrich, C. G., 111, 115, 117, 119, 120
Allen, G., 298, 372, 378, 380, 382, 383
Allen, J. D., 328
Allen, R. J., 368
Alper, A. E., 29
Alpers, B. J., 442, 450
Alvord, E. C., 437, 450
American Society of Human Genetics, 298
Ammons, R. B., 129
Amos, I. E., 118
Anastasi, A., 21, 31, 44, 179, 207, 293
Anderson, D. H., 410
Anderson, E. P., 316, 317
Anderson, J. W., 440, 450
Anderson, M. L., 471
Anderson, V. E., 377
Angelino, H., 148
Angus, L. R., 463, 480
Annett, J., 131
Arey, L. B., 300
Armstrong, M. D., 324, 338
Arthur, G., 19, 24, 29
Asling, C. W., 406, 407
Astin, A. W., 188
Atchison, C. O., 35
Auerbach, V. H., 113, 327, 353
Austin, J. H., 447, 450
Axline, V. M., 79

Babcock, H., 35
Badt, M. I., 122, 191
Baikie, A. G., 362, 418
Bailey, C. J., 413
Bailey, O. T., 443, 450
Baldridge, R. C., 327, 353

Baldwin, A. L., 176
Baldwin, M., 441, 450
Baldwin, W. D., 62
Baller, W. R., 238
Bancroft, M., 215
Bangs, J. L., 84
Barbera, S. E., 459
Barcroft, J., 308
Barnett, C. D., 39, 100, 101, 106, 113, 114, 119, 121, 124, 130, 131, 133
Baroff, G. S., 35, 378, 380, 382, 383
Baron, D. N., 325
Barr, M. L., 418
Barr, M. W., 469
Barron, M. L., 217
Batza, E. M., 84
Bayley, N., 178, 370
Beale, G. H., 397
Beaudry, P. H., 407, 416
Beck, H. S., 35
Beck, S. J., 42
Becker, R. F., 440, 452
Beckham, J. J., 247
Beerman, W., 397
Beier, A. L., 459, 461
Beier, D. C., 454, 470, 471
Beier, E. G., 164
Bekhterev, V. M., 102
Bellak, L., 461
Benda, C. E., 23, 47, 299, 429, 430, 431, 436, 437, 440, 449, 450, 460, 463
Bender, L., 46, 47, 49, 461, 462
Benirschke, K., 382
Bennett, A., 57, 73
Bennett, D., 399, 403
Benoit, E. P., 29, 121, 128, 135, 152, 375
Bensberg, G. J., 29, 41, 47, 80, 100, 114, 127
Benton, A. L., 22, 25, 28, 36, 41, 42, 47, 82, 466
Beres, D., 196
Berg, I., 107, 122
Berger, A., 101, 103

Bergler, E., 24
Bergman, M., 459, 464
Bergman, P., 464
Berkson, G., 121, 127
Berman, P. W., 324
Bernstein, B., 192, 204
Berry, H. K., 339, 340, 368
Bessman, S. P., 314
Bialer, I., 114, 149, 169
Bice, H. V., 480
Bickel, H., 336
Bicknell, E., 217
Biesele, J. J., 361
Bigelow, E. B., 234
Bijou, S. W., 24, 31, 32, 86, 160, 454, 468, 481
Billingham, R. E., 401, 410
Binet, A., 67
Bingham, W. E., 201
Birch, J. W., 27, 38
Bishop, J., 396
Blacketer-Simmonds, D. A., 38, 44
Blackman, L. S., 109, 135
Blake, K. A., 123, 124, 128, 129, 133, 134
Blatt, B., 58, 145
Blizzard, R. M., 410
Block, R. J., 334, 340
Bobroff, A., 246
Boehm, A. E., 34, 47
Böök, J. A., 267, 298, 366, 377, 380, 384
Bogaert, L. van, 437, 452
Boggs, D. A., 338
Bogoch, S., 312
Boldt, R. F., 129
Bolles, M. M., 35
Bongiovanni, A. M., 417
Bonnevie, K., 404
Bornstein, B., 24
Bossio, V., 192, 197
Bourne, H., 458
Bourquin, J., 438, 452
Bowman, M. S., 331, 446, 450
Brace, D. K., 129
Brachet, J., 397, 398, 401, 409
Braden, A. W., 402

SUBJECT INDEX

Abilities, organization of, 33
Abstraction test, 127
Achievement level, 160
Acids: amino, 312, 322, 351; 5-hydroxytrypto-phan, 314; gamma amino butyric acid (GABA), 313; glutamic acid, 313, 477; glutamine, 313; glycine, 314; histidine, 315, 353; hydroxybutyric, 334; isoleucine, 315; leucine, 315; other, 340; paper chromatography of, 336; phenolic, 338; phenylalanine, 314; 3, 4-dihydroxyphenylalanine (DOPA), 314; tryptophan, 314; valine, 315; *see also* Urea cycle, acids of
Activity, 115
Adjustment, 144, 221 ff., 233 ff.; in military service, 144, 234; in school, 145
Adopted children, studies of, 185 ff.
Agenesis of corpus callosum, 435
Aggressivity, 149
Agnosia, finger, 41
Agyria, 432
Amaurotic familial idiocy, 179, 318 ff., 356 ff., 445 f.
Amino acid metabolism, 351
Aminoacidurias, 331
Ammon's horn sclerosis, 442
Androgens, 416
Anemia, sickle-cell, 396
Anencephaly, 408, 416
Angiomatosis, 448
Animal research, 198 ff.
Anoxia, 440, 441, 442, 443; natal or prenatal, 108; in rats, 105
Anoxics, 118
Antibodies, 400, 401, 410
Antimetabolites, 409, 416
Anxiety, 30, 164, 165
Anxiety pictures, of children, 43
Aphasia, congenital, 36
Argininosuccinic aciduria, 328
Arhinencephaly, 433
Arithmetic, 80; achievement and mental age, 80; and finger localizing ability, 82; processes in, 81; teaching methods for the retarded, comparisons of, 82; vocabulary of the retarded, 82
Army, adjustment to, 234
Arnold-Chiari deformity, 434

Artistic expression, in the retarded, 88, 89, 90
Asphyxia, 413, 431, 433, 440
Aspiration, level of, 169
Association, word, 134
Ataxia-telangiectasia, 366
Atresia, of the foramina of Magendie or Luschka, 434
Attention, 110; deficit, 114, 134, 135; lack of, 113
Attitudes, patterns of, 146
Audition, 38
Autism: childhood, 16, 28, 47; early infantile, 462

Batten-Speilmeyer-Vogt's disease, 445, 446
Behavior, 26; adaptive, 26; genetics, 385 ff.; motor, 126; perseverative, 105; rigid, 170; verbal control of, 104 ff., 125 ff.; visuoconstructive, 39
Behavioral disturbances, 453; effects of, 474; as a factor in institutionalization, 457; historical views, 454 ff.; hypotheses about, 454; incidence of, 144, 454, 457, 463; medical treatment of, 477; sensitivities of sensory modalities in, 464
Behavioral pattern, adaptive significance of, 472
Behaviorally disturbed, description of, 454
Bibalismus, 447
Bielschowsky-Jansky's disease, 445, 446
Birth injury, 367
Birth trauma; *see* Trauma, birth
Branched-chain ketoaciduria (maple syrup urine disease), 326

Calcification: in cytomegalic inclusion encephalitis, 445; in Fahr's disease, 446; in mongolism, 437; in Sturge-Weber syndrome, 448; in toxoplasmosis, 444; in tuberous sclerosis, 447; in Western equine encephalitis, 444
Carbohydrates, 309, 315, 335
Cells, 397
Central nervous system: abnormalities of, 404; development of, 401; malformations of, 402, 407
Cerebellar degenerative disorders, 445, 447
Cerebral atrophy, 439, 440, 441, 442
Cholesterol, 311

497